' WEST KENT CO

iOS 8 Swift Programming
Cookbook

Vandad Nahavandipoor

Beijing · Cambridge · Farnham · Köln · Sebastopol · Tokyo   O'REILLY®

iOS 8 Swift Programming Cookbook

by Vandad Nahavandipoor

Published by O'Reilly Media, Inc., 1005 Gravenstein Highway North, Sebastopol, CA 95472.

O'Reilly books may be purchased for educational, business, or sales promotional use. Online editions are also available for most titles (*http://safaribooksonline.com*). For more information, contact our corporate/institutional sales department: 800-998-9938 or *corporate@oreilly.com*.

Editors: Andy Oram and Rachel Roumeliotis
Production Editor: Nicole Shelby
Proofreader: Gillian McGarvey
Indexer: Lucie Haskins
Cover Designer: Ellie Volckhausen
Interior Designer: David Futato
Illustrator: Rebecca Demarest

November 2014:   First Edition

Revision History for the First Edition:

2014-11-06:   First release

2014-12-05:   Second release

See *http://oreilly.com/catalog/errata.csp?isbn=9781491908693* for release details.

ISBN: 978-1-491-90869-3

[LSI]

Table of Contents

Preface.   ix

1. The Basics.   1
     1.1. Adding Blur Effects to Your Views   9
     1.2. Presenting Temporary Information on the Screen with Popovers   12
     1.3. Displaying Images with UIImageView   17
     1.4. Displaying Static Text with UILabel   21
     1.5. Adding Buttons to the User Interface with UIButton   27
     1.6. Displaying Alerts and Action Sheets   31
     1.7. Creating, Using, and Customizing Switches with UISwitch   37
     1.8. Picking Values with the UIPickerView   41
     1.9. Picking the Date and Time with UIDatePicker   46
     1.10. Implementing Range Pickers with UISlider   49
     1.11. Grouping Compact Options with UISegmentedControl   53
     1.12. Presenting Sharing Options with UIActivityViewController   57
     1.13. Presenting Custom Sharing Options with UIActivityViewController   63
     1.14. Displaying an Image on a Navigation Bar   68
     1.15. Adding Buttons to Navigation Bars Using UIBarButtonItem   70
     1.16. Accepting User Text Input with UITextField   75
     1.17. Displaying Long Lines of Text with UITextView   83
     1.18. Creating Scrollable Content with UIScrollView   88
     1.19. Loading Web Pages with WebKit   91
     1.20. Loading Web Pages with UIWebView   94
     1.21. Displaying Progress with UIProgressView   97
     1.22. Creating a Provision Profile   99

2. Extensions.   107
     2.1. Adding New Photo Editing Capabilities to the Photos App   110
     2.2. Providing a Custom Sharing Extension to iOS   118

    2.3. Building Custom Keyboards   129
    2.4. Creating a Service Within Your App with Action Extensions   137
    2.5. Adding Widgets to the Notification Center   144

3. **Managing Health Data with HealthKit**. **155**
    3.1. Setting Up Your App for HealthKit   155
    3.2. Retrieving and Modifying the User's Weight Information   160
    3.3. Accessing and Modifying the User's Height Information   165
    3.4. Retrieving User Characteristics   172
    3.5. Observing Changes to the User's Health Information   177
    3.6. Reading and Modifying the User's Total Calories Burned   183
    3.7. Converting Between Units   196

4. **Managing Home Appliances with HomeKit**. **201**
    4.1. Simulating HomeKit Accessories   203
    4.2. Managing the User's Home in HomeKit   212
    4.3. Adding Rooms to the User's Home   219
    4.4. Specifying Zones in the User's Home   224
    4.5. Discovering and Managing HomeKit Enabled Accessories   229
    4.6. Interacting with HomeKit Accessories   234
    4.7. Grouping Services of HomeKit Accessories   242

5. **Creating Dynamic and Interactive User Interfaces**. **247**
    5.1. Adding Gravity to Your UI Components   249
    5.2. Detecting and Reacting to Collisions Between UI Components   250
    5.3. Animating Your UI Components with a Push   257
    5.4. Attaching Multiple Dynamic Items to Each Other   262
    5.5. Adding a Dynamic Snap Effect to Your UI Components   266
    5.6. Assigning Characteristics to Your Dynamic Effects   269

6. **Table and Collection Views**. **275**
    6.1. Populating a Table View with Data   277
    6.2. Enabling Swipe Deletion of Table View Cells   281
    6.3. Constructing Headers and Footers in Table Views   282
    6.4. Displaying a Refresh Control for Table Views   288
    6.5. Providing Basic Content to a Collection View   292
    6.6. Feeding Custom Cells to Collection Views Using .xib Files   297
    6.7. Handling Events in Collection Views   303
    6.8. Providing Header and Footer in a Collection View   307
    6.9. Adding Custom Interactions to Collection Views   312

7. Concurrency and Multitasking... 315

7.1. Performing UI-Related Tasks   319
7.2. Performing Non-UI Related Tasks   321
7.3. Performing Tasks After a Delay   329
7.4. Performing a Task Only Once   331
7.5. Grouping Tasks Together   332
7.6. Creating Simple Concurrency with Operations   335
7.7. Creating Dependency Between Operations   340
7.8. Firing Periodic Tasks   342
7.9. Completing a Long-Running Task in the Background   345
7.10. Adding Background Fetch Capabilities to Your Apps   348
7.11. Playing Audio in the Background   357
7.12. Handling Location Changes in the Background   360
7.13. Handling Network Connections in the Background   363

8. Security.. 367

8.1. Authenticating the User with Touch ID   373
8.2. Enabling Security and Protection for Your Apps   376
8.3. Storing Values in the Keychain   381
8.4. Finding Values in the Keychain   383
8.5. Updating Existing Values in the Keychain   386
8.6. Deleting Existing Values in the Keychain   390
8.7. Sharing Keychain Data Between Multiple Apps   392
8.8. Writing to and Reading Keychain Data from iCloud   397
8.9. Storing Files Securely in the App Sandbox   399
8.10. Securing Your User Interface   403

9. Core Location, iBeacon, and Maps... 407

9.1. Detecting Which Floor the User Is on in a Building   407
9.2. Defining and Processing iBeacons   409
9.3. Pinpointing the Location of a Device   415
9.4. Displaying Pins on a Map View   420
9.5. Displaying Custom Pins on a Map View   423
9.6. Searching on a Map View   429
9.7. Displaying Directions on the Map   434
9.8. Customizing the View of the Map with a Camera   440

10. Gesture Recognizers.. 445

10.1. Detecting Swipe Gestures   447
10.2. Detecting Rotation Gestures   449
10.3. Detecting Panning and Dragging Gestures   452
10.4. Detecting Long Press Gestures   455

10.5. Detecting Tap Gestures 458
10.6. Detecting Pinch Gestures 460
10.7. Detecting Screen Edge Pan Gestures 462

11. **Networking and Sharing**. **465**
11.1. Downloading Data Using NSURLSession 465
11.2. Downloading Data in the Background Using NSURLSession 473
11.3. Uploading Data Using NSURLSession 477
11.4. Downloading Asynchronously with NSURLConnection 479
11.5. Handling Timeouts in Asynchronous Connections 483
11.6. Downloading Synchronously with NSURLConnection 484
11.7. Customizing URL Requests 487
11.8. Sending HTTP Requests with NSURLConnection 488
11.9. Serializing and Deserializing JSON Objects 491
11.10. Integrating Social Sharing into Your Apps 495

12. **Multimedia**. **499**
12.1. Playing Audio Files 499
12.2. Recording Audio 501
12.3. Playing Video Files 509
12.4. Capturing Thumbnails from Video Files 513
12.5. Accessing the Music Library 516

13. **Address Book**. **525**
13.1. Retrieving a Person Entity with System UI 527
13.2. Retrieving a Property of a Person Entity with System UI 531
13.3. Requesting Access to the Address Book 534
13.4. Retrieving All the People in the Address Book 537
13.5. Retrieving Properties of Address Book Entries 538
13.6. Inserting a Person Entry into the Address Book 541
13.7. Inserting a Group Entry into the Address Book 544
13.8. Adding Persons to Groups 547
13.9. Searching the Address Book 549
13.10. Retrieving and Setting a Person's Address Book Image 552

14. **Files and Folder Management**. **555**
14.1. Finding the Paths of the Most Useful Folders on Disk 557
14.2. Writing to and Reading from Files 559
14.3. Creating Folders on Disk 564
14.4. Enumerating Files and Folders 565
14.5. Deleting Files and Folders 571
14.6. Saving Objects to Files 574

15. **Camera and the Photo Library**. 577

    15.1. Detecting and Probing the Camera   579

    15.2. Taking Photos with the Camera   583

    15.3. Taking Videos with the Camera   587

    15.4. Storing Photos in the Photo Library   590

    15.5. Storing Videos in the Photo Library   595

    15.6. Searching for and Retrieving Images and Videos   597

    15.7. Reacting to Changes in Images and Videos   602

    15.8. Editing Images and Videos Right on the Device   608

16. **Notifications**. 615

    16.1. Sending Notifications   616

    16.2. Listening for and Reacting to Notifications   618

    16.3. Listening and Reacting to Keyboard Notifications   621

    16.4. Scheduling Local Notifications   630

    16.5. Listening for and Reacting to Local Notifications   636

    16.6. Handling Local System Notifications   639

    16.7. Setting Up Your App for Push Notifications   642

    16.8. Delivering Push Notifications to Your App   648

    16.9. Reacting to Push Notifications   656

17. **Core Data**. 659

    17.1. Performing Batch Updates on Core Data   661

    17.2. Writing to Core Data   664

    17.3. Reading Data from Core Data   666

    17.4. Deleting Data from Core Data   668

    17.5. Sorting Data in Core Data   670

    17.6. Boosting Data Access in Table Views   672

    17.7. Implementing Relationships in Core Data   680

    17.8. Fetching Data in the Background   686

    17.9. Using Custom Data Types in Your Core Data Model   690

18. **Dates, Calendars, and Events**. 697

    18.1. Constructing Date Objects   698

    18.2. Retrieving Date Components   699

    18.3. Requesting Permission to Access Calendars   700

    18.4. Retrieving Calendar Groups on an iOS Device   705

    18.5. Adding Events to Calendars   707

    18.6. Accessing the Contents of Calendars   712

    18.7. Removing Events from Calendars   714

    18.8. Adding Recurring Events to Calendars   718

    18.9. Retrieving the Attendees of an Event   722

18.10. Adding Alarms to Calendars   725

19. Graphics and Animations. **729**
19.1. Drawing Text   734
19.2. Drawing Images   736
19.3. Constructing Resizable Images   739
19.4. Drawing Lines   745
19.5. Constructing Paths   751
19.6. Drawing Rectangles   755
19.7. Adding Shadows to Shapes   759
19.8. Drawing Gradients   764
19.9. Transforming Views   770
19.10. Animating Views   776

20. Core Motion. **787**
20.1. Retrieving Altitude Data   788
20.2. Retrieving Pedometer Data   790
20.3. Detecting the Availability of an Accelerometer   794
20.4. Detecting the Availability of a Gyroscope   796
20.5. Retrieving Accelerometer Data   797
20.6. Detecting Shakes on an iOS Device   801
20.7. Retrieving Gyroscope Data   802

21. Cloud. **805**
21.1. Setting Up Your App for CloudKit   807
21.2. Storing Data with CloudKit   812
21.3. Retrieving Data with CloudKit   820
21.4. Querying the Cloud with CloudKit   826
21.5. Observing Changes to Records in CloudKit   831
21.6. Retrieving User Information from CloudKit   839
21.7. Storing and Synchronizing Dictionaries in iCloud   846
21.8. Creating and Managing Files and Folders in iCloud   851
21.9. Searching for Files and Folders in iCloud   855

Index. **863**

Preface

About a year ago, noticing that Apple had not updated Objective-C much over the past few years, I got intimations that they were working on a new language or framework for iOS development, and even suggested it to my friends at work. They laughed and said, "Then you will have to write your book from scratch." They were right; this edition is almost a whole new book.

The previous edition of the book had already seemed like a very big job because I added so many recipes as well as updated all the Objective-C code for iOS 7. But the task was dwarfed by this edition, where everything had to be rewritten in Swift. Furthermore, so many recipes are new that I have lost count. I can affirm that this edition of the book is the most extensive effort since my initial effort to write the first edition. All the code has been written in Swift. Not just translated line by line, but rewritten to take advantage of awesome features in Swift, like extensions.

None of us quite expected Swift to come out from Apple's Worldwide Developers Conference (WWDC) 2014. We thought it would be a normal WWDC with tons of new APIs and just some additions to Objective-C like previous years at WWDC. But we were all surprised. At least I was.

I think Swift is a great language and has been needed for iOS development for a long time. Those of us who grew up with the first iOS SDK or—as it was called back then—the iPhone SDK, know how painful it was to do reference counting manually. Explaining those concepts in early editions of this book, I felt they were sometimes unnecessary and "got in the way" when developing iOS apps. Instead of focusing on writing great apps, we had to focus much of our attention on writing apps that wouldn't crash because of memory management issues. Swift has fixed a lot of those issues and has left us with a lot more complicated things to deal with.

Swift seems like a programming language that is intended for more than iOS development, because so many of its features are unneeded in basic applications and are more appropriate for something complicated and demanding such as a game. When it comes to iOS development, the frameworks seem to be more important than the language, and the frameworks are usually what we struggle with. The difficulty is exacerbated by a lack of documentation for APIs. Many development companies, Apple included, seem to think they can just put out documentation for each API in isolation. They don't understand that programmers need to use a series of APIs together to achieve something. Apple tells you: here is a carrot, it has X number of calories, it weighs this much, its color is orange, and it has been produced in this country. This book tells you: here is a carrot and this is how you can make a carrot soup with it.

Apple doesn't provide basic instructions on how to use their APIs. But they are not alone in this. It is a very big job to document the APIs and they have done a great job with that. I will help you use those APIs to deliver amazing apps to your customers.

I hope you'll enjoy reading this book, and if there is anything that I have not explained, you can contact me through Facebook or Twitter or just send me an email. I will be more than happy to help fellow developers out.

Audience

I assume you know your way around Xcode and have written a few lines of Swift code before. This book does not offer a tutorial about how to write Swift code, but will show you interesting and powerful iOS apps using Swift. There is a big difference. I don't explain the Swift language in this book, because Apple has already done that quite thoroughly with the Swift Programming Language guide, which is about 500 pages long! There is no need for a book to re-explain what Apple has already explained. So if you are not comfortable with Swift yet, I suggest that you read the aforementioned guide published and made freely available by Apple—just do a web search.

This book is also *not* going to teach you the very basics of iOS development. I expect you to know the basics of software engineering and algorithms. Please do not purchase this book in the hopes that it will make you a software engineer, because that is not its goal. If you already know about functions, the stack, arrays, dictionaries or hash-tables, etc., this book is good for you. Otherwise, I suggest that you first become a software engineer of some sort (even if your language is not Swift), and then pick this book up to learn how to write awesome iOS apps.

Organization of This Book

Here is a concise breakdown of the material each chapter covers:

Chapter 1, *The Basics*

> This chapter explains the fundamental building blocks of iOS development, such as messages, labels, sliders, buttons, text fields and views, navigation bars, etc. I suggest that you read the recipes in this chapter and try them out before moving on to more advanced subjects.

Chapter 2, *Extensions*

Finally! Apple allows us to extend iOS with these little binaries that ship with our apps, get integrated into iOS, and can live by themselves without the need for our apps to be running in the background. For instance, we can now create custom keyboards that can get installed on the user's device and the user can use those keyboards even if our app is not running. This feature has been in Android pretty much since its beginning, so when Apple allowed this feature on iOS, I said not "Oh, great" but "Finally." Have a look at this chapter and make up your own mind about its value for you.

Chapter 3, *Managing Health Data with HealthKit*

The HealthKit framework allows iOS apps to integrate with the health-information that is stored on the user's device. This information belongs to the current user of the device and can contain very detailed information, such as the amount of fat that the user burned in the last running session they did. This chapter teaches you how to integrate your apps with HealthKit and read and write to this health database.

Chapter 4, *Managing Home Appliances with HomeKit*

HomeKit is another awesome framework in the SDK. It allows iOS apps to speak to accessories that are HomeKit enabled, so to speak. You will learn to discover these accessories, configure them, talk to them, and so on.

Chapter 5, *Creating Dynamic and Interactive User Interfaces*

Creating a lively user interface takes more than a table view and a label placed on a navigation bar! You need to simulate real-life physics. This chapter teaches you such things as how to model gravity and other dynamic behaviors, and how to attach those to your UI components.

Chapter 6, *Table and Collection Views*

A lot of the information that we want to display to the user is hierarchichal, in that it can be separated into specific cells on the screen and eventually displayed to the user. Table views and collection views are used pretty much everywhere in iOS. From the Photos app to the Settings, you can see collection and table views at work everywhere. This chapter teaches you all you need to know to create great functionality with these components in the SDK.

Chapter 7, *Concurrency and Multitasking*

When your app runs, by default, you will be on the main thread in your app delegate so that you can perform UI-related tasks. But you do not want to perform heavy downloading tasks and heavy calculations on the UI thread because you'll trash your users' experience. In fact, iOS will actually kill your app if you block the UI thread for more than five seconds. Concurrency and multithreading is taught in this chapter to allow you to create fluid apps that do all the work they need, without stepping on the UI thread too much.

Chapter 8, *Security*

Do you store usernames and passwords using `NSUserDefaults`? If your answer is yes, you desperately need to read this chapter. We will talk about Touch ID authentication and many Keychain-related functionalities. You will also learn how to make your user interfaces more secure.

Chapter 9, *Core Location, iBeacon, and Maps*

All the sensors in an iOS device are helpful when you try to find your way to the supermarket or find out which floor of a building you are currently on (seriously, iOS almost always knows this). So you can learn about iBeacons and maps and core location in this chapter.

Chapter 10, *Gesture Recognizers*

When Steve Jobs introduced the iPhone, he showed the world how to scroll through an iPod music library by swiping up and down the page. I still remember people clapping and going "Ooooh." Apple engineers had placed a swipe gesture on the view, which allowed Mr. Jobs to scroll up and down the page so smoothly. This chapter teaches you all about gestures.

Chapter 11, *Networking and Sharing*

What is an iOS device with no Internet connection? A simple phone or a tablet. Network connectivity really adds another dimension to smartphones. This chapter teaches you how to do background and foreground networking to download and upload files using various classes in the SDK.

Chapter 12, *Multimedia*

Inside an iOS app, with the user's permission, you can access their audio and video files and play those files for the user, or simply grab the data for those files for whatever processing you need to do. If you are creating a game, for instance, you might want to play some background music for the user to add some excitement to your game. This chapter teaches you how to load and play audio and video files.

Chapter 13, *Address Book*

The Address Book framework still consists of C APIs. Some people say this is for performance reasons, but I believe Apple has just assigned a low priority to the framework and they just have not brought it up to date with the latest technologies in the SDK. So this chapter teaches you how to use Swift to integrate the Address Book framework into your apps in order to access the user's contacts' information, after the user has given you permission to do so.

Chapter 14, *Files and Folder Management*

You can easily write iOS apps that do not need to work with files and folders. But as soon as you find the need to store information in files and categorize them into folders, you can start reading this chapter. I will teach you how to write to files, read from them, enumerate them, and so on.

Chapter 15, *Camera and the Photo Library*

iOS keeps a library of all the videos and photos that the user has on her device. The app that allows the user to see these photos and videos is called Photos (obviously!). In this chapter, we will learn how to access the raw data for the photos and videos stored on the device, so that you can integrate this functionality into your apps without having to redirect the user to the Photos app.

Chapter 16, *Notifications*

Different parts of iOS interact with each other through notifications. For instance, when the app goes to the background, iOS sends a notification into your application memory space. You can catch this notification in any object inside your app to get notified when the app has gone to the background, in order to do whatever there is that you want to do. This chapter teaches you all about local, push, and app notifications.

Chapter 17, *Core Data*

Core Data is Apple's database technology. You can store data, read it back, sort it, display it, create relationships between different pieces of data, and so on. What is there not to like? Core Data is an amazingly simple technology but requires a certain understanding of its underlying architecture. I will walk you through that in this chapter.

Chapter 18, *Dates, Calendars, and Events*

Dates are important, whether we are talking about editable dates or a date with a partner-to-be or just dates as they are in a calendar. Even though I won't be handing out dating advice, you can learn about calendar dates in this chapter. You will learn to construct date objects, read events from the user's calendar, and so on.

Chapter 19, *Graphics and Animations*

Every now and then you might want to impress your users with some cool graphics and animations. This chapter is all about that. You can draw images on the screen, animate them, rotate them, and so on. Dazzle your users.

Chapter 20, *Core Motion*

A pedometer is a wonderful device that can count the user's steps-taken from time to time. As soon as you have the user's steps data and you know their age and other simple information, you can start counting the calories that they are burning, display them motivating messages, and so on. In this chapter you will learn about the pedometer, accelerometer, and gyroscope, which are some great sensors that Apple has built into pretty much all iOS devices in the market today.

Chapter 21, *Cloud*

Imagine being able to store data in the cloud just as easily as you would store data in Core Data. CloudKit allows you to do precisely that. It is another layer on top of iCloud. You will also learn about iCloud in this chapter.

Additional Resources

Swift is a relatively new language with which you'll want to familiarize yourself if you care about iOS development. As I mentioned before, I recommend that you read Apple's guide on the Swift Programming Language. You won't be disappointed.

From time to time, I refer to official Apple documentation. Some of Apple's descriptions are right on the mark, and there is no point in trying to restate them. Throughout this book, I have listed the most important documents and guides in the official Apple documentation that every professional iOS developer should read.

For starters, I suggest that you have a look at the iOS Human Interface Guidelines (*http://bit.ly/QbdY0B*) for all iOS devices. This document will tell you everything you need to know about developing engaging and intuitive user interfaces for all iOS devices. Every iOS programmer should read this document. In fact, I believe this should be required reading for the product design and development teams of any company that develops iOS applications.

I also suggest that you skim through the "iOS App Programming Guide" in the iOS Developer Library (*http://bit.ly/Qi7JaZ*) for some tips and advice on how to make great iOS applications.

Conventions Used in This Book

The following typographical conventions are used in this book:

Italic
> Indicates new terms, URLs, email addresses, filenames, and file extensions.

`Constant width`
> Used for program listings, as well as within paragraphs to refer to program elements such as variable or function names, databases, data types, environment variables, statements, and keywords.

`Constant width bold`
> Shows commands or other text that should be typed literally by the user.

`Constant width italic`
> Shows text that should be replaced with user-supplied values or by values determined by context.

 This icon signifies a tip, suggestion, or general note.

This icon indicates a warning or caution.

Using Code Examples

Supplemental material (code examples, exercises, etc.) is available for download at *https://github.com/vandadnp/iOS-8-Swift-Programming-Cookbook*.

This book is here to help you get your job done. In general, if example code is offered with this book, you may use it in your programs and documentation. You do not need to contact us for permission unless you're reproducing a significant portion of the code. For example, writing a program that uses several chunks of code from this book does not require permission. Selling or distributing a CD-ROM of examples from O'Reilly books does require permission. Answering a question by citing this book and quoting example code does not require permission. Incorporating a significant amount of example code from this book into your product's documentation does require permission.

We appreciate, but do not require, attribution. An attribution usually includes the title, author, publisher, and ISBN. For example: *"iOS 8 Swift Programming Cookbook* by Vandad Nahavandipoor (O'Reilly). Copyright 2015 Vandad Nahavandipoor, 978-1-4919-0869-3."

If you feel your use of code examples falls outside fair use or the permission given here, feel free to contact us at *permissions@oreilly.com*.

Safari® Books Online

 Safari Books Online (*www.safaribooksonline.com*) is an on-demand digital library that delivers expert content in both book and video form from the world's leading authors in technology and business.

Technology professionals, software developers, web designers, and business and creative professionals use Safari Books Online as their primary resource for research, problem solving, learning, and certification training.

Safari Books Online offers a range of product mixes and pricing programs for organizations, government agencies, and individuals. Subscribers have access to thousands of books, training videos, and prepublication manuscripts in one fully searchable database from publishers like O'Reilly Media, Prentice Hall Professional, Addison-Wesley Professional, Microsoft Press, Sams, Que, Peachpit Press, Focal Press, Cisco Press, John Wiley & Sons, Syngress, Morgan Kaufmann, IBM Redbooks, Packt, Adobe Press, FT

Press, Apress, Manning, New Riders, McGraw-Hill, Jones & Bartlett, Course Technology, and dozens more. For more information about Safari Books Online, please visit us online.

How to Contact Us

Please address comments and questions concerning this book to the publisher:

O'Reilly Media, Inc.
1005 Gravenstein Highway North
Sebastopol, CA 95472
800-998-9938 (in the United States or Canada)
707-829-0515 (international or local)
707-829-0104 (fax)

We have a web page for this book, where we list errata, examples, and any additional information. You can access this page at *http://bit.ly/ios8-swift-prog-ckbk*.

To comment or ask technical questions about this book, send email to *bookquestions@oreilly.com*.

For more information about our books, courses, conferences, and news, see our website at *http://www.oreilly.com*.

Find us on Facebook: *http://facebook.com/oreilly*

Follow us on Twitter: *http://twitter.com/oreillymedia*

Watch us on YouTube: *http://www.youtube.com/oreillymedia*

Acknowledgments

Andy Oram, as always, has been such an amazing editor for this edition of the book. He has worked at the speed of light to deliver this material to you. He has gone through everything that I've written, word by word, and has ensured that my content is digestible by a much wider audience than I could ever imagine writing for. I thank you for your hard work. Thank you to Niklas Saers, who did a great job technically reviewing this book.

Rachel Roumeliotis has also been a fantastic help at O'Reilly. She has supported me throughout my work. She was very happy when I decided to rewrite this book for Swift so it is great having her on my side when the time came to make a big decision like that.

Thanks to Sara, my lovely partner, for her patience while I wrote this book. I cannot imagine having a more loving and patient partner. I genuinly appreciate all you've done for me throughout this period.

Also thank you to Heather Scherer and Amy Jollymore of O'Reilly for sorting out many aspects of this book and my upcoming video series. I appreciate your help.

Thanks to Ulla, Leif, Bella, David, and the kids for every second we spend together. These times mean a lot to me and I am forever grateful. Last but not least, I want to acknowledge Molly's presence and support as well and for the lovely faces that she gives me every day when we go on walks. Even though you are quite a lot of work, I still love you. "Duktig tjej"!

CHAPTER 1

The Basics

1.0. Introduction

In order to write apps for iOS, you need to know some of the basics of the Swift programming language that we will use throughout this book. Swift is Apple's new programming language introduced in Xcode 6 and iOS 8 SDK. Objects and classes are fundamental in object-oriented programming (OOP) languages such as Swift, Objective-C, Java, C++, and many others.

All iOS applications essentially use the model-view-controller (MVC) architecture. Model, view, and controller are the three main components of an iOS application from an architectural perspective.

The *model* is the brain of the application. It does the calculations and creates a virtual world for itself that can live without the views and controllers. In other words, think of a model as a virtual copy of your application, without a face!

A *view* is the window through which your users interact with your application. It displays what's inside the model most of the time, but in addition to that, it accepts users' interactions. Any interaction between the user and your application is sent to a view, which then can be captured by a view controller and sent to the model.

The *controller* in iOS programming usually refers to the view controllers I just mentioned. Think of a view controller as a bridge between the model and your views. This controller interprets what is happening on one side and uses that information to alter the other side as needed. For instance, if the user changes a field in a view, the controller makes sure the model changes in response. And if the model gets new data, the controller tells the view to reflect it.

In this chapter, you will learn how to create the structure of an iOS application and how to use views and view controllers to create intuitive applications.

I also want to teach you a few basics of the Swift programming language—but before we begin, I want to make it absolutely obvious that the goal of this book is not to teach you how to program in Swift. Apple has already released a full book more than 500 pages long that teaches you how to use Swift. But in case you're using this book in parallel with some other resource to learn Swift, I will go over a few basics.

Defining Constants and Variables in Swift

We define constants with the `let` keyword like so:

```
let integerValue = 10
let stringValue = "Swift"
let doubleValue = 10.0
```

The value that we assign to a constant (or later to a variable) defines its type. In the examples I gave, we did not have to define the data type of the constants at all because the Swift compiler can figure out the proper type from the values we assigned. However, if you want to define the data type manually, you can do so using the following syntax:

```
let integerFromDouble = 10.7 as Int
/* The value of this variable is 10
because the compiler truncated the value to an integer*/
```

When a constant is defined and a value is assigned to it, it cannot be changed later. If you need to change a value, use a variable instead, with the `var` keyword:

```
var myString = "Swi"
myString += "ft"
/* myString is now "Swift" */
```

Variables can be mutable or immutable. An immutable variable cannot be changed or appended to. Mutable variables can be changed.

Creating and Using Arrays in Swift

The `[DataType]` syntax can create an array. This is an example of creating an immutable array:

```
let allStrings = ["Swift", "Objective-C"]
```

If you want to create a mutable array, initialize an empty mutable array and then append values to it like so. Use `var` so your `allStrings` array is a variable, not a constant:

```
var allStrings = [String]()
allStrings.append("Swift")
allStrings.append("Objective-C")
/* Our array is now ["Swift", "Objective-C" */
```

If you want to access values inside an array, use subscripting with the [ ] syntax:

```
var allStrings = [String]()
allStrings.append("Swift")
```

```
allStrings.append("Objective-C")

println(allStrings[0]) /* Prints out "Swift" */

allStrings.insert("C++", atIndex: 0)

println(allStrings[0]) /* Prints out "C++" */
```

Defining and Accessing Dictionaries in Swift

A dictionary is a hash table. Each entry in a dictionary specifies one object as a key and another object as its value. Dictionaries in Swift are dynamically typed, based on what we feed them, and are created with the [key: value] syntax, as shown here:

```
let allFullNames = [
  "Vandad"   : "Nahavandipoor",
  "Andy"     : "Oram",
  "Molly"    : "Lindstedt"
]
```

To access the value of a key, use subscripting like so:

```
println(allFullNames["Vandad"]) /* Prints out "Nahavandipoor" */
```

The dictionary that we created was immutable because of the let keyword. To create a mutable version of the same dictionary, use the var keyword like so:

```
var allFullNames = [
  "Vandad"   : "Nahavandipoor",
  "Andy"     : "Oram",
  "Molly"    : "Lindstedt"
]

allFullNames["Rachel"] = "Roumeliotis"
```

This dictionary is of type [String: String] because of the values that we provided to it. You can add any type of value or key to the dictionary to see how the data type changes:

```
let personInformation = [
  "numberOfChildren"  : 2,
  "age"               : 32,
  "name"              : "Random person",
  "job"               : "Something cool",
] as [String : AnyObject]
```

The AnyObject type, as its name implies, represents an instance of any class type. In this case, we are saying that the keys to our dictionary are strings but the values are a mix of various class types. Dictionaries and arrays in Swift can be freely bridged to their Cocoa Touch counterparts of NSDictionary and NSArray.

Grouping Functionality with Classes and Structures in Swift

Structures are value types. That means that when they are passed around from one function to another, for instance, a new instance of them is created and then passed to the function. Classes are reference types, so that they can be passed around without having to be copied.

Imagine having the following structure:

```
struct Person{
  var firstName, lastName: String

  mutating func setFirstNameTo(firstName: String){
    self.firstName = firstName
  }

}
```

This structure has a method that can cause the structure to mutate, so it is prefixed with the keyword mutating. Now we can create a function that can change the value of any Person instance to any given string:

```
@UIApplicationMain
class AppDelegate: UIResponder, UIApplicationDelegate {

  var window: UIWindow?

  func changeFirstNameOf(var person: Person, to: String){
    person.setFirstNameTo(to)
    /* person.firstName is VANDAD now and only in this function */
  }

  func application(application: UIApplication,
    didFinishLaunchingWithOptions
    launchOptions: [NSObject : AnyObject]?) -> Bool {

      var vandad = Person(firstName: "Vandad", lastName: "Nahavandipoor")
      changeFirstNameOf(vandad, to: "VANDAD")
      /* vandad.firstName is still Vandad */

    return true
  }

}
```

Note that the value of the firstName property of the person instance is changed only in the context of the function, not outside it. That means when the instance of the Person structure was passed to the function to change the first name to a given string, the structure as a whole was copied into the stack and passed to the function. Therefore, even though we called the mutating function on it, the first name of the vandad variable did not change.

Now off to classes. Classes are reference types and when passed to functions, are passed just as references to a single copy held in memory. Have a look at the following example:

```swift
class Person{
  var (firstName, lastName) = ("", "")
  init (firstName: String, lastName: String){
    self.firstName = firstName
    self.lastName = lastName
  }
}

@UIApplicationMain
class AppDelegate: UIResponder, UIApplicationDelegate {

  var window: UIWindow?

  func changeFirstNameOf(person: Person, to: String){
    person.firstName = to
  }

  func application(application: UIApplication,
    didFinishLaunchingWithOptions
    launchOptions: [NSObject : AnyObject]?) -> Bool {

      var vandad = Person(firstName: "Vandad", lastName: "Nahavandipoor")
      changeFirstNameOf(vandad, to: "VANDAD")
      /* vandad.firstName is now VANDAD */

      return true
  }

}
```

You can see that the first name of the `vandad` variable is indeed changed in its original context after it was passed to a function that changed the first name. Classes can also have inheritance, but structures cannot have inheritance.

Diving into Operators in Swift

There are many valid operators in Swift. Here are a few examples:

```swift
typealias byte = UInt8

@UIApplicationMain
class AppDelegate: UIResponder, UIApplicationDelegate {

  var window: UIWindow?

  func application(application: UIApplication,
    didFinishLaunchingWithOptions launchOptions: [NSObject : AnyObject]?) -> Bool {

      /* Bitwise OR operator */
```

```
    let byte3 = 0b01010101 | 0b10101010 /* = 0b11111111 */

    /* plus operator */
    let plus = 10 + 20 /* = 30 */

    /* minus operator */
    let minus = 20 - 10 /* = 10 */

    /* multiplication operator */
    let multiplied = 10 * 20 /* = 200 */

    /* division operator */
    let division = 10.0 / 3.0 /* = 3.33333333333333 */

    return true
  }

}
```

You can also override operators. As we saw before, we had a class called `Person`. The two-character == operator checks whether two things are equal in the sense of having the same value, whereas the three-character === operator checks for instance equality. That means the first operator checks whether the two instances are equal (in whatever way that makes sense in the context of your app). The === operator is very strict: it makes sure that the two things you pass are occupying the same position in memory.

Let's explore the first type of equality. With our `Person` class, it makes sense to declare two instances of this class equal if they have the same first and last name. Therefore, using the operator overloader for the == operator, we can define this functionality:

```
func == (left: Person, right: Person) -> Bool{
  if left.firstName == right.firstName &&
    left.lastName == right.lastName{
      return true
  }
  return false
}
```

And now, if we define two people with the same first name and last name and check whether they are the same, even though the instances are different, they will come out the same:

```
let andy = Person(firstName: "Andy", lastName: "Oram")
let someoneElse = Person(firstName: "Andy", lastName: "Oram")

if andy == someoneElse{
  /* This will be printed */
  println("They are the same")
} else {
  /* We won't get here in this case */
  println("They are not the same")
}
```

The three-character === operator would say they're different, because they are separate variables and you can change one without changing the other.

Now let's say that we want to add a postfix ++ operator to our Person class. To create some numerical data it can operate on, we'll add a age property of type Int to the class:

```
class Person{
  var age: Int
  var fullName: String
  init(fullName: String, age: Int){
    self.fullName = fullName
    self.age = age
  }
}
```

Our goal is to allow the programmer to perform the prefix and the postfix operators of ++ on our person instances just like we would perform the prefix and postfix operator of ++ on integer values in C:

```
postfix func ++ (inout person: Person) -> Person{
  let newPerson = Person(fullName: person.fullName, age: person.age)
  person.age++
  return newPerson
}

prefix func ++ (inout person: Person) -> Person{
  person.age++
  let newPerson = Person(fullName: person.fullName, age: person.age)
  return newPerson
}
```

And now we can use them like so:

```
var vandad = Person(fullName: "Vandad Nahavandipoor", age: 29)
var sameAgeVandad = vandad++
/*
  vandad.age = 30
  sameAgeVandad.age = 29
*/

let olderVandad = ++sameAgeVandad

/*
  vandad.age = 30
  sameAgeVandad.age = 30
  olderVandad.age = 30
*/
```

In the same way, you can define prefix and postfix operators for any class or structure you like. Just ensure that your operator overloaders are public functions and not defined inside any specific class or structure.

Declaring and Using Enumerations in Swift

Enumerations are very sophisticated in Swift indeed. They can be of any given type. For instance, they can be strings:

```
enum CarClassification: String{
  case Estate = "Estate"
  case Hatchback = "Hatchback"
  case Saloon = "Saloon"
}

struct Car{
  let classification: CarClassification
}
```

And then you can use them without having to point to the enumeration type. Just use the values:

```
let volvoV50 = Car(classification: .Estate)
```

You can then use the switch statement to find each case of an enumeration:

```
let volvoV50 = Car(classification: .Estate)

switch volvoV50.classification{
case .Estate:
  println("This is a good family car")
case .Hatchback:
  println("Nice car, but not big enough for a family")
default:
  println("I don't understand this classification")
}
```

You can also get the raw value of an enumeration item using the rawValue property:

```
let volvoV50 = Car(classification: .Estate)
println(volvoV50.classification.rawValue) /* Prints out "Estate" */
```

Alternatively, you can construct a value of type of a specific structure using the initializer:

```
if let classification = CarClassification(rawValue: "Estate"){
  let volvoV50 = Car(classification: classification)
}
```

You can use the where clause inside a switch statement to add logic to case statements. For instance, if we have our Car type defined like so:

```
enum CarClassification: String{
  case Estate = "Estate"
  case Hatchback = "Hatchback"
  case Saloon = "Saloon"
}

struct Car{
  let classification: CarClassification
```

```
    let year: Int
  }
```

We can have a function that classifies our cars and, for each classification, decides how old the car should be and still be considered in good condition:

```
func classifyCar(car: Car){
  switch car.classification{
  case .Estate where car.year >= 2013:
    println("This is a good and usable estate car")
  case .Hatchback where car.year >= 2010:
    println("This is an okay hatchback car")
  default:
    println("Unhandled case")
  }
}
```

And we can use the function like so:

```
let oldEstate = Car(classification: .Estate, year: 1980)
let estate = Car(classification: .Estate, year: 2010)
let newEstate = Car(classification: .Estate, year: 2015)
let hatchback = Car(classification: .Hatchback, year: 2013)
let newSaloon = Car(classification: .Saloon, year: 2015)

classifyCar(oldEstate)   /* Will go to the default case */
classifyCar(estate)      /* Will go to the default case */
classifyCar(newEstate)   /* Will be picked up in the function */
classifyCar(hatchback)   /* Will be picked up in the function */
classifyCar(newSaloon)   /* Will go to the default case */
```

1.1. Adding Blur Effects to Your Views

Problem

You want to add blur effects to various UI components on your application.

Solution

Use the following two classes:

UIBlurEffect

> This is a class that represents a blur effect. You can initialize an instance of this class with its designated constructor and pass a value of type UIBlurEffectStyle to it. This value will then decide what type of blur effect you want to create.

UIVisualEffectView

> This is a simple UIView subclass that can accept and apply a visual effect of type UIVisualEffect. Because the UIBlurEffect class is a subclass of the UIVisualEffect, you can simply create a blur effect and pass it to your visual effect view. Once

you have the visual effect view, you can add it to any other existing view that you have on or off screen.

Figure 1-1 shows Safari's icon rendered with a visual effect view that includes a blur effect, blurring the center of that image.

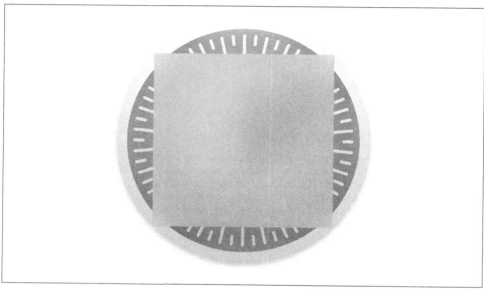

Figure 1-1. Applying a blur effect on a view

Discussion

For the purpose of this discussion, I have already added an image view on my view controller. The image is Safari.app's icon. I have explained the process of extracting this icon in Recipe 19.2, so if you are curious and don't have any other icon to use on your view controller, you can have a look at the aforementioned section of the book to learn how to extract Safari's icon (or any other app's icon for that matter). My view controller looks like Figure 1-2 at the moment.

Figure 1-2. View controller with Safari's icon on it

What I want to do now is add a blurred view on top of this image view. As we learned in the Solution section of this recipe, we are going to create our blur effect and then create a visual effect view on top of our current view, like so:

```
import UIKit

class ViewController: UIViewController {

  override func viewDidLoad() {
    super.viewDidLoad()

    let blurEffect = UIBlurEffect(style: .Light)
    let blurView = UIVisualEffectView(effect: blurEffect)
    blurView.frame.size = CGSize(width: 200, height: 200)
    blurView.center = view.center

    view.addSubview(blurView)

  }

}
```

The UIBlurEffect class can be initialized with any of the blur styles that are specified in the UIBlurEffectStyle enumeration like so:

```
enum UIBlurEffectStyle : Int {
    case ExtraLight
    case Light
    case Dark
}
```

In our example code, we used a light blur effect, but you can use any of the ones just listed. Once you have your blur effect, you can add it to the UIVisualEffectView class. This class itself can accept any visual effect of type UIVisualEffect. Another class of the aforementioned type is the UIVibrancyEffect. This class is very similar to the UIBlurEffect class, and in fact under the hood uses a blur effect as well. UIVibran cyEffect brings out the colors on the layers that are behind it. For instance, if you have a popup window that is about to appear on top of another view that contains many colorful photos on it, it is best to add a UIVibrancyEffect to a visual effect view and construct your popup using this visual effect view. That way, the colors underneath the popup (colors that come from the photos) will be more appealing to the user and the user will be able to get a better understanding of the content under your popup.

1.2. Presenting Temporary Information on the Screen with Popovers

Problem

You want to display a temporary view to the user on the screen and allow them to interact with it. When they are done, this view will need to get dismissed. On an iPad, you would like this information to take up only a bit of the screen real estate, not the whole.

Solution

Use a popup controller of type UIPopoverController and display it on your view controllers using the presentPopoverFromBarButtonItem:permittedArrowDirections:animated: method of the popup controller. A popup controller has to originate from a specific rectangular space on the screen. This is usually a button or a control on the screen where the user taps and expects to see the popover. This item could be of type UIBarButtonItem, in which case you can display the popover using its presentPopo verFromBarButtonItem:permittedArrowDirections:animated: method. Otherwise, you can display and originate a popover from any rectangular spot on the screen using the presentPopoverFromRect:permittedArrowDirections:animated: method.

Discussion

Popovers are used to display temporary information on the screen. They can be used both on regular and on compact size devices such as iPads and iPhones. In this recipe, we want to build an application with a main view controller embedded inside a navigation bar. On the navigation bar we show a plus (+) button which, upon pressing, will display a table view that is populated with 100 items. This table view will be embedded inside its own navigation bar with a Cancel button on it. When the user selects an item in the table view, the popover will be dismissed and the selected item will be passed to the root view controller for processing (see Figure 1-3).

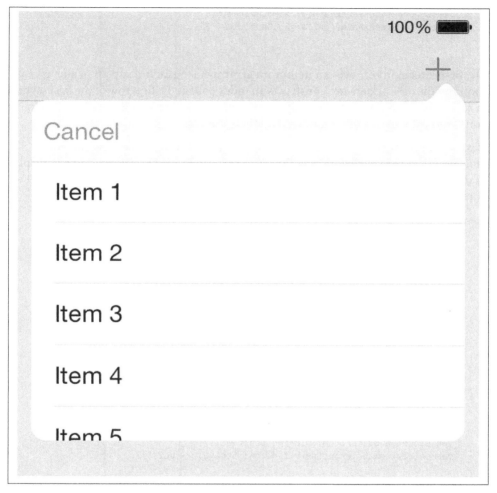

Figure 1-3. Our popover is displayed on the iPad screen

The table view controller has its own class and works with a completion handler. When an item is selected, this controller takes the selected item and passes it to its completion handler. Therefore, processing is very decoupled and it is best to start our implementation of this controller first. Before we begin, we need to define a few handy extensions:

```
extension Array{
  subscript(path: NSIndexPath) -> T{
    return self[path.row]
```

```
      }
    }

    extension NSIndexPath{
      class func firstIndexPath() -> NSIndexPath{
        return NSIndexPath(forRow: 0, inSection: 0)
      }
    }
```

The first extension retrieves an item from an array using an index path, which is really cool, and the other extension constructs an index path at the first row of the first section to relieve us from doing it manually every time. We will be using these quite soon, so don't worry if you don't fully understand their use yet.

Next we are going to define the most useful variables for our table view controller. The most useful one out of all these variables is the array of items that we are going to display to the user in the table view, so they can select one. This is an array of strings and we populate it lazily:

```
    class PopoverTableViewController: UITableViewController {

      struct TableViewValues{
        static let identifier = "Cell"
      }

      /* This variable is defined as lazy so that its memory is allocated
      only when it is accessed for the first time. If we don't use this variable,
      no computation is done and no memory is allocated for this variable */
      lazy var items: [String] = {
        var returnValue = [String]()
        for counter in 1...100{
          returnValue.append("Item \(counter)")
        }
        return returnValue
      }()

      var cancelBarButtonItem: UIBarButtonItem!
      var selectionHandler: ((selectedItem: String) -> Void!)?

      <# rest of the code #>

    }
```

When the table view is displayed to the user, we will also construct our bar button items and show them on the navigation bar without an animation:

```
    required init(coder aDecoder: NSCoder) {
      super.init(coder: aDecoder)
    }

    override init(nibName nibNameOrNil: String!, bundle nibBundleOrNil: NSBundle!) {
      super.init(nibName: nibNameOrNil, bundle: nibBundleOrNil)
```

```
    tableView.registerClass(UITableViewCell.classForCoder(),
      forCellReuseIdentifier: TableViewValues.identifier)
}

override init(style: UITableViewStyle) {
  super.init(style: style)
}

override func viewDidLoad() {
  super.viewDidLoad()

  cancelBarButtonItem = UIBarButtonItem(title: "Cancel", style: .Plain,
    target: self, action: "performCancel")
  navigationItem.leftBarButtonItem = cancelBarButtonItem

}
```

When the Cancel button is pressed, we should simply dismiss our controller:

```
func performCancel(){
  dismissViewControllerAnimated(true, completion: nil)
}
```

And when an item is selected, we will pass the item to our selection handler, which is an optional closure:

```
override func tableView(tableView: UITableView,
  didSelectRowAtIndexPath indexPath: NSIndexPath) {
    let selectedItem = items[indexPath]
    selectionHandler?(selectedItem: selectedItem)
    dismissViewControllerAnimated(true, completion: nil)
}
```

This way the root view controller can become the selection handler and get notified whenever the user has selected an item. As soon as our table view appears on the screen, we will set the preferred size of the popover controller:

```
override func viewWillAppear(animated: Bool) {
  super.viewWillAppear(animated)
  preferredContentSize = CGSize(width: 300, height: 200)
}
```

Last but not least, we will display the items that we have prepared, inside the table view:

```
override func tableView(tableView: UITableView,
  numberOfRowsInSection section: Int) -> Int {
  return items.count
}

override func tableView(tableView: UITableView,
  cellForRowAtIndexPath indexPath: NSIndexPath) -> UITableViewCell {

  let cell = tableView.dequeueReusableCellWithIdentifier(
    TableViewValues.identifier, forIndexPath: indexPath) as UITableViewCell
```

```
    cell.textLabel.text = items[indexPath]

    return cell

  }
```

Now let's go to our root view controller and construct an instance of our popover controller. We place it inside a navigation bar so that the popover controller has a place to put the bar button items:

```
import UIKit

class ViewController: UIViewController {

  var selectedItem: String?

  lazy var popoverContentController: UINavigationController = {
    let controller = PopoverTableViewController(style: .Plain)
    controller.selectionHandler = self.selectionHandler
    let navigationController = UINavigationController(
      rootViewController: controller)
    return navigationController
    }()

  lazy var popoverController: UIPopoverController = {
    return UIPopoverController(contentViewController:
      self.popoverContentController)
    }()

  <# rest of the code #>

}
```

As you saw, the selectionHandler closure of our root view controller has become the selection handler of the popover controller, so we can implement this closure like this:

```
func selectionHandler(selectedItem: String){
  self.selectedItem = selectedItem

  /* Do something with the selected item */

}
```

I've left the implementation quite open, as you may want to do something special with the value that the table view passed to you. For instance, you may want to display an alert view to the user using what you have learned in Recipe 1.6. The plus (+) button on the navigation bar of the root view controller is hooked to a method named displayPop over: that simply displays the popover:

```
@IBAction func displayPopover(sender: UIBarButtonItem){
  popoverController.presentPopoverFromBarButtonItem(sender,
```

```
          permittedArrowDirections: .Any,
          animated: true)
}
```

Please note the `permittedArrowDirections` parameter of the `presentPopoverFrom` `BarButtonItem:permittedArrowDirections:animated` method of the popover controller. This parameter dictates the direction of the arrow that originates from the source of the popover. Have another look at Figure 1-3. Can you see the arrow that is originating from the plus (+) button? That is the source of the popover. In this case, the arrow is pointing upwards towards the button, but you can change this behavior by changing the value of the `permittedArrowDirections` parameter of the aforementioned method to any of the values inside the `UIPopoverArrowDirection` structure.

See Also

Recipe 1.6

1.3. Displaying Images with UIImageView

Problem

You would like to display images on your app's UI.

Solution

Use the `UIImageView` class.

Discussion

The `UIImageView` is one of the least-complicated classes in the iOS SDK. As you know, an image view is responsible for displaying images. There are no tips or tricks involved. All you have to do is instantiate an object of type `UIImageView` and add it to your views. Now, I have a photo of Safari's icon and I would like to display it in an image view. Let's start with our view controller's implementation file:

```
import UIKit

class ViewController: UIViewController {

  let image = UIImage(named: "Safari")
  var imageView: UIImageView

  required init(coder aDecoder: NSCoder){
    imageView = UIImageView(image: image)
    super.init(coder: aDecoder)
  }
```

```
}
```

Go ahead and add the image view to your view controller's view:

```
override func viewDidLoad() {
  super.viewDidLoad()
  imageView.center = view.center
  view.addSubview(imageView)
}
```

Now if we run the app, we will see something similar to Figure 1-4.

Figure 1-4. An image view that is too big to fit on the screen

I should mention that the Safari image that I'm loading into this image view is 512×512 pixels, and as you can see, it certainly doesn't fit into the screen. So how do we solve this problem? First, we need to make sure that we are initializing our image view using the `initWithFrame:` method, instead of the `initWithImage:` method, as the latter will set the width and height of the image view to the exact width and height of the image. So let's remedy that first:

```
import UIKit

class ViewController: UIViewController {

  let image = UIImage(named: "Safari")
  var imageView: UIImageView!

  override func viewDidLoad() {
    super.viewDidLoad()
```

```
    imageView = UIImageView(frame: view.bounds)
    imageView.image = image
    imageView.center = view.center
    view.addSubview(imageView)
  }

}
```

So how does the app look now? See Figure 1-5.

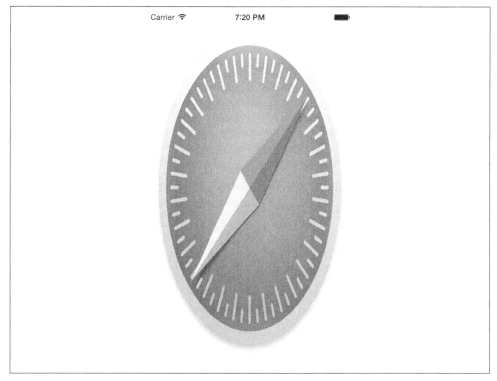

Figure 1-5. An image whose width is squished to fit the width of the screen

This isn't really what we wanted to do, is it? Of course, we got the frame of the image view right, but the way the image is rendered in the image view isn't quite right. So what can we do? We can rectify this by setting the contentMode property of the image view. This property is of type UIContentMode.

Here is an explanation of some of the most useful values in the UIViewContentMode enumeration:

UIViewContentModeScaleToFill

This will scale the image inside the image view to fill the entire boundaries of the image view.

UIViewContentModeScaleAspectFit

This will make sure the image inside the image view will have the right aspect ratio and fit inside the image view's boundaries.

UIViewContentModeScaleAspectFill

This will make sure the image inside the image view will have the right aspect ratio and fill the entire boundaries of the image view. For this value to work properly, make sure that you have set the clipsToBounds property of the image view to true.

 The clipsToBounds property of UIView denotes whether the subviews of that view should be clipped if they go outside the boundaries of the view. You use this property if you want to be absolutely certain that the subviews of a specific view will not get rendered outside the boundaries of that view (or that they do get rendered outside the boundaries, depending on your requirements).

So to make sure the image fits into the image view's boundaries and that the aspect ratio of the image is right, we need to use the UIViewContentModeScaleAspectFit content mode:

```
import UIKit

class ViewController: UIViewController {

  let image = UIImage(named: "Safari")
  var imageView: UIImageView!

  override func viewDidLoad() {
    super.viewDidLoad()
    imageView = UIImageView(frame: view.bounds)
    imageView.contentMode = .ScaleAspectFit
    imageView.image = image
    imageView.center = view.center
    view.addSubview(imageView)
  }

}
```

1.4. Displaying Static Text with UILabel

Problem

You want to display text to your users. You would also like to control the text's font and color.

 Static text is text that is not directly changeable by the user at runtime.

Solution

Use the UILabel class.

Discussion

Labels are everywhere in iOS. You can see them in practically every application, except for games, where the content is usually rendered with OpenGL ES instead of the core drawing frameworks in iOS.

To create a label, instantiate an object of type UILabel. Setting or getting the text of a label can be done through its text property. So let's first define a label in our view controller:

```
import UIKit

class ViewController: UIViewController {
  var label: UILabel!
}
```

Now in the viewDidLoad method, instantiate the label and tell the runtime where the label has to be positioned (through its frame property) on the view to which it will be added (in this case, our view controller's view):

```
import UIKit

class ViewController: UIViewController {
  var label: UILabel!

  override func viewDidLoad() {
    super.viewDidLoad()

    label = UILabel(frame: CGRect(x: 20, y: 100, width: 100, height: 23))
    label.text = "iOS Programming Cookbook"
    label.font = UIFont.boldSystemFontOfSize(14)
    view.addSubview(label)
```

```
    }

  }
```

Now let's run our app and see what happens (see Figure 1-6).

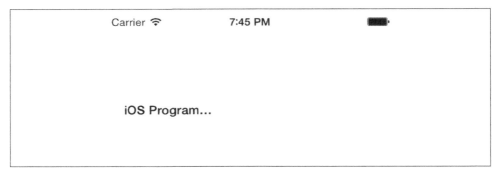

Figure 1-6. A label that is too small in width to contain its contents

You can see that the contents of the label are truncated, with a trailing ellipsis, because the width of the label isn't long enough to contain the whole contents. One solution would be to make the width longer, but how about the height? What if we wanted the text to wrap to the next line? OK, go ahead and change the height from 23.0f to 50.0f:

```
label = UILabel(frame: CGRect(x: 20, y: 100, width: 100, height: 50))
```

If you run your app now, you will get *exactly* the same results that you got in Figure 1-6. You might ask, "I increased the height, so why didn't the content wrap to the next line?" It turns out that the UILabel class has a property called numberOfLines that needs to be adjusted to the number of lines the label has to wrap the text to, in case it runs out of horizontal space. If you set this value to 3, it tells the label that you want the text to wrap to a maximum of three lines if it cannot fit the text into one line:

```
import UIKit

class ViewController: UIViewController {
  var label: UILabel!

  override func viewDidLoad() {
    super.viewDidLoad()

    label = UILabel(frame: CGRect(x: 20, y: 100, width: 100, height: 70))
    label.numberOfLines = 3
    label.lineBreakMode = .ByWordWrapping
    label.text = "iOS Programming Cookbook"
    label.font = UIFont.boldSystemFontOfSize(14)
    view.addSubview(label)
```

```
    }

  }
```

If you run the app now, you will get the desired results (see Figure 1-7).

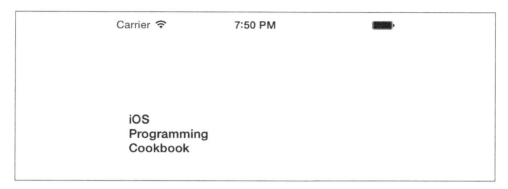

Figure 1-7. A label wrapping its contents to three lines

 In some situations, you might not know how many lines are required to display a certain text in a label. In those instances, you need to set the `numberOfLines` property of your label to 0.

If you want your label's frame to stay static and you want the font inside your label to adjust itself to fit into the boundaries of the label, you need to set the `adjustsFontSizeToFitWidth` property of your label to `true`. For instance, if the height of our label was 23.0f, as we see in Figure 1-6, we could adjust the font of the label to fit into the boundaries. Here is how it works:

```
import UIKit

class ViewController: UIViewController {
  var label: UILabel!

  override func viewDidLoad() {
    super.viewDidLoad()

    label = UILabel(frame: CGRect(x: 20, y: 100, width: 100, height: 23))
    label.adjustsFontSizeToFitWidth = true
    label.text = "iOS Programming Cookbook"
    label.font = UIFont.boldSystemFontOfSize(14)
    view.addSubview(label)

  }
```

}

Rich text is a thing of legend! A lot of us programmers have had the requirement to display mixed-style strings in one line of text on our UI. For instance, in one line of text you might have to display straight and italic text together, where one word is italic and the rest of the words are regular text. Or you might have had to underline a word inside a sentence. For this, some of us had to use Web Views, but that is not the optimal solution because Web Views are quite slow in rendering their content, and that will definitely impact the performance of your app.

Before we begin, I want to clearly show you what I mean by attributed strings, using Figure 1-8. Then we will set out on the journey to write the program to achieve exactly this.

Figure 1-8. An attributed string is displayed on the screen inside a simple label

Just to be explicit, this text is rendered inside a *single* instance of the UILabel class.

So what do we see in this example? I'll list the pieces:

The text "iOS" with the following attributes:
- Bold font with size of 60 points
- Background color of black
- Font color of red

The text "SDK" with the following attributes:
- Bold font with size of 60 points

- White text color

- Light-gray shadow

- Red background color

The best way to construct attributed strings is to use the `initWithString:` method of the mutable variant of the `NSMutableAttributedString` class and pass an instance of the `NSString` to this method. This will create our attributed string without any attributes. Then, to assign attributes to different parts of the string, we will use the `setAttributes:range:` method of the `NSMutableAttributedString` class. This method takes in two parameters:

`setAttributes`

A dictionary whose keys are character attributes and the value of each key depends on the key itself. Here are the most important keys that you can set in this dictionary:

`NSFontAttributeName`

The value of this key is an instance of `UIFont` and defines the font for the specific range of your string.

`NSForegroundColorAttributeName`

The value for this key is of type `UIColor` and defines the color for your text for the specific range of your string.

`NSBackgroundColorAttributeName`

The value of this key is of type `UIColor` and defines the background color on which the specific range of your string has to be drawn.

`NSShadowAttributeName`

The value of this key must be an instance of the `NSShadow` and defines the shadow that you want to use under the specific range of your string.

`range`

A value of type `NSRange` that defines the starting point and the length of characters to which you want to apply the attributes.

To see all the different keys that you can pass to this method, simply browse the Apple documentation online for the `NSMutableAttributedString` class. I will not put the direct URL to this documentation here because Apple may change the URL at some point, but a simple search online will do the trick.

We'll break our example down into two dictionaries of attributes. The dictionary of attributes for the word "iOS" can be constructed in this way in code:

```
let attributesForFirstWord = [
  NSFontAttributeName : UIFont.boldSystemFontOfSize(60),
  NSForegroundColorAttributeName : UIColor.redColor(),
  NSBackgroundColorAttributeName : UIColor.blackColor()
]
```

And the word "SDK" can be constructed using the following attributes:

```
let shadow = NSShadow()
shadow.shadowColor = UIColor.darkGrayColor()
shadow.shadowOffset = CGSize(width: 4, height: 4)

let attributesForSecondWord = [
  NSFontAttributeName : UIFont.boldSystemFontOfSize(60),
  NSForegroundColorAttributeName : UIColor.whiteColor(),
  NSBackgroundColorAttributeName : UIColor.redColor(),
  NSShadowAttributeName : shadow,
]
```

Putting it together, we get the following code that not only creates our label, but also sets its attributed text:

```
import UIKit

class ViewController: UIViewController {
  var label: UILabel!

  func attributedText() -> NSAttributedString{

    let string = "iOS SDK" as NSString

    let result = NSMutableAttributedString(string: string)

    let attributesForFirstWord = [
      NSFontAttributeName : UIFont.boldSystemFontOfSize(60),
      NSForegroundColorAttributeName : UIColor.redColor(),
      NSBackgroundColorAttributeName : UIColor.blackColor()
    ]

    let shadow = NSShadow()
    shadow.shadowColor = UIColor.darkGrayColor()
    shadow.shadowOffset = CGSize(width: 4, height: 4)

    let attributesForSecondWord = [
      NSFontAttributeName : UIFont.boldSystemFontOfSize(60),
      NSForegroundColorAttributeName : UIColor.whiteColor(),
      NSBackgroundColorAttributeName : UIColor.redColor(),
      NSShadowAttributeName : shadow,
    ]

    /* Find the string "iOS" in the whole string and set its attribute */
    result.setAttributes(attributesForFirstWord,
      range: string.rangeOfString("iOS"))
```

```
    /* Do the same thing for the string "SDK" */
    result.setAttributes(attributesForSecondWord,
      range: string.rangeOfString("SDK"))

    return NSAttributedString(attributedString: result)

  }

  override func viewDidLoad() {
    super.viewDidLoad()

    label = UILabel()
    label.backgroundColor = UIColor.clearColor()
    label.attributedText = attributedText()
    label.sizeToFit()
    label.center = CGPoint(x: view.center.x, y: 100)
    view.addSubview(label)

  }

}
```

1.5. Adding Buttons to the User Interface with UIButton

Problem

You want to display a button on your UI and handle the touch events for that button.

Solution

Use the UIButton class.

Discussion

Buttons allow users to initiate an action in your app. For instance, the iCloud Settings bundle in the Settings app presents a Sign Out button, as you can see in Figure 1-9. If you press this button, the iCloud app will take action. The action depends on the app. Not all apps act the same when a Sign Out button is pressed by the user. Buttons can have images in them as well as text, as we will soon see.

Figure 1-9. The Sign Out button is visible at the bottom of the page

A button can assign actions to different triggers. For instance, a button can fire one action when the user puts her finger on the button and another action when she lifts her finger off the button. These become actions, and the objects implementing the actions become targets. Let's go ahead and define a button in our view controller:

```
import UIKit

class ViewController: UIViewController {
  var button: UIButton!
}
```

Next, we move on to the implementation of the button (Figure 1-10):

```
import UIKit

class ViewController: UIViewController {
  var button: UIButton!

  func buttonIsPressed(sender: UIButton){
    println("Button is pressed.")
  }

  func buttonIsTapped(sender: UIButton){
    println("Button is tapped.")
  }

  override func viewDidLoad() {
```

```
super.viewDidLoad()

button = UIButton.buttonWithType(.System) as? UIButton

button.frame = CGRect(x: 110, y: 70, width: 100, height: 44)

button.setTitle("Press Me", forState: .Normal)
button.setTitle("I'm Pressed", forState: .Highlighted)

button.addTarget(self,
  action: "buttonIsPressed:",
  forControlEvents: .TouchDown)

button.addTarget(self,
  action: "buttonIsTapped:",
  forControlEvents: .TouchUpInside)

view.addSubview(button)

  }
}
```

Figure 1-10. A system button is shown here

In this example code, we are using the `setTitle:forState:` method of our button to set two different titles for the button. The title is the text that gets displayed on the button. A button can be in different states at different times—such as normal and high-lighted (pressed down)—and can display a different title in each state. So in this case, when the user sees the button for the first time, he will read "Press Me." After he presses the button, the title of the button will change to "I'm Pressed."

We did a similar thing with the actions that the button fires. We used the `addTarget:ac tion:forControlEvents:` method to specify two actions for our button:

1. An action to be fired when the user presses the button down.

2. Another action to be fired when the user has pressed the button and has lifted his finger off the button. This completes a *touch-up-inside* action.

The other thing that you need to know about UIButton is that it must always be assigned a type, which you do by initializing it with a call to the class method buttonWithType, as shown in the example code. As the parameter to this method, pass a value of type UIButtonType.

A button can also render an image. An image will replace the default look and feel of the button. When you have an image or a series of images that you want to assign to different states of a button, make sure your button is of type UIButtonTypeCustom. I have prepared two images here: one for the normal state of the button and the other for the highlighted (pressed) state. I will now create my custom button and assign the two images to it.

```
import UIKit

class ViewController: UIViewController {
  var button: UIButton!

  override func viewDidLoad() {
    super.viewDidLoad()

    let normalImage = UIImage(named: "NormalBlueButton")
    let highlightedImage = UIImage(named: "HighlightedBlueButton")

    button = UIButton.buttonWithType(.Custom) as? UIButton
    button.frame = CGRect(x: 110, y: 70, width: 100, height: 44)

    button.setTitle("Normal", forState: .Normal)
    button.setTitle("Pressed", forState: .Highlighted)

    button.setBackgroundImage(normalImage, forState: .Normal)
    button.setBackgroundImage(highlightedImage, forState: .Highlighted)

    view.addSubview(button)

  }
}
```

Figure 1-11 shows what the app looks like when we run it in iOS Simulator. We are using the setBackgroundImage:forState: method of the button to set a background image. With a background image, we can still use the setTitle:forState: methods to render text on top of the background image. If your images contain text and you don't need the title for a button, you can instead use the setImage:forState: method or simply remove the titles from the button.

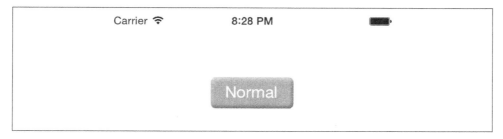

Figure 1-11. A button with a background image

1.6. Displaying Alerts and Action Sheets

Problem

You want to display alert views and/or action sheets to the user.

Solution

Use the `UIAlertController` class to create alert views and action sheets. To get an understanding of what an alert view looks like, take a look at Figure 1-12.

Figure 1-12. Simple alert view

You can also see an example of an action sheet in Figure 1-13. Both action sheets and alert views can easily be created using the `UIAlertController` class. This class provides you with an instance of `UIViewController` that you can present on your own view controllers using the `presentViewController:animated:completion:` method of `UIViewController`.

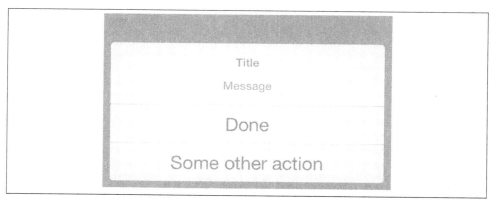

Figure 1-13. Simple action sheet

A few steps are involved in creating a simple alert view or action sheet:

1. Create an instance of the UIAlertController class and specify whether you want an alert view or an action sheet.

2. For every action that you want to add to your alert view or action sheet (actions are usually represented by a button), create an instance of the UIAlertAction class.

3. Add your UIAlertAction actions to your alert controller using the addAction: method of your alert controller.

4. Now that you are all set up, when you are ready to display your alert controller, do so using the presentViewController:animated:completion: method of your host view controller. The host view controller is the view controller that is a part of your application. Every instance of UIViewController inherits the aforementioned method, so you can use that method to display your alert controller. Bear in mind that as we mentioned before, an alert controller is an instance of UIView Controller itself, so you can display it like you would a normal view controller.

Discussion

Let's have a look at constructing a simple alert view using the alert controller that we talked about. The first thing that we have to do, obviously, is define the variable that will hold our alert controller.

```
import UIKit

class ViewController: UIViewController {

    var controller:UIAlertController?

}
```

Next we are going to start constructing a simple alert view controller using the alert view style:

```
controller = UIAlertController(title: "Title",
  message: "Message",
  preferredStyle: .Alert)
```

Now that the alert controller is created, we are going to create an action that will simply print out a text to the console when pressed.

```
let action = UIAlertAction(title: "Done",
  style: UIAlertActionStyle.Default,
  handler: {(paramAction:UIAlertAction!) in
  println("The Done button was tapped")
  })
```

The only thing that is left now in order to construct the alert controller is to add the action that we created to the alert controller like so:

```
controller!.addAction(action)
```

When our view appears on the screen, we will attempt to present the alert controller, that holds an alert view, to the user:

```
override func viewDidAppear(animated: Bool) {
  super.viewDidAppear(animated)
  self.presentViewController(controller!, animated: true, completion: nil)
}
```

So by now, the code for our view controller will look like this:

```
import UIKit

class ViewController: UIViewController {

  var controller:UIAlertController?

  override func viewDidLoad() {
    super.viewDidLoad()

    controller = UIAlertController(title: "Title",
      message: "Message",
      preferredStyle: .Alert)

    let action = UIAlertAction(title: "Done",
      style: UIAlertActionStyle.Default,
      handler: {(paramAction:UIAlertAction!) in
      println("The Done button was tapped")
      })

    controller!.addAction(action)

  }
```

```
override func viewDidAppear(animated: Bool) {
  super.viewDidAppear(animated)
  self.presentViewController(controller!, animated: true, completion: nil)
}

}
```

Let's talk a bit about how we constructed our alert controller. The constructor for `UIAlertController` is `alertControllerWithTitle:message:preferredStyle`. The title is a simple string that will usually be displayed on top of the alert or the action view. The message is an optional message that you would like to display to the user. This message usually appears under the title. Last but not least is the style of the alert controller, which you can set to either an alert (`.Alert`) or an action sheet (`.ActionSheet`). This style must be of type `UIAlertControllerStyle`.

We have now seen how we can construct a simple alert view. There is one more thing that I would like to show you before we conclude speaking about alert views, and that is adding text fields to alert views. Sometimes you want to capture some text in your app from the user—for instance, their username or some sort of an ID—using a popup dialog. You can do this easily using the alert controller. All you have to do is use the `addTextFieldWithConfigurationHandler:` method of your alert controller to add a text field to your alert view. Figure 1-14 shows you an example of how an alert view looks with a text field configured in it.

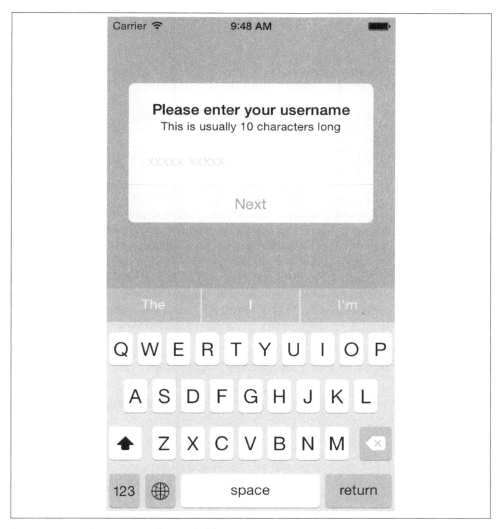

Figure 1-14. Alert view with text field

This is how we added the text field to our alert controller:

```
controller!.addTextFieldWithConfigurationHandler(
  {(textField: UITextField!) in
    textField.placeholder = "XXXXXXXXXX"
  })
```

And then, in our action closure that we constructed before, we can access the text fields in our alert controller using its `textFields` property. This is an array of text fields, and we want the text field in the zeroeth place because we have only one. So the code for the action to our alert view becomes so:

```
let action = UIAlertAction(title: "Next",
  style: UIAlertActionStyle.Default,
  handler: {[weak self] (paramAction:UIAlertAction!) in

    if let textFields = self!.controller?.textFields{
      let theTextFields = textFields as [UITextField]
      let userName = theTextFields[0].text
      println("Your username is \(userName)")
    }

})
```

Now let's have a look at constructing action sheets. Action sheets are also very similar to alert views, but the way in which they appear on the screen is different and they cannot contain text fields in them. They also have a concept of a *destructive button* that is visually very distinct. A destructive button is a button that usually terminates the alert view or the action sheet by doing something that is irreversible. For instance, if a delete or remove button causes an irreversible action such as losing information previously entered by the user, the button is said to be destructive. Alert views also have destructive buttons, but the way a destructive button is presented in an alert view is not as prominent as in an action sheet.

Now we want to display an action sheet similar to that shown in Figure 1-15.

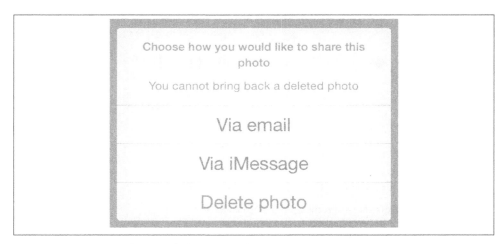

Figure 1-15. Action sheet with destructive button

First we will start by creating our alert controller:

```
controller = UIAlertController(
  title: "Choose how you would like to share this photo",
```

```
    message: "You cannot bring back a deleted photo",
    preferredStyle: .ActionSheet)
```

And then we will create our actions:

```
let actionEmail = UIAlertAction(title: "Via email",
  style: UIAlertActionStyle.Default,
  handler: {(paramAction:UIAlertAction!) in
    /* Send the photo via email */
  })

let actionImessage = UIAlertAction(title: "Via iMessage",
  style: UIAlertActionStyle.Default,
  handler: {(paramAction:UIAlertAction!) in
    /* Send the photo via iMessage */
  })

let actionDelete = UIAlertAction(title: "Delete photo",
  style: UIAlertActionStyle.Destructive,
  handler: {(paramAction:UIAlertAction!) in
    /* Delete the photo here */
  })
```

Once the actions are created, we add them to our alert controller like so:

```
controller!.addAction(actionEmail)
controller!.addAction(actionImessage)
controller!.addAction(actionDelete)
```

Everything is now set up for us to show our alert controller to the user, which we do when our view controller is displayed on the screen:

```
override func viewDidAppear(animated: Bool) {
  super.viewDidAppear(animated)
  self.presentViewController(controller!, animated: true, completion: nil)
}
```

See Also

Recipe 1.5

1.7. Creating, Using, and Customizing Switches with UISwitch

Problem

You would like to give your users the ability to turn an option on or off.

Solution

Use the `UISwitch` class.

Discussion

The `UISwitch` class provides an On/Off control like the one shown in Figure 1-16 for Auto-Capitalization, Auto-Correction, and so on.

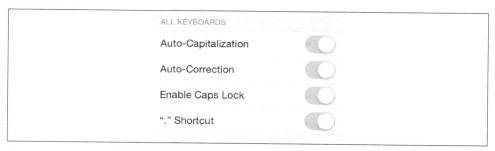

Figure 1-16. UISwitch in the Settings app

In order to create a switch, you can either use Interface Builder or simply create your instance in code. Let's do it through code. Let's create a property of type `UISwitch`:

```
import UIKit

class ViewController: UIViewController {

  var mainSwitch:UISwitch!

}
```

We can go ahead now and create our switch:

```
import UIKit

class ViewController: UIViewController {

  var mainSwitch:UISwitch!

  override func viewDidLoad() {
    super.viewDidLoad()

    mainSwitch = UISwitch(frame: CGRect(x: 100, y: 100, width: 0, height: 0))
    view.addSubview(mainSwitch)

  }

}
```

So we are allocating an object of type UISwitch and using the initWithFrame: constructor to initialize our switch. Note that the parameter that we have to pass to this method is of type CGRect. A CGRect denotes the boundaries of a rectangle using the (*x,y*) position of the top-left corner of the rectangle and its width and height. After we've created the switch, we simply add it to our view controller's view.

Now let's run our app on iOS Simulator. Figure 1-17 shows what happens.

Figure 1-17. A switch placed on a view

As you can see, the switch's default state is off. We can change this by changing the value of the on property of the switch. Alternatively, you can call the setOn: method on the switch, as shown here:

```
mainSwitch.setOn(true, animated: true)
```

You can prettify the user interaction by using the setOn:animated: method of the switch. The animated parameter accepts a Boolean value. If this Boolean value is set to true, the change in the switch's state (from on to off or off to on) will be animated, just as if the user were interacting with it.

Obviously, you can read from the on property of the switch to find out whether the switch is on or off at the moment. Alternatively, you can use the isOn method of the switch, as shown here:

```
if mainSwitch.on{
  /* Switch is on */
} else {
  /* Switch is off */
}
```

If you want to get notified *when* the switch gets turned on or off, you will need to add your class as the *target* for the switch, using the addTarget:action:forCon trolEvents: method of UISwitch, as shown here:

```
mainSwitch.addTarget(self,
  action: "switchIsChanged:",
  forControlEvents: .ValueChanged)
```

Then implement the `switchIsChanged:` method. When the runtime calls this method for the `UIControlEventValueChanged` event of the switch, it will pass the switch as the parameter to this method so you can find out which switch fired this event:

```
func switchIsChanged(sender: UISwitch){
  println("Sender is = \(sender)")

  if sender.on{
    println("The switch is turned on")
  } else {
    println("The switch is turned off")
  }
}
```

There are two main ways of customizing a switch:

Tint Colors

> Tint colors are colors that you can apply to a UI component such as a `UISwitch`. The tint color will be applied on top of the current color of the component. For instance, in a normal `UISwitch`, you will be able to see different colors. When you apply the tint color on top, the normal color of the control will be mixed with the tint color, giving a *flavor* of the tint color on the UI control.

Images

> A switch has two images:

> *On Image*

>> The image that represents the *on* state of the switch. The width of this image is 77 points, and its height is 22.

> *Off Image*

>> The image that represents the switch in its *off* state. This image, like the *on* state of the switch, is 77 points in width and 22 points in height.

Let's get started by learning how we can change the tint color of the switch UI component. This can be achieved by using three important properties of the `UISwitch` class. Each of these properties is of type `UIColor`.

`tintColor`

> This is the tint color that will be applied to the off state of the switch. Unfortunately, Apple has not taken the time to name this property `offTintColor` instead of `tint Color` to make it more explicit.

`thumbTintColor`

> This is the tint color that will be applied to the little knob on the switch.

`onTintColor`

> This tint color will be applied to the switch in its on state.

Here is a simple code snippet that will change the on-mode tint color of the switch to red, the off-mode tint color to brown, and the knob's tint color to green. It is not the best combination of colors but will demonstrate what this recipe is trying to explain:

```
override func viewDidLoad() {
  super.viewDidLoad()

  mainSwitch = UISwitch(frame: CGRect(x: 100, y: 100, width: 0, height: 0))

  /* Adjust the off-mode tint color */
  mainSwitch.tintColor = UIColor.redColor()
  /* Adjust the on-mode tint color */
  mainSwitch.onTintColor = UIColor.brownColor()
  /* Also change the knob's tint color */
  mainSwitch.thumbTintColor = UIColor.greenColor()

  view.addSubview(mainSwitch)

}
```

1.8. Picking Values with the UIPickerView

Problem

You want to allow the users of your app to select from a list of values.

Solution

Use the UIPickerView class.

Discussion

A picker view is a graphical element that allows you to display a series of values to your users and allow them to pick one. The Timer section of the Clock app on the iPhone is a great example of this (Figure 1-18).

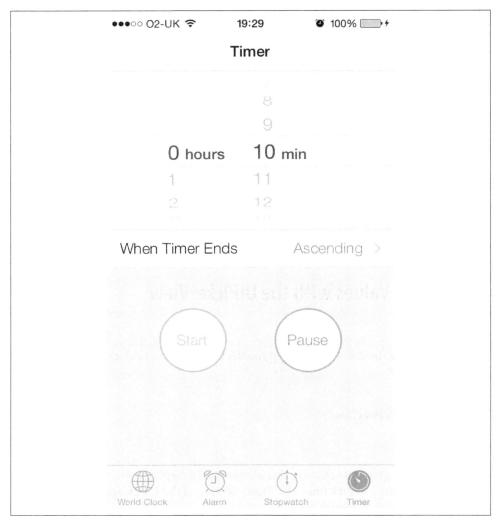

Figure 1-18. A picker view on top of the screen

As you can see, this specific picker view has two separate and independent visual elements. One is on the left, and one is on the right. The element on the left is displaying hours (such as 0, 1, 2 hours, etc.) and the one on the right is displaying minutes (such as 10, 11, 12 mins, etc.). These two items are called *components*. Each component has rows. Any item in any of the components is in fact represented by a row, as we will soon see. For instance, in the left component, "0 hours" is a row, "1" is a row, etc.

Let's go ahead and create a picker view on our view controller's view.

```
import UIKit

class ViewController: UIViewController {

  var picker: UIPickerView!

}
```

Now let's create the picker view in the `viewDidLoad` method of our view controller:

```
import UIKit

class ViewController: UIViewController {

  var picker: UIPickerView!

  override func viewDidLoad() {
    super.viewDidLoad()

    picker = UIPickerView()
    picker.center = view.center
    view.addSubview(picker)
  }

}
```

It's worth noting that in this example, we are centering our picker view at the center of our view. When you run this app on the simulator, you will see a blank screen because the picker is white and so is the view controller's background.

The reason this picker view is showing up as a plain white color is that we have not yet populated it with any values. Let's do that. We do that by specifying a data source for the picker view and then making sure that our view controller sticks to the protocol that the data source requires. The data source of an instance of `UIPickerView` must conform to the `UIPickerViewDataSource` protocol, so let's go ahead and make our view controller conform to this protocol:

```
class ViewController: UIViewController, UIPickerViewDataSource
```

Good. Let's now change our code to make sure we select the current view controller as the data source of the picker view:

```
override func viewDidLoad() {
  super.viewDidLoad()

  picker = UIPickerView()
  picker.dataSource = self
  picker.center = view.center
  view.addSubview(picker)
}
```

After this, if you try to compile your application, you will get errors from the compiler telling you that you have *not* yet implemented some of the methods that the UIPicker ViewDataSource protocol wants you to implement. The way to fix this is to press Command+Shift+O, type UIPickerViewDataSource, and press the Enter key on your keyboard. That will send you to the place in your code where this protocol is defined. Let's go and implement them in our view controller:

```
func numberOfComponentsInPickerView(pickerView: UIPickerView) -> Int {
    if pickerView == picker{
        return 1
    }
    return 0
}

func pickerView(pickerView: UIPickerView,
    numberOfRowsInComponent component: Int) -> Int {
    if pickerView == picker{
        return 10
    }
    return 0
}
```

So what is happening here? Let's have a look at what each one of these data source methods expects:

numberOfComponentsInPickerView:
> This method passes you a picker view object as its parameter and expects you to return an integer, telling the runtime how many components you want that picker view to render.

pickerView:numberOfRowsInComponent:
> For each component that gets added to a picker view, you will need to tell the system how many rows you want to render in that component. This method passes you an instance of picker view, and you will need to return an integer indicating the number of rows to render for that component.

So in the previous code listing, we are asking the system to display 1 component with only 10 rows for a picker view that we have created before.

Compile and run your application now. Ewww, what is that? Yes, indeed, we can now see the picker view, but all the items are populated incorrectly and not with the values that we have in mind. Actually, that doesn't have to worry you too much. The reason behind this is that the picker view knows the number of sections and items that we want to display but doesn't precisely know the items we need to show. That is something that we need to do now, and we do that by providing a delegate to the picker view. The delegate of an instance of UIPickerView has to conform to the UIPickerView Delegate protocol and must implement all the @required methods of that protocol.

There is only one method in the `UIPickerViewDelegate` we are interested in: the `pick`
`erView:titleForRow:forComponent:` method. This method will pass you the index of
the current section and the index of the current row in that section for a picker view,
and it expects you to return an instance of `NSString`. This string will then get rendered
for that specific row inside the component. In here, I would simply like to display the
first row as Row 1, and then continue to Row 2, Row 3, etc., until the end. Remember,
we also have to set the `delegate` property of our picker view:

```
picker!.delegate = self
```

And now we will handle the delegate method we just learned about:

```
func pickerView(pickerView: UIPickerView,
  titleForRow row: Int,
  forComponent component: Int) -> String!{
  return "\(row + 1)"
}
```

Now let's run our app and see what happens (Figure 1-19).

Figure 1-19. A picker view with one section and a few rows

Now imagine that you created this picker view in your final application. What is the use
of a picker view if we cannot detect what the user has actually selected in each one of
its components? Well, it's good that Apple has already thought of that and given us the
ability to ask the picker view what is selected. Call the `selectedRowInComponent:`
method of a `UIPickerView` and pass the zero-based index of a component. The method
will return an integer indicating the zero-based index of the row that is currently selected
in that component.

If you need to modify the values in your picker view at runtime, you need to make sure
that your picker view reloads its data from its data source and delegate. To do that, you
can either force all the components to reload their data, using the `reloadAllCompo`

nents method, or you can ask a specific component to reload its data, using the `reload` `Component:` method and passing the index of the component that has to be reloaded.

See Also

Recipe 1.7

1.9. Picking the Date and Time with UIDatePicker

Problem

You want to allow the users of your app to select a date and time using an intuitive and ready-made user interface.

Solution

Use the `UIDatePicker` class.

Discussion

`UIDatePicker` is very similar to the `UIPickerView` class. The date picker is in fact a prepopulated picker view. A good example of the date picker control is in the Calendar app on the iPhone.

Let's get started by first declaring a property of type `UIDatePicker`. Then we'll allocate and initialize this property and add it to the view of our view controller:

```
import UIKit

class ViewController: UIViewController {

  var datePicker: UIDatePicker!

  override func viewDidLoad() {
    super.viewDidLoad()

    datePicker = UIDatePicker()
    datePicker.center = view.center
    view.addSubview(datePicker)

  }

}
```

Now let's run the app and see how it looks in Figure 1-20.

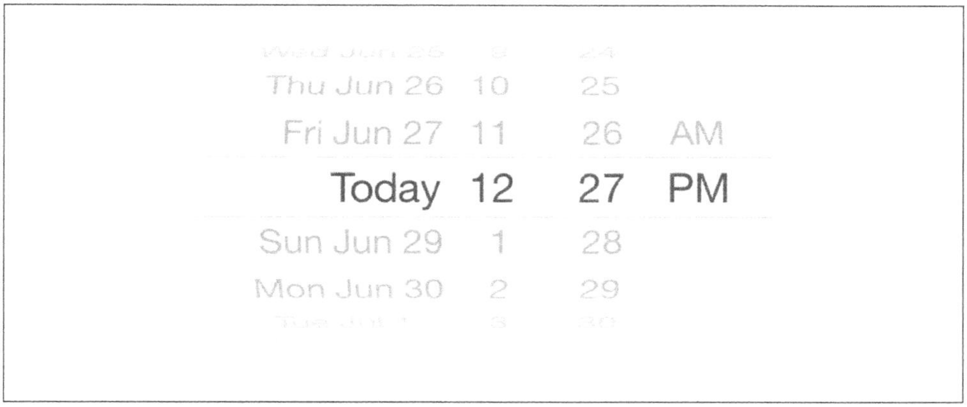

Figure 1-20. A simple date picker

You can see that the date picker, by default, has picked today's date. The first thing that we need to know about date pickers is that they can have different styles or modes. This mode can be changed through the `datePickerMode` property, which is of type `UIDate PickerMode`.

Depending on what you need, you can set the mode of your date picker to any of the values listed in the `UIDatePickerMode` enumeration. I'll show some of these as we go along.

Now that you have successfully displayed a date picker on the screen, you can attempt to retrieve its currently selected date using its `date` property. Alternatively, you can call the `date` method on the date picker, like so:

```
let currentDate = datePicker.date
println(currentDate)
```

Just like the `UISwitch` class, a date picker sends action messages to its targets whenever the user has selected a different date. To respond to these messages, the receiver must add itself as the target of the date picker, using the `addTarget:action:forControlE vents:` method, like so:

```
import UIKit

class ViewController: UIViewController {

  var datePicker: UIDatePicker!

  func datePickerDateChanged(datePicker: UIDatePicker){
    println("Selected date = \(datePicker.date)")
  }

  override func viewDidLoad() {
    super.viewDidLoad()
```

```
        datePicker = UIDatePicker()
        datePicker.center = view.center
        view.addSubview(datePicker)

        datePicker.addTarget(self,
          action: "datePickerDateChanged:",
          forControlEvents: .ValueChanged)

    }

}
```

Now, every time the user changes the date, you will get a message from the date picker.

A date picker also lets you set the minimum and the maximum dates that it can display. For this, let's first switch our date picker mode to UIDatePickerModeDate and then, using the maximumDate and the minimumDate properties, adjust this range:

```
import UIKit

class ViewController: UIViewController {

    var datePicker: UIDatePicker!

    override func viewDidLoad() {
        super.viewDidLoad()

        datePicker = UIDatePicker()
        datePicker.center = view.center
        view.addSubview(datePicker)

        let oneYearTime:NSTimeInterval = 365 * 24 * 60 * 60
        let todayDate = NSDate()

        let oneYearFromToday = todayDate.dateByAddingTimeInterval(oneYearTime)

        let twoYearsFromToday = todayDate.dateByAddingTimeInterval(2 * oneYearTime)

        datePicker.minimumDate = oneYearFromToday
        datePicker.maximumDate = twoYearsFromToday

    }

}
```

With these two properties, we can then limit the user's selection on the date to a specific range. In this example code, we limited the user's input of dates to the range of one year to two years from now.

If you want to use the date picker as a countdown timer, you must set your date picker mode to UIDatePickerModeCountDownTimer and use the countDownDuration property

---

of the date picker to specify the default countdown duration. For instance, if you want to present a countdown picker to the user and set the default countdown duration to two minutes, write code like this:

```
import UIKit

class ViewController: UIViewController {

  var datePicker: UIDatePicker!

  override func viewDidLoad() {
    super.viewDidLoad()

    datePicker = UIDatePicker()
    datePicker.center = view.center
    datePicker.datePickerMode = .CountDownTimer
    let twoMinutes = (2 * 60) as NSTimeInterval
    datePicker.countDownDuration = twoMinutes
    view.addSubview(datePicker)

  }

}
```

The results are shown in Figure 1-21.

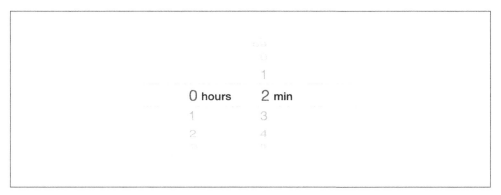

Figure 1-21. A two-minute countdown duration set on a date picker

1.10. Implementing Range Pickers with UISlider

Problem

You want to allow your users to specify a value within a range, using an easy-to-use and intuitive UI.

Solution

Use the UISlider class.

Discussion

You've certainly seen sliders before. Figure 1-22 shows an example.

Figure 1-22. The volume slider

To create a slider, instantiate an object of type UISlider. Let's dive right in and create a slider and place it on our view controller's view. First, let's go to the viewDidLoad method and create our slider component. In this code, we are going to give our slider a range between 0 and 100 and set its default position to be halfway between start and end.

The range of a slider has *nothing* to do with its appearance. We use the range specifiers of a slider to tell the slider to calculate its value based on the relative position within the range. For instance, if the range of a slider is provided as 0 to 100, when the knob on the slider is on the leftmost part, the value property of the slider is 0, and if the knob is to the rightmost side of the slider, the value property is 100.

```
import UIKit

class ViewController: UIViewController {

  var slider: UISlider!

  override func viewDidLoad() {
    super.viewDidLoad()

    slider = UISlider(frame: CGRect(x: 0, y: 0, width: 200, height: 23))
    slider.center = view.center
    slider.minimumValue = 0
    slider.maximumValue = 100
    slider.value = slider.maximumValue / 2.0
    view.addSubview(slider)

  }

}
```

What do the results look like? You can now run the app on the simulator and you'll get results like those shown in Figure 1-23.

Figure 1-23. A simple slider at the center of the screen

We used a few properties of the slider to get the results we wanted. What were they?

minimumValue
> Specifies the minimum value of the slider's range.

maximumValue
> Specifies the maximum value of the slider's range.

value
> The current value of the slider. This is a read/write property, meaning that you can both read from it and write to it. If you want the slider's knob to be moved to this value in an animated mode, you can call the setValue:animated: method of the slider and pass true as the animated parameter.

The little knob on a slider is called the *thumb*. If you wish to receive an event whenever the slider's thumb has moved, you must add your object as the target of the slider, using the slider's addTarget:action:forControlEvents: method:

```
import UIKit

class ViewController: UIViewController {

  var slider: UISlider!

  func sliderValueChanged(slider: UISlider){
    println("Slider's new value is \(slider.value)")
  }

  override func viewDidLoad() {
    super.viewDidLoad()

    slider = UISlider(frame: CGRect(x: 0, y: 0, width: 200, height: 23))
    slider.center = view.center
    slider.minimumValue = 0
    slider.maximumValue = 100
    slider.value = slider.maximumValue / 2.0

    slider.addTarget(self,
      action: "sliderValueChanged:",
      forControlEvents: .ValueChanged)

    view.addSubview(slider)

  }

}
```

If you run the application on the simulator now, you will notice that the sliderValue
Changed: target method gets called *whenever and as soon as* the slider's thumb moves.
This might be what you want, but in some cases, you might need to get notified only
after the user has let go of the thumb on the slider and let it settle. If you want to wait
to be notified, set the continuous property of the slider to false. This property, when
set to true (its default value), will call the slider's targets continuously *while* the thumb
moves.

The iOS SDK also gives you the ability to modify how a slider looks. For instance, the
thumb on the slider can have a different image. To change the image of the thumb,
simply use the setThumbImage:forState: method and pass an image along with a second parameter that can take any of these values:

UIControlStateNormal
    The normal state of the thumb, with no user finger on this component.

UIControlStateHighlighted
    The image to display for the thumb while the user is moving her finger on this
    component.

I have prepared two images: one for the normal state of the thumb and the other one for the highlighted (touched) state of the thumb. Let's go ahead and add them to the slider:

```
import UIKit

class ViewController: UIViewController {

  var slider: UISlider!

  override func viewDidLoad() {
    super.viewDidLoad()

    slider = UISlider(frame: CGRect(x: 0, y: 0, width: 200, height: 23))
    slider.center = view.center
    slider.minimumValue = 0
    slider.maximumValue = 100
    slider.value = slider!.maximumValue / 2.0

    slider.setThumbImage(UIImage(named: "ThumbNormal"), forState: .Normal)
    slider.setThumbImage(UIImage(named: "ThumbHighlighted"), forState: .Highlighted)

    view.addSubview(slider)

  }

}
```

And now let's have a look and see how our normal thumb image looks in the simulator (Figure 1-24).

Figure 1-24. A slider with a custom thumb image

1.11. Grouping Compact Options with UISegmentedControl

Problem

You would like to present a few options to your users from which they can pick an option through a UI that is compact, simple, and easy to understand.

Solution

Use the `UISegmentedControl` class, an example of which is shown in Figure 1-25.

Figure 1-25. A segmented control displaying four options

Discussion

A segmented control is a UI component that allows you to display, in a compact UI, a series of options for the user to choose from. To show a segmented control, create an instance of `UISegmentedControl`. First, we will create the segmented control in the `viewDidLoad` method of your view controller:

```
import UIKit

class ViewController: UIViewController {

  var segmentedControl:UISegmentedControl!

  override func viewDidLoad() {
    super.viewDidLoad()

    let segments = [
      "iPhone",
      "iPad",
      "iPod",
      "iMac"]

    segmentedControl = UISegmentedControl(items: segments)
    segmentedControl.center = view.center
    self.view.addSubview(segmentedControl)

  }

}
```

We are simply using an array of strings to provide the different options that our segmented control has to display. We initialize our segmented control using the `in itWithObjects:` constructor and pass the array of strings and images to the segmented control. The results will look like what we saw in Figure 1-25.

Now the user can pick *one* of the options in the segmented control. Let's say she picked *iPad*. The segmented control will then change its user interface to show the user the option she has selected, as depicted in Figure 1-26.

Figure 1-26. User has selected one of the items in a segmented control

Now the question is, how do you recognize when the user selects a new option in a segmented control? The answer is simple. Just as with a UISwitch or a UISlider, use the addTarget:action:forControlEvents: method of the segmented control to add a target to it. Provide the value of UIControlEventValueChanged for the forControlE vents parameter, because that is the event that gets fired when the user selects a new option in a segmented control:

```swift
import UIKit

class ViewController: UIViewController {

  var segmentedControl:UISegmentedControl!

  func segmentedControlValueChanged(sender: UISegmentedControl){

    let selectedSegmentIndex = sender.selectedSegmentIndex

    let selectedSegmentText =
    sender.titleForSegmentAtIndex(selectedSegmentIndex)

    println("Segment \(selectedSegmentIndex) with text" +
      " of \(selectedSegmentText) is selected")
  }
  override func viewDidLoad() {
    super.viewDidLoad()

    let segments = [
      "iPhone",
      "iPad",
      "iPod",
      "iMac"]

    segmentedControl = UISegmentedControl(items: segments)
    segmentedControl.center = view.center

    segmentedControl.addTarget(self,
      action: "segmentedControlValueChanged:",
      forControlEvents: .ValueChanged)

    self.view.addSubview(segmentedControl)

  }

}
```

If the user starts from the left side and selects each of the options in Figure 1-25, all the way to the right side of the control, the following text will print out to the console:

```
Segment 0 with text of iPhone is selected
Segment 1 with text of iPad is selected
Segment 2 with text of iPod is selected
Segment 3 with text of iMac is selected
```

As you can see, we used the selectedSegmentIndex method of the segmented control to find the index of the currently selected item. If no item is selected, this method returns the value −1. We also used the titleForSegmentAtIndex: method. Simply pass the index of an option in the segmented control to this method, and the segmented control will return the text for that item. Simple, isn't it?

As you might have noticed, when the user selects an option in a segmented control, that option will get selected and *remain* selected, as shown in Figure 1-26. If you want the user to be able to select an option but you want the button for that option to bounce back to its original shape after it has been selected (just like a normal button that bounces back up after it is tapped), you need to set the momentary property of the segmented control to true:

```
segmentedControl.momentary = true
```

One of the really neat features of segmented controls is that they can contain images instead of text. To do this, simply use the initWithObjects: constructor method of the UISegmentedControl class and pass the strings and images that will be used to initialize the segmented UI control:

```
import UIKit

class ViewController: UIViewController {

    var segmentedControl:UISegmentedControl!
    override func viewDidLoad() {
      super.viewDidLoad()

      let segments = NSArray(objects:
        "Red",
        UIImage(named: "blueDot")!,
        "Green",
        "Yellow")

      segmentedControl = UISegmentedControl(items: segments)
      segmentedControl.center = view.center
      self.view.addSubview(segmentedControl)

    }

}
```

In this example, the *blueDot* file is simply a blue circle image with the dimensions of 32x32@2x and 16x16@1x.

1.12. Presenting Sharing Options with UIActivityViewController

Problem

You want to be able to allow your users to share content inside your apps with their friends via an interface similar to that shown in Figure 1-27 that provides different sharing options available in iOS, such as Facebook and Twitter.

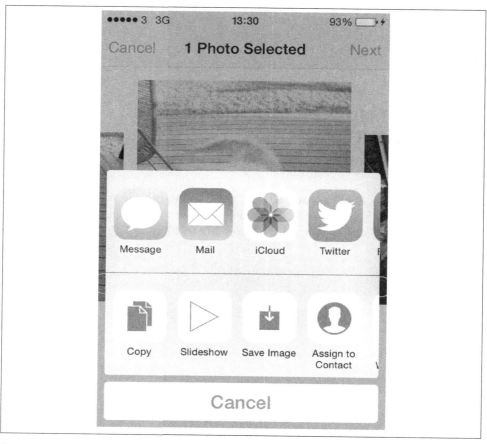

Figure 1-27. The activity view controller

Solution

Create an instance of the `UIActivityViewController` class and share your content through this class, as we will see in the Discussion section of this recipe.

The instances of `UIActivityViewController` must be presented modally on the iPhone and inside a popover on an iPad. For more information about popovers, refer to Recipe 1.2.

Discussion

There are many sharing options inside iOS, all built into the core of the OS. For instance, Facebook and Twitter integration is an integral part of the core of iOS, and you can share pretty much any content from anywhere you want. Third-party apps like ours can also use all the sharing functionalities available in iOS without having to think about the low-level details of these services and how iOS provides these sharing options. The beauty of this whole thing is that you mention *what* you want to share, and iOS will pick the sharing options that are capable of handling those items. For instance, if you want to share images and text, iOS will display many more items to you than if you want to share an audio file.

Sharing data is very easy in iOS. All you have to do is instantiate the `UIActivityView` `Controller` class using its `initWithActivityItems:applicationActivities:` constructor. Here are the parameters to this method:

`initWithActivityItems`

> The array of items that you want to share. These can be instances of `NSString`, `UIImage`, or instances of any of your custom classes that conform to the `UIActivi` `tyItemSource` protocol. We will talk about this protocol later in detail.

`applicationActivities`

> An array of instances of `UIActivity` that represent the activities that your own application supports. For instance, you can indicate here whether your application can handle its own sharing of images and strings. We will not go into detail about this parameter for now and will simply pass `nil` as its value, telling iOS that we want to stick to the system sharing options.

So let's say that you have a text field where the user can enter text to be shared, and a Share button near it. When the user presses the Share button, you will simply pass the text of the text field to your instance of the `UIActivityViewController` class. We are writing this code for iPhone, so we will present our activity view controller as a modal view controller.

Because we are putting a text field on our view controller, we need to make sure that we are handling its delegate messages, especially the `textFieldShouldReturn:` method of the `UITextFieldDelegate` protocol. Therefore, we are going to elect our view controller as the delegate of the text field. Also, we are going to attach an action method to our Share button. When the button is tapped, we want to make sure there is something in the text field to share. If there isn't, we will simply display an alert to the user telling him why we cannot share the content of the text field. If there is some text in the text field, we will pop up an instance of the `UIActivityViewController` class.

We start off with writing two methods for our view controller, each of which is able to create one of our UI components and place it on our view controller's view. One will create the text field, and the other will create the button next to it:

```
import UIKit

class ViewController: UIViewController, UITextFieldDelegate {

    var textField:UITextField!
    var buttonShare:UIButton!

    func createTextField(){
      textField = UITextField(frame:
        CGRect(x: 20, y: 35, width: 280, height: 30))
      textField.borderStyle = .RoundedRect;
      textField.placeholder = "Enter text to share..."
      textField.delegate = self
      view.addSubview(textField)
    }

    func createButton(){
      buttonShare = UIButton.buttonWithType(.System) as? UIButton
      buttonShare.frame = CGRect(x: 20, y: 80, width: 280, height: 44)
      buttonShare.setTitle("Share", forState:.Normal)

      buttonShare.addTarget(self,
        action:"handleShare:",
        forControlEvents:.TouchUpInside)

      view.addSubview(buttonShare)
    }

}
```

When we are done with that, we just have to call these two methods in the viewDid
Load method of our view controller. This will allow the UI components to be placed on
the view of our view controller:

```
override func viewDidLoad() {
  super.viewDidLoad()
  createTextField()
  createButton()
}
```

In the textFieldShouldReturn: method, all we do is dismiss the keyboard in order to
resign the text field's active state. This simply means that when a user has been editing
the text field and then presses the Return or Enter key on the keyboard, the keyboard
should be dismissed. Bear in mind that the createTextField method that we just coded
has set our view controller as the delegate of the text field. So we have to implement the
aforementioned method as follows:

```
func textFieldShouldReturn(textField: UITextField!) -> Bool{
  textField.resignFirstResponder()
  return true
}
```

Last but not least is the handler method of our button. As you saw, the `createButton` method creates the button for us and elects the `handleShare:` method to handle the touch down inside action of the button. So let's code this method:

```
func handleShare(sender: UIButton){

  if (textField.text.isEmpty){
    let message = "Please enter a text and then press Share"

    let alertController = UIAlertController(title: nil,
      message: message,
      preferredStyle: .Alert)

    alertController.addAction(
      UIAlertAction(title: "OK", style: .Default, handler: nil))

    presentViewController(alertController, animated: true, completion: nil)

    return
  }

  /* it is VERY important to cast your strings to NSString
  otherwise the controller cannot display the appropriate sharing options */
  activityViewController = UIActivityViewController(
    activityItems: [textField.text as NSString],
    applicationActivities: nil)

  presentViewController(activityViewController,
    animated: true,
    completion: {
    })
}
```

If you want to present sharing options for textual items, you need to ensure that your strings are typecast to strings of type `NSString`. Swift's string of type `String` cannot be handled by an activity view controller.

Now if you run the app, enter some text in the text field, and then press the Share button, you will see something similar to Figure 1-28.

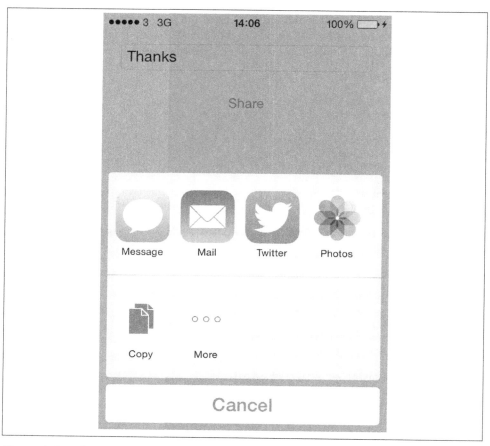

Figure 1-28. Sharing options displayed for the instance of string that we are trying to share

You can also have sharing options displayed as soon as your view controller is displayed on the screen. The viewDidAppear method of your view controller will be called when the view of your view controller is displayed on the screen and is guaranteed to be in the view hierarchy of your app, meaning that you can now display other views on top of your view controller's view.

 Do not attempt to present the activity view controller in the view DidLoad method of your view controller. At that stage in the app, your view controller's view is still not attached to the view hierarchy of the application, so attempting to present a view controller on the view will not work. Your view must be present in the hierarchy of the views for your modal views to work.

For this reason, you need to present the sharing view controller in the `viewDidAppear` method of your view controller.

See Also

Recipe 1.2

1.13. Presenting Custom Sharing Options with UIActivityViewController

Problem

You want your app to participate in the list of apps that can handle sharing in iOS and appear in the list of available activities displayed in the activity view controller (see Figure 1-27).

For example, you might need something like this if you have a text-editing app and you want a custom item that says "Archive" to appear in the activity view controller when the user presses the Share button. When the user presses the Archive button, the text inside your app's editing area will get passed to your custom activity, and your activity can then archive that text on the iOS device.

Solution

Create a class of type `UIActivity`. In other words, subclass the aforementioned class and give a name (whatever you like) to your new class. Instances of the subclasses of this class can be passed to the `initWithActivityItems:applicationActivities:` constructor of the `UIActivityViewController` class, and if they implement all the required methods of the `UIActivity` class, iOS will display them in the activity view controller.

Discussion

The `initWithActivityItems:applicationActivities:` method's first parameter accepts values of different types. These values can be strings, numbers, images, etc.—any object, really. When you present an activity controller with an array of arbitrary objects passed to the `initWithActivityItems` parameter, iOS will go through all the available system activities, like Facebook and Twitter, and ask the user to pick an activity that suits her needs best. After the user picks an activity, iOS will pass the *type* of the objects in your array to the registered system activity that the user picked. Those activities can then check the type of the objects you are trying to share and decide whether they can handle those objects or not. They communicate this to iOS through a specific method that they will implement in their classes.

So let's say that we want to create an activity that can reverse any number of strings that are handed to it. Remember that when your app initializes the activity view controller through the `initWithActivityItems:applicationActivities:` method, it can pass an array of arbitrary objects to the first parameter of this method. So our activity is going to peek at all these objects in this arbitrary array, and if they are all strings, it is going to reverse them and then display all the reversed strings in the console.

1. Subclass `UIActivity` as shown here:

```
import UIKit

class StringReverserActivity: UIActivity {

    /*
    This will aggregate all the activity items that are acceptable by us.
    We will be passed an array of various class types and we will go through
    them all and only select the string items and put them in this array.
    */
    var activityItems = [NSString]()

}
```

2. Next, override the `activityType` method of your activity. The return value of this method is an object of type `NSString` that is a unique identifier of your activity. This value will not be displayed to the user and is just for iOS to keep track of your activity's identifier. There are no specific values that you are asked to return from this method and no guidelines available from Apple, but we will follow the reverse-domain string format and use our app's bundle identifier and append the name of our class to the end of it. So if our bundle identifier is equal to *com.pixoli ty.ios.cookbook.myapp* and our class name is `StringReverserActivity`, we will return *com.pixolity.ios.cookbook.myapp.StringReverserActivity* from this method, like so:

```
override func activityType() -> String {
  return NSBundle.mainBundle().bundleIdentifier! + ".StringReverserActivity"
}
```

3. The next method to override is the `activityTitle` method, which should return a string to be displayed to the user in the activity view controller. Make sure this string is short enough to fit into the activity view controller:

```
override func activityTitle() -> String {
  return "Reverse String"
}
```

4. The next method is `activityImage`, which has to return an instance of `UIImage` that gets displayed in the activity view controller. Make sure that you provide both

Retina and non-Retina versions of the image for both iPad and iPhone/iPod. The iPad Retina image has to be 110×110 pixels and the iPhone Retina image has to be 86×86 pixels. Obviously, divide these dimensions by 2 to get the width and the height of the non-Retina images. iOS uses only the alpha channel in this image, so make sure your image's background is transparent and that you illustrate your image with the color white or the color black. I have already created an image in my app's image assets section, and I've named the image "Reverse," as you can see in Figure 1-29. Here is our code, then:

```
override func activityImage() -> UIImage {
  return UIImage(named: "Reverse")!
}
```

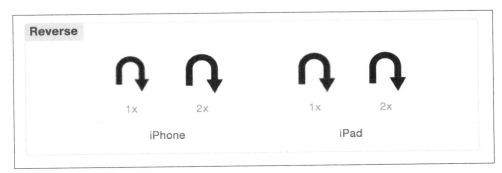

Figure 1-29. Our asset category contains images for our custom activity

5. Implement the `canPerformWithActivityItems:` method of your activity. This method's parameter is an array that will be set when an array of activity items is passed to the constructor of the activity view controller. Remember, these are objects of arbitrary type. The return value of your method will be a Boolean indicating whether you can perform your actions on any of the given items or not. For instance, our activity can reverse any number of strings that it is given. So if we find one string in the array, that is good enough for us because we know we will later be able to reverse that string. If we are given an array of 1,000 objects that contains only 2 strings, we will still accept it. But if we are given an array of 1,000 objects, none of which are of our acceptable type, we will reject this request by returning `false` from this method:

```
override func canPerformWithActivityItems(
    activityItems: [AnyObject]) -> Bool {

    for object:AnyObject in activityItems{
      if object is String{
        return true
      }
```

```
    }

        return false

    }
```

6. Now implement the `prepareWithActivityItems:` method of your activity, whose parameter is of type `NSArray`. This method gets called if you returned `true` from the `canPerformWithActivityItems:` method. You have to retain the given array for later use or you may choose to retain only the objects that you need in this array, such as the string objects. You may choose to retain only the objects you need in this array, such as the string objects.

```
override func prepareWithActivityItems(paramActivityItems: [AnyObject]) {

    for object:AnyObject in paramActivityItems{
      if object is String{
        activityItems.append(object as String)
      }
    }

}
```

7. Last but not least, you need to implement the `performActivity` method of your activity, which gets called when iOS wants you to actually perform your actions on the list of previously-provided arbitrary objects. In this method, basically, you have to perform your work. In our activity, we are going to go through the array of string objects that we extracted from this arbitrary array, reverse all of them, and display them in the console. You can come up with a better way of displaying these items or doing something more useful with them perhaps. But for the purpose of this recipe, we are simply going to display them in the console.

```
func reverseOfString(string: NSString) -> NSString{

    var result = ""
    var characters = [Character]()

    for character in string as String{
      characters.append(character)
    }

    for character in characters.reverse(){
      result += "\(character)"
    }

    return result

}
```

```
override func performActivity() {

  var reversedStrings = ""

  for string in activityItems{
    reversedStrings += reverseOfString(string) + "\n"
  }

  /* Do whatever you need to do with all these
  reversed strings */
  println(reversedStrings)

}
```

We are done with the implementation of our activity class. Now let's go to our view controller's implementation file and display the activity view controller with our custom activity in the list:

```
import UIKit

class ViewController: UIViewController {

  override func viewDidAppear(animated: Bool) {
    super.viewDidAppear(animated)

    let itemsToShare = [
      "Item 1" as NSString,
      "Item 2" as NSString,
      "Item 3" as NSString
    ]

    let activityController = UIActivityViewController(
      activityItems: itemsToShare,
      applicationActivities:[StringReverserActivity()])

    presentViewController(activityController, animated: true, completion: nil)

  }

}
```

When the app runs for the first time, you will see something similar to Figure 1-30 on the screen.

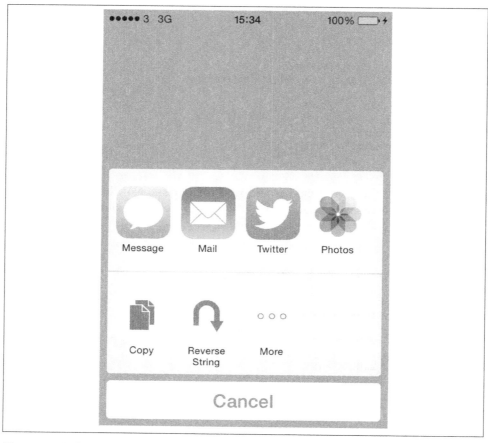

Figure 1-30. Our custom Reverse String activity is showing in the list of available activities

See Also

Recipe 1.12

1.14. Displaying an Image on a Navigation Bar

Problem

You want to display an image instead of text as the title of the current view controller on the navigation controller.

Solution

Use the `titleView` property of the view controller's navigation item:

```swift
import UIKit

class ViewController: UIViewController {

  override func viewDidLoad() {
    super.viewDidLoad()

    /* Create an Image View to replace the Title View */
    let imageView = UIImageView(
      frame: CGRect(x: 0, y: 0, width: 100, height: 40))

    imageView.contentMode = .ScaleAspectFit

    let image = UIImage(named:"Logo")

    imageView.image = image

    /* Set the Title View */
    navigationItem.titleView = imageView

  }

}
```

The preceding code must be executed in a view controller that is placed inside a navigation controller.

I have already loaded an image into my project's assets group and named it "Logo." When you run this app with the given code snippet, you'll see something similar to that shown in Figure 1-31.

Figure 1-31. An image view in our navigation bar

Discussion

The navigation item of every view controller can display two types of content in the title area of the view controller to which it is assigned:

- Simple text
- A view

If you want to use text, you can use the `title` property of the navigation item. However, if you want more control over the title or if you simply want to display an image or any other view on the navigation bar, you can use the `titleView` property of the navigation item of a view controller. You can assign any object that is a subclass of the `UIView` class. In our example, we created an image view and assigned an image to it. Then we displayed it as the title of the current view controller on the navigation controller.

The `titleView` property of the navigation bar is just a simple view, but Apple recommends that you limit the height of this view to no more than 128 points. So think about it in terms of the image. If you are loading an image that is 128 *pixels* in height, that will translate to *64 points on a Retina display*, so in that case you are fine. But if you are loading an image that is 300 pixels in height, on a Retina display, that will translate to 150 points in height, so you'll be well over the 128-point limit that Apple recommends for the title bar view height. To remedy this situation, you need to ensure that your title view is never taller than 128 points height-wise and set the view's content mode to fill the view, instead of stretching the view to fit the content. This can be done by setting the `contentMode` property of your title bar view to `UIViewContentModeScaleAspect Fit`.

1.15. Adding Buttons to Navigation Bars Using UIBarButtonItem

Problem

You want to add buttons to a navigation bar.

Solution

Use the `UIBarButtonItem` class.

Discussion

A navigation bar can contain different items. Buttons are often displayed on the left and the right sides. These buttons are of class `UIBarButtonItem` and can take many different shapes and forms. Let's have a look at an example in Figure 1-32.

Figure 1-32. Different buttons displayed on a navigation bar

Navigation bars are of class UINavigationBar and can be created at any time and added to any view. Just look at all the different buttons with different shapes that have been added to the navigation bar in Figure 1-32. The ones on the top right have up and down arrows, and the one on the top left has an arrow pointing to the left. We will have a look at creating some of these buttons in this recipe.

In order to create a navigation button, we must do the following:

1. Create an instance of UIBarButtonItem.
2. Add that button to the navigation bar of a view controller using the view controller's navigationItem property. The navigationItem property allows us to interact with the navigation bar. This property has two properties: rightBarButtonItem and leftBarButtonItem. Both of these properties are of type UIBarButtonItem.

Let's have a look at an example where we add a button to the right side of our navigation bar. In this button, we will display the text "Add":

```
import UIKit

class ViewController: UIViewController {

  func performAdd(sender: UIBarButtonItem){
    println("Add method got called")
  }

  override func viewDidLoad() {
    super.viewDidLoad()

    navigationItem.rightBarButtonItem = UIBarButtonItem(
      title: "Add",
      style: .Plain,
      target: self,
      action: "performAdd:")

  }

}
```

Now when we run our app we will see something similar to Figure 1-33.

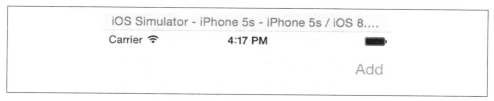

Figure 1-33. A navigation button added to a navigation bar

That was easy. But if you are an iOS user, you have probably noticed that the system apps that come preconfigured on iOS have a different Add button. Figure 1-34 shows an example in the Alarm section of the Clock app on the iPhone (notice the + button on the top right of the navigation bar).

Figure 1-34. The proper way of creating an Add button

It turns out that the iOS SDK allows us to create *system* buttons on the navigation bar. We do that by using the initWithBarButtonSystemItem:target:action: constructor of the UIBarButtonItem class:

```
import UIKit

class ViewController: UIViewController {

  func performAdd(sender: UIBarButtonItem){
    println("Add method got called")
  }

  override func viewDidLoad() {
    super.viewDidLoad()

    navigationItem.rightBarButtonItem = UIBarButtonItem(
      barButtonSystemItem: .Add,
      target: self,
      action: "performAdd:")

  }

}
```

And the results are exactly what we were looking for (Figure 1-35).

Figure 1-35. A system Add button

The first parameter of the `initWithBarButtonSystemItem:target:action:` constructor method of the navigation button can have any of the values listed in the `UIBarButtonSystemItem` enumeration.

One of the really great constructors of the `UIBarButtonItem` class is the `initWithCustomView:` method. As its parameter, this method accepts any view. This means we can even add a `UISwitch` (see Recipe 1.7) as a button on the navigation bar. This won't look very good, but let's give it a try:

```
import UIKit

class ViewController: UIViewController {

  func switchIsChanged(sender: UISwitch){
    if sender.on{
      println("Switch is on")
    } else {
      println("Switch is off")
    }
  }

  override func viewDidLoad() {
    super.viewDidLoad()

    let simpleSwitch = UISwitch()
    simpleSwitch.on = true

    simpleSwitch.addTarget(self,
      action: "switchIsChanged:",
      forControlEvents: .ValueChanged)

    self.navigationItem.rightBarButtonItem =
      UIBarButtonItem(customView: simpleSwitch)

  }

}
```

And Figure 1-36 shows the results.

Figure 1-36. A switch added to a navigation bar

You can create pretty amazing navigation bar buttons. Just take a look at what Apple has done with the up and down arrows on the top-right corner of Figure 1-32. Let's do the same thing, shall we? Well, it looks like the button actually contains a segmented control (see Recipe 1.11). So we should create a segmented control with two segments, add it to a navigation button, and finally place the navigation button on the navigation bar. Let's get started:

```
import UIKit

class ViewController: UIViewController {

  let items = ["Up", "Down"]

  func segmentedControlTapped(sender: UISegmentedControl){

    if sender.selectedSegmentIndex < items.count{
      println(items[sender.selectedSegmentIndex])
    } else {
      println("Unknown button is pressed")
    }

  }

  override func viewDidLoad() {
    super.viewDidLoad()

    let segmentedControl = UISegmentedControl(items: items)
    segmentedControl.momentary = true

    segmentedControl.addTarget(self,
      action: "segmentedControlTapped:",
      forControlEvents: .ValueChanged)

    navigationItem.rightBarButtonItem =
      UIBarButtonItem(customView: segmentedControl)

  }

}
```

And Figure 1-37 shows what the output looks like.

Figure 1-37. A segmented control inside a navigation button

The `navigationItem` of every view controller also has two very interesting methods:

`setRightBarButtonItem:animated:`
Sets the navigation bar's right button.

`setLeftBarButtonItem:animated:`
Sets the navigation bar's left button.

Both methods allow you to specify whether you want the placement to be animated. Pass the value of `true` to the `animated` parameter if you want the placement to be animated. Here is an example:

```
let rightBarButton =
UIBarButtonItem(customView:segmentedControl)

navigationItem.setRightBarButtonItem(rightBarButton, animated: true)
```

See Also

Recipe 1.7; Recipe 1.11

1.16. Accepting User Text Input with UITextField

Problem

You want to accept text input in your user interface.

Solution

Use the `UITextField` class.

Discussion

A text field is very much like a label in that it can display text, but a text field can also accept text entry at runtime.

A text field allows only a single line of text to be input/displayed. As a result, the default height of a text field is system defined. In Interface Builder, this height cannot be modified, but if you are creating your text field in code, you can change the text field's height. A change in height, though, will *not* change the number of lines you can render in a text field, which is always 1.

Let's start to define our text field:

```
import UIKit

class ViewController: UIViewController {

    var textField: UITextField!

}
```

And then let's create the text field:

```
import UIKit

class ViewController: UIViewController {

    var textField: UITextField!

    override func viewDidLoad() {
        super.viewDidLoad()

        textField = UITextField(frame: CGRect(x: 0, y: 0, width: 200, height: 31))

        textField.borderStyle = .RoundedRect

        textField.contentVerticalAlignment = .Center

        textField.textAlignment = .Center

        textField.text = "Sir Richard Branson"
        textField.center = view.center
        view.addSubview(textField)

    }

}
```

Before looking at the details of the code, let's first have a look at the results (Figure 1-38).

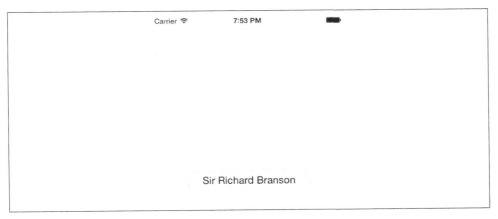

Figure 1-38. A simple text field with center-aligned text

In order to create this text field, we used various properties of `UITextField`.

borderStyle
: This property is of type `UITextBorderStyle` and specifies how the text field should render its borders.

contentVerticalAlignment
: This value is of type `UIControlContentVerticalAlignment` and tells the text field how the text should appear, vertically, in the boundaries of the control. If we didn't center the text vertically, it would appear on the top-left corner of the text field by default.

textAlignment
: This property is of type `NSTextAlignment` and specifies the horizontal alignment of the text in a text field. In this example, we centered the text horizontally.

text
: This is a read/write property: you can both read from it and write to it. Reading from it will return the text field's current text, and writing to it will set the text field's text to the value that you specify.

A text field sends delegate messages to its delegate object. These messages get sent, for instance, when the user starts editing the text inside a text field, when the user enters any character into the text field (changing its contents in any way), and when the user finishes editing the field (by leaving the field). To get notified of these events, set the `delegate` property of the text field to your object. The delegate of a text field must conform to the `UITextFieldDelegate` protocol, so let's first take care of this:

```
import UIKit

class ViewController: UIViewController, UITextFieldDelegate {
```

```
<# the rest of your code goes here #>

}
```

Hold down the Command key on your computer and click the `UITextFieldDelegate` protocol in Xcode. You will see all the methods that this protocol gives you control over. Here are those methods with descriptions of when they get called:

`textFieldShouldBeginEditing:`

A method that returns a `BOOL` telling the text field (the parameter to this method) whether it should start getting edited by the user or not. Return `false` if you don't want the user to edit your text field. This method gets fired as soon as the user taps on the text field with the goal of editing its content (assuming the text field allows editing).

`textFieldDidBeginEditing:`

Gets called when the text field starts to get edited by the user. This method gets called when the user has already tapped on the text field and the `textFieldShould BeginEditing:` delegate method of the text field returned `true`, telling the text field it is OK for the user to edit the content of the text field.

`textFieldShouldEndEditing:`

Returns a `BOOL` telling the text field whether it should end its current editing session or not. This method gets called when the user is about to leave the text field or the first responder is switching to another data entry field. If you return `false` from this method, the user will not be able to switch to another text entry field, and the keyboard will stay on the screen.

`textFieldDidEndEditing:`

Gets called when the editing session of the text field ends. This happens when the user decides to edit some other data entry field or uses a button provided by the supplier of the app to dismiss the keyboard shown for the text field.

`textField:shouldChangeCharactersInRange:replacementString:`

Gets called whenever the text inside the text field is modified. The return value of this method is a Boolean. If you return `true`, you say that you allow the text to be changed. If you return `false`, the change in the text of the text field will *not* be confirmed and will not happen.

`textFieldShouldClear:`

Each text field has a *clear* button that is usually a circular X button. When the user presses this button, the contents of the text field will automatically get erased. We need to manually enable the clear button, though. If you have enabled the clear button and you return `false` to this method, that gives the user the impression that your app isn't working, so make sure you know what you are doing. It is a very poor user experience if the user sees a clear button and presses it but doesn't see the text in the text field get erased.

textFieldShouldReturn:

Gets called when the user has pressed the Return/Enter key on the keyboard, trying to dismiss the keyboard. You should assign the text field as the first responder in this method.

Let's mix this recipe with Recipe 1.4 and create a dynamic text label under our text field. We'll also display the total number of characters entered in our text field in the label.

```
import UIKit

class ViewController: UIViewController, UITextFieldDelegate {

  var textField: UITextField!
  var label: UILabel!

}
```

We skip implementing many of the UITextFieldDelegate methods, because we don't need all of them in this example:

```
import UIKit

class ViewController: UIViewController, UITextFieldDelegate {

  var textField: UITextField!
  var label: UILabel!

  func calculateAndDisplayTextFieldLengthWithText(text: String){

    var characterOrCharacters = "Character"
    if countElements(text) != 1{
      characterOrCharacters += "s"
    }

    let stringLength = countElements(text)

    label.text = "\(stringLength) \(characterOrCharacters)"

  }


  func textField(paramTextField: UITextField,
    shouldChangeCharactersInRange range: NSRange,
    replacementString string: String) -> Bool{

    let text = paramTextField.text as NSString

    let wholeText =
    text.stringByReplacingCharactersInRange(
```

```
        range, withString: string)

        calculateAndDisplayTextFieldLengthWithText(wholeText)

        return true

    }

    func textFieldShouldReturn(paramTextField: UITextField) -> Bool{
      paramTextField.resignFirstResponder()
      return true
    }

    override func viewDidLoad() {
      super.viewDidLoad()

      textField = UITextField(frame:
        CGRect(x: 38, y: 30, width: 220, height: 31))

      textField.delegate = self
      textField.borderStyle = .RoundedRect
      textField.contentVerticalAlignment = .Center
      textField.textAlignment = .Center
      textField.text = "Sir Richard Branson"
      view.addSubview(textField)

      label = UILabel(frame: CGRect(x: 38, y: 61, width: 220, height: 31))
      view.addSubview(label)
      calculateAndDisplayTextFieldLengthWithText(textField.text)

    }

  }
```

One important calculation we are doing takes place in the textField:shouldChange
CharactersInRange:replacementString: method. There, we declare and use a variable called wholeText. When this method gets called, the replacementString parameter specifies the string that the user has entered into the text field. You might be thinking
that the user can enter only one character at a time, so why can't this field be a char?
But don't forget that the user can paste a whole chunk of text into a text field, so this
parameter needs to be a string. The shouldChangeCharactersInRange parameter specifies where, in terms of location inside the text field's text, the user is entering the text.
So using these two parameters, we will create a string that first reads the whole text
inside the text field and then uses the given range to place the new text inside the old
text. With this, we will come up with the text that will appear in the text field *after* the
textField:shouldChangeCharactersInRange:replacementString: method returns
true. Figure 1-39 shows how our app looks when it gets run on the simulator.

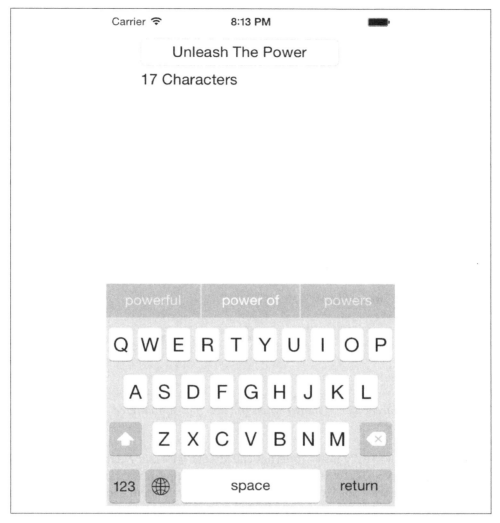

Figure 1-39. Responding to delegate messages of a text field

In addition to displaying text, a text field can also display a *placeholder*. A placeholder is the text displayed *before* the user has entered any text in the text field, while the text field's text property is empty. This can be any string that you wish, and setting it will help give the user an indication as to what this text field is for. Many use this placeholder to tell the user what type of value she can enter in that text field. You can use the `placeholder` property of the text field to set or get the current placeholder. Here is an example:

```
import UIKit

class ViewController: UIViewController {

  var textField: UITextField

  override func viewDidLoad() {
    super.viewDidLoad()

    textField = UITextField(frame:
      CGRect(x: 38, y: 30, width: 220, height: 31))

    textField.borderStyle = .RoundedRect
    textField.contentVerticalAlignment = .Center
    textField.textAlignment = .Center
    textField.placeholder = "Enter your text here..."
    view.addSubview(textField)

  }

}
```

The results are shown in Figure 1-40.

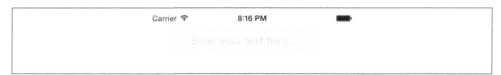

Figure 1-40. A placeholder is shown when the user has not entered any text in a text field

Text fields have two really neat properties called leftView and rightView. These two properties are of type UIView and are read/write. They appear, as their names imply, on the left and the right side of a text field if you assign a view to them. One place you might use a left view, for instance, is if you are displaying a currency text field where you would like to display the currency of the user's current country in the left view as a UILabel. Here is how we can accomplish that:

```
let currencyLabel = UILabel(frame: CGRectZero)
currencyLabel.text = NSNumberFormatter().currencySymbol
currencyLabel.font = theTextField.font
currencyLabel.textAlignment = .Right
currencyLabel.sizeToFit()
/* Give more width to the label so that it aligns properly on the
   text field's left view when the label's text itself is right aligned
*/
currencyLabel.frame.size.width += 10
theTextField.leftView = currencyLabel
```

```
    theTextField.leftViewMode = .Always
    view.addSubview(theTextField)
```

If we simply assign a view to the `leftView` or to the `rightView` properties of a text field, those views will not appear automatically by default. When they show up on the screen depends on the mode that governs their appearance, and you can control that mode using the `leftViewMode` and `rightViewMode` properties, respectively. These modes are of type `UITextFieldViewMode`.

So if, for instance, you set the left view mode to `UITextFieldViewModeWhileEditing` and assign a value to it, it will appear only while the user is editing the text field. Conversely, if you set this value to `UITextFieldViewModeUnlessEditing`, the left view will appear only while the user is *not* editing the text field. As soon as editing starts, the left view will disappear. Let's have a look at our code now in the simulator (Figure 1-41).

Figure 1-41. A text field with a left view

See Also

Recipe 1.4

1.17. Displaying Long Lines of Text with UITextView

Problem

You want to display multiple lines of text in your UI inside one scrollable view.

Solution

Use the `UITextView` class.

Discussion

The `UITextView` class can display multiple lines of text and contain scrollable content, meaning that if the contents run off the boundaries of the text view, the text view's internal components allow the user to scroll the text up and down to see different parts of the text. An example of a text view is shown in Figure 1-42.

Figure 1-42. A text view is displayed on the screen

Let's create a text view and see how it works. We start off by declaring the text view in our view controller:

```
import UIKit

class ViewController: UIViewController {

    var textView: UITextView?

}
```

Now it's time to create the text view itself. We will make the text view as big as the view controller's view:

```
import UIKit

class ViewController: UIViewController {

    var textView: UITextView?

    override func viewDidLoad() {
      super.viewDidLoad()

      textView = UITextView(frame: view.bounds)
```

```
    if let theTextView = textView{
      theTextView.text = "Some text goes here..."

      theTextView.contentInset =
        UIEdgeInsets(top: 10, left: 0, bottom: 0, right: 0)

      theTextView.font = UIFont.systemFontOfSize(16)
      view.addSubview(theTextView)
    }

  }

}
```

Now let's run the app and see how it looks (Figure 1-43).

Carrier 📶	8:43 PM	▬
Some text goes here...		

Figure 1-43. A text view consuming the entire boundary of the screen

If you tap on the text field, you will notice a keyboard pop up from the bottom of the screen, concealing almost half the entire area of the text view. That means if the user starts typing text and gets to the middle of the text view, the rest of the text that she types will *not* be visible to her.

To remedy this, we have to listen for certain notifications:

UIKeyboardWillShowNotification
  Gets sent by the system whenever the keyboard is brought up on the screen for any component, be it a text field, a text view, etc.

UIKeyboardDidShowNotification
  Gets sent by the system when the keyboard has already been displayed.

UIKeyboardWillHideNotification
  Gets sent by the system when the keyboard is about to hide.

UIKeyboardDidHideNotification
  Gets sent by the system when the keyboard is now fully hidden.

The keyboard notifications contain a dictionary, accessible through the userInfo property, that specifies the boundaries of the keyboard on the screen. This property is of type NSDictionary. One of the keys in this dictionary is UIKeyboardFrameEndUserInfoKey, which contains an object of type NSValue that itself contains the rectangular boundaries of the keyboard when it is fully shown. This rectangular area is denoted with a CGRect.

So our strategy is to find out when the keyboard is getting displayed and then somehow resize our text view. For this, we will use the `contentInset` property of `UITextView` to specify the margins of contents in the text view from top, left, bottom, and right:

```
import UIKit

class ViewController: UIViewController {

  var textView: UITextView?

  let defaultContentInset =
  UIEdgeInsets(top: 10, left: 0, bottom: 0, right: 0)

  func handleKeyboardDidShow (notification: NSNotification){

    /* Get the frame of the keyboard */
    let keyboardRectAsObject =
    notification.userInfo![UIKeyboardFrameEndUserInfoKey] as NSValue

    /* Place it in a CGRect */
    var keyboardRect = CGRectZero

    keyboardRectAsObject.getValue(&keyboardRect)

    /* Give a bottom margin to our text view that makes it
    reach to the top of the keyboard */
    textView!.contentInset =
      UIEdgeInsets(top: defaultContentInset.top,
        left: 0, bottom: keyboardRect.height, right: 0)
  }

  func handleKeyboardWillHide(notification: NSNotification){
    textView!.contentInset = defaultContentInset
  }

  override func viewDidLoad() {
    super.viewDidLoad()

    textView = UITextView(frame: view.bounds)
    if let theTextView = textView{
      theTextView.text = "Some text goes here..."
      theTextView.font = UIFont.systemFontOfSize(16)
      theTextView.contentInset = defaultContentInset

      view.addSubview(theTextView)

      NSNotificationCenter.defaultCenter().addObserver(
        self,
        selector: "handleKeyboardDidShow:",
        name: UIKeyboardDidShowNotification,
        object: nil)
```

```
    NSNotificationCenter.defaultCenter().addObserver(
      self,
      selector: "handleKeyboardWillHide:",
      name: UIKeyboardWillHideNotification,
      object: nil)

  }

}

deinit{
  NSNotificationCenter.defaultCenter().removeObserver(self)
}

}
```

In this code, we start looking for keyboard notifications in `viewWillAppear:` and we stop listening to keyboard notifications in `viewWillDisappear:`. Removing your view controller as the listener is important, because when your view controller is no longer displayed, you probably don't want to receive keyboard notifications fired by any other view controller. There may be times when a view controller in the background needs to receive notifications, but these are rare, and you must normally make sure to stop listening for notifications in `viewWillDisappear:`. I've seen many programmers break their apps by not taking care of this simple logic.

 If you intend to change your UI structure when the keyboard gets displayed and when the keyboard is dismissed, the only method that you can rely on is to use the keyboard notifications. Delegate messages of `UITextField` get fired when the text field is getting edited, whether there is a soft keyboard on the screen or not. Remember, a user can have a Bluetooth keyboard connected to his iOS device and use it to edit the content of text fields and any other data entry in your apps. In the case of a Bluetooth keyboard, no soft keyboard will be displayed on the screen—and if you change your UI when your text fields start to get edited, you might unnecessarily change the UI while the Bluetooth keyboard user is editing text.

Now, if the user tries to enter some text into the text view, the keyboard will pop up, and we take the height of the keyboard and assign that value as the bottom margin of the contents inside the text view. This makes our text view's contents smaller in size and allows the user to enter as much text as she wishes without the keyboard blocking her view.

1.18. Creating Scrollable Content with UIScrollView

Problem

You have content that needs to get displayed on the screen, but it requires more real estate than what the device's screen allows for.

Solution

Use the `UIScrollView` class.

Discussion

Scroll views are one of the features that make iOS a really neat operating system. They are practically everywhere. You've been to the Clock or the Contacts apps, haven't you? Have you seen how the content can be scrolled up and down? Well, that's the magic of scroll views.

There really is one basic concept you need to learn about scroll views: the *content size*, which lets the scroll view conform to the size of what it's displaying. The content size is a value of type `CGSize` that specifies the width and the height of the contents of a scroll view. A scroll view, as its name implies, is a subclass of `UIView`, so you can simply add your views to a scroll view using its `addSubview:` method. However, you need to make sure that the scroll view's content size is set properly; otherwise, the contents inside the scroll view *won't* scroll.

As an example, let's find a big image and load it to an image view. I will add the same image that I used in Recipe 1.3: Safari's icon. I will add it to an image view and place it in a scroll view. Then I will use the `contentSize` of the scroll view to make sure this content size is equal to the size of the image (width and height). First, let's define our image view and the scroll view:

```
import UIKit

class ViewController: UIViewController {
  var imageView: UIImageView!
  var scrollView: UIScrollView!
  let image = UIImage(named: "Safari")
}
```

And let's place the image view inside the scroll view:

```
import UIKit

class ViewController: UIViewController {
  var imageView: UIImageView!
  var scrollView: UIScrollView!
  let image = UIImage(named: "Safari")
```

```
    override func viewDidLoad() {
      super.viewDidLoad()

      imageView = UIImageView(image: image)
      scrollView = UIScrollView(frame: view.bounds)

      scrollView.addSubview(imageView)
      scrollView.contentSize = imageView.bounds.size
      view.addSubview(scrollView)

    }

  }
```

If you now load up the app in iOS Simulator, you will see that you can scroll the image horizontally and vertically. The challenge here, of course, is to provide an image that is bigger than the screen's boundaries. For example, if you provide an image that is 20×20 pixels, the scroll view won't be of much use to you. In fact, it would be wrong to place such an image into a scroll view, as the scroll view would practically be useless in that scenario. There would be nothing to scroll because the image is smaller than the screen size.

One of the handy features of UIScrollView is support for delegation, so that it can report really important events to the app through a delegate. A delegate for a scroll view must conform to the UIScrollViewDelegate protocol. Here are some of the methods defined in this protocol:

scrollViewDidScroll:
  Gets called whenever the contents of a scroll view get scrolled.

scrollViewWillBeginDecelerating:
  Gets called when the user scrolls the contents of a scroll view and lifts his finger off the screen as the scroll view scrolls.

scrollViewDidEndDecelerating:
  Gets called when the scroll view has finished scrolling its contents.

scrollViewDidEndDragging:willDecelerate:
  Gets called when the user finishes dragging the contents of the scroll view. This method is very similar to the scrollViewDidEndDecelerating: method, *but* you need to bear in mind that the user can drag the contents of a scroll view without scrolling the contents. She can simply put her finger on the content, move her finger to any location on the screen, and lift her finger without giving the contents any momentum to move. This is dragging as opposed to scrolling. Scrolling is similar to dragging, but the user will give momentum to the contents' movement by lifting her finger off the screen while the content is being dragged around, and not waiting for the content to stop before lifting her finger off the screen. Dragging is compa-

rable to holding down the accelerator in a car or pedaling on a bicycle, whereas scrolling is comparable to coasting in a car or on a bicycle.

So let's add some fun to our previous app. Now the goal is to set the alpha level of the image inside our image view to 0.50f (half transparent) when the user starts to scroll the scroll view and set this alpha back to 1.0f (opaque) when the user finishes scrolling. Let's begin by conforming to the UIScrollViewDelegate protocol:

```
import UIKit

class ViewController: UIViewController, UIScrollViewDelegate {
  var imageView: UIImageView!
  var scrollView: UIScrollView!
  let image = UIImage(named: "Safari")
}
```

Then let's implement this functionality:

```
func scrollViewDidScroll(scrollView: UIScrollView){
/* Gets called when user scrolls or drags */
  scrollView.alpha = 0.50
}

func scrollViewDidEndDecelerating(scrollView: UIScrollView){
/* Gets called only after scrolling */
  scrollView.alpha = 1
}

func scrollViewDidEndDragging(scrollView: UIScrollView!,
  willDecelerate decelerate: Bool){
    scrollView.alpha = 1
}

override func viewDidLoad() {
  super.viewDidLoad()

  imageView = UIImageView(image: image)
  scrollView = UIScrollView(frame: view.bounds)

  if let theScrollView = scrollView{
    theScrollView.addSubview(imageView!)
    theScrollView.contentSize = imageView!.bounds.size
    theScrollView.delegate = self
    view.addSubview(theScrollView)
  }

}
```

As you might have noticed, scroll views have *indicators*. An indicator is the little tracking line that appears on the sides of a scroll view when its contents are getting scrolled and moved.

Indicators simply show the user where the current view is in relation to the content (top, halfway down, etc.). You can control what the indicators look like by changing the value of the `indicatorStyle` property. For instance, here I have changed the indicator style of my scroll view to white:

```
theScrollView.indicatorStyle = .White
```

1.19. Loading Web Pages with WebKit

Problem

You want to display web pages to your user and be able to customize the user's interaction and experience with the web pages.

Solution

Use a blend of the following classes and protocols to load web pages to your UI:

WKWebView
> This is a web view that can load web contents. We will need to create an instance of NSURL to contain the URL that we want to load and then place that URL inside an instance of NSURLRequest that will encapsulate our request to the web view. Once the request is ready, we will ask the web view to load it.

WKPreferences
> This class will encapsulate our preferences for rendering web views. For instance, you can specify in your preferences that you do not want JavaScript to be loaded as part of loading the web page. When you are done creating your preferences, you should place them inside a web view configuration object.

WKWebViewConfiguration
> After the preferences are created, you must place them inside a configuration object and pass the configuration to the web view.

WKNavigationDelegate
> Whatever instance is assigned to the `navigationDelegate` property of your web view must confirm to this protocol. Using this protocol, you can, for instance, detect when the user taps on a link in the web view and then either accept or reject that request. There are many other things that you can do with the navigation delegate, as we shall soon see.

Let's start off by conforming to the WKNavigationDelegate protocol:

```
class ViewController: UIViewController, WKNavigationDelegate
```

Then we define our web view as a property of our controller:

```
var webView: WKWebView?
```

After that, we create our web view preferences, followed by the configuration objects, stating that we don't want our web view to process any JavaScript:

```
/* Create our preferences on how the web page should be loaded */
let preferences = WKPreferences()
preferences.javaScriptEnabled = false

/* Create a configuration for our preferences */
let configuration = WKWebViewConfiguration()
configuration.preferences = preferences
```

The next step is to create and configure the web view and add it to our view hierarchy:

```
/* Now instantiate the web view */
webView = WKWebView(frame: view.bounds, configuration: configuration)

if let theWebView = webView{
  /* Load a web page into our web view */
  let url = NSURL(string: "http://www.apple.com")
  let urlRequest = NSURLRequest(URL: url!)
  theWebView.loadRequest(urlRequest)
  theWebView.navigationDelegate = self
  view.addSubview(theWebView)

}
```

Our web view, depending on what page it is loading and which device it is loading the page on, may take a while to process our request. This calls for displaying the default system activity indicator to the user while the web view is processing the page for her. For that, we will implement two of the most important methods that are defined in the WKNavigationDelegate protocol, like so:

```
/* Start the network activity indicator when the web view is loading */
func webView(webView: WKWebView!,
  didStartProvisionalNavigation navigation: WKNavigation!){
    UIApplication.sharedApplication().networkActivityIndicatorVisible
      = true
}

/* Stop the network activity indicator when the loading finishes */
func webView(webView: WKWebView!,
  didFinishNavigation navigation: WKNavigation!){
    UIApplication.sharedApplication().networkActivityIndicatorVisible
      = false
}
```

The webView:didStartProvisionalNavigation: method gets called on the navigation delegate of your web view whenever a navigation has been provisioned to happen, before the web view asks you whether it is OK to make that navigation. We will give the answer to that question later. But for now, we see that the web view lets us know that a navigation is about to happen. The webView:didFinishNavigation: method of the navigation delegate gets called on our view controller when the web view has finished doing whatever navigation was requested of it. Here, we will use the opportunity to hide the network activity indicator that was previously displayed to the user.

The next thing we have to look at is the webView:decidePolicyForNavigationAction:decisionHandler: method of our web view's navigation delegate, which gets called whenever a navigation of any sort is about to happen in the web view. The navigationAction parameter will give you more information about what type of navigation is about to happen. If you inspect the navigationType property of the navigationAction parameter, you will be able to tell between the various types of navigations that can occur on a web view. One sort of navigation is when the user taps on a link—any link! The other is when the user submits a form for processing on a server or (for instance) when the user reloads a page.

We are now going to take advantage of the presence of this method on the navigation delegate of our web view and block the user from tapping on any link in the web page that we are displaying. Whenever she attempts to tap on a link, we will display an alert informing her that she is not allowed to tap on a link inside our application. This is for demonstration purposes, to give an example of how you can tap into the power of WebKit to control how your users interact with a web view. You may not necessarily be interested in blocking your user from tapping on various links on a web page.

```
/* Do not allow links to be tapped */
func webView(webView: WKWebView!,
  decidePolicyForNavigationAction navigationAction: WKNavigationAction!,
  decisionHandler: ((WKNavigationActionPolicy) -> Void)!){

    /* Do not allow links to be tapped */
    if navigationAction.navigationType == .LinkActivated{

      decisionHandler(.Cancel)

      let alertController = UIAlertController(
        title: "Action not allowed",
        message: "Tapping on links is not allowed. Sorry!",
        preferredStyle: .Alert)

      alertController.addAction(UIAlertAction(
        title: "OK", style: .Default, handler: nil))

      presentViewController(alertController,
        animated: true,
        completion: nil)

      return

    }

    decisionHandler(.Allow)
```

```
    }
```

Discussion

One of the really powerful frameworks in the iOS SDK is the WebKit framework. Using this framework, you can tap into many preferences and settings that Apple has enabled us to take control of. For instance, you can detect when the user wants to go back to the previous page or go forward to the next page. After you detect the type of event, you can then choose whether to allow it or to reject it.

As you saw earlier in the Solution section of this recipe, you can instantiate an instance of WKWebView using its constructor. This method takes the frame for the web view and the configuration, which must be of type WKWebViewConfiguration. You can leave this configuration empty, or create a proper instance of the aforementioned class and create your configuration as you will. Configurations for WebKit web views allow you to customize how users are able to interact with the web view. For instance, you can decide what happens if the user taps on a link that opens a new window.

Another handy navigation method that has been defined in the WKNavigationDelegate protocol is the webView:decidePolicyForNavigationResponse:decisionHandler: method. This method gets called when the navigation of a certain request on the web view has been finished and the results are now known by the web view. For instance, if the user taps on a link, the web view won't know what the content will be and what type it will have, whether it will be a media file, etc. until the content is loaded. But after the request is sent to the server and the response has been received, the aforementioned method gets called on the navigation delegate of the web view, informing it of content that is about to be loaded on the web view. You can implement this method to understand what content your web view is loading, such as the MIME type of the content. You can also allow or cancel the loading of these contents into your web view.

See Also

Recipe 1.20

1.20. Loading Web Pages with UIWebView

Problem

You want to load a web page dynamically right inside your iOS app.

Solution

Use the UIWebView class.

Discussion

A web view is what the Safari browser uses on iOS to load web content. You have the whole power of Safari in your iOS apps through the UIWebView class. All you have to do is place a web view on your UI and use one of its loading methods:

loadData:MIMEType:textEncodingName:baseURL:
    Loads an instance of NSData into the web view.

loadHTMLString:baseURL:
    Loads an instance of NSString into the web view. The string should be valid HTML, or in other words, something that a web browser can render.

loadRequest:
    Loads an instance of NSURLRequest. This is useful when you want to load the contents of a remote URL into a web view inside your application.

Let's see an example. I would like to load the string *iOS Programming* into the web view. To prove things are working as expected and that our web view is capable of rendering rich text, I will go ahead and make the *Programming* part bold while leaving the rest of the text intact:

```
import UIKit

class ViewController: UIViewController {

  override func viewDidLoad() {
    super.viewDidLoad()

    let webView = UIWebView(frame: view.bounds)
    let htmlString = "<br/>iOS <strong>Programming</strong>"
    webView.loadHTMLString(htmlString, baseURL: nil)
    view.addSubview(webView)

  }

}
```

Another way to use a web view is to load a remote URL into it. For this purpose, we can use the loadRequest: method. Let's go ahead and look at an example where we will load Apple's main page into a web view in our iOS app:

```
import UIKit

class ViewController: UIViewController {

  /* Hide the status bar to give all the screen real estate */
  override func prefersStatusBarHidden() -> Bool {
    return true
  }
```

```
override func viewDidLoad() {
  super.viewDidLoad()

  let webView = UIWebView(frame: view.bounds)
  webView.scalesPageToFit = true
  view.addSubview(webView)

  let url = NSURL(string: "http://www.apple.com")
  let request = NSURLRequest(URL: url!)

  webView.loadRequest(request)

  view.addSubview(webView)

  }

}
```

It might take quite a while for a web view to load the contents that you pass to it. You might have noticed that when loading content in Safari, you get a little activity indicator in the top-left corner of the screen telling you that the device is busy loading the contents. Figure 1-44 shows an example.

Figure 1-44. A progress bar indicating a loading process

iOS accomplishes this through delegation. We will subscribe as the delegate of a web view, and the web view will notify us when it starts to load content. When the content is fully loaded, we get a message from the web view informing us about this. We do this through the `delegate` property of the web view. A delegate of a web view must conform to the `UIWebViewDelegate` protocol.

Let's go ahead and implement the little activity indicator in our view controller. Please bear in mind that the activity indicator is already a part of the application and we don't have to create it. We can control it using the `setNetworkActivityIndicatorVisible:` method of `UIApplication`. So let's start:

```
import UIKit

class ViewController: UIViewController, UIWebViewDelegate
```

Then do the implementation. Here we will use three of the methods declared in the `UIWebViewDelegate` protocol:

webViewDidStartLoad:

This method gets called as soon as the web view starts loading content.

webViewDidFinishLoad:

This method gets called as soon as the web view finishes loading content.

webView:didFailLoadWithError:

This method gets called when the web view stops loading content, for instance because of an error or a broken network connection.

```
func webViewDidStartLoad(webView: UIWebView!){
  UIApplication.sharedApplication().networkActivityIndicatorVisible = true
}

func webViewDidFinishLoad(webView: UIWebView!){
  UIApplication.sharedApplication().networkActivityIndicatorVisible = false
}

func webView(webView: UIWebView!, didFailLoadWithError error: NSError!){
  UIApplication.sharedApplication().networkActivityIndicatorVisible = false
}

override func viewDidLoad() {
  super.viewDidLoad()

  /* Render the web view under the status bar */
  var frame = view.bounds
  frame.origin.y = UIApplication.sharedApplication().statusBarFrame.height
  frame.size.height -= frame.origin.y

  let webView = UIWebView(frame: frame)
  webView.delegate = self
  webView.scalesPageToFit = true
  view.addSubview(webView)

  let url = NSURL(string: "http://www.apple.com")
  let request = NSURLRequest(URL: url!)

  webView.loadRequest(request)

  view.addSubview(webView)

}
```

1.21. Displaying Progress with UIProgressView

Problem

You want to display a progress bar on the screen depicting the progress of a certain task; for instance, the progress of downloading a file from a URL.

Solution

Instantiate a view of type UIProgressView and place it on another view.

Discussion

A progress view is what programmers generally call a progress bar. An example of a progress view is depicted in Figure 1-45.

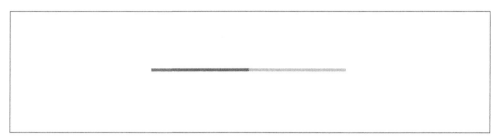

Figure 1-45. A simple progress view

Progress views are generally displayed to users to show them the progress of a task that has a well-defined starting and ending point. For instance, downloading 30 files is a well-defined task with a specific starting and ending point. This task obviously finishes when all 30 files have been downloaded. A progress view is an instance of UIProgress View and is initialized using the designated constructor of this class, the initWithProg ressViewStyle: method. This method takes in the style of the progress bar to be created as a parameter. This parameter is of type UIProgressViewStyle and can therefore be one of the following values:

UIProgressViewStyleDefault
> This is the default style of the progress view. An example of this is the progress view shown in Figure 1-45.

UIProgressViewStyleBar
> This is similar to the UIProgressViewStyleDefault but is meant to be used for progress views that are to be added to a toolbar.

An instance of UIProgressView defines a property called progress (of type float). This property tells iOS how the bar inside the progress view should be rendered. This value must be in the range +0 to +1.0. If the value of +0 is given, the progress bar won't appear to have started yet. A value of +1.0 shows progress of 100%. The progress depicted in Figure 1-45 is 0.5 (or 50%).

To get used to creating progress views, let's create one similar to what we saw in Figure 1-45. Instantiate an object of type UIProgressView:

```
import UIKit

class ViewController: UIViewController {

  override func viewDidLoad() {
    super.viewDidLoad()

    let progressView = UIProgressView(progressViewStyle: .Bar)
    progressView.center = view.center
    progressView.progress = 1/2
    progressView.trackTintColor = UIColor.lightGrayColor()
    progressView.tintColor = UIColor.blueColor()
    view.addSubview(progressView)

  }

}
```

Obviously, creating a progress view is very straightforward. All you really need to do is display your progress correctly, because the `progress` property of a progress view should be in the range +0 to +1.0, which is a normalized value. So if you have 30 tasks to take care of and you have completed 20 of them so far, you need to assign the result of the following equation to the `progress` property of your progress view:

```
progressView.progress = 20.0/30.0
```

In this code, we are explicitly creating two double values, 20 and 30, and then dividing the 20 by 30 in order to create the resulting value as a double value as well. Because the `progress` property of the progress view itself is a floating point value, the result of this division will be created as a floating point value instead of an integer. So we don't really have to worry about type casting or loss of precision in this division.

1.22. Creating a Provision Profile

Problem

You want to to set up a provision profile that you can use for your app development. You might also be interested in setting up an Ad Hoc or a distribution provision profile for deploying your app to an enterprise or series of testers, or for submitting your app to the App Store.

Solution

Follow these steps:

1. Create a certificate request using Keychain Access.
2. Create a development or a distribution certificate.

3. Create an App ID that corresponds to your application.

4. Create a provision profile that is linked to your certificate and your App ID, as is explained in the Discussion section of this recipe.

Discussion

Throughout the years that I've been working as an iOS engineer, I have seen many engineers who do not really understand the whole flow of creating provision profiles, or sometimes even what provision profiles are and what they do. That is not their fault. Apple has made this extremely difficult. Even though Xcode has tried to make this process easier, it still fails often and can't really read the developer's mind. For this reason, I've decided to explain the whole thing once and for all so that we are all on the same page.

Xcode's flow for creating provision profiles looks deceptively simple and fun, but don't be fooled. Xcode has a long way to go before it can really read your mind and create your profiles exactly how you would want them to be created. For this reason, Apple has kept the "Certificates, Identifiers & Profiles" section of the developer page updated regularly.

So let's get cracking. In this recipe, we are going to focus on creating a provision profile for debugging our app. This is also called a *development profile*. It's a profile that can only be used for development purposes and for debugging your apps on test devices.

The first thing that we need to do is to create a certificate signing request. Every profile is linked to a certificate and every certificate is linked to a private key. When you use Keychain (as we will soon see) to create a certificate signing request to send to Apple, your Keychain will create a private key for you and keep it ready for later. After we send our signing request to Apple, Apple will create a certificate for us. We will then need to import this certificate into our Keychain by double-clicking it. Once imported, Keychain will find the relevant private key that was generated before and will hook it up to the certificate so they become a pair.

So open up Keychain Access on your computer now, go to the Keychain Access menu, then Certificate Assistant, and choose "Request a Certificate From a Certificate Authority." You will then be presented with a screen similar to that shown in Figure 1-46. Enter your email address and your full name, then choose the "Save to disk" option. When you are done, press the Continue button and save the resulting code signing request file to your desktop.

Figure 1-46. Creating a certificate signing request in Keychain Access

At this point, Keychain Access has already created a private key for you, but that private key is not yet associated with any certificates. That's OK, though, because soon we are going to download a certificate from Apple and import it into Keychain.

Now you have a file named *CertificateSigningRequest.certSigningRequest* on your desktop. Navigate to the iOS Dev Center website and log in there if you are not already logged in. Then move to the "Certificates, Identifiers & Profiles" section of the portal and choose Certificates. On the lefthand side, under Certificates, choose Development as shown in Figure 1-47.

Figure 1-47. On our way to create a development certificate

Now press the plus button (+) to create a new development certificate. You can only have one development certificate, so if you have already created one, you might decide to revoke it and create a new one. Simply select the old certificate and press the Revoke button as shown in Figure 1-48.

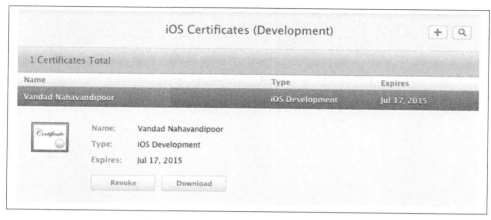

Figure 1-48. Revoking an old certificate

After pressing the plus (+) button, choose the option indicating that you want to create a development certificate and then move to the next step. You will be prompted to upload your code signing request file, which is currently saved on your desktop, to Apple's web site. Then wait a few seconds. After the wait is over, you will be given the ability to download the certificate. Please do so, and after your download is complete, double-click on your certificate to import it into Keychain Access.

Now navigate to the certificates section of your Keychain, find the certificate that was imported, and note that it is associated with the private key that was generated for you when you created the certificate signing request earlier, as shown in Figure 1-49.

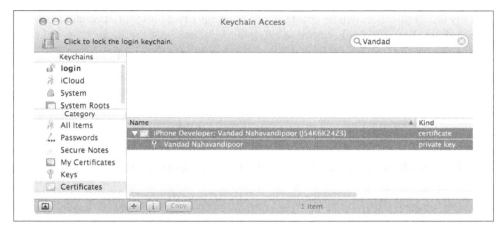

Figure 1-49. The certificate is associated with the private key

Now in the same Certificates, Identifiers & Profiles page of iOS Dev Center, move to the Identifiers section and then choose App IDs, as shown in Figure 1-50.

Figure 1-50. App IDs section of the portal

Press the plus (+) button to create a new App ID. In the App ID Description section, enter a description for your application. For instance, I have entered "iOS Cookbook App." This name will appear only in this list and not in Xcode, so if you are working in a team where a lot of people have access to one portal, make sure that you give meaningful names to your apps.

In the App ID Prefix section, ensure the default value of "Team ID" is selected. In the App ID Suffix section, ensure that the Explicit App ID is selected and in the Bundle ID: section, enter a reverse-domain-style identifier for your bundle. This identifier needs to uniquely identify your application and you have to use the same identifier in the bundle-identifier section of your app's plist. I have chosen the value of "com.pixolity.ios.cookbook.app" for this section.

Under the App Services section, choose all the services that you want your application to be able to use. For the purpose of this recipe, I have chosen every item in this list so that my test application will be able to take advantage of all these functionalities should I need them, but you can be more selective and choose only the items that make the most sense to you and your app. After you are done, press the Continue button.

Now you are on the Confirm your App ID page. Simply review your settings for your App ID and press the Submit button. When you are done, your App ID is ready. Bear in mind that an App ID is not something you can download or import. It is just an identifier for your app that will be associated with your provision profile in the portal.

Before you move on to creating your profile, you might want to register a few devices on which your app is able to run. You can do so by navigating to the All item under the Devices section of the portal. Now press the plus (+) button to add a new device. Enter a descriptive name for your device and the UDID of your device. You can find the UDID of the device by connecting it to your computer and then looking at the UDID in iTunes. Alternatively, if the device doesn't belong to you, you can ask the owner to use iTunes or the iPhone Configuration Utility to find the device's UDID. When you are done with that, press the Continue button to go to the review section. If all the details are correct, move past the review section to add the device to your portal.

Please note that any device added to your portal will count towards your total device quota for your membership. Most members can only add 100 devices per year, and any device that is deleted during this period will still count towards your quota until the membership period is over, upon which you can reset your list. This is to prevent people from adding billions of devices to their portal and creating an App Store competitor on their own where they can sign their apps with their own profiles and avoid having to send their apps to Apple for approval.

Next stop is creating the profile. In the same Certificates, Identifiers & Profiles page of iOS Dev Center, navigate to the Development item of the Provision Profiles section, as shown in Figure 1-51.

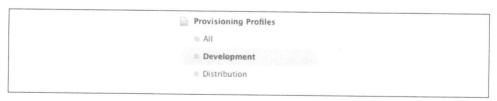

Figure 1-51. Development profiles

Press the plus (+) button to start generating a new development provision profile. Then choose the iOS App Development option and move on to the next stage. In the Select App ID section, choose the App ID that you just generated and move to the next stage. In the "Select certificates" section, choose the development certificate that you just created and move on to the next stage. When you get to the "Select devices" section, choose the devices that you want your app to be able to run on. After this, give a meaningful name to your profile and press the Generate button. This profile name will be visible in Xcode, so please, just like all the other names, ensure that this name is descriptive and not something similar to My Profile.

After you are done generating the profile, you can download it to your computer. After the profile is downloaded, install it by dragging it and dropping it into iTunes. Do not double-click on this profile because doing so will install the profile in your system with its MD5 hash value as its name. Thus, when you move to the *~/Library/MobileDevice/ Provisioning Profiles* folder on your computer to see the list of your profiles, you will see really cryptic names like that shown in Figure 1-52. As you can see, only one of the profiles has a meaningful name. The others have cryptic names because they were either installed on this sytem by Xcode or installed when the user double-clicked on them. If you want to see meaningful names on your computer and be able to manage these profiles easily, I suggest that you either copy and paste the profile directly to the afore-mentioned folder or drag and drop the profile onto iTunes for installation.

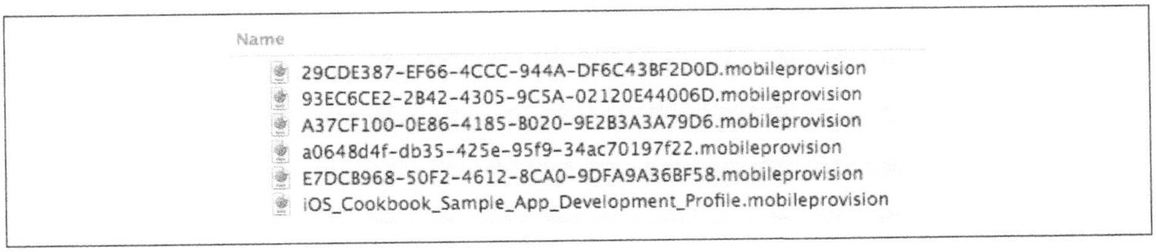

Name

29CDE387-EF66-4CCC-944A-DF6C43BF2D0D.mobileprovision
93EC6CE2-2B42-4305-9C5A-02120E44006D.mobileprovision
A37CF100-0E86-4185-B020-9E2B3A3A79D6.mobileprovision
a0648d4f-db35-425e-95f9-34ac70197f22.mobileprovision
E7DCB968-50F2-4612-8CA0-9DFA9A36BF58.mobileprovision
iOS_Cookbook_Sample_App_Development_Profile.mobileprovision

Figure 1-52. Only one of the profiles has a proper name

Congratulations. You have now created your profile. All you have to do in order to use it is to go to your app in Xcode and ensure that your *info.plist* has the same bundle identifier as the one that you designated in your profile, as shown in Figure 1-53.

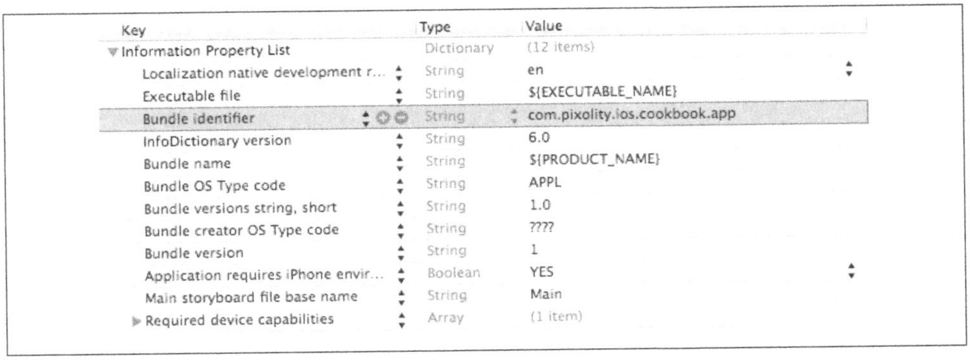

Key	Type	Value
▼ Information Property List	Dictionary	(12 items)
Localization native development r...	String	en
Executable file	String	${EXECUTABLE_NAME}
Bundle identifier	String	com.pixolity.ios.cookbook.app
InfoDictionary version	String	6.0
Bundle name	String	${PRODUCT_NAME}
Bundle OS Type code	String	APPL
Bundle versions string, short	String	1.0
Bundle creator OS Type code	String	????
Bundle version	String	1
Application requires iPhone envir...	Boolean	YES
Main storyboard file base name	String	Main
▶ Required device capabilities	Array	(1 item)

Figure 1-53. The bundle identifier in our plist has to match our profile

As the last step, move to the Build Settings of your project and set the correct certificate and the profile, as shown in Figure 1-54.

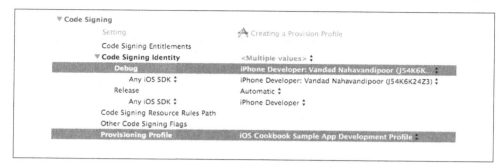

Figure 1-54. Setting the certificate and profile of the project

Build your project and ensure that it builds without errors. If it doesn't, make sure that you have followed all the steps explained in this recipe and attempt to build again until you get it right.

CHAPTER 2

Extensions

2.0. Introduction

Since the introduction of iOS, Apple has been very cautious about opening it up to developers to extend the system. The reason, at least officially, was that Apple wanted to find the right way of allowing access without compromising the security of user content and the system as a whole. In version 8 of iOS, developers are given a bit more control over how we can use iOS to provide content to the user. For instance, you can build custom keyboards or provide custom sharing extensions to the user.

To make an extension available to users, your app instantiates an object of type `UIActi vityViewController` and displays it on the screen like you would display any other view controller. When this view controller is displayed on the screen, iOS will look at all the extensions that are currently installed on the system and will display a sheet similar to that shown in Figure 2-1.

These are simply extensions provided by the system and third-party providers. The ones on top are sharing extensions and the ones on the bottom are action extensions. *Sharing extensions*, as the term suggests, take in content, such as a photo or text, and allow the user to share that item with others. For instance, if you open a photo, you can then directly share that with your followers on Twitter. *Action extensions* are those that perform some work on the item that is being shared and return immediately. For instance, you might want to provide a action extension that is called "Rotate 90 Degrees" that can take in a photo, rotate it 90 degrees, and immediately save it back.

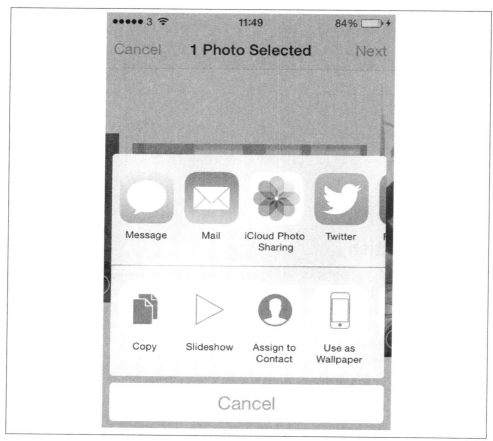

Figure 2-1. Activity controller

Extensions are not apps. They are separate binaries that are shipped with your app and are sent to Apple for review before Apple puts your app on the App Store. Extensions are separate targets in your apps and do not, by default, share any code or data with your application. However, you can enable them so that they can share data with your application, as we will see later in this chapter. Importantly, extensions that you create as part of your app can be executed by the system even when your app is not running. iOS will spin off a separate process to launch your extension when needed, and your extension has to perform its work then. When complete, iOS may tear off that process and go back to the user immediately.

Here are some rules to live by when providing extensions to the user:

- Make your extensions useful. Ensure that they actually provide exciting and valuable functionality; otherwise they are not worth the effort.

- Ensure your extensions work gracefully and quickly without crashing or taking too much of the CPU time.

- Use `NSURLSession` when

  you do networking in your extension. See Chapter 11 for more information.

As mentioned before, extensions are shipped with your app and become separate targets in your project. That means they have their own data storage as well as their own plist files and build settings. You can share information between your main app and your extension using the Keychain, `NSUserDefaults`, or `CoreData`, as we will see later.

An app that carries an extension with it is known as the *container app* from the extension's point of view. So when I refer to an *extension container* in this chapter, I mean the app that contains the extension. We also consider *host applications* in this picture. Host apps are those that cause your extension to launch. For instance, you may provide a sharing extension for sharing photos on your own social media website. When the user taps the photo in the Photos app and selects your extension to share that photo with her friends, there are four players in the picture:

Host app
    The Photos app in this scenario. The host app causes your extension to be launched.

Container app
    The app you wrote that owns the extension. This app may or may not be running while the extension is running.

Extension
    The extension itself, which will carry out the work for the host app.

iOS
    iOS will coordinate all activities between the other pieces of this picture.

In this scenario, where the user has opened a photo in the Photos app and then taps on your extension, control comes to your extension. The photo that the user was working on will also be made available to your extension to operate on. This coordination is performed by iOS through what is known as the *extension context*. The extension context is of type `NSExtentionContext` and is your way of getting your inputs from the host app, performing your work on them, and sending them back (if you want to) to the host app.

The extension context has a property called `inputItems` that is an array of `NSExtensionItem`. These are the items that the host app passed to your app, wrapped in this instance. You can use this instance (or these instances, if multiple items were passed to your extension) to retrieve the actual item's data and metadata, as we will see soon.

There are a few things you will need to do before you can go ahead and ship an application that contains an extension:

1. Ensure that you have designed appropriate icons for your application. It is best to assign the same icon to your app uses and your extension, because the user will be more likely to recognize who the provider of the extension is and whether to use it or not. If you are using asset catalogs to store your container app's icons, you can use the same icons for your extension by going to the General tab of your extension's project settings.

2. Ensure that your app is signed with a valid provision profile (see Recipe 1.22 for more information).

3. Ensure that your extension is also signed with a valid provision profile (see Recipe 1.22 for more information).

Bear in mind that when a container app is deleted, its associated extensions are deleted along with it.

2.1. Adding New Photo Editing Capabilities to the Photos App

Problem

You found a really cool image effect that you can apply to any image in the system, and you would like to expose that functionality to the user.

Solution

Follow these steps:

1. Add a new Photo Editing Extension target to your app.

2. Ensure that your extension is signed with a valid provision profile.

3. By default, your extension's view controller will conform to the PHContentEditing Controller protocol. So ensure that the canHandleAdjustmentData: method is implemented. We will discuss all of the methods mentioned in this list soon.

4. Implement your view controller's startContentEditingWithInput:placeholder Image: method. The input will be of type PHContentEditingInput and you can use that to construct your output of type PHContentEditingOutput as we will see soon. The placeholder image is the image that the user is currently editing. You can do what you will with this image, but usually, you would just take this image in and display it on your extension view controller while you apply your edits to the image in the background.

5. Implement the finishContentEditingWithCompletionHandler: method of your view controller and tell the completion handler the output that you produced.

6. Also implement the `cancelContentEditing` method of your view controller and ensure that you clean up after your editing operations if the user cancels your photo editing view controller before you are done.

Discussion

Every photo editing extension that you create will give you a view controller with some boilerplate code already baked in. You can read the comments that Apple has left in the view controller to understand the structure a bit better, but there is a lot to do before this view controller can actually be usable.

In this recipe, we are going to present our photo editing extension to the user to allow them to apply a "posterize" filter to their photos. So here is how we will get started. After you have created your main iOS app (the container app), go to the File menu in Xcode and choose New and then Target. Under the iOS category and Application Extensions subcategory, choose the Photo Editing Extension target and proceed to add it to your project (see Figure 2-2).

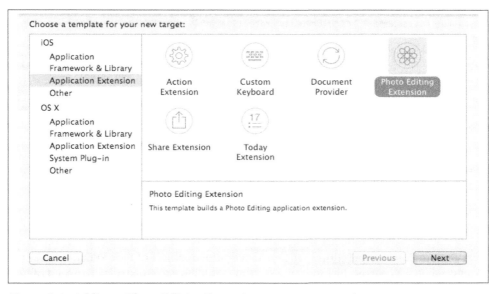

Figure 2-2. Adding a Photo Editing Extension target to our project

Now that you have a new target, look into your project structure to notice that a new folder has been added for you. I named my extension "PosterizeExtension" and the folder is also called the same. Under this folder, you will find a class called `PhotoEditingViewController`, which is the main view controller for your extension. Now I am going to provide the list of variables that my view controller needs with some comments so that you understand them better:

```swift
import UIKit
import Photos
import PhotosUI
import OpenGLES

class PhotoEditingViewController: UIViewController,
PHContentEditingController {

    /* An image view on the screen that first shows the original
    image to the user; after we are done applying our edits to the image,
    it will show the edited image */
    @IBOutlet weak var imageView: UIImageView!

    /* The input that the system will give us */
    var input: PHContentEditingInput!

    /* We give our edits to the user in this way */
    var output: PHContentEditingOutput!

    /* The name of the image filter that we will apply to the input image */
    let filterName = "CIColorPosterize"

    /* These two values are our way of telling the Photos framework about
    the identifier of the changes that we are going to make to the photo */
    let editFormatIdentifier = NSBundle.mainBundle().bundleIdentifier!

    /* Just an application specific editing version */
    let editFormatVersion = "0.1"

    /* A queue that will execute our edits in the background */
    let operationQueue = NSOperationQueue()

    let shouldShowCancelConfirmation: Bool = true

    <# rest of the code #>

}
```

Every photo editing operation is encapsulated into an object of type PHContentEditingInput when iOS passes the input image to you. You have to construct an output of type PHContentEditingOutput that will contain your edits. Constructing this output is pretty easy, as you will see soon.

If you've noticed, I am using OpenGLES in this project. The reason behind that is to retrieve an instance of NSData for a Core Image content of type CIImage. This is explained in Recipe 15.8, so I suggest that you have a look at that recipe to understand how we are doing the conversion. We are going to use Core Image to apply our filter to the UIImage instance that we will be given by iOS, so let's write a method that retrieves

---

the data from the `CIImage` instance. We will save this data to disk and ask iOS to pick it up from a specific location when our extension is done. This whole process was also explained in Recipe 15.8, so I highly recommend that you read that recipe before proceeding with this.

```
/* This turns an image into its NSData representation */
func dataFromCiImage(image: CIImage) -> NSData{
  let glContext = EAGLContext(API: .OpenGLES2)
  let context = CIContext(EAGLContext: glContext)
  let imageRef = context.createCGImage(image, fromRect: image.extent())
  let image = UIImage(CGImage: imageRef, scale: 1.0, orientation: .Up)
  return UIImageJPEGRepresentation(image, 1.0)
}
```

The core of our extension is the ability to take in an image and apply our filter on top of it. As mentioned before, the input to our extension will be of type `PHContentEditingInput` and the output has to be of type `PHContentEditingOutput`. We will therefore write a method that can take the input and translate it to the output that we need.

When iOS passes the image to you, it doesn't pass the real image that the user is seeing on her device. It will copy the image content into a location that is readable by your application. You can find the URL to this image by accessing the `fullSizeImageURL` property of your input. After you are done reading this image from the given URL, you can do your edits to it and then construct an instance of the `PHContentEditingOutput` class by providing the input to the constructor of this class. So now you have a valid and initialized instance of the `PHContentEditingOutput` class.

After you are done with your edits, convert the resulting image to its data equivalent of type `NSData` and save that data to the location specified by the `renderedContentURL` property of your output instance. Also ensure that you set the value of the `adjustmentData` property of your output to a valid instance of the `PHAdjustmentData` class. We will look at that in a moment.

```
/* This takes the input and converts it to the output. The output
has our posterized content saved inside it */
func posterizedImageForInput(input: PHContentEditingInput) ->
  PHContentEditingOutput{

    /* Get the required information from the asset */
    let url = input.fullSizeImageURL
    let orientation = input.fullSizeImageOrientation

    /* Retrieve an instance of CIImage to apply our filter to */
    let inputImage =
    CIImage(contentsOfURL: url,
      options: nil).imageByApplyingOrientation(orientation)

    /* Apply the filter to our image */
    let filter = CIFilter(name: filterName)
    filter.setDefaults()
```

```
filter.setValue(inputImage, forKey: kCIInputImageKey)
let outputImage = filter.outputImage

/* Get the data of our edited image */
let editedImageData = dataFromCiImage(outputImage)

/* The results of editing our image are encapsulated here */
let output = PHContentEditingOutput(contentEditingInput: input)

/* Here we are saving our edited image to the URL that is dictated
by the content editing output class */
editedImageData.writeToURL(output.renderedContentURL,
  atomically: true)

output.adjustmentData =
  PHAdjustmentData(formatIdentifier: editFormatIdentifier,
    formatVersion: editFormatVersion,
    data: filterName.dataUsingEncoding(NSUTF8StringEncoding,
      allowLossyConversion: false))

return output

}
```

iOS will keep track of all the edits that have ever been applied to an image and, when passing an image to an editing extension, will ask the extension whether it needs the original and unedited image or wants the image as it looks with the other filters applied. So we will implement the canHandleAdjustmentData: method to tell iOS that we are interested only in the original image and not any edits that have already been applied to it:

```
/* We just want to work with the original image */
func canHandleAdjustmentData(adjustmentData: PHAdjustmentData?) -> Bool {
  return false
}
```

Because we will have to be able to cancel our editing at any point when the user decides to cancel the whole editing session, we need to ensure that we have a way to stop our editing operation. The best way to do this is to encapsulate our edits in a closure and then submit that closure to an operation queue to execute as a block operation. If the user decides to cancel the edits, we will simply cancel all the operations in queue. Here is our closure that does the edits for us:

```
/* This is a closure that we will submit to our operation queue */
func editingOperation(){

  output = posterizedImageForInput(input)

  dispatch_async(dispatch_get_main_queue(), {[weak self] in
    let strongSelf = self!
```

```
    let data = NSData(contentsOfURL: strongSelf.output.renderedContentURL,
      options: .DataReadingMappedIfSafe,
      error: nil)

    let image = UIImage(data: data!)

    strongSelf.imageView.image = image
    })
}
```

We also need to implement the `startContentEditingWithInput:placeholder`
`Image:` method of our view controller now. This method will get called whenever our
extension view controller is about to be displayed on the screen. In this particular extension that we are creating, we need to ensure that the user will see how our posterize
filter will affect their image. So as soon as this method is called, we display the original
image on the screen. Then we kick off the filter in the background, and after the filter
is applied, we display the modified image to the user:

```
func startContentEditingWithInput(
  contentEditingInput: PHContentEditingInput?,
  placeholderImage: UIImage) {

    imageView.image = placeholderImage
    input = contentEditingInput

    /* Start the editing in the background */
    let block = NSBlockOperation(block: editingOperation)
    operationQueue.addOperation(block)

}
```

The `finishContentEditingWithCompletionHandler:` method of your view controller
will also get called when the user confirms that they are happy with your extension's
output and want to keep your changes. In here, you will have a completion handler that
you have to call and pass your output value to:

```
func finishContentEditingWithCompletionHandler(
  completionHandler: ((PHContentEditingOutput!) -> Void)!) {
    /* Report our output */
    completionHandler(output)
}
```

Last but not least, remember that the user can cancel the edits at any point, so ensure
that you've implemented the `cancelContentEditing` method of your view controller:

```
/* The user cancelled the editing process */
func cancelContentEditing() {
  /* Make sure we stop our operation here */
  operationQueue.cancelAllOperations()
}
```

Make sure that both your app and your extension are signed with valid provision profiles, and run your app on a device. Now switch to the Photos app and start editing a photo. You will now see the extensions button on the interface as shown in Figure 2-3. Press that button.

Figure 2-3. Photo extensions button is displayed on the top left corner

After pressing that button, you should be able to see your extension in the list of available extensions, as shown in Figure 2-4.

Figure 2-4. Our photo editing extension is displayed in the list

Press the extension and wait until the processing completes, whereupon you should see the posterized results as shown in Figure 2-5.

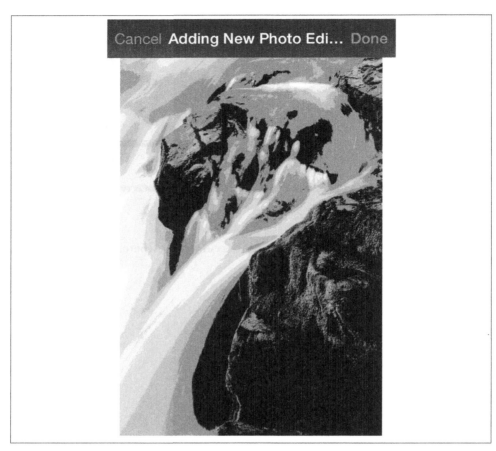

Figure 2-5. Our filter is applied to the image

You can now proceed to the next stage and save our extension's edits on the original image.

See Also

Recipe 2.0; Recipe 15.8; Recipe 1.22

2.2. Providing a Custom Sharing Extension to iOS

Problem

You want your application to be displayed in the list of apps that are able to handle a specific file type when the user is trying to share that file or files.

Solution

Add a Share Extension target to your application and configure it so that it can handle incoming data.

Discussion

A share extension is an extension to iOS that will appear in every activity view controller when the user presses the share button. This isn't limited to system applications. Any custom application that presents an instance of the UIActivityViewController class will be able to see your sharing extension if you built your extension so that it can handle a given file type, as we will soon see.

When you create a new sharing extension target for your project in Xcode, you will be able to see a new view controller called ShareViewController added to your project. This view controller subclasses the SLComposeServiceViewController class, which does all the heavy lifting to present your view controller. All you really have to do is provide implementations of a few functions and you are done.

Let's say that we want to create an image sharing extension whereby a user can select an image in any other app on the system, such as the Photos app, and then bring up the sharing sheet to use our extension. Our extension will ask for some comments on the text and then upload the image to our social media website (a hypothetical website, obviously).

So the first thing you have to do is to add the Sharing Extension target to your Xcode project. In Xcode, go to File menu, then New, and then Target. Under the iOS category and Application Extension subcategory, choose the Sharing Extension target as shown in Figure 2-6.

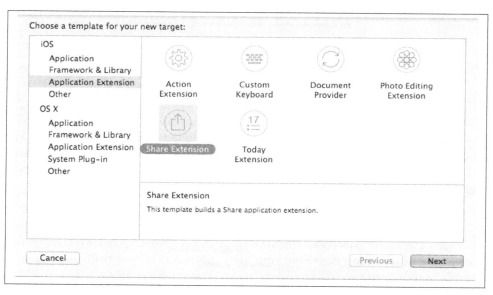

Figure 2-6. Adding a sharing extension to your app

You now have your `ShareViewController` class that we talked about. There is some boilerplate code that has been written for you by Apple, but we aren't going to need it so feel free to remove it.

Before proceeding any further, it probably helps if I could show you the end result that we are trying to achieve. When a user browses an image anywhere in the system and presses the share button, she will see our app in the list, as shown in Figure 2-7.

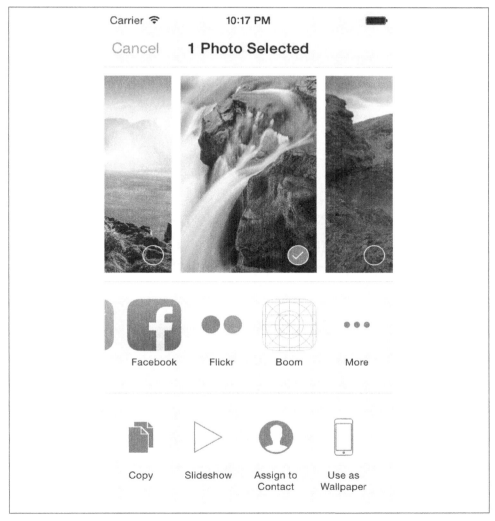

Figure 2-7. Our extension is called Boom and is displayed to the user

I have named this extension Boom under the assumption that our hypothetical social networking website is called that. When the user taps on our extension, she will see our `ShareViewController` instance, as shown in Figure 2-8.

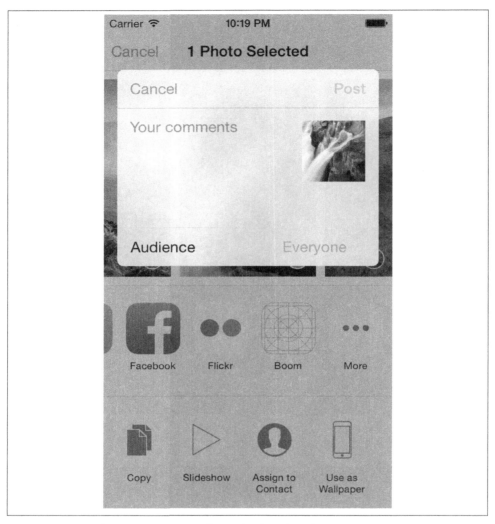

Figure 2-8. Our sharing view controller is displayed to the user

She can also limit the audience to her post by tapping on the Audience button to see a screen similar to that shown in Figure 2-9.

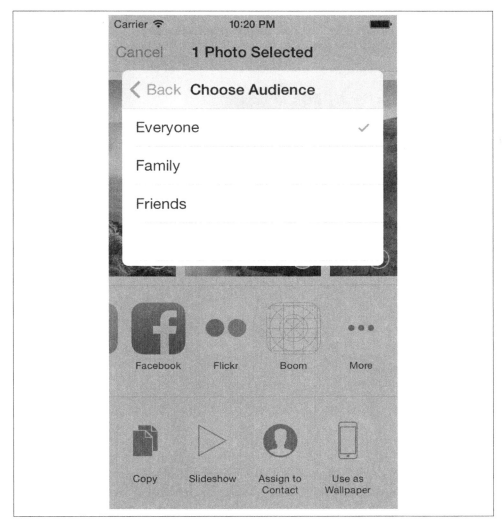

Figure 2-9. The user can choose the audience to the photo

When a comment has been entered in the comments section, our Post button will be enabled and the user can press that button. Upon pressing the post button, we will upload the selected image to our network alongside the entered text.

Brilliant! Now that we know what we are building, let's carry on with our `ShareView Controller` implementation. Let's begin by defining our variables:

```
import UIKit
import Social
import MobileCoreServices
```

```
class ShareViewController: SLComposeServiceViewController,
AudienceSelectionViewControllerDelegate, NSURLSessionDelegate {

  var imageData: NSData?

  <# rest of the code #>

}
```

The `AudienceSelectionViewControllerDelegate` is a protocol that we are going to
define in our audience selection view controller to allow the user to change the audience
of the uploaded photo. We will get to that soon, but for now all you have to know is that
we are conforming to this particular delegate and will write the code soon. The `image`
`Data` property is the data that we are going to extract from the image the user wants to
share. If we cannot load this data, we will not enable the Post button.

Let's go ahead and implement the `isContentValid` method of our view controller. This
method gets called whenever iOS wants to ask your view controller whether to enable
the Post button. Return a Boolean value here to enable or disable the Post button:

```
override func isContentValid() -> Bool {
  /* The post button should be enabled only if we have the image data
  and the user has entered at least one character of text */
  if let data = imageData{
    if countElements(contentText) > 0{
      return true
    }
  }

  return false
}
```

Now we need to implement the `presentationAnimationDidFinish` method of our view
controller. This method gets called just as our view controller is fully displayed on the
screen. You can use this method to take in the attachments that the system has sent you,
and then validate them. To do so, use the `inputItems` property of your extension context.
This property is an array of `NSExtensionItem` instances, which are the same items that
caused your extension to be shown on screen. In our example, we are going to want to
only allow the user to share one image at a time, so we will read the first item in this
array. Then we will read the content of the attached image and, if the data could be
loaded, ask the view controller to be validated again by calling its `validateContent`
method.

```
override func presentationAnimationDidFinish() {
  super.presentationAnimationDidFinish()

  placeholder = "Your comments"

  let content = extensionContext!.inputItems[0] as NSExtensionItem
```

```
let contentType = kUTTypeImage as NSString

for attachment in content.attachments as [NSItemProvider]{
  if attachment.hasItemConformingToTypeIdentifier(contentType){

    let dispatchQueue =
    dispatch_get_global_queue(DISPATCH_QUEUE_PRIORITY_DEFAULT, 0)

    dispatch_async(dispatchQueue, {[weak self] in

      let strongSelf = self!

      attachment.loadItemForTypeIdentifier(contentType,
        options: nil,
        completionHandler: {(content: NSSecureCoding!, error: NSError!) in
          if let data = content as? NSData{
            dispatch_async(dispatch_get_main_queue(), {
              strongSelf.imageData = data
              strongSelf.validateContent()
              })
          }
        })

    })

  }

  break
}

}
```

Then we need to implement the didSelectPost method. This method gets called whenever the user taps the Post button. Here we are going to post the data of the image that was being shared through our application and then use the NSURLSession class to upload that content to our website:

```
override func didSelectPost() {

  let identifier = NSBundle.mainBundle().bundleIdentifier! + "." +
    NSUUID().UUIDString

  let configuration =
  NSURLSessionConfiguration.backgroundSessionConfigurationWithIdentifier(
    identifier)

  let session = NSURLSession(configuration: configuration,
    delegate: self,
    delegateQueue: nil)

  let url = NSURL(string: "https://<# your url goes here#>/&text=" +
    self.contentText)
```

```
let request = NSMutableURLRequest(URL: url!)
request.HTTPMethod = "POST"
request.HTTPBody = imageData!

let task = session.uploadTaskWithRequest(request,
  fromData: request.HTTPBody)

task.resume()

extensionContext!.completeRequestReturningItems([], completionHandler: nil)
}
```

 To learn how to upload content to a URL using NSURLSession, please refer to Recipe 11.3.

Great stuff. The next method we have to implement is configurationItems, which has to return an array of SLComposeSheetConfigurationItem instances. These instances will determine what the sharing extension displays as extra configuration items. Our only configuration item is the Audience configuration item that allows the user to choose the audience, as we saw in Figure 2-8.

```
lazy var audienceConfigurationItem: SLComposeSheetConfigurationItem = {
  let item = SLComposeSheetConfigurationItem()
  item.title = "Audience"
  item.value = AudienceSelectionViewController.defaultAudience()
  item.tapHandler = self.showAudienceSelection
  return item
  }()

override func configurationItems() -> [AnyObject]! {
  return [audienceConfigurationItem]
}
```

You can see that the tap handler of our configuration item is set to the showAudience Selection closure of our view controller so that when the Audience option is tapped on the share controller, we can take action and display our audience selection view controller like so:

```
func showAudienceSelection(){
  let controller = AudienceSelectionViewController(style: .Plain)
  controller.audience = audienceConfigurationItem.value
  controller.delegate = self
  pushConfigurationViewController(controller)
}
```

As we will soon see, in our audience picker view controller, we will have a delegate property that will be called by us whenever the user has finished picking the required audience from a list that is presented as a table view. We will then call the `audienceSe lectionViewController:selectedValue:` method of the delegate. So we have to implement this method of the `AudienceSelectionViewControllerDelegate` protocol in our main extension view controller to pop the configuration view controller. This may sound strange, but all we want to do is to pop back to the main sharing extension view controller when the user is done picking her desired audience:

```
func audienceSelectionViewController(sender: AudienceSelectionViewController,
  selectedValue: String) {
    audienceConfigurationItem.value = selectedValue
    popConfigurationViewController()
}
```

Now let us start implementing the `AudienceSelectionViewController` class. First, we want to have a delegate for this class so that the delegate would be informed whenever an audience is selected in the list:

```
@objc(AudienceSelectionViewControllerDelegate)
protocol AudienceSelectionViewControllerDelegate{
  optional func audienceSelectionViewController(
    sender: AudienceSelectionViewController,
    selectedValue: String)
}
```

For the audience that we want to display in the table view, we are going to define a structure and then have a default audience value as well. When our view controller is initialized, we will register a class for reusable table view cells just like we should, and then set our view controller's title:

```
class AudienceSelectionViewController: UITableViewController {

  struct TableViewValues{
    static let identifier = "Cell"
  }

  enum Audience: String{
    case Everyone = "Everyone"
    case Family = "Family"
    case Friends = "Friends"
    static let allValues = [Everyone, Family, Friends]
  }

  var delegate: AudienceSelectionViewControllerDelegate?

  var audience = Audience.Everyone.rawValue

  class func defaultAudience() -> String{
    return Audience.Everyone.rawValue
  }

  required init(coder aDecoder: NSCoder) {
```

```
    super.init(coder: aDecoder)
  }

  override init(style: UITableViewStyle) {
    super.init(style: style)
    tableView.registerClass(UITableViewCell.classForCoder(),
      forCellReuseIdentifier: TableViewValues.identifier)
    title = "Choose Audience"
  }

  override init(nibName nibNameOrNil: String!, bundle nibBundleOrNil: NSBundle!){
    super.init(nibName: nibNameOrNil, bundle: nibBundleOrNil)
  }

  <# rest of the code #>

}
```

Last but not least, we need to provide the cells to our table view for every item that we have in our Audience enumeration:

```
override func tableView(tableView: UITableView,
  numberOfRowsInSection section: Int) -> Int {
    return Audience.allValues.count
}

override func tableView(tableView: UITableView,
  cellForRowAtIndexPath indexPath: NSIndexPath) -> UITableViewCell {
    let cell = tableView.dequeueReusableCellWithIdentifier(
      TableViewValues.identifier,
      forIndexPath: indexPath) as UITableViewCell

    let text = Audience.allValues[indexPath.row].rawValue

    cell.textLabel.text = text

    if text == audience{
      cell.accessoryType = .Checkmark
    } else {
      cell.accessoryType = .None
    }

    return cell
}

override func tableView(tableView: UITableView,
  didSelectRowAtIndexPath indexPath: NSIndexPath) {

    if let theDelegate = delegate{
      let selectedAudience = Audience.allValues[indexPath.row].rawValue
      theDelegate.audienceSelectionViewController!(self,
        selectedValue: selectedAudience)
```

```
        }

    }
```

Fantastic! We are almost done. There is one thing remaining, though. We need to tell iOS that our extension can handle only one image a time because our uploading mechanism can only support that. So what we need to do is to go into the plist file of our extension and find the `NSExtension` key. Under that key you will be able to see the `NSExtensionAttributes` key and under that, you need to create a new key called `NSEx tensionAttributes` of type `Dictionary`. This key's values specify exactly how you would like iOS to interact with your extension: specifically, how many items your extension can handle and when iOS is allowed to show your extension in the list of extensions that can handle a certain file type. Add the `NSExtensionActivationSupport sImageWithMaxCount` key under the `NSExtensionActivationRule` key and set its type to `Number` and give it a value of 1. This tells iOS that we can only handle images and only 1 image at a time. For now, this is enough information to get started with sharing extensions.

See Also

Recipe 2.0; Recipe 1.22

2.3. Building Custom Keyboards

Problem

You want to implement a keyboard that the user of the current iOS device can use on any iOS app in the system, not just your own app.

Solution

Add a Custom Keyboard extension (see Figure 2-10) to your app. This will cause Xcode to generate a view controller of type `UIInputViewController`. This view controller's view is your keyboard canvas. You can construct your keyboard in whatever way you want. The view is of type `UIView`, so you have to lay out your keyboard the way you imagine it looking like, and you need to implement it to work flawlessly in landscape and portrait mode on various iOS devices regardless of their screen size.

Figure 2-10. Adding a Custom Keyboard extension target to your project

Discussion

Users of iOS can use various keyboards that are provided by the system: for instance, US English, UK English, a Swedish keyboard, or even Emoji. iOS developers can also create keyboard extensions to be shipped alongside their apps and installed system-wide so users can use them in other applications as well.

When an app has a custom keyboard extension installed on the user's device, the user must go to her iOS device's Settings page and manually add the keyboard to the system (see Figure 2-11).

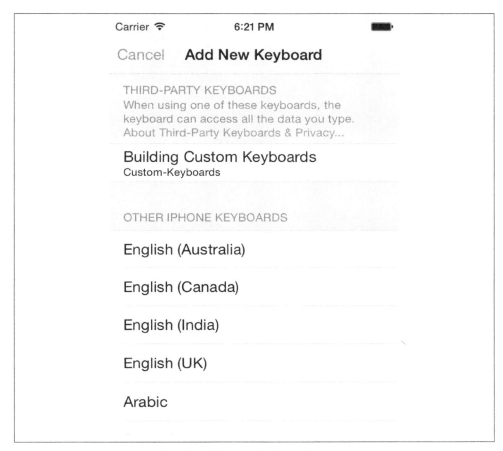

Figure 2-11. User must explicitly add a new keyboard

Begin creating your custom keyboard by adding a Custom Keyboard target to your app using Xcode. Now you have a new target and a new class in that target. This class is called KeyboardViewController by default. What we want to achieve in this recipe is to create a custom keyboard that, for the sake of simplicity, works only in portrait mode of an iPhone device and looks like that shown in Figure 2-12. However, if you are shipping a real app to the App Store, please ensure that your custom keyboard works flawlessly on various devices with different resolutions and in all orientations.

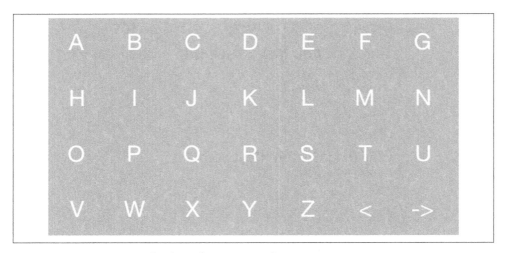

Figure 2-12. Our custom keyboard is very simplistic

Peek inside the KeyboardViewController class and you will notice that it subclasses the UIInputViewController class. This controller gives us access to some very important objects. For instance, we can get a proxy object to talk to the control on the current app that is using our keyboard. We will then be able to insert text into that control or delete text. We will need all this control in order to create a functional keyboard thauiint is able to allow the user to type with the keyboard and have the results appear in the control that currently has keyboard focus, on any app in the system.

One of the properties of this view controller that is going to be our gateway to the current control using our keyboard is the textDocumentProxy property. This is a proxy to the text input that our keyboard class is interacting with, as Apple puts it. In this view controller, we are going to load up our own view, which will be our keyboard view, so I have done that here:

```
import UIKit

class KeyboardViewController: UIInputViewController {

  /* Load our custom keyboard view up here */
  override func loadView() {
    let loadedView = KeyboardView(frame: CGRectZero)
    loadedView.textDocumentProxy = (textDocumentProxy as UITextDocumentProxy)
    loadedView.nextKeyboardButton.button.addTarget(self,
      action: "advanceToNextInputMode", forControlEvents: .TouchUpInside)
    view = loadedView

  }

}
```

There are a few things happening here that I would like to explain. One is that we are setting the text document proxy of our keyboard view to allow it to directly interact with the current control. The other thing is that we are getting the reference to the "Next Keyboard" button of our keyboard and hooking it up to the advanceToNextInput Mode method of our controller. This is a system method that Apple provides on the current instance of our view controller. Calling it will switch the current keyboard to the next keyboard that the user has configured for her device. As you know, the user can have multiple keyboards, and we should always allow her to switch from our keyboard to the next keyboard in her list. This method does exactly that.

As you saw, the view controller is loading a view of type KeyboardView and is assigning it as its own view. This is a class that we are going to write. The class will display keyboard buttons of type KeyboardButton, which again is a class that we are going to write. Please don't get confused here. There is nothing complicated going on. We have a keyboard view and we are going to display buttons on it. That's it! Nothing complicated, really. I promise.

Let's have a look at the implementation of the KeyboardButton class. This is going to be a subclass of the UIView class that contains an instance of the UIButton, so it is not a button itself, but a view that contains a button. The reason behind this is that this approach gives us more flexibility in case you want to add more than just a button to your keyboard button class.

In the button class's implementation, we are just going to have the button transform to a larger button when it is tapped in order to give the user feedback that they have tapped the button, and then move the button back to how it was originally when the tap is finished. This is how the system-wide keyboard also works in iOS. When you tap on a button, the button visually gets larger to let you know which button you are currently holding your finger on. So first we are going to write an extension on the UIView class that allows us to scale it up, and then reset the scaling to its default value:

```
extension UIView{
  func scaleByFactor(factor: CGFloat, animationDuration: NSTimeInterval){
    UIView.animateWithDuration(animationDuration, animations: {[weak self] in
      let strongSelf = self!
      strongSelf.transform = CGAffineTransformMakeScale(factor, factor)
      })
  }

  func resetScalingWithAnimationDuration(duration: NSTimeInterval){
    scaleByFactor(1.0, animationDuration: duration)
  }
}
```

Next up is the button class. This button class has really nothing interesting except that it creates a view with a button on it. When the button is held down, it will scale up to give the user a visual indication that they have held their finger on it:

```
class KeyboardButton : UIView{

  var button: UIButton!

  required init(coder aDecoder: NSCoder) {
    super.init(coder: aDecoder)
  }

  init(buttonTitle: String){
    super.init(frame: CGRectZero)
    button = UIButton(frame: bounds)
    button.autoresizingMask = .FlexibleWidth | .FlexibleHeight
    addSubview(button)
    button.setTitle(buttonTitle, forState: .Normal)
    button.addTarget(self, action: "enlargeForTouchDown",
      forControlEvents: .TouchDown)
    button.addTarget(self, action: "goToNormalSize",
      forControlEvents: .AllEvents ^ (.TouchDown))
  }

  func goToNormalSize(){
    self.resetScalingWithAnimationDuration(0.1)
  }

  func enlargeForTouchDown(){
    self.scaleByFactor(3.0, animationDuration: 0.1)
  }

}
```

Then we are going to start implementing our KeyboardView class. Let's begin with the
basic variables and constants:

```
class KeyboardView: UIView {

  var buttons = [KeyboardButton]()
  let characters = "ABCDEFGHIJKLMNOPQRSTUVWXYZ"
  var nextKeyboardButton: KeyboardButton!
  let buttonWidth = 45.0 as CGFloat
  let buttonHeight = 45.0 as CGFloat

  weak var textDocumentProxy: UITextDocumentProxy?{
  willSet(newValue){
    if let proxy = newValue{
      if proxy.keyboardAppearance! == .Dark{
        backgroundColor = UIColor.darkGrayColor()
      } else {
        backgroundColor = UIColor.lightGrayColor()
      }
    }
  }
  }
}
```

```
    <# rest of the code #>

}
```

The really important thing to note from this code is the textDocumentProxy optional property that we defined for our class. Whenever this variable is set, we are retrieving the keyboard appearance of the control using our custom keyboard. If the appearance is dark, we are also using a dark color for our keyboard. Otherwise, we are using a light color. As you know, every control that conforms to the UITextInputTraits class has a property named keyboardAppearance that lets the user decide the appearance of the keyboard for that control. This appearance can be light or dark or any other value that Apple may decide to add to the SDK in the later versions. This value is defined for every text control that conforms to the aforementioned protocol and is set by the programmer of the app. So we need to adhere to what that programmer expects from our keyboard and be kind enough to adjust our keyboard's appearance as well.

After our view is created, we are going to create all our keys. Two special keys exist on our keyboard:

Backspace
 Pressing the back key will clear the previous character or, if text is selected, remove the selected text.

Next keyboard
 Pressing this key will switch the current keyboard to the next keyboard that the user has configured in her system settings, like so:

```
required init(coder aDecoder: NSCoder) {
  super.init(coder: aDecoder)
}

override init(frame: CGRect) {
  super.init(frame: frame)

  backgroundColor = UIColor.lightGrayColor()

  /* Create all the buttons */
  for character in characters{
    let keyboardButton = KeyboardButton(buttonTitle: "\(character)")
    buttons.append(keyboardButton)
    keyboardButton.button.addTarget(self, action: "handleTapOnButton:",
      forControlEvents: .TouchUpInside)
    addSubview(keyboardButton)
  }

  /* Create the backspace button */
  let backspaceButton = KeyboardButton(buttonTitle: "<")
  backspaceButton.button.addTarget(self, action: "handleBackSpace",
    forControlEvents: .TouchUpInside)
  buttons.append(backspaceButton)
```

```
addSubview(backspaceButton)

/* Create the next button */
nextKeyboardButton = KeyboardButton(buttonTitle: "->")
nextKeyboardButton.button.addTarget(self, action: "goToNextKeyboard",
  forControlEvents: .TouchUpInside)
buttons.append(nextKeyboardButton)
addSubview(nextKeyboardButton)

}
```

For the backspace key, we need only call the `deleteBackward` method of our document proxy:

```
func handleBackSpace(){
  if let proxy = textDocumentProxy{
    proxy.deleteBackward()
  }
}
```

The next-keyboard key's action has already been configured by the `KeyboardViewCon troller` class, as we saw earlier, to call the `advanceToNextInputMode` method of our view controller.

Except for these two special buttons, we hooked all the other buttons (such as A, B, etc.) to the `handleTapOnButton:` method of our view controller. In this method, we will take the button that was tapped, read its title, and then insert that title into the active text control that is using our keyboard, using the `insertText:` method of our proxy:

```
func handleTapOnButton(button: UIButton){
  let buttonText = button.titleForState(.Normal)
  if let text = buttonText{
    if let proxy = textDocumentProxy{
      proxy.insertText(text)
    }
  }
}
```

Because we have not yet written any code to position our buttons on the screen, let's do that now. Here I am assuming that the whole screen is a grid and we start from top left and start putting our buttons on the view until we reach the right edge of the screen. As soon as we do, we will move one row down and start laying the rest of the buttons down:

```
override func layoutSubviews() {
  super.layoutSubviews()

  var xPosition = 0.0 as CGFloat
  var yPosition = 0.0 as CGFloat

  for button in buttons{
    button.frame = CGRect(x: xPosition,
      y: yPosition,
```

```
            width: buttonWidth,
            height: buttonHeight)

    xPosition += buttonWidth

    if xPosition + buttonWidth >= bounds.size.width{
      xPosition = 0.0
      yPosition += buttonHeight
    }

  }

}
```

You might be surprised, but that was really it. Give this a go for yourself and check out how our keyboard looks on your iOS device.

2.4. Creating a Service Within Your App with Action Extensions

Problem

You want to create a service to help the user in some other applications in addition to your app. For instance, you might want to develop a service that can take some text as input and turn it to uppercase text. This may be used not only in your app, but any other app that handles text. To gain access to your extension, another app has to display action extensions on the system using an instance of the UIActivityViewController class.

Solution

Add an Action Extension target to your project (Figure 2-13).

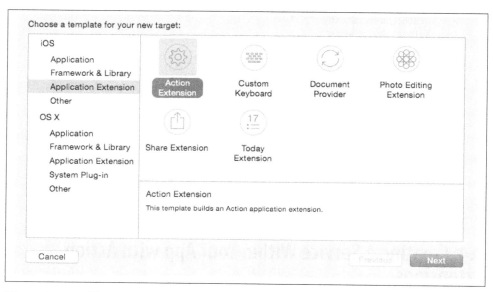

Figure 2-13. Adding an Action Extension target to your project

Discussion

Action extensions extend iOS with additional services. This means that they can take in any number of items of any type, transform them in whatever way they want, and then return those items to the calling application. The calling application must first display a view controller of type UIActivityViewController to the user and pass the items that it wants to be transformed to it. For instance, if you have a text field on your view and you want to see which services in the system can work on that text, you have to display an instance of the UIActivityViewController and pass the text of your text field to that controller. iOS will then detect the type of item that you are trying to expose from your app and find various services in the system that can handle that item.

In this recipe, we are going to have a look at a service that we call "Uppercase Extension." This extension can take in text of type kUTTypeText and turn that text into uppercase text. Once the user is happy with the transformed text, she can press a button on the extension's UI, the extension will report the transformed value back to iOS, and iOS will give that value back to the app if it is interested in it. The app can then take appropriate action to handle the transformed value.

Please go ahead and create a single-view application in Xcode, then add a text field and a navigation bar button item to your view controller. Embed your view controller in the navigation bar. This is all easily done through Storyboards. Then hook your bar button item to an IBAction method on your view controller that will display the sharing items:

```
@IBAction func performShare(){
  let controller = UIActivityViewController(activityItems: [textField.text],
    applicationActivities: nil)
  controller.completionWithItemsHandler = activityCompletionHandler
  presentViewController(controller, animated: true, completion: nil)
}
```

We are setting the `completionWithItemsHandler` property of the container controller to the `activityCompletionHandler` closure in our view controller. This closure is invoked when the action extension finishes and returns values to your app, and takes the following parameters:

activityType
: The type of activity that this completion handler was called on. You can specify here any of the `kUTType` values, such as `kUTTypeText` to indicate that the action was performed on a text item.

completed
: A Boolean value that will let you know whether the action extension that performed its work finished successfully.

returnedItems
: An array of `NSExtensionItem` instances that the action extension returned to your application. Action extensions can return values of this type and encapsulate the returned values in them. For instance, if you pass a text to the activity view controller and ask it to show all action extensions that can perform their work on that text, and the user picks one of the actions, the action can then do its work. When it is done, it will return this array of results. We will discuss this in detail quite soon.

activityError
: An error object that the action extension can return to you.

Every instance of the `NSExtensionItem` class has a property called `attachments`, which is an array of `NSItemProvider` instances. These are the items that actually returned from the extension. Call the `hasItemConformingToTypeIdentifier:` method on the item provider instance to find out whether it contains an item of type *X*, where *X* is any of the `kUTType` values. For instance, you can ask the provider whether it contains text, or an image, or a URL.

Once you are sure that the instance contains your required type, load the value of that type using the `loadItemForTypeIdentifier:options:completionHandler:` method of the provider to get your data. The data that comes back will be an object that conforms to the `NSSecureCoding` protocol. This could be a string, an instance of `NSData`, or any other class that conforms to this protocol.

So in our example, I am going to get the text that came back from the extension and place it back in my text field:

```
    let type = kUTTypeText as NSString as String

func activityCompletionHandler(activityType: String!,
  completed: Bool,
  returnedItems: [AnyObject]!,
  activityError: NSError!){

    if completed && activityError == nil{

      let item = returnedItems[0] as NSExtensionItem

      if let attachments = item.attachments{

        let attachment = attachments[0] as NSItemProvider

        if attachment.hasItemConformingToTypeIdentifier(type){
          attachment.loadItemForTypeIdentifier(type, options: nil,
            completionHandler: {[weak self]
              (item: NSSecureCoding!, error: NSError!) in

                let strongSelf = self!
                if error != nil{
                  strongSelf.textField.text = "\(error)"
                } else {
                  if let value = item as? NSString{
                    strongSelf.textField.text = value
                  }
                }
            })
        }

      }

    }

  }
}
```

Now go to the plist file of your extension and ensure that it accepts only text content by setting the value of the NSExtensionActivationSupportsText key to true like so:

```
<key>NSExtension</key>
<dict>
  <key>NSExtensionAttributes</key>
  <dict>
    <key>NSExtensionActivationRule</key>
    <dict>
      <key>NSExtensionActivationSupportsFileWithMaxCount</key>
      <integer>0</integer>
      <key>NSExtensionActivationSupportsImageWithMaxCount</key>
      <integer>0</integer>
      <key>NSExtensionActivationSupportsMovieWithMaxCount</key>
      <integer>0</integer>
```

```
        <key>NSExtensionActivationSupportsText</key>
        <true/>
        <key>NSExtensionActivationSupportsWebURLWithMaxCount</key>
        <integer>0</integer>
      </dict>
      <key>NSExtensionPointName</key>
      <string>com.apple.ui-services</string>
      <key>NSExtensionPointVersion</key>
      <string>1.0</string>
    </dict>
    <key>NSExtensionMainStoryboard</key>
    <string>MainInterface</string>
    <key>NSExtensionPointIdentifier</key>
    <string>com.apple.ui-services</string>
  </dict>
```

The storyboard file of your extension contains a view controller that has a navigation bar. Place two buttons on the navigation bar, calling one of them Done and the other one Cancel. When the cancel button is pressed, make sure that you call the `cancelRequestWithError:` method of your `extensionContext` property, which is your bridge to the application that actually called you. We don't get direct access to the calling app or its private data, but using the `extensionContext` property, we can pass data to the calling app. By calling the `cancelRequestWithError:` method, we tell the calling app that the user has cancelled our extension and that we have no data to pass to the app.

```
@IBAction func cancel(){
  let userInfo = [NSLocalizedDescriptionKey : "User cancelled"]
  let error = NSError(domain: "Extension", code: -1, userInfo: userInfo)
  extensionContext!.cancelRequestWithError(error)
}
```

When our view was loaded, we placed a text view on the view of out extension, so now we load the text that the calling app shared with us, translate it to uppercase letters, and place it in the text view so that the user can see a preview of how we are transforming the text they shared with us.

```
import UIKit
import MobileCoreServices

class ActionViewController: UIViewController {

  @IBOutlet weak var textView: UITextView!

  let type = kUTTypeText as NSString as String

  override func viewDidLoad() {
    super.viewDidLoad()

    for item in extensionContext!.inputItems as [NSExtensionItem]{
      for provider in item.attachments as [NSItemProvider]{
        if provider.hasItemConformingToTypeIdentifier(type){
```

```
        provider.loadItemForTypeIdentifier(type, options: nil,
          completionHandler: {[weak self]
            (item: NSSecureCoding!, error: NSError!) in

            let strongSelf = self!

            if error != nil{
              strongSelf.textView.text = "\(error)"
            } else {
              if let loadedItem = item as? String{
                strongSelf.textView.text = loadedItem.uppercaseString
              }
            }

          })
      }
    }
  }

}

<# rest of the code #>

}
```

When the user presses the Done button, we will take the uppercase text in our text view and place it inside an object of type NSExtensionItem. Once that is done, we will pass this object to the calling application by calling the completeRequestReturningI tems:completionHandler: method of our extensionContext property:

```
@IBAction func done() {

  let extensionItem = NSExtensionItem()
  let text = textView.text as NSString
  let itemProvider = NSItemProvider(item: text,
    typeIdentifier: type)
  extensionItem.attachments = [itemProvider]
  let itemsToShare = [extensionItem]

  extensionContext!.completeRequestReturningItems(itemsToShare,
    completionHandler: nil)
}
```

Perfect. Now when I run the app, the main app's view controller contains a text field. I enter some text in there and press the Share button, which is placed in the navigation bar to see what's shown in Figure 2-14.

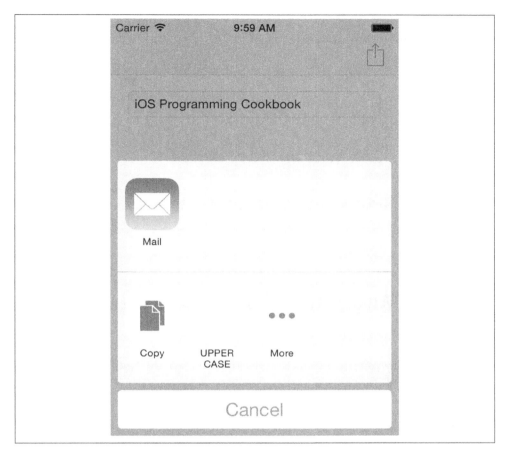

Figure 2-14. Our extension is shown in the list

Then, after pressing on our extension in the list, the user will see the uppercase text in the extension as shown in Figure 2-15.

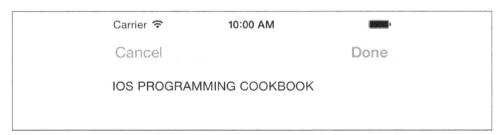

Figure 2-15. The text is transformed to uppercase in our extension

When the user presses the Done button, they will go back to the main app and see that the text has changed there as well (see Figure 2-16).

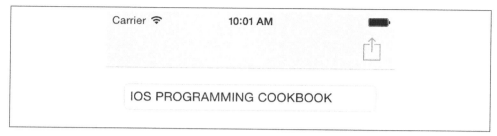

Figure 2-16. The text has changed to uppercase in the main app now

See Also

Recipe 2.0

2.5. Adding Widgets to the Notification Center

Problem

You want to display your own widgets in the Today view of the Notification Center on an iOS device.

Solution

Use Xcode's Today Extension target. Follow these steps:

1. After you have created a project to which you want to attach a widget, in Xcode, add a new target to your own target. Choose the Application Extension and then the Today Extension in the New Target window.

2. After your target has been created, ensure that you have imported the Notification Center framework by writing the following code on top of your newly-created view controller:

```
import UIKit
import NotificationCenter
```

3. Ensure that your newly created view controller (for your new target) conforms to the NCWidgetProviding protocol like so:

```
class TodayViewController: UITableViewController, NCWidgetProviding {

  <# rest of the code #>
}
```

4. Implement the `widgetPerformUpdateWithCompletionHandler:` method of your view controller that comes from the `NCWidgetProviding` protocol, and call the completion block with an appropriate value depending on whether your widget could fetch new data or not.

Discussion

The Today view in the notification presents the most useful items for the user that correspond to the activities that are relevant to the user's day: for instance, a shopping list, things to do before leaving the house, things to do do before leaving work, the weather, etc. Your app can also add an item to this list. By default, this list is similar to that shown in Figure 2-17:

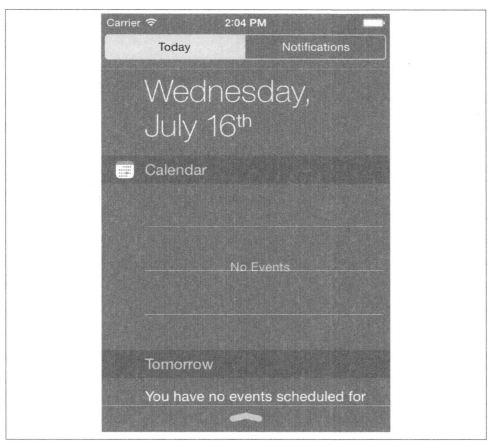

Figure 2-17. Today view on the notification center

It is very important to understand how the Today view actually works in terms of the lifecycle of extensions and widgets that can be added to it. Every widget is a view controller and has the same lifecycle as other view controllers in the system. The widget view controllers have to conform to the NCWidgetProviding protocol and should implement the widgetPerformUpdateWithCompletionHandler: method of this protocol. This method will get called on your view controller whenever the system wants your widget to update its contents.

A closure is passed to this method as a completion block parameter. Your application has to call the closure and pass a value of type NCUpdateResult. If you could fetch new content to display to the user, pass the value of NCUpdateResultNewData to this closure. If you could not fetch new data, pass the value of NCUpdateResultNoData, and if you encountered an error (such as a connection error), pass the value of NCUpdateResult Failed.

We are now going to look at an example of adding our own widget to the Today view in the notification center. Follow these steps:

 I am assuming that you have already created a project in Xcode before proceeding to the following steps. This project is a single-view application in this recipe.

1. After you have your current project set up, from the File menu in Xcode, add a new target to your project. When asked to select the Target type, choose the iOS category from the lefthand side and then Application Extension. Under the Application Extension, choose Today Extension, as shown in Figure 2-18.

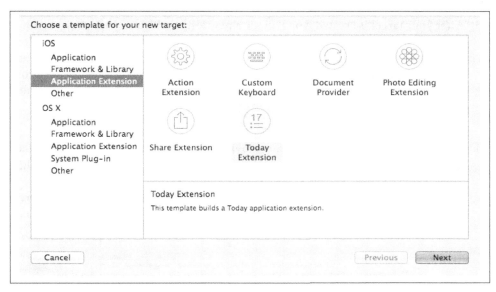

Figure 2-18. Choose the Today Extension in Xcode

2. Now you will be asked to choose a name for your target. Set the target name to Widget as shown in Figure 2-19.

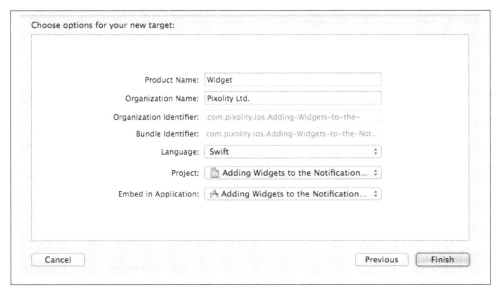

Figure 2-19. Choose your target name

3. After your target is created, you will see a new target added to your project named Widget. Under this target, you will see two new files: one called TodayViewController and the other called MainInterface. The interface is the UI of your content on the screen and the view controller is the code behind your interface. Go to your view controller and make sure it subclasses the `UITableViewController` class and that it conforms to the `NCWidgetProviding` protocol like so:

```
class TodayViewController: UITableViewController, NCWidgetProviding
```

4. Now you have a table view that can provide contents to the Today view. Populate your table view as you would other table views. When you are done, set the height of your content in the Today view using the `preferredContentSize` property of your view controller. Any width that you provide to this property will be ignored, because the width of all widgets on the Today view are determined by the system. The height, however, is determined by your view controller.

 Whenever your view controller is displayed to the user, you need to ensure that you set the height of your view controller by using the `preferredContentSize` property of your view controller. Put your resizing code in the `awakeFromNib` method of your view controller, which gets called whenever the nib file/storyboard associated with your view controller gets unpacked and loaded into memory.

So let's begin with the implementation of our view controller first:

```
import UIKit
import NotificationCenter

class TodayViewController: UITableViewController, NCWidgetProviding {

  /* The same identifier is saved in our storyboard for the prototype
  cells for this table view controller */
  struct TableViewConstants{
    static let cellIdentifier = "Cell"
  }

  /* List of items that we want to display in our table view */
  var items: [String] = []

  <# rest of the code goes here #>

}
```

Nothing strange here. We are now going to tell the system how many rows of information we want to display to the user in the Today view of the notification center:

```
override func tableView(tableView: UITableView,
  numberOfRowsInSection section: Int) -> Int {
```

```
        return items.count
    }
```

And now let's also provide our cells to the table view controller:

```
override func tableView(tableView: UITableView,
    cellForRowAtIndexPath indexPath: NSIndexPath) -> UITableViewCell {

        let cell = tableView.dequeueReusableCellWithIdentifier(
            TableViewConstants.cellIdentifier,
            forIndexPath: indexPath) as UITableViewCell

        cell.textLabel.text = items[indexPath.row]

        return cell

    }
```

Every time our view controller is displayed to the user, we must set the height of our widget properly. The height will be determined by the height of our table view like so:

```
func resetContentSize(){
    self.preferredContentSize = tableView.contentSize
}

override func awakeFromNib() {
    super.awakeFromNib()
    resetContentSize()
}

override func viewDidAppear(animated: Bool) {
    super.viewDidAppear(animated)
    resetContentSize()
}
```

Now on to writing the code for the widgetPerformUpdateWithCompletionHandler: delegate method of the NCWidgetProviding protocol to which our view controller conforms. We will create a method that is able to perform fetches and, based on whether it could get new data or not, call the completion handler of this method with relevant information as explained before. For the sake of simplicity, we are going to fake this call and always generate new results like so:

```
func performFetch() -> NCUpdateResult{

    for counter in 0..<arc4random_uniform(10){
        items.append("Item \(counter)")
    }

    return .NewData
}

func widgetPerformUpdateWithCompletionHandler(
    completionHandler: ((NCUpdateResult) -> Void)!) {
```

```
    let result = performFetch()

    if result == .NewData{
      tableView.reloadData()
      resetContentSize()
    }

    completionHandler(result)
  }
```

And also, when the user taps on a cell in our table view, we want to open our application and do something with the tapped cell. So let's implement the `tableView:didSelectRowAtIndexPath:` method of our table view's delegate:

```
override func tableView(tableView: UITableView,
  didSelectRowAtIndexPath indexPath: NSIndexPath) {
    let urlAsString = "widget://" + "\(indexPath.section)-\(indexPath.row)"
    let url = NSURL(string: urlAsString)
    self.extensionContext!.openURL(url!, completionHandler: nil)
    tableView.deselectRowAtIndexPath(indexPath, animated: false)
  }
```

As you can see, we are using the `extensionContext` property of our view controller to open a custom URL with the prefix of `widget://`. This is a custom URL scheme that upcoming code will make our main app understand. We are taking the index of the cell that was tapped, attaching it to the end of our custom URL scheme, and then telling the extension context to open that URL whenever the cell is tapped. For instance, if cell 1 is tapped (the first cell in the first section of the table view), considering that we have only one section in our table view, the resulting URL will be *widget://0-1*. iOS will then attempt to open the URL, and after our app is made to handle this type of URL, iOS will open our app and pass this URL to it.

Now let's go to our main app's *info.plist* file and ensure that it can handle the custom URL scheme that we just talked about. We do this by adding the `CFBundleURLTypes` key to our *info.plist* file like so:

```
<key>CFBundleURLTypes</key>
<array>
  <dict>
    <key>CFBundleURLName</key>
    <string>com.pixolity.ios.widgeturlidentifier</string>
    <key>CFBundleURLSchemes</key>
    <array>
      <string>widget</string>
    </array>
  </dict>
</array>
```

You can change the value of the `CFBundleURLName` key to a value that makes more sense to your application. After you are done with that, open the code file for your app delegate and implement the `application:handleOpenURL:` method like so:

```
import UIKit

/* This is an extenstion on the String class that can convert a given
string with the format of %d-%d into an NSIndexPath */
extension String{
  func toIndexPath () -> NSIndexPath{
    let components = self.componentsSeparatedByString("-")
    if components.count == 2{
      let section = components[0]
      let row = components[1]
      if let sectionValue = section.toInt(){
        if let rowValue = row.toInt(){
          return NSIndexPath(forRow: rowValue, inSection: sectionValue)
        }
      }
    }
    return NSIndexPath()
  }
}

@UIApplicationMain
class AppDelegate: UIResponder, UIApplicationDelegate {

  var window: UIWindow?
  let widgetUrlScheme = "widget"

  func application(application: UIApplication!,
    didFinishLaunchingWithOptions
    launchOptions: [NSObject : AnyObject]?) -> Bool {
      return true
  }

  func application(application: UIApplication!,
    handleOpenURL url: NSURL!) -> Bool {

      if url.scheme == widgetUrlScheme{

        /* Goes through our extension to convert
        String to NSIndexPath */
        let indexPath: NSIndexPath = url.host!.toIndexPath()

        /* Now do your work with the index path */
        println(indexPath)

      }

      return true
```

```
        }
    }
```

Now run your application. You will obviously see just an empty view on the screen because we didn't write any code for the main application. We only wrote the code for our Today Extension. Bring the notification center down by swiping down from the topmost edge of the screen and you will see something similar to that shown in Figure 2-20 on a newly-reset iOS simulator:

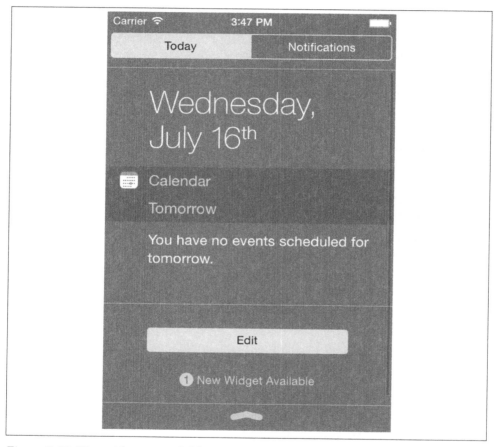

Figure 2-20. New widget is available

Now press the Edit button to edit the number of widgets that are displayed in your view. You should see something similar to that shown in Figure 2-21.

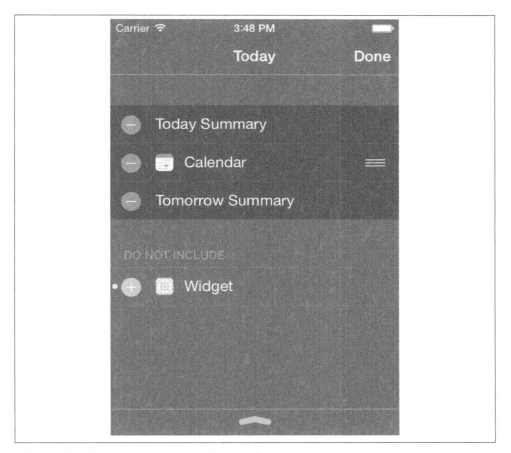

Figure 2-21. Our widget is displayed on the list

Add our widget to the list and press the Done button. Now you should be able to see our widget on the Today view as shown in Figure 2-22.

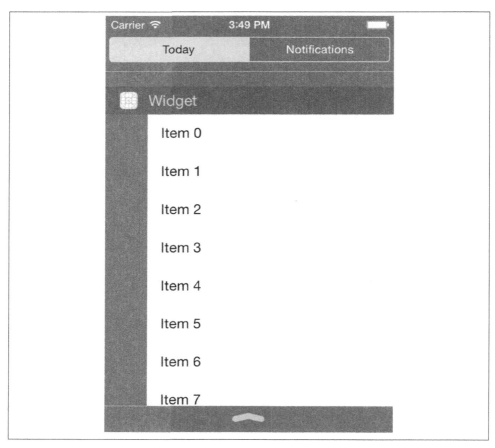

Figure 2-22. Our widget is working

CHAPTER 3

Managing Health Data with HealthKit

3.0. Introduction

Apple has created a health management application, appropriately called Health, which allows the user to enter their health-related information. This application is backed by a database that programmers don't have direct access to. However, a layer that is called HealthKit gives us access only to the information that we are authorized to use. Therefore, we need to ask the user for authorization before we can access their information.

There are more than 15 classes that we need to learn about in the HealthKit framework, and one of the most important is HKUnit. This class is responsible for representing units in various measures. For instance, one kilogram can be expressed as grams, milligrams, tons, etc. Also, this class allows you to convert units with ease. Let's say that in your country, a person's weight is measured in kilograms. But when you go to England, people ask you "How many stones do you weigh?" because they count weight in stones. The aforementioned class will help us a lot in working with various units, as we are going to see in Recipe 3.7.

3.1. Setting Up Your App for HealthKit

Problem

You want to be able to start using HealthKit in your app.

Solution

Follow these steps:

1. Set up your provision profile as explained in Recipe 1.22.
2. Import the HealthKit framework into your project.

3. Navigate to the Capabilities section of your Xcode project and enable HealthKit as shown in Figure 3-1.

4. Query the `isHealthDataAvailable` type method of the `HKHealthStore` class in order to determine whether health data is available for the app. Your app may be running on a device that has the latest version of iOS but doesn't support HealthKit, so this is our way of finding this fact out. If HealthKit isn't available, you need to ensure that your app can still function properly unless your app relies purely on HealthKit to function.

5. Use the `requestAuthorizationToShareTypes:readTypes:completion:` method of your health store to ask the user for authorization to access her medical data.

6. When your completion handler is called for the authorization, take appropriate action and make sure that you handle all errors appropriately.

Figure 3-1. Enabling HealthKit in Xcode

Discussion

The first two parameters that we submit to the `requestAuthorizationToShare Types:readTypes:completion:` method of the health store are of type `NSSet` and should contain instances of the `HKObjectType` class. This class has various subclasses (direct and indirect), such as `HKCharacteristicType`, `HKSampleType`, `HKCategoryType`, and `HKWorkoutType`. You can create instances of the various class types using the `HKObject Type` class. I know this may sound confusing, but try to focus only on one thing right now: every piece of information that is stored on HealthKit has a type. The data can be either of the following types:

Quantity type
    A type that can be specified by a numeric value such as height, weight, or body mass index.

Category type
    A type that doesn't have a value, but categorizes other data.

Characteristic type
    A user trait that is not quantitative, such as date of birth or blood type.

Correlation type

A value that correlates with another value, such as blood pressure that is dependent on the heart rate.

When we want to ask for permission to access users' health data, we need to tell iOS which one of these types we are interested in writing to and reading from. The terminology that Apple has shared for writing data is *sharing*, so if you are asked to specify which type of data you want to share, just know that you are being asked what type of data you want to write to the user's health store.

Let's see an example of reading and writing a user's weight and height data, and reading the user's heart rate information. All of these three are quantity types and all quantity types have an identifier that starts with the HKQuantityTypeIdentifier prefix. For heart rate, we will use HKQuantityTypeIdentifierHeartRate. For weight, we will use HKQuantityTypeIdentifierBodyMass and for height, we will use HKQuantityTypeIdentifierHeight.

All quantity types are divided into two categories:

Discrete

A value that has only one instance at a time. For instance, a person's weight cannot be two values at one point in time. Adding up discrete values doesn't make sense either. That's how you know a value is discrete: when you would never add instances of it all up together. Again, why would somebody add up a person's weight from day to day to create a sum of all the weights?

Cumulative

A value that accumulates over time, such as the calories a person burns per day.

In our example, the weight, height, and heart rate are all discrete values because they have one value at any given point in time and you wouldn't want to calculate the sum of all their values over time.

```
import UIKit
import HealthKit

class ViewController: UIViewController {

  let heightQuantity = HKQuantityType.quantityTypeForIdentifier(
    HKQuantityTypeIdentifierHeight)

  let weightQuantity = HKQuantityType.quantityTypeForIdentifier(
    HKQuantityTypeIdentifierBodyMass)

  let heartRateQuantity = HKQuantityType.quantityTypeForIdentifier(
    HKQuantityTypeIdentifierHeartRate)

  lazy var healthStore = HKHealthStore()
```

```
/* The type of data that we wouldn't write into the health store */
lazy var typesToShare: NSSet = {
  return NSSet(objects: self.heightQuantity,
    self.weightQuantity)
}()

/* We want to read these types of data */
lazy var typesToRead: NSSet = {
  return NSSet(objects: self.heightQuantity,
    self.weightQuantity,
    self.heartRateQuantity)
}()

/* Ask for permission to access the health store */
override func viewDidAppear(animated: Bool) {
  super.viewDidAppear(animated)

  if HKHealthStore.isHealthDataAvailable(){

    healthStore.requestAuthorizationToShareTypes(typesToShare,
      readTypes: typesToRead,
      completion: {(succeeded: Bool, error: NSError!) in

        if succeeded && error == nil{
          println("Successfully received authorization")
        } else {
          if let theError = error{
            println("Error occurred = \(theError)")
          }
        }

    })

  } else {
    println("Health data is not available")
  }

}

}
```

When you run your app, an interface similar to that shown in Figure 3-2 will be displayed to the user:

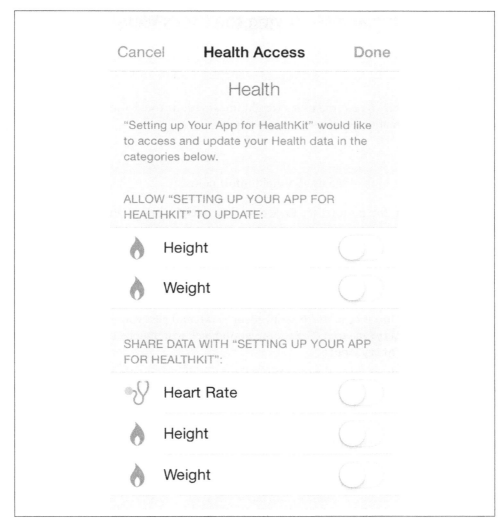

Figure 3-2. Ask the user for authorization to access her health data

When your completion handler is called, you know that the user has made her choice as to what type of data she wants to share with you from her health store. Just keep in mind that your completion handler is going to be called on a random background thread, so don't do anything in the completion handler (such as user interaction) that needs to be done on the main thread.

See Also

Recipe 1.22

3.2. Retrieving and Modifying the User's Weight Information

Problem

You want to be able to read the user's weight information. You'd also like to be able to update this information within your application.

Solution

Follow these steps to read the user's weight information:

1. Ask the user for permission to access their weight information, as shown in Recipe 3.1.

2. Instantiate an object of type `NSSortDescriptor` with the key of `HKSampleSortIdentifierEndDate` in descending order—that is, sorted so that the highest end date is on top. In this way, you'll get the last weight sample that the user has stored in her health store.

3. Construct an instance of the `HKSampleQuery` class and pass your weight quantity of type `HKQuantityType` to it. Your completion block will then be called with objects of type `HKQuantitySample`.

4. Get the sample of type `HKQuantitySample` from the completion block and access the sample's `quantity` property of type `HKQuantity`. This will be your quantity for the user's weight.

5. Use the `doubleValueForUnit:` method of the quantity to get the user's weight in a given unit. The unit is of type `HKMetricPrefix`.

6. Last but not least, run your query on the health store using the `executeQuery:` method of the health store instance.

Similarly, you can save the user's weight data to the health store by following these steps:

1. Assuming that the user's weight is specified in kilograms in your application, create a unit of type `HKUnit` using the `gramUnitWithMetricPrefix:` convenience constructor of this class and pass the `HKMetricPrefixKilo` value as the parameter to this method, to yield a kilogram unit.

2. Then create your quantity object of type `HKQuantity` with your kilogram unit that you created in the previous step and the user's weight specified in kilograms as a `Double` value.

3. Next stop, create a sample object of type `HKQuantitySample` from the quantity that you created earlier.

---

4. When you are done, call the `saveObject:` method of your health store and send your quantity sample to this method as a parameter for saving. Your completion block will give you a Boolean value and an error to indicate whether everything went well or not.

Discussion

Using HealthKit, we can create various queries to read the user's health data. One of the classes that can help us read data from the user's health store is the `HKSampleQuery` class. This class can get a sample of a specific object type in the user's health store, such as the user's heart rate, weight, or height. This class can query the health store for objects of type `HKSample`.

Several classes can represent a sample value in the health store. One is the concrete class of `HKSample` that we talked about. Two other classes, `HKQuantitySample` and `HKCate gorySample`, are subclasses of `HKSample`. We usually work with the latter two classes rather than the `HKSample` class directly, because our samples are usually categorized into more specific types such as quantity or category.

For the purpose of this recipe, I want to create an app that has a UI similar to that shown in Figure 3-3.

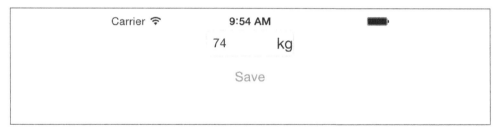

Figure 3-3. Our weight reading and writing UI

When the user opens the app, we will read her weight information and display it in the text field. Then we will let the user change the value inside this text field, and when she presses the Save button, we will save her weight information into her health store. Let's begin by defining our outlets:

```
import UIKit
import HealthKit

class ViewController: UIViewController, UITextFieldDelegate {

    @IBOutlet weak var textField: UITextField!
    @IBOutlet weak var saveButton: UIButton!
    /* This is a label that shows the user's weight unit (Kilograms) on
```

```
the righthand side of our text field */
let textFieldRightLabel = UILabel(frame: CGRectZero)

let weightQuantityType = HKQuantityType.quantityTypeForIdentifier(
  HKQuantityTypeIdentifierBodyMass)

lazy var types: NSSet = {
  return NSSet(object: self.weightQuantityType)
}()

lazy var healthStore = HKHealthStore()

<# rest of the code #>

}
```

When our view is loaded into the memory, we will set up our little label to be displayed on the righthand side of the text field. This label will show the localized value of kilograms in the user's current language:

```
override func viewDidLoad() {
  super.viewDidLoad()
  textField.rightView = textFieldRightLabel
  textField.rightViewMode = .Always
}
```

Next, when the view appears on the screen, we will ask the user for permission to access her weight information:

```
/* Ask for permission to access the health store */
override func viewDidAppear(animated: Bool) {
  super.viewDidAppear(animated)

  if HKHealthStore.isHealthDataAvailable(){

    healthStore.requestAuthorizationToShareTypes(types,
      readTypes: types,
      completion: {[weak self]
        (succeeded: Bool, error: NSError!) in

        let strongSelf = self!
        if succeeded && error == nil{
          dispatch_async(dispatch_get_main_queue(),
            strongSelf.readWeightInformation)
        } else {
          if let theError = error{
            println("Error occurred = \(theError)")
          }
        }

    })

  } else {
```

```
        println("Health data is not available")
    }

}
```

As you can see, after we are granted permission, we are calling the `readWeightInfor`
`mation` method of our view controller to read the user's weight information. We will
implement that method now:

```
func readWeightInformation(){

  let sortDescriptor = NSSortDescriptor(key: HKSampleSortIdentifierEndDate,
    ascending: false)

  let query = HKSampleQuery(sampleType: weightQuantityType,
    predicate: nil,
    limit: 1,
    sortDescriptors: [sortDescriptor],
    resultsHandler: {[weak self] (query: HKSampleQuery!,
      results: [AnyObject]!,
      error: NSError!) in

      if results.count > 0{

        /* We really have only one sample */
        let sample = results[0] as HKQuantitySample
        /* Get the weight in kilograms from the quantity */
        let weightInKilograms = sample.quantity.doubleValueForUnit(
          HKUnit.gramUnitWithMetricPrefix(.Kilo))

        /* This is the value of KG, localized in user's language */
        let formatter = NSMassFormatter()
        let kilogramSuffix = formatter.unitStringFromValue(weightInKilograms,
          unit: .Kilogram)

        dispatch_async(dispatch_get_main_queue(), {

          let strongSelf = self!


          /* Set the value of KG on the righthand side of the
          text field */
          strongSelf.textFieldRightLabel.text = kilogramSuffix
          strongSelf.textFieldRightLabel.sizeToFit()

          /* And finally set the text field's value to the user's
          weight */
          let weightFormattedAsString =
          NSNumberFormatter.localizedStringFromNumber(
            NSNumber(double: weightInKilograms),
            numberStyle: .NoStyle)
```

```
                strongSelf.textField.text = weightFormattedAsString

            })

        } else {
          print("Could not read the user's weight ")
          println("or no weight data was available")
        }


    })

    healthStore.executeQuery(query)

  }
```

The constructor that we are using for the `HKSampleQuery` class takes the following parameters:

`sampleType`
> A sample type of class `HKSampleType`. This is the type of the sample that we want to retrieve from the user's health store.

`predicate`
> This is a predicate that you can use for filtering the results. We will talk about this later. For now, we will pass nil to this parameter.

`limit`
> The number of results that you want to retrieve. We only want the latest data as we will specify soon with our sort descriptor, so we will specify the value of 1 in this parameter.

`sortDescriptors`
> This is an array of sort descriptors of type `NSSortDescriptor` that you can create using values such as `HKSampleSortIdentifierStartDate` and `HKSampleSortIden tifierEndDate`. Your results will be sorted by the order specified in your descriptors.

`resultsHandler`
> This is a completion closure that will get called whenever HealthKit retrieves or fails to retrieve your results.

When our completion handler closure is called, we will get an array of results of type `[AnyObject]`, but the values for our sample will actually be of type `HKQuantitySam ple` because we specified that when defining our `weightQuantityType` variable. After that, we will use the `quantity` property of the sample to read the weight. But how do we save the user's weight? We've already hooked the Save button with the `saveUser Weight` method of our view controller:

```
@IBAction func saveUserWeight(){

  let kilogramUnit = HKUnit.gramUnitWithMetricPrefix(.Kilo)
  let weightQuantity = HKQuantity(unit: kilogramUnit,
    doubleValue: (textField.text as NSString).doubleValue)
  let now = NSDate()
  let sample = HKQuantitySample(type: weightQuantityType,
    quantity: weightQuantity,
    startDate: now,
    endDate: now)

  healthStore.saveObject(sample, withCompletion: {
    (succeeded: Bool, error: NSError!) in

    if error == nil{
      println("Successfully saved the user's weight")
    } else {
      println("Failed to save the user's weight")
    }

  })

}
```

Last but not least, we need to ensure that our text field can stop being active when the user decides to dismiss the keyboard, so let's implement the functionality that allows the keyboard to be dismissed when the user wants it to:

```
func textFieldShouldReturn(textField: UITextField!) -> Bool {
  textField.resignFirstResponder()
  return true
}
```

See Also

Recipe 3.1; Recipe 3.3

3.3. Accessing and Modifying the User's Height Information

Problem

You want to retrieve the user's height information from HealthKit and store a new value as the height.

Solution

Follow the steps we saw in the Solution section of Recipe 3.2, but instead of pulling down an instance of HKQuantityType with a weight identifier, pull down the height identifier using the `HKQuantityTypeIdentifierHeight` value. Then use the `NSNumber Formatter` class with a style of type `NSNumberFormatterStyle` set to the value of `NSNum berFormatterDecimalStyle` to get the decimal points of a person's height as well.

Discussion

In this recipe, we are going to create an app whose UI looks like Figure 3-4.

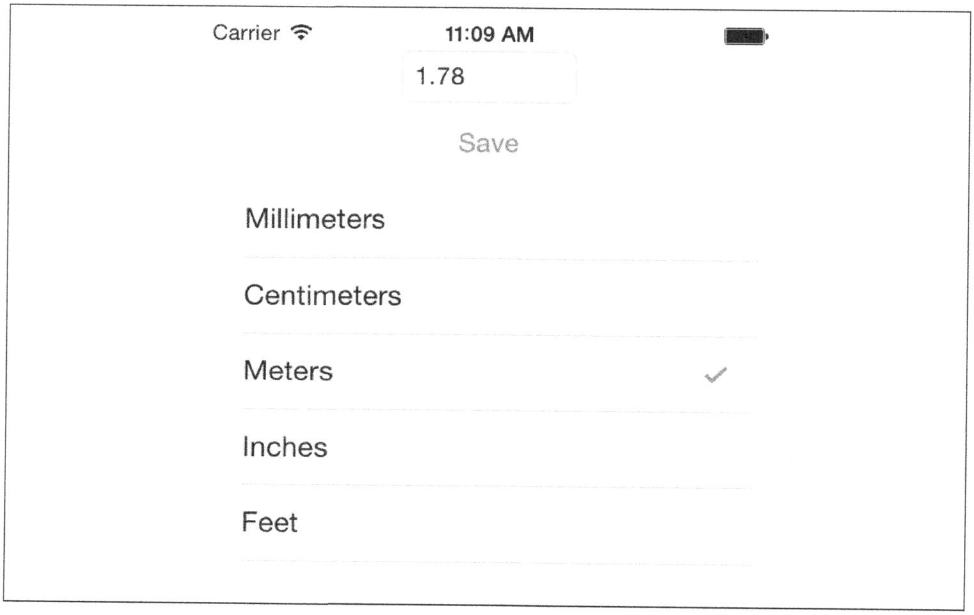

Figure 3-4. User's height is retrieved and can be saved in various units

When we launch the app, the first unit will be selected in the table view and we will attempt to retrieve the user's height in that unit. If the user then changes the value inside the text field, chooses a unit from the list, and presses the save button, we will save her height information into the health store instance of our view controller with the selected unit.

For instance, a person living in Sweden opens the app. If she has never entered her height information, she will see no data in the text field and the Millimeters value will be selected in the list. She then changes the units to Meters, enters her height of 1.78 meters into the text field, and presses the Save button. She then travels to the UK and wants to see her height in Feet. She opens the app, where we read her previously saved height in the units of Meters that she had selected. She then moves to the Feet value in the list and we will convert her height to Feet, as expected.

The first thing that we are going to do is to define a data structure whose values we will display in our table view:

```swift
enum HeightUnits: String{
  case Millimeters = "Millimeters"
  case Centimeters = "Centimeters"
  case Meters = "Meters"
  case Inches = "Inches"
  case Feet = "Feet"
  static let allValues = [Millimeters, Centimeters, Meters, Inches, Feet]

  func healthKitUnit() -> HKUnit{
    switch self{
    case .Millimeters:
      return HKUnit.meterUnitWithMetricPrefix(.Milli)
    case .Centimeters:
      return HKUnit.meterUnitWithMetricPrefix(.Centi)
    case .Meters:
      return HKUnit.meterUnit()
    case .Inches:
      return HKUnit.inchUnit()
    case .Feet:
      return HKUnit.footUnit()
    }
  }

}
```

This enumeration can give us string values that we can display in our table view and can also translate its members to items of type HKUnit so that we can use those units to read and save the user's height data. Now place a table view, a button, and a text field on your storyboard and connect them to the outlets on your view controller:

```swift
class ViewController: UIViewController, UITableViewDataSource,
UITableViewDelegate {

  @IBOutlet weak var textField: UITextField!
  @IBOutlet weak var saveButton: UIButton!
  @IBOutlet weak var tableView: UITableView!

  <# rest of the code #>

}
```

Then let us define all the other variables that we are going to need. One of the really important variables that we have in our view controller is the heightUnit variable that will be set to the currently selected height unit in our table view. As soon as this value is changed, we are going to want to convert the user's height to the selected units, so we will take advantage of the Swift runtime to find out when this variable's value is changed and then read the user's height again:

```
/* The currently selected height unit */
var heightUnit:HeightUnits = .Millimeters{
willSet{
  readHeightInformation()
}
}

/* Keep track of which index path is tapped so that we can
put a checkmark next to it */
var selectedIndexPath = NSIndexPath(forRow: 0, inSection: 0)

let heightQuantityType = HKQuantityType.quantityTypeForIdentifier(
  HKQuantityTypeIdentifierHeight)

lazy var types: NSSet = {
  return NSSet(object: self.heightQuantityType)
  }()

lazy var healthStore = HKHealthStore()

struct TableViewInfo{
  static let cellIdentifier = "Cell"
}
```

Next, for every item in our HeightUnits enumeration, we will display an item in our table view:

```
func tableView(tableView: UITableView,
  numberOfRowsInSection section: Int) -> Int {
  return HeightUnits.allValues.count
}

/* If a new cell is selected, show the selection only for that
cell and remove the selection from the previously-selected cell */
func tableView(tableView: UITableView,
  didSelectRowAtIndexPath indexPath: NSIndexPath) {

    let previouslySelectedIndexPath = selectedIndexPath
    selectedIndexPath = indexPath

    tableView.reloadRowsAtIndexPaths([previouslySelectedIndexPath,
      selectedIndexPath], withRowAnimation: .Automatic)

}

func tableView(tableView: UITableView,
  cellForRowAtIndexPath indexPath: NSIndexPath) -> UITableViewCell {

    let cell = tableView.dequeueReusableCellWithIdentifier(
      TableViewInfo.cellIdentifier, forIndexPath: indexPath)
      as UITableViewCell

    let heightUnit = HeightUnits.allValues[indexPath.row]
```

```
cell.textLabel.text = heightUnit.rawValue

if indexPath == selectedIndexPath{
  cell.accessoryType = .Checkmark
} else {
  cell.accessoryType = .None
}

return cell
}
```

When a unit is selected in the table view, we will put a checkmark next to it and read the user's height in the given unit:

```
/* If a new cell is selected, show the selection only for that
cell and remove the selection from the previously-selected cell */
func tableView(tableView: UITableView,
  didSelectRowAtIndexPath indexPath: NSIndexPath) {

    let previouslySelectedIndexPath = selectedIndexPath
    selectedIndexPath = indexPath

    tableView.reloadRowsAtIndexPaths([previouslySelectedIndexPath,
      selectedIndexPath], withRowAnimation: .Automatic)

}
```

As you saw earlier, when the value of the `heightUnit` property of our view controller changes, we call the `readHeightInformation` method of our view controller. This method will read the user's height, similar to how we read the user's weight in Recipe 3.2. The only difference is that our units in this recipe are selected by the user in the table view, unlike the constant unit of kilograms that we had in the aforementioned recipe to measure the user's weight.

```
func readHeightInformation(){

    let sortDescriptor = NSSortDescriptor(key: HKSampleSortIdentifierEndDate,
      ascending: false)

    let query = HKSampleQuery(sampleType: heightQuantityType,
      predicate: nil,
      limit: 1,
      sortDescriptors: [sortDescriptor],
      resultsHandler: {[weak self] (query: HKSampleQuery!,
        results: [AnyObject]!,
        error: NSError!) in

        let strongSelf = self!

        if results.count > 0{
```

```
        /* We really have only one sample */
        let sample = results[0] as HKQuantitySample
        /* Get the height in the currently selected unit */
        let currentlySelectedUnit = strongSelf.heightUnit.healthKitUnit()

        let heightInUnit = sample.quantity.doubleValueForUnit(
          currentlySelectedUnit)

        dispatch_async(dispatch_get_main_queue(), {

          /* And finally set the text field's value to the user's height */
          let heightFormattedAsString =
          NSNumberFormatter.localizedStringFromNumber(
            NSNumber(double: heightInUnit),
            numberStyle: .DecimalStyle)

          strongSelf.textField.text = heightFormattedAsString

        })

      } else {
        print("Could not read the user's height ")
        println("or no height data was available")
      }


    })

    healthStore.executeQuery(query)

  }
```

Our Save button is hooked to the following action, which will accept the user's current height, taking into account the currently selected weight unit, and save that data to the user's health store:

```
@IBAction func saveHeight(){
  let currentlySelectedUnit = heightUnit.healthKitUnit()
  let heightQuantity = HKQuantity(unit: currentlySelectedUnit,
    doubleValue: (textField.text as NSString).doubleValue)
  let now = NSDate()
  let sample = HKQuantitySample(type: heightQuantityType,
    quantity: heightQuantity,
    startDate: now,
    endDate: now)

  healthStore.saveObject(sample, withCompletion: {
    (succeeded: Bool, error: NSError!) in

    if error == nil{
      println("Successfully saved the user's height")
    } else {
```

```
      println("Failed to save the user's height")
    }

  })
}
```

When our view appears on the screen, we will do the usual authorization from the user to access her health store information:

```
/* Ask for permission to access the health store */
override func viewDidAppear(animated: Bool) {
  super.viewDidAppear(animated)

  if HKHealthStore.isHealthDataAvailable(){

    healthStore.requestAuthorizationToShareTypes(types,
      readTypes: types,
      completion: {[weak self]
        (succeeded: Bool, error: NSError!) in

        let strongSelf = self!
        if succeeded && error == nil{
          dispatch_async(dispatch_get_main_queue(),
            strongSelf.readHeightInformation)
        } else {
          if let theError = error{
            println("Error occurred = \(theError)")
          }
        }

    })

  } else {
    println("Health data is not available")
  }

}
```

To be extremely awesome, we will also opt into view controller restoration to ensure that even when our app is killed by the system or user, the next time our app is opened, our view controller will go exactly to the state that it was in before it was killed. So we will save the currently selected unit and the current index path into the state restoration coder like so:

```
override func encodeRestorableStateWithCoder(coder: NSCoder) {
  super.encodeRestorableStateWithCoder(coder)
  coder.encodeObject(selectedIndexPath, forKey: "selectedIndexPath")
  coder.encodeObject(heightUnit.rawValue, forKey: "heightUnit")
}

override func decodeRestorableStateWithCoder(coder: NSCoder) {
  super.decodeRestorableStateWithCoder(coder)
```

```
      selectedIndexPath = coder.decodeObjectForKey("selectedIndexPath")
        as NSIndexPath
      if let newUnit = HeightUnits(rawValue:
        coder.decodeObjectForKey("heightUnit")
        as String){
          heightUnit = newUnit
      }
    }
```

Last but not least, we need to opt into state restoration in our app delegate:

```
import UIKit

@UIApplicationMain
class AppDelegate: UIResponder, UIApplicationDelegate {

  var window: UIWindow?

  func application(application: UIApplication!,
    shouldRestoreApplicationState coder: NSCoder!) -> Bool {
    return true
  }

  func application(application: UIApplication!,
    shouldSaveApplicationState coder: NSCoder!) -> Bool {
      return true
  }

  func application(application: UIApplication!,
    didFinishLaunchingWithOptions
    launchOptions: [NSObject : AnyObject]?) -> Bool {
    return true
  }

}
```

Run your app and see how nicely you can store and retrieve height information with state restoration to allow fast restoration of your view controller. For state restoration to work, just ensure that your view controller has a restoration identifier in your storyboard.

See Also

Recipe 3.2; Recipe 3.1

3.4. Retrieving User Characteristics

Problem

You want to retrieve a user trait, such as date of birth, from her health store.

Solution

Follow these steps:

1. Create an instance of the `HKCharacteristicType` class using its `characteristic TypeForIdentifier:` convenience constructor and passing the value of `HKCharac teristicTypeIdentifierDateOfBirth` to it.

2. Request authorization to HealthKit as we learned in Recipe 3.1 and pass the characteristic type that you created in the previous step as data to read. We cannot set the user birth date, so the data that we will share will be nil.

3. After you receive your authorization, use the `dateOfBirthWithError:` method of the health store instance to retrieve the user's date of birth as an object of type `NSDate`.

Discussion

A user can set her date of birth by opening the Health app on her iOS device and then navigating to the Health Data section and editing her date of birth as shown in Figure 3-5.

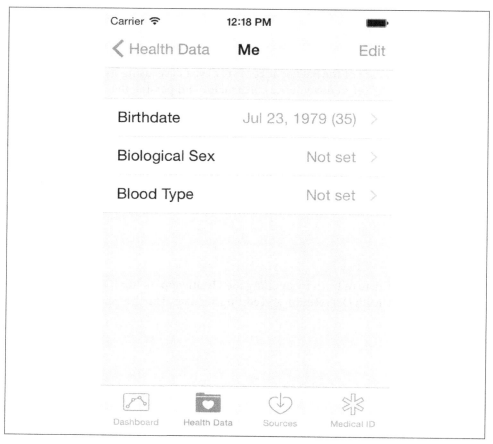

Figure 3-5. The user has set her date of birth in the Health app

An app cannot change the value of the user's date of birth in the health store. When your app opens and you use the technique that you learned in Recipe 3.1 to gain access to the uer's date of birth information, she will see a dialog similar to that shown in Figure 3-6.

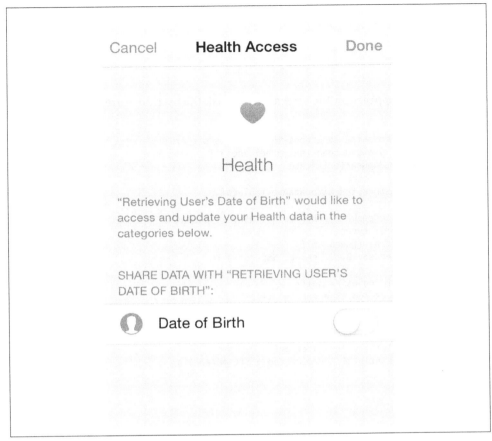

Figure 3-6. The user is asked if she wants to let our app access her date of birth

Once you have permission, you can call the `dateOfBirthWithError:` method of the health store to retrieve the user's date of birth. Let's first define the characteristic type that we want to read from the health store:

```
import UIKit
import HealthKit

class ViewController: UIViewController {

  let dateOfBirthCharacteristicType =
  HKCharacteristicType.characteristicTypeForIdentifier(
    HKCharacteristicTypeIdentifierDateOfBirth)

  lazy var types: NSSet = {
    return NSSet(object: self.dateOfBirthCharacteristicType)
    }()
```

```
lazy var healthStore = HKHealthStore()

<# rest of the code #>

}
```

When our view appears on the screen, we will ask the user if we are allowed to access her date of birth:

```
/* Ask for permission to access the health store */
override func viewDidAppear(animated: Bool) {
  super.viewDidAppear(animated)

  if HKHealthStore.isHealthDataAvailable(){

    healthStore.requestAuthorizationToShareTypes(nil,
      readTypes: types,
      completion: {[weak self]
        (succeeded: Bool, error: NSError!) in

        let strongSelf = self!
        if succeeded && error == nil{
          dispatch_async(dispatch_get_main_queue(),
            strongSelf.readDateOfBirthInformation)
        } else {
          if let theError = error{
            println("Error occurred = \(theError)")
          }
        }

    })

  } else {
    println("Health data is not available")
  }

}
```

Note how we are passing nil as the first parameter of the requestAuthorizationToSh areTypes:readTypes:completion: method. We are telling the health store that we are not going to want to change the value of the user's date of birth. If you attempt to ask HealthKit to modify the user's date of birth, HealthKit will throw an exception at you. All we are saying is that we are interested in reading the user's date of birth. Once we are given permission, we are calling the readDateOfBirthInformation method of our view controller.

```
func readDateOfBirthInformation(){

  var dateOfBirthError: NSError?
  let birthDate = healthStore.dateOfBirthWithError(&dateOfBirthError)
    as NSDate?
```

```
    if let error = dateOfBirthError{
      println("Could not read user's date of birth")
    } else {

      if let dateOfBirth = birthDate{
        let formatter = NSNumberFormatter()
        let now = NSDate()
        let components = NSCalendar.currentCalendar().components(
          .YearCalendarUnit,
          fromDate: dateOfBirth,
          toDate: now,
          options: .WrapComponents)

        let age = components.year

        println("The user is \(age) years old")
      } else {
        println("User has not specified her date of birth yet")
      }

    }

  }
```

Often, what you want in a health app is not the date of birth, but the user's current age. It's easy, luckily, to calculate the user's age by subtracting her date of birth from the current date and taking the year value, techniques you can read about in Chapter 18.

See Also

Recipe 3.2; Recipe 3.1; Recipe 3.3

3.5. Observing Changes to the User's Health Information

Problem

You do not want to constantly poll data from HealthKit, but instead be notified about changes in data of a specific type, such as the user's weight.

Solution

Create an observer query of type HKObserverQuery and submit it to your health store instance. To start the query, simply call the executeQuery: method of your health store. When you no longer are interested in watching for changes for a specific type, call the stopQuery: method of your health store.

Discussion

When you issue a normal query, it polls the health store that is assigned to the current user. That's great for one-time operations, but we all know that for data that changes rapidly or at inconsistent times, you might want to sit back and be told about changes as they happen instead of polling it all the time. For this reason, we can use the HKOb serverQuery class instead of HKQuery. The observer query is initialized by passing it a sample type of class HKSampleType, a predicate of type NSPredicate, and an update handler. This update handler is a closure that you need to specify, which will get called whenever the requested data type is changed in the user's health store.

Let's assume that we want to write an app that can monitor the changes to the user's weight from yesterday to today, even in the background. First, we have to define the most basic variables that we are going to need: the health store instance and the types of data that we need access to in the health store:

```
import UIKit
import HealthKit

class ViewController: UIViewController {

  let weightQuantityType = HKQuantityType.quantityTypeForIdentifier(
    HKQuantityTypeIdentifierBodyMass)

  lazy var types: NSSet = {
    return NSSet(object: self.weightQuantityType)
    }()

  lazy var healthStore = HKHealthStore()

  <# rest of the code #>

}
```

Because we want all the changes in the user's weight from yesterday to today, we will create a predicate of type NSPredicate using the predicateForSamplesWithStart Date:endDate:options: method of the HKQuery class:

```
lazy var predicate: NSPredicate = {
  let now = NSDate()
  let yesterday =
  NSCalendar.currentCalendar().dateByAddingUnit(.DayCalendarUnit,
    value: -1,
    toDate: now,
    options: .WrapComponents)

  return HKQuery.predicateForSamplesWithStartDate(yesterday,
    endDate: now,
    options: .StrictEndDate)
  }()
```

Then we need our actual query of type `HKObserverQuery`. This query will be initialized with the weight quantity type that we created earlier and the predicate that we just created. The completion handler of the query of this query is set to the `weightChanged Handler` closure of our view controller, which we are going to soon implement:

```
lazy var query: HKObserverQuery = {[weak self] in
  let strongSelf = self!
  return HKObserverQuery(sampleType: strongSelf.weightQuantityType,
    predicate: strongSelf.predicate,
    updateHandler: strongSelf.weightChangedHandler)
}()
```

When our view appears on the screen, we will first ask the user for permission to observe their weight information in the health store, and when the view disappears, we will stop watching for changes.

```
/* Ask for permission to access the health store */
override func viewDidAppear(animated: Bool) {
  super.viewDidAppear(animated)

  if HKHealthStore.isHealthDataAvailable(){

    healthStore.requestAuthorizationToShareTypes(nil,
      readTypes: types,
      completion: {[weak self]
        (succeeded: Bool, error: NSError!) in

        let strongSelf = self!
        if succeeded && error == nil{
          dispatch_async(dispatch_get_main_queue(),
            strongSelf.startObservingWeightChanges)
        } else {
          if let theError = error{
            println("Error occurred = \(theError)")
          }
        }

    })

  } else {
    println("Health data is not available")
  }

}

override func viewDidDisappear(animated: Bool) {
  super.viewDidDisappear(animated)
  stopObservingWeightChanges()
}
```

When the user is asked to give or reject permission to our app to access her weight data, she will see a dialog similar to that shown in Figure 3-7.

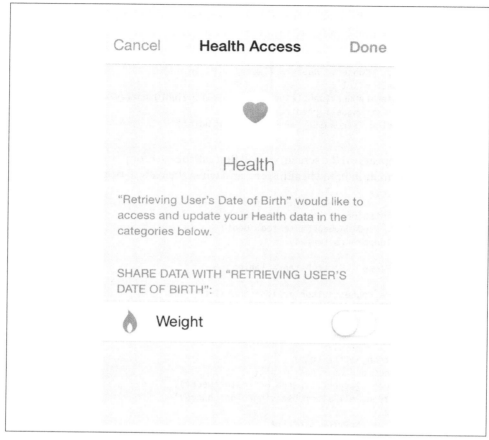

Figure 3-7. We request permission to read user's weight

When our view appeared on the screen and we succeeded in getting permission, we called the `startObservingWeightChanges` method of our view controller. In this method, we start our observer query and invoke the `enableBackgroundDeliveryForType:frequency:withCompletion:` method of the health store. This method will allow our app to start observing changes in the health store even in the background, which is just what we need. The frequency that you pass to this method has to be of type `HKUpdateFrequency` and your completion handler will be a closure that takes in a Boolean and an error value of type `NSError`. This completion handler will be called to inform you whether your request to observe the user's health store in the background was granted by the system.

```
func startObservingWeightChanges(){
  healthStore.executeQuery(query)
  healthStore.enableBackgroundDeliveryForType(weightQuantityType,
```

```
      frequency: .Immediate,
      withCompletion: {(succeeded: Bool, error: NSError!) in

        if succeeded{
          println("Enabled background delivery of weight changes")
        } else {
          if let theError = error{
            print("Failed to enable background delivery of weight changes. ")
            println("Error = \(theError)")
          }
        }

      })
  }
```

And when our view controller disappears, we stop watching for changes in the health store in the background and stop our query:

```
func stopObservingWeightChanges(){
  healthStore.stopQuery(query)
  healthStore.disableAllBackgroundDeliveryWithCompletion{
    (succeeded: Bool, error: NSError!) in

    if succeeded{
      println("Disabled background delivery of weight changes")
    } else {
      if let theError = error{
        print("Failed to disable background delivery of weight changes. ")
        println("Error = \(theError)")
      }
    }

  }
}
```

If you look at the way we created our query earlier, the update handler of that query was set to the `weightChangedHandler` closure of your view controller. Here you will be informed that the health store now has some changes that have been applied to the type that you asked for (weight). In this method, HealthKit will not tell you what the new data is, only that there have been some changes. So now we have to query the health store for the changes that happened between yesterday to today:

```
func fetchRecordedWeightsInLastDay(){

  let sortDescriptor = NSSortDescriptor(key: HKSampleSortIdentifierEndDate,
    ascending: true)

  let query = HKSampleQuery(sampleType: weightQuantityType,
    predicate: predicate,
    limit: Int(HKObjectQueryNoLimit),
    sortDescriptors: [sortDescriptor],
    resultsHandler: {[weak self] (query: HKSampleQuery!,
```

```
        results: [AnyObject]!,
        error: NSError!) in

        if results.count > 0{

            for sample in results as [HKQuantitySample]{
                /* Get the weight in kilograms from the quantity */
                let weightInKilograms = sample.quantity.doubleValueForUnit(
                    HKUnit.gramUnitWithMetricPrefix(.Kilo))

                /* This is the value of "KG", localized in user's language */
                let formatter = NSMassFormatter()
                let kilogramSuffix = formatter.unitStringFromValue(
                    weightInKilograms, unit: .Kilogram)

                dispatch_async(dispatch_get_main_queue(), {

                    let strongSelf = self!

                    println("Weight has been changed to " +
                        "\(weightInKilograms) \(kilogramSuffix)")
                    println("Change date = \(sample.startDate)")

                })
            }

        } else {
            print("Could not read the user's weight ")
            println("or no weight data was available")
        }


    })

    healthStore.executeQuery(query)

}

func weightChangedHandler(query: HKObserverQuery!,
    completionHandler: HKObserverQueryCompletionHandler!,
    error: NSError!){

    /* Be careful, we are not on the UI thread */
    fetchRecordedWeightsInLastDay()

    completionHandler()

}
```

Give this a go for yourself and observe what values get printed to the background. If you have no weight values stored in the health store, use what you learned in Recipe 3.2

---

to add some weight samples to the health store and run this app again when you are done.

See Also

Recipe 3.2; Recipe 3.1

3.6. Reading and Modifying the User's Total Calories Burned

Problem

You want to retrieve the calories that the user has burned over a certain period of time and also store samples in the health store for calories burned.

Solution

Read and write into the contents of the health store for the `HKQuantityTypeIdentifierActiveEnergyBurned` quantity type.

Discussion

In this recipe, we want to develop a simple app that shows the calories that the user has burned from the beginning of today until now. So we will become an observer of the `HKQuantityTypeIdentifierActiveEnergyBurned` quantity type. For information about observing changes in the health store, please have a look at Recipe 3.5. We will display all the calories burned along with information of how those calories were burned, in the form of the type of the exercise that was performed. The first view controller is going to look like Figure 3-8.

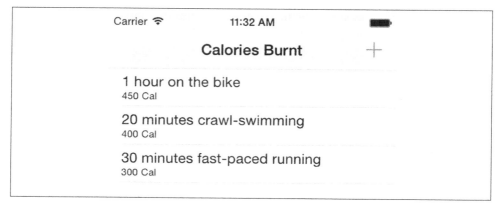

Figure 3-8. *List of exercises that burned calories*

The list that appears here is the list of all the exercises that the user has performed from the beginning of the day. As you can see, each item has the name of the exercise and the number of calories burned by it. When the user presses the add (+) button on the navigation bar, she will be shown a screen that looks like Figure 3-9.

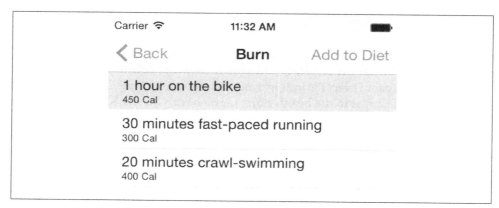

Figure 3-9. *Adding an exercise to the health store*

The two view controllers work through delegation. When the user chooses an exercise in Figure 3-9 and then presses the add button, our view controller will send a message to its delegate saying that the user chose an exercise. The root view controller will become the delegate of the second view controller and will receive the delegate message. The second view controller lists all the exercises and allows the user to add them to her health store.

Because the root controller depends on the second view controller, but the second view controller is independent, let's start by talking about the second view controller. We will call this `AddBurnedCaloriesToDietViewController`. For the `AddBurnedCaloriesTo` `DietViewController` class, we need to define a structure that allows us to store information about any exercise that causes calories to be burned. This has a name, the number of calories burned, a start date, and an end date.

```
import UIKit

extension NSDate{
  func dateByAddingMinutes(minutes: Double) -> NSDate{
    return self.dateByAddingTimeInterval(minutes * 60.0)
  }
}

struct CalorieBurner{
  var name: String
  var calories: Double
  var startDate = NSDate()
  var endDate = NSDate()

  init(name: String, calories: Double, startDate: NSDate, endDate: NSDate){
    self.name = name
    self.calories = calories
    self.startDate = startDate
    self.endDate = endDate
  }

  init(name: String, calories: Double, minutes: Double){
    self.name = name
    self.calories = calories
    self.startDate = NSDate()
    self.endDate = self.startDate.dateByAddingMinutes(minutes)
  }
}
```

Then we will define our protocol for the view controller that can inform the first view controller of the user's action when she decides to add an exercise to her list for today:

```
@objc(AddBurnedCaloriesToDietViewControllerDelegate)
protocol AddBurnedCaloriesToDietViewControllerDelegate{
  optional func addBurnedCaloriesToDietViewController(
    sender: AddBurnedCaloriesToDietViewController,
    addedCalorieBurnerWithName: String,
    calories: Double,
    startDate: NSDate,
    endDate: NSDate)
}
```

For the implementation of our view controller, we need a few things:

1. An identifier for all the cells that are to be displayed in the table view. This identifier is obviously previously defined in the storyboard file.

2. An energy formatter of type `NSEnergyFormatter` that can convert the number of calories for every calorie burner (exercise) into a human readable string. See Recipe 3.7 for more information about formatters.

3. A pre-populated array of calorie burners that we can display in the table view.

Knowing this, we will start implementing our second view controller like so:

```
class AddBurnedCaloriesToDietViewController: UITableViewController {

  struct TableViewValues{
    static let identifier = "Cell"
  }

  lazy var formatter: NSEnergyFormatter = {
    let theFormatter = NSEnergyFormatter()
    theFormatter.forFoodEnergyUse = true
    return theFormatter
    }()

  /* This is our delegate that gets notified whenever the user
  chooses to add a calorie burner to her list */
  var delegate: AddBurnedCaloriesToDietViewControllerDelegate?

  /* An array of calorie burners that we will display
  in our table view */
  lazy var allCalorieBurners: [CalorieBurner] = {

    let cycling = CalorieBurner(name: "1 hour on the bike",
      calories: 450,
      minutes: 60)
    let running = CalorieBurner(name: "30 minutes fast-paced running",
      calories: 300,
      minutes: 30
    )
    let swimming = CalorieBurner(name: "20 minutes crawl-swimming",
      calories: 400,
      minutes: 20
    )

    return [cycling, running, swimming]

  }()

  <# rest of the code #>

}
```

We set the forFoodEnergyUse property of our energy formatter to true. As you may know, when we say "I ate 200 calories," we actually mean kilocalories. However, because that is a longer word, people have opted to just say calories when they mean kilocalories. Food packages and labels, for instance, use calories in this colloquial sense. If you set this property, the energy formatter also gives you labeling for calories, not kilocalories.

Perfection! When our second view controller appears on the screen, by default we will select the first exercise in the list to make it more convenient for the user:

```
override func viewWillAppear(animated: Bool) {
  super.viewWillAppear(animated)
  tableView.selectRowAtIndexPath(
    NSIndexPath(forRow: 0, inSection: 0),
    animated: false,
    scrollPosition: .None)
}
```

In our table view, we only display the exercises that we have stored in the allCalorie Burners variable:

```
override func tableView(tableView: UITableView,
  numberOfRowsInSection section: Int) -> Int {
  return allCalorieBurners.count
}

override func tableView(tableView: UITableView,
  cellForRowAtIndexPath indexPath: NSIndexPath) -> UITableViewCell {

    let cell = tableView.dequeueReusableCellWithIdentifier(
      TableViewValues.identifier, forIndexPath: indexPath)
      as UITableViewCell

    let burner = allCalorieBurners[indexPath.row]

    let caloriesAsString = formatter.stringFromValue(burner.calories,
      unit: .Kilocalorie)

    cell.textLabel.text = burner.name
    cell.detailTextLabel!.text = caloriesAsString

    return cell
}
```

When the user chooses an exercise and presses the add button on the navigation bar to add the exercise to her exercise list for today, we call our delegate to inform it of this fact and pass the selected exercise's information to that view controller for saving:

```
@IBAction func addToDiet(){
```

```
    let burner = allCalorieBurners[tableView.indexPathForSelectedRow()!.row]

    if let theDelegate = delegate{
      theDelegate.addBurnedCaloriesToDietViewController?(self,
        addedCalorieBurnerWithName: burner.name,
        calories: burner.calories,
        startDate: burner.startDate,
        endDate: burner.endDate)
    }

    navigationController!.popViewControllerAnimated(true)

  }
```

Now on to the root view controller. Here we need a few handy things to be defined before we begin. One is the metadata that we want to add to the exercise samples that we store to the health store. Another is an extension on the NSDate class that allows us to calculate the beginning of a specific day. For instance, if you instantiate an NSDate class, you will also get the time, which could be the middle of the day or the end of the day. This extension sets the hour, minutes, and seconds to 0 to reset the time to the beginning of that specific day. We will use this extension to find the stored exercises in the user's health store from beginning of today until end of the day. The reason that we do not check the exercises from the beginning of today to now is that "now" refers to the moment in time when we take our instance from NSDate. So if we go and add an exercise after that, our "now" is not really now anymore, but the time in past when we instantiated our date.

```
import UIKit
import HealthKit

/* We will store this as metadata for the exercise in the health store */
let HKMetadataKeyExerciseName = "ExerciseName"

extension NSDate{
  func beginningOfDay() -> NSDate{
    return NSCalendar.currentCalendar().dateBySettingHour(0,
      minute: 0,
      second: 0,
      ofDate: self,
      options: .WrapComponents)!
  }
}
```

Then we will start the implementation of the view controller. The most important variable in our view controller is an array of CalorieBurner items. When we read a new exercise sample from the health store, we will convert it to an instance of the Calorie Burner type that we defined earlier. This mutable array will hold all those values for us.

```
class ListCaloriesBurnedTableViewController: UITableViewController,
AddBurnedCaloriesToDietViewControllerDelegate {
```

```
/* The array of all the exercises that the user performed
today */
var allCaloriesBurned = [CalorieBurner]()
/* To format the calorie values */
lazy var formatter: NSEnergyFormatter = {
  let theFormatter = NSEnergyFormatter()
  theFormatter.forFoodEnergyUse = true
  return theFormatter
}()
/* Find out when the user wants to add a new calorie burner
to the list and set our view controller as the delegate of the second
view controller */
let segueIdentifier = "burnCalories"
var isObservingBurnedCalories = false

/* When people say calories, they are actually talking about kilocalories
but I guess because kilocalories is difficult to say, we have opted to
say calories instead over the years */
lazy var unit = HKUnit.kilocalorieUnit()

struct TableViewValues{
  static let identifier = "Cell"
}

<# rest of the code #>

}
```

Also, we are going to add energy-burner items of type `HKQuantityTypeIdentifierAc` `tiveEnergyBurned` to the health store and read all of those types back from the health store as well, so let's form that quantity type now:

```
let burnedEnergyQuantityType = HKQuantityType.quantityTypeForIdentifier(
  HKQuantityTypeIdentifierActiveEnergyBurned)

lazy var types: NSSet = {
  return NSSet(object: self.burnedEnergyQuantityType)
  }()
```

The next thing we have to do is form our query to read all the exercises in the health store of the `HKQuantityTypeIdentifierActiveEnergyBurned` type. You can read more about queries in Recipe 3.2.

```
lazy var query: HKObserverQuery = {[weak self] in
  let strongSelf = self!
  return HKObserverQuery(sampleType: strongSelf.burnedEnergyQuantityType,
    predicate: strongSelf.predicate,
    updateHandler: strongSelf.burnedCaloriesChangedHandler)
  }()
```

Let's also form our predicate, which will allow us to query exercises from the beginning until the end of today:

```
lazy var healthStore = HKHealthStore()

lazy var predicate: NSPredicate = {

  let options: NSCalendarOptions = .WrapComponents

  let nowDate = NSDate()
  let beginningOfToday = nowDate.beginningOfDay()

  let tomorrowDate =
  NSCalendar.currentCalendar().dateByAddingUnit(.DayCalendarUnit,
    value: 1, toDate: NSDate(), options: options)

  let beginningOfTomorrow = tomorrowDate!.beginningOfDay()

  return HKQuery.predicateForSamplesWithStartDate(beginningOfToday,
    endDate: beginningOfTomorrow,
    options: .StrictEndDate)
}()
```

In our table view, we will display all the exercises that we saved in our `allCalories Burned` property:

```
override func tableView(tableView: UITableView,
  numberOfRowsInSection section: Int) -> Int {
    return allCaloriesBurned.count
}

override func tableView(tableView: UITableView,
  cellForRowAtIndexPath indexPath: NSIndexPath) -> UITableViewCell {

    let cell = tableView.dequeueReusableCellWithIdentifier(
      TableViewValues.identifier, forIndexPath: indexPath)
      as UITableViewCell

    let burner = allCaloriesBurned[indexPath.row]

    let caloriesAsString = formatter.stringFromValue(burner.calories,
      unit: .Kilocalorie)

    cell.textLabel.text = burner.name
    cell.detailTextLabel!.text = caloriesAsString

    return cell
}
```

I set my storyboard up so that the little add (+) button on the navigation bar will push the second view controller on the stack with a segue whose name is stored in the `se gueIdentifier` property of our view controller. So we will intercept that segue and set our root view controller as the delegate of the second view controller:

```
override func prepareForSegue(segue: UIStoryboardSegue,
  sender: AnyObject!) {
```

```
    if segue.identifier == segueIdentifier{
      let controller = segue.destinationViewController
        as AddBurnedCaloriesToDietViewController

      controller.delegate = self
    }

  }
```

When the user adds a new exercise to the list, the one and only method of the `AddBur nedCaloriesToDietViewControllerDelegate` protocol will be fired, and here we will add the exercise to the health store:

```
func addBurnedCaloriesToDietViewController(
  sender: AddBurnedCaloriesToDietViewController,
  addedCalorieBurnerWithName: String,
  calories: Double,
  startDate: NSDate,
  endDate: NSDate) {

    let quantity = HKQuantity(unit: unit, doubleValue: calories)
    let metadata = [
      HKMetadataKeyExerciseName: addedCalorieBurnerWithName
    ]

    let sample = HKQuantitySample(type: burnedEnergyQuantityType,
      quantity: quantity,
      startDate: startDate,
      endDate: endDate,
      metadata: metadata)

    healthStore.saveObject(sample, withCompletion: {[weak self]
      (succeeded: Bool, error: NSError!) in

      let strongSelf = self!

      if succeeded{
        println("Successfully saved the calories...")
        strongSelf.tableView.reloadData()
      } else {
        println("Failed to save the calories")
        if let theError = error{
          println("Error = \(theError)")
        }
      }

    })

  }
```

In this code, we are forming an instance of the `HKQuantitySample` class and storing it in the health store. We've discussed this class in recipes such as Recipe 3.2, but there is one part of the initialization of this class that we didn't really talk about before: the metadata. This is a dictionary of pretty much any data that you want to add to the sample as metadata. I am storing the name of the exercise in the metadata and the other properties like the start and the end date in the sample itself.

When the root view controller is displayed to the user, we will ask her whether we have permission to access and write to her Active Energy Burned health store category of type `HKQuantityTypeIdentifierActiveEnergyBurned`. If the user grants us permission, we will also start observing this category and update our UI whenever there is a new value stored there.

```
deinit{
  stopObservingBurnedCaloriesChanges()
}

func stopObservingBurnedCaloriesChanges(){

  if isObservingBurnedCalories == false{
    return
  }

  healthStore.stopQuery(query)
  healthStore.disableAllBackgroundDeliveryWithCompletion{[weak self]
    (succeeded: Bool, error: NSError!) in

    if succeeded{
      self!.isObservingBurnedCalories = false
      println("Disabled background delivery of burned energy changes")
    } else {
      if let theError = error{
        print("Failed to disable background delivery of " +
          "burned energy changes. ")
        println("Error = \(theError)")
      }
    }

  }
}

/* Ask for permission to access the health store */
override func viewDidAppear(animated: Bool) {
  super.viewDidAppear(animated)

  if HKHealthStore.isHealthDataAvailable(){

    healthStore.requestAuthorizationToShareTypes(types,
      readTypes: types,
      completion: {[weak self]
        (succeeded: Bool, error: NSError!) in
```

```
          let strongSelf = self!
          if succeeded && error == nil{
            dispatch_async(dispatch_get_main_queue(),
              strongSelf.startObservingBurnedCaloriesChanges)
          } else {
            if let theError = error{
              println("Error occurred = \(theError)")
            }
          }

        })

    } else {
      println("Health data is not available")
    }

    if allCaloriesBurned.count > 0{
      let firstCell = NSIndexPath(forRow: 0, inSection: 0)
      tableView.selectRowAtIndexPath(firstCell,
        animated: true,
        scrollPosition: UITableViewScrollPosition.Top)
    }

  }
```

We are calling the startObservingBurnedCaloriesChanges method of the view controller whenever the permission is granted and our view has appeared on the screen,
and we will also call the stopObservingBurnedCaloriesChanges method when the view
controller is deallocated in order to stop observing changes in the aforementioned category:

```
func startObservingBurnedCaloriesChanges(){

  if isObservingBurnedCalories{
    return
  }

  healthStore.executeQuery(query)
  healthStore.enableBackgroundDeliveryForType(burnedEnergyQuantityType,
    frequency: .Immediate,
    withCompletion: {[weak self] (succeeded: Bool, error: NSError!) in

      if succeeded{
        self!.isObservingBurnedCalories = true
        println("Enabled background delivery of burned energy changes")
      } else {
        if let theError = error{
          print("Failed to enable background delivery " +
            "of burned energy changes. ")
          println("Error = \(theError)")
        }
```

```
    }

  })
}

func stopObservingBurnedCaloriesChanges(){

  if isObservingBurnedCalories == false{
    return
  }

  healthStore.stopQuery(query)
  healthStore.disableAllBackgroundDeliveryWithCompletion{[weak self]
    (succeeded: Bool, error: NSError!) in

    if succeeded{
      self!.isObservingBurnedCalories = false
      println("Disabled background delivery of burned energy changes")
    } else {
      if let theError = error{
        print("Failed to disable background delivery of " +
          "burned energy changes. ")
        println("Error = \(theError)")
      }
    }

  }
}
```

When we constructed our query earlier, we made sure that its completion handler is set
to the burnedCaloriesChangedHandler:completionHandler:error: closure of our
view controller. In this closure, we will simply call the fetchBurnedCaloriesInLast
Day method, which we are going to write in order to fetch all the calories burned in the
past day and add them to our table view:

```
func addBurnedCaloriesToDietViewController(
    sender: AddBurnedCaloriesToDietViewController,
    addedCalorieBurnerWithName: String,
    calories: Double,
    startDate: NSDate,
    endDate: NSDate) {

    let quantity = HKQuantity(unit: unit, doubleValue: calories)
    let metadata = [
      HKMetadataKeyExerciseName: addedCalorieBurnerWithName
    ]

    let sample = HKQuantitySample(type: burnedEnergyQuantityType,
      quantity: quantity,
      startDate: startDate,
      endDate: endDate,
      metadata: metadata)
```

```
      healthStore.saveObject(sample, withCompletion: {[weak self]
        (succeeded: Bool, error: NSError!) in

      let strongSelf = self!

      if succeeded{
        println("Successfully saved the calories...")
        strongSelf.tableView.reloadData()
      } else {
        println("Failed to save the calories")
        if let theError = error{
          println("Error = \(theError)")
        }
      }

      })

}

func fetchBurnedCaloriesInLastDay(){

  let sortDescriptor = NSSortDescriptor(
    key: HKSampleSortIdentifierStartDate,
    ascending: false)

  let query = HKSampleQuery(sampleType: burnedEnergyQuantityType,
    predicate: predicate,
    limit: Int(HKObjectQueryNoLimit),
    sortDescriptors: [sortDescriptor],
    resultsHandler: {[weak self] (query: HKSampleQuery!,
      results: [AnyObject]!,
      error: NSError!) in

    println("Received new data from the query. Processing...")

    let strongSelf = self!

    if results.count > 0{

      strongSelf.allCaloriesBurned = [CalorieBurner]()

      for sample in results as [HKQuantitySample]{

        let burnerName = sample.metadata[HKMetadataKeyExerciseName]
          as? NSString
        let calories = sample.quantity.doubleValueForUnit(strongSelf.unit)
        let caloriesAsString =
        strongSelf.formatter.stringFromValue(calories, unit: .Kilocalorie)

        let burner = CalorieBurner(name: burnerName!,
          calories: calories,
```

```
                    startDate: sample.startDate,
                    endDate: sample.endDate)
                strongSelf.allCaloriesBurned.append(burner)

            }

            dispatch_async(dispatch_get_main_queue(), {
                strongSelf.tableView.reloadData()
                })

        } else {
            print("Could not read the burned calories ")
            println("or no burned calories data was available")
        }


    })

    healthStore.executeQuery(query)

}
```

That was it, really. Now give this a go for yourself and start adding exercises to the health store using the second view controller. When you add a new exercise, you will automatically come to the root view controller and see the added exercise on top of the list. The view controller will also highlight the added exercise for you, just to be nice!

See Also

Recipe 3.2; Recipe 3.1

3.7. Converting Between Units

Problem

You want to be able to convert various measurements units. For instance, you want to convert kilograms to grams, grams to stones, or meters to miles.

Solution

Follow these steps:

1. Create a unit of type HKUnit for your source unit.

2. Create another unit of type HKUnit for your destination unit.

3. Provide the quantity of your source as an object of type HKQuantity. So in converting grams to kilograms for example, provide your gram value as an object of type HKQuantity.

---

4. Convert your source to your destination unit using the `doubleValueForUnit:` method of your quantity object.

Let's say that you want to convert from grams to kilograms. Create your gram unit first:

```
let gramUnit = HKUnit(fromMassFormatterUnit: .Gram)
```

Then create your kilogram unit:

```
let kilogramUnit = HKUnit(fromMassFormatterUnit: .Kilogram)
```

And then say how many grams you want to convert to kilograms:

```
let weightInGrams:Double = 74_250
```

Create a quantity object out of your weight in grams:

```
let weightQuantity = HKQuantity(unit: gramUnit,
        doubleValue: weightInGrams)
```

When you are done, convert the quantity to your kilograms unit in this way:

```
let weightInKilograms = weightQuantity.doubleValueForUnit(kilogramUnit)
```

At the end, print out the results to the console:

```
println("Your weight is \(weightInKilograms) kilograms")
println("Your weight is \(weightInGrams) grams")
```

Discussion

Units are extremely important in HealthKit. We will be using them alot. In normal daily use, units are not very easy to convert, and calculations often need long implementations that are easy to get wrong. Thanks to HealthKit, you don't really have to do much. Just use the units and the quantity class and convert between your units.

You saw that we initialized both our gram and kilogram units using the `unitFromMass FormatterUnit:` constructor of the `HKUnit` class. This constructor takes in a parameter of type `NSMassFormatterUnit`, which specifies the unit in which we want to specify our value: for instance, `.Gram` for grams or `.Kilogram` for kilograms.

So far I've covered units for specifying mass. What if you want to specify length, such as meters or miles? Well, then you would need to use the `unitFromLengthFormatterU nit:` constructor of the same class. This constructor takes in a parameter of type `NSLengthFormatterUnit` so that you can pass values such as `NSLengthFormatterUnit Millimeter` and `NSLengthFormatterUnitCentimeter`.

To specify values for energy such as calories, use the `unitFromEnergyFormatterU nit:` constructor of this class that takes in a parameter of type `NSEnergyFormatterU nit`. Let's say we want to convert the energy used up through exercise from 1,500 calories to kilojoules, and we want to be able to print the results out to the console like so:

```
You've burned 1,500 cal
You've burned 6.276 kJ
```

Note how the "cal" and "kJ" are formatted. In another region of the world, "cal" might be expressed as "Calories" or "Cal" with a capital C, and the same for "kJ". We need a way not only to convert calories to kilojoules but also to localize our returned values. For that we will use the NSEnergyFormatter class. This class can convert a value of type Double to any unit of type NSEnergyFormatterUnit using its stringFromVal ue:unit: method. We will also use the calorieUnit and the jouleUnitWithMetric Prefix: convenience constructors of our HKUnit class to specify our units:

```
let caloriesValue:Double = 1_500

let caloriesUnit = HKQuantity(unit: HKUnit.calorieUnit(),
  doubleValue: caloriesValue)

let kilojoulesValue = caloriesUnit.doubleValueForUnit(
  HKUnit.jouleUnitWithMetricPrefix(.Kilo))

let energyFormatter = NSEnergyFormatter()

let caloriesString = energyFormatter.stringFromValue(
  caloriesValue, unit: .Calorie)
let kilojoulesString = energyFormatter.stringFromValue(kilojoulesValue,
  unit: .Kilojoule)

println("You've burned \(caloriesString)")
println("You've burned \(kilojoulesString)")
```

The NSLengthFormatter, NSMassFormatter, and NSEnergyFormatter classes format length, mass, and energy related units respectively. So let's also have a look at length conversion. Say that you want to convert 1,234 meters to feet and print out values to the console like so:

```
You've driven 1,234 m
You've driven 4,048.556 ft
```

We have to define the distance first:

```
let distanceInMeters:Double = 1_234
```

And then present our meters in HKUnit:

```
let metersUnit = HKQuantity(unit: HKUnit.meterUnit(),
  doubleValue: distanceInMeters)
```

Then we convert the meters to feet:

```
let feetValue = metersUnit.doubleValueForUnit(
  HKUnit.footUnit())
```

Eventually, we will retrieve the values as formatted and localized strings using the NSLengthFormatter class:

```
let lengthFormatter = NSLengthFormatter()

let metersString = lengthFormatter.stringFromValue(distanceInMeters,
    unit: .Meter)
let feetString = lengthFormatter.stringFromValue(feetValue,
    unit: .Foot)
```

And print out our values to the console with ease:

```
println("You've driven \(metersString)")
println("You've driven \(feetString)")
```

CHAPTER 4

Managing Home Appliances with HomeKit

4.0. Introduction

A variety of accessories have been built that can interact with iOS over the years. Many of these accessories work in a home environment. For instance, the projector in a cinema room inside the house or an accessory that adjusts the temperature of the water in a swimming pool can be controlled via Apple's new technology, appropriately named HomeKit. This is a framework that allows us to initiate contact with these accessories in the context of a home.

Now let's have a look at a simple home setup. This house has four floors: a basement and the ground, first, and the second floors. The house has seven bedrooms on two different floors. The underground floor has a few things that excite us. One is a cinema room with a fantastic projector and some comfortable cinema seats. The chairs are reclining chairs whose positions can be adjusted to suit each viewer's needs. In front of the projector, a few meters away, a white screen can descend from the ceiling to cover the wall so that the projector can project there, giving us a great picture while playing games or watching TV and videos.

We open the door from inside the cinema room and reach the indoor pool. There is a device that allows us to cover the swimming pool with a hard material that reclines as well, so that we can cover the pool when we don't need it and makes sure the kids won't fall into it at night or when not under supervision of an adult. We also have a Jacuzzi with a few switches to light up inside in various colors and to control the heat for the water.

All of these devices in the underground level of this house are rather complex to work with and require some sort of "techy-ness" before anybody can really adjust their settings. This is where HomeKit comes in. It allows us to build apps that can work with HomeKit-ready appliances inside the premises of our home and control them with ease.

Throughout this chapter, I am going to use examples that come back to this basement setup.

Everything in this house can be controlled with a single iOS device. And this is not just inside the house. All these appliances can be controlled remotely. Let's say you are on vacation and you have forgotten to turn the cinema room's projector off. You can simply open up an app on your phone, which has been programmed to talk to all the appliances in your home, and turn that projector off. Alternatively, the company from whom you bought the projector might provide an app on the App Store that you can download to control the projector inside your cinema room.

HomeKit has more than 10 classes that we will learn about in this chapter. The master class in HomeKit is named HMHomeManager. This is our entry point to all the appliances inside our house. Every house is represented by the HMHome class and then divided into rooms, and every room (of type HMRoom) has appliances, or, as HomeKit calls them, *accessories* represented by the HMAccessory class.

Every accessory then has *services* that it can provide to the user. In the case of the Jacuzzi in the house, one of the services can be the bubble generator or the lights that can be adjusted to various colors. Services are represented by the HMService class.

Every zone has characteristics as well. For instance, take the projector in the cinema room. One of its services is to "project a movie on the white wall." However, is this service on or off at the moment? This is a *characteristic* of that service. Another characteristic of this service might be "needs repair." This may be a Boolean and, if set to true, indicates that the projector needs to be repaired because the "project movie on the white wall" service isn't working as expected.

You can also define *zones* for this house. For instance, we can have a zone called "floor 1" and then many accessories under that zone so that we can, for instance, turn all the lights off in that particular zone. Zones are represented by the HMZone class. You can also define service groups in HomeKit, represented by the HMServiceGroup class. Service groups are great for giving a logical order to services from different accessories. For instance, if you have a "turn off" service for various appliances in your house, such as lights, computers, projectors, oven, and so on, you might decide to group that service together into a "turn off all appliances" service group. And when going outside the house, you can just run that service group to turn everything off—except for your fridge and freezer, that is. I have made that mistake before. Never again!

HomeKit integrates very well with Siri. That is why everything that you define using HomeKit has to have a unique name so that when you tell Siri, "Turn off the projector," it knows that "projector" is a unique item in the house and can then call its "turn off" service. Therefore, you cannot have two accessories with the same name defined in the context of your house.

Integrating your app with HomeKit APIs requires a bit of setup, which we are going to see how to do in this chapter. One thing that you have to do before proceeding further with this chapter is to set up your provision profile to support HomeKit and then turn on HomeKit in the Capabilities section of your project. You can learn about setting up provision profiles that support HomeKit by reading Recipe 1.22.

4.1. Simulating HomeKit Accessories

Problem

You want to be able to use the HomeKit APIs without having to purchase a third-party appliance that is built to work with HomeKit, or alternatively, you want to speed up your development of an app that can speak with a third-party appliance that will eventually integrate with HomeKit at some point—but for the time being, you need to do some development of your own.

 This recipe uses the example house that we talked about in Recipe 4.0, so make sure you read that introduction before proceeding with this recipe to get a better understanding of what we are trying to achieve.

Solution

Download the HomeKit Accessory Simulator from Apple's Developer website.

Discussion

The HomeKit Accessory Simulator has been very wisely developed by Apple to allow us to test our apps on simulated third-party accessories and be able to proceed with our development before purchasing an accessory that works with HomeKit. This is great stuff because not everybody can afford to purchase a real HomeKit integrated device while developing a simple application. However, you will always need to test your apps on real devices and with real accessories before sending them to Apple for approval, so I highly discourage working only with the iOS simulator and the HomeKit Accessory Simulator without trying your app with real devices.

Open the HomeKit Accessory Simulator, press the little add (+) button, and choose New Accessory from the list. This will allow you to create a new accessory in the simulator. We are going to create the cinema room's projector right now. You will be presented with a dialog similar to that shown in Figure 4-1, so please enter the same values that I did and then press the Finish button. You can change the Manufacturer to whatever you want. I have used my limited company's name for that.

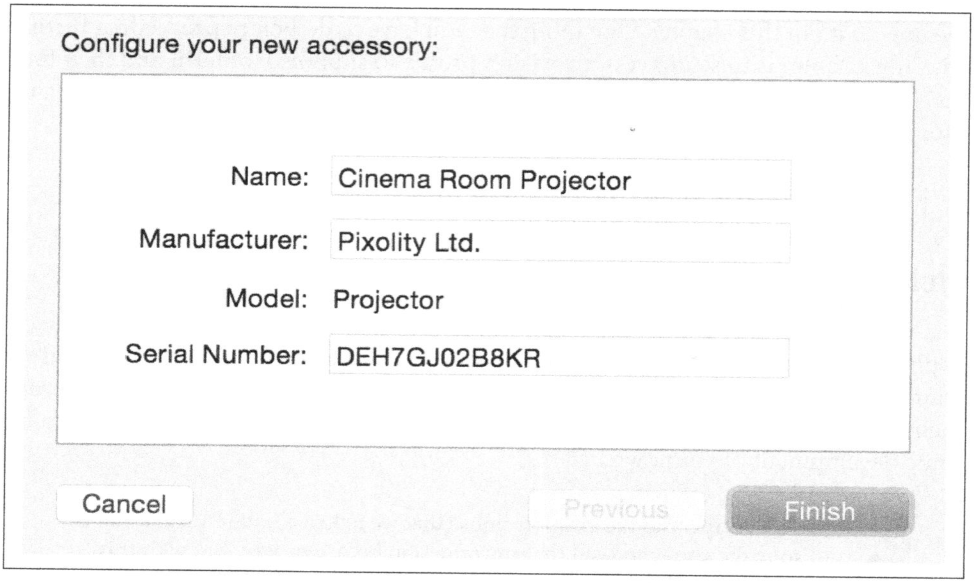

Figure 4-1. Adding a new accessory to the HomeKit Accessory Simulator

Now you will see the information for your accessory that has been generated by the HomeKit Accessory Simulator (Figure 4-2).

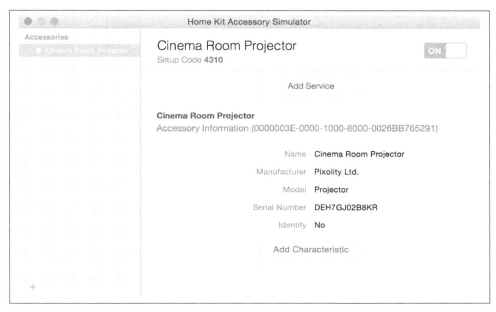

Figure 4-2. Information for our accessory is shown in the HomeKit Accessory Simulator

Let's go and add a service to our projector. Press the Add Service button and then choose the Add Switch option. This is the switch that turns our projector on or off. Change the On value of this service to No and rename it to `Cinema Room Projector Switch`. Now your simulator should look like that shown in Figure 4-3.

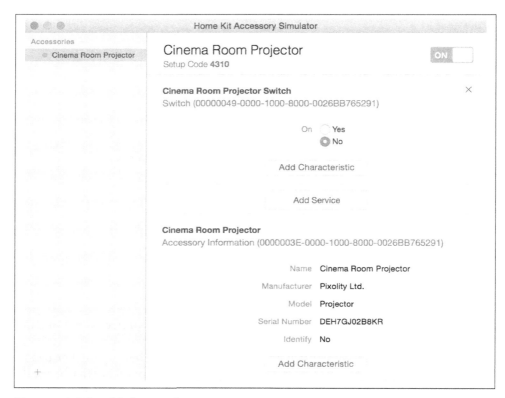

Figure 4-3. We added a switch service to our projector accessory

Now, under the Cinema Room Projector accessory, press the Add Characteristic button. A new page will appear on your screen where you will be able to change the characteristic that you are about to add to the accessory. From the Characteristic Type menu, choose Brightness and then enter a description of "This changes the projector's brightness on the wall." To allow users to raise the brightness to the screen's maximum value, ensure the maximum value here is 100, while the minimum value must be 0. Use 1 as the step value. Your screen must now look like that shown in Figure 4-4. When you are done, press the Finish button to add the brightness characteristic to your projector accessory.

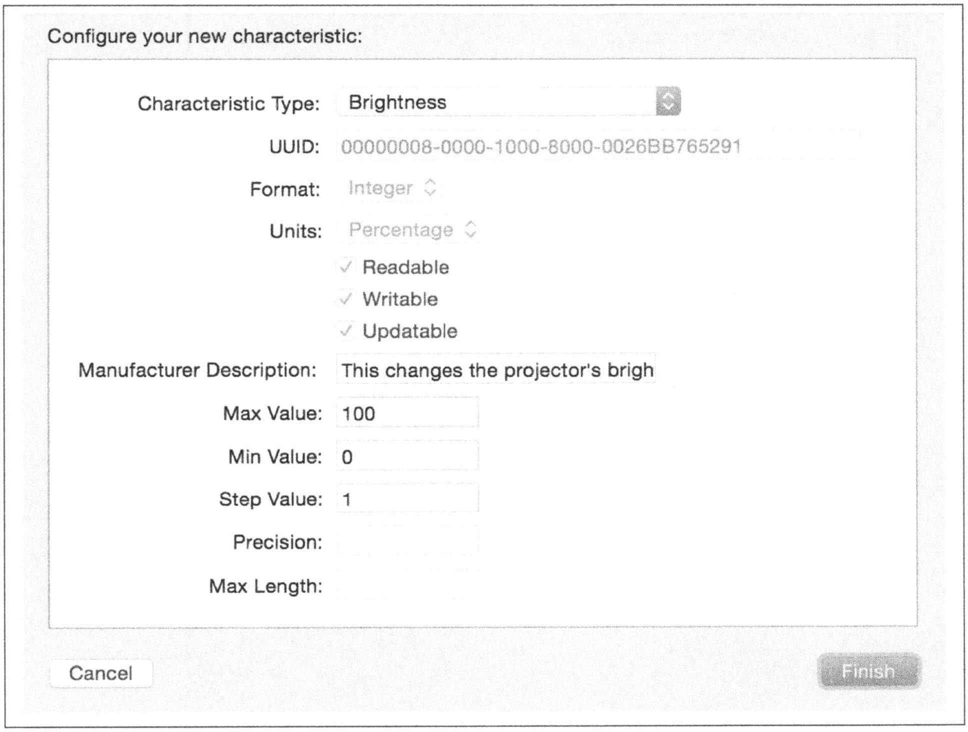

Configure your new characteristic:

Characteristic Type:	Brightness
UUID:	00000008-0000-1000-8000-0026BB765291
Format:	Integer
Units:	Percentage
	✓ Readable
	✓ Writable
	✓ Updatable
Manufacturer Description:	This changes the projector's brigh
Max Value:	100
Min Value:	0
Step Value:	1
Precision:	
Max Length:	

Cancel   Finish

Figure 4-4. We created a brightness characteristic for the projector

Return to the main screen of the HomeKit Accessory Simulator and change the current value of the Brightness characteristic of your projector to a value right in the middle, 50. We are going to play with this value later in this chapter. Now add another characteristic to the projector and this time, set the type of the characteristic to Custom. You will then be asked to provide a UUID for this characteristic. You can use the `NSUUID` class in your project to create a new UUID and use it here:

```
println(NSUUID().UUIDString)
```

Choose Float for the format of the characteristic and choose Celcius for its Units section. Ensure that the Readable and the Updatable checkmarks are checked, but uncheck the Writable checkmark. This means that we want to be able to read this characteristic but do not want to allow app programmers to write to it.

For the manufacturer description, enter "Current Heat Level." For the maximum value, enter 60; for the minimum value, enter -10; and for the step value, enter 1. Your HomeKit Accessory Simulator should now look like that shown in Figure 4-5.

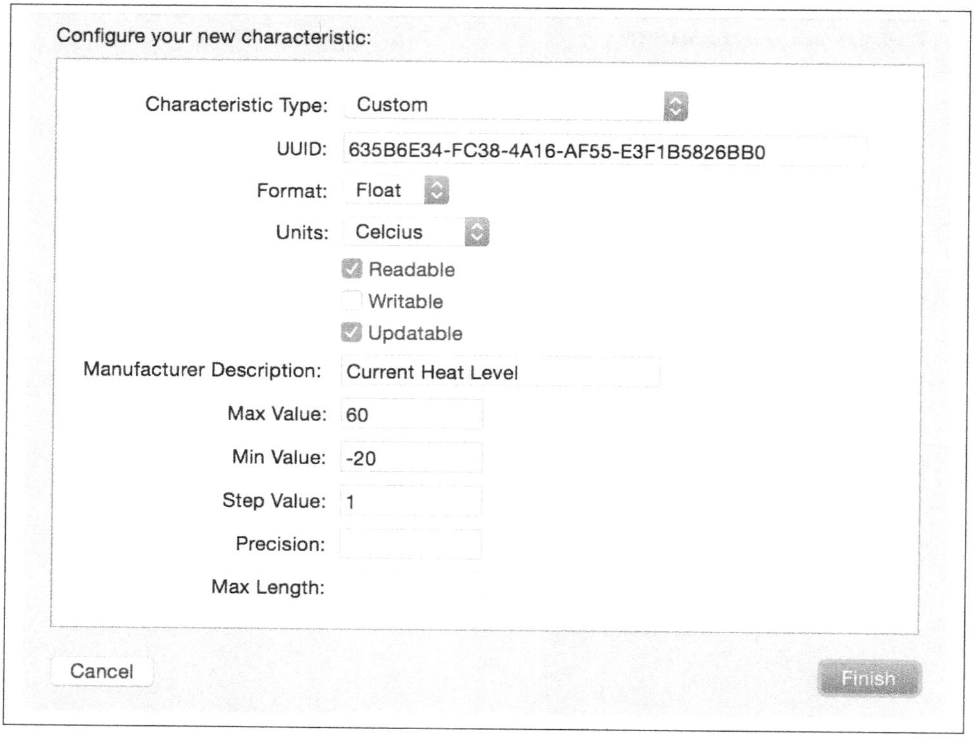

Configure your new characteristic:

Characteristic Type: Custom

UUID: 635B6E34-FC38-4A16-AF55-E3F1B5826BB0

Format: Float

Units: Celcius

☑ Readable
☐ Writable
☑ Updatable

Manufacturer Description: Current Heat Level

Max Value: 60

Min Value: -20

Step Value: 1

Precision:

Max Length:

Cancel   Finish

Figure 4-5. Adding a heat level characteristic to our projector

Now press the Finish button and change the current value of the heat level to 20 as shown in Figure 4-6.

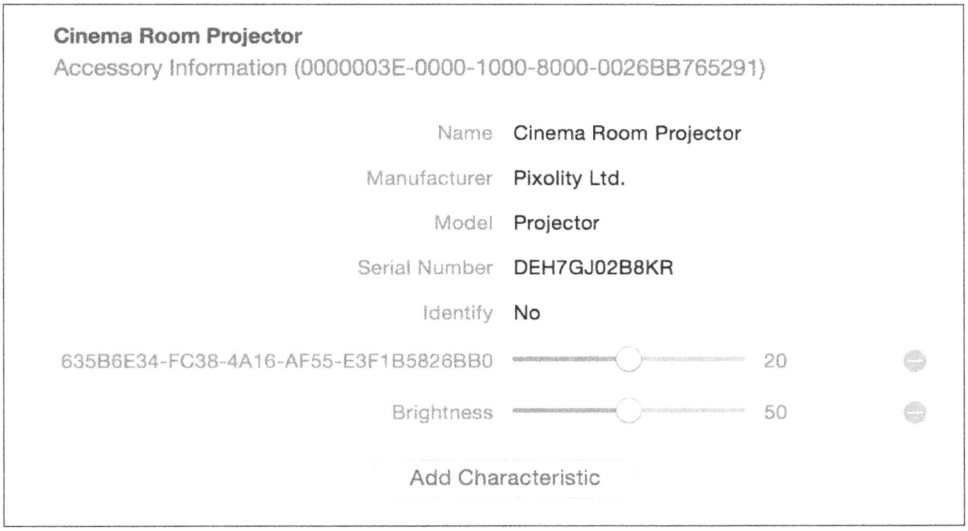

Cinema Room Projector
Accessory Information (0000003E-0000-1000-8000-0026BB765291)

Name	Cinema Room Projector
Manufacturer	Pixolity Ltd.
Model	Projector
Serial Number	DEH7GJ02B8KR
Identify	No
635B6E34-FC38-4A16-AF55-E3F1B5826BB0	20
Brightness	50

Add Characteristic

Figure 4-6. We set default values for both our characteristics

Now that you have learned how to add accessories, services, and characteristics, create a Pool Area Cover accessory, add a Switch service to it, and set its value to Yes for now. Then add a characteristic to the switch of type Locked and give it a description that makes sense to you. We are going to pretend that this is the parental lock we have on the pool cover. So the pool cover has a switch that can be on or off, and it is set to on by default so that the pool is covered. We have also applied a parental lock characteristic on this switch so that we can lock it and prevent the kids from opening the pool cover if we don't want them to. The default value of this lock is on, meaning that the parental lock has been applied. So now you should have something that looks like Figure 4-7.

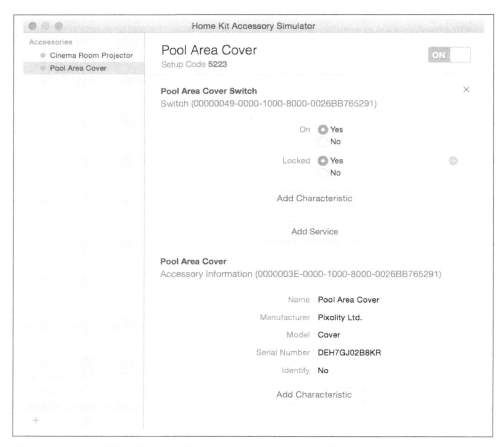

Figure 4-7. We defined our pool area cover accessory in the HomeKit Accessory Simulator

The last thing we are going to do is add a new accessory to the list in HomeKit Accessory Simulator and call it *Jacuzzi*. Then add a switch service to it to identify whether the Jacuzzi is currently on or off. Add a custom characteristic of type Bool to the Jacuzzi itself, and give it a description of "Does the Jacuzzi have enough water?". Make this property readable and updatable but not writable. Set the default value of this property to Yes to indicate that currently there is enough water in the Jacuzzi for it to function normally. Now your HomeKit Accessory Simulator screen should look like that shown in Figure 4-8:

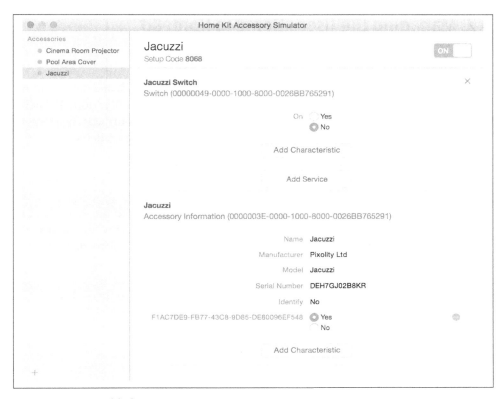

Figure 4-8. We added a Jacuzzi as an accessory

Okay, that is perfect for now. We are going to base the rest of this chapter on what we have created in this recipe, so this was a very important step in getting you started with the HomeKit Accessory Simulator. Just as a side note, since it is really easy to mess up what we have created in the HomeKit Accessory Simulator, I suggest that you export all the accessories that you have created so far in the simulator and save them on disk. Simply select an accessory on the lefthand side of the HomeKit Accessory Simulator, choose File, and then choose the Export Accessory menu option. Do this for all three of the accessories that we created in this recipe and keep a copy of all of them in case something goes wrong in the HomeKit Accessory Simulator or you accidentally delete an accessory or its services or characteristics.

4.2. Managing the User's Home in HomeKit

Problem

You want to be able to work with the user's home objects in HomeKit and define a home if one does not exist. You would also like to be able to work with various HomeKit delegate methods pertaining to the user's home, so that you can be notified when various aspects of the user's home change, such as an accessory becoming available.

Solution

Instantiate an object of type `HMHomeManager`. After the home manager signals to you (through delegation) that the list of homes is ready to be read, read the instance's `primaryHome` or `homes` propeties. If a home is defined for the user, you may want to become the delegate of the home manager object by conforming to the `HMHomeManagerDelegate` protocol.

 This recipe uses the example house that we talked about in Recipe 4.0, so to get a better understanding of what we are trying to achieve, please read that introduction before proceeding with this recipe.

Discussion

As soon as you instantiate an object of type `HMHomeManager`, ensure that you set its delegate property. This delegate must conform to the `HMHomeManagerDelegate` protocol. As soon as you do this, the user will be prompted to grant or reject access to HomeKit for your app. The dialog that the user will see will be similar to that shown in Figure 4-9.

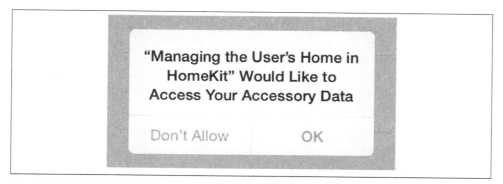

Figure 4-9. The user is asked for permission to grant or reject access to our app to HomeKit

Once you are granted permission to work with the HomeKit APIs, the first delegation call you may want to implement in the `HMHomeManagerDelegate` protocol is the `home ManagerDidUpdateHomes:` method. This method gets called whenever the home manager object detects a change to the list of homes that are registered for the user. You cannot begin reading the values of the `primaryHome` or the `homes` properties of the home manager until this delegate method is called on your delegate object. Before that, the state of the home manager is unknown.

In this recipe, let's start building an app that can list the currently-registered homes for the user in a table view and allow the user to add homes to the list with another view controller. We will call the first view controller the `ListHomesViewController` and the second one `AddHomeViewController`. We want the first view controller to look like Figure 4-10.

Figure 4-10. List of homes is displayed on the first view controller

So let's begin with the most important variables that our view controller needs:

```
import UIKit
import HomeKit

class ListHomesViewController: UITableViewController, HMHomeManagerDelegate{

  let segueIdentifier = "addHome"

  struct TableViewValues{
    static let identifier = "Cell"
  }

  <# rest of the code #>

}
```

The segue name is a variable I defined to contain the name of the segue between this view controller and the next. Whenever this segue is triggered, I will catch that action and set the home manager property of the second view controller so that the view controller can save a home into HomeKit with the name that the user chooses. Don't worry about this for now. We will see how it works in practice.

Then we need to define our home manager:

```
lazy var homeManager: HMHomeManager = {
  let manager = HMHomeManager()
  manager.delegate = self
  return manager
}()
```

Then, for every home that we can find in the home manager, we will display a cell:

```
override func tableView(tableView: UITableView,
  numberOfRowsInSection section: Int) -> Int {
  return homeManager.homes.count
}

override func tableView(tableView: UITableView,
  cellForRowAtIndexPath indexPath: NSIndexPath) -> UITableViewCell {

    let cell = tableView.dequeueReusableCellWithIdentifier(
      TableViewValues.identifier, forIndexPath: indexPath)
    as UITableViewCell

    let home = homeManager.homes[indexPath.row] as HMHome

    cell.textLabel.text = home.name

    return cell

}
```

As soon as the home manager is ready with the list of homes, we will update our table view:

```
func homeManagerDidUpdateHomes(manager: HMHomeManager!) {
  tableView.reloadData()
}
```

Last but not least, as soon as the segue between our plus (+) button is tapped on the navigation bar, we will set the home manager property of the second view controller so that it can save a new home in the manager:

```
override func prepareForSegue(segue: UIStoryboardSegue,
  sender: AnyObject!) {

    if segue.identifier == segueIdentifier{

      let controller = segue.destinationViewController
        as AddHomeViewController
      controller.homeManager = homeManager

    }
```

```
    super.prepareForSegue(segue, sender: sender)

}
```

OK, great stuff! Now let's begin with the implementation of the second view controller, named AddHomeViewController. Here, we will have a reference to the home manager and our text field outlet:

```
import UIKit
import HomeKit

class AddHomeViewController: UIViewController {

    @IBOutlet weak var textField: UITextField!
    var homeManager: HMHomeManager!

    <# rest of the code #>

}
```

The text field is on the screen to allow the user to enter a name for the home they are about to add to HomeKit and the UI is going to look like that shown in Figure 4-11.

Figure 4-11. The user can add a new home to HomeKit

As soon as the view controller is displayed to the user, we will make the keyboard pop up for the text field, ready for the user to start typing:

```swift
override func viewDidAppear(animated: Bool) {
  super.viewDidAppear(animated)

  textField.becomeFirstResponder()

}
```

We have linked the Save button on our navigation bar with the addHome method of our view controller. Here, we will use the addHomeWithName:completionHandler: method of the home manager. This method adds a new home with a given name and then calls the completion handler on the current thread. In the completion handler, you will be given an error object that you can check to ensure that the home was added successfully:

```swift
func displayAlertWithTitle(title: String, message: String){
  let controller = UIAlertController(title: title,
    message: message,
    preferredStyle: .Alert)

  controller.addAction(UIAlertAction(title: "OK",
    style: .Default,
    handler: nil))

  presentViewController(controller, animated: true, completion: nil)

}

@IBAction func addHome(){

  if countElements(textField.text) == 0{
    displayAlertWithTitle("Home name", message: "Please enter the home name")
    return
  }

  homeManager.addHomeWithName(textField.text,
    completionHandler: {[weak self] (home: HMHome!, error: NSError!) in

      let strongSelf = self!

      if error != nil{
        strongSelf.displayAlertWithTitle("Error happened",
          message: "\(error)")
      } else {
        strongSelf.navigationController!.popViewControllerAnimated(true)
      }

  })

}
```

The next thing we are going to do is to add deletion capabilities to the first view controller so that the user can delete homes if she wants to. In order to delete a home from the home manager, invoke the `removeHome:completionHandler:` method of the home manager. The completion handler will be a closure that gets an instance of the `NSError` indicating whether the home was successfully removed. So let's modify our first view controller to make it look more like that shown in Figure 4-12.

Figure 4-12. We can now remove homes from the list

We want to allow the user to push the Edit button on the navigation bar and start deleting homes from the list if she wants to. Since we are going to use the `UIAlertController` class every now and then, I am going to create an extension on this class to give us a type method that we can use to display alert messages to the user with ease:

```
extension UIAlertController{
  class func showAlertControllerOnHostController(
    hostViewController: UIViewController,
    title: String,
    message: String,
    buttonTitle: String){

      let controller = UIAlertController(title: title,
        message: message,
        preferredStyle: .Alert)

      controller.addAction(UIAlertAction(title: buttonTitle,
        style: .Default,
        handler: nil))

      hostViewController.presentViewController(controller,
        animated: true,
        completion: nil)

  }
}
```

Then I am going to display an Edit button to the user on the navigation bar. When the Edit button is pressed, I will disable the add (+) button so that the user can focus only on the task of editing the list of homes:

```
override func setEditing(editing: Bool, animated: Bool) {
  super.setEditing(editing, animated: animated)

  /* Don't let the user add another home while they are editing
  the list of homes. This makes sure the user focuses on the task
  at hand */
  self.navigationItem.rightBarButtonItem!.enabled = !editing
}

override func viewWillAppear(animated: Bool) {
  super.viewWillAppear(animated)

  navigationItem.leftBarButtonItem = editButtonItem()

}
```

When the user presses the Delete action on any of the cells, we will intercept that action and delete the selected home from the list of homes using the removeHome:completionHandler: of the home manager:

```
override func tableView(tableView: UITableView,
    commitEditingStyle editingStyle: UITableViewCellEditingStyle,
    forRowAtIndexPath indexPath: NSIndexPath) {

    if editingStyle == .Delete{

      let home = homeManager.homes[indexPath.row] as HMHome
      homeManager.removeHome(home, completionHandler: {[weak self]
        (error: NSError!) in

        let strongSelf = self!

        if error != nil{
          UIAlertController.showAlertControllerOnHostController(strongSelf,
            title: "Error",
            message: "An error occurred = \(error)",
            buttonTitle: "OK")
        } else {

          tableView.deleteRowsAtIndexPaths([indexPath],
            withRowAnimation: .Automatic)

        }

      })

    }

}
```

```
      }
```

Also, when we have no homes in the home manager, we should disable the Edit button because it makes no sense to have it there:

```
override func tableView(tableView: UITableView,
  numberOfRowsInSection section: Int) -> Int {
    let numberOfRows = homeManager.homes.count

    if numberOfRows == 0 && editing{
      setEditing(!editing, animated: true)
    }

    editButtonItem().enabled = (numberOfRows > 0)

    return numberOfRows
}
```

This code snippet will also take the view controller out of editing mode if the last cell has just been deleted. Great stuff! Now give this a go in your simulator or on a device and see how you get on.

See Also

Recipe 4.0; Recipe 1.22

4.3. Adding Rooms to the User's Home

Problem

You want to be able to add rooms to a home that you have already defined for the user.

Solution

Use the `addRoomWithName:completionHandler:` method of your home object (see Recipe 4.2) and you will receive either an error or the created room of type `HMRoom`.

 In this recipe, I am going to base our solution on what we learned in Recipe 4.2 and just expand the same app to allow the user to add rooms to houses. So it is beneficial to read the aforementioned recipe first, before proceeding with this one.

Discussion

Every home can have rooms. Every room is represented by the `HMRoom` class in HomeKit. You can read the list of rooms that every home can have by checking the value of the rooms property of the home. Every home object also has a delegate of type `HMHomeDele` `gate`. This delegate will receive updates on the state of the home. One of the important methods that this delegate has is the `home:didAddRoom:` method that gets called whenever a new room is added to the home. The other method is the `home:didRemove` `Room:` method which, as you can guess, gets called whenever a room is removed from a home.

In this recipe, we are going to expand the same app that we wrote in Recipe 4.2, but this time allow the user to add rooms to a home and delete those rooms if she wants to. So we are going to have two new view controllers. One is going to show the list of rooms for a home and the other is going to allow us to add a room to a home by entering the room's name. The first view controller will be called `ListRoomsTableViewController` and all it has to do is to read the list of the rooms that a home has and display it on the table view. I am assuming that the `ListHomesViewController` class that we coded in the previously mentioned recipe is passing the home manager reference, along with the home object that was tapped, to this view controller so that we have a reference to both and will be able to add rooms to the home if needed.

```
import UIKit
import HomeKit

class ListRoomsTableViewController: UITableViewController, HMHomeDelegate {

  var homeManager: HMHomeManager!
  var home: HMHome!{
  didSet{
    home.delegate = self
  }
  }

  struct TableViewValues{
    static let identifier = "Cell"
  }

  let addRoomSegueIdentifier = "addRoom"

  <# rest of the code #>

}
```

Can you see how I am setting the delegate of the home object? This delegate is getting set to our view controller as soon as the value of the home object changes. This value is passed to us from the `ListHomesViewController` class like so:

```
override func prepareForSegue(segue: UIStoryboardSegue,
  sender: AnyObject!) {

    if segue.identifier == addHomeSegueIdentifier{
```

```
    let controller = segue.destinationViewController
        as AddHomeViewController
    controller.homeManager = homeManager

}

else if segue.identifier == showRoomsSegueIdentifier{
    let controller = segue.destinationViewController
        as ListRoomsTableViewController
    controller.homeManager = homeManager

    let home = homeManager.homes[tableView.indexPathForSelectedRow()!.row]
        as HMHome

    controller.home = home
}

super.prepareForSegue(segue, sender: sender)

}
```

We can also add the delegate methods for our home to get notified whenever a room gets added or deleted:

```
func home(home: HMHome!, didAddRoom room: HMRoom!) {
    println("Added a new room to the home")
}

func home(home: HMHome!, didRemoveRoom room: HMRoom!) {
    println("A room has been removed from the home")
}
```

When the table view is displayed, we will read the value of the rooms property of the home variable and then display all the rooms that have currently been saved in the home, in our table view:

```
override func tableView(tableView: UITableView,
    numberOfRowsInSection section: Int) -> Int {
    return home.rooms.count

}

override func tableView(tableView: UITableView,
    cellForRowAtIndexPath indexPath: NSIndexPath) -> UITableViewCell{

    let cell = tableView.dequeueReusableCellWithIdentifier(
        TableViewValues.identifier, forIndexPath: indexPath)
        as UITableViewCell

    let room = home.rooms[indexPath.row] as HMRoom

    cell.textLabel.text = room.name
```

```
        return cell

    }
```

We will also allow the user to delete a room in the selected home. To delete a room, we will use the removeRoom:completionHandler: method of the instance of the HMHome object:

```
override func tableView(tableView: UITableView,
  commitEditingStyle editingStyle: UITableViewCellEditingStyle,
  forRowAtIndexPath indexPath: NSIndexPath) {

    if editingStyle == .Delete{

      let room = home.rooms[indexPath.row] as HMRoom
      home.removeRoom(room, completionHandler: {[weak self]
        (error: NSError!) in

        let strongSelf = self!

        if error != nil{
          UIAlertController.showAlertControllerOnHostController(strongSelf,
            title: "Error",
            message: "An error occurred = \(error)",
            buttonTitle: "OK")
        } else {

          tableView.deleteRowsAtIndexPaths([indexPath],
            withRowAnimation: .Automatic)

        }

      })

    }

}
```

So our "list rooms" view controller is going to look like Figure 4-13.

When the user taps on the little add (+) button on the navigation bar, we will display the Add Room view controller, which is going to look like Figure 4-14.

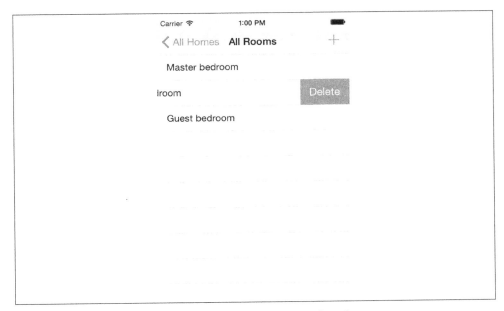

Figure 4-13. We can now see and edit the list of rooms for a home

Figure 4-14. We can add rooms to a home

In this view controller, we will simply use the `addRoomWithName:completionHandler:` method of our home instance and add the room to it:

```
@IBAction func addRoom(){

  if countElements(textField.text) == 0{
    UIAlertController.showAlertControllerOnHostController(self,
      title: "Room name", message: "Please enter the room name",
      buttonTitle: "OK")
    return
  }

  home.addRoomWithName(textField.text, completionHandler: {[weak self]
    (room: HMRoom!, error: NSError!) in

    let strongSelf = self!

    if error != nil{
      UIAlertController.showAlertControllerOnHostController(strongSelf,
        title: "Error happened", message: "\(error)",
        buttonTitle: "OK")
    } else {
      strongSelf.navigationController!.popViewControllerAnimated(true)
    }

    })

}
```

See Also

Recipe 4.2; Recipe 4.4; Recipe 4.0

4.4. Specifying Zones in the User's Home

Problem

You want to define virtual zones in the user's home to group various rooms into logical groups. For instance, you want to group all kids' rooms into a zone called Kids' Rooms and all the bathrooms into a zone called Bathrooms so that you can later interact with accessories only in these zones.

Solution

Use the `addZoneWithName:completionHandler:` method of your home object to add a new zone to the home. To remove a zone, use the `removeZone:completionHandler:` method of the home. The created zone will be of type `HMZone` and you can interact with the various methods that it provides.

Every zone has a `name` and a `rooms` property. The `name` property is a string and the `rooms` property is an array of `HMRoom` instances. To add a room to a zone, use its `addRoom:com pletionHandler:` method and to remove a room (correct, you guessed it!), use the `removeRoom:completionHandler:` method. Both these methods accept a completion handler whose only parameter is an instance of `NSError`, which indicates whether the room could be added or removed successfully.

Discussion

Zones are very useful if you want to bring more logic than rooms into a house. We can categorize "things" inside a house into zones. These "things" are usually appliances but can also be rooms. For instance, let's say that you defined all the rooms in the house using what we learned in Recipe 4.3. Now the user wants to turn off all the lights in the kids' bedrooms, but not in other rooms. This is where zones are really useful. You can add the kids' bedrooms to a zone with a name similar to Kids' Bedrooms, for instance, and then see that zone in your app and allow the user to interact with various accessories that are present in rooms added to that zone.

So let's have a look at an example. We want to do the following:

1. Create a home object with a random name.
2. Add three rooms to the home, two of which are bedrooms and the other one a gaming room.
3. Add a Bedrooms zone to the home and add the two bedrooms to the zone.
4. At the end, delete the zones and the home altogether.

Let's start with the most basic variables that we need in our view controller:

```
import UIKit
import HomeKit

class ViewController: UIViewController, HMHomeManagerDelegate{

    /* We use this name to search in the list of rooms added to the home
    and read their names and find this string in them. If we
    find this string, we are sure that the room is a bedroom indeed */
    let bedroomKeyword = "bedroom"
    var numberOfBedroomsAddedSoFar = 0
    let numberOfBedroomsToAdd = 2
    var home: HMHome!
    var bedroomZone: HMZone!

    <# rest of the code #>

}
```

Then we will generate a random name for the house:

```
var randomHomeName: String = {
  return "Home \(arc4random_uniform(UInt32.max))"
}()

var homeManager: HMHomeManager!
```

As soon as our view is loaded, we will start up the home manager:

```
override func viewDidLoad() {
  super.viewDidLoad()

  homeManager = HMHomeManager()
  homeManager.delegate = self

}
```

This will then go through all the homes that have been defined for the current user and call our homeManagerDidUpdateHomes: method. In that method, I am going to add a home to the home manager's database using what we learned in Recipe 4.2. Then if that goes well, I will add a Bedrooms zone to the home:

```
func homeManagerDidUpdateHomes(manager: HMHomeManager!) {

  manager.addHomeWithName(randomHomeName, completionHandler: {
    [weak self](home: HMHome!, error :NSError!) in

    let strongSelf = self!

    if error != nil{
      println("Failed to add the home. Error = \(error)")
      return
    }

    strongSelf.home = home

    /* Now let's add the Bedrooms zone to the home */
    home.addZoneWithName("Bedrooms", completionHandler:
      strongSelf.addZoneCompletionHandler)

  })

}
```

The completion handler for adding the zone is set to the addZoneCompletionHandler closure of this view controller. That closure has to take in a parameter of type HMZone, which will be the zone that we added to the home and an error parameter of type NSError. In this closure, if the zone could be created, we will add three rooms to the home before we add them to the zone. It is important to note that rooms that you are trying to add to a zone must have already been added to a home to which the zone also belongs.

```
func addZoneCompletionHandler(zone: HMZone!, error: NSError!){

  if error != nil{
    println("Failed to add the zone. Error = \(error)")
    return
  } else {
    println("Successfully added the zone")
    println("Adding bedrooms to the home now...")
  }

  bedroomZone = zone

  /* Now add rooms to this home */
  home.addRoomWithName("Master bedroom",
    completionHandler: self.roomAddedToHomeCompletionHandler)

  home.addRoomWithName("Kids' bedroom",
    completionHandler: self.roomAddedToHomeCompletionHandler)

  home.addRoomWithName("Gaming room",
    completionHandler: self.roomAddedToHomeCompletionHandler)
}
```

The completion handler of the `addRoomWithName:completionHandler:` method of the home is set to the `roomAddedToHomeCompletionHandler` closure of this view controller. This closure must take in a parameter of type `HMRoom` and one of type `NSError`. After the rooms are added to the home, we will check for the ones that have the name "bedroom" in them and then if we find them, we will add them to the Bedrooms zone:

```
func roomAddedToHomeCompletionHandler(room: HMRoom!, error: NSError!){

  if error != nil{
    println("Failed to add room to home. Error = \(error)")
  } else {
    if (room.name as NSString).rangeOfString(bedroomKeyword,
      options: .CaseInsensitiveSearch).location != NSNotFound{
        println("A bedroom is added to the home")
        println("Adding it to the zone...")
        bedroomZone.addRoom(room, completionHandler:
          self.roomAddedToZoneCompletionHandler)
    } else {
      println("The room that is added is not a bedroom")
    }
  }

}
```

Now when we add the rooms to our zone, the completion handler of the `addRoom:com pletionHandler:` of the zone is set to the `roomAddedToZoneCompletionHandler` closure of our view controller. In that closure, we will check to make sure we have added all the bedrooms that we intended to add (numberOfBedroomsToAdd), and if yes, we will then start removing the zone and subsequently the home from the HomeKit database:

```
func roomAddedToZoneCompletionHandler(error: NSError!){

    if error != nil{
      println("Failed to add room to zone. Error = \(error)")
    } else {
      println("Successfully added a bedroom to the Bedroom zone")
      numberOfBedroomsAddedSoFar++
    }

    if numberOfBedroomsAddedSoFar == numberOfBedroomsToAdd{
      home.removeZone(bedroomZone, completionHandler: {[weak self]
        (error: NSError!) in

        let strongSelf = self!

        if error != nil{
          println("Failed to remove the zone")
        } else {
          println("Successfully removed the zone")
          println("Removing the home now...")

          strongSelf.homeManager.removeHome(strongSelf.home,
            completionHandler: {(error: NSError!) in

              if error != nil{
                println("Failed to remove the home")
              } else {
                println("Removed the home")
              }

          })

        }

      })
    }

}
```

If you now run this on your simulator or on a device, you will see results similar to this printed to the console:

```
Successfully added the zone
Adding bedrooms to the home now...
A bedroom is added to the home
Adding it to the zone...
A bedroom is added to the home
Adding it to the zone...
The room that is added is not a bedroom
Successfully added a bedroom to the bedroom zone
```

```
Successfully added a bedroom to the bedroom zone
Successfully removed the zone
Removing the home now...
Removed the home
```

See Also

Recipe 4.2; Recipe 4.3

4.5. Discovering and Managing HomeKit Enabled Accessories

Problem

You want to write an app that is able to discover all HomeKit-enabled accessories on the current network to which the user's iOS device is connected.

Solution

Instantiate an object of type `HMAccessoryBrowser` and then assign your own view controller or any other object as the delegate of the accessory browse. Once you are ready to start discovering accessories that are reachable on the network, call the `startSearch ingForNewAccessories` method of your accessory browser. This will then call the `ac cessoryBrowser:didFindNewAccessory:` delegate method of the `HMAccessoryBrows erDelegate` protocol for every accessory that has been found. Equally, it will call the `accessoryBrowser:didRemoveNewAccessory:` method for accessories that are either not discoverable anymore or have now been added to a home.

Discussion

Accessories that are HomeKit compatible are connected to a network and can be discovered by an instance of the `HMAccessoryBrowser` class. For an instance of this class to work, the current device running your app must have an active and enabled Internet connection. Sometimes your device might seem like it is connected to the Internet but in reality is stuck behind a firewall. For instance, you might go to a hotel and see that your phone is connected to the "free" Wifi. Then you attempt to open a web page and you see a login screen from the hotel asking for your username and password. Even though you thought you were on the Internet, you are still on a closed network.

In this recipe, we are going to have a look at a simple application that is based on the accessories we set up in Recipe 4.1, in the HomeKit Accessory Simulator. As soon as our app runs, we will use the home manager to get access to the user's HomeKit database and then create a home object with a random name. Then we will create a room and add it to the home. After that, we will add a few accessories to the home and then assign them to the room using the `assignAccessory:toRoom:completionHandler:` method of the home. After the accessories are assigned to a room, we will go through the services that they offer. In each service, we will find all the characteristics of the service and print the information to the screen.

Let us begin by defining our accessory browser, the home manager, and the home and room name variables:

```
import UIKit
import HomeKit

class ViewController: UIViewController, HMHomeManagerDelegate,
HMAccessoryBrowserDelegate {

  var accessories = [HMAccessory]()
  var home: HMHome!
  var room: HMRoom!

  lazy var accessoryBrowser: HMAccessoryBrowser = {
    let browser = HMAccessoryBrowser()
    browser.delegate = self
    return browser
    }()

  var randomHomeName: String = {
    return "Home \(arc4random_uniform(UInt32.max))"
    }()

  let roomName = "Bedroom 1"

  var homeManager: HMHomeManager!

  <# rest of the code #>

}
```

As soon as our view is created, we will start our home manager to ask the user for permission to use HomeKit in our app:

```
override func viewDidLoad() {
  super.viewDidLoad()
  homeManager = HMHomeManager()
  homeManager.delegate = self
}
```

When the home manager has finished finding all the homes in the user's HomeKit database, it will call the `homeManagerDidUpdateHomes:` method of its delegate (our view controller). In this method, we will add our home to the list of homes that already exist. If the home can be added, we will add a room to it as well:

```
func homeManagerDidUpdateHomes(manager: HMHomeManager!) {
```

```
manager.addHomeWithName(randomHomeName, completionHandler: {[weak self]
  (home: HMHome!, error: NSError!) in

  if error != nil{
    println("Could not add the home")
  } else {
    let strongSelf = self!
    strongSelf.home = home
    println("Successfully added a home")
    println("Adding a room to the home...")
    home.addRoomWithName(strongSelf.roomName, completionHandler: {
      (room: HMRoom!, error: NSError!) in

      if error != nil{
        println("Failed to add a room...")
      } else {
        strongSelf.room = room
        println("Successfully added a room.")
        println("Discovering accessories now...")
        strongSelf.accessoryBrowser.startSearchingForNewAccessories()
      }

    })

  }

})

}
```

You can see that as soon as our room can be added to the home, we use the start
SearchingForNewAccessories method of our accessory browser. As soon as the accessory browser finds a new accessory in reach, it calls the accessoryBrowser:did
FindNewAccessory: method of our view controller. This method is defined in the HMAc
cessoryBrowserDelegate protocol, which our view controller conforms to. In this
method, as soon as the accessory is found, we add it to the home using the addAcces
sory:completionHandler: method of the home object. After the accessory is added to
the home, we will use the assignAccessory:toRoom:completionHandler: of our home
object to assign the accessory to the room we created:

```
func accessoryBrowser(browser: HMAccessoryBrowser!,
  didFindNewAccessory accessory: HMAccessory!) {

  println("Found a new accessory")
  println("Adding it to the home...")
  home.addAccessory(accessory, completionHandler: {[weak self]
    (error: NSError!) in

    let strongSelf = self!

    if error != nil{
```

```
        println("Failed to add the accessory to the home")
        println("Error = \(error)")
    } else {
        println("Successfully added the accessory to the home")
        println("Assigning the accessory to the room...")
        strongSelf.home.assignAccessory(accessory,
          toRoom: strongSelf.room,
          completionHandler: {(error: NSError!) in

            if error != nil{
                println("Failed to assign the accessory to the room")
                println("Error = \(error)")
            } else {
                println("Successfully assigned the accessory to the room")

                strongSelf.findServicesForAccessory(accessory)

            }

        })
    }

})

}
```

When the accessory is successfully assigned to the room, we are calling the `findServi cesForAccessory:` method of our view controller. This method goes through all the services that this accessory has and prints their information to the screen.

```
func findServicesForAccessory(accessory: HMAccessory){
    println("Finding services for this accessory...")
    for service in accessory.services as [HMService]{
        println(" Service name = \(service.name)")
        println(" Service type = \(service.serviceType)")

        println(" Finding the characteristics for this service...")
        findCharacteristicsOfService(service)
    }
}
```

When a new service is found in this code, we will call the `findCharacteristicsOfSer vice:` method of the view controller to go through the characteristic of each one of the services:

```
func findCharacteristicsOfService(service: HMService){
    for characteristic in service.characteristics as [HMCharacteristic]{
        println("   Characteristic type = " +
          "\(characteristic.characteristicType)")
    }
}
```

We will also implement the `accessoryBrowser:didRemoveNewAccessory:` method of the view controller, which is defined in the `HMAccessoryBrowserDelegate` protocol:

```
func accessoryBrowser(browser: HMAccessoryBrowser!,
  didRemoveNewAccessory accessory: HMAccessory!){

    println("An accessory has been removed")

}
```

This method gets called on the delegate of the accessory browser whenever an accessory is moved out of range and/or cannot be accessed anymore. It will also get called if the accessory has just been added to a home.

Having created all the accessories that we talked about in Recipe 4.1, I run this code on my simulator and first see the screen in Figure 4-15.

Figure 4-15. iOS asking for pairing code for an accessory

Every HomeKit accessory has a code that is similar to Bluetooth pairing codes that you are probably familiar with. Before an app on a device can start working with an accessory, the user has to enter this code. In the HomeKit Accessory Simulator earlier, when we created the accessories (see Recipe 4.1), you might have noticed that every accessory had a setup code generated for it (Figure 4-16).

Figure 4-16. The accessory setup code is displayed on top of the screen

This code will be different for you, so please have a look at your HomeKit Accessory Simulator and then enter the relevant codes for every accessory that is being discovered. As you carry out this experiment for yourself in Xcode, have a look at the logs that are being printed to the console. You will then be able to see information for every accessory and its services and the characteristics of every service. Later in this chapter, we will talk more about services and characteristics of services for accessories.

See Also

Recipe 4.1; Recipe 4.4; Recipe 4.3

4.6. Interacting with HomeKit Accessories

Problem

You want to be able to discover and modify the value of the characteristics of a service inside an accessory. For instance, you may want to change the brightness (a characteristic) of a cinema room projector (an accessory). The cinema room projector that we created in Recipe 4.1 is both a service and an accessory, and the brightness of the projector was a characteristic of the projector accessory. You can change the value of any characteristic of any service as long as that value is writable.

Solution

First, find the characteristic of a service inside an accessory whose value you want to change. Then go through the `properties` property of the characteristic and look for the `HMCharacteristicPropertyReadable` value. If this value exists, it means that you can read the value of the characteristic. When you are sure you can read the value of the characteristic, issue the `readValueWithCompletionHandler:` method of the characteristic to prepare its value for reading. Then read the value from the `value` property of the characteristic.

To be able to write to a characteristic, you need to ensure that the `HMCharacteristic PropertyWritable` property exists for this characteristic. When you are sure that you can write a value, issue the `writeValue:completionHandler:` method of the characteristic to change the value.

Discussion

What we are going to do in this recipe is quite simple: we are going to create a home in the user's HomeKit database and then add a room to it. Then we are going to add the Cinema Room Projector accessory that we created in Recipe 4.1 to the home and assign it to the room. The second time the user opens the app, we are going to retrieve the same home, room, and accessory instead of creating a new home. So the first time, we will set a random name on the home and store that name in the user defaults. The next time the user opens the app, we will read the home name from user defaults and attempt to find it. If it doesn't exist, we will create it.

If you remember from Recipe 4.1, our projector accessory had a brightness characteristic, which was a floating point value. In this recipe, we will find that characteristic and reduce its value by 1. So if the brightness is currently set to 50, our app will change it to 49. Every time the app runs, it will reduce this value by 1 until the value reaches the minimum value that was specified for it.

As part of this recipe, we will read the value of the brightness characteristic and reduce it. Before we read the value, we need to find out whether this characteristic is readable and before writing to it, we need to make sure it is writable. You can find this information out by going through the `properties` property of the characteristic instance as mentioned in the Solution of this recipe. Since this is a very important part of the project, I've decided to extend the `HMCharacteristic` class and add two functions that allow us to find out with ease whether a characteristic is readable and/or writable:

```
import UIKit
import HomeKit

extension HMCharacteristic{

  func containsProperty(paramProperty: String) -> Bool{
```

```
        if let propeties = self.properties{
          for property in properties as [String]{
            if property == paramProperty{
              return true
            }
          }
        }
        return false
    }

    func isReadable() -> Bool{
      return containsProperty(HMCharacteristicPropertyReadable)
    }

    func isWritable() -> Bool{
      return containsProperty(HMCharacteristicPropertyWritable)
    }

}
```

Now in your view controller, define your home, room, and projector accessory variables:

```
class ViewController: UIViewController, HMHomeManagerDelegate,
HMAccessoryBrowserDelegate {

    var home: HMHome!
    var room: HMRoom!
    var projectorAccessory: HMAccessory!

    <# rest of the code #>

}
```

Then let's create a computed property that can generate a random home name for our home, if we have to create one. This property has to be able to persist its value between app runs, so it has to save the value and be able to read it back:

```
/* The first time it is read, it will generate a random string.
The next time it is read, it will give you the string that it created
the first time. Works between application runs and persist the
data in user defaults */
var homeName: String = {
  let homeNameKey = "HomeName"

  let defaults = NSUserDefaults.standardUserDefaults()

  /* Can we find the old value? */
  if let name = defaults.stringForKey(homeNameKey){
    if countElements(name) > 0 {
      return name
    }
  }
```

```
/* Create a new name */
let newName = "Home \(arc4random_uniform(UInt32.max))"
defaults.setValue(newName, forKey: homeNameKey)
return newName
}()
```

We will also define our room name, which is part of the home, and the accessory name that we are going to be looking for. Again, remember that we created this accessory as part of Recipe 4.1:

```
lazy var accessoryBrowser: HMAccessoryBrowser = {
  let browser = HMAccessoryBrowser()
  browser.delegate = self
  return browser
  }()

let roomName = "Bedroom"
let accessoryName = "Cinema Room Projector"

var homeManager: HMHomeManager!
```

As soon as our view is loaded into memory, we start looking for existing home objects:

```
override func viewDidLoad() {

    homeManager = HMHomeManager()
    homeManager.delegate = self


}
```

This will call the homeManagerDidUpdateHomes: method of the home manager delegate. In that method, we will try to find the existing home and the bedroom in it.

```
func homeManagerDidUpdateHomes(manager: HMHomeManager!) {

  for home in manager.homes as [HMHome]{
    if home.name == homeName{

      println("Found the home")
      self.home = home

      for room in home.rooms as [HMRoom]{
        if room.name == roomName{
          println("Found the room")
          self.room = room
          findCinemaRoomProjectorAccessory()
        }
      }

      if self.room == nil{
        /* We have to create the room */
        println("The room doesn't exist. Creating it...")
        createRoom()
```

```
        }

      }
    }

    if home == nil{
      println("Home doesn't exist. Creating it...")
      createHome()
    }

  }
```

If we could not find the home, we created it by calling the createHome method of our view controller. If we found the home but couldn't find the bedroom in it, we called the createRoom method of our view controller. And if we found both the home and the bedroom, we called the findCinemaRoomProjectorAccessory method. First let's see how we create a home if one doesn't exist:

```
func createHome(){

  homeManager.addHomeWithName(homeName, completionHandler: {
    [weak self](home: HMHome!, error: NSError!) in

    if error != nil{
      println("Failed to create the home")
    } else {
      println("Successfully created the home")
      let strongSelf = self!
      strongSelf.home = home
      println("Creating the room...")
      strongSelf.createRoom()
    }

  })

}
```

This is what we have already learned in Recipe 4.2, so it isn't new to us. If the home doesn't exist, it means that its bedroom doesn't exist either, so let's create the room now.

```
func createRoom(){

  home.addRoomWithName(roomName, completionHandler: {
    [weak self](room: HMRoom!, error: NSError!) in

    if error != nil{
      println("Failed to create the room")
    } else {
      println("Successuflly created the room")
      let strongSelf = self!
      strongSelf.room = room
      strongSelf.findCinemaRoomProjectorAccessory()
```

```
        }
    })

}
```

When we have the home and the room, we will reach the `findCinemaRoomProjector`
`Accessory` function. In this method, we will find the "Cinema Room Projector" accessory that we had created in Recipe 4.1 by going through `accessories` properties of the
room which we found. If we cannot find this accessory, we have to start looking for that
accessory by using the accessory browser, which we learned about in Recipe 4.5:

```
func findCinemaRoomProjectorAccessory(){

    if let accessories = room.accessories{
        for accessory in accessories as [HMAccessory]{
            if accessory.name == accessoryName{
                println("Found the projector accessory in the room")
                self.projectorAccessory = accessory
            }
        }
    }

    /* Start searching for accessories */
    if self.projectorAccessory == nil{
        println("Could not find the projector accessory in the room")
        println("Starting to search for all available accessories")
        accessoryBrowser.startSearchingForNewAccessories()
    } else {
        lowerBrightnessOfProjector()
    }

}
```

If we can find the accessory attached to the room, we immediately attempt to lower its
brightness by 1. But if we cannot find it in the room, our accessory browser will find it
in the HomeKit Accessory Simulator. The browser will then call the `accessoryBrows`
`er:didFindNewAccessory:` method of its delegate (our view controller) and let us know
that an accessory was found. Then we will check the name of the accessory to make sure
that we found the projector because there may be other accessories that are being discovered, but we are interested only in the projector.

```
func accessoryBrowser(browser: HMAccessoryBrowser!,
    didFindNewAccessory accessory: HMAccessory!) {

    println("Found an accessory...")

    if accessory.name == accessoryName{
        println("Discovered the projector accessory")
        println("Adding it to the home")
        home.addAccessory(accessory, completionHandler: {
```

```
      [weak self](error: NSError!) in

      if error != nil{
        println("Failed to add it to the home")
      } else {
        println("Successfully added it to home")
        println("Assigning the projector to the room...")
        let strongSelf = self!
        strongSelf.home.assignAccessory(accessory,
          toRoom: strongSelf.room,
          completionHandler: {(error: NSError!) in

            if error != nil{
              println("Failed to assign the projector to the room")
            } else {
              strongSelf.projectorAccessory = accessory
              println("Successfully assigned the projector to the room")
              strongSelf.lowerBrightnessOfProjector()
            }

        })

      }

    })
  }

}
```

Now off to the `lowerBrightnessOfProjector` method of our view controller. When we get to this method, we already have the home, the room, and the projector accessory as properties of our view controller. All we have to do is this:

1. Go through the services of the projector using its `services` array property and find the characteristic of type `HMCharacteristicTypeBrightness`.

2. After the brightness characteristic is found, find out whether it is readable. If it is readable, read its value.

3. If we can read the value, find out whether the characteristic is writable. If writable, reduce the read value by 1 and write the value back to the characteristic.

4. Ensure that we handle all the errors appropriately.

```
    func lowerBrightnessOfProjector(){

      var brightnessCharacteristic: HMCharacteristic!

      println("Finding the brightness characteristic of the projector...")

      for service in projectorAccessory.services as [HMService]{
        for characteristic in service.characteristics as [HMCharacteristic]{
```

```
      if characteristic.characteristicType == HMCharacteristicTypeBrightness{
        println("Found it")
        brightnessCharacteristic = characteristic
      }
    }
  }

  if brightnessCharacteristic == nil{
    println("Cannot find it")
  } else {

    if brightnessCharacteristic.isReadable() == false{
      println("Cannot read the value of the brightness characteristic")
      return
    }

    println("Reading the value of the brightness characteristic...")

    brightnessCharacteristic.readValueWithCompletionHandler{[weak self]
      (error: NSError!) in

      if error != nil{
        println("Cannot read the brightness value")
      } else {
        println("Read the brightness value. Setting it now...")

        if brightnessCharacteristic.isWritable(){
          let newValue = (brightnessCharacteristic.value as Float) - 1.0
          brightnessCharacteristic.writeValue(newValue,
            completionHandler: {(error: NSError!) in

              if error != nil{
                println("Failed to set the brightness value")
              } else {
                println("Successfully set the brightness value")
              }

          })
        } else {
          println("The brightness characteristic is not writable")
        }

      }

    }

    if brightnessCharacteristic.value is Float{

    } else {
      println("The value of the brightness is not Float. Cannot set it")
    }
```

```
        }
    }
```

Run this code for yourself and experiment a little bit with the characteristic's value. Note that if the value of the brightness characteristic of the projector is already set to its minimum, our code will fail to set the value and will print an appropriate message to the console informing you of this fact.

See Also

Recipe 4.1

4.7. Grouping Services of HomeKit Accessories

Problem

You want to group a few services together for easy access later, or you want to allow the user to access those services with ease using Siri on their iOS devices.

Solution

Go through all the service groups of type `HMServiceGroup` in the `serviceGroups` property of the home object of type `HMHome`. If you cannot find one, create one using the `addServiceGroupWithName:completionHandler:` method of the home. This will either give you an error in the completion handler or a service group of type `HMServiceGroup`. If you successfully add a service group to the home, you can start adding services to it using its `addService:completionHandler:` method.

After the service group has some services, you can then enumerate through its services using its `services` property and perform actions on those services as you wish.

Discussion

Service groups are useful if you want to perform actions on services that are similar to each other. Let's say that you have a "Switch" service on all your HomeKit accessories and when you go on holidays, you want to switch everything off. You can therefore create a service group and call it, for example, "Switches off all accessories." Then you can go through the services in this group in one go and turn all the switches off instead of finding all accessories in the home and then finding their services.

I am going to base my example now on the code that we wrote in Recipe 4.6 except here, after we get our home and room reference, I am going to try to find my "All Switches" service group. If I cannot find it, I will create it:

```
func findOrCreateSwitchServiceGroup(){

  /* Find out whether we already have our switch service group */
  if let groups = home.serviceGroups{
    for serviceGroup in groups as [HMServiceGroup]{
      if serviceGroup.name == switchServiceGroupName{
        switchServiceGroup = serviceGroup
      }
    }
  }

  if switchServiceGroup == nil{
    println("Cannot find the switch service group. Creating it...")
    home.addServiceGroupWithName(switchServiceGroupName,
      completionHandler: {[weak self ]
        (group: HMServiceGroup!, error: NSError!) in

        if error != nil{
          println("Failed to create the switch service group")
        } else {
          let strongSelf = self!
          println("The switch service group was created successfully")
          strongSelf.switchServiceGroup = group
          strongSelf.discoverServicesInServiceGroup(group)
        }

      })
  } else {
    println("Found an existing switch service group")
    discoverServicesInServiceGroup(switchServiceGroup)

  }

  /* First, start finding new accessories */
  println("Finding new accessories...")
  accessoryBrowser.startSearchingForNewAccessories()

}
```

When the switch has been found or created, I call the `discoverServicesInServi`
`ceGroup:` method of my view controller, which will go through all the accessories in the
only room in the house. If any of those accessories has a switch, it will attempt to add
that switch to the group. Eventually, it will enumerate all the services in the group:

```
func discoverServicesInServiceGroup(serviceGroup: HMServiceGroup){

  addAllSwitchesToServiceGroup(serviceGroup, completionHandler: {
    [weak self](error: NSError!) in

    if error != nil{
      println("Failed to add the switch to the service group")
    } else {
```

```
    let strongSelf = self!
    strongSelf.enumerateServicesInServiceGroup(serviceGroup)
  }

})

enumerateServicesInServiceGroup(serviceGroup)

}
```

The enumeration of services in the group is purely done by accessing the `services` property of the group:

```
func enumerateServicesInServiceGroup(serviceGroup: HMServiceGroup){
  println("Discovering all the services in this service group...")
  if let services = serviceGroup.services{
    for service in services as [HMService]{
      println(service)
    }
  }
}
```

We find all the switch services in all accessories of the room by enumerating the accessories in the room, finding the switch services, and adding them to the group using the group's `addService:completionHandler:` method.

```
func addAllSwitchesToServiceGroup(serviceGroup: HMServiceGroup,
  completionHandler: ((NSError!) -> Void)?){

  if let accessories = room.accessories{
    for accessory in accessories as [HMAccessory]{
      if let services = accessory.services{
        for service in services as [HMService]{
          if (service.name as NSString).rangeOfString("switch",
            options: .CaseInsensitiveSearch).location != NSNotFound{
            /* This is a switch, add it to the service group */
            println("Found a switch service. Adding it to the group...")
            serviceGroup.addService(service,
              completionHandler: completionHandler)
          }
        }
      }
    }
  }

}
```

Give this a go for yourself and see how it goes. You will then have a service group that contains all the switch services of all accessories that we could find in reach:

```
let switchServiceGroupName = "All Switches"
```

See Also

Recipe 4.6; Recipe 4.1

CHAPTER 5

Creating Dynamic and Interactive User Interfaces

5.0. Introduction

There are a few classes in the iOS SDK that you can use to add very interesting physics to your app to make it even more interactive. For instance, if you look at the new iOS, you'll notice that background images that you can use as wallpapers are more lively than before because they can move and slide around as you move your device to the left, right, etc. These are some of the various behaviors that the new SDK allows you to add to your apps as well.

Let me give you another example. Let's say that you have a photo-sharing application that runs on the iPad. On the lefthand side of the screen, you have some pictures that your app has pulled onto the screen from the user's photo album, and on the right you have a basket-like component where every photo that is placed into the basket will be batch-shared on a social networking service like Facebook. You want to provide interactivity on your UI with an animation so that the user can flick the pictures onto the basket from the left, and the pictures will snap into the basket. This was all possible in the past, but you had to know a fair bit about Core Animation and have a rather good understanding of physics. With UI Dynamics, Apple's new technology, a lot of these things can be attached to your apps very easily. In fact, you can attach very interesting physics and behaviors to your views with just a few lines of code.

Apple has categorized these actions into *behavior* classes that you can attach to an *animator*. Behaviors are simple classes that you can configure, while animators group and manage various behaviors. For instance, you can add a *gravity* behavior to a button on your view, and this will cause the button to fall from the top of the screen (if that's where you placed it) all the way down and even outside the boundaries of your view. Now, if you want to prevent that from happening and you allow your button to fall into the view but snap to the bottom and go no farther than that, you will need to attach a *collision* behavior to your animator as well. The animator will manage all the behaviors that you've added to various views in your app, as well as their interactions. You won't have to worry about that. Here are a few classes that provide different behaviors for your UI components:

UICollisionBehavior
   Provides collision detection.

UIGravityBehavior
   As its name implies, provides gravity behavior for your views.

UIPushBehavior
   Allows you to simulate a push behavior on your views. Imagine placing your finger on the screen and then moving your finger gradually toward the top of the screen. If a button with the push behavior is attached to the view, you can cause it to move up as you move your finger up the screen, as if you are pushing it in the real world.

UISnapBehavior
   Allows views to snap to a specific point on the screen.

For every dynamic behavior, as discussed before, we will need an animator of type UIDynamicAnimator. This animator needs to be initialized with what Apple calls a *reference view*. The animator uses the reference view's coordinate system to calculate output of various behaviors. For instance, if you pass a view controller's view as the reference view of a dynamic animator, when you add a collision behavior to the animator, you can ask the collision behavior to ensure that the items that are added to it will not go outside the boundaries of the reference view. That means you can put all your UI components within your reference view, even if they have gravity applied to them.

The reference view is also used as the context of the animations that the animator manages. For instance, if the animator wants to figure out whether two squares will collide with each other, it uses Core Graphics methods to find where those two squares overlap with each other in the context of their superview—in this case, the reference view.

In this chapter, we are going to explore the different combinations of these behaviors and how you can add more interactivity to your apps with UIKit behaviors and animators. We will start with simple examples and gradually build on top of what we've learned and dig a bit deeper into more exciting examples.

5.1. Adding Gravity to Your UI Components

Problem

You want your UI components to have gravity so that if they are dragged up to the top of the screen, they will descend on their own. Combining this with the collision behavior that you will learn later, you can create UI components that fall from their current location until they collide with a path that you'll specify.

Solution

Initialize an object of type `UIGravityBehavior` and add your UI components that need gravity to this object. After you are done, create an instance of `UIDynamicAnimator`, add your gravity behavior to the animator, and let the animator take care of the rest of the work for you.

Discussion

For the purpose of this recipe, we are going to create a simple colored square view in our single-view application and place that view at the center of the screen. We will then add gravity to that view and watch it fall from the center all the way down and eventually outside the bounds of the screen.

So let's start by defining our animator and the view:

```
import UIKit

class ViewController: UIViewController {
  var squareView: UIView?
  var animator: UIDynamicAnimator?
}
```

Next, we are going to create our little view, assign a color to it, and place it at the center of our view controller's view. Then we will create an instance of the `UIGravityBehav ior` class using its `initWithItems:` constructor. This constructor takes in an array of objects that conform to the `UIDynamicItem` protocol. By default, all instances of `UI View` conform to this protocol, so as long as you have a view, you are good to go.

```
override func viewDidAppear(animated: Bool) {
  super.viewDidAppear(animated)

  /* Create our little square view and add it to self.view */
  squareView = UIView(frame: CGRect(x: 0, y: 0, width: 100, height: 100))

  if let theSquareView = squareView{
    theSquareView.backgroundColor = UIColor.greenColor()
    theSquareView.center = view.center
    view.addSubview(theSquareView)
```

```
    animator = UIDynamicAnimator(referenceView: view)

    if let theAnimator = animator{
      let gravity = UIGravityBehavior(items: [theSquareView])
      theAnimator.addBehavior(gravity)
    }

  }

}
```

 If you don't want to add all your views to the gravity behavior as soon as you initialize the behavior, you can add them later using the addI tem: instance method of the UIGravityBehavior class. This method also accepts any object that conforms to the aforementioned protocol.

Now if you run your app, as soon as your view controller's view appears on screen, you will see the colored view drop from the center of the screen all the way down and out of the screen. It fails to stop because we have not given any collision boundaries to our animator. The gravity behavior, just like real gravity, will pull the items down until they hit a boundary, but in the absence of an existing boundary, the items will just keep dropping for all eternity. We will remedy that later in this chapter by adding collision behaviors to our items.

See Also

Recipe 5.0, "Introduction"

5.2. Detecting and Reacting to Collisions Between UI Components

Problem

You want to specify collision boundaries between your UI components on the screen so that they will not overlap one another.

Solution

Instantiate an object of type UICollisionBehavior and attach it to your animator object. Set the translatesReferenceBoundsIntoBoundary property of your collision behavior to true and ensure that your animator is initialized with your superview as its reference value. This will ensure that the subviews that are the targets of your collision behavior (as will be discussed soon) will not go outside the boundaries of your superview.

Discussion

A collision behavior of type UICollisionBehavior takes in objects that conform to the UIDynamicItem protocol. All views of type UIView already conform to this protocol, so all you have to do is instantiate your views and add them to the collision behavior. A collision behavior requires you to define the boundaries that the items in the animator will not be able to pass. For instance, if you define a line that runs from the bottom-left edge to the bottom-right edge of your reference view (the bottommost horizontal line of your reference view), and add a gravity behavior to your view, those views will be pulled down by gravity to the bottom of the view but will not go further because they will collide with the bottom edge of the view, defined by the collision behavior.

If you want your reference view's boundaries to be considered as the boundaries of your collision detection behavior, just set the translatesReferenceBoundsIntoBoundary property of the collision behavior's instance to true. If you want to add custom lines as boundaries to your collision behavior, simply use the addBoundaryWithIdentifi er:fromPoint:toPoint: instance method of the UICollisionBehavior class.

In this recipe, we are going to create two colored views, one on top of the other, and then add gravity to our animator so that the views fall down from the center of the view controller's view. Then we are going to add a collision behavior to the mix so that the views will not overlap each other. In addition, they won't go outside the boundaries of the reference view (the view controller's view).

So let's begin by defining an array of our views and our animator:

```
import UIKit

class ViewController: UIViewController {
  var squareViews = [AnyObject]()
  var animator: UIDynamicAnimator?
}
```

Then when our view appears on the screen, we will set up the collision and the gravity behaviors and add them to an animator:

```
override func viewDidAppear(animated: Bool) {
  super.viewDidAppear(animated)

  let colors = [UIColor.redColor(), UIColor.greenColor()]

  /* Create the views */
  var currentCenterPoint = view.center
  let eachViewSize = CGSize(width: 50, height: 50)
  for counter in 0..<2{
```

```
let newView = UIView(frame:
  CGRect(x: 0,
    y: 0,
    width: eachViewSize.width,
    height: eachViewSize.height))

newView.backgroundColor = colors[counter]
newView.center = currentCenterPoint
currentCenterPoint.y += eachViewSize.height + 10
squareViews.append(newView)
view.addSubview(newView)

}

animator = UIDynamicAnimator(referenceView: self.view)

/* Create gravity */
let gravity = UIGravityBehavior(items: squareViews)
animator!.addBehavior(gravity)

/* Create collision detection */
let collision = UICollisionBehavior(items: squareViews)
collision.translatesReferenceBoundsIntoBoundary = true
animator!.addBehavior(collision)

}
```

The result will look similar to that shown in Figure 5-1; this example shows that the collision behavior works perfectly when the translatesReferenceBoundsIntoBoun dary property's value is set to true. But what if we want to specify custom boundaries? This is where we will use the addBoundaryWithIdentifier:fromPoint:toPoint: instance method of the collision behavior. Here are the parameters that you should pass to this method:

addBoundaryWithIdentifier

A string identifier for your boundary. This is used so that if you want to get the collision behavior back for your boundary later, you can pass the same identifier to the boundaryWithIdentifier: method and get your boundary object back. The object is of type UIBezierPath, which can support quite complicated, curved boundaries. But most programmers are likely to specify simple horizontal or vertical boundaries, which we'll do here.

fromPoint

The starting point of your boundary, of type CGPoint.

toPoint

The ending point of your boundary, of type CGPoint.

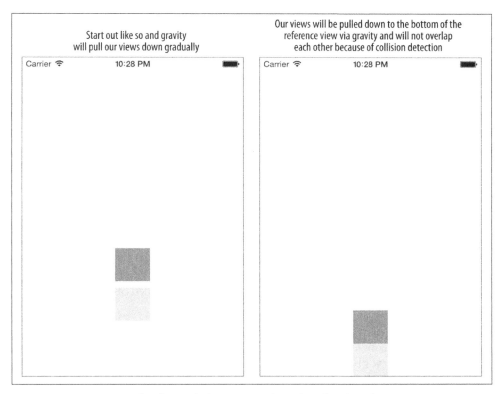

Figure 5-1. Gravity and collision behaviors working hand in hand

So let's imagine that you want to add a boundary to the bottom of your reference view (in this case, the view of our view controller), but you don't want this boundary to be at the bottommost point of your view. Instead, you want this boundary to be 100 points away from the bottommost point of the view. In that case, setting the `translatesRe ferenceBoundsIntoBoundary` property of the collision behavior is not going to help you, because you want a different boundary than the boundary provided by the reference view. Instead, we will use the `addBoundaryWithIdentifier:fromPoint:toP oint:` method like so:

```
/* Create collision detection */
let collision = UICollisionBehavior(items: squareViews)

let fromPoint = CGPoint(x: 0, y: view.bounds.size.height - 100)

let toPoint = CGPoint(x: view.bounds.size.width,
  y: view.bounds.size.height - 100)

collision.addBoundaryWithIdentifier("bottomBoundary",
  fromPoint: fromPoint,
```

```
    toPoint: toPoint)

  animator!.addBehavior(collision)
```

Now, when we mix this up with gravity as before, our square views will fall to the bottom of the reference view but won't quite hit the bottom because our boundary is positioned a bit higher. As part of this recipe, I am also going to demonstrate the ability to detect collisions between various items that have been added to your collision behavior. The UICollisionBehavior class has a property called collisionDelegate that will be the delegate whenever a collision is detected on the items that have been added to the collision behavior. This delegate object has to conform to the UICollisionBehaviorDelegate protocol, which has a few methods that you can implement. Here are two of the most important methods in this protocol:

collisionBehavior:beganContactForItem:withBoundaryIdentifier:atPoint:
    Gets called on the delegate when an item in your collision behavior collides with one of the boundaries that you've added to the behavior.

collisionBehavior:endedContactForItem:withBoundaryIdentifier:atPoint:
    Gets called when the item that hit the boundary has bounced off the boundary and no longer collides with that boundary.

To demonstrate the delegate's activities to you and show you how you could use it, we are going to expand on our previous example. As soon as our square views hit the bottom of our reference view's boundary, we will set their color to red, enlarge them by 200% in size, and then fade them out to simulate an explosion:

```
import UIKit

class ViewController: UIViewController, UICollisionBehaviorDelegate {

  let bottomBoundary = "bottomBoundary"
  var squareViews = [AnyObject]()
  var animator: UIDynamicAnimator?

  func collisionBehavior(behavior: UICollisionBehavior!,
    beganContactForItem item: UIDynamicItem!,
    withBoundaryIdentifier identifier: NSCopying!,
    atPoint p: CGPoint){

      if identifier as? String == bottomBoundary{
        UIView.animateWithDuration(1, animations: {
          let view = item as UIView
          view.backgroundColor = UIColor.redColor()
          view.alpha = 0
          view.transform = CGAffineTransformMakeScale(2, 2)
          }, completion:{(finished: Bool) in
            let view = item as UIView
            behavior.removeItem(item)
            view.removeFromSuperview()
```

```
      })
    }

}

override func viewDidAppear(animated: Bool) {
  super.viewDidAppear(animated)

  let colors = [UIColor.redColor(), UIColor.greenColor()]

  /* Create the views */
  var currentCenterPoint = CGPoint(x: view.center.x, y: 0)
  let eachViewSize = CGSize(width: 50, height: 50)
  for counter in 0..<2{

    let newView = UIView(frame:
      CGRect(x: 0,
        y: 0,
        width: eachViewSize.width,
        height: eachViewSize.height))

    newView.backgroundColor = colors[counter]
    newView.center = currentCenterPoint
    currentCenterPoint.y += eachViewSize.height + 10
    squareViews.append(newView)
    view.addSubview(newView)

  }

  animator = UIDynamicAnimator(referenceView: self.view)

  /* Create gravity */
  let gravity = UIGravityBehavior(items: squareViews)
  animator!.addBehavior(gravity)

  /* Create collision detection */
  let collision = UICollisionBehavior(items: squareViews)

  let fromPoint = CGPoint(x: 0, y: view.bounds.size.height - 100)

  let toPoint = CGPoint(x: view.bounds.size.width,
    y: view.bounds.size.height - 100)

  collision.addBoundaryWithIdentifier(bottomBoundary,
    fromPoint: fromPoint,
    toPoint: toPoint)

  collision.collisionDelegate = self

  animator!.addBehavior(collision)

}
```

}

I'll explain what is happening in our code here. First, we create two views and place them on top of each other. These views are just two simple, colored squares, the second on top of the first, added to the view of our view controller. As in our previous examples, we are adding gravity to our animator so that when the animation kicks in, our views will be dragged toward the bottom of the screen as if descending to the ground. Then, instead of setting the boundaries of our reference view as the boundaries of collision, we are using the addBoundaryWithIdentifier:fromPoint:toPoint method of our collision behavior to create a boundary near the bottom of the screen—specifically, 100 points away from the bottommost point. This will create an invisible line segment that runs from the left side to the right side of the screen, and prevents the views from falling all the way down and out of the reference view.

Also, as you can see, we are setting our view controller as the delegate of the collision behavior. This means that we get updates from the collision behavior telling us when a collision has occurred. When you learn that one has occurred, you will probably want to find out whether it was with a boundary (such as the one we've created) or an item on the scene. For instance, if you have various virtual walls that you've created on your reference view and your small square views collide with one of those walls, you might want to create a different effect (such as an explosion) based on which boundary they hit. You can find out what the item collided with from the delegate method that gets called on your view controller, which gives you the identifier of the boundary that the item collided with. Knowing what the object is, you can then make a decision about what to do with it.

In our example, we compare the identifier that comes back from the collision behavior with our kBottomBoundary constant, which we assigned to our barrier when we created it. We create an animation for the object that moves a square view down the screen, using the gravity and the boundary that we set up. The boundary ensures that the view won't go past the 100-point limit that we created at the bottom of the screen.

One of the interesting properties of the UIGravityBehavior class is collisionMode. This property dictates how the collision should be managed in the animator. For instance, in our previous example, we saw a typical collision behavior added to an animator without modifying the value of the collisionMode. In this case, the collision behavior was detecting collisions between our small square views and the boundaries that we set around the reference view. However, this behavior can be changed by modifying the value of the aforementioned property. Here are the values that you can set for this property:

UICollisionBehaviorModeItems

Setting this value means that the collision behavior will detect collisions between dynamic items, such as our small square views.

`UICollisionBehaviorModeBoundaries`

> This tells the collision behavior that it has to detect collisions of dynamic items with the boundaries that we set up, such as the boundaries around our reference view.

`UICollisionBehaviorModeEverything`

> This dictates to the collision behavior that it has to detect all types of collisions, regardless of whether they are boundaries, items, or something else. This is the default value of this property.

 The values that we just talked about can be mixed together using bitwise OR operators so that you can create a combination of collision modes that comply with your business requirements.

I suggest that you go on and change the value of the `collisionMode` property of the collision behavior in our previous example to `UICollisionBehaviorModeBoundaries` and then run the app. You will see that both of the square views will drop down to the bottom of the screen near the boundaries that we set up, but instead of the items colliding with each other, they will move into each other because the collision behavior doesn't care about or even notice the collision between them.

See Also

Recipe 5.1

5.3. Animating Your UI Components with a Push

Problem

You want to "flick" your views from one point to another.

Solution

Initialize a behavior object of type `UIPushBehavior` using its `initWithItems:mode:` method, and for the mode, pass the value of `UIPushBehaviorModeContinuous`. When you are ready to start pushing the items toward an angle, issue the `setAngle:` method on the push behavior to set the angle (in radians) for the behavior. After that, you will need to set the *magnitude*, or the force behind the push. You can set this force using the `setMagnitude:` method of the push behavior. The magnitude is calculated in this way: each magnitude of 1 point will result in acceleration of 100 points per second squared for your target views.

Discussion

Push behaviors, especially continuous pushes, are very useful. Let's say you are working on a scrapbook iPad app, and on top of the screen, you have created three slides, each representing one of the scrapbook pages that the user has created. On the bottom of the screen, you have various pictures that the user can drag and drop into the pages. One way to allow the user to do this is to add a tap gesture recognizer (see Recipe 10.5) to your reference view to track the tap and allow the pictures to be moved onto the target slide, which will, in turn, simulate the dragging. The other, and perhaps better, way of doing this is to use the push behavior that Apple has introduced into UIKit.

The push behavior is of type `UIPushBehavior` and has a magnitude and an angle. The angle is measured in radians, and a magnitude of 1 point will result in acceleration of 100 points per second squared. We create push behaviors like we create any other behaviors: we need to initialize them and then add them to an animator of type `UIDyna micAnimator`.

For this example, we are going to create a view and place it at the center of our view controller's view. We are going to incorporate a collision behavior into our animator, which will prevent our little view from going outside the bounds of our view controller's view. You learned this technique in Recipe 5.2. We are then going to add a tap gesture recognizer (see Recipe 10.5) to our view controller's view so that we will be notified whenever a tap occurs.

When a tap is detected, we will calculate the angle between the tap point and the center of our small square view. This will give us the angle, in radians, toward which we can push the small square view. Then we will calculate the distance between the tap point and the center of our small square view, which will then give us a value that can be used as the magnitude of the push. This means that the magnitude will be larger the farther away from each other the tap point and the center of the small square view are.

In this recipe, I'm assuming that you are already familiar with the basics of trigonometry. If you aren't, that's OK because all you really need are the formulas that I describe in the example code for this recipe. In Figure 5-2, you can see how the angle between two points is calculated, so I'm hoping that this will give us enough information to write our solution to this problem.

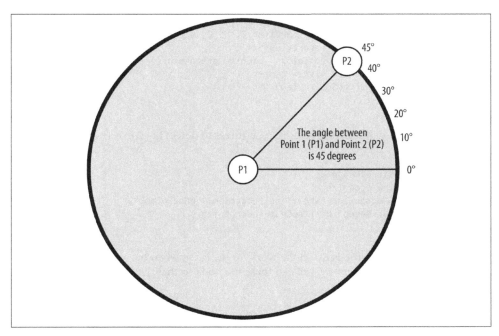

Figure 5-2. Calculating the angle between two points

So let's get started by declaring the relevant properties of our view controller:

```
import UIKit

class ViewController: UIViewController {
  var squareView: UIView?
  var animator: UIDynamicAnimator?
  var pushBehavior: UIPushBehavior?
}
```

 Our example adds a collision and a push behavior to our animator. The push behavior is added as a property to our class, whereas the collision behavior is just a local variable. The reason behind this is that when we are done adding the collision behavior to our animator, we leave the animator to calculate all collisions with the boundaries of our reference view and we no longer need to reference that collision behavior. However, in the case of our push behavior, when we handle taps, we want to update the push behavior so that it pushes our item toward the tap point. That is why we need to have a reference to the push behavior but not the collision.

The next stop is a method that creates a small square view and places it on our view controller's view:

```
func createSmallSquareView(){
  squareView = UIView(frame: CGRect(x: 0, y: 0, width: 80, height: 80))
  if let theSquareView = squareView{
    theSquareView.backgroundColor = UIColor.greenColor()
    theSquareView.center = view.center
    view.addSubview(theSquareView)
  }
}
```

Right after that, we will use a tap gesture recognizer to detect taps on our view controller's view:

```
func createGestureRecognizer(){
  let tapGestureRecognizer =
  UITapGestureRecognizer(target: self, action: "handleTap:")
  view.addGestureRecognizer(tapGestureRecognizer)
}
```

 These methods do all the work for us. Later, when our view displays on the screen, we will call these methods so that they can carry out their work.

And let's not forget a method to set up our collision and push behaviors:

```
func createAnimatorAndBehaviors(){
  animator = UIDynamicAnimator(referenceView: view)

  if let theSquareView = squareView{
    /* Create collision detection */
    let collision = UICollisionBehavior(items: [theSquareView])
    collision.translatesReferenceBoundsIntoBoundary = true
    pushBehavior = UIPushBehavior(items: [theSquareView], mode: .Continuous)
    animator!.addBehavior(collision)
    animator!.addBehavior(pushBehavior)
  }

}
```

To learn more about collision behaviors, please have a look at Recipe 5.2. After we set up all these methods, we need to call them when our view appears on the screen:

```
override func viewDidAppear(animated: Bool) {
  super.viewDidAppear(animated)
  createGestureRecognizer()
  createSmallSquareView()
  createAnimatorAndBehaviors()
}
```

Brilliant. Now if you look at our implementation of the createGestureRecognizer method, you will notice that we are installing our tap gesture recognizer on a method in our view controller called `handleTap:`. In this method, we calculate the distance between the center point of the small square view and the point where the user tapped on the reference view. This also calculates the angle between the center of the small square view and the tap point to figure out the angle of the push.

```
func handleTap(tap: UITapGestureRecognizer){

  /* Get the angle between the center of the square view
  and the tap point */

  let tapPoint = tap.locationInView(view)
  let squareViewCenterPoint = self.squareView!.center

  /* Calculate the angle between the center point of the square view and
  the tap point to find out the angle of the push

  Formula for detecting the angle between two points is:

  arc tangent 2((p1.x - p2.x), (p1.y - p2.y)) */
  let deltaX = tapPoint.x - squareViewCenterPoint.x
  let deltaY = tapPoint.y - squareViewCenterPoint.y
  let angle = atan2(deltaY, deltaX)

  pushBehavior!.angle = angle

  /* Use the distance between the tap point and the center of our square
  view to calculate the magnitude of the push

  Distance formula is:
  square root of ((p1.x - p2.x)^2 + (p1.y - p2.y)^2) */
  let distanceBetweenPoints =
    sqrt(pow(tapPoint.x - squareViewCenterPoint.x, 2.0) +
      pow(tapPoint.y - squareViewCenterPoint.y, 2.0))

  pushBehavior!.magnitude = distanceBetweenPoints / 200.0

}
```

 I am not going to dive into trigonometry here, but this code uses a basic formula taught in high school trigonometry to calculate the angle between two points in radians, along with the Pythagorean theorem to get the distance between two points. You can find these formulas by looking at the comments that I've left in the code, but if you want a deeper understanding of things such as radians and angles, please obtain a basic text on trigonometry.

Now if you run your app, you will first see a green small square view at the center of your screen. Tap anywhere on the area around this view (the white area) to start moving your green view. In this example, I am dividing the distance between the tap point and the center point of the small square view by 200 to get a realistic push magnitude, but you can increase the acceleration of your push behavior, such as by reducing this number from 200 to 100. It's best to experiment with different numbers to get the right feel for *your* app.

See Also

Recipe 5.2

5.4. Attaching Multiple Dynamic Items to Each Other

Problem

You want to attach dynamic items, such as views, so that the movements in one will cascade to the second view automatically. Alternatively, you want to attach a dynamic item to an anchor point so that when that point moves (because your app or the user moves it), the item will automatically move with it.

Solution

Instantiate an attachment behavior of type `UIAttachmentBehavior`, using the `initWithItem:point:attachedToAnchor:` instance method of this class. Add this behavior to an animator (see Recipe 5.0, "Introduction"), which will take care of the dynamics and the physics of movement.

Discussion

The attachment behavior is at first a bit difficult to understand. In simple terms, you can set an anchor and then have a point follow that anchor. But I'd like to give you more details.

Let's say that you have a large photo on a flat desk. Now if you place your index finger on the upper-right corner of the photo and start moving it around, the picture may rotate around your fingertip, and may not go exactly straight toward the direction you are moving it to. But if you move your finger to the center of the photo and move it around, the photo will not rotate around your fingertip. You can create the same real-life behavior using the attachment behavior in UIKit.

In this recipe, we want to create an effect similar to that explained in Figure 5-3.

In Figure 5-3 you can see that we have three views on our screen. The main view is in the center and includes another small view at its top-right corner. The small view is the point that will follow our anchor point, as explained in my photo example. Last but not least, we have the anchor point, which will be moved around the screen with a pan gesture recognizer (see Recipe 10.3). The movements on this view will then cause our view at the center of the screen to move as well. First, let's declare the necessary properties of our view controller:

```
import UIKit

class ViewController: UIViewController {

  var squareView: UIView?
  var squareViewAnchorView: UIView?
  var anchorView: UIView?
  var animator: UIDynamicAnimator?
  var attachmentBehavior: UIAttachmentBehavior?

}
```

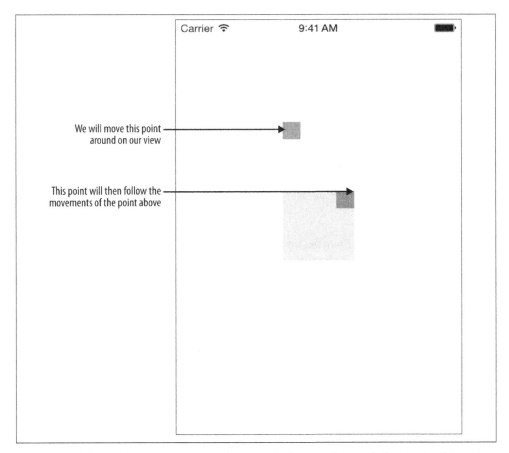

Figure 5-3. This is what we want to achieve with the attachment behavior in this recipe

The next thing we have to do is create our small square view, but this time we are going to put another view inside it. The smaller view, which will be at the top-right corner of the parent view, will be virtually connected to the anchor point of the attachment behavior, as explained in the photo example:

```
unc createSmallSquareView(){

  squareView = UIView(frame: CGRect(x: 0, y: 0, width: 80, height: 80))

  if let theSquareView = squareView{
    theSquareView.backgroundColor = UIColor.greenColor()
    theSquareView.center = view.center

    squareViewAnchorView = UIView(frame:
      CGRect(x: 60, y: 0, width: 20, height: 20))

    squareViewAnchorView!.backgroundColor = UIColor.brownColor()
    theSquareView.addSubview(squareViewAnchorView!)
    view.addSubview(theSquareView)
  }

}
```

Next up, the creation of the anchor point view:

```
func createAnchorView(){

  anchorView = UIView(frame: CGRect(x: 120, y: 120, width: 20, height: 20))
  anchorView!.backgroundColor = UIColor.redColor()
  view.addSubview(anchorView!)

}
```

Then we need to create our pan gesture recognizer and the animator, as we have already seen in other recipes in this chapter:

```
func createGestureRecognizer(){
  let panGestureRecognizer = UIPanGestureRecognizer(target: self,
    action: "handlePan:")
  view.addGestureRecognizer(panGestureRecognizer)
}

func createAnimatorAndBehaviors(){

  animator = UIDynamicAnimator(referenceView: view)

  /* Create collision detection */
  let collision = UICollisionBehavior(items: [squareView!])
  collision.translatesReferenceBoundsIntoBoundary = true

  attachmentBehavior = UIAttachmentBehavior(item: squareView!,
    offsetFromCenter: UIOffset(horizontal: 30, vertical: -40),
    attachedToAnchor: anchorView!.center)
```

```
  animator!.addBehavior(collision)
  animator!.addBehavior(attachmentBehavior!)

}

override func viewDidAppear(animated: Bool) {
  super.viewDidAppear(animated)

  createGestureRecognizer()
  createSmallSquareView()
  createAnchorView()
  createAnimatorAndBehaviors()

}
```

You can see how we are initializing our anchor behavior, using its `initWithI
tem:point:attachedToAnchor:` instance method. This method takes in the following
parameters:

`initWithItem`
> The dynamic item (or in our example, the view) that has to be connected to the
> anchor point.

`point`
> The point inside the dynamic item that has to be connected to the anchor point.
> This behavior uses the center point of the item to establish a connection to the
> anchor point. But you can change that by providing a different value to this pa-
> rameter.

`attachedToAnchor`
> The anchor point itself, measured as a `CGPoint` value.

Now that we have connected the square view's top-right corner to an anchor point
(represented by the anchor point view), we need to demonstrate that by moving the
anchor point, we also indirectly move the square view. If you look at the `createGestur
eRecognizer` method that we wrote earlier, we created a pan gesture recognizer that
tracks the user's finger movements on the screen. We have chosen the `handlePan:`
method of our view to handle the gesture recognizer, and we will implement that method
like so:

```
func handlePan(pan: UIPanGestureRecognizer){

  let tapPoint = pan.locationInView(view)
  attachmentBehavior!.anchorPoint = tapPoint
  anchorView!.center = tapPoint

}
```

What we are doing here is detecting the point of movement on our view and then moving the anchor point to that point. After we do this, the attachment behavior will then move our small square view as well.

See Also

Recipe 10.3; Recipe 5.0, "Introduction"

5.5. Adding a Dynamic Snap Effect to Your UI Components

Problem

Using an animation, you want to snap a view in your UI to a specific point on the screen, with the elasticity of a real-world snap effect. This means that when your UI component snaps to the given point, you will feel that it has elasticity built into it.

Solution

Instantiate an object of type `UISnapBehavior` and add it to an animator of type `UIDynamicAnimator`.

Discussion

To really understand how the snap dynamic behavior works, think about a small amount of jelly covered in oil with a string attached to it, sitting on a very smooth table. I know that sentence sounds really odd, but bear with me. Now imagine, pulling on that string from another point on the table to get the jelly to move from its initial point to the point you ordered it to move to. With the oil all around it, the jelly will move smoothly from that point to where you want it to go, and because it is jelly, it will wiggle when it snaps to position. This behavior is exactly what you can achieve with the `UISnapBehavior` class.

One of the use cases for this is when you have an app and some views on the screen, such as images, and you want the user to be able to dictate where those views have to be moved to create a customized UI for the user. One way of handling this is using the technique that we learned in Recipe 5.3, but that solution is quite rigid and has its own use cases. Here in this recipe, we have a view on our screen, and we want to allow the user to tap anywhere on the screen to relocate the view. We will then snap that view to the point where that tap originated.

So what we are going to do in this recipe is create a small view in the center of our view controller's view and then attach a tap gesture recognizer (Recipe 10.5) to our view controller's view. Whenever the user taps anywhere on the screen, we will snap the small square view to that point. So let's begin by defining the required properties of our view controller:

```
import UIKit

class ViewController: UIViewController {
  var squareView: UIView?
  var animator: UIDynamicAnimator?
  var snapBehavior: UISnapBehavior?
}
```

The next thing to do is create a method that will create our tap gesture recognizer for us:

```
func createGestureRecognizer(){

  let tap = UITapGestureRecognizer(target: self, action: "handleTap:")
  view.addGestureRecognizer(tap)

}
```

Just like the previous recipes, we also need to create a small view in the center of the screen. I've chosen the center arbitrarily, so you can create it at a different point if you want to. We will then snap this view to where the user taps on the screen. So here is our method for creating this view:

```
func createSmallSquareView(){
  squareView = UIView(frame: CGRect(x: 0, y: 0, width: 80, height: 80))

  squareView!.backgroundColor = UIColor.greenColor()
  squareView!.center = view.center
  view.addSubview(squareView!)

}
```

The next step is to create our animator (see Recipe 5.0, "Introduction") and attach our snap behavior to it. We will initialize the snap behavior of type UISnapBehavior using its initWithItem:snapToPoint: method. This method takes two parameters:

initWithItem

> The dynamic item (in this case, our view) that the snap behavior has to be applied to. Just like all the other dynamic UI behaviors, this item has to conform to the UIDynamicItem protocol. By default, all UIView instances conform to this protocol so we are good to go.

snapToPoint

> The point on the reference view (see Recipe 5.0, "Introduction") that the dynamic item has to snap to.

There is one very important thing to note about the snap behavior: for it to work on a specific item, you need to have at least one instance of the snap behavior for that item already added to the animator but snapping the item to its current position. After that, subsequent snaps will work properly. Let me demonstrate this to you. We will now implement a method that creates the snap behavior and the animator and adds the snap behavior to the animator:

```
func createAnimatorAndBehaviors(){
    animator = UIDynamicAnimator(referenceView: view)

    let collision = UICollisionBehavior(items: [squareView!])
    collision.translatesReferenceBoundsIntoBoundary = true

    animator!.addBehavior(collision)

    /* For now, snap the square view to its current center */
    snapBehavior = UISnapBehavior(item: squareView!,
      snapToPoint: squareView!.center)
    /* Medium oscillation */
    snapBehavior!.damping = 0.5

    animator!.addBehavior(snapBehavior!)
}
```

As you can see, we are currently snapping the small square view to its current center, essentially not moving it at all from its position. Later, when we detect tap gestures on our screen, we will update the snap behavior. Also note that we are setting the damp ing property of our snap behavior. This property controls the elasticity with which your item snaps to place. Higher values mean less elasticity and therefore less wiggle motion. This value can be anything from 0 to 1. Now when our view appears on the screen, we will call all these methods to instantiate our small square view, set up the tap gesture recognizer, and set up the animator and the snap behavior:

```
override func viewDidAppear(animated: Bool) {
    super.viewDidAppear(animated)

    self.createGestureRecognizer()
    self.createSmallSquareView()
    self.createAnimatorAndBehaviors()

}
```

When we created the tap gesture recognizer in the createGestureRecognizer method of our view controller, we asked the recognizer to report the taps to the handleTap: method of our view controller. In this method, we will get the point where the user tapped on the screen, and then we will update our snap behavior.

The important thing to note here is that you cannot just update the existing behavior without reinstantiating it. So before we instantiate a new instance of the snap behavior, we have to remove the old one (if any) and then add a new one to our animator. Each animator can have only one snap behavior attached to a specific dynamic item, in this case, our small square view. If you add multiple snap behaviors for the same dynamic item to the same animator, the animator will ignore all your snap behaviors for that item, because it won't know which one to execute first. So to make the behavior work, first remove all the snap behaviors for that item from your animator using its `remove Behavior:` method, and then add a new snap behavior like so:

```
func handleTap(tap: UITapGestureRecognizer){

    /* Get the angle between the center of the square view
    and the tap point */

    let tapPoint = tap.locationInView(view)

    if let theSnap = snapBehavior{
        animator!.removeBehavior(theSnap)
    }

    snapBehavior = UISnapBehavior(item: squareView!, snapToPoint: tapPoint)
    /* Medium oscillation */
    snapBehavior!.damping = 0.5
    animator!.addBehavior(snapBehavior!)
}
```

See Also

Recipe 10.5; Recipe 5.0, "Introduction"

5.6. Assigning Characteristics to Your Dynamic Effects

Problem

You like the default physics built into the dynamic behaviors of UIKit, but you want to be able to assign different characteristics, such as mass and elasticity, to various items that you control using dynamic behaviors.

Solution

Instantiate an object of type `UIDynamicItemBehavior` and assign your dynamic items to it. Once instantiated, use the various properties of this class to change the characteristics of your dynamic items. Then add this behavior to your animator (see Recipe 5.0, "Introduction") and let the animator take care of the rest for you.

Discussion

Dynamic behaviors are great for adding real-life physics to items that conform to the `UIDynamicItem` protocol, such as all views of type `UIView`. In some apps, though, you might wish to explicitly specify the characteristics of a specific item. For instance, in an app where you are using gravity and collision behaviors (see Recipe 5.1 and Recipe 5.2), you may wish to specify that one of the items on your screen affected by this gravity and the collision has to bounce harder than the other item when it collides with a boundary. Another example is when you want to specify that an item should not rotate during all the different dynamic animations that will be applied to it with an animator.

These are all easily doable when you use instances of the `UIDynamicItemBehavior` class. These instances are dynamic behaviors too, and you can add them to an animator using the `addBehavior:` instance method of the `UIDynamicAnimator` class, as you have already seen in this chapter. When you initialize an instance of this class, you can call the `initWithItems:` constructor and pass your view, or any object that conforms to the `UIDynamicItem` protocol. Alternatively, initialize your dynamic item behavior instance using the `init` method and later add different objects to the behavior using the `addItem:` method.

Instances of the `UIDynamicItemBehavior` have properties that you can adjust in order to customize the behavior of your dynamic items (views, for instance). Some of the most important properties of this class are listed and explained here:

`allowsRotation`

A Boolean value that, when set to `true`, as its name implies, allows your dynamic items to get rotated by the animator during the animations that get applied to them. You would ideally want the value of this property to be set to `true` if you want to mimic real-life physics, but if for any reason you need to ensure that a specific item never rotates, set this property to `false` and attach the item to this behavior.

`resistance`

The resistance of the item to movement. This can be from 0 to `CGFLOAT_MAX`. The higher the value, the more resistant that item becomes to forces that you'll apply to it. For instance, if you add a gravity behavior to your animator and create a view in the center of the screen with the resistance of `CGFLOAT_MAX`, the gravity won't be able to force that view down toward its center. The view will just be stuck where you create it.

`friction`

A floating point value from 0.0 to 1.0 that specifies how much friction should be applied to the edges of this item when other items hit it or slide by its edges. The higher the value, the more friction applied to that item.

The more friction you put on an item, the more *sticky* that item becomes. This stickiness will be contagious in that, when other items collide with the sticky item, it will feel as if those items are sticking to the target item a bit more than usual. Just think about the friction of tires on a car. The more friction between the tires and the asphalt, the slower the car will move, but the better the grip it will have on slippery roads. This is exactly the type of friction that this property allows you to assign to your items.

elasticity

> A floating point from 0.0 to 1.0 that specifies how elastic an item should be. The higher this value, the more elastic and jelly-like this item will appear to the eyes of the animator. See Recipe 5.5 for an explanation of elasticity.

density

> A floating point value between 0 and 1 (the default value is 1) that isn't directly used to affect your dynamic item's behaviors but is used by the animator to calculate the mass of your objects and to find out how that mass will affect your animations. For instance, if you flick two items onto each other (see Recipe 5.3), and one of them has a density of 1 and the other has a density of 0.5, the former item's mass will be more than the latter, given that both items are of the same width and height. The animator calculates the mass of items using their density and size on screen. So if you flick a small view with a high density at a big view with a very low density, the small view may, depending on its size and the value of the density, be seen by your animator as the item with more mass. The animator might push away the item that appears larger on screen harder than the larger item will push the small item.

Let's have a look at an example. This is loosely based on the example that we saw in Recipe 5.2. In this example, we are going to place two views on top of each other, but we are going to make the view on the bottom have a very high elasticity and the view on top have quite a low elasticity. This way, when both views hit the bottom of the screen, where they collide with the bottom bounds of the screen, the view on the bottom will jump around and bounce much more, due to its high elasticity, than the view on the top. So let's get started by defining the animator and other properties of our view controller:

```
import UIKit

class ViewController: UIViewController {
  var animator: UIDynamicAnimator?
}
```

Next, we will code a handy method to create views for us with a specific center point and background colors. We will use this method to create two very similar views with different background colors and center points:

```
func newViewWithCenter(center: CGPoint, backgroundColor: UIColor) -> UIView{

  let newView = UIView(frame: CGRect(x: 0, y: 0, width: 50, height: 50))
  newView.backgroundColor = backgroundColor
  newView.center = center
  return newView

}
```

Now when our view gets displayed on the screen, we will create these two views and add them to the screen:

```
let topView = newViewWithCenter(CGPoint(x: 100, y: 0),
    backgroundColor: UIColor.greenColor())

let bottomView = newViewWithCenter(CGPoint(x: 100, y: 50),
    backgroundColor: UIColor.redColor())

view.addSubview(topView)
view.addSubview(bottomView)
```

Now we are going to add a gravity behavior to our views, as we learned about in Recipe 5.1:

```
animator = UIDynamicAnimator(referenceView: view)

/* Create gravity */
let gravity = UIGravityBehavior(items: [topView, bottomView])
animator!.addBehavior(gravity)
```

We don't want our views to fall off the bottom of the screen, so we are going to use what we learned in Recipe 5.2 to set a boundary and collision behavior for our animator:

```
/* Create collision detection */
let collision = UICollisionBehavior(items: [topView, bottomView])
collision.translatesReferenceBoundsIntoBoundary = true

animator!.addBehavior(collision)
```

Last but not least, we are going to add the dynamic behavior to our views, making the view on top less elastic than the one on the bottom:

```
/* Now specify the elasticity of the items */
let moreElasticItem = UIDynamicItemBehavior(items: [bottomView])
moreElasticItem.elasticity = 1

let lessElasticItem = UIDynamicItemBehavior(items: [topView])
lessElasticItem.elasticity = 0.5
animator!.addBehavior(moreElasticItem)
animator!.addBehavior(lessElasticItem)
```

Now you can run your app and watch your views bounce off the bottom of the screen when they hit it (see Figure 5-4).

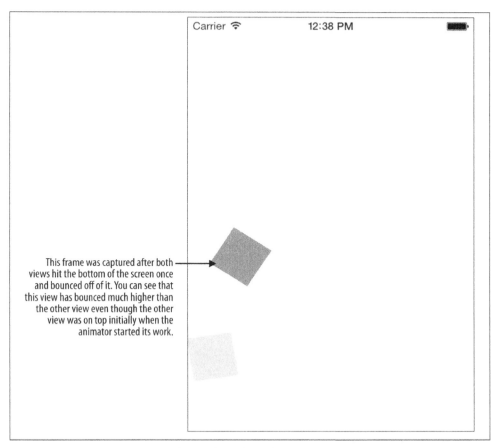

This frame was captured after both views hit the bottom of the screen once and bounced off of it. You can see that this view has bounced much higher than the other view even though the other view was on top initially when the animator started its work.

Figure 5-4. One view is more elastic than the other

See Also

Recipe 5.0, "Introduction"

CHAPTER 6

Table and Collection Views

6.0. Introduction

A table view is simply a scrolling view that is separated into sections, each of which is further separated into rows. Each row is an instance of the UITableViewCell class, and you can create custom table view rows by *subclassing* this class.

Using table views is an ideal way to present a list of items to users. You can embed images, text, and other objects into your table view cells; you can customize their height, shape, grouping, and much more. The simplicity of the structure of table views is what makes them highly customizable.

A table view can be fed with data using a table view data source, and you can receive various events and control the physical appearance of table views using a table view delegate object. These are defined, respectively, in the UITableViewDataSource and UITableViewDelegate protocols.

Although an instance of UITableView subclasses UIScrollView, table views can only scroll vertically. This is more a feature than a limitation. In this chapter, we will discuss the different ways of creating, managing, and customizing table views.

Table views are great. They really are. However, they are very rigid in that they always render their content vertically. They aren't grids and weren't meant to act like grids. However, as a programmer, you may find yourself in a situation where you want to draw a grid-like component with columns and rows, and put different types of UI objects in each one, or make each one interactive. In a table view, you essentially have one column containing multiple rows. If you want to create an illusion of multiple columns, you need to provide a custom cell and make that cell look like it is constructed out of multiple columns.

Collection views, just like table views, are based on the concept of cells, with each cell containing an item or view that it renders on the screen. Cells in collection views are reusable, just like in table views, and they can be dequeued and brought back to the screen whenever necessary. But the layout can be almost anything you can think of that works in two dimensions.

For this reason, Apple introduced collection views in version 6 of the iOS SDK. A collection view is simply a scroll view on steroids. It has a data source and a delegate, just like a table view, but it has one property that sets it apart from table views or scroll views: the *layout object*.

What the layout object does is essentially calculate where each item in the collection view has to be placed. Apple has made this a *bit* complicated, though, by introducing a concrete layout class for collection views that cannot be used by direct instantiation. Instead, you have to instantiate a subclass of this class named `UICollectionView FlowLayout`.

The flow layout arranges collection view cells on the screen in sections. Each section is a group of collection view cells, just as in table views. However, in a collection view, a section can be laid out on the screen in many ways, not necessarily vertically. For instance, you might have three rectangles, each containing its own little grid, as in Figure 6-1.

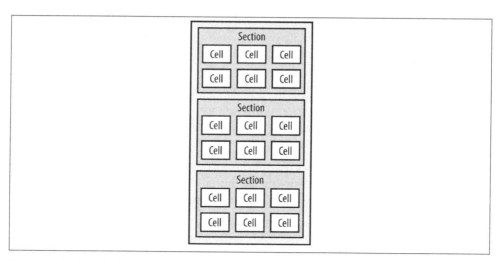

Figure 6-1. A typical flow layout in a collection view

A typical way of laying sections out on the screen is in a grid-like fashion with rows and columns, and that's what the flow layout class does. If you want to stretch the limits of the layout further, you have to modify the properties of the flow layout. And if what you want differs quite a lot from what the flow layout provides, you will need to create your own layout class. For instance, you would need a custom layout class to create the collection view in Figure 6-2. Here a custom layout class has laid out three sections and their corresponding cells in quite a different way from a grid.

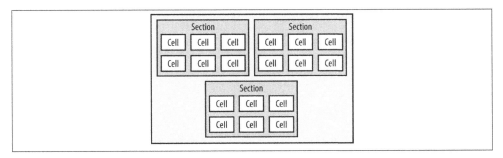

Figure 6-2. A custom layout in a collection view

6.1. Populating a Table View with Data

Problem

You would like to populate your table view with data.

Solution

Conform to the UITableViewDataSource protocol in an object and assign that object to the dataSource property of a table view.

Discussion

Create an object that conforms to the UITableViewDataSource protocol and assign it to a table view instance. Then, by responding to the data source messages, provide information to your table view.

Now let's have a look at an example. In the viewDidLoad method of our view controller, we create the table view and assign our view controller as its data source:

```
import UIKit

class ViewController: UIViewController, UITableViewDataSource {

  var tableView: UITableView?

  override func viewDidLoad() {
    super.viewDidLoad()
    tableView = UITableView(frame: view.bounds, style: .Plain)

    if let theTableView = tableView{
```

```
theTableView.registerClass(UITableViewCell.classForCoder(),
    forCellReuseIdentifier: "identifier")

theTableView.dataSource = self
theTableView.autoresizingMask = .FlexibleWidth | .FlexibleHeight

view.addSubview(theTableView)
    }
  }

    <# Rest of the code goes here #>

}
```

Everything is very simple in this code snippet except for the `registerClass:forCe`
`llReuseIdentifier:` method that we are calling on the instance of our table view. What
does this method do, you ask? The `registerClass` parameter of this method simply
takes a class name that denotes the type of object that you want your table view to load
when it renders each cell. Cells inside a table view all have to be direct or indirect an-
cestors of the `UITableViewCell` class. This class on its own provides a lot of functionalities to programmers, but if you want to extend this class, you can simply subclass it
and add your new functionalities to your own class. So going back to the `register`
`Class` parameter of the aforementioned method, you have to pass the class name of
your cells to this parameter and then pass an identifier to the `forCellReuseIdentifi`
`er` parameter. The reason behind associating table view cell classes with identifiers is
that later, when you populate your table view, you can simply pass the same identifier
to the table view's `dequeueReusableCellWithIdentifier:forIndexPath:` method and
have the table view instantiate the cell for you if one cannot be reused.

Now we need to make sure our table view responds to the required methods of the
`UITableViewDataSource` protocol. Press the Command+Shift+O key combination on
your keyboard, type this protocol name in the dialog, and then press the Enter key. This
will show you the required methods for this protocol.

The `UITableView` class defines a property called `dataSource`. This is an untyped object
that must conform to the `UITableViewDataSource` protocol. Every time a table view is
refreshed and reloaded using the `reloadData` method, the table view will call various
methods in its data source to find out about the data you intend to populate it with. A
table view data source can implement three important methods, two of which are
mandatory for every data source:

`numberOfSectionsInTableView:`

   This method allows the data source to inform the table view of the number of
   sections that must be loaded into the table.

`tableView:numberOfRowsInSection:`
This method tells the view controller how many cells or rows have to be loaded for each section. The section number is passed to the data source in the `numberOfRows InSection` parameter. The implementation of this method is mandatory in the data source object.

`tableView:cellForRowAtIndexPath:`
This method is responsible for returning instances of the `UITableViewCell` class as rows that have to be populated into the table view. The implementation of this method is mandatory in the data source object.

So let's go ahead and implement these methods in our view controller, one by one. First, let's tell the table view that we want it to render three sections:

```
func numberOfSectionsInTableView(tableView: UITableView) -> Int {
  return 3
}
```

Then we tell the table view how many rows we want it to render for each section:

```
func tableView(tableView: UITableView,
  numberOfRowsInSection section: Int) -> Int {

    switch section{
    case 0:
      return 3
    case 1:
      return 5
    case 2:
      return 8
    default:
      return 0
    }

}
```

So up to now, we have asked the table view to render three sections with three rows in the first, five rows in the second, and eight rows in the third section. What's next? We have to return instances of `UITableViewCell` to the table view—the cells that we want the table view to render:

```
func tableView(tableView: UITableView,
  cellForRowAtIndexPath indexPath: NSIndexPath) -> UITableViewCell{

    let cell = tableView.dequeueReusableCellWithIdentifier("identifier",
      forIndexPath: indexPath) as UITableViewCell

    cell.textLabel.text = "Section \(indexPath.section), " +
    "Cell \(indexPath.row)"

    return cell
```

```
    }

    override func prefersStatusBarHidden() -> Bool {
      return true
    }
```

Now if we run our app in iPhone Simulator, we see the results of our work (Figure 6-3).

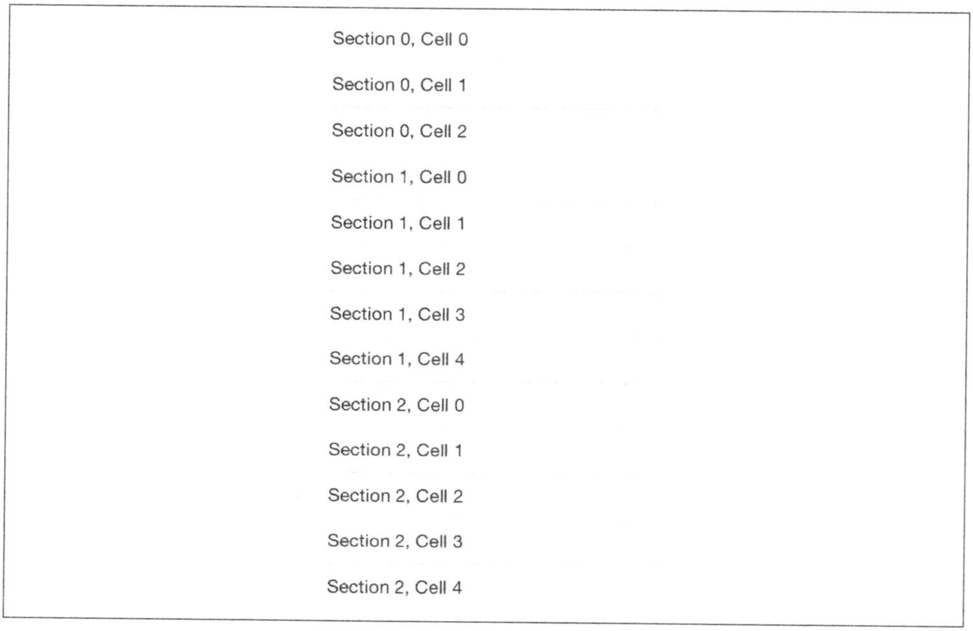

Section 0, Cell 0
Section 0, Cell 1
Section 0, Cell 2
Section 1, Cell 0
Section 1, Cell 1
Section 1, Cell 2
Section 1, Cell 3
Section 1, Cell 4
Section 2, Cell 0
Section 2, Cell 1
Section 2, Cell 2
Section 2, Cell 3
Section 2, Cell 4

Figure 6-3. A plain table view with three sections

When a table view is reloaded or refreshed, it queries its data source through the UITableViewDataSource protocol, asking for various bits of information. Among the important methods previously mentioned, the table view first asks for the number of sections. Each section is responsible for holding rows or cells. After the data source specifies the number of sections, the table view asks for the number of rows that have to be loaded into each section. The data source gets the zero-based index of each section and, based on this, can decide how many cells have to be loaded into each section.

The table view, after determining the number of cells in the sections, continues to ask the data source about the view that will represent each cell in each section. You can allocate instances of the UITableViewCell class and return them to the table view. There are, of course, properties that can be set for each cell, including the title, subtitle, and color of each cell, among other properties.

6.2. Enabling Swipe Deletion of Table View Cells

Problem

You want your application users to be able to delete rows from a table view easily.

Solution

Implement the `tableView:editingStyleForRowAtIndexPath:` selector in the delegate and the `tableView:commitEditingStyle:forRowAtIndexPath:` selector in the data source of your table view:

```
override func tableView(tableView: UITableView,
  editingStyleForRowAtIndexPath indexPath: NSIndexPath)
  -> UITableViewCellEditingStyle {
  return .Delete
}

override func setEditing(editing: Bool, animated: Bool) {
  super.setEditing(editing, animated: animated)
  tableView!.setEditing(editing, animated: animated)
}

func tableView(tableView: UITableView,
  commitEditingStyle editingStyle: UITableViewCellEditingStyle,
  forRowAtIndexPath indexPath: NSIndexPath){

    if editingStyle == .Delete{
      /* First remove this object from the source */
      allRows.removeAtIndex(indexPath.row)
      tableView.deleteRowsAtIndexPaths([indexPath], withRowAnimation: .Left)
    }

}
```

The `tableView:editingStyleForRowAtIndexPath:` method can enable deletions. It is called by the table view, and its return value determines what the table view allows the user to do (insertion, deletion, etc.). The `tableView:commitEditingStyle:forRowAtIndexPath:` method carries out the user's requested deletion. The latter method is defined in the delegate, but its functionality is a bit overloaded: not only do you use the method to delete data, but you also have to delete rows from the table here.

Discussion

The table view responds to the swipe by showing a button on the right side of the targeted row (Figure 6-4). As you can see, the table view is *not* in editing mode, but the button allows the user to delete the row.

This mode is enabled by implementing the `tableView:editingStyleForRowAtIndex Path:` method (declared in the `UITableViewDelegate` protocol), whose return value indicates whether the table should allow insertions, deletions, both, or neither. By implementing the `tableView:commitEditingStyle:forRowAtIndexPath:` method in the data source of a table view, you can then get notified if a user has performed an insertion or deletion.

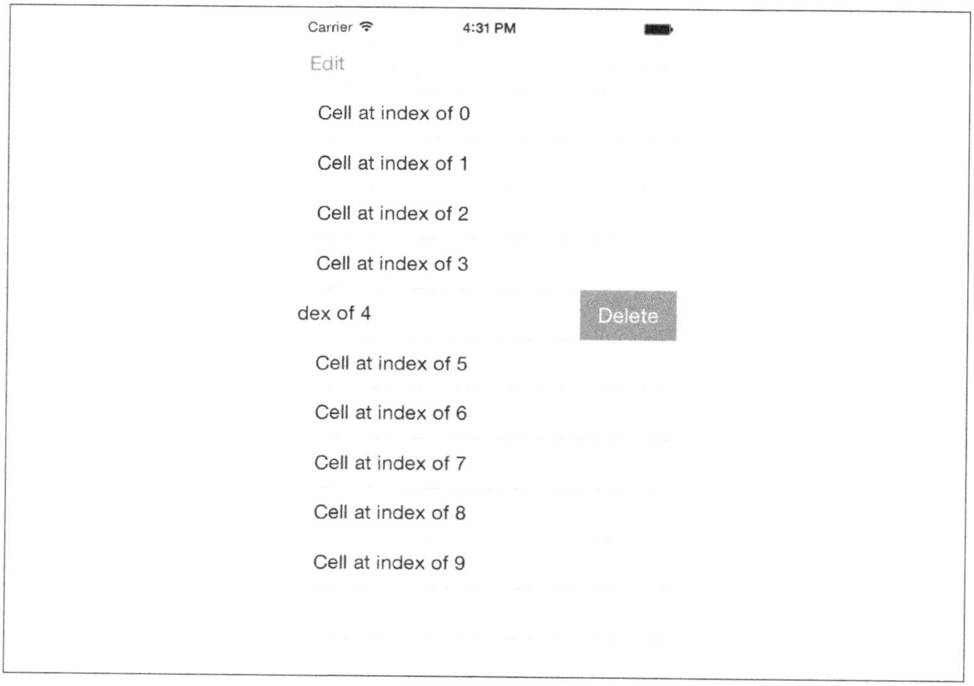

Figure 6-4. Delete button appearing on a table view cell

The second parameter of the `deleteRowsAtIndexPaths:withRowAnimation:` method allows you to specify an animation method that will be performed when rows are deleted from a table view. Our example specifies that we want rows to disappear by moving from right to left when deleted.

6.3. Constructing Headers and Footers in Table Views

Problem

You want to create a header and/or a footer for a table view.

Solution

Create a view (could be a label, image view, etc.—anything that directly or indirectly subclasses `UIView`), and assign that view to the header and/or the footer of a section of a table view. You can also allocate a specific number of points in height for a header or a footer, as we will soon see.

Discussion

A table view can have multiple headers and footers. Each section in a table view can have its own header and footer, so if you have three sections in a table view, you can have a maximum of three headers and a maximum of three footers. You are *not* obliged to provide headers and footers for any of these sections. It is up to you to tell the table view whether you want a header and/or a footer for a section, and you pass these views to the table view through its delegate, should you wish to provide header(s)/footer(s) for section(s) of your table view. Headers and footers in a table view become a part of the table view, meaning that when the table view's contents scroll, so do the header(s) and footer(s) inside that table view.

 Specifying the height of a header and footer in a section inside a table view is done through methods defined in the `UITableViewData` `Source`. Specifying the actual view that has to be displayed for the header/footer of a section in a table view is done through methods defined in the `UITableViewDelegate` protocol.

Let's go ahead and create a simple app with one table view in it. Then let's provide two labels of type `UILabel`, one as the header and the other as the footer of the only section in our table view, and populate this one section with only three cells. In the header we will place the text "Section 1 Header," and in the footer label we will place the text "Section 1 Footer." Starting with our root view controller, we define a table view:

```
import UIKit

class ViewController: UIViewController,
  UITableViewDelegate, UITableViewDataSource {

    var tableView: UITableView?

}
```

Now we create a grouped table view and load three cells into it:

```
override func viewDidLoad() {
  super.viewDidLoad()
  tableView = UITableView(frame: view.bounds, style: .Grouped)

  if let theTableView = tableView{
```

```
    theTableView.registerClass(UITableViewCell.classForCoder(),
      forCellReuseIdentifier: "identifier")

    theTableView.dataSource = self
    theTableView.delegate = self
    theTableView.autoresizingMask = .FlexibleWidth | .FlexibleHeight

    view.addSubview(theTableView)
  }
}

func tableView(tableView: UITableView,
  numberOfRowsInSection section: Int) -> Int {
    return 3
}

func tableView(tableView: UITableView,
  cellForRowAtIndexPath indexPath: NSIndexPath) -> UITableViewCell{

    let cell = tableView.dequeueReusableCellWithIdentifier("identifier",
      forIndexPath: indexPath) as UITableViewCell

    cell.textLabel.text = "Cell \(indexPath.row)"

    return cell

}
```

Here is the exciting part. We can now use two important methods (which are defined in UITableViewDelegate) to provide a label for the header and another label for the footer of the one section that we loaded into our table view:

tableView:viewForHeaderInSection:

> This method expects a return value of type UIView. The view returned from this method will be displayed as the header of the section specified by the viewForHeaderInSection parameter.

tableView:viewForFooterInSection:

> This method expects a return value of type UIView. The view returned from this method will be displayed as the footer of the section specified by the viewForFooterInSection parameter.

Our task now is to implement these methods and return an instance of UILabel. On the header label we enter the text "Section 1 Header," and on the footer label we enter the text "Section 1 Footer," as we had planned:

```
func newLabelWithTitle(title: String) -> UILabel{
  let label = UILabel()
  label.text = title
  label.backgroundColor = UIColor.clearColor()
```

```
        label.sizeToFit()
        return label
    }

    func tableView(tableView: UITableView,
        heightForHeaderInSection section: Int) -> CGFloat{
            return 30
    }

    func tableView(tableView: UITableView,
        viewForHeaderInSection section: Int) -> UIView?{
            return newLabelWithTitle("Section \(section) Header")
    }

    func tableView(tableView: UITableView,
        viewForFooterInSection section: Int) -> UIView?{
            return newLabelWithTitle("Section \(section) Footer")
    }

    override func prefersStatusBarHidden() -> Bool {
        return true
    }
```

If you run your app now, you will see something similar to Figure 6-5.

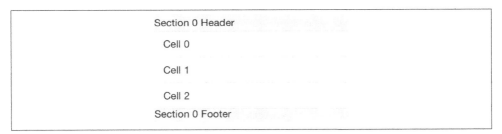

Figure 6-5. The header and footer labels of a table view are not aligned properly

To specify the height of the header and footer views, you need to use the following two methods, which are defined in the UITableViewDelegate protocol:

tableView:heightForHeaderInSection:
> The return value of this method, of type CGFloat, specifies the height of the header for a section in a table view. The section's index is passed through the heightFo rHeaderInSection parameter.

tableView:heightForFooterInSection:
> The return value of this method, of type CGFloat, specifies the height of the footer for a section in a table view. The section's index is passed through the heightFo rHeaderInSection parameter.

There is still something wrong with the code we've written—the left margin of our header and footer labels. Take a look for yourself. The labels are aligned to the left and are pretty much sticking to the lefthand side of the view. The reason for this is that the table view, by default, places header and footer views at *x* point 0.0f. You might think that changing the frame of your header and footer labels will fix this issue, but unfortunately it doesn't. The solution to this problem is to create a generic UIView and place your header and footer labels on that view. Return the generic view as the header/footer, but change the *x* position of your labels within the generic view. The following snippet makes that modification to our implementation of the tableView:viewForHeaderIn Section: and the tableView:viewForFooterInSection: methods:

```
func newLabelWithTitle(title: String) -> UILabel{
  let label = UILabel()
  label.text = title
  label.backgroundColor = UIColor.clearColor()
  label.sizeToFit()
  return label
}

func newViewForHeaderOrFooterWithText(text: String) -> UIView{
  let headerLabel = newLabelWithTitle(text)

  /* Move the label 10 points to the right */
  headerLabel.frame.origin.x += 10
  /* Go 5 points down in y axis */
  headerLabel.frame.origin.y = 5

  /* Give the container view 10 points more in width than our label
  because the label needs a 10 extra points left-margin */
  let resultFrame = CGRect(x: 0,
    y: 0,
    width: headerLabel.frame.size.width + 10,
    height: headerLabel.frame.size.height)

  let headerView = UIView(frame: resultFrame)
  headerView.addSubview(headerLabel)

  return headerView
}

func tableView(tableView: UITableView,
  heightForHeaderInSection section: Int) -> CGFloat{
    return 30
}

func tableView(tableView: UITableView,
  viewForHeaderInSection section: Int) -> UIView?{
    return newViewForHeaderOrFooterWithText("Section \(section) Header")
}
```

```
func tableView(tableView: UITableView,
  viewForFooterInSection section: Int) -> UIView?{
    return newViewForHeaderOrFooterWithText("Section \(section) Footer")
}
```

Now if you run your app, you will get results similar to Figure 6-6.

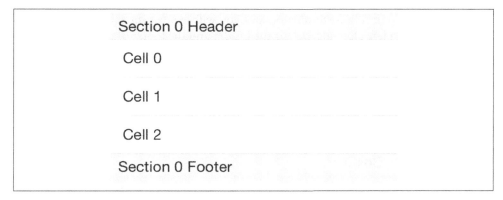

Figure 6-6. Our header and footer labels displayed in a table view

With the methods you just learned, you can even place images as the header/footer of
your table views. Instances of `UIImageView` have `UIView` as their superclass, so you can
easily place your images in image views and return them as headers/footers of a table
view. If all you want to place is text as the header/footer of table views, you can use two
handy methods defined in the `UITableViewDataSource` protocol, which will save you
a lot of hassle. Instead of creating your own labels and returning them as headers/footers
of your table view, you can simply use these methods:

`tableView:titleForHeaderInSection:`
> The return value of this method is of type `NSString`. This string will automatically
> be placed inside a label by the table view and displayed as the header of the section,
> which is specified in the `titleForHeaderInSection` parameter.

`tableView:titleForFooterInSection:`
> The return value of this method is of type `NSString`. This string will automatically
> be placed inside a label by the table view and displayed as the footer of the section,
> which is specified in the `titleForFooterInSection` parameter.

So to make our app's code simpler, let's get rid of our implementation of the `table
View:viewForHeaderInSection:` and the `tableView:viewForFooterInSection:`
methods and replace them with the implementation of the `tableView:titleForHea
derInSection:` and the `tableView:titleForFooterInSection:` methods:

```
func tableView(tableView: UITableView,
  titleForHeaderInSection section: Int) -> String?{
```

```
    return "Section \(section) Header"
}

func tableView(tableView: UITableView,
  titleForFooterInSection section: Int) -> String?{
  return "Section \(section) Footer"
}
```

Now run your app in iPhone Simulator, and you will see that the table view has auto-matically created a left-aligned label for the header and the footer of the only section in our table view. In iOS 8, by default, the header and the footer are left-aligned. In earlier versions of iOS, the header is left-aligned but the footer is center-aligned. In every version, the table view can set the alignment of these labels (see Figure 6-7).

Figure 6-7. A table view rendering text in headers and footers

6.4. Displaying a Refresh Control for Table Views

Problem

You want to display a nice refresh UI control on top of your table views that allows your users to intuitively pull down the table view in order to update its contents. An example of a refresh control is shown in Figure 6-8.

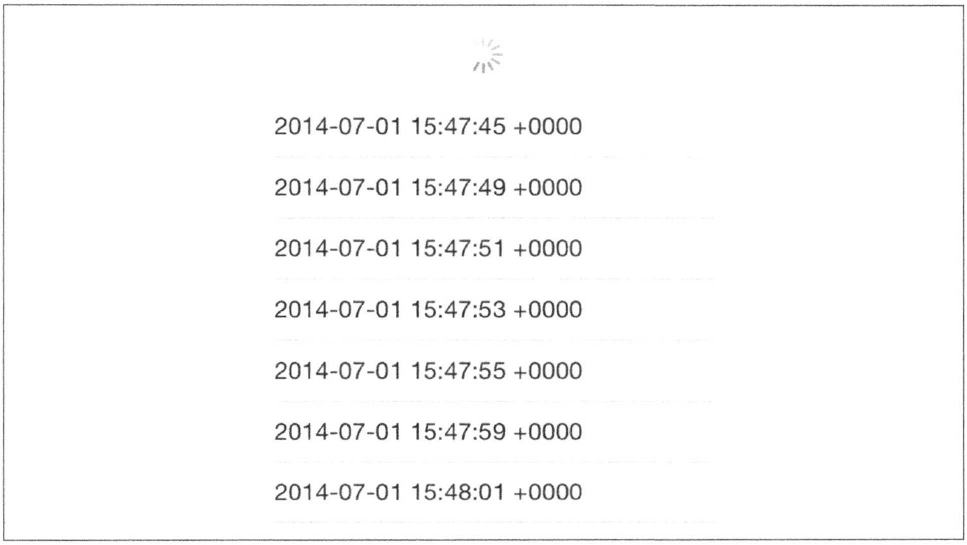

2014-07-01 15:47:45 +0000

2014-07-01 15:47:49 +0000

2014-07-01 15:47:51 +0000

2014-07-01 15:47:53 +0000

2014-07-01 15:47:55 +0000

2014-07-01 15:47:59 +0000

2014-07-01 15:48:01 +0000

Figure 6-8. A refresh control is displayed on top of a table view

Solution

Simply create a table view controller and add an instance of the UIRefreshControl to the table view as a subview.

```
override func viewDidLoad() {

  super.viewDidLoad()

  allTimes.append(NSDate())

  tableView = UITableView(frame: view.bounds, style: .Plain)

  if let theTableView = tableView{

    theTableView.registerClass(UITableViewCell.classForCoder(),
      forCellReuseIdentifier: "identifier")

    theTableView.dataSource = self
    theTableView.autoresizingMask = .FlexibleWidth | .FlexibleHeight

    /* Create the refresh control */
    refreshControl = UIRefreshControl()
    refreshControl!.addTarget(self,
      action: "handleRefresh:",
      forControlEvents: .ValueChanged)

    theTableView.addSubview(refreshControl!)
```

```
        view.addSubview(theTableView)
    }
}
```

Discussion

Refresh controls are simple visual indicators that appear on top of table views and tell the user that something is about to get updated. For instance, prior to iOS 6, in order to refresh your mailbox in the Mail app, you had to press a refresh button. In the new iOS, now you can simply drag the list of your emails down, as if you wanted to see what's above there in the list that you haven't read already. When iOS detects this gesture, it triggers a refresh. Isn't that cool? Twitter's iPhone app started this whole thing when they added a refresh control to their apps, so kudos to them for this. Apple has realized that this is in fact a really nice and intuitive way of updating table views and has since added a dedicated component to the SDK to implement it. The class name for this component is `UIRefreshControl`.

Create a new instance of this class simply by calling its `init` method. When you are done, add this instance to your table view controller, as described in the Solution section of this recipe.

Now you'll want to know when the user has triggered a refresh on your table view. To do this, simply call the `addTarget:action:forControlEvents:` instance method of your refresh control and pass the target object and a selector on that object that takes care of the refresh for you. Pass `UIControlEventValueChanged` to the `forControlE vents` parameter of this method.

Here—I want to demonstrate this to you. In this example, we will have a table view controller that displays the date and time formatted as strings. When the user refreshes the list by pulling it down, we add the current date and time again to the list and refresh our table view. This way, every time the user pulls the list down, it triggers a refresh that allows us to add the current date and time to the list and refresh the table view to display the new date and time. So let's start with our table view controller and define our refresh control and our data source:

```
import UIKit

class ViewController: UIViewController, UITableViewDataSource {
    var tableView: UITableView?
    var allTimes = [NSDate]()
    var refreshControl: UIRefreshControl?

    <# rest of the code goes here #>
```

The `allTimes` property is a simple mutable array that contains all the instances of `NSDate` in it as the user refreshes the table view. We have already seen the initialization of our table view controller in the Solution section of this recipe, so I won't write it again here.

But as you saw there, we hooked the UIControlEventValueChanged event of our refresh control to a method called handleRefresh:. In this method, all we are going to do is add the current date and time to our array of dates and times and then refresh the table view:

```
func handleRefresh(paramSender: AnyObject){

  /* Put a bit of delay between when the refresh control is released
  and when we actually do the refreshing to make the UI look a bit
  smoother than just doing the update without the animation */

  let popTime = dispatch_time(DISPATCH_TIME_NOW, Int64(NSEC_PER_SEC))
  dispatch_after(popTime,
    dispatch_get_main_queue(), {

      /* Add the current date to the list of dates that we have
      so that when the table view is refreshed, a new item appears
      on the screen so that the user sees the difference between
      the before and the after of the refresh */
      self.allTimes.append(NSDate())
      self.refreshControl!.endRefreshing()
      let indexPathOfNewRow = NSIndexPath(forRow: self.allTimes.count - 1,
        inSection: 0)

      self.tableView!.insertRowsAtIndexPaths([indexPathOfNewRow],
        withRowAnimation: .Automatic)

  })

}
```

Last but not least, we provide the date to our table view through the table view's delegate and data source methods:

```
func tableView(tableView: UITableView,
  numberOfRowsInSection section: Int) -> Int {

    return allTimes.count

}

func tableView(tableView: UITableView,
  cellForRowAtIndexPath indexPath: NSIndexPath) -> UITableViewCell{

    let cell = tableView.dequeueReusableCellWithIdentifier("identifier",
      forIndexPath: indexPath) as UITableViewCell

    cell.textLabel.text = "\(allTimes[indexPath.row])"

    return cell

}
```

Give this a go in either the simulator or the device. When you open the app, at first you will see only one date/time added to the list. Keep dragging the table view down to get more items in the list (see Figure 6-8).

6.5. Providing Basic Content to a Collection View

Problem

You already set up a flow layout for your collection view, but you don't know how to render cells in your collection view.

Solution

Either use the `UICollectionViewCell` class directly to present your cells, or subclass this class and provide further implementation on top of that class. In addition, you can have a *.xib* file associated with your cell, as we will soon see.

Discussion

Let's take this one step at a time and start with the fastest and easiest way of creating our cells: instantiate objects of type `UICollectionViewCell` and feed them to our collection view in our data source. The `UICollectionViewCell` class has a content view property named `contentView`, where you can add your own views for display. You can also set various other properties of the cell, such as its background color, which is what we are going to do in this example. But before we begin, let's first set the expectations of what we are going to achieve in this example code and explain the requirements.

We are going to program a collection view with a flow layout that displays three sections, each of which contains anywhere between 20 and 40 cells, with the first section's cells all being red, the second section's cells all being green, and the third section's cells all being blue, as shown in Figure 6-9.

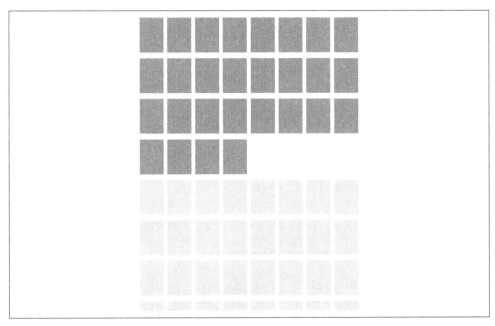

Figure 6-9. A simple collection view with flow layout displaying three sections with different colors

So let's get started. In your collection view controller, create an array of three colors, which you will then assign to the cells for each section:

```
import UIKit

class ViewController: UICollectionViewController {

  let allSectionColors = [
    UIColor.redColor(),
    UIColor.greenColor(),
    UIColor.blueColor()]

}
```

After that, override the `initWithCollectionViewLayout:` designated constructor of your collection view controller and register the `UICollectionViewCell` with a specific identifier. Don't worry if this makes no sense yet, but look at it this way: for every cell that your collection view has to render, it will first look into a queue of reusable cells and find out if a reusable cell exists. If so, the collection view pulls the cell from the queue, and if not, it creates a new cell and return that to you for configuration.

```
override init(collectionViewLayout layout: UICollectionViewLayout!) {
  super.init(collectionViewLayout: layout)
```

```
collectionView.registerClass(UICollectionViewCell.classForCoder(),
  forCellWithReuseIdentifier: "cell")

collectionView.backgroundColor = UIColor.whiteColor()
}

convenience required init(coder aDecoder: NSCoder) {

  let flowLayout = UICollectionViewFlowLayout()

  flowLayout.minimumLineSpacing = 20
  flowLayout.minimumInteritemSpacing = 10
  flowLayout.itemSize = CGSize(width: 80, height: 120);
  flowLayout.scrollDirection = .Vertical

  flowLayout.sectionInset =
    UIEdgeInsets(top: 10, left: 20, bottom: 10, right: 20)

  self.init(collectionViewLayout: flowLayout)
}
```

You can register a cell with a table or a collection view, and when you have to configure a new cell, you simply ask the table or the collection view to give you a new cell of that kind. If the cell exists in the reusable queue, it will be given to you. If not, the table or the collection view will automatically create that cell for you. This is called *registering a reusable cell*, and you can do it in two ways:

- Register a cell using a class name
- Register a cell using a *.xib* file

Both of these ways of registering reusable cells work perfectly with collection views. To register a new cell with a collection view using the cell's class name, use the `register Class:forCellWithReuseIdentifier:` method of the `UICollectionView` class, where the identifier is a simple string that you provide to the collection view. When you then attempt to retrieve reusable cells, you ask the collection view for the cell with a given identifier. To register a *.xib* file with the collection view, you need to use the `register Nib:forCellWithReuseIdentifier:` instance method of your collection view. The identifier of this method also works, as explained earlier in this paragraph. The nib is an object of type `UINib`, which we get to use later in this chapter.

The default implementation of your collection view will have one section unless you implement the `numberOfSectionsInCollectionView:` method in your data source. We want three sections for our collection view, so let's implement this method:

```
override func numberOfSectionsInCollectionView(
  collectionView: UICollectionView) -> Int{
    return allSectionColors.count
}
```

Part of the requirement for our application was for each cell to contain at least 20 and at most 40 cells. We can achieve this using the `arc4random_uniform(x)` function. It returns positive integers between 0 and *x*, where *x* is the parameter that you provide to this function. Therefore, to generate a number between 20 and 40, all we have to do is add 20 to the return value of this function while setting *x* to 20 as well. With this knowledge, let's implement the `collectionView:numberOfItemsInSection:` method of our collection view's data source:

```
override func collectionView(collectionView: UICollectionView,
  numberOfItemsInSection section: Int) -> Int{
    /* Generate between 20 to 40 cells for each section */
    return Int(arc4random_uniform(21)) + 20
}
```

Last but not least, we want to provide the cells to the collection view. For that we need to implement the `collectionView:cellForItemAtIndexPath:` method of our collection view's data source:

```
override func collectionView(collectionView: UICollectionView,
  cellForItemAtIndexPath indexPath: NSIndexPath) -> UICollectionViewCell{

    let cell = collectionView.dequeueReusableCellWithReuseIdentifier(
      "cell",
      forIndexPath: indexPath) as UICollectionViewCell

    cell.backgroundColor = allSectionColors[indexPath.section]

    return cell

}
```

 Index paths simply contain a section number and a row number. So an index path of *0, 1* means the first section's second row, since the indexes are zero-based. Or to denote the fifth row of the tenth section, the index path would be *9, 4*. Index paths are extensively used in table and collection views because they intrinsically embody the notion of sections and of cells in each section. Delegates and data sources for tables and collection views work by communicating the target cell to you using its index path. For instance, if the user taps a cell in a collection view, you will receive its index path. Using the index path, you can look at that cell's underlying data structure (the data that was used to construct that cell originally in your class).

As you can see, we are using the `dequeueReusableCellWithReuseIdentifier:forIndexPath:` instance method of our collection view to pull reusable cells out of the queue. This method expects two parameters: the identifier of the cell that you registered earlier with the collection view, and the index path at which that cell should be rendered. The index path is given to you in the same `collectionView:cellForItemAtIndexPath:` method as a parameter, so the only thing that you have to provide is the identifier of the cell.

The return value of this method will be a cell of type `UICollectionViewCell`, which you can configure. In this implementation, the only thing we have done is to set the background color of the cell to the background color that we chose earlier for all the cells in that section.

 An instance of `UICollectionViewController` has a view of type `UIView` that can be accessed using its `view` property. Don't confuse this view with the `collectionView` property of your controller, which is where the collection view itself sits.

The great thing about our solution in this recipe is that it works perfectly on both the iPad and the iPhone. We saw how it looks on the iPad in Figure 6-9, and on the iPhone, it looks like what's shown in Figure 6-10.

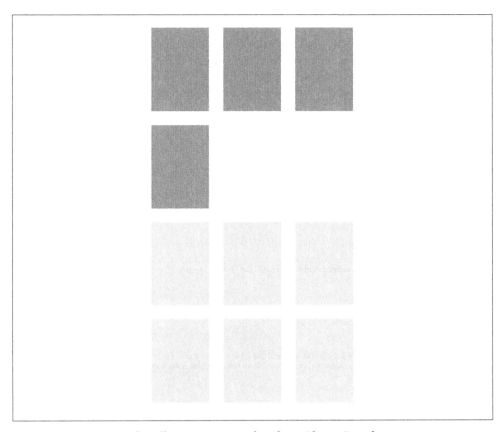

Figure 6-10. Our simple collection view rendered on iPhone Simulator

6.6. Feeding Custom Cells to Collection Views Using .xib Files

Problem

You want to configure collection view cells in Interface Builder and feed those cells to your collection view for rendering.

Solution

Follow these steps:

1. Create a subclass of the UICollectionViewCell and give it a name (we'll use My CollectionViewCell for this example).

2. Create an empty *.xib* file and name it *MyCollectionViewCell.xib*.

3. Drop a Collection View Cell from the Objects Library in Interface Builder onto your empty *.xib* file and change the class name of the dropped object in Interface Builder to `MyCollectionViewCell` (see Figure 6-11). Because you make this association, when you load the *.xib* file programmatically, your custom class of `MyCollectionViewCell` will automatically be loaded into memory. This is pure magic!

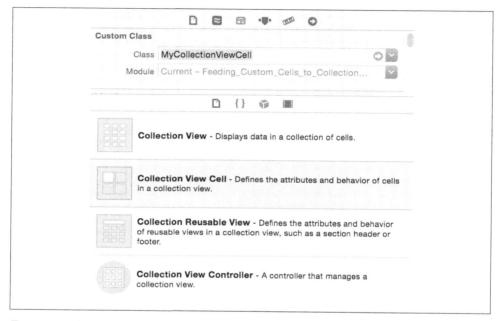

Figure 6-11. Assigning our custom class to the .xib file of our custom collection view cell

4. Customize your cell in Interface Builder. For every UI component that you drop on your cell, ensure that you create an associated `IBOutlet` either in the header or the implementation file of your class (`MyCollectionViewCell`).

5. Register your nib with your collection view using the `registerNib:forCellWi thReuseIdentifier:` instance method of your collection view. You can load your nib into memory using the `nibWithNibName:bundle:` class method of the `UINib` class, as we will see soon.

Discussion

As you read earlier in this recipe, you need to create a *.xib* file for your custom cell and call that file *MyCollectionViewCell.xib*. Please do bear in mind that your *.xib* file doesn't

---

necessarily have to be called that. It can be called anything you like. However, for the sake of simplicity and so that readers can follow the same naming convention throughout this chapter, we will use the aforementioned name. So go ahead and create an empty *.xib* file using the following steps:

1. In File → New → File...

2. On the lefthand side, under the iOS category, choose User Interface, and under the righthand side, pick Empty.

3. You are now asked for the device family of your *.xib* file. Simply choose iPhone for device family.

4. You are now asked to save your *.xib* file to disk. Save your file as *MyCollectionView Cell.xib*.

You also need to create a class that you can link to your *.xib* file's contents. The class will be named `MyCollectionViewCell` and will subclass `UICollectionViewCell`. You can do this by following these steps:

1. In Xcode, choose File → New → File...

2. In the new file dialog, under the iOS category, choose Source. On the righthand side, select "Cocoa Touch Class."

3. Name your class `MyCollectionViewCell` and choose `UICollectionViewCell` as its superclass. Ensure that the language is set to Swift.

4. When asked to do so, save your file to disk.

Now you have to associate the class with your *.xib* file. To do this, follow these steps:

1. Open your *MyCollectionViewCell.xib* file in Interface Builder. In the Object Library, simply find the Collection View Cell and drop it into your *.xib* file. By default, this cell will be very small (50×50 points) and will have a black background color.

2. Explicitly select the cell on your *.xib* file by clicking on it. Open the Identity Inspector in Interface Builder and change the Class field's value to `MyCollection ViewCell`, as shown earlier in Figure 6-11.

The next thing you need to do is add some UI components to your cell. Later, when you populate your collection view, your can change the value of those components. The best component for this demonstration is an image view, so while you have your *MyCollec tionViewCell.xib* file open in Interface Builder, drop an instance of `UIImageView` onto it. Connect that image view to your collection view cell class file and name it `image ViewBackgroundImage` so that your cell's class file will look like this:

```
import UIKit
```

```
class MyCollectionViewCell: UICollectionViewCell {

    @IBOutlet weak var imageViewBackgroundImage: UIImageView!

}
```

We are going to populate this image view with various images. For this recipe, I created three simple images that I'm going to use, each one 50×50 points in size. You can use any image you want, simply by doing a quick search on the Internet. Once you've found your images, add them to your project. Ensure that the images are named *1.png*, *2.png*, and *3.png*, and that their @2x Retina counterparts are named *1@2x.png*, *2@2x.png*, and *3@2x.png*.

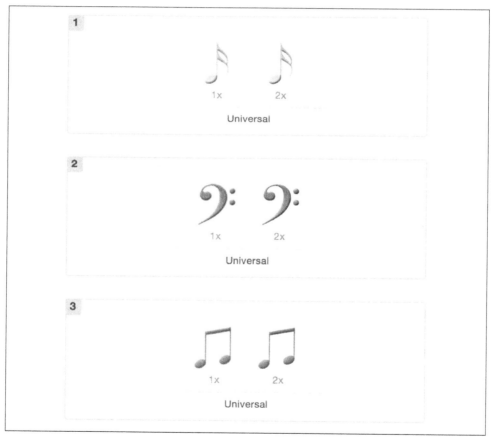

Figure 6-12. The images that we want to load into our cells

In this example, we are going to display a user interface similar to that shown in Figure 6-9, but instead of colors for cells, we are going to set the background image view's image to a random image. So it makes sense to base our code on what we wrote for Recipe 6.5 because the output will be very similar.

The first modification that we have to make is to prepare a method in our view controller that can return a random image to us. We have an array of images, as explained before. So after instantiating the array, we need a handy little method that can grab a random image out of the array for us:

```
let allImages = [
  UIImage(named: "1"),
  UIImage(named: "2"),
  UIImage(named: "3")
]


func randomImage() -> UIImage{
  return allImages[Int(arc4random_uniform(UInt32(allImages.count)))]!
}
```

Next, we need to override our collection view controller's designated constructor to register our MyCollectionViewCell nib with our collection view:

```
import UIKit

class ViewController: UICollectionViewController {

  let allImages = [
    UIImage(named: "1"),
    UIImage(named: "2"),
    UIImage(named: "3")
  ]


  func randomImage() -> UIImage{
    return allImages[Int(arc4random_uniform(UInt32(allImages.count)))]!
  }

  override init(collectionViewLayout layout: UICollectionViewLayout!) {
    super.init(collectionViewLayout: layout)

    let nib = UINib(nibName: "MyCollectionViewCell", bundle: nil)

    collectionView.registerNib(nib, forCellWithReuseIdentifier: "cell")
    collectionView.backgroundColor = UIColor.whiteColor()
  }

  convenience required init(coder aDecoder: NSCoder) {
    let flowLayout = UICollectionViewFlowLayout()

    flowLayout.minimumLineSpacing = 20
    flowLayout.minimumInteritemSpacing = 10
    flowLayout.itemSize = CGSize(width: 80, height: 120);
```

```
        flowLayout.scrollDirection = .Vertical

        flowLayout.sectionInset =
          UIEdgeInsets(top: 10, left: 20, bottom: 10, right: 20)

        self.init(collectionViewLayout: flowLayout)
    }

}
```

Also, when asked how many sections we have, we return a random number between 3 and 6. This is not really required—we could go with one section, but it won't hurt to have more. Also for each section, we want to have between 10 and 15 cells:

```
override func numberOfSectionsInCollectionView(
  collectionView: UICollectionView) -> Int {
    /* Between 3 to 6 sections */
    return Int(3 + arc4random_uniform(4))
}

override func collectionView(collectionView: UICollectionView,
  numberOfItemsInSection section: Int) -> Int {
    /* Each section has between 10 to 15 cells */
    return Int(10 + arc4random_uniform(6))
}
```

Last but not least, we ask the collection view for the cells and configure them with a random image:

```
override func collectionView(collectionView: UICollectionView,
  cellForItemAtIndexPath indexPath: NSIndexPath) -> UICollectionViewCell {

    let cell = collectionView.dequeueReusableCellWithReuseIdentifier(
      "cell", forIndexPath: indexPath) as MyCollectionViewCell

    cell.imageViewBackgroundImage.image = randomImage()
    cell.imageViewBackgroundImage.contentMode = .ScaleAspectFit

    return cell

}
```

Run your app and you will see something similar to that shown in Figure 6-13. Of course if you use different images from the ones I chose, your images will show up instead of mine.

Figure 6-13. A collection view with custom cells loaded from a nib

See Also

Recipe 6.5

6.7. Handling Events in Collection Views

Problem

You want to be able to handle collection view events, such as taps.

Solution

Assign a delegate to your collection view. In some other cases, you may not even have to do that. All you may need to do is listen for those events in your cell classes and handle them right there.

Discussion

Collection views have `delegate` properties that have to conform to the `UICollection` `ViewDelegate` protocol. The delegate object will then receive various delegation calls from the collection view informing the delegate of various events, such as a cell becoming highlighted or selected. You need to know the difference between the highlighted and selected state of a collection view cell. When the user presses her finger down on a cell in a collection view but doesn't lift her finger up, the cell under her finger is *highlighted*. When she presses her finger down and lifts her finger up to say she wants to perform an action on the cell, that cell will then be *selected*.

Collection view cells of type `UICollectionViewCell` have two very useful properties, `highlighted` and `selected`, that get set to `true` when the cell becomes highlighted or selected.

If all you want to do is change your cell's visual presentation when it becomes selected, you're in luck, because cells of type `UICollectionViewCell` expose a property named `selectedBackgroundView` of type `UIView` that you can set to a valid view. This view will then get displayed on the screen when your cell is selected. Let's demonstrate this by building on top of what we created in Recipe 6.6. If you remember, in that example, we created a custom cell that had a background image view property named `imageView BackgroundImage`, which covered the whole of the cell. We were loading custom image instances into that image view. What we want now is to set the background *color* of our cell to blue when the cell becomes selected. Because the image view is sitting on top of everything else on our collection view, before we set the background color of our cell, we need to ensure that our image view is transparent by changing the background color of the image view to a clear color. The reason behind this is that an image view is opaque by default, so if you place it on a view that has a background color, you won't be able to see the color of the view because the image view is opaque. Thus, in order for us to see the color of our image view's super view, we will set the image view's background color to a clear and transparent color. So let's get started:

```swift
import UIKit

class MyCollectionViewCell: UICollectionViewCell {

    @IBOutlet weak var imageViewBackgroundImage: UIImageView!

    override func awakeFromNib() {
      super.awakeFromNib()

      imageViewBackgroundImage.backgroundColor = UIColor.clearColor()
      selectedBackgroundView = UIView(frame: bounds)
      selectedBackgroundView.backgroundColor = UIColor.blueColor()

    }

}
```

That's all, really! Now if you tap on any of the cells in your program, you will see that the background color of the cell becomes blue.

There are more things that you can do with your collection view by listening to various events that it sends. For instance, you might want to play a sound or an animation when a cell is selected. Imagine that when the user taps on a cell, that we want to use an animation to momentarily hide the cell and then show it again, creating a fading-out and fading-in animation. If this is the type of thing you want to do, start by setting the delegate object of your collection view, because that's really where you get a lot of events reported back to you. Your delegate object, as mentioned before, has to conform to the `UICollectionViewDelegate` protocol. This protocol contains a lot of useful methods that you can implement. The following are some of the most important methods in this protocol:

 The `UICollectionViewDelegateFlowLayout` protocol lets you provide information about your items, such as width and height, to the flow layout. You can either provide a generic size for all the flow layout item sizes in one go so that all items have the same size, or you can respond to the relevant messages that you receive from the flow layout delegate protocol, asking you to provide a size for individual cells in the layout.

`collectionView:didHighlightItemAtIndexPath:`
Gets called on the delegate when a cell becomes highlighted.

`collectionView:didUnhighlightItemAtIndexPath:`
Gets called on the delegate when a cell comes out of the highlighted state. This method gets called when the user successfully finishes the tap event (pushes her finger on the item and lifts her finger off it, generating the tap gesture) or it can get called if the user cancels her earlier highlighting of the cell by dragging her finger out of the boundaries of the cell.

`collectionView:didSelectItemAtIndexPath:`
This method gets called on the delegate object when a given cell becomes selected. The cell is always highlighted before it is selected.

`collectionView:didDeselectItemAtIndexPath:`
Gets called on the delegate object when the cell comes out of the selected state.

So let's build an app according to our earlier requirements. We want to fade out the cell and fade it back in when it becomes selected. In your `UICollectionViewController` instance, implement the `collectionView:didSelectItemAtIndexPath:` method like so:

Our code is written inside our collection view controller, which by default is automatically chosen by the system as both the data source and the delegate of its collection view. It conforms to both the UICollectionViewDataSource and the UICollectionViewDelegate protocols. Therefore, you can simply implement any data source or delegate method directly in your collection view controller's implementation file.

```
import UIKit

class ViewController: UICollectionViewController {

  override func collectionView(collectionView: UICollectionView,
    didSelectItemAtIndexPath indexPath: NSIndexPath){

    let selectedCell = collectionView.cellForItemAtIndexPath(indexPath)
    as UICollectionViewCell!

    UIView.animateWithDuration(animationDuration, animations: {
      selectedCell.alpha = 0
      }, completion: {[weak self] (finished: Bool) in
        UIView.animateWithDuration(self!.animationDuration, animations: {
          selectedCell.alpha = 1
          })
      })

  }

  <# rest of your code goes here #>
```

We are using animations here in our example, but this is not the right place to explain how animations work. If you require more information about composing simple animations in iOS, refer to Chapter 19.

OK! That was easy. How about another example? Let's say you want to make a cell four times as big as its normal size when it becomes highlighted and then take it back to its original size when it loses its highlighted state. That means, when the user presses her finger down on the cell (before releasing her finger), the cell enlarges to twice its size and then, when she releases her finger, the cell goes back to its original size. For this, we have to implement the collectionView:didHighlightItemAtIndexPath: and collectionView:didUnhighlightItemAtIndexPath: methods of the UICollectionViewDelegate protocol in our collection view controller (remember, collection view controllers, by default, conform to the UICollectionViewDelegate and the UICollectionViewDataSource protocols):

```
override func collectionView(collectionView: UICollectionView,
  didHighlightItemAtIndexPath indexPath: NSIndexPath) {
```

```
let selectedCell = collectionView.cellForItemAtIndexPath(indexPath)
  as UICollectionViewCell!

UIView.animateWithDuration(animationDuration, animations: {
  selectedCell.transform = CGAffineTransformMakeScale(4, 4)
  })

}

override func collectionView(collectionView: UICollectionView,
  didUnhighlightItemAtIndexPath indexPath: NSIndexPath){

  let selectedCell = collectionView.cellForItemAtIndexPath(indexPath)
    as UICollectionViewCell!

  UIView.animateWithDuration(animationDuration, animations: {
    selectedCell.transform = CGAffineTransformIdentity
    })

}
```

As you can see, we are using the CGAffineTransformMakeScale Core Graphics function to create an affine transformation, and then assigning that to the cell itself to create the visual effect of the cell growing twice as large and then shrinking back to its original size. To learn more about this function, please read through Recipe 19.9.

See Also

Recipe 6.6; Recipe 19.9

6.8. Providing Header and Footer in a Collection View

Problem

You want to provide header and footer views for your collection view, just as in table views, while using the flow layout.

Solution

Follow these steps:

1. Create an *.xib* file for your header and another one for your footer.

2. Drag and drop, from Interface Builder's Object Library, an instance of *Collection Reusable View* into your *.xib* files. Ensure that the collection reusable view that you dropped into your *.xib* file is the only view in your *.xib* file. This makes the reusable view the root view of your *.xib* file, exactly the way that you should provide headers and footers to the collection view.

3. If you want more control over how your *.xib* file behaves, create an Objective-C class and associate your *.xib* file's root view to your class. This ensures that when your *.xib* file's contents are loaded from disk by iOS, the associated class will also be loaded into memory, giving you access to the view hierarchy in the *.xib* file.

4. Instantiate the `registerNib:forSupplementaryViewOfKind:withReuseIdentifi er:` instance method of your collection view and register your nib files for the `UICollectionElementKindSectionHeader` and `UICollectionElementKindSec tionFooter` view kinds.

5. To customize your header and footer views when they are about to be displayed, implement the `collectionView:viewForSupplementaryElementOfKind:atIndex Path:` method of your collection view's data source, and in there, issue the `de queueReusableSupplementaryViewOfKind:withReuseIdentifier:forIndex Path:` method of your collection view to dequeue a reusable header/footer of a given kind.

6. Last but not least, ensure that you set the size for your headers and footers by setting the value of the `headerReferenceSize` and the `footerReferenceSize` properties of your flow layout object. This step is very important: if you forget to do this, you will not see your header or footer.

Discussion

All right, so now we have to create the *.xib* files for our custom headers and footers. Let's call these *.xib* files *Header.xib* and *Footer.xib*. We create them in the same exact way described in Recipe 6.6, so I won't explain that again here. Ensure that you have also created a class for your header and one for your footer. Name those `Header` and `Foot er`, respectively, and ensure that they subclass `UICollectionReusableView`. Then configure a label and a button in Interface Builder, and drag and drop the label into your Header file and the button into your Footer *.xib* file, and link them up to your classes as shown in Figure 6-14 and Figure 6-15.

Figure 6-14. Configuring a header cell for a collection view in Interface Builder

Figure 6-15. Configuring a footer cell for a collection view in Interface Builder

I linked my header's label up to my Header class through an outlet property in the *Header* file and named the outlet simply *label*:

```
import UIKit

class Header: UICollectionReusableView {
  @IBOutlet weak var label: UILabel!
}
```

I did the same thing for the footer, linking the button on my Footer *.xib* file to an outlet in my *Footer* file and naming the outlet *button*:

```
import UIKit

class Footer: UICollectionReusableView {
  @IBOutlet weak var button: UIButton!
}
```

Now, in the constructor method of your collection view, register the collection view's cell, header cell, and footer cell using the nib files that we load into memory:

```
override init(collectionViewLayout layout: UICollectionViewLayout!) {
    super.init(collectionViewLayout: layout)

    /* Register the nib with the collection view for easy retrieval */
    let nib = UINib(nibName: "MyCollectionViewCell", bundle: nil)
    collectionView.registerNib(nib, forCellWithReuseIdentifier: "cell")

    /* Register the header's nib */
    let headerNib = UINib(nibName: "Header", bundle: nil)
    collectionView.registerNib(headerNib,
      forSupplementaryViewOfKind: UICollectionElementKindSectionHeader,
      withReuseIdentifier: "header")

    /* Register the footer's nib */
    let footerNib = UINib(nibName: "Footer", bundle: nil)
    collectionView.registerNib(footerNib,
      forSupplementaryViewOfKind: UICollectionElementKindSectionFooter,
      withReuseIdentifier: "footer")

    collectionView.backgroundColor = UIColor.whiteColor()
}

convenience required init(coder aDecoder: NSCoder) {
    let flowLayout = UICollectionViewFlowLayout()

    flowLayout.minimumLineSpacing = 20
    flowLayout.minimumInteritemSpacing = 10
    flowLayout.itemSize = CGSize(width: 80, height: 120);
    flowLayout.scrollDirection = .Vertical

    flowLayout.sectionInset =
      UIEdgeInsets(top: 10, left: 20, bottom: 10, right: 20)

    self.init(collectionViewLayout: flowLayout)
}
```

The next thing you have to do is implement the collectionView:viewForSupplemen taryElementOfKind:atIndexPath: method of your collection view to configure the headers and footers and provide them back to the collection view:

```
override func collectionView(collectionView: UICollectionView,
  viewForSupplementaryElementOfKind kind: String,
  atIndexPath indexPath: NSIndexPath) -> UICollectionReusableView {

    var identifier = "header"
    if kind == UICollectionElementKindSectionFooter{
      identifier = "footer"
    }

    let view = collectionView.dequeueReusableSupplementaryViewOfKind(kind,
      withReuseIdentifier: identifier,
      forIndexPath: indexPath) as UICollectionReusableView

    if kind == UICollectionElementKindSectionHeader{
      if let header = view as? Header{
        header.label.text = "Section Header \(indexPath.section+1)"
      }
    }
    else if kind == UICollectionElementKindSectionFooter{
      if let footer = view as? Footer{
        let title = "Section Footer \(indexPath.section+1)"
        footer.button.setTitle(title, forState: .Normal)
      }
    }

    return view

}
```

Last but not least, ensure that your flow layout knows the dimensions of your collection view's header and footer cells:

```
convenience required init(coder aDecoder: NSCoder) {
  let flowLayout = UICollectionViewFlowLayout()

  flowLayout.minimumLineSpacing = 20
  flowLayout.minimumInteritemSpacing = 10
  flowLayout.itemSize = CGSize(width: 80, height: 120);
  flowLayout.scrollDirection = .Vertical

  flowLayout.sectionInset =
    UIEdgeInsets(top: 10, left: 20, bottom: 10, right: 20)

  /* Set the reference size for the header and the footer views */
  flowLayout.headerReferenceSize = CGSize(width: 300, height: 50)
  flowLayout.footerReferenceSize = CGSize(width: 300, height: 50)
```

```
    self.init(collectionViewLayout: flowLayout)
  }
```

All ready to go! If you launch your app on an iPad, you will see something similar to that shown in Figure 6-16.

Figure 6-16. Headers and footers rendered in the collection view

See Also

Recipe 6.6

6.9. Adding Custom Interactions to Collection Views

Problem

You want to add your own gesture recognizers, such as pinch gesture recognizers, to a collection view in order to enable custom behaviors on top of the existing ones.

Solution

Instantiate your gesture recognizer and then go through all the existing collection view gesture recognizers to see whether a gesture recognizer similar to yours already exists. If so, call the `requireGestureRecognizerToFail:` method on the existing gesture recognizer and pass your own recognizer as the parameter to this method. This ensures that the collection view's gesture recognizer that is similar to yours will grab the gestures only if your gesture recognizer fails to process its data or its requirements/criteria aren't met. That means that if your gesture recognizer can process the gesture, it will, but if it cannot, the gesture will be sent to the collection view's existing gesture recognizers for processing.

After this is done, add your gesture recognizer to your collection view. Remember, in an instance of `UICollectionViewController`, your collection view object is accessible through the `collectionView` property of the controller and *not* the `view` property.

Discussion

The iOS API has already added a few gesture recognizers to collection views. So in order to add your own gesture recognizers on top of the existing collection, you first need to make sure that your gesture recognizers will not interfere with the existing ones. To do that, you have to first instantiate your own gesture recognizers and, as explained before, look through the existing array of gesture recognizers on the collection view and call the `requireGestureRecognizerToFail:` method on the one that is of the same class type of gesture recognizer as the one you are attempting to add to the collection view.

Let's have a look at an example. Our objective for this example is to add pinching for zooming in and zooming out functionality to our collection view. We are going to build this example on top of what we have already done in Recipe 6.6. So the first thing we are going to do is add a pinch gesture recognizer to the collection of gesture recognizers in our collection view, which must be done in the `viewDidLoad` method of the collection view controller:

```
override func viewDidLoad() {
  super.viewDidLoad()

  let pinch = UIPinchGestureRecognizer(target: self,
    action: "handlePinches:")

  for recognizer in collectionView.gestureRecognizers as
    [UIGestureRecognizer]{
      if recognizer is UIPinchGestureRecognizer{
        recognizer.requireGestureRecognizerToFail(pinch)
      }
  }

  collectionView.addGestureRecognizer(pinch)

}
```

The pinch gesture recognizer is set up to call the `handlePinches:` method of our view controller. We'll write this method now:

```
func handlePinches(pinch: UIPinchGestureRecognizer){
```

```
        let defaultLayoutItemSize = CGSize(width: 80, height: 120)

        let layout = collectionView.collectionViewLayout
          as UICollectionViewFlowLayout

        layout.itemSize =
          CGSize(width: defaultLayoutItemSize.width * pinch.scale,
            height: defaultLayoutItemSize.height * pinch.scale)

        layout.invalidateLayout()

    }
```

There are two very important parts to this code:

1. We assume that the default item size on our collection view's flow layout was set to have a width of 80 points and a height of 120 points. We then take the scale factor that came back from the pinch gesture recognizer and multiply the size of the items in our collection view by the pinch scale factor, which can cause our items to become bigger or smaller in dimension, depending on how the user is controlling the pinching on the screen.

2. After we change the default item size in our flow layout, we need to refresh the layout. In table views, we refreshed the sections, the rows, or the whole table view, but here, we refresh or invalidate the layout that is attached to the collection view in order to ask the collection view to redraw itself after a layout change. Since a collection view can contain only one layout object at a time, invalidating that layout object will force the whole collection view to reload. If we could have one layout per section, we would be able to reload only the section(s) that is linked to that layout, but for now, the whole collection view will be repainted when the layout object is invalidated.

Now if you run your code, you will notice that you can use two fingers on the screen to pinch inward and enlarge the size of the items on your collection view, or pinch outward to make them smaller.

See Also

Recipe 6.6

CHAPTER 7

Concurrency and Multitasking

7.0. Introduction

Concurrency is achieved when two or more tasks are executed at the same time. Modern operating systems have the ability to run tasks concurrently, even on one CPU. They achieve this by giving every task a certain time slice from the CPU. For instance, if there are 10 tasks to be executed in one second, all with the same priority, the operating system will divide 1,000 milliseconds by 10 (tasks) and will give each task 100 milliseconds of the CPU time. That means that all these tasks will be executed in the same second, and will appear to have been executed concurrently.

However, with advances in technology, now we have CPUs with more than one core. This means that the CPU is truly capable of executing tasks at the same time. The operating system will dispatch the tasks to the CPU and wait until they are done. It's that simple!

Grand Central Dispatch, or GCD for short, is a low-level C API that works with block objects. The real use for GCD is to dispatch tasks to multiple cores without making you, the programmer, worry about which core is executing which task. On Mac OS X, multicore devices, including laptops, have been available to users for quite some time. With the introduction of multicore devices such as the new iPad, programmers can write amazing multicore-aware multithreaded apps for iOS.

At the heart of GCD are dispatch queues. Dispatch queues, as we will soon see, are pools of threads managed by GCD on the host operating system, whether iOS or Mac OS X. You will not be working with these threads directly. You will just work with dispatch queues, dispatching *tasks* to these queues and asking the queues to invoke your tasks. GCD offers several options for running tasks: synchronously, asynchronously, after a certain delay, etc.

To start using GCD in your apps, you don't have to import any special library into your project. Apple has already incorporated GCD into various frameworks, including Core Foundation and Cocoa/Cocoa Touch. All methods and data types available in GCD start with a *dispatch_* keyword. For instance, `dispatch_async` allows you to dispatch a task on a queue for asynchronous execution, whereas `dispatch_after` allows you to run a block of code after a given delay.

Before GCD and operations, programmers had to create their own threads to perform tasks in parallel. The programmer has to start the thread manually and then create the required structure for the thread (entry point, autorelease pool, and thread's main loop). When we write the same code with GCD, we really won't have to do much. We will simply place our code in a block object and dispatch that block object to GCD for execution. Whether that code gets executed on the main thread or any other thread depends on us. In this chapter, you will learn all there is to know about GCD and how to use it to write modern multithreaded apps for iOS and Mac OS X that will achieve blazing performance on multicore devices such as the iPad 2.

We will be working with dispatch queues a lot, so please make sure that you fully understand the concept behind them. There are three types of dispatch queues:

Main queue

> This queue performs all its tasks on the main thread, which is where Cocoa and Cocoa Touch require programmers to call all UI-related methods. Use the `dispatch_get_main_queue` function to retrieve the handle to the main queue.

Concurrent queues

> These are queues that you can retrieve from GCD in order to execute asynchronous or synchronous tasks. Multiple concurrent queues can execute multiple tasks in parallel without breaking a sweat. No more thread management—yippee! Use the `dispatch_get_global_queue` function to retrieve the handle to a concurrent queue.

Serial queues

> These are queues that, no matter whether you submit synchronous or asynchronous tasks to them, will always execute their tasks in a first-in-first-out (FIFO) fashion, meaning that they can only execute one block object at a time. However, they do *not* run on the main thread and therefore are perfect for a series of tasks that have to be executed in strict order without blocking the main thread. Use the `dispatch_queue_create` function to create a serial queue.

Block objects that get passed to GCD functions don't always follow the same structure. Some must accept parameters and some shouldn't, but none of the block objects submitted to GCD return a value.

At any moment during the lifetime of your application, you can use multiple dispatch queues at the same time. Your system has only one main queue, but you can create as many serial dispatch queues as you want (within reason, of course), for whatever functionality you require for your app. You can also retrieve multiple concurrent queues and dispatch your tasks to them.

Block objects are *packages* of code that usually appear in the form of methods. Block objects, together with Grand Central Dispatch (GCD), create a harmonious environment in which you can deliver high-performance multithreaded apps in iOS and Mac OS X. What's so special about block objects and GCD, you might ask? It's simple: no more threads! All you have to do is put your code in block objects and ask GCD to take care of the execution of that code for you.

 Perhaps the most important difference between block objects (sometimes referred to as *closures*) and traditional function pointers is that block objects copy the values of local variables accessed inside the block objects and keep those copies for local use. If the values of those variables change outside the scope of the block object, you can be sure that the block object keeps a copy of the variable. We will discuss this in more detail soon.

Constructing block objects is similar to constructing traditional C functions. Block objects can have return values and can accept parameters. Block objects can be defined inline or treated as a separate block of code, similar to a C function. When created inline, the scope of variables accessible to block objects is considerably different from when a block object is implemented as a separate block of code.

GCD works with block objects. When performing tasks with GCD, you can pass a block object whose code can get executed synchronously or asynchronously, depending on which methods you use in GCD. Thus, you can create a block object that is responsible for downloading a URL passed to it as a parameter. That single block object can then be used synchronously or asynchronously in various places in your app, depending on how you would like to run it. You don't have to make the block object synchronous or asynchronous per se; you simply call it with synchronous or asynchronous GCD methods and the block object *just works*.

This chapter is dedicated entirely to constructing and using block objects in iOS and Mac OS X apps, using GCD for dispatching tasks to the operating system, threads and timers. I would like to stress that the only way to get used to block objects' syntax is to write a few of them for yourself. Have a look at the sample code in this chapter and try implementing your own block objects.

Operations can be configured to run a block of code synchronously or asynchronously. You can manage operations manually or place them on *operation queues*, which facilitate concurrency so that you do not need to think about the underlying thread management.

In this chapter, you will see how to use operations and operation queues, as well as basic threads and timers, to synchronously and asynchronously execute tasks in applications.

Cocoa provides three different types of operations:

Block operations
> These facilitate the execution of one or more block objects.

Invocation operations
> These allow you to invoke a method in another, existing object.

Plain operations
> These are plain operation classes that need to be subclassed. The code to be executed will be written inside the `main` method of the operation object.

Operations, as mentioned before, can be managed with operation queues, which have the data type `NSOperationQueue`. After instantiating any of the aforementioned operation types (block, invocation, or plain operation), you can add them to an operation queue and have the queue manage the operation.

An operation object can have dependencies on other operation objects and be instructed to wait for the completion of one or more operations before executing the task associated with it. Unless you add a dependency, you have no control over the order in which operations run. For instance, adding them to a queue in a certain order does not guarantee that they will execute in that order, despite the use of the term *queue*.

There are a few important things to bear in mind when working with operation queues and operations:

- By default, operations run on the thread that starts them, using their `start` instance method. If you want the operations to work asynchronously, you have to use either an operation queue or a subclass `NSOperation` and detach a new thread on the `main` instance method of the operation.

- An operation can wait for the execution of another operation to finish before it starts itself. Be careful not to create interdependent operations, a common mistake known as a *deadlock*. In other words, do not tell operation A to depend on operation B if B already depends on A; this will cause both to wait forever, taking up memory and possibly hanging your application.

- Operations can be cancelled. So, if you subclassed `NSOperation` to create custom operation objects, you have to make sure to use the `isCancelled` instance method to check whether the operation has been cancelled before executing the task associated with the operation. For instance, if your operation's task is to check for the availability of an Internet connection every 20 seconds, it must call the `isCancelled` instance method at the beginning of each run to make sure it has not been cancelled before attempting to check for an Internet connection again. If the operation takes more than a few seconds (such as when you download a file), you should also check isCancelled periodically while running the task.

- Operation objects comply with key-value observing (KVO) on various key paths such as isFinished, isReady, and isExecuting. We will be discussing Key Value Coding and Key Value Observing in a later chapter.

- If you plan to subclass NSOperation and provide a custom implementation for the operation, you must create your own autorelease pool in the main method of the operation, which gets called from the start method. We will discuss this in detail later in this chapter.

- Always keep a reference to the operation objects you create. The concurrent nature of operation queues might make it impossible for you to retrieve a reference to an operation after it has been added to the queue.

7.1. Performing UI-Related Tasks

Problem

You are using GCD for concurrency, and you would like to know the best way of working with UI-related APIs.

Solution

Use the dispatch_get_main_queue function.

Discussion

UI-related tasks have to be performed on the main thread, so the main queue is the only candidate for UI task execution in GCD. We can use the dispatch_get_main_queue function to get the handle to the main dispatch queue.

The correct way to dispatch tasks to the main queue is by using the dispatch_async function, which executes a block object on a dispatch queue.

 The dispatch_sync method *cannot* be called on the main queue because it will block the thread indefinitely and cause your application to deadlock. All tasks submitted to the main queue through GCD must be submitted asynchronously.

Let's have a look at using the dispatch_async function. It accepts two parameters:

Dispatch queue handle
   The dispatch queue on which the task has to be executed

Block object

The block object to be sent to the dispatch queue for asynchronous execution

Here is an example. This code will display an alert in iOS to the user, using the main queue:

```
import UIKit

class ViewController: UIViewController {

  override func viewDidLoad() {
    super.viewDidLoad()

    dispatch_async(dispatch_get_main_queue(), {[weak self] in

      let alertController = UIAlertController(title: "GCD",
        message: "GCD is amazing!",
        preferredStyle: .Alert)

      alertController.addAction(UIAlertAction(title: "OK",
        style: .Default,
        handler: nil))

      self!.presentViewController(alertController,
        animated: true,
        completion: nil)

    })

  }

}
```

 As you've noticed, the dispatch_async GCD function has no parameters or return value. The block object that is submitted to this function must gather its own data in order to complete its task. In the code snippet that we just saw, the alert view has all the values it needs to finish its task. However, this might not always be the case. In such instances, you must make sure the block object submitted to GCD has access in its scope to all the values that it requires.

This might not seem very impressive, if you think about it. So what makes the main queue truly interesting? The answer is simple: when you are getting the maximum performance from GCD to do some heavy calculation on concurrent or serial threads, you might want to display the results to your user or move a component on the screen. For that, you *must* use the main queue, because it is UI-related work. The functions shown in this section are the *only* ways to get out of a serial or concurrent queue while still utilizing GCD to update your UI, so you can imagine how important they are.

If you invoke the `currentThread` class method of the `NSThread` class, you will find out that the block objects you dispatch to the main queue are indeed running on the main thread:

```
import UIKit

class ViewController: UIViewController {

  override func viewDidLoad() {
    super.viewDidLoad()

    dispatch_async(dispatch_get_main_queue(), {
      println("Current thread = \(NSThread.currentThread())")
      println("Main thread = \(NSThread.mainThread())")
      })

  }

}
```

Now that you know how to perform UI-related tasks using GCD, it is time we moved to other subjects, such as performing tasks in parallel using concurrent queues (see Recipe 7.2) and mixing the code with UI-related code if need be.

7.2. Performing Non-UI Related Tasks

Problem

You want to perform non-UI related tasks with GCD.

Solution

Use the `dispatch_sync` or the `dispatch_async` functions on a queue that is not the main queue.

Discussion

 In this recipe, we start by discussing synchronous calls and then advance to asynchronous calls that allow us to perform tasks that do not block the current thread.

There are times when you want to perform tasks that have nothing to do with the UI or that interact with the UI as well as doing other tasks that take up a lot of time. For instance, you might want to download an image and display it to the user after it is downloaded. The downloading process has absolutely nothing to do with the UI.

For any task that doesn't involve the UI, you can use global concurrent queues in GCD. These allow either synchronous or asynchronous execution. But synchronous execution does *not* mean your program waits for the code to finish before continuing. It simply means that the concurrent queue will wait until your task has finished before it continues to the next block of code on the queue. When you put a block object on a concurrent queue, your own program *always* continues right away without waiting for the queue to execute the code. This is because concurrent queues, as their name implies, run their code on threads other than the main thread. (There is one exception to this: when a task is submitted to a concurrent or serial queue using the dispatch_sync function, iOS will, if possible, run the task on the *current* thread, which *might* be the main thread, depending on where the code path is at the moment. This is an optimization that has been programmed on GCD, as we shall soon see.)

If you submit a task to a concurrent queue synchronously, and at the same time submit another synchronous task to *another* concurrent queue, these two synchronous tasks will run asynchronously in relation to each other because they are running two *different concurrent queues*. It's important to understand this because sometimes, as we'll see, you want to make sure task A finishes before task B starts. To ensure that, submit them synchronously to the *same* queue.

You can perform synchronous tasks on a dispatch queue using the dispatch_sync function. All you have to do is provide the handle of the queue that has to run the task and a block of code to execute on that queue.

Let's look at an example. It prints the integers 1 to 1,000 twice, one complete sequence after the other, without blocking the main thread. We can create a block object that does the counting for us and synchronously call the same block object twice:

```
func printFrom1To1000(){

  for counter in 0..<1000{
    println("Counter = \(counter) - Thread = \(NSThread.currentThread())")
  }

}
```

Now let's go and invoke this block object using GCD:

```
override func viewDidLoad() {
  super.viewDidLoad()

  let queue = dispatch_get_global_queue(DISPATCH_QUEUE_PRIORITY_DEFAULT, 0)
  dispatch_sync(queue, printFrom1To1000)
  dispatch_sync(queue, printFrom1To1000)

}
```

If you run this code, you might notice the counting taking place on the main thread, even though you've asked a concurrent queue to execute the task. It turns out this is an optimization by GCD. The `dispatch_sync` function will use the current thread—the thread you're using when you dispatch the task—whenever possible, as a part of an optimization that has been programmed into GCD. Here is what Apple says about it:

> As an optimization, this function invokes the block on the current thread when possible.
>
> —Grand Central Dispatch (GCD) Reference

The first parameter of the `dispatch_get_global_queue` function specifies the priority of the concurrent queue that GCD has to retrieve for the programmer. The higher the priority, the more CPU timeslices will be provided to the code getting executed on that queue. You can use any of these values for the first parameter to the `dispatch_get_glob al_queue` function:

`DISPATCH_QUEUE_PRIORITY_LOW`
Fewer timeslices will be applied to your task than normal tasks.

`DISPATCH_QUEUE_PRIORITY_DEFAULT`
The default system priority for code execution will be applied to your task.

`DISPATCH_QUEUE_PRIORITY_HIGH`
More timeslices will be applied to your task than normal tasks.

 The second parameter of the `dispatch_get_global_queue` function is reserved, and you should always pass the value 0 to it.

After learning how to dispatch tasks to a queue synchronously, it is now time to learn how to execute the same blocks asynchronously, without blocking the current queue.

Executing tasks asynchronously is where GCD can show its true power: specifically, executing blocks of code asynchronously on the main, serial, or concurrent queues. I promise that, by the end of this section, you will be completely convinced that GCD is the future of multithread applications, completely replacing threads in modern apps.

In order to execute asynchronous tasks on a dispatch queue, you must use `dis patch_async`, which submits a block object to a dispatch queue (both specified by parameters) for asynchronous execution.

Discussion

Let's have a look at a real example. We'll write an iOS app that is able to download an image from a URL on the Internet. After the download is finished, the app should display the image to the user. Here is the plan and how we will use what we've learned so far about GCD in order to accomplish it:

1. We are going to launch a block object asynchronously on a concurrent queue.

2. In this block, we will launch another block object *synchronously*, using the dis patch_sync function, to download the image from a URL. We do this because we want the rest of the code in this concurrent queue to wait until the image is downloaded. Therefore, we are only making the concurrent queue wait; not the rest of the queues. Synchronously downloading a URL from an asynchronous code block holds up just the queue running the synchronous function, not the main thread. The whole operation is still asynchronous when we look at it from the main thread's perspective. All we care about is that we are not blocking the main thread while downloading the image.

3. Right after the image is downloaded, we synchronously execute a block object on the *main queue* (see Recipe 7.1) in order to display the image on the UI.

The skeleton for the plan is as simple as this:

```
import UIKit

class ViewController: UIViewController {

  override func viewDidAppear(animated: Bool) {
    super.viewDidAppear(animated)

    let queue = dispatch_get_global_queue(DISPATCH_QUEUE_PRIORITY_DEFAULT, 0)
    dispatch_async(queue, {

      dispatch_sync(queue, {
        /* Download the image here */
      })

      dispatch_sync(dispatch_get_main_queue(), {
        /* Show the image to the user here on the main queue */
      })

    })
  }

}
```

The second dispatch_sync call, which displays the image, will be executed on the queue after the first synchronous call, which downloads the image. That's exactly what we want, because we *have* to wait for the image to be fully downloaded before we can display it to the user. So after the image is downloaded, we execute the second block object, but this time on the main queue.

Let's download the image and display it to the user now. We will do this in the `viewDi dAppear:` instance method of a view controller displayed in an iPhone app:

```swift
import UIKit

class ViewController: UIViewController {

  override func viewDidAppear(animated: Bool) {
    super.viewDidAppear(animated)

    let queue = dispatch_get_global_queue(DISPATCH_QUEUE_PRIORITY_DEFAULT, 0)
    dispatch_async(queue, {[weak self] in

      var image: UIImage?

      dispatch_sync(queue, {
        /* Download the image here */

        /* Put your own URL here */
        let urlAsString = "https://www.apple.com/iphone-5s/features/" +
        "images/wireless_hero.jpg"

        let url = NSURL(string: urlAsString)
        let urlRequest = NSURLRequest(URL: url!)
        var downloadError: NSError?

        let imageData = NSURLConnection.sendSynchronousRequest(urlRequest,
          returningResponse: nil, error: &downloadError)

        if let error = downloadError{
          println("Error happened = \(error)")
        } else {

          if imageData.length > 0{
            image = UIImage(data: imageData)
            /* Now we have the image */
          } else {
            println("No data could get downloaded from the URL")
          }

        }

      })

      dispatch_sync(dispatch_get_main_queue(), {
        /* Show the image to the user here on the main queue */

        if let theImage = image{
          let imageView = UIImageView(frame: self!.view.bounds)
          imageView.contentMode = .ScaleAspectFit
          imageView.image = theImage
          self!.view.addSubview(imageView)
```

```
            }
        })
    })
}
}
```

As you can see in Figure 7-1, we have successfully downloaded the image and also created an image view to display the image to the user on the UI.

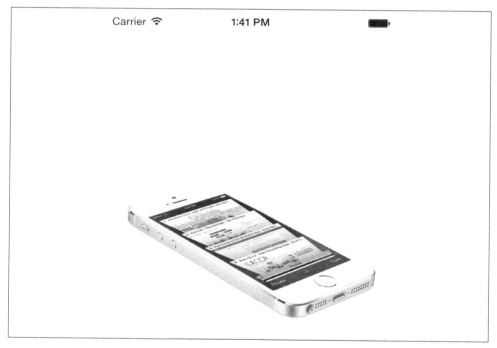

Figure 7-1. Downloading and displaying images to users, using GCD

Let's move on to another example. Let's say that we have an array of 10,000 random numbers that have been stored in a file on disk and we want to load this array into memory, sort the numbers in an ascending fashion (with the smallest number appearing first in the list), and then display the list to the user. The control used for the display depends on whether you are coding this for iOS (ideally, you'd use an instance of UITableView) or Mac OS X (NSTableView would be a good candidate). Because we don't have an array, let's create one first, load it, and then display it.

Here are two methods that will help us find the location where we want to save the array of 10,000 random numbers on disk on the device:

```
func fileLocation() -> String?{

  /* Get the document folder(s) */
  let folders = NSSearchPathForDirectoriesInDomains(.DocumentDirectory,
    .UserDomainMask,
    true) as [String]

  /* Did we find anything? */
  if folders.count == 0{
    return nil
  }

  /* Get the first folder */
  let documentsFolder = folders[0]

  /* Append the filename to the end of the documents path */
  return documentsFolder.stringByAppendingPathComponent("list.txt")

}

func hasFileAlreadyBeenCreated() -> Bool{
  let fileManager = NSFileManager()
  if let theLocation = fileLocation(){
    return fileManager.fileExistsAtPath(theLocation)
  }
  return false
}
```

Now the important part: we want to save an array of 10,000 random numbers to disk *if and only if* we have not created this array before on disk. If we have, we will load the array from disk immediately. If we have not created this array before on disk, we will first create it and then move on to loading it from disk. At the end, if the array was successfully read from disk, we will sort the array in an ascending fashion and finally display the results to the user on the UI. I will leave displaying the results up to you:

```
override func viewDidAppear(animated: Bool) {
  super.viewDidAppear(animated)

  let concurrentQueue =
    dispatch_get_global_queue(DISPATCH_QUEUE_PRIORITY_DEFAULT, 0)

  /* If we have not already saved an array of 10,000
  random numbers to the disk before, generate these numbers now
  and then save them to the disk in an array */
  dispatch_async(concurrentQueue, {[weak self] in

    let numberOfValuesRequired = 10000


    if self!.hasFileAlreadyBeenCreated() == false{
      dispatch_sync(concurrentQueue, {
```

```
          var arrayOfRandomNumbers = [Int]()

          for _ in 0..<numberOfValuesRequired{
            let randomNumber = Int(arc4random())
            arrayOfRandomNumbers.append(randomNumber)
          }

          /* Now let's write the array to disk */
          let array = arrayOfRandomNumbers as NSArray
          array.writeToFile(self!.fileLocation()!, atomically: true)

        })
      }

    var randomNumbers: NSMutableArray?

    /* Read the numbers from disk and sort them in an
    ascending fashion */
    dispatch_sync(concurrentQueue, {
      /* If the file has been created, we have to read it */
      if self!.hasFileAlreadyBeenCreated(){
        randomNumbers = NSMutableArray(
          contentsOfFile: self!.fileLocation()!)

        /* Now sort the numbers */
        randomNumbers!.sortUsingComparator({
          (obj1: AnyObject!, obj2: AnyObject!) -> NSComparisonResult in
          let number1 = obj1 as NSNumber
          let number2 = obj2 as NSNumber
          return number1.compare(number2)
          })
      }
      })


    dispatch_async(dispatch_get_main_queue(), {
      if let numbers = randomNumbers{

        if numbers.count > 0{
          /* Refresh the UI here using the numbers in the
          randomNumbers array */
          println("The sorted array was read back from disk = \(numbers)")
        } else {
          println("The numbers array is emtpy")
        }

      }
      })

    })

}
```

There is a lot more to GCD than synchronous and asynchronous block or function execution. In Recipe 7.5, you will learn how to group block objects together and prepare them for execution on a dispatch queue. I also suggest that you have a look at Recipe 7.3 and Recipe 7.4 to learn about other functionalities that GCD can provide to programmers.

7.3. Performing Tasks After a Delay

Problem

You want to be able to execute code, after a certain amount of delay, which you specify using GCD.

Solution

Use the `dispatch_after` function.

Discussion

The `dispatch_after` function dispatches a block object to a dispatch queue after a given period of time, specified in nanoseconds. These are the parameters that this function requires:

Delay in nanoseconds
> The number of nanoseconds GCD has to wait on a given dispatch queue (specified by the second parameter) before it executes the given block object (specified by the third parameter).

Dispatch queue
> The dispatch queue on which the block object (specified by the third parameter) has to be executed after the given delay (specified by the first parameter).

Block object
> The block object to be invoked after the specified number of nanoseconds on the given dispatch queue. This block object should have no return value and should accept no parameters.

Although the delays are in nanoseconds, it is up to iOS to decide the granularity of dispatch delay, and this delay might not be as precise as what you hope when you specify a value in nanoseconds.

Let's have a look at an example for `dispatch_after` first:

```
import UIKit

class ViewController: UIViewController {

  override func viewDidLoad() {
    super.viewDidLoad()

    let delayInSeconds = 2.0

    let delayInNanoSeconds =
    dispatch_time(DISPATCH_TIME_NOW,
      Int64(delayInSeconds * Double(NSEC_PER_SEC)))

    let concurrentQueue =
    dispatch_get_global_queue(DISPATCH_QUEUE_PRIORITY_DEFAULT, 0)

    dispatch_after(delayInNanoSeconds, concurrentQueue, {
      /* Perform your operations here */
      })

  }

}
```

As you can see, the nanoseconds delay parameter for both the dispatch_after and dispatch_after_f functions has to be of type dispatch_time_t, which is an abstract representation of absolute time. To get the value for this parameter, you can use the dispatch_time function as demonstrated in this sample code. Here are the parameters that you can pass to the dispatch_time function:

Base time

If this value was denoted with *B* and the delta parameter was denoted with *D*, the resulting time from this function would be equal to *B* + *D*. You can set this parameter's value to DISPATCH_TIME_NOW to denote *now* as the base time and then specify the delta from now using the delta parameter.

Delta to add to base time

This parameter is the nanoseconds that will get added to the base time parameter to create the result of this function.

For example, to denote a time three seconds from now, you could write your code like so:

```
let delay = dispatch_time(DISPATCH_TIME_NOW,
  Int64(3.0 * Double(NSEC_PER_SEC)));
```

Or to denote half a second from now:

```
let delay = dispatch_time(DISPATCH_TIME_NOW,
  Int64((1.0 / 2.0) * Double(NSEC_PER_SEC)));
```

Recipe 7.1

7.4. Performing a Task Only Once

Problem

You want to make sure a piece of code gets executed only once during the lifetime of your application, even if it gets called more than once from different places in your code (such as the constructor for a singleton).

Solution

Use the dispatch_once function.

Discussion

Allocating and initializing a singleton is one of the tasks that has to happen exactly once during the lifetime of an app. I am sure you know of other scenarios where you had to make sure a piece of code was executed only once during the lifetime of your application.

GCD lets you specify an identifier for a piece of code when you attempt to execute it. If GCD detects that this identifier has been passed to the framework before, it won't execute that block of code again. The function that allows you to do this is dispatch_once, which accepts two parameters:

Token

A token of type dispatch_once_t that holds the token generated by GCD when the block of code is executed for the first time. If you want a piece of code to be executed at most once, you must specify the same token to this method whenever it is invoked in the app. We will see an example of this soon.

Block object

The block object to get executed at most once. This block object returns no values and accepts no parameters.

 dispatch_once always executes its task on the current queue being used by the code that issues the call, be it a serial queue, a concurrent queue, or the main queue.

Here is an example:

```
import UIKit

class ViewController: UIViewController {

  var token: dispatch_once_t = 0
  var numberOfEntries = 0

  func executedOnlyOnce(){
    numberOfEntries++;
    println("Executed \(numberOfEntries) time(s)")
  }

  override func viewDidLoad() {
    super.viewDidLoad()

    dispatch_once(&token, executedOnlyOnce)
    dispatch_once(&token, executedOnlyOnce)

  }

}
```

As you can see, although we are attempting to invoke the executedOnlyOnce block object twice, using the dispatch_once function, in reality GCD is executing this block object only once, since the identifier passed to the dispatch_once function is the same both times.

7.5. Grouping Tasks Together

Problem

You want to group blocks of code together and ensure that all of them get executed by GCD one by one, as dependencies of one another.

Solution

Use the dispatch_group_create function to create groups in GCD.

Discussion

GCD lets us create *groups*, which allow you to place your tasks in one place, run all of them, and get a notification at the end from GCD. This has many valuable applications. For instance, suppose you have a UI-based app and want to reload the components on your UI. You have a table view, a scroll view, and an image view. You want to reload the contents of these components using these methods:

```
func reloadTableView(){
  /* Reload the table view here */
  println(__FUNCTION__)
}

func reloadScrollView(){
  /* Do the work here */
  println(__FUNCTION__)
}

func reloadImageView(){
  /* Reload the image view here */
  println(__FUNCTION__)
}
```

At the moment these methods are empty, but you can put the relevant UI code in them later. Now we want to call these three methods, one after the other, and we want to know when GCD has finished calling these methods so that we can display a message to the user. For this, we should be using a group. You should know about three functions when working with groups in GCD:

dispatch_group_create
> Creates a group handle.

dispatch_group_async
> Submits a block of code for execution on a group. You must specify the dispatch queue on which the block of code has to be executed *as well as* the group to which this block of code belongs.

dispatch_group_notify
> Allows you to submit a block object that should be executed after all tasks added to the group for execution have finished their work. This function also allows you to specify the dispatch queue on which that block object has to be executed.

Let's have a look at an example. As explained, in the example we want to invoke the reloadTableView, reloadScrollView, and reloadImageView methods one after the other and then display a message to the user when we are done. We can utilize GCD's powerful grouping facilities in order to accomplish this:

```
import UIKit

class ViewController: UIViewController {

  func reloadTableView(){
    /* Reload the table view here */
    println(__FUNCTION__)
  }

  func reloadScrollView(){
    /* Do the work here */
```

```
    println(__FUNCTION__)
  }

  func reloadImageView(){
    /* Reload the image view here */
    println(__FUNCTION__)
  }

  override func viewDidLoad() {
    super.viewDidLoad()

    let taskGroup =  dispatch_group_create()
    let mainQueue =  dispatch_get_main_queue()

    /* Reload the table view on the main queue */
    dispatch_group_async(taskGroup, mainQueue, {[weak self] in
      self!.reloadTableView()
      });

    /* Reload the scroll view on the main queue */
    dispatch_group_async(taskGroup, mainQueue, {[weak self] in
      self!.reloadScrollView()
      });

    /* Reload the image view on the main queue */
    dispatch_group_async(taskGroup, mainQueue, {[weak self] in
      self!.reloadImageView()
      });

    /* When we are done, dispatch the following block */
    dispatch_group_notify(taskGroup, mainQueue, {[weak self] in
      /* Do some processing here */

      let controller = UIAlertController(title: "Finished",
        message: "All tasks are finished",
        preferredStyle: .Alert)


      controller.addAction(UIAlertAction(title: "OK",
        style: .Default,
        handler: nil))

      self!.presentViewController(controller, animated: true, completion: nil)

      });

  }

}
```

When all the given tasks are finished, the user will see a result similar to that shown in
Figure 7-2.

Figure 7-2. Managing a group of tasks with GCD

See Also

Recipe 7.1

7.6. Creating Simple Concurrency with Operations

Problem

You want to put a block of independent code, which can be executed in a queue, into a class file and execute it concurrently so that it does not block the main thread.

Solution

Subclass the NSOperation class, override the main method of the new class, and place your code in it. This will be the code that you can later put inside a queue of type NSOperationQueue to execute in parallel to the rest of the code being executed at any point in the application's life.

Let's have a look at an example. Say that you want to create an operation that can count from *startingCount* to *endingCount*, where *startingCount* and *endingCount* will be parameters provided by the programmer who instantiates your operation class. First, we subclass NSOperation like so:

```
import UIKit

class CountingOperation: NSOperation
```

After this, we introduce two properties to our class to record the starting and ending counts that should be provided by the programmer who will instantiate our class:

```
var startingCount: Int = 0
var endingCount: Int = 0
```

Then we introduce the constructor for our class:

```
init(startCount: Int, endCount: Int){
  startingCount = startCount
  endingCount = endCount
}

convenience override init(){
  self.init(startCount: 0, endCount: 3)
}
```

And the next step is to override the `main` method of this operation, where we will have the chance to perform our task:

```
override func main() {

  var isTaskFinished = false

  while isTaskFinished == false &&
    self.finished == false{
      for counter in startingCount..<endingCount{
        println("Count = \(counter)")
        println("Current thread = \(NSThread.currentThread())")
        println("Main thread = \(NSThread.mainThread())")
        println("------------------------------")
      }

      isTaskFinished = true
  }

}
```

Here we are just counting from the start to the end number that we are given. As you can see, this is not complicated at all. Now we will instantiate this operation as well as an operation queue, and add the operation to the queue like so:

```
import UIKit

class ViewController: UIViewController {

  override func viewDidLoad() {
    super.viewDidLoad()
    /* This is the convenience constructor of the operation */
    let operation = CountingOperation()
    let operationQueue = NSOperationQueue()
    operationQueue.addOperation(operation)
  }

}
```

And the results will be printed to the console like so:

```
Count = 0
Current thread = <NSThread: 0x10bd68ec0>{number = 2, name = (null)}
Main thread = <NSThread: 0x10bd00550>{number = 1, name = (null)}
```

```
--------------------------------
Count = 1
Current thread = <NSThread: 0x10bd68ec0>{number = 2, name = (null)}
Main thread = <NSThread: 0x10bd00550>{number = 1, name = (null)}
--------------------------------
Count = 2
Current thread = <NSThread: 0x10bd68ec0>{number = 2, name = (null)}
Main thread = <NSThread: 0x10bd00550>{number = 1, name = (null)}
--------------------------------
```

Discussion

Operations can be constructed in many different ways. You don't necessarily have to subclass NSOperation in order to run your operations. One of the most common ways of creating an operation is through closures: create your closure and place your operations code in there. After you have your code, create a block operation out of your code using the NSBlockOperation class. Then send your block operation to an operation queue using the addOperation: method of your operation queue. This will then dispatch the operation to the queue, which will in turn run your block object or closure for you asynchronously.

Let's have a look at an example. Say we want to create a closure that can count from m to n, and then asynchronously dispatch this closure to an operation queue. We do that in this way:

First, we define the closure which will do the job for us:

```
func operationCode(){
  for _ in 0..<100{
    println("Thread = \(NSThread.currentThread())")
  }
}
```

Then we create the block operations (as many as you want) from the closure:

```
let operation1 = NSBlockOperation(block: operationCode)
let operation2 = NSBlockOperation(block: operationCode)
```

Last but not least, we instantiate our operation queue and then add the operations to it:

```
let operationQueue = NSOperationQueue()
operationQueue.addOperation(operation1)
operationQueue.addOperation(operation2)
```

Give this a go for yourself and see what happens when you run your application.

Of course, operations have important effects on your application's performance. For instance, if you want to download a lot of content from the Internet, you might want to do so only when it is absolutely necessary. Also, you might decide to ensure that only a specific number of operations can run at the same time. If you do decide to limit the number of concurrent operations in a queue, you can change the maxConcurrentOper ationCount property of your operation queue. This is an integer property that allows you to specify how many operations, at most, can run in a queue at a given time.

In addition to the number of concurrent operations that can run at any instance, you can also change the quality of service of an operation queue. Let me explain this by giving you an example. Think about downloading the contents of a URL from the Internet. You can start the downloading of the URL for many different reasons. One reason might be that the user has initialized this action herself (user-initiated). Another reason might be that your application wants to download the content in order to use it internally (background). And yet another reason might be that the user initiated the action but does not want to wait for the results to come back immediately (utility).

To accommodate these different use cases, iOS provides different quality of services for difference operation queues. You can change the quality of service of an operation queue using its qualityOfService property. Let's look at an example.

Let's assume that we are writing an application that displays the list of people who are friends with our user. Each one of these people has a thumbnail image that the user may be immediately interested in seeing as she scrolls the list. You want to create an operation that can download the data for an array of URLs that can be passed to it as a parameter. The operation will then store the downloaded data in a temporary directory. The action of scrolling is user initiated, so we can set the quality of service on our operation queue accordingly. Also, we don't want to put too much pressure on the system to download too many of those URLs at the same time. For this reason, we will limit the maximum concurrent number of operations in the queue.

So first let's have a look at the code that will download an array of URLs for us:

```
func downloadUrls(urls: Array<NSURL>){

  for url in urls{

    let request = NSURLRequest(URL: url!)
    NSURLConnection.sendAsynchronousRequest(request,
      queue: NSOperationQueue.currentQueue(),
      completionHandler: {(response: NSURLResponse!,
        data: NSData!,
        error: NSError!) in

      if error{
        /* An error occurred */
        println("Failed to download data. Error = \(error)")
      } else {
        println("Data is downloaded. Save it to disk...")
      }

    })

  }

}
```

```
}
```

You can see that we are going through a loop to download all the URLs one by one, but we are not doing this synchronously like we had done before. Because we want all the operations to be fired asynchronously, we are asking the connection to fire them off for us accordingly. The next step is to define our URLs somewhere and then download them in a group:

```
func downloadUrls(){

  /* You can add your own URLs here as strings */
  let urlsAsString = [
    "http://goo.gl/BYih4G",
    "http://goo.gl/ErcCAa",
    "http://goo.gl/pJW9xK",
  ]

  /* Convert all the string URLs to URL objects */
  var urls = Array<NSURL>()
  for string in urlsAsString{
    urls.append(NSURL(string: string))
  }

  /* And then pass them to the function that will
  eventually download the items */
  downloadUrls(urls)

}
```

This function has an array of strings that I have personally shortened using Google's URL shortener (just so they won't look so ugly in this book). I also have created an array of NSURL objects out of the strings. When the array of URLs is ready, I submit it to the actual function that will do the downloading job.

Now on to the very exciting part: creating a block operation out of our code and submitting that operation to a queue with the "user-initiated" quality of service:

```
/* Define our operation here using a block operation */
let operation = NSBlockOperation(block: downloadUrls)

let operationQueue = NSOperationQueue()
/* We assume that the reason we are downloading the content
to disk is that the user wanted us to and that it was "user initiated" */
operationQueue.qualityOfService = .UserInitiated
/* We will avoid overloading the system with too many URL downloads
and download only a few simultaneously */
operationQueue.maxConcurrentOperationCount = 3
operationQueue.addOperation(operation)
```

Give it a go on your own device or simulator and see how it goes.

See Also

Recipe 7.1

7.7. Creating Dependency Between Operations

Problem

You want to start a certain task after another task has finished executing.

Solution

If operation B has to wait for operation A before it can run the task associated with it, operation B has to add operation A as its dependency using the addDependency: instance method of NSOperation.

Discussion

An operation will not start executing until all the operations on which it depends have successfully finished executing the tasks associated with them. By default, an operation, after initialization, has no dependency on other operations.

Now let's have a look at an example. We want to create two invocation operations, each of which will invoke a selector. Each one of these selectors corresponds to a closure in our code, which will simply take in an optional parameter of type AnyObject and print the value of that parameter to the console. It will also print out the current thread and the main thread so that we can see visually in the console whether we are on the main thread or a secondary thread when our closures get called. Here are our closures:

```
func performWorkForParameter(param: AnyObject?, operationName: String){
  if let theParam: AnyObject = param{
    println("First operation - Object = \(theParam)")
  }

  println("\(operationName) Operation - " +
    "Main Thread = \(NSThread.mainThread())")

  println("\(operationName) Operation - " +
    "Current Thread = \(NSThread.currentThread())")
}
func firstOperationEntry(param: AnyObject?){
  performWorkForParameter(param, operationName: "First")
}

func secondOperationEntry(param: AnyObject?){

  performWorkForParameter(param, operationName: "Second")
```

```
}
```

The work is very simple, as I said; I am not trying to demonstrate performing a very complicated task here. All I want to do is to create dependency between operations. Now let's create our operations out of our closures:

```
let firstNumber = 111
let secondNumber = 222

let firstOperation = NSBlockOperation {[weak self] () -> Void in
  if let strongSelf = self{
    strongSelf.firstOperationEntry(firstNumber)
  }
}

let secondOperation = NSBlockOperation {[weak self] () -> Void in
  if let strongSelf = self{
    strongSelf.secondOperationEntry(secondNumber)
  }
}
```

What we need to do now is create an operation queue and then add the second operation as the dependency on the first operation. That means our second operation must be executed first in order for the first operation to begin its work:

```
let operationQueue = NSOperationQueue()

firstOperation.addDependency(secondOperation)

operationQueue.addOperation(firstOperation)
operationQueue.addOperation(secondOperation)

println("Main thread is here")
```

Now if you run your application, you will see something similar to this printed to the console:

```
Main thread is here
First operation - Object = 222
Second Operation - Main Thread =
  <NSThread: 0x10bc026c0>{number = 1, name = (null)}
Second Operation - Current Thread =
  <NSThread: 0x10bb76d30>{number = 2, name = (null)}
First operation - Object = 111
First Operation - Main Thread =
  <NSThread: 0x10bc026c0>{number = 1, name = (null)}
First Operation - Current Thread =
  <NSThread: 0x10bb76d30>{number = 2, name = (null)}
```

It's quite obvious that although the operation queue attempted to run both operations in parallel, the first operation had a dependency on the second operation, and therefore the second operation had to finish before the first operation could run.

If at any time you want to break the dependency between two operations, you can use the `removeDependency:` instance method of an operation object.

7.8. Firing Periodic Tasks

Problem

You would like to perform a specific task repeatedly with a certain delay. For instance, you want to update a view on your screen every second that your application is running.

Solution

Use a timer:

```
import UIKit

@UIApplicationMain
class AppDelegate: UIResponder, UIApplicationDelegate {

  var paintingTimer: NSTimer?
  var window: UIWindow?

  func paint(paramTimer: NSTimer){
    println("Painting")
  }

  func startPainting(){
    stopPainting()
    println("Starting painting...")
    paintingTimer = NSTimer.scheduledTimerWithTimeInterval(1.0,
      target: self,
      selector: "paint:",
      userInfo: nil,
      repeats: true)
  }

  func stopPainting(){
    if let timer = paintingTimer{
      timer.invalidate()
      paintingTimer = nil
    }
  }

  func application(application: UIApplication,
    didFinishLaunchingWithOptions
    launchOptions: [NSObject : AnyObject]?) -> Bool {
    return true
  }

  func applicationWillResignActive(application: UIApplication) {
```

```
        stopPainting()
    }

    func applicationDidBecomeActive(application: UIApplication) {
        startPainting()
    }

}
```

 The `invalidate` method will also release the timer, so that we don't
have to do that manually.

Discussion

A timer is an object that fires an event at specified intervals. An `NSTimer` object creates
a nonscheduled timer that does nothing but is available to the program when you want
to schedule it. When you issue a call, e.g. `scheduledTimerWithTimeInterval:tar`
`get:selector:userInfo:repeats:`, the time becomes a scheduled timer and will fire
the event you request. A scheduled timer is a timer that is added to a run loop. To get
any timer to fire its target event, we must schedule that timer on a run loop. This is
demonstrated in a later example where we create a nonscheduled timer and then manually schedule it on the main run loop of the application.

After a timer is created and added to a run loop, either explicitly or implicitly, the timer
will start calling a method in its target object (as specified by the programmer) every *n*
seconds (*n* is specified by the programmer as well). Because *n* is floating-point, you can
specify a fraction of a second.

There are various ways to create, initialize, and schedule timers. One of the easiest ways
is through the `scheduledTimerWithTimeInterval:target:selector:userInfo:re`
`peats:` class method of `NSTimer`. Here are the different parameters of this method:

`scheduledTimerWithTimeInterval`
> This is the number of seconds the timer has to wait before it fires an event. For
> example, if you want the timer to call a method in its target object twice per second,
> you have to set this parameter to 0.5 (1 second divided by 2); if you want the target
> method to be called four times per second, this parameter should be set to 0.25 (1
> second divided by 4).

`target`
> This is the object that will receive the event.

`selector`
> This is the method signature in the target object that will receive the event.

userInfo

This is the object that will be retained in the timer for later reference (in the target method of the target object).

repeats

This specifies whether the timer must call its target method repeatedly (in which case this parameter has to be set to `true`), or just once and then stop (in which case this parameter has to be set to `false`).

 Once a timer is created and added to a run loop, you can stop and release that timer using the `invalidate` instance method of the NSTimer class. This not only releases the timer, but also the object, if any, that was passed for the timer to retain during its lifetime (e.g., the object passed to the userInfo parameter of the scheduledTimer WithTimeInterval:target:selector:userInfo:repeats: class method of NSTimer). If you pass `false` to the `repeats` parameter, the timer invalidates itself after the first pass and subsequently releases the object it had retained (if one exists).

Scheduling a timer can be compared to starting a car's engine. A scheduled timer is a running car engine. A nonscheduled timer is a car engine that is ready to be started but is not running yet. We can schedule and unschedule timers whenever we want in the application, just like we might need the engine of a car to be on or off depending on the situation we are in.

The target method of a timer receives the instance of the timer that calls it as its parameter. For instance, the `paint:` method introduced initially in this recipe demonstrates how the timer gets passed to its target method, by default, as the target method's one and only parameter:

```
func paint(paramTimer: NSTimer){
  println("Painting")
}
```

This parameter provides a reference to the timer that is firing this method. You can, for instance, prevent the timer from running again using the `invalidate` method, if needed. You can also invoke the `userInfo` method of the NSTimer instance in order to retrieve the object being retained by the timer (if any). This object is just an object passed to the initialization methods of NSTimer, and it gets directly passed to the timer for future reference.

7.9. Completing a Long-Running Task in the Background

Problem

You want to borrow some time from iOS to complete a long-running task when your application is being sent to the background.

Solution

Use the `beginBackgroundTaskWithExpirationHandler:` instance method of `UIApplication`. After you have finished the task, call the `endBackgroundTask:` instance method of `UIApplication`.

Discussion

When an iOS application is sent to the background, its main thread is paused. The threads you create within your application are also suspended. If you are attempting to finish a long-running task when your application is being sent to the background, you must call the `beginBackgroundTaskWithName:expirationHandler:` instance method of `UIApplication` to borrow some time from iOS. The `backgroundTimeRemaining` property of `UIApplication` contains the number of seconds the application has to finish its job. If the application doesn't finish the long-running task before this time expires, iOS will terminate the application. Every call to the `beginBackgroundTaskWithName:expirationHandler:` method must have a corresponding call to `endBackgroundTask:` (another instance method of `UIApplication`). In other words, if you ask for more time from iOS to complete a task, you must tell iOS when you are done with that task. When this is done and no more tasks are requested to be running in the background, your application will be fully put into the background with all threads paused.

When your application is in the foreground, the `backgroundTimeRemaining` property of `UIApplication` is equal to the `DBL_MAX` constant, which is the largest value that a value of type `double` can contain (the integer equivalent of this value is normally equal to −1 in this case). After iOS is asked for more time before the application is fully suspended, this property will indicate the number of seconds the application has before it finishes running its task(s).

You can call the `beginBackgroundTaskWithName:expirationHandler:` method as many times as you wish inside your application. The important thing to keep in mind is that whenever iOS returns a token or a task identifier to your application with this method, you must call the `endBackgroundTask:` method to mark the end of that task when you are finished running the task. Failing to do so might cause iOS to terminate your application.

While in the background, applications are not supposed to be fully functioning and processing heavy data. They are indeed only supposed to *finish* a long-running task. An example could be an application that is calling a web service API and has not yet received the response of that API from the server. During this time, if the application is sent to the background, the application can request more time until it receives a response from the server. When the response is received, the application must save its state and mark that task as finished by calling the endBackgroundTask: instance method of UIApplication.

Let's have a look at an example. I will start by defining a property of type UIBackgroundTaskIdentifier in the app delegate. Also, let's define a timer of type NSTimer, which we will use to print a message to the console window every second when our app is sent to the background:

```
import UIKit

@UIApplicationMain
class AppDelegate: UIResponder, UIApplicationDelegate {

  var window: UIWindow?

  var backgroundTaskIdentifier: UIBackgroundTaskIdentifier =
  UIBackgroundTaskInvalid

  var myTimer: NSTimer?
```

Now let's move on to creating and scheduling our timer when the app gets sent to the background:

```
func isMultitaskingSupported() -> Bool{
  return UIDevice.currentDevice().multitaskingSupported
}

func timerMethod(sender: NSTimer){

  let backgroundTimeRemaining =
  UIApplication.sharedApplication().backgroundTimeRemaining

  if backgroundTimeRemaining == DBL_MAX{
    println("Background Time Remaining = Undetermined")
  } else {
    println("Background Time Remaining = " +
      "\(backgroundTimeRemaining) Seconds")
  }

}

func applicationDidEnterBackground(application: UIApplication) {

  if isMultitaskingSupported() == false{
    return
```

```
    }

    myTimer = NSTimer.scheduledTimerWithTimeInterval(1.0,
      target: self,
      selector: "timerMethod:",
      userInfo: nil,
      repeats: true)

    backgroundTaskIdentifier =
      application.beginBackgroundTaskWithName("task1",
        expirationHandler: {[weak self] in
        self!.endBackgroundTask()
        })

}
```

You can see that in the completion handler for our background task, we are calling the endBackgroundTask method of our app delegate. This is a method that we have written, and it looks like this:

```
func endBackgroundTask(){

  let mainQueue = dispatch_get_main_queue()

  dispatch_async(mainQueue, {[weak self] in
    if let timer = self!.myTimer{
      timer.invalidate()
      self!.myTimer = nil
      UIApplication.sharedApplication().endBackgroundTask(
        self!.backgroundTaskIdentifier)
      self!.backgroundTaskIdentifier = UIBackgroundTaskInvalid
    }
  })
}
```

There are a couple of things we need to do to clean up after a long-running task:

1. End any threads or timers, whether they are foundation timers or they are created with GCD.

2. End the background task by calling the endBackgroundTask: method of UIApplication.

3. Mark our task as ended by assigning the value of UIBackgroundTaskInvalid to our task identifiers.

Last but not least, when our app is brought to the foreground, if we still have our background task running, we need to ensure that we get rid of it:

```
func applicationWillEnterForeground(application: UIApplication) {
  if backgroundTaskIdentifier != UIBackgroundTaskInvalid{
    endBackgroundTask()
```

```
    }
  }
```

In our example, whenever the application is put into the background, we ask for more time to finish a long-running task (in this case, for instance, our timer's code). In our time, we constantly read the value of the backgroundTimeRemaining property of UIApplication 's instance and print that value out to the console. In the beginBackgroundTaskWithExpirationHandler: instance method of UIApplication, we provided the code that will be executed just before our application's extra time to execute a long-running task finishes (usually about 5 to 10 seconds before the expiration of the task). In here, we can simply end the task by calling the endBackgroundTask: instance method of UIApplication.

 When an application is sent to the background and the application has requested more execution time from iOS, before the execution time is finished, the application could be revived and brought to the foreground by the user again. If you had previously asked for a long-running task to be executed in the background when the application was being sent to the background, you must end the long-running task using the endBackgroundTask: instance method of UIApplication.

7.10. Adding Background Fetch Capabilities to Your Apps

Problem

You want your app to be able to fetch content in the background by using the new capabilities introduced in iOS SDK.

Solution

Add the Background Fetch capability to your app.

Discussion

A lot of the apps that get submitted on a daily basis to the App Store have connectivity to some servers. Some fetch data, some post data, etc. For a while, in iOS, the only way for apps to fetch content in the background was to borrow some time from iOS, as you can read about in Recipe 7.9, and the apps could use that time to complete their work in the background. But this is a very active way of going about doing this. There is a passive way as well, where your app sits there and then iOS gives your app time to do some processing in the background. So all you have to do is hook into this capability and let iOS wake your app at a quiet moment and ask it to do some processing. This is usually used for background fetches.

For instance, you might need to download some new content. Imagine the Twitter app. All you are interested in when you open that app is to see new tweets. Up until now, the only way to do this was for you to open the app and then let the app refresh the list of tweets. But now iOS is able to wake the Twitter app in the background and ask it to refresh its feed so that when you open the app, all the tweets on the screen are already up to date.

The first thing that we have to do to enable background-fetching capabilities for our app is to go to the Capabilities tab of the project settings, and under the Background Modes slice, enable the "Background fetch" item, as shown in Figure 7-3.

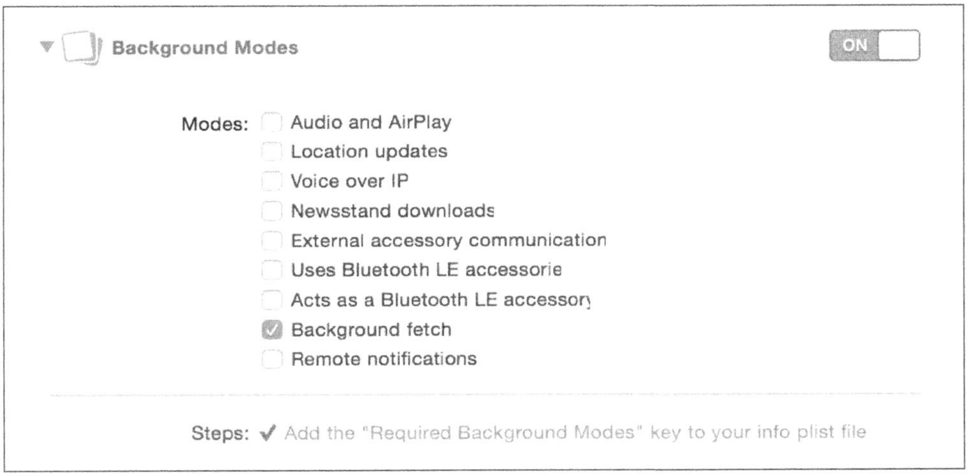

Figure 7-3. Enabling background fetch for our app

There are two ways your app could use background fetches. One is when your app is in the background and iOS wakes your app (without making it visible to the user) and asks it to fetch some content. The other time is when your app is dormant and iOS wakes your app (again in the background), asking it to look for content to fetch. But how does iOS know which apps to wake up and which ones not to? Well, the programmer has to help iOS.

The way we do that is by calling the `setMinimumBackgroundFetchInterval:` instance method of the `UIApplication` class. The parameter that you pass to this method is the interval and the frequency at which you want iOS to wake up your app in the background and ask it to fetch new data. The default value for this property is `UIApplicationBackgroundFetchIntervalNever`, meaning that iOS will never wake your app in the background. But you can set this property's value manually by passing the number of interval seconds, or you can simply pass the value of `UIApplicationBackgroundFetchInter` valMinimum to ask iOS to put minimal effort into waking up your app by not doing the process too frequently.

```
func application(application: UIApplication,
  didFinishLaunchingWithOptions
  launchOptions: [NSObject : AnyObject]?) -> Bool {

    newsItems.append(NewsItem(date: NSDate(), text: "News Item 1"))

    application.setMinimumBackgroundFetchInterval(
      UIApplicationBackgroundFetchIntervalMinimum)

    return true
}
```

After you've done that, you will need to implement the application:performFetch WithCompletionHandler: instance method of your app delegate. The performFetch WithCompletionHandler: parameter of this method will give you a block object that you will have to call once your app is finished fetching data. This method, in general, gets called in your app delegate when iOS wants your app to fetch new content in the background, so you respond to it and call the completion handler when you are done. The block object that you have to call will accept a value of type UIBackgroundFetchRe sult.

So if iOS asks your app to fetch new content and you try to fetch the data but there is no new data available, you have to call the completion handler and pass the value of UIBackgroundFetchResultNoData to it. This way, iOS will know that there was no new content available for your app and can adjust its scheduling algorithm and AI in order to not call your app so frequently. iOS is very smart about this indeed. Let's imagine that you ask iOS to call your app in the background so that you can retrieve new content. If your server doesn't give you any new updates, and for a whole week of your app being woken up in the background on the user's device you could not fetch any new data and always passed UIBackgroundFetchResultNoData to the completion block of the afore-mentioned method, iOS will not wake your app as frequently. That preserves processing power and, subsequently, battery.

For the purpose of this recipe, we are going to create a simple app that retrieves news items from a server. To avoid overcomplicating the recipe with server code, we are going to fake the server calls. Let's first create a struct named NewsItem that has a date and a text as its properties:

```
import Foundation

struct NewsItem{
  var date: NSDate
  var text: String
}
```

The struct won't have any implementation and will only carry information through its properties. Now, back in the app delegate, we define a mutable array of news items so that we can hook into that array and display the news items in our table view controller:

```
import UIKit

@UIApplicationMain
class AppDelegate: UIResponder, UIApplicationDelegate {

  var window: UIWindow?
  var newsItems = [NewsItem]()

  <# rest of your code goes here #>
```

Now as soon as our application starts, we are going to insert one news item into our array like so:

```
/* The name of the notification that we will send when our news
items are changed */
class func newsItemsChangedNotification() -> String{
  return "\(__FUNCTION__)"
}

func application(application: UIApplication,
  didFinishLaunchingWithOptions
  launchOptions: [NSObject : AnyObject]?) -> Bool {

    newsItems.append(NewsItem(date: NSDate(), text: "News Item 1"))

    application.setMinimumBackgroundFetchInterval(
      UIApplicationBackgroundFetchIntervalMinimum)

    return true
}
```

We will now implement a method in our app that fakes a server call. Basically, it tosses a coin. More precisely, it gets a random integer between 0 and 1, inclusively. If that number is 1, it pretends there is new server content, and if that value is 0, it pretends there are no new server items to download. If this value turns out to be 1, it adds a new item to the list as well:

```
/* Returns true if it could get some news items from the server */
func fetchNewsItems () -> Bool{

  if (arc4random_uniform(2) != 1){
    return false
  }

  /* Generate a new item */
  let item = NewsItem(date: NSDate(),
    text: "News Item \(newsItems.count + 1)")
```

```
    newsItems.append(item)

    /* Send a notification to observers telling them that a news item
    is now available */
    NSNotificationCenter.defaultCenter().postNotificationName(
      self.classForCoder.newsItemsChangedNotification(),
      object: nil)

    return true

  }
```

The Boolean return value of this method tells us whether there was any new content that was added to the array. Now let's implement the background fetching mechanism of our app delegate as explained before:

```
func application(application: UIApplication,
  performFetchWithCompletionHandler completionHandler:
  ((UIBackgroundFetchResult) -> Void)!){

    if self.fetchNewsItems(){
      completionHandler(.NewData)
    } else {
      completionHandler(.NoData)
    }

}
```

Beautiful. In our table view controller, we watch for changes to this array of items in the app delegate, and as soon as the array's contents are changed, we refresh our table view. We will be smart about this, though. If our app is in the foreground, we refresh the table view, but if our app is in the background, we delay the refresh of the table view until the app is brought back to the foreground:

```
import UIKit

class ViewController: UITableViewController {

  var mustReloadView = false

  /* Our news items comes from the app delegate */
  var newsItems: [NewsItem]{
  let appDelegate = UIApplication.sharedApplication().delegate as AppDelegate
  return appDelegate.newsItems
  }

  override func viewDidLoad() {
    super.viewDidLoad()

    /* Listen to when the news items are changed */
    NSNotificationCenter.defaultCenter().addObserver(self,
      selector: "handleNewsItemsChanged:",
```

```
      name: AppDelegate.newsItemsChangedNotification(),
      object: nil)

    /* Handle what we need to do when the app comes back to the
    foreground */
    NSNotificationCenter.defaultCenter().addObserver(self,
      selector: "handleAppIsBroughtToForeground:",
      name: UIApplicationWillEnterForegroundNotification,
      object: nil)

  }

  /* If there is need to reload after we come back to the foreground,
  do it here */
  func handleAppIsBroughtToForeground(notification: NSNotification){
    if mustReloadView{
      tableView.reloadData()
    }
  }

  /* We are being told that new news items are available.
  Reload the table view */
  func handleNewsItemsChanged(notification: NSNotification) {
    if self.isBeingPresented(){
      tableView.reloadData()
    } else {
      mustReloadView = true
    }
  }
```

Last but not least, we will write the required methods of our table view data source to feed the news items to the table view:

 In this example code, we are dequeueing table view cells with the identifier of *Cell*. The reason that the dequeueReusableCellWithI dentifier:forIndexPath: method of our table view returns valid cells instead of returning nil is that in our storyboard file, we have already defined this identifier for the cell prototype of our table view. At runtime, our storyboard is registering this prototype cell for iOS with the given identifier, so that you can simply dequeue the cells with the given identifier without having to register the cells in advance.

```
override func tableView(tableView: UITableView,
  numberOfRowsInSection section: Int) -> Int {
    return newsItems.count
}

override func tableView(tableView: UITableView,
  cellForRowAtIndexPath indexPath: NSIndexPath) -> UITableViewCell {
```

```
    let cell = tableView.dequeueReusableCellWithIdentifier("Cell",
        forIndexPath: indexPath) as UITableViewCell

    cell.textLabel.text = newsItems[indexPath.row].text

    return cell
}

deinit{
    NSNotificationCenter.defaultCenter().removeObserver(self)
}
```

 For more information about table views, please refer to Chapter 6.

So now run your app and press the Home button to send your app to the background. Go back to Xcode, and from the Debug menu, choose Simulate Background Fetch (see Figure 7-4). Now open your app again without terminating it and see whether any new content shows up in your table view. If not, it's because we put the logic in our app that basically tosses a coin and randomly decides whether there is new content on the server. This is to fake the server calls. If you don't get any new content, simply repeat the simulation of background fetch in the Debug menu until you get new content.

Up until now, we have been processing background fetch requests by iOS while our app was in the background, but what if our app has been completely terminated and is not in the background anymore? How do we simulate that situation to find out whether our app will still work? Well, it turns out that Apple has already thought about this. All you have to do is choose the Manage Schemes menu item of the Product menu in Xcode, and from there, duplicate the main scheme of your app by pressing the little (+) button and then choosing Duplicate Scheme (see Figure 7-5).

Pause	⌃⌘Y
Continue To Current Line	⌃⌘C
Step Over	F6
Step Into	F7
Step Out	F8
Step Over Instruction	⌃F6
Step Over Thread	⌃⇧F6
Step Into Instruction	⌃F7
Step Into Thread	⌃⇧F7
Capture GPU Frame	
Simulate Location	▶
Simulate Background Fetch	
iCloud	▶
View Debugging	▶
Deactivate Breakpoints	⌘Y
Breakpoints	▶
Debug Workflow	▶
Attach to Process	▶
Detach	

Figure 7-4. Simulating a background fetch in Xcode

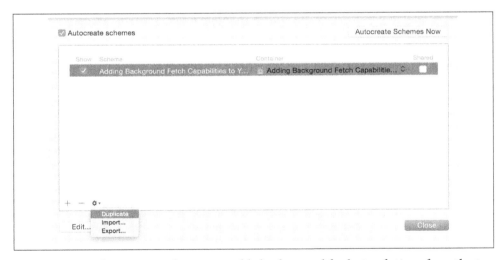

Figure 7-5. Duplicate your scheme to enable background fetch simulations from the terminated app state

Now a new dialog appears in front of you, similar to that shown in Figure 7-6, and asks you to set the various properties of the new scheme. In this dialog, enable the "Launch due to a background fetch event" item and press the OK button.

Figure 7-6. Enabling your scheme to launch your app for background fetches

Now you have two schemes in the Xcode for your app (see Figure 7-7). All you have to do to launch your app for background fetches is to select the second scheme that you just created and run your app in the simulator or on the device. This does not bring your app to the foreground. Instead, it sends it a signal to fetch data in the background, and that, in turn, invokes the `application:performFetchWithCompletionHandler:` method of your app delegate. If you followed all the steps explained in this recipe, you should have a fully working app in both scenarios: when iOS wakes up your app from the background, and when your app is started afresh to fetch data in the background.

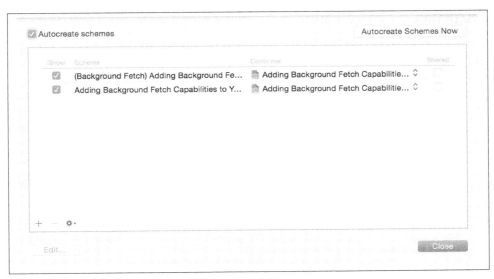

Figure 7-7. Use the new scheme to start your app by simulating a background fetch

See Also

Recipe 7.9

7.11. Playing Audio in the Background

Problem

You are writing an application that plays audio files (such as a music player) and you would like the audio files to be played even if your application is running in the background.

Solution

Select your project file in the Navigator of Xcode. Then, from the Capabilities section, switch on the Background Modes subsection. After the list of background modes is given to you, tick on the Audio & Airplay switch.

Now you can use the AV Foundation to play audio files, and your audio files will be played even if your application is in the background. (Please bear in mind that playing audio in the background might not work in iOS Simulator. You need to test this recipe on a real device. On the simulator, chances are that the audio will stop playing once your application is sent to the background.)

Discussion

In iOS, applications can request that their audio files continue playing even if the application is sent to the background. AV Foundation's `AVAudioPlayer` is an easy-to-use audio player that we will employ in this recipe. Our mission is to start an audio player and play a simple song, and while the song is playing, send the application to the background by pressing the Home button. If you successfully enabled the Audio background mode (as explained in the Solution of this recipe) in our target, iOS will continue playing the music from our app's audio player, even in the background. While in the background, we should only play music and provide our music player with the data that is necessary for it to run. We should not be performing any other tasks, such as displaying new screens.

Here is the declaration of a simple app delegate that starts an `AVAudioPlayer`:

```
import UIKit
import AVFoundation

@UIApplicationMain
class AppDelegate: UIResponder, UIApplicationDelegate, AVAudioPlayerDelegate {

  var window: UIWindow?
  var audioPlayer: AVAudioPlayer?

  <# rest of the code #>

}
```

When our app opens, we allocate and initialize our audio player, read the contents of a file named *MySong.mp3* into an instance of `NSData`, and use that data in the initialization process of our audio player:

```
func application(application: UIApplication,
  didFinishLaunchingWithOptions
  launchOptions: [NSObject : AnyObject]?) -> Bool {

    let dispatchQueue =
    dispatch_get_global_queue(DISPATCH_QUEUE_PRIORITY_DEFAULT, 0)

    dispatch_async(dispatchQueue, {[weak self] in

      var audioSessionError: NSError?
      let audioSession = AVAudioSession.sharedInstance()
      NSNotificationCenter.defaultCenter().addObserver(self!,
        selector: "handleInterruption:",
        name: AVAudioSessionInterruptionNotification,
        object: nil)

      audioSession.setActive(true, error: nil)

      if audioSession.setCategory(AVAudioSessionCategoryPlayback,
```

```
        error: &audioSessionError){
          println("Successfully set the audio session")
      } else {
        println("Could not set the audio session")
      }

      let filePath = NSBundle.mainBundle().pathForResource("MySong",
        ofType:"mp3")

      let fileData = NSData(contentsOfFile: filePath!,
        options: .DataReadingMappedIfSafe,
        error: nil)

      var error:NSError?

      /* Start the audio player */
      self!.audioPlayer = AVAudioPlayer(data: fileData, error: &error)

      /* Did we get an instance of AVAudioPlayer? */
      if let theAudioPlayer = self!.audioPlayer{
        theAudioPlayer.delegate = self;
        if theAudioPlayer.prepareToPlay() &&
          theAudioPlayer.play(){
            println("Successfully started playing")
        } else {
          println("Failed to play")
        }
      } else {
        /* Handle the failure of instantiating the audio player */
      }
    })

    return true
  }
```

In this example code, we are using AV audio sessions to silence music playback from
other applications (such as the Music application) before starting to play the audio. For
more information about audio sessions, please refer to Recipe 12.2. When in the background, you are not limited to playing only the current audio file. If the currently playing
audio file (in the background) finishes playing, you can start another instance of
AVAudioPlayer and play a completely new audio file. iOS will adjust the processing
required for this, but there is no guarantee that while in the background, your application will be given permission to allocate enough memory to accommodate the data of
the new sound file.

You've probably noticed that in our code, we are electing our app delegate to become
the delegate of our audio player. We will implement the notification method like so:

```
func handleInterruption(notification: NSNotification){
  /* Audio Session is interrupted. The player will be paused here */
```

```
let interruptionTypeAsObject =
notification.userInfo![AVAudioSessionInterruptionTypeKey] as NSNumber

let interruptionType = AVAudioSessionInterruptionType(rawValue:
  interruptionTypeAsObject.unsignedLongValue)

if let type = interruptionType{
  if type == .Ended{

    /* resume the audio if needed */

  }
}

}
```

For more information about playing audio and video, please refer to Chapter 12.

Another important thing to keep in mind is that while your application is running an audio file in the background, the value returned by the `backgroundTimeRemaining` property of `UIApplication` will not be changed. In other words, an application that requests to play audio files in the background is not implicitly or explicitly asking iOS for extra execution time.

7.12. Handling Location Changes in the Background

Problem

You are writing an application whose main functionality is processing location changes using Core Location. You want the application to retrieve the iOS device location changes even if the application is sent to the background.

Solution

Select your project file in the Navigator of Xcode. Then, from the Capabilities section, switch on the Background Modes subsection. After the list of background modes is given to you, tick on the Location updates switch.

Discussion

When your application is running in the foreground, you can receive delegate messages from an instance of `CLLocationManager` telling you when iOS detects that the device is at a new location. However, if your application is sent to the background and is no longer active, the location delegate messages will not be delivered normally to your application. They will instead be delivered in a batch when your application again becomes the foreground application.

If you still want to be able to receive changes in the location of the user's device while running in the background, you must enable the Location updates capability of your app, as described in the Solution section of this recipe. Once in the background, your application will continue to receive the changes in the device's location. Let's test this in a simple app with just the app delegate.

What I intend to do in this app is to keep a Boolean value in the app delegate, called *executingInBackground*. When the app goes to the background, I will set this value to `true`; when the app comes back to the foreground, I will set this value to `false`. When we get location updates from CoreLocation, we will check this flag. If this flag is set to `true`, then we won't do any heavy calculations or any UI update because, well, our app is in the background and as responsible programmers, we should not do heavy processing while our app is in the background.

If our app is in the foreground, however, we have all the device's processing power for the normal processing that we wish to do. We will also attempt to get the best location change accuracy when our app is in the foreground; when the app is sent to the background, we will be sure to ask for less accuracy in location updates to ease the strain on the location sensors. So let's go ahead and define our app delegate:

```
import UIKit
import CoreLocation

@UIApplicationMain
class AppDelegate: UIResponder, UIApplicationDelegate,
CLLocationManagerDelegate {

  var window: UIWindow?
  var locationManager: CLLocationManager! = nil
  var isExecutingInBackground = false

  <# rest of the code goes here #>
}
```

Now let's go ahead and create and start our location manager when our app starts:

```
func application(application: UIApplication,
  didFinishLaunchingWithOptions
  launchOptions: [NSObject : AnyObject]?) -> Bool {
  locationManager = CLLocationManager()
  locationManager.desiredAccuracy = kCLLocationAccuracyBest
  locationManager.delegate = self
  locationManager.startUpdatingLocation()
  return true
}
```

You can see that we set the desired accuracy of our location manager to a high level. However, when we go to the background, we want to lower this accuracy to give iOS a bit of a rest:

```
func applicationDidEnterBackground(application: UIApplication) {
  isExecutingInBackground = true

  /* Reduce the accuracy to ease the strain on
  iOS while we are in the background */
  locationManager.desiredAccuracy = kCLLocationAccuracyHundredMeters
}
```

When our app is awakened from the background, we can change this accuracy back to
a high level:

```
func applicationWillEnterForeground(application: UIApplication) {
  isExecutingInBackground = false

  /* Now that our app is in the foreground again, let's increase the location
  detection accuracy */
  locationManager.desiredAccuracy = kCLLocationAccuracyBest
}
```

Additionally, we would like to avoid doing any intense processing when we get a new
location from the location manager while our app is in the background, so we need to
handle the locationManager:didUpdateToLocation:fromLocation: delegate method
of our location manager in this way:

```
func locationManager(manager: CLLocationManager!,
  didUpdateToLocation newLocation: CLLocation!,
  fromLocation oldLocation: CLLocation!){
    if isExecutingInBackground{
      /* We are in the background. Do not do any heavy processing */
    } else {
      /* We are in the foreground. Do any processing that you wish */
    }
}
```

The simple rule here is that if we are in the background, we should be using the smallest
amount of memory and processing power to satisfy our application's needs. So, by de-
creasing the accuracy of the location manager while in the background, we are decreas-
ing the amount of processing iOS has to do to deliver new locations to our application.

 Depending on the version of iOS Simulator you are testing your applications with, as well as the settings of your network connection and
many other factors that affect this process, background location processing might not work for you. Please test your applications, including the source code in this recipe, on a real device.

7.13. Handling Network Connections in the Background

Problem

You are using instances of NSURLConnection to send and receive data to and from a web server and are wondering how you can allow your application to work in the multitasking environment of iOS without connection failures.

Solution

Make sure you support connection failures in the block objects that you submit to your connection objects.

Discussion

For applications that use NSURLConnection but do not borrow extra time from iOS when they are sent to the background, connection handling is truly simple. Let's go through an example to see how an asynchronous connection will act if the application is sent to the background and brought to the foreground again. For this, let's send an asynchronous connection request to retrieve the contents of a URL (say, Apple's home page):

```
func application(application: UIApplication,
    didFinishLaunchingWithOptions
    launchOptions: [NSObject : AnyObject]?) -> Bool {

    let urlAsString = "http://www.apple.com"
    let url = NSURL(string: urlAsString)
    let urlRequest = NSURLRequest(URL: url!)
    let queue = NSOperationQueue()

    NSURLConnection.sendAsynchronousRequest(urlRequest,
        queue: queue,
        completionHandler: {(response: NSURLResponse!,
            data: NSData!,
            error: NSError!) in

        if data.length > 0 && error == nil{
            /* Date did come back */
        }
        else if data.length == 0 && error == nil{
            /* No data came back */
        }
        else if error != nil{
            /* Error happened. Make sure you handle this properly */
        }
        })

    return true
}
```

I advise you to replace the Apple home page URL in this example with the URL to a rather large file on the Internet. The reason is that if your app is downloading a large file, you will have more time to play with the app and send it to the background and bring it to the foreground. Whereas, if you are on a rather fast Internet connection and you are just downloading Apple's home page, chances are the connection is going to retrieve the data for you in a second or two.

In the foreground, our application will continue downloading the file. While downloading, the user can press the Home button and send the application to the background. What you will observe is true magic! iOS automatically puts the download process into a paused state for you. When the user brings your application to the foreground again, the downloading resumes without you writing a single line of code to handle multitasking.

Now let's see what happens with synchronous connections. We are going to download a very big file on the main thread (a very bad practice—do not do this in a production application!) as soon as our application launches:

```swift
func application(application: UIApplication,
  didFinishLaunchingWithOptions
  launchOptions: [NSObject : AnyObject]?) -> Bool {

  let urlAsString = "http://www.apple.com"
  let url = NSURL(string: urlAsString)
  let urlRequest = NSURLRequest(URL: url!)
  let queue = NSOperationQueue()
  var error: NSError?

  let data = NSURLConnection.sendSynchronousRequest(urlRequest,
    returningResponse: nil,
    error: &error)

  if data != nil && error == nil{
    /* Date did come back */
  }
  else if data!.length == 0 && error == nil{
    /* No data came back */
  }
  else if error != nil{
    /* Error happened. Make sure you handle this properly */
  }

  return true
}
```

If you run this application and send it to the background, you will notice that the application's GUI is sent to the background, but the application's core is never sent to the background and the appropriate delegate messages—applicationWillResignAc tive: and applicationDidEnterBackground:—will never be received. I conducted this test on an iPhone.

The problem with this approach is that we are consuming the main thread's time slice by downloading files synchronously. We can fix this by either downloading the files asynchronously on the main thread, as mentioned before, or downloading them synchronously on separate threads.

Take the previous sample code, for example. If we download the same big file synchronously on a global concurrent queue, the connection pauses when the application is sent to the background, and resumes once it is brought to the foreground again:

```swift
func application(application: UIApplication,
  didFinishLaunchingWithOptions
  launchOptions: [NSObject : AnyObject]?) -> Bool {

    let dispatchQueue =
    dispatch_get_global_queue(DISPATCH_QUEUE_PRIORITY_DEFAULT, 0)

    dispatch_async(dispatchQueue, {
      /* Replace this URL with the URL of a file that is
      rather big in size */
      let urlAsString = "http://www.apple.com"
      let url = NSURL(string: urlAsString)
      let urlRequest = NSURLRequest(URL: url!)
      let queue = NSOperationQueue()
      var error: NSError?

      let data = NSURLConnection.sendSynchronousRequest(urlRequest,
        returningResponse: nil,
        error: &error)

      if data != nil && error == nil{
        /* Date came back */
      }
      else if data!.length == 0 && error == nil{
        /* No data came back */
      }
      else if error != nil{
        /* Error happened. Make sure you handle this properly. */
      }
    })

    return true
}
```

See Also

Recipe 7.9

CHAPTER 8

Security

8.0. Introduction

Security is at the heart of iOS and OS X. You can use security functions in iOS to store data or files securely in different storage spaces. For instance, you can ask iOS to lock and secure your app's data files stored on disk if the user has enabled a passcode for her device and her device is locked. If you do not explicitly ask for this, iOS will not use any secure storage for your app, and your app data will be available to be read by a process that has access to read your device's filesystem. There are a variety of Mac applications out there that can explore an iOS device's filesystem *without* the iOS device being jail-broken.

Jailbreaking is the process of enabling root access and removing many protection layers built on top of an operating system, such as iOS. For instance, on a jailbroken device, an application can execute an un-signed binary. However, on a normal iOS device, for an app to be able to get executed on the device, it has to be signed either by Apple through the App Store, or through a verified iOS developer portal.

Apple has had Keychain Access in OS X for a long time. Keychain Access is a program that allows OS X users to store data securely on their computers. Built on top of the Common Data Security Architecture, or CDSA, the Keychain Access and other security functionalities in OS X are available to programmers like us. Keychain Access can manage various keychains. Every keychain itself can contain secure data such as passwords. For instance, on your OS X machine, when you log into a website using Safari, you will be prompted to either request for your password to be remembered by Safari or ignore that request. If you ask Safari to remember your password, Safari will then store the given password securely in your default keychain.

The OS X and iOS keychains differ in various ways, as listed here:

- In OS X, the user can have multiple keychains. In iOS, there is a single global keychain.

- In OS X, a keychain can be locked by the user. In iOS, the default keychain gets locked and unlocked as the device gets locked and unlocked.

- OS X has the concept of a *default keychain* that gets automatically unlocked by OS X when the user logs in, as long as the default keychain has the same password as the user's account password. iOS, as just mentioned, has only one keychain and this keychain, is unlocked by iOS by default.

To get a better understanding of the keychain on OS X, before we dig deeper into the keychain and security concepts in iOS, I would like to demonstrate something to you. Open Terminal on your Mac, type the following command, and press Enter:

```
security list-keychains
```

The output, depending on your machine's setup and your username, might be very similar to that shown here:

```
"/Users/vandadnp/Library/Keychains/login.keychain"
"/Library/Keychains/System.keychain"
```

You can see that I have two keychains, the first being the login keychain and the second being the system keychain. To find out which keychain is the default keychain, type the following command in Terminal, and then press Enter:

```
security default-keychain
```

On a typical OS X installation, this command will return a result similar to this:

```
"/Users/vandadnp/Library/Keychains/login.keychain"
```

The output indicates that my default keychain is the login keychain. So by default, all passwords that I have asked various programs in my OS X installation to remember will get stored in the default keychain unless the app in question decides that it needs to store the password in a different keychain. The app will have to create that keychain if it's not already there.

Now let's try something exciting. To find out what passwords are already stored in your default keychain, assuming that the default keychain as we found out earlier was the login.keychain, type the following command in Terminal and press Enter:

```
security dump-keychain login.keychain | grep "password" -i
```

The dump-keychain argument to the security command in Terminal will dump the whole contents of a keychain to the standard output. We used the grep command to search for the passwords. The output of this command may be similar to the following, depending on your computer's remembered passwords:

```
security dump-keychain login.keychain | grep "password" -i
"icmt"<blob>="Used to decode the encrypted file that contains
  non-password data previously entered in web page forms."
0x00000007 <blob>="iTunes iAd password"
"desc"<blob>="iTunes iAd password"
"desc"<blob>="iWork Document Password"
```

OK, well, this is all great, but why am I talking about it, and how is it related to iOS? It turns out that the architecture of the keychain in iOS is *very* similar to OS X, because iOS was based on OS X's source code. A lot of the concepts in iOS are similar to those in OS X, and the keychain is no exception. There are some really important things to note about the keychain in iOS, such as access groups and services. To ease you into the subject, I will demonstrate how they apply to OS X, and then I will talk more about the iOS implementation of the keychain.

On your Mac, press Command+Space to open the Spotlight, or simply click the Spotlight icon on the top menu bar on your screen.

When the Spotlight opens, type in "Keychain Access" and press the Enter key to open Keychain Access. On the lefthand side of Keychain Access, under the Keychains section, click the *login* keychain and then, under the Category section on the lefthand side, choose *Passwords*. Now you should see an interface similar to that shown in Figure 8-1.

Figure 8-1. The Keychain Access on Mac OS X

Keychain Access is the graphical user interface that sits on top of the keychain and security APIs in OS X, giving you a nice, clean interface that hides a lot of the complexity underneath the security frameworks in OS X. Now, if you have any passwords remembered by apps such as Safari, double-click one of the password items on the righthand side of the Keychain Access screen to open a dialog similar to that shown in Figure 8-2.

Figure 8-2. Keychain Access dialog displaying information for a saved password

We need to know some of the properties of the password shown in Figure 8-2:

Name

> The name of the password, which was assigned by the application that stored the item. For instance, this one is a WiFi password for a network named *206-NET*. This name is also sometimes referred to as the *label*.

Kind

> The kind of item that this is. In this case, the kind is *AirPort network password*. This is a plain string and can be used to query the keychain later, as we will see.

Account

> This is usually the key for the value that we want to store. The keychain uses a key-value store, just as dictionaries do in Objective-C. The key is an arbitrary string, and most applications that store items in the keychain store the key of the value in this section.

Where

> Often referred to as the *service*, this is the identifier of the service that stored this item in the keychain. This identifier is something for you to remember, and the keychain doesn't really care about it too much as long as it makes sense to you. In iOS, we usually set this service name to the bundle identifier of our apps to distinguish our app's stored values from other apps' stored data. We will talk about this in a short while.

You can also see the *Show password* checkbox in Figure 8-2. Pressing this checkbox will ask for your permission to display the password for the item in question. If you enter your password and give permission to display the password for this item, Keychain Access will retrieve the secure password for you and display it on-screen.

We can use the `security` command in Terminal to fetch the exact same information. If you type the following command in Terminal:

```
security find-generic-password -help
```

You will get an output similar to this:

```
security find-generic-password -help
Usage: find-generic-password [-a account] [-s service]
[options...] [-g] [keychain...]
    -a  Match "account" string
    -c  Match "creator" (four-character code)
    -C  Match "type" (four-character code)
    -D  Match "kind" string
    -G  Match "value" string (generic attribute)
    -j  Match "comment" string
    -l  Match "label" string
    -s  Match "service" string
    -g  Display the password for the item found
    -w  Display only the password on stdout
If no keychains are specified to search, the default search list is used.
        Find a generic password item.
```

In iOS, even though the whole operating system has one global keychain area, an application can still just read from and write to a sandboxed area of the global keychain. Two apps written by the same developer (signed by a provision profile from the same iOS Developer Portal) can access a shared area of the keychain, but they still maintain their own sandboxed access to their own keychain. Therefore, two apps named App X and App Y, developed by the same iOS developer, can access the following keychain areas:

1. App X can access App X's keychain area.

2. App Y can access App Y's keychain area.

3. App X and App Y can both access a shared keychain area (using access groups, if the programmer configures the app's entitlements appropriately).

4. App X cannot read App Y's keychain data, and App Y cannot read App X's keychain data.

iOS looks at an app's *entitlements* to figure out what type of access it requires. Entitlements of an app are encoded inside the provision profile that is used to sign the app. Assume you have just created a new provision profile called *KeychainTest_Dev.mobile provision* and placed it on your desktop. Using the following command, you can extract the entitlements inside the profile, as follows:

```
cd ~/Desktop
```

That command will take you to your desktop, where you can issue the following command to read the entitlements of your provision profile:

```
security cms -D -i KeychainTest_Dev.mobileprovision | grep -A12 "Entitlements"
```

 The `security` command shown here will decode the whole provision profile, after which the `grep` command will look for the Entitlements section in the profile and read 12 lines of text at the beginning of it. If your entitlements contain more or less text, you might need to adjust the `-A12` argument to read more lines or fewer.

The output of that command will potentially look like this, depending on your profile:

```
<key>Entitlements</key>
<dict>
  <key>application-identifier</key>
  <string>F3FU372W5M.com.pixolity.ios.cookbook.KeychainTest</string>
  <key>com.apple.developer.default-data-protection</key>
  <string>NSFileProtectionComplete</string>
  <key>com.apple.developer.team-identifier</key>
  <string>F3FU372W5M</string>
  <key>get-task-allow</key>
  <true/>
  <key>keychain-access-groups</key>
  <array>
    <string>F3FU372W5M.*</string>
  </array>
</dict>
```

The important section that we are looking for is the *keychain-access-groups* section that specifies the access groups for our keychain items. This is the group identifier of the shared keychain for all apps developed by the same developer. In this case, the *F3FU372W5M* is my iOS portal's team ID, and the asterisk after that shows what access groups in the keychain I can place my securely stored items in later. The asterisk in this case means *any group*, so by default, this app will be able to access the keychain items for any app that belongs to the aforementioned team. Don't worry if this doesn't make that much sense now. I can guarantee that by reading more about this subject in this chapter, you will get to know all a programmer needs to use keychain in iOS.

It is absolutely crucial that you add the Security framework to your app before continuing to read the recipes in this chapter. Most of the recipes in this chapter work with the keychain services in iOS, which require the presence of the Security framework. The iOS SDK 7 introduced the idea of modules, so that if you simply import the security framework's umbrella header into your project, LLVM will link your application to the relevant security module; you won't have to do the link manually. All you have to do is ensure that the Enable Modules feature is enabled in your build settings and that you import the following header file into your project:

```
import Security
```

Xcode 5 also added support for Capabilities, a new tab near the Build Settings tab. There, you can easily add entitlements to your app or even enable the keychain without much hassle. However, this hides almost every detail from you and doesn't allow you to create your own provision profiles. All you will be able to use are Wildcard provision profiles, which is not what we usually use when adding push notifications and other capabilities to our apps. I suggest that you have a look at this new tab simply by clicking on your project file in Xcode, looking to the righthand side of the screen, and selecting Capabilities. You can then easily turn on or off features such as iCloud and Keychain Access.

8.1. Authenticating the User with Touch ID

Problem

You would like to harvest the power of Touch ID in your application to authenticate the user through his or her fingerprint.

Solution

Use the `LocalAuthentication` framework in your application.

First, you need to create an instance of the `LAContext` class. This is just a handle to the Touch ID APIs you are going to use. When you have the handle to this object, invoke its `canEvaluatePolicy:error:` method to determine the availability of Touch ID for your application. Pass the value `LAPolicyDeviceOwnerAuthenticationWithBiometrics` as the first parameter. You can also optionally pass a handle to an error object as the second parameter, so the method can notify you whether an error has occurred. The return value of the method is a Boolean indicating whether Touch ID is available on the device on which your code is running. Please bear in mind that Touch ID is currently not available for the simulator, so you will need a real device that supports Touch ID to test this recipe out for yourself.

Assuming that Touch ID is available, you can now use the `evaluatePolicy:localizedReason:reply:` method of the `LAContext` local authentication context you created to authenticate the user using their Touch ID data. Note that the actual fingerprint information of the user is not exposed to any application. The only data you will receive from the local authentication framework is a true or a false value stating whether the user's fingerprint was correct or not. That's it!

As a setup for this recipe, I prepared a very simple user interface for an app that we can use in order to test the Touch ID functionality. Figure 8-3 shows what this app's UI looks like.

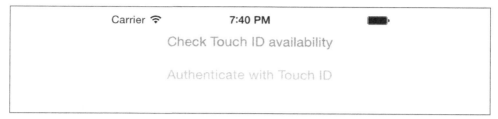

Figure 8-3. A simple Touch ID app UI

I have also connected the two buttons to their corresponding outlets in our view controller:

```
import UIKit

class ViewController: UIViewController {

    @IBOutlet weak var buttonCheckTouchId: UIButton!
    @IBOutlet weak var buttonUseTouchId: UIButton!

}
```

The first button (which is also on the top of our view on our UI) will check the availability of touch UI when it is pressed. If Touch UI is available on the current device, pressing this button will enable the second button, which as you can see is disabled by default.

Pressing the second button will then use the Touch ID APIs to authenticate the user. Here is our code for the first button:

```
import UIKit
import LocalAuthentication

class ViewController: UIViewController {

    @IBOutlet weak var buttonCheckTouchId: UIButton!
    @IBOutlet weak var buttonUseTouchId: UIButton!

    @IBAction func checkTouchIdAvailability(sender: AnyObject) {

        let context = LAContext()
        var error: NSError?

        let isTouchIdAvailable = context.canEvaluatePolicy(
          .DeviceOwnerAuthenticationWithBiometrics,
          error: &error)
```

```
buttonUseTouchId.enabled = isTouchIdAvailable

/* Touch ID is not available */
if isTouchIdAvailable == false{

  let alertController = UIAlertController(title: "Touch ID",
    message: "Touch ID is not available",
    preferredStyle: .Alert)

  alertController.addAction(UIAlertAction(title: "OK",
    style: .Default,
    handler: nil))

  presentViewController(alertController, animated: true, completion: nil)

  }

  }

@IBAction func useTouchId(sender: AnyObject) {
  /* We will code this soon */
  }

}
```

This is very simple, isn't it? We are just checking the availability of Touch ID and enabling or disabling the "Use Touch ID" button on our interface based on the availability of Touch ID. Now we have to work on actually using the Touch ID APIs. We will do so using the evaluatePolicy:localizedReason:reply: method of LAContext. The policy will be the same as we saw before. The localizedReason is the text that will be displayed to the user in a message when they are asked to provide their biometrics to be authenticated into your app. Here is your chance to let the user know why you need this authentication to take place. For instance, you can let the user know that they need to provide their biometrics data in order to access some sensitive information.

```
@IBAction func useTouchId(sender: AnyObject) {
  /* We will code this soon */

  let context = LAContext()
  var error: NSError?
  let reason = "Please authenticate with Touch ID " +
  "to access your private information"

  context.evaluatePolicy(.DeviceOwnerAuthenticationWithBiometrics,
    localizedReason: reason, reply: {(success: Bool, error: NSError!) in

      if success{
        /* The user was successfully authenticated */
      } else {
        /* The user could not be authenticated */
      }
```

```
    })

  }
```

Discussion

Please be mindful when asking the user for authentication using Touch ID. The reason is that this is an inconvenience for the user, as it takes their attention away from the task at hand and focuses it on carefully placing their fingers on the Touch ID sensors. Also, not every iOS device is equipped with Touch ID sensors. So ensure that your app has another method of authentication for users on iOS devices that have no access to Touch ID sensors.

Another thing to bear in mind is that the block object that you provide to the `reply` parameter of the `evaluatePolicy:localizedReason:reply:` method of `LAContext` may not be executed on the main thread or the thread that you call this method on. So if you do need to perform some work on the main thread, please ensure that you do so using the technique that you learned in Recipe 7.1.

See Also

Recipe 7.1

8.2. Enabling Security and Protection for Your Apps

Problem

You want to store values in the keychain and enable secure file storage for your app.

Solution

Create a provision profile for your app that has file protection enabled.

Discussion

Provision profiles, as discussed earlier in Recipe 8.0, "Introduction", contain entitlements that dictate to iOS how your app utilizes the security functionalities in the operating system. On iOS Simulator, apps do not get codesigned and, therefore, these concepts will not make sense. But for debugging your app on a device or submitting your app to the App Store, you need to ensure that your app is signed with the correct provision profile for both the Debug and the Release schemes.

I will show you the steps required to create a valid provision profile for your development, as well as Ad Hoc and the App Store. Follow these steps to create a valid development provision profile (with debugging enabled) for the apps that we are going to be working on in this chapter of the book. We start by creating an App ID:

 I am assuming that you have already created valid development and distribution certificates for yourself.

1. Navigate to the iOS Dev Center (*http://bit.ly/ios-dev-center*) and sign in with your username and password.

2. Find the iOS Developer Program section and choose Certificates, Identifiers & Profiles.

3. On the lefthand side of the screen, find and navigate to the App IDs section of the portal and press the plus button (+) to create a new App ID.

4. In the Name section, enter the name "Security App." You can actually enter anything you want, but to avoid confusion in this chapter, it's best to stick with the afore-mentioned name, which I will be using in examples.

5. Under the App Services section, check the Data Protection box and ensure that the Complete Protection option is selected. Leave the rest of the settings intact.

6. Under the App ID Suffix section, ensure that the Explicit App ID option is selected, and in the Bundle ID box, enter the dot-separated name of a service. I recommend `com.NAME.REST`, where `NAME` is your company's name. If you don't have a company, make up a name! I am using `com.pixolity.ios.cookbook.app` in examples, but you need a unique name, so you can't use mine.

7. After you are done, press the Continue button.

8. You should now be asked to confirm your settings before your App ID is created, similar to the screen depicted in Figure 8-4.

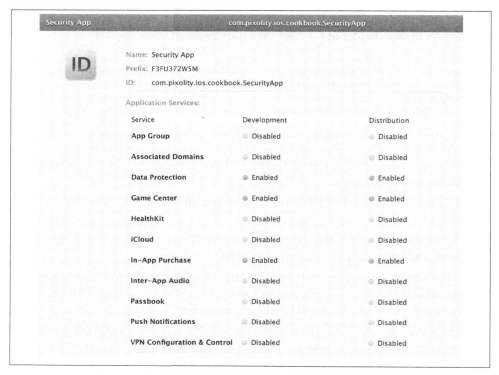

Figure 8-4. Confirming your App ID settings before creating the App ID

9. When you are happy with your settings, press the Submit button to create your App ID.

Beautiful! Now we have an App ID, but we still need to create our provision profiles. I am going to walk you through creating your development provision profile, and I will let you create the Ad Hoc and your App Store profiles on your own because the process is almost identical. Follow these steps to create your development provision profile:

1. In the Certificates, Identifiers & Profiles section of the Developer Portal, choose the Development section of the Provisioning Profiles category and press the plus button (+).

2. In the screen that appears, under the Development section, choose the iOS App Development option and press the Continue button.

3. When asked to choose your App ID, select the App ID that you created earlier. For me, this would be the App ID shown in Figure 8-5. When you are happy with your selection, press the Continue button.

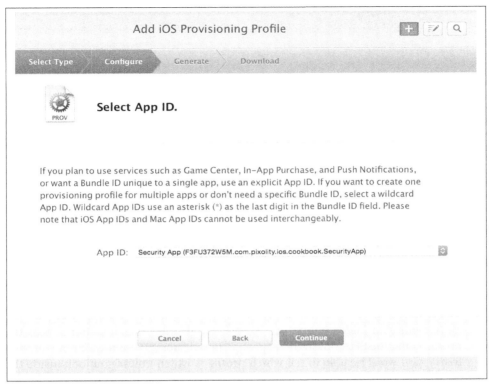

Figure 8-5. Choosing our new App ID for the new development provision profile

4. Choose the development certificate(s) to which you want to link your profile. Then press the Continue button.

5. Choose the list of devices on which your profile is allowed to be installed (only for Development and Ad Hoc profiles, not for App Store). Press the Continue button.

6. On the next screen, where you are asked to specify a name for your profile, enter something along the lines of "App Dev Profile" and then press the Generate button to create your provision profile.

7. Your profile is now ready to be downloaded (see Figure 8-6). Press the Download button to download your profile.

Figure 8-6. A development profile is generated and ready to be downloaded

8. To install the profile, drag and drop the downloaded profile into iTunes. This will install the profile with its original name into the *~/Library/MobileDevice/Provision ing Profiles/* folder. I have seen many iOS developers install a provision profile by double-clicking on it. While this does work in that it installs the profile into the aforementioned folder, it destroys the original profile's filename and installs the profile using the SHA1 hash of the profile. If you later go into the aforementioned folder, you won't be able to tell which profile is which unless you look inside the profiles for their names, so I strongly discourage this way of installing profiles. It's best to either drag and drop the downloaded profiles into iTunes or manually paste the profiles into the aforementioned folder.

Brilliant. You now have the provision profile installed on your computer. Use the build settings of your project to make sure that the correct profile is selected for the Debug scheme. After you follow the same process for creating your Ad Hoc and App Store profiles, you can ensure that your app is built with the correct Ad Hoc or App Store profile for the Release scheme.

The provision profile that you created now will allow you to debug your apps on an iOS device and store data onto the disk or into the keychain with ease.

See Also

Recipe 8.0, "Introduction"

8.3. Storing Values in the Keychain

Problem

You want to securely store sensitive data in the keychain.

Solution

Ensure that your app is linked against the Security framework. Then use the `SecI temAdd` function to add a new item to your app's keychain.

Discussion

Keychain APIs in both iOS and OS X are C APIs. That means we don't have an Objective-C bridge or layer on top of the C APIs, so they are a bit more difficult to use than normal APIs. The key to learning the APIs is that the requests that we send to the keychain APIs are usually packed inside dictionaries. For instance, if you want to ask the keychain services to securely store a piece of data, you put your request—including the data that you want to store, the key for that data, the identifer of your app, etc.—inside a dictionary and submit that dictionary to an API such as the `SecItemAdd` function. To store a piece of value in the keychain, construct a dictionary with the following keys:

`kSecClass`
> The value of this key is usually equal to `kSecClassGenericPassword` for storage of secure pieces of data, such as strings.

`kSecAttrService`
> The value of this key is usually a string. This string usually is our app bundle identifier.

`kSecAttrAccount`
> The value of this key is a string that specifies the key to the value that we want to store. This is an arbitrary string that should make sense to you and your app.

`kSecValueData`
> The value of this key is an instance of `NSData` that you want to store for a given key (`kSecAttrAccount`.)

The return value of the `SecItemAdd` function is of type `OSStatus`. The different values that you can receive from this function are defined inside the *SecBase* file in your SDK, so simply press the Command+Shift+O keys on your keyboard while in Xcode, type in *SecBase*, and try to find the value `errSecSuccess`. After you find `errSecSuccess` in an enumeration, you will be able to see the rest of the values that can be returned inside a value of type `OSStatus`.

If the SecItemAdd function succeeds, you will receive the errSecSuccess value as the return value of this function. Otherwise, this function is indicating failure. So let's put all this together and write a small piece of code that can write a string value to the keychain:

```
import UIKit

@UIApplicationMain
class AppDelegate: UIResponder, UIApplicationDelegate{

  var window: UIWindow?

  func application(application: UIApplication,
    didFinishLaunchingWithOptions
    launchOptions: [NSObject : AnyObject]?) -> Bool {

      let key = "Full Name"

      let value = "Steve Jobs"
      let valueData = value.dataUsingEncoding(NSUTF8StringEncoding,
        allowLossyConversion: false)

      let service = NSBundle.mainBundle().bundleIdentifier!

      let secItem = [
        kSecClass as NSString :
      kSecClassGenericPassword as NSString,

        kSecAttrService as NSString : service,
        kSecAttrAccount as NSString : key,
        kSecValueData as NSString : valueData!,
        ] as NSDictionary

      var result: Unmanaged<AnyObject>? = nil
      let status = Int(SecItemAdd(secItem, &result))

      switch status{
      case Int(errSecSuccess):
        println("Successfully stored the value")
      case Int(errSecDuplicateItem):
        println("This item is already saved. Cannot duplicate it")
      default:
        println("An error occurred with code \(status)")
      }

      return true
  }

}
```

If you run this app for the first time, assuming that you have followed the advice in previous sections of this chapter to set up your profile correctly, you will receive the errSecSuccess value from the SecItemAdd function. However, if you run the same app again, you will receive the errSecDuplicateItem value. This is Keychain's way of telling you that you cannot overwrite the existing value. What you *can* do, though, is update the existing value, as we will see later in this chapter.

See Also

Recipe 8.2

8.4. Finding Values in the Keychain

Problem

You want to query the keychain to find an existing item.

Solution

Use the SecItemCopyMatching function. Follow these steps:

1. Construct a dictionary to pass to the aforementioned function. Add the kSec Class key to the dictionary. Set the key's value to reflect the type of item that you are looking for. Usually the value should be kSecClassGenericPassword.

2. Add the kSecAttrService key to the dictionary. Set the key's value to the service string of the item you are looking for. In this chapter, for service names, we use our app's bundle identifier and we set the bundle identifiers of all our apps to the same string, so that one can write to the keychain, another can read the same data, etc.

3. Add the kSecAttrAccount key to the dictionary and set its value to the actual key of the value that you previously stored in the keychain. If you followed the example that we wrote in Recipe 8.3, the account name in this case would be the string "Full Name."

4. Add the kSecReturnAttributes attribute to the dictionary and set its value to kCFBooleanTrue if you want to retrieve the attributes, such as the creation and modification date, of the existing value in the keychain. If you want to retrieve the actual value of the item you stored in the keychain, instead of the kSecReturnAt tributes key, add the kSecReturnData key to your dictionary and set its value to kCFBooleanTrue.

When your dictionary is ready, you can pass it as the first parameter to the SecItemCo pyMatching function. The second parameter is a pointer to an object that will be returned by this function. This pointer must be of type CFTypeRef *. This is a generic data type, and the type depends on what you pass as the first parameter to the SecItem CopyMatching function. For instance, if your dictionary contains the kSecReturnAt tributes key, the second parameter to this function must be either nil or a pointer to a `CFDictionaryRef` opaque type. If you instead pass the `kSecReturnData` key to your dictionary, the second parameter to this function must be of type `CFDataRef`, which is an opaque type that will receive the actual data of the existing item. You can then convert this data to an instance of `NSString` and work with it.

Discussion

Suppose you want to read the *properties* of the string that you wrote to the keychain in Recipe 8.3. You can write your code in this way:

```
import UIKit

@UIApplicationMain
class AppDelegate: UIResponder, UIApplicationDelegate {

  var window: UIWindow?

  func application(application: UIApplication,
    didFinishLaunchingWithOptions
    launchOptions: [NSObject : AnyObject]?) -> Bool {

    let keyToSearchFor = "Full Name"
    let service = NSBundle.mainBundle().bundleIdentifier!

    let query = [
      kSecClass as NSString :
    kSecClassGenericPassword as NSString,

      kSecAttrService as NSString : service,
      kSecAttrAccount as NSString : keyToSearchFor,
      kSecReturnAttributes as NSString : kCFBooleanTrue,
    ] as NSDictionary


    var valueAttributes: Unmanaged<AnyObject>? = nil
    let results = Int(SecItemCopyMatching(query, &valueAttributes))

    if results == Int(errSecSuccess){

      let attributes = valueAttributes!.takeRetainedValue() as NSDictionary

      let key = attributes[kSecAttrAccount as NSString]
        as String

      let accessGroup = attributes[kSecAttrAccessGroup as NSString] as String

      let creationDate = attributes[kSecAttrCreationDate as NSString] as NSDate

      let modifiedDate = attributes[
        kSecAttrModificationDate as NSString] as NSDate
```

```
    let serviceValue = attributes[kSecAttrService as NSString] as String

    println("Key = \(key)")
    println("Access Group = \(accessGroup)")
    println("Creation Date = \(creationDate)")
    println("Modification Date = \(modifiedDate)")
    println("Service = \(serviceValue)")

  } else {
    println("Error happened with code: \(results)")
  }

  return true
}

}
```

When you run the app, results similar to the following print to the console:

```
Key = Full Name
Access Group = F3FU372W5M.com.pixolity.ios.cookbook.app
Creation Date = 2014-07-07 14:01:58 +0000
Modification Date = 2014-07-07 14:01:58 +0000
Service = com.pixolity.ios.cookbook.app
```

That is great, but how can you now read the actual data of the value? The Solution section of this recipe already answered this: you have to include the kSecReturnData in your query. When you do that, the second parameter to the SecItemCopyMatching function will need to either be nil or a pointer to a CFDataRef opaque variable, like so:

```
func application(application: UIApplication,
  didFinishLaunchingWithOptions
  launchOptions: [NSObject : AnyObject]?) -> Bool {

    let keyToSearchFor = "Full Name"
    let service = NSBundle.mainBundle().bundleIdentifier!

    let query = [
      kSecClass as NSString :
      kSecClassGenericPassword as NSString,

      kSecAttrService as NSString : service,
      kSecAttrAccount as NSString : keyToSearchFor,
      kSecReturnData as NSString : kCFBooleanTrue,
      ] as NSDictionary

    var returnedData: Unmanaged<AnyObject>? = nil
    let results = Int(SecItemCopyMatching(query, &returnedData))

    if results == Int(errSecSuccess){

      let data = returnedData!.takeRetainedValue() as NSData
```

```
        let value = NSString(data: data, encoding: NSUTF8StringEncoding)

        println("Value = \(value)")

    } else {
        println("Error happened with code: \(results)")
    }

    return true
}
```

By default, the SecItemCopyMatching function looks for the first match in the keychain. Let's say that you stored 10 secure items of class kSecClassGenericPassword in the keychain and you want to query them all. How can you do that? The answer is simple. Just add the kSecMatchLimit key into your query dictionary and provide the maximum number of matching items that the keychain services have to look for in the keychain or, alternatively, set the value of this key to kSecMatchLimitAll to find all matching items. When you include the kSecMatchLimit key in your query dictionary to the SecItemCopyMatching function, the second parameter to this method will then require a pointer to a CFArrayRef opaque type, and the items in this array will then be the items that you asked for. If you include the kSecReturnData key in your dictionary with the value of true, the items in this array will be of type CFDataRef. However, if instead of the kSecReturnData key, you included the kSecReturnAttributes key in your query dictionary with the value of true, the items in your array will be of type CFDictionar yRef and contain the dictionary object that describes the found item.

See Also

Recipe 8.3

8.5. Updating Existing Values in the Keychain

Problem

You have already stored a value in the keychain but now want to update it to a new value.

Solution

Given that you have been able to find the value in the keychain (see Recipe 8.4), you can issue the SecItemUpdate function with your query dictionary as its first parameter and a dictionary describing the change that you want to make to the existing value as its second parameter. Usually this update dictionary (the second parameter to the method) contains just one key (kSecValueData) and the value of this dictionary key is the data to set for the existing key in the keychain.

Discussion

Following the advice given in Recipe 8.3, let's assume that you stored the string *Steve Jobs* with the key *Full Name* in your app's keychain, but want to update that value now. The first thing that you have to do is find out whether the existing value is already in the keychain. For that, construct a simple query, as we have seen earlier in this chapter:

```
let keyToSearchFor = "Full Name"
let service = NSBundle.mainBundle().bundleIdentifier!

let query = [
  kSecClass as NSString :
  kSecClassGenericPassword as NSString,

  kSecAttrService as NSString : service,
  kSecAttrAccount as NSString : keyToSearchFor,
] as NSDictionary
```

Then query for that dictionary and see whether you can find the existing item in the keychain:

```
var result: Unmanaged<AnyObject>? = nil
let found = Int(SecItemCopyMatching(query, &result))
```

 You don't necessarily have to check for an existing value before trying to update it. You can just attempt to update the value, and if the item doesn't exist, the SecItemUpdate function returns the value of errSecItemNotFound to you. The choice is whether to search in the keychain yourself or let SecItemUpdate do the check for you.

If this function returns the value of errSecSuccess, you know that your value is already there. Note that we passed nil as the second parameter. The reason behind this is that we are not interested in retrieving the old value from the keychain. We just want to find out whether the value exists, and we can find that out by checking the function's return value. If the return value is errSecSuccess, then we know the value has already been stored and can be updated. So all we have to do is update it like so:

```
if found == Int(errSecSuccess){

  let newData = "Mark Tremonti".dataUsingEncoding(NSUTF8StringEncoding,
    allowLossyConversion: false)

  let update = [
    kSecValueData as NSString : newData!,
    kSecAttrComment as NSString : "My comments"
  ] as NSDictionary

  let updated = Int(SecItemUpdate(query, update))
```

```
  if updated == Int(errSecSuccess){
    println("Successfully updated the existing value")
    readExistingValue()
  } else {
    println("Failed to update the value. Error = \(updated)")
  }

} else {
  println("Error happened. Code = \(found)")
}
```

The update dictionary that we pass to the second parameter of the SecItemUpdate function can contain more keys than the kSecValueData key that we used in our example. This dictionary can indeed contain any update to the existing item. For instance, if you want to add a comment to the existing value (a comment is a string), you can issue your update like so:

```
import UIKit
import Security

@UIApplicationMain
class AppDelegate: UIResponder, UIApplicationDelegate {

  var window: UIWindow?

  func readExistingValue(){
    let keyToSearchFor = "Full Name"
    let service = NSBundle.mainBundle().bundleIdentifier!

    let query = [
      kSecClass as NSString :
      kSecClassGenericPassword as NSString,

      kSecAttrService as NSString : service,
      kSecAttrAccount as NSString : keyToSearchFor,
      kSecReturnAttributes as NSString : kCFBooleanTrue,

    ] as NSDictionary

    var returnedAttributes: Unmanaged<AnyObject>? = nil
    let results = Int(SecItemCopyMatching(query, &returnedAttributes))

    if results == Int(errSecSuccess){

      let attributes = returnedAttributes!.takeRetainedValue() as NSDictionary

      let comments = attributes[kSecAttrComment as NSString] as String

      println("Comments = \(comments)")

    } else {
      println("Error happened with code: \(results)")
```

```
    }
  }

  func application(application: UIApplication,
    didFinishLaunchingWithOptions
    launchOptions: [NSObject : AnyObject]?) -> Bool {

    let keyToSearchFor = "Full Name"
    let service = NSBundle.mainBundle().bundleIdentifier!

    let query = [
      kSecClass as NSString :
    kSecClassGenericPassword as NSString,

      kSecAttrService as NSString : service,
      kSecAttrAccount as NSString : keyToSearchFor,
    ] as NSDictionary

    var result: Unmanaged<AnyObject>? = nil
    let found = Int(SecItemCopyMatching(query, &result))

    if found == Int(errSecSuccess){

      let newData = "Mark Tremonti".dataUsingEncoding(NSUTF8StringEncoding,
        allowLossyConversion: false)

      let update = [
        kSecValueData as NSString : newData!,
        kSecAttrComment as NSString : "My comments"
      ] as NSDictionary

      let updated = Int(SecItemUpdate(query, update))

      if updated == Int(errSecSuccess){
        println("Successfully updated the existing value")
        readExistingValue()
      } else {
        println("Failed to update the value. Error = \(updated)")
      }

    } else {
      println("Error happened. Code = \(found)")
    }


    return true
  }

}
```

The important thing to note about this example code is the inclusion of the `kSecAttr`
`Comment` key in our update dictionary. After the update is done, we read our comment
back using the same reading technique that we learned in Recipe 8.4.

See Also

Recipe 8.4; Recipe 8.3

8.6. Deleting Existing Values in the Keychain

Problem

You want to delete a keychain item.

Solution

Use the `SecItemDelete` function.

Discussion

In Recipe 8.3, we learned how to store values in the keychain. In order to delete those
values, you will need to use the `SecItemDelete` function. This function takes only one
parameter: a dictionary of type `CFDictionaryRef`. The dictionary that you'll pass to this
method has to contain the following keys:

kSecClass
> The type of item that you want to delete. For instance, `kSecClassGenericPassword`.

kSecAttrService
> The service that this item is hooked to. When you stored the item, you chose the
> service for it, so you'll need to provide the same service here. For instance, in pre-
> vious examples, we set the value of this key to our app's bundle identifier. If that's
> what you did as well, simply provide your app's bundle identifier for the value of
> this key.

kSecAttrAccount
> The value of this key is the key that has to be deleted.

Assuming you have followed Recipe 8.3, the keychain now has a generic password
(`kSecClassGenericPassword`) with the service name (`kSecAttrService`) equal to our
app's bundle ID and the key (`kSecAttrAccount`) equal to *Full Name*. To delete this key,
here is what you'll have to do:

```
import UIKit
import Security

@UIApplicationMain
```

```
class AppDelegate: UIResponder, UIApplicationDelegate {

  var window: UIWindow?

  func application(application: UIApplication,
    didFinishLaunchingWithOptions
    launchOptions: [NSObject : AnyObject]?) -> Bool {

      let keyToSearchFor = "Full Name"
      let service = NSBundle.mainBundle().bundleIdentifier!

      let query = [
        kSecClass as NSString :
      kSecClassGenericPassword as NSString,

        kSecAttrService as NSString : service,
        kSecAttrAccount as NSString : keyToSearchFor,
        ] as NSDictionary


      var result: Unmanaged<AnyObject>? = nil
      let foundExisting = Int(SecItemCopyMatching(query, &result))

      if foundExisting == Int(errSecSuccess){

        let deleted = Int(SecItemDelete(query))
        if deleted == Int(errSecSuccess){
          println("Successfully deleted the item")
        } else {
          println("Failed to delete the item")
        }

      } else {
        println("Error happened with code: \(foundExisting)")
      }

    return true
  }

}
```

After you run this program, assuming that you've followed the instructions in Recipe 8.3, you should see the log on the console for a successful deletion. If not, you can always read the return value of the SecItemDelete function to determine what the issue was.

See Also

Recipe 8.3

8.7. Sharing Keychain Data Between Multiple Apps

Problem

You want two of your apps to be able to share keychain storage.

Solution

When storing your keychain data, specify the `kSecAttrAccessGroup` key in the dictionary that gets passed to the `SecItemAdd` function. The value of this key has to be the access group, which you can find in the Entitlements section of your provision profile, as explained in this chapter's Introduction.

Discussion

Multiple apps from the same developer portal can share a keychain area. To avoid complications, we are going to limit our thoughts to only two apps for now, but this same technique applies to any number of apps.

In order for two apps to be able to share a keychain area, the following criteria must be met:

1. Both apps must have been signed using a provision profile originated from the same iOS Developer Portal.

2. Both apps have to have the same Group ID in their provision profile. This is usually the Team ID as selected by Apple. I suggest that you *don't* change this group ID when you create your own provision profiles.

3. The first app that stores the value in the keychain must specify the `kSecAttrAccessGroup` attribute for the keychain item that is getting stored. This access group must be the same access group that is mentioned in your provision profile. Have a look at this chapter's Introduction to learn how to extract this value from your provision profiles.

4. The value stored in the keychain should have been stored with the `kSecAttrService` attribute set to a value that the two apps know about. This is usually the bundle identifier of the app that actually stored the value. If both apps are created by you, you know the bundle identifier of the app that stored the value. So you can read the value in your other app by providing the bundle identifier of the first app for the aforementioned key.

5. Both apps have to have a codesigning identity. This is a *plist* that contains the exact same contents from the Entitlements section of your provision profile. You then

have to set the path of this file in the Code Signing Entitlements of your build settings. We will talk about this in greater detail in a short while.

Even though your app is signed with provision profiles that have entitlements in them (please see this chapter's Introduction), you will still need to explicitly tell Xcode about your entitlements. The entitlements are nothing but a *plist* file with contents similar to these, which I took from the Entitlements that I showed you how to print in the Introduction.

Note the `keychain-access-groups` key. That key's value specifies the keychain group to which the current app has access: `F3FU372W5M.*`. You will have to find your own keychain access group in your Entitlements and use it in the example code in this recipe. We are going to write two apps. The first will write information to the keychain, referring to the keychain access group, and the second will read that information. The apps are going to have different bundle identifiers and are generally two completely separate apps, yet they will be able to share a keychain area.

 The *F3FU372W5M.** access group is my team ID's keychain access group. This value will certainly be different for you. Use the technique that you learned in the Introduction section of this chapter to extract the entitlements of your provision profiles.

I am going to use the following settings for the first iOS app. You should replace them with your own:

Bundle identifier
> `com.pixolity.ios.cookbook.SharingKeychainData.Writer`

Keychain access group
> `F3FU372W5M.*`

Provision profile
> A provision profile specifically created for the bundle ID of this app

And here are my settings for the second app, or the app that can read the values stored in the keychain by the first app:

Bundle identifier
> `com.pixolity.ios.cookbook.SharingKeychainData.Reader`

Keychain access group
> `F3FU372W5M.*`

Provision profile
> A provision profile specifically created for the bundle ID of this app, which differs from the provision profile that was created for the first app

The most important thing that differentiates the first app (the keychain storing app) from the second app (the keychain reading app) is the bundle identifiers. The first app will use its own bundle identifier to store a value in the keychain and the second app will use the first app's bundle identifier to read that same value back from the keychain. So let's write the code for the first app. This code is very similar to what we saw in Recipe 8.3. The only difference is that this new code will specify a keychain access group when storing the data to the keychain:

```swift
import UIKit
import Security

@UIApplicationMain
class AppDelegate: UIResponder, UIApplicationDelegate {

  var window: UIWindow?

  func application(application: UIApplication,
    didFinishLaunchingWithOptions
    launchOptions: [NSObject : AnyObject]?) -> Bool {

    let key = "Full Name";
    let service = NSBundle.mainBundle().bundleIdentifier!
    /* TODO: Place your own team ID here */
    let accessGroup = "F3FU372W5M.*"

    /* First delete the existing one if it exists. We don't have to do this
    but SecItemAdd will fail if an existing value is in the keychain. */
    let query = [
      kSecClass as NSString :
      kSecClassGenericPassword as NSString,

      kSecAttrService as NSString : service,
      kSecAttrAccessGroup as NSString : accessGroup,
      kSecAttrAccount as NSString : key
      ] as NSDictionary


    SecItemDelete(query)

    /* Then write the new value in the keychain */
    let value = "Steve Jobs"
    let valueData = value.dataUsingEncoding(NSUTF8StringEncoding,
      allowLossyConversion: false)

    let secItem = [
      kSecClass as NSString :
      kSecClassGenericPassword as NSString,

      kSecAttrService as NSString : service,
      kSecAttrAccount as NSString : key,
      kSecAttrAccessGroup as NSString : accessGroup,
```

```
      kSecValueData as NSString : valueData!,
      ] as NSDictionary

    var result: Unmanaged<AnyObject>? = nil
    let status = Int(SecItemAdd(secItem, &result))

    switch status{
    case Int(errSecSuccess):
      println("Successfully stored the value")
    case Int(errSecDuplicateItem):
      println("This item is already saved. Cannot duplicate it")
    default:
      println("An error occurred with code \(status)")
    }

    return true
  }

}
```

This starts by querying the keychain to find an existing item with a given key, service name, and keychain access group. If one exists, it deletes it from the keychain. We are doing this just to ensure that later we can add the new value successfully. The SecIte mAdd fails if you attempt to overwrite an existing value. So we delete the existing value (if it exists) and write a new one. You could just as well attempt to find an existing value, update it if it exists, and write a new one if it doesn't exist. The latter approach is more complicated and not necessary for our demonstration.

Before you can run this app, though, you need to set up your code signing entitlements. To set the code signing entitlements of you app, follow these steps:

1. Select your project file in Xcode. Then, under the Capabilities section, turn the switch for the Keychain Sharing to on.

2. Look in your file list in Xcode for your project. You will notice that Xcode has added a new entitlements file to it automatically. Click on this file and find the first item under the Keychain Access Groups item. Change the value of this item to *TEAM ID.**, where *TEAMID* is your own team ID.

Now that we have the writing app done, we can focus on the iOS app that can read the data. These two are completely separate signed apps, each with its own provision profile:

```
import UIKit

@UIApplicationMain
class AppDelegate: UIResponder, UIApplicationDelegate {

  var window: UIWindow?

  func application(application: UIApplication,
```

```
didFinishLaunchingWithOptions
launchOptions: [NSObject : AnyObject]?) -> Bool {

  let key = "Full Name"

  /* This is the bundle ID of the app that wrote the data to the keychain.
  This is NOT this app's bundle ID */
  let service = "com.pixolity.ios.cookbook.app"

  let accessGroup = "F3FU372W5M.*"

  let query = [
    kSecClass as NSString :
    kSecClassGenericPassword as NSString,

    kSecAttrService as NSString : service,
    kSecAttrAccessGroup as NSString : accessGroup,
    kSecAttrAccount as NSString : key,
    kSecReturnData as NSString : kCFBooleanTrue,
    ] as NSDictionary


  var returnedData: Unmanaged<AnyObject>? = nil
  let results = Int(SecItemCopyMatching(query, &returnedData))

  if results == Int(errSecSuccess){

    let data = returnedData!.takeRetainedValue() as NSData

    let value = NSString(data: data, encoding: NSUTF8StringEncoding)

    println("Value = \(value)")

  } else {
    println("Error happened with code: \(results)")
  }

  return true
}


}
```

Getting used to how the keychain works takes a while, but don't worry if things don't
work right out the box. Simply read the instructions given in this chapter, especially this
chapter's Introduction, to get a better understanding of the keychain access group and
how that relates to your app's entitlements.

See Also

Recipe 8.0, "Introduction"; Recipe 8.3

8.8. Writing to and Reading Keychain Data from iCloud

Problem

You want to store data in the keychain and have that data stored in the user's iCloud keychain so that it will be available on all her devices.

Solution

When adding your item to the keychain using the `SecItemAdd` function, add the `kSecAttrSynchronizable` key to the dictionary that you pass to that function. For the value of this key, pass `kCFBooleanTrue`.

Discussion

When items are stored in the keychain with their `kSecAttrSynchronizable` key set to `kCFBooleanTrue`, they will be stored in the user's iCloud keychain. This means that the items will be available on all the user's devices as long as she is logged into them using her iCloud account. If you want to simply read a value that you know is synchronized to the user's iCloud keychain, you need to specify the aforementioned key and the `kCFBooleanTrue` for this key as well, so that iOS will retrieve that value from the cloud if it hasn't already done so.

The example that we are going to see here is 99% similar to the example code that we saw in Recipe 8.7. The difference is that, when we store or try to read from the keychain, we specify the `kSecAttrSynchronizable` in our dictionary and set the value of this key to `kCFBooleanTrue`. So let's have a look at how we can store the value in the keychain first:

```
import UIKit
import Security

@UIApplicationMain
class AppDelegate: UIResponder, UIApplicationDelegate {

  var window: UIWindow?

  func application(application: UIApplication,
    didFinishLaunchingWithOptions
    launchOptions: [NSObject : AnyObject]?) -> Bool {

      let key = "Full Name"
      let accessGroup = "F3FU372W5M.*"
      let value = "Steve Jobs"
      let valueData = value.dataUsingEncoding(NSUTF8StringEncoding,
        allowLossyConversion: false)

      let service = NSBundle.mainBundle().bundleIdentifier!
```

```
/* First delete the existing one if one exists. We don't have to do this,
but SecItemAdd will fail if an existing value is in the keychain. */
let query = [
  kSecClass as NSString :
  kSecClassGenericPassword as NSString,

  kSecAttrService as NSString : service,
  kSecAttrAccessGroup as NSString : accessGroup,
  kSecAttrAccount as NSString : key,
  kSecAttrSynchronizable as NSString : kCFBooleanTrue
  ] as NSDictionary

SecItemDelete(query)

let secItem = [
  kSecClass as NSString :
  kSecClassGenericPassword as NSString,

  kSecAttrService as NSString : service,
  kSecAttrAccessGroup as NSString : accessGroup,
  kSecAttrAccount as NSString : key,
  kSecValueData as NSString : valueData!,
  kSecAttrSynchronizable as NSString : kCFBooleanTrue
  ] as NSDictionary

var result: Unmanaged<AnyObject>? = nil
let status = Int(SecItemAdd(secItem, &result))

switch status{
case Int(errSecSuccess):
  println("Successfully stored the value")
case Int(errSecDuplicateItem):
  println("This item is already saved. Cannot duplicate it")
default:
  println("An error occurred with code \(status)")
}

return true
  }

}
```

 Please read the notes in Recipe 8.7. You should now know that the access group that has been provided in all these examples will be different from developer to developer. This is usually the team ID that Apple's iOS Developer Portal will generate for each developer, which is a random ID for that development team. You will need to change this for your app to make sure it matches *your* team ID.

There are a few things that you have to note about working with the iCloud keychain:

- Only passwords can be stored.
- The iCloud keychain is ubiquitous, meaning that it appears on multiple devices belonging to the same iCloud user. If you write to one iCloud keychain, the same item will be synchronized to all of her devices. Similarly, if you delete an item, it will be deleted from all of her devices, so take extra caution.

It's worth mentioning that all the other techniques that you learned in this chapter (such as updating an existing keychain item; see Recipe 8.5) work with the iCloud keychain as well.

See Also

Recipe 8.0, "Introduction";Recipe 8.7

8.9. Storing Files Securely in the App Sandbox

Problem

You want iOS to protect the files in your app sandbox from being read without permission, perhaps by iOS file explorers available on the Internet.

Solution

Follow these steps:

1. Follow the steps in this chapter's Introduction to create a provision profile that is linked to an App ID that has Data Protection enabled (see Figure 8-7).

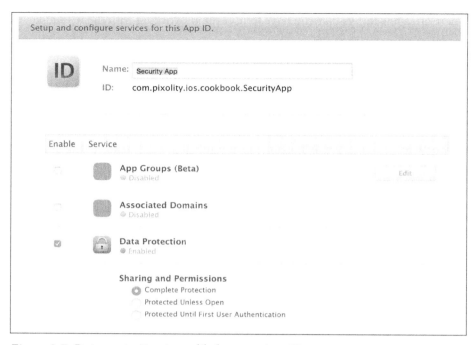

Figure 8-7. Data protection is enabled on our App ID

2. Sign your app with the provision profile.

3. Set the Code Signing Entitlements of your app by following the instructions given in Recipe 8.7.

4. Use the `createFileAtPath:contents:attributes:` method of an instance of `NSFileManager` to store your file. For the `attributes` property, pass a dictionary that contains the `NSFileProtectionKey` key. The value of this key can be one of the following:

`NSFileProtectionNone`

   This dictates that there should be no file protection on the stored file. A file that is stored using this protection is available to the app that writes it to disk and to any free or commercially accessible file explorer apps on the Internet that can expose the filesystem of an iOS device, even if the user's device is locked with a passcode. If you specify this key, you can read from and write to your file, even if the user's device is locked.

`NSFileProtectionComplete`

   This is the strongest protection that you can give to your files. By doing so, your app can read from and write to this file as long as the device is unlocked. As soon as the device is locked, you won't be able to read from or write to the file.

When you use this type of protection, free or commercial file system explorers cannot read the contents of your files, even if the user's device is unlocked.

NSFileProtectionCompleteUnlessOpen

Very similar to NSFileProtectionComplete. The only difference is that, as its name suggests, you can access the file if you have already opened it, even if the user subsequently locks the device. So after you first open the file, you are ensured access to it as long as your app doesn't exit.

NSFileProtectionCompleteUntilFirstUserAuthentication

This means that your app can read from and write to the file as soon as the user unlocks her device for the first time. After that, you can continue accessing the file, even if the user subsequently locks her device again.

Here is an example:

```
import UIKit

@UIApplicationMain
class AppDelegate: UIResponder, UIApplicationDelegate {

  var window: UIWindow?

  var filePath: String?{

    let fileManager = NSFileManager()

    var error:NSError?

    let documentFolderUrl = fileManager.URLForDirectory(.DocumentDirectory,
      inDomain: .UserDomainMask,
      appropriateForURL: nil,
      create: true,
      error: &error)

    if error == nil && documentFolderUrl != nil{

      let fileName = "MyFile.txt"
      let filePath =
      documentFolderUrl!.path!.stringByAppendingPathComponent(fileName)

      return filePath
    }

    return nil

  }

  func application(application: UIApplication,
    didFinishLaunchingWithOptions
    launchOptions: [NSObject : AnyObject]?) -> Bool {
```

```
/*
Prerequisites:

1) Sign with a valid provision profile.
2) Your profile has to have complete-file-protection enabled.
3) Add Code Signing Entitlements to your project.
*/

let fileManager = NSFileManager()

if let path = filePath{

  let dataToWrite = "Hello, World".dataUsingEncoding(
    NSUTF8StringEncoding,
    allowLossyConversion: false)

  let fileAttributes = [
    NSFileProtectionKey : NSFileProtectionComplete
  ]

  let wrote = fileManager.createFileAtPath(path,
    contents: dataToWrite,
    attributes: fileAttributes)

  if wrote{
    println("Successfully and securely stored the file")
  } else {
    println("Failed to write the file")
  }

}

    return true
  }

}
```

Discussion

Your users trust your apps. That means that if you ask them for information such as their first name and last name, they expect you to store those values in a secure place and protect them from being retrieved by a hacker or somebody who has temporary access to their iOS devices.

Let's imagine that you are working on a photo-editing application where the user can hook up her camera to her iOS device, import her photos into your app, and use your app to edit, save, and share those photos. You can do what a lot of app developers do, which is import those photos into the Documents folder of your app, ready for editing. The issue with this approach is that any freely available iOS device explorer on the

Internet can read the contents of the Documents folder on any app, even if the device is locked. In order to protect the user's data, you are expected to enable file protection on the files that you store in your app's sandbox. The file protection goes hand in hand with the user's device security, specifically her device's passcode/password. If she set a passcode for her device, even if it is a simple passcode, and she locks her device, the files that have been stored in your app sandbox with the `NSFileProtectionComplete` key will not be accessible to outsiders, even those who may try to read the file using an iOS device explorer.

So, when shipping your application, or even while developing it, set up your development and distribution provision profiles with file protection enabled and ensure that the files that you store on disk are protected. Obviously, you don't want to protect *every* file if there is no need to. Just find out which files need to be protected from prying eyes, apply your file protections on those files, and leave the rest of the files unprotected on disk.

See Also

Recipe 8.0, "Introduction"; Recipe 8.7

8.10. Securing Your User Interface

Problem

You want to ensure that your UI conforms to some of the most common security guidelines in iOS.

Solution

Follow these guidelines:

- Ensure that all passwords and secure fields are entered, by the user, into instances of `UITextField` with their `secureTextEntry` properties set to `true`.
- If the user is on a screen that contains personal information, such as the user's credit card number or home address, set the `hidden` property of your app's main window to `true` in the `applicationWillResignActive:` method of your app delegate, and set the same property to `false` (to show the window) in the `applicationDidBecomeActive:` app delegate method. This will ensure that the screenshot that iOS takes of your app's UI when going to the background will not contain any of your window's contents in it. This method is recommended by Apple.
- Ensure that you validate the user's input in your text fields/views before sending them to a server.

- Using the mechanisms that you've learned in this chapter, secure the user's entry if you are storing it in files on disk or in the keychain.

- On screens where you accept a password or a numerical code for authentication, once the view controller is no longer on the screen, clear those password/code fields because the user won't need them anymore. If you are not relinquishing ownership of those view controllers, their contents will stay in the memory. This includes the secure text field entries on those view controllers. It's best to dispose of memory that contains sensitive information as soon as you are done with that data.

Discussion

The only item in the list that requires more explanation is the second. When the user is looking at an app on the screen of her iOS device and sends the app to the background by pressing the Home screen, iOS puts the app into the inactive state and sends it to the background. When the app is sent to the background, iOS takes a screenshot of the app's user interface as it appears on the screen and saves that file in the *Library/Caches/Snap shots/* folder inside your app's sandbox. When the user brings the app back to the foreground, iOS momentarily displays that screenshot to the user until the app comes back alive and takes control of the screen. This makes the transition from background to foreground look very smooth. Even though this adds value from the UX point of view, it raises a security concern that if the screen that was in the screenshot contained sensitive information, that information will be present in the screenshot and subsequently saved on disk. We cannot really disable this functionality in iOS, but we can neutralize its negative security aspects for our app. The way to do this, and the way Apple recommends we do it, is to cover our app's main window with another view or hide our app's window by setting its `hidden` property to `true` when our app becomes inactive and setting this property back to `false` (to make the window visible again) when our app becomes active.

 A common mistake made by iOS developers trying to meet this security requirement is to attempt to set the value of the `hidden` property of the `keyWindow` of their application to `true` or `false`. Even though the `keyWindow` of your application instance will be a valid window when your app is becoming inactive, it will be `nil` (or pointing to nothing) when your app becomes active. Therefore, to avoid this mistake, simply use the `window` property of your app delegate to hide or show the window.

The other security concern raised was the lingering personal data in our view controllers. Suppose you have a login view controller where the user can enter her username and password. When the Login button is tapped (for instance), you send the user's credentials to a server using HTTPS network connections, and when the user is authenticated, you push another view controller on the screen. The problem with this approach is that the username and password that the user entered on the previous screen are still in memory because the view controller is still in memory (remember, it is in the stack of view controllers of your navigation controller).

The way to solve this and increase the security of your UI is to set the `text` property of your (secure) text fields to `nil` just as you are pushing the second view controller on the screen. Alternatively, override the `viewWillDisappear:` instance method of your login view controller and set the text fields' `text` property to `nil` right there. However, you should be careful with this approach because the aforementioned instance method of your view controller gets called *anytime* your view controller disappears—such as when the user switches from the tab on which your view controller sits into another tab, and then comes back to your tab. That means your view controller disappeared and then reappeared. So if you clear your text fields in this case, when the user switches from the second tab back to the tab that contains your view controller, all the values that she may have entered into your text fields disappear and she has to type them all over again. You need to develop according to your business requirements, and there is no single right way of handling this situation.

See Also

Recipe 8.3; Recipe 8.9

CHAPTER 9

Core Location, iBeacon, and Maps

9.0. Introduction

The Core Location and Map Kit frameworks can be used to create location-aware and map-based applications. The Core Location framework uses the device's internal hardware to determine the current location of the device. The Map Kit framework enables your application to display maps to your users, put custom annotations on the maps, and so on. The availability of location services purely from a programming perspective depends on the availability of hardware on the device; if the hardware is there, it must be enabled and switched on for the Map Kit and Core Location frameworks to work. An iOS device with GPS services can use 2G, EDGE, 3G, 4G, and other technologies to determine the user's location. Presently, almost all iOS devices support location services, but it is good programming practice to check the availability of location services before starting to use them, as we cannot predict whether in the future Apple will release a device with all hardware required to support location services.

In order to start using Core Location and Map Kit, all you have to do is to import these frameworks into your code like so:

```
import CoreLocation
import MapKit
```

9.1. Detecting Which Floor the User Is on in a Building

Problem

You want your application to be able to detect not only the user's location, but also which floor they are on if they are inside a large and densely inhabited structure, such as the Empire State Building.

Solution

Use an instance of `CLLocationManager` just as we saw in Recipe 9.3, and then implement the `locationManager:didUpdateLocations:` method of your location manager delegate. This method will give you an array of location objects of type `CLLocation`, each of which has a property called `floor` of type `CLFloor`. Depending on the user's location in the world and which building she is located in, this property may or may not be set by core location. If this property is set, you can get its value and then use the `level` property of the floor to access the logical representation of the level inside the building where the user is. A level value of 0 represents the ground floor. Anything over that represents floors 1 and higher, whereas anything below that (minus levels) represents basements or floors below the ground floor.

```
func locationManager(manager: CLLocationManager!,
  didUpdateLocations locations: [AnyObject]!) {

    println("Updated locations... \(__FUNCTION__)")

    if locations.count > 0{
      let location = (locations as [CLLocation])[0]
      println("Location found = \(location)")
      if let theFloor = location.floor{
        println("The floor information is = \(theFloor)")
      } else {
        println("No floor information is available")
      }
    }

}
```

Discussion

Apple is adding detailed information, such as the floor number where the user is, to the world's most popular buildings. The list of the buildings where this data will be available has not been provided by Apple, but we can expect that this information will be added to some of the most important buildings, and that Apple will probably—and not surprisingly—start with locations in the United States of America.

Please ensure that you program your application so that it can work whether or not floor information is available as part of the `CLLocation` values that you will receive from your location manager. There will certainly be times where floor information will not be available to your location manager and your application has to be able to handle that scenario.

See Also

Recipe 9.3

9.2. Defining and Processing iBeacons

Problem

You want to be able to define iBeacons, find them, and communicate with them. An iBeacon can be any device with any operating system that has access to Bluetooth Low Energy (BLE).

Solution

 For this recipe to really make sense, we need to run our app on two devices, both of which have access to (BLE).

First, use the `CBPeripheralManager` class to ensure that Bluetooth is turned on, both on the source and on the destination device. The source device is going to act as your beacon, while the destination device is going to be the device that finds the source device and communicates with it.

Then you have to create an instance of the `CLBeaconRegion` class that defines the region in which your beacon will work. This region will require values such as a unique identifier, a major and minor value that identifies your beacon (very similar to a software version with major and minor values), and an identifier for your beacon. The identifier is a UUID for which you can simply use your app bundle ID, or register another UUID if you prefer.

Then call the `peripheralDataWithMeasuredPower:` method on your region object to determine the data that you can use to advertise our beacon. This data will then be picked up by the destination device when it starts looking for iBeacons in its range. After you have this data (which will be structured as a dictionary), use the `startAdvertising:` method of your peripheral manager of type `CBPeripheralManager` to start advertising your beacon.

On your destination device, create beacon regions of type `CLBeaconRegion` using the identifiers that your source beacons have, and then start monitoring them using the `startRangingBeaconsInRegion:` of your core location manager of type `CLLocationManager`.

Discussion

I know that what you have heard about iBeacons may sound very fancy and mysterious, but there really isn't anything magical about iBeacons that should scare you from touching one or exploring them. A beacon is simply a device that can be installed by a person, anywhere, as long as it supports BLE. When this device is powered on, it will broadcast information about itself to devices around it.

Let's have a look at a real-life example. Say that you create an iBeacon in your kitchen using an iPhone device. All your other iOS devices will then detect this beacon and connect to it while you are at home. You can program your app to pop up a window to tell you to "Remember to take your mass transit card with you" when you exit the region of the iBeacon in your kitchen, so that the message appears as leave home. You can also shop around for very small iBeacon devices, program them, and attach them to your pets so when they go too far from you, you'll get notified on your phone. Isn't that cool?!

For the purpose of this recipe, I created two projects in Xcode: *Defining and Process ing iBeacons - Source* and *Defining and Processing iBeacons - Destination*. The source project will act as the beacon, and the destination project will look for the source.

In the first project, we will create our peripheral manager and then start advertising our beacon. So let's begin by defining all the variables and constants that we need to finish this part of the puzzle:

```
import UIKit
import CoreLocation
import CoreBluetooth

class ViewController: UIViewController, CBPeripheralManagerDelegate {

  var peripheralManager : CBPeripheralManager?

  /* A newly-generated UUID for our beacon */
  let uuid = NSUUID()

  /* The identifier of our beacon is the identifier of our bundle here */
  let identifier = NSBundle.mainBundle().bundleIdentifier!

  /* Made up major and minor versions of our beacon region */
  let major: CLBeaconMajorValue = 1
  let minor: CLBeaconMinorValue = 0

  <# rest of the code goes here #>
}
```

Now when our view appears to the user, we will create our peripheral manager so that we can start finding out the state of the Bluetooth service on the device:

```
override func viewDidAppear(animated: Bool) {
  super.viewDidAppear(animated)

  let queue = dispatch_get_global_queue(DISPATCH_QUEUE_PRIORITY_DEFAULT, 0)
  peripheralManager = CBPeripheralManager(delegate: self, queue: queue)
```

```
    if let manager = peripheralManager{
      manager.delegate = self
    }

  }
```

You can see that we are setting the delegate of our peripheral manager to our view controller. The delegate object receives the `peripheralManagerDidUpdateState:` method on itself when the peripheral manager's state has changed. This state can be powered off, powered on, authorized, and set to some other values that we will see soon. If Bluetooth is not powered on, we display a dialog to the user asking them to turn Bluetooth on.

If Bluetooth is available, we start advertising our beacon. The way to do that is to create an instance of the `CLBeaconRegion` class. We initialize this class using its `initWithProx imityUUID:major:minor:identifier:` method. This method accepts a UUID of type `NSUUID`, which is the unique identifier of our iBeacon. In our example, every time our view controller is instantiated, we are creating a new unique identifier that we can pass to our beacon region. The other parameters to this method are the major and the minor values of the beacon service that we are going to advertise. Remember that these are just numbers that have to make sense to you and your beacons. For instance, in a two-floor house, you may decide that the major value of your beacons is 0 and the minor value is 0 for the ground floor and 1 for the first floor. This is completely up to you.

Last but not least, you have to pass an identifier to your beacon's constructor. This identifier can be your bundle identifier. This is, again, really dependent on you and how you would like to set it up. I chose to use the bundle identifier to initialize the beacon.

The `startAdvertising:` method of our peripheral manager accepts an optional dictionary that can be set up to define our beacon a bit better. Here are some of the keys and values that you can place in this dictionary:

CBAdvertisementDataLocalNameKey
  This is the name of the beacon you are creating.

CBAdvertisementDataManufacturerDataKey
  The value of this key is an instance of `NSData` that represents the manufacturer of the beacon. You can place any data in here.

CBAdvertisementDataServiceUUIDsKey
  This is the UUID of your beacon, of type `CBUUID`. You can create a `CBUUID` out of an `NSUUID` using the `UUIDWithNSUUID:` type method of the `CBUUID` class.

```
  func peripheralManagerDidUpdateState(peripheral: CBPeripheralManager!){

    peripheral.stopAdvertising()

    print("The peripheral state is ")
    switch peripheral.state{
```

```
      case .PoweredOff:
        println("Powered off")
      case .PoweredOn:
        println("Powered on")
      case .Resetting:
        println("Resetting")
      case .Unauthorized:
        println("Unauthorized")
      case .Unknown:
        println("Unknown")
      case .Unsupported:
        println("Unsupported")
      }

      /* Make sure Bluetooth is powered on */
      if peripheral.state != .PoweredOn{

        let controller = UIAlertController(title: "Bluetooth",
          message: "Please turn Bluetooth on",
          preferredStyle: .Alert)

        controller.addAction(UIAlertAction(title: "OK",
          style: .Default,
          handler: nil))

        presentViewController(controller, animated: true, completion: nil)

      } else {

        let region = CLBeaconRegion(proximityUUID: uuid,
          major: major,
          minor: minor,
          identifier: identifier)

        let manufacturerData = identifier.dataUsingEncoding(
          NSUTF8StringEncoding,
          allowLossyConversion: false)

        let theUUid = CBUUID(NSUUID: uuid)

        let dataToBeAdvertised:[String: AnyObject!] = [
          CBAdvertisementDataLocalNameKey : "Sample peripheral",
          CBAdvertisementDataManufacturerDataKey : manufacturerData,
          CBAdvertisementDataServiceUUIDsKey : [theUUid],
          ]

        peripheral.startAdvertising(dataToBeAdvertised)

      }

  }
```

We will also implement the `peripheralManagerDidStartAdvertising:error:` method of our peripheral manager delegate to be notified of when advertisement of our beacon succeeds or fails:

```
func peripheralManagerDidStartAdvertising(peripheral: CBPeripheralManager!,
  error: NSError!){

    if error == nil{
      println("Successfully started advertising our beacon data")

      let message = "Successfully set up your beacon. " +
      "The unique identifier of our service is: \(uuid.UUIDString)"

      let controller = UIAlertController(title: "iBeacon",
        message: message,
        preferredStyle: .Alert)

      controller.addAction(UIAlertAction(title: "OK",
        style: .Default,
        handler: nil))

      presentViewController(controller, animated: true, completion: nil)

    } else {
      println("Failed to advertise our beacon. Error = \(error)")
    }

}
```

Now when you run the source application to set up your beacon, if Bluetooth is enabled and you are able to set up the beacon, you will see an alert on the screen telling you about the successful start. You will also get to see your beacon's UUID, which you will use in the destination application to discover the source beacon.

First, we import all the necessary frameworks and define our required values:

```
import UIKit
import CoreBluetooth
import CoreLocation

class ViewController: UIViewController, CLLocationManagerDelegate {
  var locationManager: CLLocationManager!

  /* Place your beacon UUID here. This is the UUID of the source
  application that we have already written. I ran that app
  on a device and copied and pasted the UUID here in the destination
  application */
  let uuid = NSUUID(UUIDString: "1FBF369D-6E55-4F3C-A4DA-CDE6155920A1")
  /* This is the identifier of the beacon that we just wrote. The identifier
  of the beacon was chosen to be the same as the bundle id of
  that app. */
  let identifier = "com.pixolity.ios.Defining-and-Processing-iBeacons---Source"
```

```
<# rest of the code goes here #>

}
```

Then we instantiate our location manager and start monitoring the beacon that we created previously in the source application:

```
init(coder aDecoder: NSCoder!) {
  locationManager = CLLocationManager()
  super.init(coder: aDecoder)
  locationManager.delegate = self
}

override func viewDidAppear(animated: Bool) {
  super.viewDidAppear(animated)

  let region = CLBeaconRegion(proximityUUID: uuid, identifier: identifier)
  locationManager.startRangingBeaconsInRegion(region)

}
```

Now that we have started looking for a specific beacon and have chosen our view controller to become the delegate of the location manager we created, we will create a locationManager:didRangeBeacons:inRegion: method on our view controller to take action whenever a beacon is found in range. Our implementation of this delegate method is rather simple:

```
/* We will know when we have made contact with a beacon here */
func locationManager(manager: CLLocationManager!,
  didRangeBeacons beacons: [AnyObject]!,
  inRegion region: CLBeaconRegion!){

    print("Found a beacon with the proximity of = ")

    /* How close are we to the beacon? */
    for beacon in beacons as [CLBeacon]{
      switch beacon.proximity{
      case .Far:
        println("Far")
      case .Immediate:
        println("Immediate")
      case .Near:
        println("Near")
      default:
        println("Unknown")
      }
    }

}
```

When we have contact with a beacon and know it is in range, we can exit that range whenever we want. Our core location manager informs us that we are exiting a region using the `locationManager:didExitRegion:` delegate method, which we implement quite simply like so:

```
/* This lets us know when we are exiting the region of the beacon */
func locationManager(manager: CLLocationManager!,
  didExitRegion region: CLRegion!){

    println("You are exiting the region of a beacon " +
      "with an identifier of \(region.identifier)")

}
```

Now it is your turn to run both the source and the destination apps on two BLE-enabled devices and see the results for yourself. You can be creative with iBeacon to create some really amazing tools and projects. One example that I am thinking of building using iBeacon is to purchase a small iBeacon-enabled device—an Arduino for example—and program it so I can attach it to my dog's collar and control how far she gets from me off-leash when we are out on a walk. Then I can use the command "come" if I understand that the proximity of her beacon is "far."

9.3. Pinpointing the Location of a Device

Problem

You want to find the latitude and longitude of a device.

Solution

Use the `CLLocationManager` class.

Discussion

The Core Location framework in the SDK provides functionality for programmers to detect the current spatial location of an iOS device. Because the user is allowed to disable location services using Settings in iOS, it is best to first determine whether location services are enabled on the device before instantiating an object of type `CLLocation Manager`.

 The delegate object of an instance of `CLLocationManager` must conform to the `CLLocationManagerDelegate` protocol.

When an application wants to use location services to determine the user's location, it must first ask for the user's authorization. If the user doesn't want to allow the app, she is free to deny access to location services. We must program our apps to be flexible enough to deal with the fact that users are in charge and they are the ones that decide how an application can use a service such as location services.

Before you can even start to use location services, you need to find out whether they are available on the target device. You can do so using the locationServicesEnabled type method of the CLLocationManager class. This type method returns a Boolean value indicating whether location services are enabled on the target device. If location services are enabled, you should next find out whether you are authorized to use these services. Do that by using the authorizationStatus type method of the CLLocationManager class. This type method returns a value of type CLAuthorizationStatus that allows you to determine whether you are authorized to access location services. Various values can come back from this method:

Authorized
This status means that your app has unlimited access to location services whenever it is run.

AuthorizedWhenInUse
This indicates that your app has access to location services only when running right now. The permissions will be reset when your app is closed and opened again. Then you will have to ask for permission again.

Denied
This means that the user has denied access from your app to location services.

NotDetermined
This value indicates that you have not yet asked the user for permission to access location services and you must do so before the authorization status changes.

Restricted
This value means that there are some parental controls or other restrictions on the device that have prevented your application from accessing location services.

When you are ready to ask the user for location services, use either the requestWhenI nUseAuthorization or the requestAlwaysAuthorization method of the CLLocation Manager class. The former method requests access to location services only during this run of your app. The latter method requests permission to use location services for your app permanently, until the user changes her settings on her device.

An instance of the CLLocationManager class can also set a delegate object that receives messages relevant to the location manager, such as when the authorization status of the location manager has been modified by the user. This delegate must confirm to the CLLocationManagerDelegate protocol. One of the really important methods that is specified in this protocol is the locationManager:didChangeAuthorizationStatus:

method. This method, as its name implies, gets called on the delegate as soon as the authorization status of your location manager is changed by the user. Here is a simple implementation of this method:

```swift
func locationManager(manager: CLLocationManager!,
  didChangeAuthorizationStatus status: CLAuthorizationStatus){

    print("The authorization status of location services is changed to: ")

    switch CLLocationManager.authorizationStatus(){
    case .Authorized:
      println("Authorized")
    case .AuthorizedWhenInUse:
      println("Authorized when in use")
    case .Denied:
      println("Denied")
    case .NotDetermined:
      println("Not determined")
    case .Restricted:
      println("Restricted")
    default:
        println("Unhandled")
    }

}
```

The other method in this protocol that you may want to implement is the `location Manager:didFailWithError:` method, which will get called whenever an error occurs on your location manager, such as a failure to retrieve the user's location. Here is our implementation of this method for now:

```swift
func locationManager(manager: CLLocationManager!,
  didFailWithError error: NSError!){
    println("Location manager failed with error = \(error)")
}
```

Another really handy method that you may want to implement in your delegate is the `locationManager:didUpdateToLocation:fromLocation:` method, which gets called on the delegate whenever the location manager object has received a location update for the user. You will get a handle to the old and the new location for the user in this method. Here is our implementation:

```swift
func locationManager(manager: CLLocationManager!,
  didUpdateToLocation newLocation: CLLocation!,
  fromLocation oldLocation: CLLocation!){

    println("Latitude = \(newLocation.coordinate.latitude)")
    println("Longitude = \(newLocation.coordinate.longitude)")

}
```

Whenever iOS asks the user to give or deny permission to access location services for an app, it reads the contents of the `NSLocationWhenInUseUsageDescription` key in your *info.plist* and display that string to the user as the reason why your application is requesting location services. For instance, I set the value of this key in my plist file to `Testing location services`. When the user is prompted for location services by iOS, she will see a dialog similar to that shown in Figure 9-1.

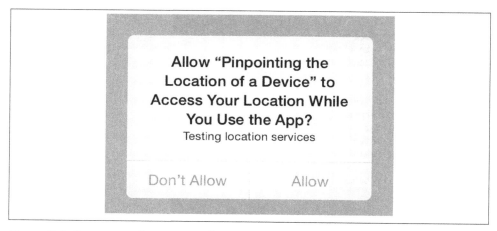

Figure 9-1. Our reason for accessing location services is displayed to the user

It is of utmost importance that you set the value of this key in your plist file. In fact, it is so important that if you do not do this, iOS will not display a permission dialog to the user at all and your app will never gain access to location services. So it is not just important, but necessary. Before we jump into asking the user for permission to access location services, I listened to the relevant protocols in our view controller and defined a property of type `CLLocationManager`, which I will use to check the user's location like so:

```
import UIKit
import CoreLocation
import MapKit

class ViewController: UIViewController, CLLocationManagerDelegate {

    var locationManager: CLLocationManager?

    <# rest of the code goes here #>
```

It's also handy to create a method that displays an alert view to the user with a specific title and message. We will use the following method to display an alert view to the user whenever there is a problem with the authorization status of location services on her device:

```
func displayAlertWithTitle(title: String, message: String){
  let controller = UIAlertController(title: title,
    message: message,
    preferredStyle: .Alert)

  controller.addAction(UIAlertAction(title: "OK",
    style: .Default,
    handler: nil))

  presentViewController(controller, animated: true, completion: nil)

}
```

And now on to the fun part. We are going to ask the user for permission to access location services:

```
func createLocationManager(#startImmediately: Bool){
  locationManager = CLLocationManager()
  if let manager = locationManager{
    println("Successfully created the location manager")
    manager.delegate = self
    if startImmediately{
      manager.startUpdatingLocation()
    }
  }
}

override func viewDidAppear(animated: Bool) {
  super.viewDidAppear(animated)

  /* Are location services available on this device? */
  if CLLocationManager.locationServicesEnabled(){

    /* Do we have authorization to access location services? */
    switch CLLocationManager.authorizationStatus(){
    case .Authorized:
      /* Yes, always. */
      createLocationManager(startImmediately: true)
    case .AuthorizedWhenInUse:
      /* Yes, only when our app is in use. */
      createLocationManager(startImmediately: true)
    case .Denied:
      /* No. */
      displayAlertWithTitle("Not Determined",
        message: "Location services are not allowed for this app")
    case .NotDetermined:
      /* We don't know yet; we have to ask */
      createLocationManager(startImmediately: false)
      if let manager = self.locationManager{
        manager.requestWhenInUseAuthorization()
      }
    case .Restricted:
      /* Restrictions have been applied; we have no access
```

```
        to location services. */
        displayAlertWithTitle("Restricted",
          message: "Location services are not allowed for this app")
    }


    } else {
      /* Location services are not enabled.
      Take appropriate action: for instance, prompt the
      user to enable the location services. */
      println("Location services are not enabled")
    }
  }
}
```

Go ahead and try this out for yourself. Just note that the reason I put our code in the viewDidAppear: method of our view controller instead of viewDidLoad is that under certain authorization statuses of the location services, we want to display an alert controller to the user. An alert controller cannot be presented to the user inside the view DidLoad method of our view controller because the host view controller of an alert controller has to have its view already presented to the user and our view controller's view will not yet be on the screen when the viewDidLoad method is being called. Our best bet is to place it under the viewDidAppear method for this example.

9.4. Displaying Pins on a Map View

Problem

You want to point out a specific location on a map to the user.

Solution

Use built-in map view annotations. Follow these steps:

1. Create a new class, subclassing NSObject, and call it MyAnnotation.
2. Make sure this class conforms to the MKAnnotation protocol.
3. Define a property for this class of type CLLocationCoordinate2D and name it coordinate. Make sure you set it as a readonly property because the coordinate property is defined as readonly in the MKAnnotation protocol.
4. Optionally, define two properties of type NSString, namely title and subtitle, which can carry the title and the subtitle information for your annotation view. Both of these properties are readonly as well.
5. Create an constructor method for your class that accepts a parameter of type CLLo cationCoordinate2D. In this method, assign the passed location parameter to the property that we defined in step 3. Because this property is readonly, it cannot be

assigned by code outside the scope of this class. Therefore, the constructor of this class acts as a bridge here and allows us to indirectly assign a value to this property. We will do the same thing for the `title` and `subtitle` properties.

6. Instantiate the `MyAnnotation` class and add it to your map using the `addAnnotation:` method of the `MKMapView` class.

Discussion

As explained in this recipe's Solution, we must create an object that conforms to the `MKAnnotation` protocol and later instantiate this object and pass it to the map to be displayed. We declare the header of this object like so:

```
import UIKit
import MapKit

class MyAnnotation: NSObject, MKAnnotation {
  var coordinate: CLLocationCoordinate2D = CLLocationCoordinate2DMake(0, 0)
  var title: String!
  var subtitle: String!

  init(coordinate: CLLocationCoordinate2D, title: String, subtitle: String){
    self.coordinate = coordinate
    self.title = title
    self.subtitle = subtitle
    super.init()
  }

}
```

Later, we will instantiate this class and add it to our map, for instance, in our view controller that creates and displays a map view:

```
import UIKit
import MapKit

class ViewController: UIViewController, MKMapViewDelegate {
  var mapView: MKMapView!

  required init(coder aDecoder: NSCoder) {
    super.init(coder: aDecoder)
    mapView = MKMapView()
  }

  /* We have a pin on the map; now zoom into it and make that pin
  the center of the map */
  func setCenterOfMapToLocation(location: CLLocationCoordinate2D){
    let span = MKCoordinateSpan(latitudeDelta: 0.01, longitudeDelta: 0.01)
    let region = MKCoordinateRegion(center: location, span: span)
    mapView.setRegion(region, animated: true)
  }
```

```
func addPinToMapView(){

  /* This is just a sample location */
  let location = CLLocationCoordinate2D(latitude: 58.592737,
    longitude: 16.185898)

  /* Create the annotation using the location */
  let annotation = MyAnnotation(coordinate: location,
    title: "My Title",
    subtitle: "My Sub Title")

  /* And eventually add it to the map */
  mapView.addAnnotation(annotation)

  /* And now center the map around the point */
  setCenterOfMapToLocation(location)

}

/* Set up the map and add it to our view */
override func viewDidLoad() {
  super.viewDidLoad()
  mapView.mapType = .Standard
  mapView.frame = view.frame
  mapView.delegate = self
  view.addSubview(mapView)
}

/* Add the pin to the map and center the map around the pin */
override func viewDidAppear(animated: Bool) {
  super.viewDidAppear(animated)
  addPinToMapView()
}

}
```

Figure 9-2 depicts the output of the program when run in the simulator.

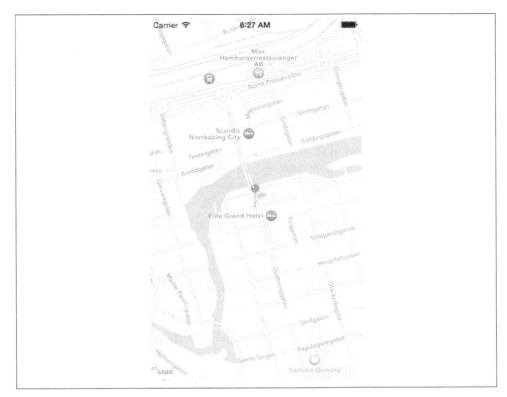

Figure 9-2. A built-in pin dropped on a map

9.5. Displaying Custom Pins on a Map View

Problem

Instead of the default iOS SDK pins, you would like to display your own images as pins on a map view.

Solution

Load an arbitrary image into an instance of the `UIImage` class and assign it to the `image` property of the `MKAnnotationView` instance that you return to your map view as a pin.

Annotation views on a map view are similar to table view cells in that they have to be instantiated and dequeued from a reusable queue whenever possible. You can of course subclass your own annotation views from the `MKAnnotationView` class. Once you have subclassed this class, you can add your own properties and methods to your annotation view. The important thing for a map view is that you return an instance of the afore-mentioned class, either directly or as a subclass of the method.

You can dequeue an annotation view using the dequeueReusableAnnotationViewWithIdentifier: of the map view. This method returns either an instance of MKPinAnnotationView or nil. If nil is returned, that's your chance to go and instantiate a new annotation view and return it to the map view.

Whenever you add a new annotation to a map view, as we saw in Recipe 9.4, you can also work through delegation to provide an annotation view for the pin. The delegate of the map view gets called on its mapView:viewForAnnotation: method and is given a chance to provide a custom annotation view to be displayed on the map view. If you do not implement this method, the map view displays a system annotation view.

We are going to build on top of what we did in Recipe 9.4 by creating our own annotation class called MyAnnotation. But this time we are also going to allow the annotation class to carry a pin color, which we will use as a custom enumeration. The pin color can be green, red, purple, or blue. The first three of these colors are already defined by iOS in MKPinAnnotationColor, but the blue color is something that we need to add to the mix. For every annotation that has a pin color of blue, we will create a new annotation view and set its image to a custom blue annotation image. If the color of the annotation is green, red, or purple, we will just change the value of the pinColor property of the MKPinAnnotationView instances that we are going to plot on the map view. So let's begin by implementing our MyAnnotation class:

```
import UIKit
import MapKit

/* This allows us to check for equality between two items
of type PinColor */
func == (left: PinColor, right: PinColor) -> Bool{
  return left.rawValue == right.rawValue
}

/* The various pin colors that our annotation can have */
enum PinColor : String{
  case Blue = "Blue"
  case Red = "Red"
  case Green = "Green"
  case Purple = "Purple"

  /* We convert our pin color to the system pin color */
  func toPinColor() -> MKPinAnnotationColor{
    switch self{
    case .Red:
      return .Red
    case .Green:
      return .Green
    case .Purple:
```

```
      return .Purple
    default:
      /* For the blue pin, this returns .Red but we need
      to return *a* value in this function. For this case, we
      ignore the return value */
      return .Red
    }
  }
}

class MyAnnotation: NSObject, MKAnnotation {
  var coordinate: CLLocationCoordinate2D = CLLocationCoordinate2DMake(0, 0)
  var title: String!
  var subtitle: String!
  var pinColor: PinColor!

  init(coordinate: CLLocationCoordinate2D,
    title: String,
    subtitle: String,
    pinColor: PinColor){
      self.coordinate = coordinate
      self.title = title
      self.subtitle = subtitle
      self.pinColor = pinColor
      super.init()
  }

  convenience init(coordinate: CLLocationCoordinate2D,
    title: String,
    subtitle: String){
      self.init(coordinate: coordinate,
        title: title,
        subtitle: subtitle,
        pinColor: .Blue)
  }

}
```

After we are done with this annotation class, we are going to focus our attention on our view controller code. We will build on top of what we did in the Recipe 9.4 recipe, expanding the addPinToMapView method to create four different pins of different colors. And then we will add all of them to the map view like so:

```
func addPinToMapView(){

  /* These are just sample locations */
  let purpleLocation = CLLocationCoordinate2D(latitude: 58.592737,
    longitude: 16.185898)

  let blueLocation = CLLocationCoordinate2D(latitude: 58.593038,
    longitude: 16.188129)
```

```
let redLocation = CLLocationCoordinate2D(latitude: 58.591831,
    longitude: 16.189073)

let greenLocation = CLLocationCoordinate2D(latitude: 58.590522,
    longitude: 16.185726)

/* Create the annotations using the location */
let purpleAnnotation = MyAnnotation(coordinate: purpleLocation,
    title: "Purple",
    subtitle: "Pin",
    pinColor: .Purple)

/* This calls the convenience constructor which will, by default,
create a blue pin for us */
let blueAnnotation = MyAnnotation(coordinate: blueLocation,
    title: "Blue",
    subtitle: "Pin")

let redAnnotation = MyAnnotation(coordinate: redLocation,
    title: "Red",
    subtitle: "Pin",
    pinColor: .Red)

let greenAnnotation = MyAnnotation(coordinate: greenLocation,
    title: "Green",
    subtitle: "Pin",
    pinColor: .Green)

/* And eventually add them to the map */
mapView.addAnnotations([purpleAnnotation,
    blueAnnotation,
    redAnnotation,
    greenAnnotation])

/* And now center the map around the point */
setCenterOfMapToLocation(purpleLocation)

}
```

The `setCenterOfMapToLocation:` method stays the same as it was in the Recipe 9.4 recipe. After this is done and dusted off, we will start with providing custom annotation views to our map view. Our plan is to return instances of the `MKAnnotationView` class to our map view for every annotation. For the red, green, and purple annotations, we will just change the `pinColor` property of our annotation view to the respective colors. However, for any annotation whose pin color is set to blue, we will change the `image` property of our annotation view to a custom blue pin image like so:

```
func mapView(mapView: MKMapView!,
    viewForAnnotation annotation: MKAnnotation!) -> MKAnnotationView!{

    if annotation is MyAnnotation == false{
```

```
      return nil
    }

    /* First, typecast the annotation for which the Map View
    fired this delegate message */
    let senderAnnotation = annotation as MyAnnotation

    /* We will attempt to get a reusable
    identifier for the pin we are about to create */
    let pinReusableIdentifier = senderAnnotation.pinColor.rawValue

    /* Using the identifier we retrieved above, we will
    attempt to reuse a pin in the sender Map View */
    var annotationView =
    mapView.dequeueReusableAnnotationViewWithIdentifier(
      pinReusableIdentifier) as? MKPinAnnotationView

    if annotationView == nil{
      /* If we fail to reuse a pin, we will create one */
      annotationView = MKPinAnnotationView(annotation: senderAnnotation,
        reuseIdentifier: pinReusableIdentifier)

      /* Make sure we can see the callouts on top of
      each pin in case we have assigned title and/or
      subtitle to each pin */
      annotationView!.canShowCallout = true
    }

    if senderAnnotation.pinColor == .Blue{
      let pinImage = UIImage(named:"BluePin")
      annotationView!.image = pinImage
    } else {
      annotationView!.pinColor = senderAnnotation.pinColor.toPinColor()
    }

    return annotationView

}
```

And the results can be seen in Figure 9-3.

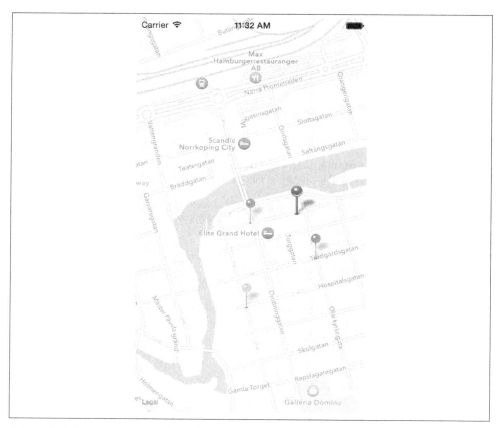

Figure 9-3. System pins mixed with a custom blue pin are displayed on a map

Discussion

The delegate object of an instance of the MKMapView class must conform to the MKMap ViewDelegate protocol and implement the mapView:viewForAnnotation: method. The return value of this method is an instance of the MKAnnotationView class. Any object that subclasses the aforementioned class, by default, inherits a property called image. Assigning a value to this property replaces the default image provided by the Map Kit framework, as shown in Figure 9-4.

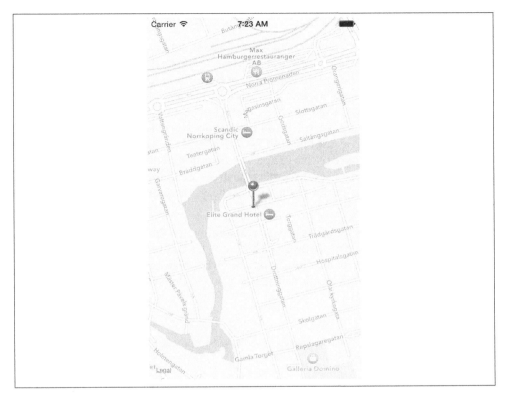

Figure 9-4. A custom image displayed on a map view

9.6. Searching on a Map View

Problem

You want to be able to provide search functionality to your users while they are viewing a map view. For instance, you may want to allow your users to search for all restaurants or gyms in a given region inside the map. So if the person is in the center of the town and she can see her location on the map, she can simply type "restaurants" in the search box and get your app to do the search for her.

Solution

Instantiate an object of type `MKLocalSearchRequest` and provide your search query, such as "restaurants," for the request. Then you can submit your request to the iOS SDK using the `MKLocalSearch` class. The response that you get will be of type `MKLocalSear chResponse`.

Discussion

Map views are great, they really are. But what use do they have for the user if all she can see is the map itself? The user might as well buy a traditional map on a piece of paper. Users like their smartphones' map capabilities because they are interactive. The user can find things, search for locations, and get directions to an address. Apple has included three really handy classes in the iOS SDK that allow us to search for locations on the map. The searching is really easy. All you have to do is provide a text of what you are actually looking for, such as "restaurants" or "cafes," and the SDK will do the rest of the job for you. For the purpose of this recipe, we are going to display a map view on our view controller, ask the map view to display the user's location, and track the user as she moves around so that the center of the map is always the location of where the user is right now.

Once our map view finds the user's location (assuming that the user gives us permission to find her location), we will issue a call to the `MKLocalSearch` class to fetch all the restaurants around the user's location. So let's begin by creating a map view on the screen and start tracking the user's location. The first thing to do is define the map view:

```
import UIKit
import MapKit

class ViewController: UIViewController, MKMapViewDelegate {
  var mapView: MKMapView!

  <# rest of the code goes here #>

}
```

Next, we have to create the map view:

```
init(coder aDecoder: NSCoder!) {
  super.init(coder: aDecoder)
  mapView = MKMapView()
}


/* Set up the map and add it to our view */
override func viewDidLoad() {
  super.viewDidLoad()
  mapView.mapType = .Standard
  mapView.frame = view.frame
  mapView.delegate = self
  view.addSubview(mapView)
}
```

We want to display the user's location on the map using the `showsUserLocation` property of our map view. However, because this will attempt to use a built-in core location manager to track the user's location, we must first ask the user whether they allow this.

Using what we learned in Recipe 9.3, we will ask the user whether we are allowed to find her current location:

```
/* The authorization status of the user has changed; we need to react
to that so that if she has authorized our app to to view her location,
we will accordingly attempt to do so */
func locationManager(manager: CLLocationManager!,
  didChangeAuthorizationStatus status: CLAuthorizationStatus){

    print("The authorization status of location services is changed to: ")

    switch CLLocationManager.authorizationStatus(){
    case .Denied:
      println("Denied")
    case .NotDetermined:
      println("Not determined")
    case .Restricted:
      println("Restricted")
    default:
      showUserLocationOnMapView()
    }

}

/* Just a little method to help us display alert dialogs to the user */
func displayAlertWithTitle(title: String, message: String){
  let controller = UIAlertController(title: title,
    message: message,
    preferredStyle: .Alert)

  controller.addAction(UIAlertAction(title: "OK",
    style: .Default,
    handler: nil))

  presentViewController(controller, animated: true, completion: nil)

}

/* We call this method when we are sure that the user has given
us access to her location */
func showUserLocationOnMapView(){
  mapView.showsUserLocation = true
  mapView.userTrackingMode = .Follow
}

override func viewDidAppear(animated: Bool) {
  super.viewDidAppear(animated)

  /* Are location services available on this device? */
  if CLLocationManager.locationServicesEnabled(){

    /* Do we have authorization to access location services? */
```

```
    switch CLLocationManager.authorizationStatus(){
    case .Denied:
      /* No */
      displayAlertWithTitle("Not Determined",
        message: "Location services are not allowed for this app")
    case .NotDetermined:
      /* We don't know yet; we have to ask */
      locationManager = CLLocationManager()
      if let manager = locationManager{
        manager.requestWhenInUseAuthorization()
      }
    case .Restricted:
      /* Restrictions have been applied; we have no access
      to location services */
      displayAlertWithTitle("Restricted",
        message: "Location services are not allowed for this app")
    default:
      showUserLocationOnMapView()
    }


  } else {
    /* Location services are not enabled.
    Take appropriate action: for instance, prompt the
    user to enable the location services. */
    println("Location services are not enabled")
  }
}
```

We are using the `showsUserLocation` property of the map view. It's a Boolean value, which, when set to `true`, makes the map view find the user's location, assuming that she has given us permission to do so. That is all good, but the default behavior of the map view is to find the location and display an annotation on the map, but not to move the map's center location to zoom on the user's location. In other words, if the current view on the map view is on the United Kingdom and the user's current location is somewhere in New York, the user will still see her view of the United Kingdom on the map. We can remedy this by setting the value of the `userTrackingMode` property of our map view to `MKUserTrackingModeFollow`, which forces the map view to always keep the center of the map view as the user's location and adjust the map as the user moves.

Now that we have asked the map view to track the user's location, we need to implement the following map view delegates' methods:

`mapView:didFailToLocateUserWithError:`
  Gets called on the delegate when the map view has trouble finding the user's location. In this method, we are going to display an alert to the user to let her know that we had trouble finding her location.

`mapView:didUpdateUserLocation:`

Gets called on the delegate of the map whenever the user's location is updated. So this is always the successful path of our logic, and we can implement our local search functionality in this method.

Let's implement the `mapView:didFailToLocateUserWithError:` method first:

```
func mapView(mapView: MKMapView!,
  didFailToLocateUserWithError error: NSError!) {
  displayAlertWithTitle("Failed",
    message: "Could not get the user's location")
}
```

Plain and simple. Next up, the `mapView:didUpdateUserLocation:` method:

```
func mapView(mapView: MKMapView!,
  didUpdateUserLocation userLocation: MKUserLocation!) {

    let request = MKLocalSearchRequest()
    request.naturalLanguageQuery = "restaurants";

    let span = MKCoordinateSpan(latitudeDelta: 0.1, longitudeDelta: 0.1)

    request.region = MKCoordinateRegion(
      center: userLocation.location.coordinate,
      span: span)

    let search = MKLocalSearch(request: request)

    search.startWithCompletionHandler{
      (response: MKLocalSearchResponse!, error: NSError!) in

      for item in response.mapItems as [MKMapItem]{

        println("Item name = \(item.name)")
        println("Item phone number = \(item.phoneNumber)")
        println("Item url = \(item.url)")
        println("Item location = \(item.placemark.location)")

      }

    }
}
```

What we are doing in this method is simple. We create a local search request and setting its `naturalLanguageQuery` property to the actual items that we want to find on the map; in this case, restaurants. Then, we retrieve the user's location and creating a region of type `MKCoordinateRegion` out of that. The purpose of this is that we want to find the region around the user and do our local search in there. The region tells the location search engines that we want to limit our search to the given region. After the region is created, we set that as the `region` property of the local search. As soon as that is done,

we can begin the search by sending our local search request to the `startWithComple`
`tionHandler:` instance method of the `MKLocalSearch` class. This method accepts a
block as a parameter. This block is called when the search results come back or an error
occurs.

The found items are in the `mapItems` property of the response parameter of your block
object, and these map items are of type `MKMapItem`. Each item has properties such as
`name`, `phoneNumber`, and `url` that help you plot those points of interest on the map, using
the techniques that you learned in this chapter for displaying pins on the map (see
Recipe 9.4).

See Also

Recipe 9.4; Recipe 9.5

9.7. Displaying Directions on the Map

Problem

You want to display directions on a map to show the user how to get from point A to
point B.

Solution

Instantiate an object of type `MKDirections` and issue the `calculateDirectionsWith`
`CompletionHandler:` instance method of that object. The completion handler is called
and passes you an object of type `MKDirectionsResponse`. Use the directions response
object to open the Maps app on your device, as you will soon learn.

Discussion

Directions to walk or drive can be displayed only in the Maps app on a device, so you
cannot display them inside an instance of a map view in your app. The way we go about
displaying directions is very straightforward. In order to display the directions on the
Maps app, we need to create an instance of the `MKDirections` class. This class requires
us to have already prepared an instance of the `MKDirectionsRequest`.

In addition, to create the directions request, you need to create instances of the `MKMapI`
`tem`. Every map item represents a point on the map. So the bottom line is that if you
want to display directions from point A to point B on the map, you need to represent
them as map items, create a request out of that, and then use the `MKDirections` class to
receive the directions. After receiving the directions, you have two choices:

- Process the directions yourself. For instance, using the technique that you learned earlier in this chapter (see Recipe 9.4), you might want to retrieve all the gas stations (placemarks) that are along the way from point A to point B and drop pins for those on the map.
- Send the directions to the Maps app for rendering.

In this recipe, we are going to explore the second option. So let's assume that we want to get *driving directions* from our current location to an arbitrary location on the map. For the purpose of this recipe, I am going to set the destination address as `Churchill Square Shopping Center, Brighton, United Kingdom`. You can convert this meaningful address to its latitude and longitude, and then use that information to create an instance of the `MKPlacemark` class, as we shall soon see.

So let's get started. The first thing that we have to do is import the Core Location framework so that we can translate the aforementioned address to its raw coordinates (latitude, longitude). We also import the MapKit framework so that we can create the directions request.

Now we convert our destination address to latitude and longitude:

```
let destination = "Godsgatan, Norrköping, Sweden"
CLGeocoder().geocodeAddressString(destination,
  completionHandler: {(placemarks: [AnyObject]!, error: NSError!) in
  <# Now we have the coordinates for the address #>
  })
```

 All the code that we write from here in this recipe will go inside the completion block object of the `geocodeAddressString:completion Handler:` method of the `CLGeocoder` class that we just wrote.

The completion block gives us a reference to an error object. You need to read this error object and, if an error comes back, handle it appropriately. I will leave that part to you. So now let's go and tell MapKit that we want the source of the directions to be where we currently are. We use the `MKDirectionsRequest` class to create a directions request and set the value of the request's `source` property to the value of the `mapItemForCur rentLocation` class method of the `MKMapItem` class:

```
if error != nil{
  /* Handle the error her perhaps by displaying an alert */
} else {
  let request = MKDirectionsRequest()
  request.setSource(MKMapItem.mapItemForCurrentLocation())
}
```

Earlier on, we created a string object that contained our destination address. Now that we have its `CLPlacemark` instance, we need to convert it to an instance of `MKPlacemark` that can be set as the value of the `Destination` property of our directions request, like so:

```
/* Convert the CoreLocation destination
placemark to a MapKit placemark */
let placemark = placemarks[0] as CLPlacemark
let destinationCoordinates =
placemark.location.coordinate
/* Get the placemark of the destination address */
let destination = MKPlacemark(coordinate: destinationCoordinates,
  addressDictionary: nil)
```

The `MKDirectionsRequest` class has a property named `transportType` that is of type `MKDirectionsTransportType`.

Because we want to display driving directions from our source to the destination, we are going to use the `MKDirectionsTransportTypeAutomobile` value in our recipe:

```
/* Set the transportation method to automobile */
request.transportType = .Automobile
```

Eventually, we will create an instance of the `MKDirections` class using its `initWithRequest:` constructor, which takes as a parameter an instance of the `MKDirectionsRequest` class. We already created and prepared this object with a map item indicating the source and destination.

We then use the `calculateDirectionsWithCompletionHandler:` instance method of our directions class to get the directions from our source to destination map items. This method takes as a parameter a block object that provides us with an object of type `MKDirectionsResponse` and an error of type `NSError` that we can use to determine whether an error occurred. The response object that gets passed to us has two very important properties: `source` and `destination`. These are the same source and destination map items that we set before. Once in this block, you can either use the direction response and handle it manually, as explained before, or pass the source and destination to the Maps app for rendering like so:

```
/* Get the directions */
let directions = MKDirections(request: request)
directions.calculateDirectionsWithCompletionHandler{
  (response: MKDirectionsResponse!, error: NSError!) in

  /* You can manually parse the response, but in here we will take
  a shortcut and use the Maps app to display our source and
  destination. We didn't have to make this API call at all,
  as we already had the map items, but this is to
  demonstrate that the directions response contains more
  information than just the source and the destination. */
```

```
  /* Display the directions on the Maps app */
  let launchOptions = [
    MKLaunchOptionsDirectionsModeKey:
    MKLaunchOptionsDirectionsModeDriving]

  MKMapItem.openMapsWithItems([response.source, response.destination],
    launchOptions: launchOptions)
}
```

 Please bear in mind that we are attempting to show directions from the user's current location to a specific point on the map. Whenever we try to attempt the user's current location, we need to ensure that the user is aware of this and agrees to it. So we need to follow the steps provided in Recipe 9.3, first asking for authorization from the user to access her location, and then provide directions from her location to another place.

So our code eventually becomes like so:

```
import UIKit
import MapKit

class ViewController: UIViewController,
MKMapViewDelegate, CLLocationManagerDelegate {

  var mapView: MKMapView!
  var locationManager: CLLocationManager?

  required init(coder aDecoder: NSCoder) {
    super.init(coder: aDecoder)
    mapView = MKMapView()

  }

  /* Set up the map and add it to our view */
  override func viewDidLoad() {
    super.viewDidLoad()
    mapView.mapType = .Standard
    mapView.frame = view.frame
    mapView.delegate = self
    view.addSubview(mapView)
  }

  func provideDirections(){
    let destination = "Godsgatan, Norrköping, Sweden"
    CLGeocoder().geocodeAddressString(destination,
      completionHandler: {(placemarks: [AnyObject]!, error: NSError!) in

        if error != nil{
          /* Handle the error here perhaps by displaying an alert */
```

```
      } else {
        let request = MKDirectionsRequest()
        request.setSource(MKMapItem.mapItemForCurrentLocation())

        /* Convert the CoreLocation destination
        placemark to a MapKit placemark */
        let placemark = placemarks[0] as CLPlacemark
        let destinationCoordinates =
        placemark.location.coordinate
        /* Get the placemark of the destination address */
        let destination = MKPlacemark(coordinate:
          destinationCoordinates,
          addressDictionary: nil)

        request.setDestination(MKMapItem(placemark: destination))

        /* Set the transportation method to automobile */
        request.transportType = .Automobile

        /* Get the directions */
        let directions = MKDirections(request: request)
        directions.calculateDirectionsWithCompletionHandler{
          (response: MKDirectionsResponse!, error: NSError!) in

          /* You can manually parse the response, but in
          here we will take a shortcut and use the Maps app
          to display our source and
          destination. We didn't have to make this API call at all,
          as we already had the map items before, but this is to
          demonstrate that the directions response contains more
          information than just the source and the destination. */

          /* Display the directions on the Maps app */
          let launchOptions = [
            MKLaunchOptionsDirectionsModeKey:
            MKLaunchOptionsDirectionsModeDriving]

          MKMapItem.openMapsWithItems(
            [response.source, response.destination],
            launchOptions: launchOptions)
        }

      }

    })
}

func locationManager(manager: CLLocationManager!,
  didChangeAuthorizationStatus status: CLAuthorizationStatus){

    print("The authorization status of location " +
      "services is changed to: ")
```

```
    switch CLLocationManager.authorizationStatus(){
    case .Denied:
      println("Denied")
    case .NotDetermined:
      println("Not determined")
    case .Restricted:
      println("Restricted")
    default:
      println("Authorized")
      provideDirections()
    }

}

func displayAlertWithTitle(title: String, message: String){
  let controller = UIAlertController(title: title,
    message: message,
    preferredStyle: .Alert)

  controller.addAction(UIAlertAction(title: "OK",
    style: .Default,
    handler: nil))

  presentViewController(controller, animated: true, completion: nil)

}

/* Add the pin to the map and center the map around the pin */
override func viewDidAppear(animated: Bool) {
  super.viewDidAppear(animated)

  /* Are location services available on this device? */
  if CLLocationManager.locationServicesEnabled(){

    /* Do we have authorization to access location services? */
    switch CLLocationManager.authorizationStatus(){
    case .Denied:
      /* No */
      displayAlertWithTitle("Not Determined",
        message: "Location services are not allowed for this app")
    case .NotDetermined:
      /* We don't know yet, we have to ask */
      locationManager = CLLocationManager()
      if let manager = self.locationManager{
        manager.delegate = self
        manager.requestWhenInUseAuthorization()
      }
    case .Restricted:
      /* Restrictions have been applied, we have no access
      to location services */
      displayAlertWithTitle("Restricted",
```

```
        message: "Location services are not allowed for this app")
      default:
        provideDirections()
      }


    } else {
      /* Location services are not enabled.
      Take appropriate action: for instance, prompt the
      user to enable the location services */
      println("Location services are not enabled")
    }

  }

}
```

See Also

Recipe 9.3

9.8. Customizing the View of the Map with a Camera

Problem

The default topdown view of the map view just doesn't do it for you and you want to be able to customize how the user sees a location on the map.

Solution

Instantiate an object of type `MKMapCamera` and set the camera location accordingly. When you are done, assign your newly-created camera object to the map view using the map view's `camera` property.

```
func mapView(mapView: MKMapView!,
  didUpdateUserLocation userLocation: MKUserLocation!){

    println("Setting the camera for our map view...")

    let userCoordinate = userLocation.coordinate

    /* Assuming my location is hardcoded to
    lat: 58.592725 and long:16.185962, the following camera
    angle works perfectly for me */
    let eyeCoordinate = CLLocationCoordinate2D(
      latitude: 58.571647,
      longitude: 16.234660)

    let camera = MKMapCamera(
```

```
        lookingAtCenterCoordinate: userCoordinate,
        fromEyeCoordinate: eyeCoordinate,
        eyeAltitude: 400.0)

    mapView.setCamera(camera, animated: true)
}
```

 In this recipe, we are going to expand on what we learned in the Recipe 9.3 recipe, so I suggest that you have a glance over that recipe if you haven't done so already.

Discussion

If we have already detected the user's location, our map view will look like Figure 9-5.

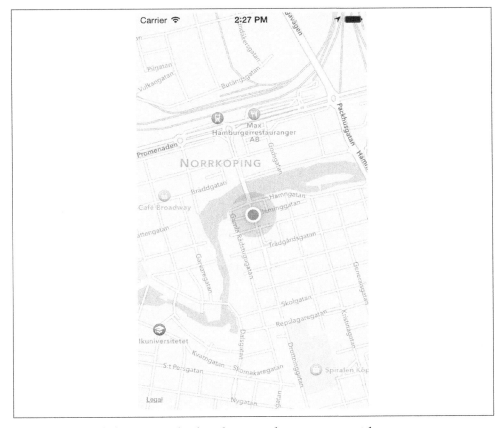

Figure 9-5. User's location is displayed in a topdown manner with no camera

Now if you attempt to place two fingers on the map and just drag down, you can see the same map tilted slightly (Figure 9-6).

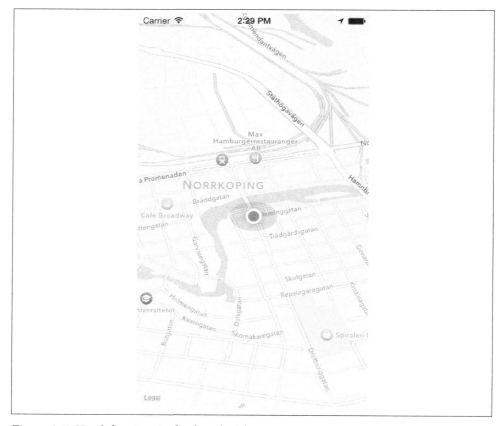

Figure 9-6. User's location is displayed with a camera

For every `MKMapCamera` instantiation, we need to provide three parameters:

The destination coordinate of the camera
> This is the location toward which the camera is pointed, or the *destination* of the camera.

The coordinate of the camera
> This is the center point of the camera, expressed as a location with latitude and longitude.

The altitude of the camera
> This defines how high up in the sky the camera has to be positioned, measured in meters.

After you are done creating your camera, you can assign it to your map view in two ways. One is to set it directly as the value of the camera property of your map view. The other way is to use the setCamera:animated: method of your map view. The second method allows you to animate the transition from the default topdown view of the map to the view of your camera, if you pass true as the animated parameter of this method.

See Also

Recipe 9.3

CHAPTER 10

Gesture Recognizers

10.0. Introduction

Gestures are a combination of touch events. An example of a gesture can be found in the default iOS Photo application, which allows the user to zoom into and out of a photo while "pinching" the photo in and out using two fingers. Some of the most common gesture event detection code is encapsulated into reusable classes built into the iOS SDK. These classes can be used to detect swipe, pinch, pan, tap, drag, long-press, and rotation gestures.

Gesture recognizers must be added to instances of the UIView class. A single view can have more than one gesture recognizer. When a view catches the gesture, that view will be responsible for passing down the same gesture to other views in the hierarchy, if needed.

Some touch events required by an application might be complicated to process and might require the same event to be detectable in other views in the same application. This introduces the requirements for reusable gesture recognizers. There are six gesture recognizers in iOS SDK 5 and above:

- Swipe
- Rotation
- Pinch
- Pan
- Long-press
- Tap

The basic framework for handling a gesture through a built-in gesture recognizer is as follows:

1. Create an object of the right data type for the gesture recognizer you want.

2. Add this object as a gesture recognizer to the view that will receive the gesture.

3. Write a method that is called when the gesture occurs and that takes the action you want.

The method associated as the target method of any gesture recognizer must follow these rules:

- It must return `void`.

- It must either accept no parameters, or accept a single parameter of type `UIGesture Recognizer` in which the system passes the gesture recognizer that calls this method.

Gesture recognizers are divided into two categories: *discrete* and *continuous*. Discrete gesture recognizers detect their gesture events and, when detected, call a method in their respective owners. Continuous gesture recognizers keep their owner objects informed of the events as they happen and call the method in their target object repeatedly as the event happens and until it ends.

For instance, a double-tap event is discrete. Even though it consists of two taps, the system recognizes that the taps occurred close enough together to be treated as a single event. The double-tap gesture recognizer calls the method in its target object when the double-tap event is detected.

An example of a continuous gesture recognizer is rotation. This gesture starts as soon as the user starts the rotation and only finishes when the user lifts his fingers off the screen. The method provided to the rotation gesture recognizer class gets called at short intervals until the event is finished.

Gesture recognizers can be added to any instance of the `UIView` class using the `addGes tureRecognizer:` method of the view, and when needed, they can be removed from the view using the `removeGestureRecognizer:` method.

The `UIGestureRecognizer` class has a property named `state`. The `state` property represents the different states the gesture recognizer can have throughout the recognition process. Discrete and continuous gesture recognizers go through different sets of states.

Discrete gesture recognizers can pass through the following states:

1. `UIGestureRecognizerStatePossible`

2. `UIGestureRecognizerStateRecognized`

3. `UIGestureRecognizerStateFailed`

Depending on the situation, a discrete gesture recognizer might send the `UIGestureR ecognizerStateRecognized` state to its target, or it might send the `UIGestureRecogni zerStateFailed` state if an error occurs during the recognition process.

Continuous gesture recognizers take a different path in the states they send to their targets:

1. `UIGestureRecognizerStatePossible`
2. `UIGestureRecognizerStateBegan`
3. `UIGestureRecognizerStateChanged`
4. `UIGestureRecognizerStateEnded`
5. `UIGestureRecognizerStateFailed`

 A gesture recognizer's state is changed to `UIGestureRecognizer StatePossible` when it is gathering information about touch events on a view and *might* at any point detect the relevant gesture. In addition to the aforementioned states of a continuous gesture recognizer, the `UIGestureRecognizerStateCancelled` state can also be generated if anything interrupts the gesture. For instance, an incoming phone call can interrupt a pan gesture. In that case, the state of the gesture recognizer is changed to `UIGestureRecognizerStateCancel led` and no further messages are called on the receiver object by that gesture recognizer unless the user restarts the gesture sequence.

Again, if the continuous gesture recognizer stumbles upon a situation that cannot be fixed internally, it ends with the `UIGestureRecognizerStateFailed` state instead of `UIGestureRecognizerStateEnded`.

10.1. Detecting Swipe Gestures

Problem

You want to be able to detect when the user performs a swipe gesture on a view—for instance, swiping a picture out of the window.

Solution

Instantiate an object of type `UISwipeGestureRecognizer` and add it to an instance of `UIView`:

```
import UIKit
```

```
class ViewController: UIViewController {

  var swipeRecognizer: UISwipeGestureRecognizer!

  required init(coder aDecoder: NSCoder) {
    super.init(coder: aDecoder)
    swipeRecognizer = UISwipeGestureRecognizer(target: self,
      action: "handleSwipes:")
  }

  func handleSwipes(sender: UISwipeGestureRecognizer){

    if sender.direction == .Down{
      println("Swiped Down")
    }
    if sender.direction == .Left{
      println("Swiped Left")
    }
    if sender.direction == .Right{
      println("Swiped Right")
    }
    if sender.direction == .Up{
      println("Swiped Up")
    }

  }

  override func viewDidLoad() {
    super.viewDidLoad()

    /* Swipes that are performed from right to
    left are to be detected */
    swipeRecognizer.direction = .Left

    /* Just one finger needed */
    swipeRecognizer.numberOfTouchesRequired = 1

    /* Add it to the view */
    view.addGestureRecognizer(swipeRecognizer)

  }

}
```

Discussion

The swipe gesture is one of the most straightforward motions that built-in iOS SDK gesture recognizers register. It is a simple movement of one or more fingers on a view from one direction to another. The UISwipeGestureRecognizer, like other gesture recognizers, inherits from the UIGestureRecognizer class and adds various functionalities to this class, such as properties that allow us to specify the direction in which the swipe gestures have to be performed in order to be detected, or how many fingers the user has to hold on the screen to be able to perform a swipe gesture. Please bear in mind that swipe gestures are discrete gestures.

Even though the `direction` property of the `UISwipeGestureRecognizer` class is documented to be able to accept a blend of swipe gesture directions—such as left mixed with right or up mixed with down—in actuality, this does not work. This is perhaps a bug in the SDK. If you want to detect swipes in multiple directions, simply create swipe gesture recognizers for each one of those directions.

Although swipe gestures are usually performed with one finger, the number of fingers required for the swipe gesture to be recognized can also be specified with the `number OfTouchesRequired` property of the `UISwipeGestureRecognizer` class.

10.2. Detecting Rotation Gestures

Problem

You want to detect when a user is attempting to rotate an element on the screen using her fingers.

Solution

Create an instance of the `UIRotationGestureRecognizer` class and attach it to your target view:

```
override func viewDidLoad() {
  super.viewDidLoad()

  helloWorldLabel.text = "Hello, World!"
  helloWorldLabel.font = UIFont.systemFontOfSize(16)
  helloWorldLabel.sizeToFit()
  helloWorldLabel.center = view.center
  view.addSubview(helloWorldLabel)

  view.addGestureRecognizer(rotationRecognizer)

}
```

Discussion

The `UIRotationGestureRecognizer`, as its name implies, is the perfect candidate among gesture recognizers to detect rotation gestures and to help you build more intuitive graphical user interfaces. For instance, when the user encounters an image on the screen in your application in full-screen mode, it is quite intuitive for him to attempt to correct the orientation by rotating the image.

The `UIRotationGestureRecognizer` class implements a property named `rotation` that specifies the total amount and direction of rotation requested by the user's gesture, in radians. The rotation is determined from the fingers' initial position (`UIGestureRecog nizerStateBegan`) and final position (`UIGestureRecognizerStateEnded`).

To rotate UI elements that inherit from `UIView` class, you can pass the `rotation` property of the rotation gesture recognizer to the `CGAffineTransformMakeRotation` function to make an affine transform, as shown in the example.

The code in this recipe's Solution passes the current object, in this case a view controller, to the target of the rotation gesture recognizer. The target selector is specified as `han dleRotations:`, a method we have to implement. But before we do that, let's have a look at the view controller's code:

```
import UIKit

class ViewController: UIViewController {

  var helloWorldLabel: UILabel!
  var rotationRecognizer: UIRotationGestureRecognizer!
  var rotationAngleInRadians = 0.0 as CGFloat

  <# rest of the code goes here #>
}
```

Before we carry on, let's have a look at what each one of these properties does and why it is declared:

`helloWorldLabel`

This is a label that we must create on the view of the view controller. Then we will write the code to rotate this label whenever the user attempts to perform rotation gestures on the view that owns this label (in this case, the view of the view controller).

`rotationRecognizer`

This is the instance of the rotation gesture recognizer that we will later allocate and initialize.

`rotationAngleInRadians`

This is the value we will query as the exact rotation angle of our label. Initially, we will set this to zero. Since the rotation angles reported by a rotation gesture recognizer are reset every time the rotation gesture is started again, we can keep the value of the rotation gesture recognizer whenever it goes into the `UIGestureRecognizer StateEnded` state. The next time the gesture is started, we will add the previous value to the new value to get an overall rotation angle.

The size and the origin of the label does not matter much. Even the position of the label isn't that important, as we will only attempt to rotate the label around its center, no matter where on the view the label is positioned. The only important thing to remember is that in universal applications, the position of a label on a view controller used in different targets (devices) must be calculated dynamically using the size of its parent view. Otherwise, on different devices such as the iPad or the iPhone, it might appear in different places on the screen.

Using the center property of the label, and setting that center location to the center of the containing view, we will center-align the contents of the label. The rotation transformation that we will apply to this label rotates the label around its center—and left-aligned or right-aligned labels whose actual frame is bigger than the minimum frame required to hold their contents without truncation will appear to be rotating in an unnatural way and not on the center. If you are curious, go ahead and left- or right-align the contents of the label and see what happens.

As we saw in this recipe's Solution, the rotation gesture recognizer that we created will send its events to a method called handleRotations:. Here is the implementation for this method:

```
func handleRotations(sender: UIRotationGestureRecognizer){

  /* Take the previous rotation and add the current rotation to it */
  helloWorldLabel.transform =
    CGAffineTransformMakeRotation(rotationAngleInRadians +
      sender.rotation)

  /* At the end of the rotation, keep the angle for later use */
  if sender.state == .Ended{
    rotationAngleInRadians += sender.rotation;
  }

}
```

The way a rotation gesture recognizer sends us the rotation angles is very interesting. This gesture recognizer is continuous, which means it starts finding the angles as soon as the user begins her rotation gesture and sends updates to the handler method at frequent intervals until the user is done. Each message treats the starting angle as zero and reports the difference between the message's starting point (which is the angle where the previous message left off) and its ending point. Thus, the complete effect of the gesture can be discovered only by adding up the angles reported by the different events. Clockwise movement produces a positive angular value, whereas counterclockwise movement produces a negative value.

If you are using iPhone Simulator instead of a real device, you can still simulate the rotation gesture by holding down the Option key in the simulator. You will see two circles appear on the simulator at the same distance from the center of the screen, representing two fingers. If you want to shift these fingers from the center to another location while holding down the Alt key, press the Shift key and point somewhere else on the screen. Where you leave your pointer will become the new center for these two fingers.

Now we will simply assign this angle to the rotation angle of the label. But can you imagine what will happen when the rotation is finished and another one starts? The second rotation gesture's angle will replace that of the first rotation in the `rotation` value reported to the handler. For this reason, whenever a rotation gesture is finished, we must keep the current rotation of the label. The value in each rotation gesture's angle must be added in turn, and we must assign the result to the label's rotation transformation as we saw before.

As we saw earlier, we used the `CGAffineTransformMakeRotation` function to create an affine transformation. Functions in the iOS SDK that start with "CG" refer to the Core Graphics framework. For programs that use Core Graphics to compile and link successfully, you must make sure the Core Graphics framework is added to the list of frameworks. New versions of Xcode link a default project against the Core Graphics framework automatically, so you don't really have to worry about that.

Now that we are sure Core Graphics is added to the target, we can compile and run the app.

See Also

Recipe 10.6

10.3. Detecting Panning and Dragging Gestures

Problem

You want the users of your application to be able to move GUI elements around using their fingers.

Pan gestures are continuous movements of fingers on the screen; recall that swipe gestures were discrete gestures. This means the method set as the target method of a pan gesture recognizer gets called repeatedly from the beginning to the end of the recognition process.

Solution

Use the `UIPanGestureRecognizer` class:

```
import UIKit

class ViewController: UIViewController {

  var helloWorldLabel: UILabel!
  var panGestureRecognizer: UIPanGestureRecognizer!

  required init(coder aDecoder: NSCoder) {
    super.init(coder: aDecoder)
    let labelFrame = CGRect(x: 0, y: 0, width: 150, height: 100)
    helloWorldLabel = UILabel(frame: labelFrame)
    /* Make sure to enable user interaction; otherwise, tap events
    won't be caught on this label */
    helloWorldLabel.userInteractionEnabled = true
    helloWorldLabel.text = "Hello World"
    helloWorldLabel.frame = labelFrame
    helloWorldLabel.backgroundColor = UIColor.blackColor()
    helloWorldLabel.textColor = UIColor.whiteColor()
    helloWorldLabel.textAlignment = .Center
    panGestureRecognizer = UIPanGestureRecognizer(target: self,
      action: "handlePanGestures:")
  }

  override func viewDidLoad() {
    super.viewDidLoad()

    /* Now make sure this label gets displayed on our view */
    view.addSubview(helloWorldLabel)

    /* At least and at most we need only one finger to activate
    the pan gesture recognizer */
    panGestureRecognizer.minimumNumberOfTouches = 1
    panGestureRecognizer.maximumNumberOfTouches = 1

    /* Add it to our view */
    helloWorldLabel.addGestureRecognizer(panGestureRecognizer)

  }

  <# rest of the code goes here #>
}
```

The pan gesture recognizer will call the `handlePanGestures:` method as its target
method. This method is described in this recipe's Discussion.

Discussion

The `UIPanGestureRecognizer`, as its name implies, can detect *pan gestures*. The pan gesture recognizer will go through the following states while recognizing the pan gesture:

1. `UIGestureRecognizerStateBegan`
2. `UIGestureRecognizerStateChanged`
3. `UIGestureRecognizerStateEnded`

We can implement the gesture recognizer target method as follows. The code will continuously move the center of the label along with the user's finger as `UIGestureRecognizerStateChanged` events are reported:

```
func handlePanGestures(sender: UIPanGestureRecognizer){

  if sender.state != .Ended && sender.state != .Failed{
    let location = sender.locationInView(sender.view!.superview!)
    sender.view!.center = location
  }

}
```

 To be able to move the label on the view of the view controller, we need the position of the finger on the view, not the label. For this reason, we call the `locationInView:` method of the pan gesture recognizer and pass the superview of the label as the target view.

Use the `locationInView:` method of the pan gesture recognizer to find the point of the current panning finger(s). To detect multiple finger locations, use the `locationOfTouch:inView:` method. Using the `minimumNumberOfTouches` and `maximumNumberOfTouches` properties of the `UIPanGestureRecognizer`, you can detect more than one panning touch at a time. In the example, for the sake of simplicity, we are trying to detect only one finger.

 During the `UIGestureRecognizerStateEnded` state, the reported *x* and *y* values might not be a number; in other words, they could be equal to NAN. That is why we need to avoid using the reported values during this particular state.

10.4. Detecting Long Press Gestures

Problem

You want to be able to detect when the user taps and holds his finger on a view for a certain period of time.

Solution

Create an instance of the `UILongPressGestureRecognizer` class and add it to the view that has to detect long-tap gestures:

```
import UIKit

class ViewController: UIViewController {

  var longPressGestureRecognizer: UILongPressGestureRecognizer!
  var dummyButton: UIButton!

}
```

Here is the code of the view controller that uses the long-press gesture recognizer that we defined earlier:

```
init(coder aDecoder: NSCoder!) {
  super.init(coder: aDecoder)

  dummyButton = UIButton.buttonWithType(.System) as UIButton
  dummyButton.frame = CGRect(x: 0, y: 0, width: 72, height: 37)
  dummyButton.setTitle("My Button", forState: .Normal)

  /* First create the gesture recognizer */
  longPressGestureRecognizer = UILongPressGestureRecognizer(target: self,
    action: "handleLongPressGestures:")

  /* The number of fingers that must be present on the screen */
  longPressGestureRecognizer.numberOfTouchesRequired = 2

  /* Maximum 100 points of movement allowed before the gesture
  is recognized */
  longPressGestureRecognizer.allowableMovement = 100

  /* The user must press 2 fingers (numberOfTouchesRequired) for
  at least 1 second for the gesture to be recognized */
  longPressGestureRecognizer.minimumPressDuration = 1

}

override func viewDidLoad() {
  super.viewDidLoad()
```

```
        dummyButton.center = view.center
        view.addSubview(dummyButton)

        /* Add this gesture recognizer to our view */
        view.addGestureRecognizer(longPressGestureRecognizer)

    }
```

 If the long-press gesture recognizer is firing events to the receiver object while the gesture continues on the user's end, and a phone call or any other interruption comes in, the state of the gesture recognizer will be changed to `UIGestureRecognizerStateCancelled`. No further messages will be sent to the receiver object from that gesture recognizer until the user initiates the actions required to start the recognition process again; in this example, holding two fingers for at least one second on the view of our view controller.

 Our code runs on a view controller with a property named `long PressGestureRecognizer` of type `UILongPressGestureRecognizer`. For more information, refer to this recipe's Discussion.

Discussion

The iOS SDK comes with a long-tap gesture recognizer class named `UILongTapGes tureRecognizer`. A long-tap gesture is triggered when the user presses one or more fingers (configurable by the programmer) on a `UIView` and holds the finger(s) for a specific amount of time. Furthermore, you can narrow the detection of gestures down to only those long-tap gestures that are performed after a certain number of fingers are tapped on a view for a certain number of times and are then kept on the view for a specified number of seconds. Bear in mind that long taps are continuous events.

Four important properties can change the way the long-tap gesture recognizer performs.

numberOfTapsRequired

> This is the number of taps the user has to perform on the target view before the gesture can be triggered. Bear in mind that a tap is *not* merely a finger positioned on a screen. A tap is the movement of putting a finger down on the screen and lifting the finger off. The default value of this property is 0.

numberOfTouchesRequired

> This property specifies the number of fingers that must be touching the screen before the gesture can be recognized. You must specify the same number of fingers to detect the taps, if the `numberOfTapsRequired` property is set to a value larger than 0.

allowableMovement

> This is the maximum number of pixels that the fingers on the screen can be moved before the gesture recognition is aborted.

minimumPressDuration

> This property dictates how long, measured in seconds, the user must press his finger(s) on the screen before the gesture event can be detected.

In the example, these properties are set as follows:

- numberOfTapsRequired: Default (we are not changing this value)
- numberOfTouchesRequired: 2
- allowableMovement: 100
- minimumPressDuration: 1

With these values, the long-tap gesture will be recognized only if the user presses on the screen and holds both fingers for 1 second (minimumPressDuration) without moving her fingers more than 100 pixels around (allowableMovement).

Now when the gesture is recognized, it will call the handleLongPressGestures: method, which we can implement in this way:

```
func handleLongPressGestures(sender: UILongPressGestureRecognizer){

    /* Here we want to find the midpoint of the two fingers
    that caused the long-press gesture to be recognized. We configured
    this number using the numberOfTouchesRequired property of the
    UILongPressGestureRecognizer that we instantiated before. If we
    find that another long-press gesture recognizer is using this
    method as its target, we will ignore it */

    if sender.numberOfTouches() == 2{

        let touchPoint1 = sender.locationOfTouch(0, inView: sender.view)
        let touchPoint2 = sender.locationOfTouch(1, inView: sender.view)

        let midPointX = (touchPoint1.x + touchPoint2.x) / 2.0
        let midPointY = (touchPoint1.y + touchPoint2.y) / 2.0

        let midPoint = CGPoint(x: midPointX, y: midPointY)

        dummyButton.center = midPoint

    } else {
        /* This is a long-press gesture recognizer with more
        or less than 2 fingers */
        let controller = UIAlertController(title: "Two fingers",
            message: "Please use two fingers",
            preferredStyle: .Alert)
```

```
      controller.addAction(UIAlertAction(title: "OK",
        style: .Default,
        handler: nil))
      presentViewController(controller, animated: true, completion: nil)
  }
}
```

 One of the applications in iOS that uses long-press gesture recognizers is the Maps application. In this application, when you are looking at different locations, press your finger on a specific location and
hold it for a while without lifting it off the screen. This will drop a pin
on that specific location.

10.5. Detecting Tap Gestures

Problem

You want to be able to detect when users tap on a view.

Solution

Create an instance of the UITapGestureRecognizer class and add it to the target view,
using the addGestureRecognizer: instance method of the UIView class. Let's have a
look at the definition of the view controller:

```
import UIKit

class ViewController: UIViewController {

  var tapGestureRecognizer: UITapGestureRecognizer!

  <# rest of the code goes here #>

}
```

The implementation of the viewDidLoad instance method of the view controller is as
follows:

```
init(coder aDecoder: NSCoder!){
  super.init(coder: aDecoder)

  /* Create the Tap Gesture Recognizer */
  tapGestureRecognizer = UITapGestureRecognizer(target: self,
    action: "handleTaps:")

  /* The number of fingers that must be on the screen */
  tapGestureRecognizer.numberOfTouchesRequired = 2

  /* The total number of taps to be performed before the
```

```
        gesture is recognized */
        tapGestureRecognizer.numberOfTapsRequired = 3

}

override func viewDidLoad() {
  super.viewDidLoad()

  /* Add this gesture recognizer to our view */
  view.addGestureRecognizer(tapGestureRecognizer)

}
```

Discussion

The tap gesture recognizer is the best candidate among gesture recognizers to detect plain tap gestures. A tap event is the event triggered by the user touching and lifting his finger(s) off the screen. A tap gesture is a discrete gesture.

The locationInView: method of the UITapGestureRecognizer class can be used to detect the location of the tap event. If the tap gesture requires more than one touch, the locationOfTouch:inView: method of the UITapGestureRecognizer class can be called to determine individual touch points. In the code, we set the numberOfTouchesRe quired property of the tap gesture recognizer to 2. With this value set, the gesture recognizer will require two fingers to be on the screen on each tap event. The number of taps that are required for the gesture recognizer to recognize this gesture is set to 3, using the numberOfTapsRequired property. We provided the handleTaps: method as the target method of the tap gesture recognizer:

```
func handleTaps(sender: UITapGestureRecognizer){

  for touchCounter in 0..<sender.numberOfTouchesRequired{

    let touchPoint = sender.locationOfTouch(touchCounter,
      inView: sender.view)

    println("Touch \(touchCounter + 1): \(touchPoint)")

  }

}
```

In this code, we go through the number of touches that the tap gesture recognizer was asked to look for. Based on that number, we find the location of each tap. Depending on where you tap on the view on your simulator, you will get results similar to this in the console window:

```
Touch 1: (163.0,356.0)
Touch 2: (157.0,212.0)
```

If you are using the simulator, you can simulate two touches at the same time by holding down the Option key and moving your mouse on the simulator's screen. You now have two concentric touch points on the screen.

10.6. Detecting Pinch Gestures

Problem

You want your users to be able to perform pinch gestures on a view.

Solution

Create an instance of the `UIPinchGestureRecognizer` class and add it to your target view, using the `addGestureRecognizer:` instance method of the `UIView` class:

```
init(coder aDecoder: NSCoder!) {
  super.init(coder: aDecoder)

  let labelRect = CGRect(x: 0, y: 0, width: 200, height: 200)
  myBlackLabel = UILabel(frame: labelRect)
  myBlackLabel.backgroundColor = UIColor.blackColor()
  /* Without this line, our pinch gesture recognizer
  will not work */
  myBlackLabel.userInteractionEnabled = true

  /* Create the Pinch Gesture Recognizer */
  pinchGestureRecognizer = UIPinchGestureRecognizer(target: self,
    action: "handlePinches:")

  /* Add this gesture recognizer to our view */
  myBlackLabel.addGestureRecognizer(pinchGestureRecognizer)
}

override func viewDidLoad() {
  super.viewDidLoad()

  myBlackLabel.center = view.center
  view.addSubview(myBlackLabel)

}
```

The view controller's properties are defined in this way:

```
var myBlackLabel: UILabel!
var pinchGestureRecognizer: UIPinchGestureRecognizer!
var currentScale = 0.0 as CGFloat
```

Discussion

Pinching allows users to scale GUI elements up and down easily. For instance, the Safari web browser on iOS allows users to pinch on a web page in order to zoom into the contents being displayed. Pinching works in two ways: scaling up and scaling down. It is a continuous gesture that must always be performed using two fingers on the screen.

The state of this gesture recognizer changes in this order:

1. `UIGestureRecognizerStateBegan`
2. `UIGestureRecognizerStateChanged`
3. `UIGestureRecognizerStateEnded`

When the pinch gesture is recognized, the action method in the target object will be called (and will continue to be called until the pinch gesture ends). Inside the action method, you can access two very important properties of the pinch gesture recognizer: `scale` and `velocity`. `scale` is the factor by which you should scale the *x*- and *y*-axes of a GUI element to reflect the size of the user's gesture. `velocity` is the velocity of the pinch in pixels per second. The velocity is a negative value if the touch points are getting closer to each other and a positive value if they are getting farther away from each other.

The value of the `scale` property can be provided to the `CGAffineTransformMakeScale` Core Graphics function in order to retrieve an affine transformation. This affine transformation can be applied to the transform property of any instance of the `UIView` class in order to change its transformation. We are using this function in this way:

```
func handlePinches(sender: UIPinchGestureRecognizer){

  if sender.state == .Ended{
    currentScale = sender.scale
  } else if sender.state == .Began && currentScale != 0.0{
    sender.scale = currentScale
  }

  if sender.scale != CGFloat.NaN && sender.scale != 0.0{
    sender.view!.transform = CGAffineTransformMakeScale(sender.scale,
      sender.scale);
  }

}
```

Because the `scale` property of a pinch gesture recognizer is reset every time a new pinch gesture is recognized, we store the last value of this property in an instance property of the view controller called `currentScale`. The next time a new gesture is recognized, we start the scale factor from the previously reported scale factor, as demonstrated in the code.

10.7. Detecting Screen Edge Pan Gestures

Problem

You want to detect the panning gesture that the user can perform by moving her finger from any edge of the screen towards the inside of your views.

Solution

Utilize the `UIScreenEdgePanGestureRecognizer` class.

```
func handleScreenEdgePan(sender: UIScreenEdgePanGestureRecognizer){

  if sender.state == .Ended{
    displayAlertWithTitle("Detected",
      message: "Edge swipe was detected")
  }

}

init(coder aDecoder: NSCoder!) {
  super.init(coder: aDecoder)

  /* Create the Pinch Gesture Recognizer */
  screenEdgeRecognizer = UIScreenEdgePanGestureRecognizer(target: self,
    action: "handleScreenEdgePan:")

  /* Detect pans from left edge to the inside of the view */
  screenEdgeRecognizer.edges = .Left
}
```

Discussion

A screen edge pan gesture recognizer subclasses the `UIPanGestureRecognizer` class and is in fact a pan gesture recognizer. However, it is solely designed to detect pan gestures from one of the edges of the screen (top, left, bottom, right) towards the inside of a view to which it is attached. Have you noticed how, on iOS, you can swipe your finger from the bottom of any view in the system (or even in third-party apps) to access the Control Center, or swipe from top to bottom to reveal the Notification Center? Detecting these pan gestures is possible with the `UIScreenEdgePanGestureRecognizer` class.

Any edge pan gesture recognizer has a property named `edges` which is of type `UIRectEdge`. This property defines the edges that you want to detect the pan gestures. You construct this gesture recognizer using its constructor and provide it with a target object and a selector that will be called when the gesture is recognized.

With this knowledge, we are going to complete the implementation of our view controller which is able to detect pan gestures from the left edge of the screen towards the center:

```swift
import UIKit

class ViewController: UIViewController {

  var screenEdgeRecognizer: UIScreenEdgePanGestureRecognizer!

  /* Just a little method to help us display alert dialogs to the user */
  func displayAlertWithTitle(title: String, message: String){
    let controller = UIAlertController(title: title,
      message: message,
      preferredStyle: .Alert)

    controller.addAction(UIAlertAction(title: "OK",
      style: .Default,
      handler: nil))

    presentViewController(controller, animated: true, completion: nil)

  }

  func handleScreenEdgePan(sender: UIScreenEdgePanGestureRecognizer){

    if sender.state == .Ended{
      displayAlertWithTitle("Detected",
        message: "Edge swipe was detected")
    }

  }

  required init(coder aDecoder: NSCoder) {
    super.init(coder: aDecoder)

    /* Create the Pinch Gesture Recognizer */
    screenEdgeRecognizer = UIScreenEdgePanGestureRecognizer(target: self,
      action: "handleScreenEdgePan:")

    /* Detect pans from left edge to the inside of the view */
    screenEdgeRecognizer.edges = .Left
  }

  override func viewDidLoad() {
    super.viewDidLoad()
    view.addGestureRecognizer(screenEdgeRecognizer)
  }

  override func viewDidAppear(animated: Bool) {
    super.viewDidAppear(animated)
```

```
        displayAlertWithTitle("Instructions",
          message: "Start swiping from the left edge of the screen " +
          "to the right, please!")
    }

  }
```

See Also

Recipe 10.3

CHAPTER 11

Networking and Sharing

11.0. Introduction

When iOS apps are connected to the Internet, they become more lively. For example, imagine an app that brings high-quality wallpapers to its users. The user can pick from a big list of wallpapers and assign any of those images as his iOS background. Now consider an app that does the same thing but adds to its list of wallpapers every day, week, or month. The user comes back to the app, and voilà! Tons of new wallpapers are dynamically added to the app. That is the magic of web services and the Internet. This can easily be achieved with basic knowledge of networking, XML, JSON, and sharing options, along with some creativity on the app developer's part.

In this chapter, we are going to explore various classes that connect our applications with the Internet and social media. Take the NSURLSession class for example. This class replaces NSURLConnection and allows us to create sophisticated upload and download tasks that use block objects and are very configurable. For instance, as you will see in this chapter, using the NSURLSession class, we will be able to download content from a URL even when our application is in the background.

We also have at our disposal the Social framework that allows us to share user-created or app-created content with various social media services, such as FaceBook and Twitter. We are going to explore this framework as well in this chapter.

11.1. Downloading Data Using NSURLSession

Problem

You want to be able to download data from a URL.

Solution

Create an instance of the NSURLSessionConfiguration class for your session configurations. After that, pass your configuration object and a delegate to the constructor of the NSURLSession class. Once you have your session, create a task to download your contents from it. A task can be of type NSURLSessionDataTask or NSURLSessionDownloadTask.

```
import UIKit

class ViewController: UIViewController, NSURLSessionDelegate {

  var session: NSURLSession!

  required init(coder aDecoder: NSCoder) {
    super.init(coder: aDecoder)

    /* Create our configuration first */
    let configuration =
    NSURLSessionConfiguration.defaultSessionConfiguration()
    configuration.timeoutIntervalForRequest = 15.0

    /* Now create our session which will allow us to create the tasks */
    session = NSURLSession(configuration: configuration,
      delegate: self,
      delegateQueue: nil)

  }

  override func viewDidLoad() {
    super.viewDidLoad()

    /* Now attempt to download the contents of the URL */
    let url = NSURL(string: "<# place a URL here #>")

    let task = session.dataTaskWithURL(url!,
      completionHandler: {[weak self] (data: NSData!,
        response: NSURLResponse!,
        error: NSError!) in

        /* We got our data here */
        println("Done")

        self!.session.finishTasksAndInvalidate()

      })

    task.resume()

  }

}
```

Discussion

The NSURLSession can handle everything you need in order to download content from a server. But before you can create a session object, you need a configuration object of type NSURLSessionConfiguration. Create this configuration object from one of the following type methods of the NSURLSessionConfiguration class:

defaultSessionConfiguration

> This type of configuration can be used to configure a session object that has a disk-based cache. This is similar to how NSURLConnection works. This configuration also asks the session object to store communication credentials in the keychain.

ephemeralSessionConfiguration

> This creates temporary RAM-based storage for all the downloaded data and for the credentials. Use this configuration only when you are downloading very small, temporary data. Your connection credentials will be disposed of as soon as you are done with the session.

backgroundSessionConfigurationWithIdentifier:

> This configuration allows you to create a session object that is able to download items using a system process even when your app is not running. We will learn more about this later in this chapter.

After we are done creating the configuration object, you can customize it even further and change the values that are already populated in your instance. For example, one of the properties of your configuration object that you might need to change every now and then is its timeoutIntervalForRequest property. This is how long your session will wait for communication between the app and the server before it times out. This value is expressed in seconds. For instance, if you create a configuration object with the defaultSessionConfiguration type method of the NSURLSessionConfiguration class, you will notice that the default timeout interval might be set to a number such as 60. This means the session will be able to wait 60 seconds for a connection to be established between the app and a server that you are attempting to download something from or upload something to. I don't know about you, but I am not willing to wait 60 seconds before I can download some content from the Internet. Therefore, I would rather change this value to something like 15 or 20, maximum.

When you have your configuration object, pass it to the constructor of the NSURLSession class to create your session. This constructor can take a configuration file, a delegate, and an operation queue. We know about the configuration file, but what is the delegate? The delegate will be informed of various communications that your session or its download/upload tasks need to use. For instance, it can give you a progress report as data is downloaded, and let you know when an error has occurred when trying to download the content. The operation queue is the queue on which the session will schedule all the delegation tasks. If you want your delegation tasks to be performed on the main thread, use the `mainQueue` type method of the `NSOperationQueue` class.

 The delegate object of your session will be retained by the session object. In order to ensure that it gets released when you are done, invoke the `finishTasksAndInvalidate` method of your session when you are done with it. This will run all the current tasks to completion and then invalidate the session. No new tasks can be added to the session after this method is called.

Now that we have a session, we can construct two really interesting tasks that can download our content for us: a data task and a download task. The data task obviously gives you the downloaded data, whereas the download task not only downloads the data for you, but also saves it on disk so that you can access it later. This is really good for us because we can create download tasks and ask the session to download the content for us into a temporary URL. When it is done, we use `NSFileManager` to move this file into a more suitable URL for our application.

Bear in mind that after every task that you create with a URL session, you need to call the `resume` method on that task to start it. Don't ask me why Apple has named this method in such a strange way! It would have been better if it was called `start` or something similar, but there you go. We cannot do anything about that unless you want to be creative and create an extension on the `NSURLSessionTask` class, which is the superclass of both the `NSURLSessionDataTask` and the `NSURLSessionDownloadTask` classes, like so:

```
extension NSURLSessionTask{
  func start(){
    self.resume()
  }
}
```

We've had a look at data tasks. Let's look now at download tasks. What we are going to do is download the contents of a URL using `NSURLSession` and a download task. After we successfully download the contents, we will move the downloaded file from the temporary folder into the caches folder of our application:

```
import UIKit

extension NSURLSessionTask{
  func start(){
    self.resume()
  }
}

class ViewController: UIViewController, NSURLSessionDelegate {
```

```
var session: NSURLSession!

required init(coder aDecoder: NSCoder) {
  super.init(coder: aDecoder)

  /* Create our configuration first */
  let configuration =
  NSURLSessionConfiguration.defaultSessionConfiguration()
  configuration.timeoutIntervalForRequest = 15.0

  /* Now create a session that allows us to create the tasks */
  session = NSURLSession(configuration: configuration,
    delegate: self,
    delegateQueue: nil)

}

/* Just a little method to help us display alert dialogs to the user */
func displayAlertWithTitle(title: String, message: String){
  let controller = UIAlertController(title: title,
    message: message,
    preferredStyle: .Alert)

  controller.addAction(UIAlertAction(title: "OK",
    style: .Default,
    handler: nil))

  presentViewController(controller, animated: true, completion: nil)

}

override func viewDidAppear(animated: Bool) {
  super.viewDidAppear(animated)

  /* Now attempt to download the contents of the URL */
  let url = NSURL(string: "<# place a URL here #>")

  let task = session.downloadTaskWithURL(url!,
    completionHandler: {[weak self] (url: NSURL!,
      response: NSURLResponse!,
      error: NSError!) in

      if error == nil{

        let manager = NSFileManager()

        /* Get the path to the caches folder */
        var error: NSError?
        var destinationPath = manager.URLForDirectory(.CachesDirectory,
          inDomain: .UserDomainMask,
          appropriateForURL: url,
          create: true,
```

```
              error: &error)!

              /* Extract the last part of the source URL, which is the name of the
              file we are downloading  */
              let componentsOfUrl =
              url.absoluteString!.componentsSeparatedByString("/")
              let fileNameFromUrl = componentsOfUrl[componentsOfUrl.count - 1]

              /* Append the name of the file in the source URL to the
              destination folder */
              destinationPath =
                destinationPath.URLByAppendingPathComponent(fileNameFromUrl)

              /* Now move the file over */
              manager.moveItemAtURL(url, toURL: destinationPath, error: nil)

              let message = "Saved the downloaded data to = \(destinationPath)"

              self!.displayAlertWithTitle("Success", message: message)
            } else {
              self!.displayAlertWithTitle("Error",
                message: "Could not download the data. An error occurred")
            }

          })

          /* Our extension on the task adds the start method */
          task.start()

      }

    }
```

So far, we have used the completion handler of our tasks, but the delegate property of our session also plays a very important role. If you do not provide completion handlers to your tasks, your session's delegate will start receiving events instead.

Let's have a look at an example. Say that we want to create a data task and then be informed of the download's progress over time. Previously, on the completion handler of our data task, we were only told when the data was completely downloaded. But now we want to be notified while it is happening. So the first thing that we have to do is to pass nil as the completion handler of our data task. Then we have to conform to the NSURLSessionDataDelegate protocol. This protocol has a really handy method called URLSession:dataTask:didReceiveData:, which you can implement so you're notified while the data task is downloading the data from its URL.

The didReceiveData parameter of this method will give you access to the NSData that is being downloaded for you. Do not copy this data. Instead, use the enumerateByteR angesUsingBlock: method of the data instance to get the bytes out of it and add them to a mutable data. Let's start by defining a mutable data and also a session:

```swift
import UIKit

extension NSURLSessionTask{
  func start(){
    self.resume()
  }
}

class ViewController: UIViewController, NSURLSessionDelegate,
NSURLSessionDataDelegate {

  var session: NSURLSession!
  /* We will download a URL one chunk at a time and append the downloaded
  data to this mutable data */
  var mutableData: NSMutableData = NSMutableData()

  <# rest of the code #>

}
```

As soon as our app runs and is displayed to the user, we will attempt to download the contents of a URL using a data task as we saw before, but this time we will not provide a completion handler and instead will attempt to listen to delegation messages:

```swift
init(coder aDecoder: NSCoder!) {
  super.init(coder: aDecoder)

  /* Create our configuration first */
  let configuration =
  NSURLSessionConfiguration.defaultSessionConfiguration()
  configuration.timeoutIntervalForRequest = 15.0

  /* Now create a session that allows us to create the tasks */
  session = NSURLSession(configuration: configuration,
    delegate: self,
    delegateQueue: nil)

}

override func viewDidLoad() {
  super.viewDidLoad()

  /* Now attempt to download the contents of the URL */
  let url = NSURL(string: "<# place your URL here #>")

  let task = session.dataTaskWithURL(url!, completionHandler: nil)

  task.start()
```

```
}

/* Just a little method to help us display alert dialogs to the user */
func displayAlertWithTitle(title: String, message: String){
  let controller = UIAlertController(title: title,
    message: message,
    preferredStyle: .Alert)

  controller.addAction(UIAlertAction(title: "OK",
    style: .Default,
    handler: nil))

  presentViewController(controller, animated: true, completion: nil)

}
```

The next step is to define the URLSession:dataTask:didReceiveData: delegate method for our class so that we are notified whenever a chunk of data is downloaded:

```
/* This method will get called on a random thread because
we have not provided an operation queue to our session */
func URLSession(session: NSURLSession,
  dataTask: NSURLSessionDataTask!,
  didReceiveData data: NSData!) {

    data.enumerateByteRangesUsingBlock{[weak self]
      (pointer: UnsafePointer<()>,
      range: NSRange,
      stop: UnsafeMutablePointer<ObjCBool>) in
      let newData = NSData(bytes: pointer, length: range.length)
      self!.mutableData.appendData(newData)
    }

}
```

And after that, we also need to find out when the download finishes so that we can stop our session, which in turn releases the session's delegate, ensuring that we won't leak memory:

```
func URLSession(session: NSURLSession,
  task: NSURLSessionTask,
  didCompleteWithError error: NSError){

    /* Now you have your data in the mutableData property */
    session.finishTasksAndInvalidate()

    dispatch_async(dispatch_get_main_queue(), {[weak self] in

      var message = "Finished downloading your content"

      if error != nil{
        message = "Failed to download your content"
      }
```

```
            self!.displayAlertWithTitle("Done", message: message)

        })

    }
```

See Also

Recipe 11.2

11.2. Downloading Data in the Background Using NSURLSession

Problem

You want your application to be able to download data even when sent to the background.

Solution

Building on top of what we learned in Recipe 11.1, you can accomplish this task by creating a session with a background configuration. Your background configuration can be instantiated using the `backgroundSessionConfigurationWithIdentifier:` type method of the `NSURLSessionConfiguration` class.

After you are done creating your configuration, create an instance of the `NSURLSession` class with a valid delegate. This delegate will then receive events on your connection whether your app is in the foreground or background.

Then create a download task from your session using its `downloadTaskWithURL:` method. When the download task is ready, call the `resume` method on it to kick it off.

Although your session delegate can receive events related to your download task, there are certain limitations. Data tasks do not support downloading content while your app is in the background. And background downloading won't happen if the user shuts down your app manually. The downloads do work, however, when your app is sent to the background by the user and even if iOS has shut your app down completely while it was in the background. Even if iOS shuts your app down—usually because of a lack of system resources, but perhaps for other reasons—your background download tasks will still happen, because a system process handles the work of downloading the content.

Discussion

One of the beauties of the NSURLSession class is that it allows downloading content in the background. You need to create a download task for that, though. You also need to create a background configuration for your session. This configuration has to have an identifier that you can use to resume a broken download later. For instance, if you are downloading content in the background and the user shuts down that app manually, you can bring back the same configuration identifier when your app is run again by the user, and resume the download of your content using the downloadTaskWithResumeData: method of your session. The only thing you have to pass to this method is the handle to the data that was previously downloaded.

For the purpose of this example, the identifier of our configuration is a computed property that will first find out if we stored the identifier for our configuration in system defaults. If not, it generates one by taking the current date and time and persists that in the system defaults. The next time this computed property is called, it will get its value from the system defaults so that from launch to launch, the identifier of our session configuration will be the same.

```
import UIKit

extension NSURLSessionTask{
  func start(){
    self.resume()
  }
}

class ViewController: UIViewController, NSURLSessionDelegate,
NSURLSessionDownloadDelegate, NSURLSessionTaskDelegate {

  var session: NSURLSession!

  /* This computed property will generate a unique identifier for our
  background session configuration. The first time it is used, it will get
  the current date and time and return that as a string to you. It will
  also save that string into the system defaults so that it can retrieve
  it the next time it is called. This computed property's value
  is persistent between launches of this app.
  */
  var configurationIdentifier: String{
  let userDefaults = NSUserDefaults.standardUserDefaults()
    /* Designate a key that makes sense to your app */
    let key = "configurationIdentifier"
    let previousValue = userDefaults.stringForKey(key) as String?

    if let thePreviousValue = previousValue{
      return previousValue!
    } else {
      let newValue = NSDate().description
      userDefaults.setObject(newValue, forKey: key)
```

```
      userDefaults.synchronize()
      return newValue
    }
  }

  <# rest of the code goes here #>
}
```

Now that we have all our variables and have conformed to the relevant protocols, we are going to start the download task of our URL and kick off the download itself:

```
init(coder aDecoder: NSCoder!) {
  super.init(coder: aDecoder)

  /* Create our configuration first */
  let configuration =
  NSURLSessionConfiguration.backgroundSessionConfigurationWithIdentifier(
    configurationIdentifier)

  configuration.timeoutIntervalForRequest = 15.0

  /* Now create a session that allows us to create the tasks */
  session = NSURLSession(configuration: configuration,
    delegate: self,
    delegateQueue: nil)

}

/* Just a little method to help us display alert dialogs to the user */
func displayAlertWithTitle(title: String, message: String){
  let controller = UIAlertController(title: title,
    message: message,
    preferredStyle: .Alert)

  controller.addAction(UIAlertAction(title: "OK",
    style: .Default,
    handler: nil))

  presentViewController(controller, animated: true, completion: nil)

}

override func viewDidAppear(animated: Bool) {
  super.viewDidAppear(animated)

  /* Now attempt to download the contents of the URL */
  let url = NSURL(string: "<# place your URL here #>")

  let task = session.downloadTaskWithURL(url!)

  /* Our own extension on the task adds the start method */
  task.start()
```

```
    }
```

We can get to know when there is incoming data using the `URLSession:download Task:didWriteData:totalBytesWritten:totalBytesExpectedToWrite:` delegate method of our session delegate:

```
func URLSession(session: NSURLSession,
  downloadTask: NSURLSessionDownloadTask,
  didWriteData bytesWritten: Int64,
  totalBytesWritten: Int64,
  totalBytesExpectedToWrite: Int64){
    println("Received data")
}
```

We also want to know when the downloading process has finished, so let's implement the `URLSession:didCompleteWithError:` delegate method:

```
/* We now get to know that the download procedure finished */
func URLSession(session: NSURLSession, task: NSURLSessionTask,
  didCompleteWithError error: NSError){

    print("Finished ")

    if error == nil{
      println("without an error")
    } else {
      println("with an error = \(error)")
    }

    /* Release the delegate */
    session.finishTasksAndInvalidate()

}
```

If the download task succeeds, it saves the downloaded data to disk and gives us the URL back. In that case, the `URLSession:downloadTask:didFinishDownloading ToURL:` method of our delegate gets called.

```
func URLSession(session: NSURLSession,
  downloadTask: NSURLSessionDownloadTask,
  didFinishDownloadingToURL location: NSURL){
    println("Finished writing the downloaded content to URL = \(location)")
}
```

Now it is your turn to put this to test and see how it works. Run this on a device, send your app to the background, and see what happens in the console while you are debugging your app.

See Also

Recipe 11.1

11.3. Uploading Data Using NSURLSession

Problem

You want to be able to upload some data from inside your application to a web server.

Solution

First, prepare a session configuration object using the `defaultSessionConfigura` `tion` type method of the `NSURLSessionConfiguration` class. Then instantiate a URL session using the constructor of the `NSURLSession` class. When you have your session, create an upload task using the `uploadTaskWithRequest:fromData:` method of your URL session. Then invoke the `resume` method on it to start it.

This recipe builds on top of what we learned in the Recipe 11.1 recipe. I strongly advise that you read the aforementioned recipe before proceeding with this one.

Discussion

Let's jump right in. Assume you want to convert a simple string to its `NSData` representation and then upload that data to a server. What we need is a url session that we define like so:

```
import UIKit

extension NSURLSessionTask{
  func start(){
    self.resume()
  }
}

class ViewController: UIViewController, NSURLSessionDelegate,
  NSURLSessionDataDelegate {

  var session: NSURLSession!

  <# rest of your code #>
}
```

Then we create our session and set the delegate of the URL session to receive delegate messages:

```
init(coder aDecoder: NSCoder!) {
  super.init(coder: aDecoder)
```

```
/* Create our configuration first */
let configuration =
NSURLSessionConfiguration.defaultSessionConfiguration()
configuration.timeoutIntervalForRequest = 15.0

/* Now create a session that allows us to create the tasks */
session = NSURLSession(configuration: configuration,
  delegate: self,
  delegateQueue: nil)

}
```

After this, we use the uploadTaskWithRequest:fromData: method of our URL session to create an upload task of type NSURLSessionUploadTask. This class subclasses the NSURLSessionDataTask class, which in turn subclasses the NSURLSessionTask class eventually. The aforementioned method takes in a request of type NSURLRequest, which can also be a mutable request of type NSMutableURLRequest. When you have created your URL request, you can submit it to this method. For its fromData parameter, you can provide the instance of NSData that you are trying to submit to the server. Here is our code:

```
override func viewDidLoad() {
  super.viewDidLoad()

  /* Now attempt to upload to the following URL */

  let dataToUpload = "Hello World".dataUsingEncoding(NSUTF8StringEncoding,
    allowLossyConversion: false)

  let url = NSURL(string: "<# place your upload URL here #>")
  let request = NSMutableURLRequest(URL: url!)
  request.HTTPMethod = "POST"
  let task = session.uploadTaskWithRequest(request, fromData: dataToUpload)

  /* The start method is an extension that we built on this class */
  task.start()

}
```

When the upload task is done, whether it fails or succeeds, your session delegate will receive the URLSession:task:didCompleteWithError: message. You can then check the error object that this method gives you to see if the upload task succeeded or not:

```
func URLSession(session: NSURLSession,
  task: NSURLSessionTask,
  didCompleteWithError error: NSError){

    /* Now you have your data in the mutableData property */
    session.finishTasksAndInvalidate()

    println("Error = \(error)")
```

```
dispatch_async(dispatch_get_main_queue(), {[weak self] in

  var message = "Finished uploading your content"

  if error != nil{
    message = "Failed to upload your content"
  }

  self!.displayAlertWithTitle("Done", message: message)

})

}
```

See Also

Recipe 11.1

11.4. Downloading Asynchronously with NSURLConnection

Problem

You want to download a file from a URL, asynchronously.

Solution

Use the NSURLConnection class with an asynchronous request.

Discussion

There are two ways of using the NSURLConnection class. One is asynchronous, and the other is synchronous. An asynchronous connection creates a new thread and does its downloading process on the new thread. A synchronous connection blocks the *calling thread* while downloading content and doing its communication.

Many developers think that a synchronous connection blocks the *main thread*, but that is incorrect. A synchronous connection always blocks the thread from which it is fired. If you fire a synchronous connection from the main thread, yes, the main thread will be blocked. But if you fire a synchronous connection from a thread other than the main thread, it will be like an asynchronous connection in that it won't block your main thread. In fact, the only difference between a synchronous and an asynchronous connection is that the runtime creates a thread for the asynchronous connection, but does not for a synchronous connection.

In order to create an asynchronous connection, we need to do the following:

1. Have our URL in an instance of NSString.
2. Convert our string to an instance of NSURL.
3. Place our URL in a URL Request of type NSURLRequest, or in the case of mutable URLs, in an instance of NSMutableURLRequest.
4. Create an instance of NSURLConnection and pass the URL request to it.

We can create an asynchronous URL connection using the sendAsynchronousRequest:queue:completionHandler: class method of NSURLConnection. Here are the parameters to this method:

sendAsynchronousRequest
A request of type NSURLRequest, as we already discussed.

queue
An operation queue. We can simply allocate and initialize a new operation queue and pass it to this method, if we wish.

completionHandler
A block object to be executed when the asynchronous connection finishes its work either successfully or unsuccessfully. This block object should accept three parameters:

1. An object of type NSURLResponse, which encapsulates the response that the server sent us, if any.
2. Data of type NSData, if any. This data will be the data that the connection fetched from the URL.
3. Error of type NSError if an error occurs.

 The sendAsynchronousRequest:queue:completionHandler: method doesn't get called on the main thread, so make sure that, if you want to perform a UI-related task, you are back on the main thread.

Enough talk. Let's have a look at an example. In this example, we try to fetch the HTML contents of a web page and then print the contents as a string to the console window:

```
import UIKit

class ViewController: UIViewController {

  override func viewDidLoad() {
    super.viewDidLoad()
```

```
/* Construct the URL and the request to send to the connection */
let urlAsString = "http://www.apple.com"
let url = NSURL(string: urlAsString)
let urlRequest = NSURLRequest(URL: url!)

/* We do the asynchronous request on our queue */
let queue = NSOperationQueue()

NSURLConnection.sendAsynchronousRequest(urlRequest,
  queue: queue,
  completionHandler: {(response: NSURLResponse!,
    data: NSData!,
    error: NSError!) in

    /* Now we may have access to the data, but check if an error came back
    first or not */
    if data.length > 0 && error == nil{
      let html = NSString(data: data, encoding: NSUTF8StringEncoding)
      println("html = \(html)")
    } else if data.length == 0 && error == nil{
      println("Nothing was downloaded")
    } else if error != nil{
      println("Error happened = \(error)")
    }

})

}

}
```

It's as simple as that. If you wanted to save the data that the connection downloaded to disk, you could simply do so using the appropriate methods of the NSData that we get from the completion block:

```
import UIKit

extension NSURL{
  /* An extension on the NSURL class that allows us to retrieve the current
  documents folder path */
  class func documentsFolder() -> NSURL{
    let fileManager = NSFileManager()
    return fileManager.URLForDirectory(.DocumentDirectory,
      inDomain: .UserDomainMask,
      appropriateForURL: nil,
      create: false,
      error: nil)!
  }
}

class ViewController: UIViewController {
```

```
override func viewDidLoad() {
  super.viewDidLoad()

  /* Construct the URL and the request to send to the connection */
  let urlAsString = "http://www.apple.com"
  let url = NSURL(string: urlAsString)
  let urlRequest = NSURLRequest(URL: url!)

  /* We do the asynchronous request on our queue */
  let queue = NSOperationQueue()

  NSURLConnection.sendAsynchronousRequest(urlRequest,
    queue: queue,
    completionHandler: {(response: NSURLResponse!,
      data: NSData!,
      error: NSError!) in

      /* Now we may have access to the data, but check if an error came back
      first or not */
      if data.length > 0 && error == nil{

        /* Append the filename to the documents directory */
        let filePath =
        NSURL.documentsFolder().URLByAppendingPathComponent("apple.html")

        if data.writeToURL(filePath, atomically: true){
          println("Successfully saved the file to \(filePath)")
        } else {
          println("Failed to save the file to \(filePath)")
        }

      } else if data.length == 0 && error == nil{
        println("Nothing was downloaded")
      } else if error != nil{
        println("Error happened = \(error)")
      }

  })

}

}
```

It's that simple, really. In older versions of iOS SDK, URL connections used the delegation model, but now it's all simply block-based, and you no longer have to worry about implementing delegate methods.

It's also a very good idea to start looking at implementing your connections using the NSURLSession class, as we saw in Recipe 11.1. URL sessions are much more intuitive and customizable, and Apple is steering programmers in general toward using these instead of URL connections to download or upload data.

11.5. Handling Timeouts in Asynchronous Connections

Problem

You want to set a wait limit—in other words, a timeout—on an asynchronous connection.

Solution

Set the timeout on the URL request that you pass to the `NSURLConnection` class.

Discussion

When instantiating an object of type `NSURLRequest` to pass to your URL connection, you can use its `requestWithURL:cachePolicy:timeoutInterval:` class method and pass the desired number of seconds of your timeout as the `timeoutInterval` parameter.

For instance, if you want to wait a maximum of 30 seconds to download the contents of a web page using a synchronous connection, create your URL request like so:

```
import UIKit

class ViewController: UIViewController {

  override func viewDidLoad() {
    super.viewDidLoad()

    /* We have a 15 second timeout for our connection */
    let timeout = 15

    /* You can choose your own URL here */
    let urlAsString = "http://www.apple.com"
    let url = NSURL(string: urlAsString)

    /* Set the timeout on our request here */
    let urlRequest = NSURLRequest(URL: url!,
      cachePolicy: .ReloadIgnoringLocalAndRemoteCacheData,
      timeoutInterval: 15.0)

    let queue = NSOperationQueue()

    NSURLConnection.sendAsynchronousRequest(urlRequest,
      queue: queue,
      completionHandler: {(response: NSURLResponse!,
        data: NSData!,
        error: NSError!) in

        /* Now we may have access to the data, but check if an error came back
        first or not */
        if data.length > 0 && error == nil{
```

```
            let html = NSString(data: data, encoding: NSUTF8StringEncoding)
            println("html = \(html)")
        } else if data.length == 0 && error == nil{
            println("Nothing was downloaded")
        } else if error != nil{
            println("Error happened = \(error)")
        }

      }
    )

  }

}
```

What happens here is that the runtime tries to retrieve the contents of the provided URL. If this can be done before the timeout has elapsed and the connection is established before the timeout occurs, then fine. If not, the runtime provides you with a timeout error in the error parameter of the completion block.

11.6. Downloading Synchronously with NSURLConnection

Problem

You want to download the contents of a URL, synchronously.

Solution

Use the `sendSynchronousRequest:returningResponse:error:` type method of `NSURLConnection`. The return value of this method is data of type `NSData`.

Discussion

Using the `sendSynchronousRequest:returningResponse:error:` class method of `NSURLConnection`, we can send a synchronous request to a URL. Now, remember: synchronous connections do *not* necessarily block the main thread! Synchronous connections block the *current thread*, and if the current thread is the main thread, then the main thread will be blocked. If you go on a global concurrent queue with GCD and then initiate a synchronous connection, then you are *not* blocking the main thread.

Let's go ahead and initiate our first synchronous connection and see what happens. In this example, we try to retrieve a website's data:

```
import UIKit

class ViewController: UIViewController {

  override func viewDidLoad() {
```

```
    super.viewDidLoad()

    println("We are here...")

    /* You can have a custom URL here */
    let urlAsString = "http://www.yahoo.com"
    let url = NSURL(string: urlAsString)

    let urlRequest = NSURLRequest(URL: url!)

    var response: NSURLResponse?
    var error: NSError?

    println("Firing synchronous url connection...")

    /* Get the data for our URL, synchronously */
    let data = NSURLConnection.sendSynchronousRequest(urlRequest,
      returningResponse: &response,
      error: &error)

    if data != nil && error == nil{
      println("\(data!.length) bytes of data was returned")
    }
    else if data!.length == 0 && error == nil{
      println("No data was returned")
    }
    else if error != nil{
      println("Error happened = \(error)");
    }

    println("We are done")

  }

}
```

If you run this app and then look at the console window, you will see something similar to this printed out:

```
We are here...
Firing synchronous url connection...
160014 bytes of data was returned
We are done
```

So it's obvious that the current thread printed the string We are here... to the console window, waited for the connection to finish (as it was a synchronous connection that blocks the current thread), and then printed the We are done. text to the console window. Now let's do an experiment. Let's place the same exact synchronous connection inside a global concurrent queue in GCD, which guarantees concurrency, and see what happens:

```
import UIKit

class ViewController: UIViewController {

  override func viewDidLoad() {
    super.viewDidLoad()

    println("We are here...")

    /* You can have a custom URL here */
    let urlAsString = "http://www.yahoo.com"
    let url = NSURL(string: urlAsString)

    let urlRequest = NSURLRequest(URL: url!)

    var response: NSURLResponse?
    var error: NSError?

    println("Firing synchronous url connection...")

    let dispatchQueue =
    dispatch_get_global_queue(DISPATCH_QUEUE_PRIORITY_DEFAULT, 0)

    dispatch_async(dispatchQueue, {

      /* Get the data for our URL, synchronously */
      let data = NSURLConnection.sendSynchronousRequest(urlRequest,
        returningResponse: &response,
        error: &error)

      if data != nil && error == nil{
        println("\(data!.length) bytes of data was returned")
      }
      else if data!.length == 0 && error == nil{
        println("No data was returned")
      }
      else if error != nil{
        println("Error happened = \(error)");
      }

    })

    println("We are done")

  }

}
```

The output will be similar to this:

```
We are here...
Firing synchronous url connection...
```

```
We are done
159254 bytes of data was returned
```

So in this example, the current thread carried on to print the `We are done.` text to the console window without having to wait for the synchronous connection to finish reading from its URL. That is interesting, isn't it? So this proves that a synchronous URL connection won't necessarily block the main thread, if managed properly. Synchronous connections are guaranteed to block the *current thread*, though.

11.7. Customizing URL Requests

Problem

You want to adjust various HTTP headers and settings of a URL request before passing it to a URL connection.

Solution

This technique is the basis of many useful recipes shown later in this chapter. Use `NSMutableURLRequest` instead of `NSURLRequest`.

Discussion

A URL request can be either *mutable* or *immutable*. A mutable URL request can be changed after it has been allocated and initialized, whereas an immutable URL request cannot. Mutable URL requests are the target of this recipe. You can create them using the `NSMutableURLRequest` class.

Let's have a look at an example in which we change the timeout interval of a URL request *after* we allocate and initialize it:

```
let urlAsString = "http://www.apple.com"
let url = NSURL(string: urlAsString)

let urlRequest = NSMutableURLRequest(URL: url)

urlRequest.timeoutInterval = 30
```

Now let's have a look at another example where we set the URL and the timeout of a URL request after it has been allocated and initialized:

```
let urlAsString = "http://www.apple.com"
let url = NSURL(string: urlAsString)
let urlRequest = NSMutableURLRequest()
urlRequest.timeoutInterval = 30
urlRequest.URL = url
```

In other recipes in this chapter, we have a look at some of the really neat tricks that we can perform using mutable URL requests.

11.8. Sending HTTP Requests with NSURLConnection

Problem

You want to send a GET, PUT, POST, or DELETE request over the HTTP protocol and perhaps pass parameters along with your request to the receiver.

Solution

Set the `HTTPMethod` property of your mutable URL request, of type `NSMutableURLRequest`, to the required HTTP method. For instance, if you want to send a GET call to the server, set the value of this property to "GET" as a string object. If you want to send a POST value, set the value of this property to "POST". Have a look at the discussion section of this recipe for more information on how to configure your mutable URL request for various HTTP methods.

Discussion

A GET request is a request to a web server to retrieve data. The request usually carries some parameters, which are sent in a query string as part of the URL.

In order to test a GET call, you need to find a web server that accepts the GET method and can send you some data back. This is simple. You might already know that when you open a web page in your browser, your browser by default sends a GET request to that end point, so you can use this recipe on any website of your liking.

To simulate sending query string parameters in a GET request to the same web service using `NSURLConnection`, use a mutable URL request and explicitly specify your HTTP method to `GET` using the `setHTTPMethod:` method of `NSMutableURLRequest` and put your parameters as part of the URL, like so:

```
import UIKit

class ViewController: UIViewController {

  override func viewDidLoad() {
    super.viewDidLoad()

    let httpMethod = "GET"

    /* We have a 15-second timeout for our connection */
    let timeout = 15

    /* You can choose your own URL here */
```

```
var urlAsString = "<# place your url here #>"

urlAsString += "?param1=First"
urlAsString += "&param2=Second"

let url = NSURL(string: urlAsString)

/* Set the timeout on our request here */
let urlRequest = NSMutableURLRequest(URL: url!,
  cachePolicy: .ReloadIgnoringLocalAndRemoteCacheData,
  timeoutInterval: 15.0)

urlRequest.HTTPMethod = httpMethod

let queue = NSOperationQueue()

NSURLConnection.sendAsynchronousRequest(urlRequest,
  queue: queue,
  completionHandler: {(response: NSURLResponse!,
    data: NSData!,
    error: NSError!) in

    /* Now we may have access to the data, but check if an error came back
    first or not */
    if data.length > 0 && error == nil{
      let html = NSString(data: data, encoding: NSUTF8StringEncoding)
      println("html = \(html)")
    } else if data.length == 0 && error == nil{
      println("Nothing was downloaded")
    } else if error != nil{
      println("Error happened = \(error)")
    }

  }
)

}

}
```

 The urlAsString variable in this code is an Xcode variable template. If you copy and paste this code into your Xcode project, the variable will get displayed as shown in Figure 11-1. Before running this example code, ensure that you assigned a valid URL to the aforementioned variable.

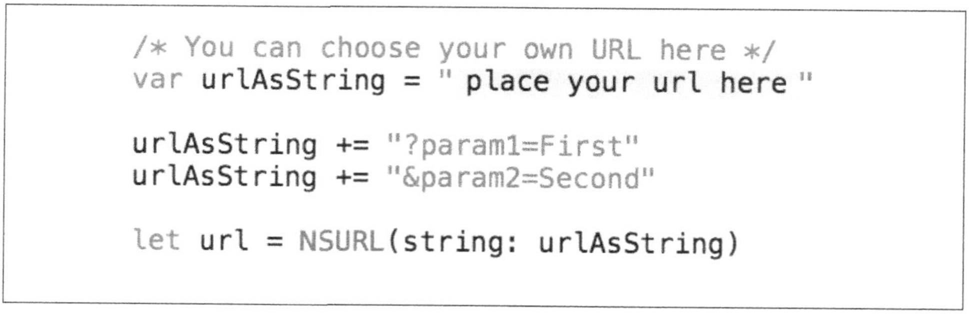

```
/* You can choose your own URL here */
var urlAsString = " place your url here "

urlAsString += "?param1=First"
urlAsString += "&param2=Second"

let url = NSURL(string: urlAsString)
```

Figure 11-1. A replaceable variable in Xcode

Just as with the GET method, we can use the POST method using NSURLConnection. We must explicitly set our URL's method to POST.

Let's write a simple app that can create an asynchronous connection and send a few parameters as a query string and a few parameters in the HTTP body to a URL:

```
import UIKit

class ViewController: UIViewController {

  override func viewDidLoad() {
    super.viewDidLoad()

    let httpMethod = "POST"

    /* We have a 15-second timeout for our connection */
    let timeout = 15

    /* You can choose your own URL here */
    var urlAsString = "<# place your url here #>"

    /* These are the parameters that will be sent as part of the URL */
    urlAsString += "?param1=First"
    urlAsString += "&param2=Second"

    let url = NSURL(string: urlAsString)

    /* Set the timeout on our request here */
    let urlRequest = NSMutableURLRequest(URL: url!,
      cachePolicy: .ReloadIgnoringLocalAndRemoteCacheData,
      timeoutInterval: 15.0)

    urlRequest.HTTPMethod = httpMethod

    /* These are the POST parameters */
    let body =
    "bodyParam1=BodyValue1&bodyParam2=BodyValue2".dataUsingEncoding(
      NSUTF8StringEncoding,
```

```
      allowLossyConversion: false)

    urlRequest.HTTPBody = body

    let queue = NSOperationQueue()

    NSURLConnection.sendAsynchronousRequest(urlRequest,
      queue: queue,
      completionHandler: {(response: NSURLResponse!,
        data: NSData!,
        error: NSError!) in

        /* Now we may have access to the data, but check if an error came back
        first or not */
        if data.length > 0 && error == nil{
          let html = NSString(data: data, encoding: NSUTF8StringEncoding)
          println("html = \(html)")
        } else if data.length == 0 && error == nil{
          println("Nothing was downloaded")
        } else if error != nil{
          println("Error happened = \(error)")
        }

      }
    )

  }

}
```

The first parameter sent in the HTTP body does not have to be prefixed with a question mark, unlike the first parameter in a query
string.

Do a bit of experimenting on your own, using the DELETE and the PUT HTTP methods
as well as the POST and GET methods as you saw earlier in this recipe. All you have to
do is to change the HTTPMethod property.

11.9. Serializing and Deserializing JSON Objects

Problem

You want to serialize a dictionary or an array into a JSON object that you can transfer
over the network or simply save to disk. Alternatively, you want to deserialize JSON-
formatted data into a dictionary or an array.

Solution

Use the `dataWithJSONObject:options:error:` method of the `NSJSONSerialization`
class to serialize a dictionary or an array into a JSON object represented by its data. You
can also use the `JSONObjectWithData:options:error:` method of the same class to
return a dictionary or an array from the data in a JSON object.

Discussion

The `dataWithJSONObject:options:error:` method of the `NSJSONSerialization` class
can serialize dictionaries and arrays that only contain instances of `NSString`, `NSNum
ber`, `NSArray`, or `NSDictionary` variables, or `NSNull` for nil values. As mentioned, the
object that you pass to this method should be either an array or a dictionary.

Now let's go ahead and create a simple dictionary with a few keys and values:

```
let dictionary:[NSString : AnyObject] =
[
  "First Name" : "Anthony",
  "Last Name" : "Robbins",
  "Age" : 51,
  "children" : [
    "Anthony's Son 1",
    "Anthony's Daughter 1",
    "Anthony's Son 2",
    "Anthony's Son 3",
    "Anthony's Daughter 2"
  ],
]
```

As you can see, this dictionary contains the first name, last name, and age of Anthony
Robbins. A key in the dictionary named children contains the names of Anthony's children. This is an array of strings with each string representing one child. So by this time,
the `dictionary` variable contains all the values that we want it to contain. It is now time
to serialize it into a JSON object:

```
var error: NSError?
let jsonData = NSJSONSerialization.dataWithJSONObject(dictionary,
  options: .PrettyPrinted,
  error: &error)

if let data = jsonData{
  if data.length > 0 && error == nil{
    println("Successfully serialized the dictionary into data \(jsonData)")
  }
  else if data.length == 0 && error == nil{
    println("No data was returned after serialization.")
  }
  else if error != nil{
    println("An error happened = \(error)")
```

```
    }
}
```

The return value of the `dataWithJSONObject:options:error:` method is data of type `NSData`. However, you can simply turn this data into a string and print it to the console using the `initWithData:encoding:` constructor of `NSString`. Here is the complete example that serializes a dictionary into a JSON object, converts that object into a string, and prints the string out to the console window:

```swift
import UIKit

class ViewController: UIViewController {

  override func viewDidLoad() {
    super.viewDidLoad()

    let dictionary:[NSString : AnyObject] =
    [
      "First Name" : "Anthony",
      "Last Name" : "Robbins",
      "Age" : 51,
      "children" : [
        "Anthony's Son 1",
        "Anthony's Daughter 1",
        "Anthony's Son 2",
        "Anthony's Son 3",
        "Anthony's Daughter 2"
      ],
    ]

    /* Convert the dictionary into a data structure */
    var error: NSError?
    let jsonData = NSJSONSerialization.dataWithJSONObject(dictionary,
      options: .PrettyPrinted,
      error: &error)

    if let data = jsonData{
      if data.length > 0 && error == nil{
        println("Successfully serialized the dictionary into data")

        /* Then convert the data into a string */
        let jsonString = NSString(data: data, encoding: NSUTF8StringEncoding)
        println("JSON String = \(jsonString)")

      }
      else if data.length == 0 && error == nil{
        println("No data was returned after serialization.")
      }
      else if error != nil{
        println("An error happened = \(error)")
      }
    }
}
```

```
    }

}
```

When you run this app, the following results print to the console window:

```
Successfully serialized the dictionary into data
JSON String = {
  "Age" : 51,
  "children" : [
    "Anthony's Son 1",
    "Anthony's Daughter 1",
    "Anthony's Son 2",
    "Anthony's Son 3",
    "Anthony's Daughter 2"
  ],
  "First Name" : "Anthony",
  "Last Name" : "Robbins"
}
```

If you already serialized your dictionary or array into a JSON object (encapsulated inside an instance of NSData, you should be able to deserialize them back into a dictionary or an array using the JSONObjectWithData:options:error: method of the NSJSONSerialization class. The object that is returned by this method will be either a dictionary or an array, depending on the data that we pass to it. Here is an example:

```
func retrieveJsonFromData(data: NSData){

  /* Now try to deserialize the JSON object into a dictionary */
  var error: NSError?

  let jsonObject: AnyObject? = NSJSONSerialization.JSONObjectWithData(data,
    options: .AllowFragments,
    error: &error)

  if error == nil{

    println("Successfully deserialized...")

    if jsonObject is NSDictionary{
      let deserializedDictionary = jsonObject as NSDictionary
      println("Deserialized JSON Dictionary = \(deserializedDictionary)")
    }
    else if jsonObject is NSArray{
      let deserializedArray = jsonObject as NSArray
      println("Deserialized JSON Array = \(deserializedArray)")
    }
    else {
      /* Some other object was returned. We don't know how to
      deal with this situation because the deserializer only
      returns dictionaries or arrays */
    }
```

```
    }
    else if error != nil{
      println("An error happened while deserializing the JSON data.")
    }

  }
```

The options parameter of the JSONObjectWithData:options:error: method accepts one or a mixture of the following values:

NSJSONReadingMutableContainers

The dictionary or the array returned by the JSONObjectWithData:options:error: method will be mutable. In other words, this method will return either an instance of NSMutableArray or NSMutableDictionary, as opposed to an immutable array or dictionary.

NSJSONReadingMutableLeaves

Leaf values will be encapsulated into instances of NSMutableString.

NSJSONReadingAllowFragments

Allows the deserialization of JSON data whose root top-level object is not an array or a dictionary.

11.10. Integrating Social Sharing into Your Apps

Problem

You want to provide sharing capabilities in your app so that your user can compose a tweet or a Facebook status update on her device.

Solution

Incorporate the Social framework into your app and use the SLComposeViewController class to compose social sharing messages, such as tweets.

Discussion

The SLComposeViewController class is available in the Social framework and with the Modules feature in the LLVM compiler. All you have to do to start using this framework is import its umbrella header file into your project like so:

```
import UIKit
import Social
```

As Apple adds new social sharing options to the SDK, you can query the Social framework to find out, at runtime, which one of the services is available on the device that runs your app. Because the particular services vary from device to device, you should not try to use one until you make sure it is running. In order to query iOS for that, you need to use the `isAvailableForServiceType:` class method of the `SLComposeViewCon` `troller` class. The parameter that you pass to this method is of type `NSString`, and you can pass any of the values that start with `SLServiceType` to this parameter.

Once you know a service is available, you can use the constructor of the `SLCompose` `ViewController` class to get a new instance of your social sharing view controller. After that, things are super easy. All you have to do is use one or more of the following methods on your social sharing view controller:

`setInitialText:`
: Sets the string that you want to share with others.

`addImage:`
: Adds an image that has to be attached to your post.

`addURL:`
: Adds a URL that you can share along with your text and image.

The instance of the `SLComposeViewController` will also have a very handy property called `completionHandler`, which is a block object of type `SLComposeViewController` `CompletionHandler`. This completion handler will be called whenever the user finishes the sharing process successfully (meaning that she sends the sharing post out to be delivered by iOS to Twitter, Facebook, etc.) or if she cancels the dialog. A parameter of type `SLComposeViewControllerResult` will be delivered to this method to denote the type of event that happened, such as success or cancellation.

OK, enough talking. Let's get to the juicy stuff. Here we are going to look at a code snippet that tries to find out whether the current device has Twitter sharing capabilities. If it does, the code composes a simple tweet with a picture and URL and displays the tweet dialog to the user, ready for tweeting:

```
import UIKit
import Social

class ViewController: UIViewController {

  override func viewDidAppear(animated: Bool) {
    super.viewDidAppear(animated)

    let serviceType = SLServiceTypeTwitter

    if SLComposeViewController.isAvailableForServiceType(serviceType){
      let controller = SLComposeViewController(forServiceType: serviceType)
      controller.setInitialText("Safari is a great browser!")
      controller.addImage(UIImage(named: "Safari"))
      controller.addURL(NSURL(string: "http://www.apple.com/safari/"))
      controller.completionHandler = {(result: SLComposeViewControllerResult) in
        println("Completed")
      }
      presentViewController(controller, animated: true, completion: nil)
```

```
    } else {
      println("The Twitter service is not available")
    }

  }

}
```

When you run this app on a device that has Twitter integration enabled in the iOS settings, the user sees something similar to that shown in Figure 11-2.

Figure 11-2. Composing a simple tweet with the Social framework

With this information, you can compose various other messages, such as Facebook updates. All you have to do, as explained earlier, is to find out at runtime whether the given service is enabled and then attempt to use it by adding text, images, and URLs to your request.

One last thing to keep in mind is that the completion handler for your composer view controllers *may* be called on a different thread from the one that you used to create the controller. So remember that and use the techniques that you learned in Chapter 7 to switch to the main thread inside the completion handler if you want to do something UI related.

See Also

Recipe 11.0, "Introduction"

CHAPTER 12

Multimedia

12.0. Introduction

The Audio and Video (AV) Foundation framework in the iOS SDK allows developers to play and/or record audio and video with ease. In addition, the Media Player framework allows developers to play audio and video files.

Before you can run the code in this chapter, you must add the *AVFoundation.frame work* and *MediaPlayer.framework* frameworks to your Xcode project. With the new LLVM compiler, the only thing you need to do to include these frameworks into your app is to import their umbrella header files like so:

```
import AVFoundation
import MediaPlayer
```

12.1. Playing Audio Files

Problem

You want to be able to play an audio file in your application.

Solution

Use the AV Foundation framework's AVAudioPlayer class.

Discussion

The AVAudioPlayer class in the AV Foundation framework can play back all audio formats supported by iOS. The delegate property of an instance of AVAudioPlayer allows you to get notified by events, such as when the audio playback is interrupted or when an error occurs as a result of playing an audio file. Let's have a look at a simple example that demonstrates how we can play an audio file from the application's bundle:

```
import UIKit
import AVFoundation

class ViewController: UIViewController, AVAudioPlayerDelegate {

  var audioPlayer: AVAudioPlayer?

  /* The delegate message that will let us know that the player
  has finished playing an audio file */
  func audioPlayerDidFinishPlaying(player: AVAudioPlayer!,
    successfully flag: Bool) {
      println("Finished playing the song")
  }

  override func viewDidLoad() {
    super.viewDidLoad()

    let dispatchQueue =
    dispatch_get_global_queue(DISPATCH_QUEUE_PRIORITY_DEFAULT, 0)

    dispatch_async(dispatchQueue, {[weak self] in
      let mainBundle = NSBundle.mainBundle()

      /* Find the location of our file to feed to the audio player */
      let filePath = mainBundle.pathForResource("MySong", ofType:"mp3")

      if let path = filePath{
        let fileData = NSData(contentsOfFile: path)

        var error:NSError?

        /* Start the audio player */
        self!.audioPlayer = AVAudioPlayer(data: fileData, error: &error)

        /* Did we get an instance of AVAudioPlayer? */
        if let player = self!.audioPlayer{
          /* Set the delegate and start playing */
          player.delegate = self
          if player.prepareToPlay() && player.play(){
            /* Successfully started playing */
          } else {
            /* Failed to play */
          }
        } else {
          /* Failed to instantiate AVAudioPlayer */
        }
      }

    })
```

```
    }
  }
```

As you can see, the file's data is loaded into an instance of `NSData` and then passed on to `AVAudioPlayer`'s `initWithData:error:` method. Because we need the actual, absolute path of the MP3 file to extract the data from that file, we invoke the `mainBundle` class method of `NSBundle` to retrieve the information from the application's configuration. The `pathForResource:ofType:` instance method of `NSBundle` can then be used to retrieve the absolute path to a resource of a specific type, as demonstrated in the example code.

The `audioPlayerDidFinishPlaying:successfully:` delegate method of the audio player is called on the delegate object of the player whenever, as the method's name indicates, the audio player finishes playing the audio file. Now, this does not necessarily mean that the whole audio file finished playing. There could have been an interruption —for instance, the audio channel might have gotten occupied by another app that came to the foreground, causing your app to stop playing. In this case, the aforementioned method gets called. This is a great place to release your audio player if you no longer need it.

In the `viewDidLoad` method, we are using GCD to asynchronously load the song's data into an instance of `NSData` and use that as a feed to the audio player. We do this because loading the data of an audio file can take a long time (depending on the length of the audio file), and if we do this on the main thread, we run the risk of stalling the UI experience. Because of this, we use a global concurrent queue to ensure that the code does *not* run on the main thread.

As you can see, we made the view controller the delegate of the audio player. This way, we can receive messages from the system whenever the audio player, for instance, is interrupted or has finished playing the song. With this information in hand, we can make appropriate decisions in the application, such as starting to play another audio file.

See Also

Chapter 7

12.2. Recording Audio

Problem

You want to be able to record audio files on an iOS device.

Solution

Use the AVAudioRecorder class in the AV Foundation framework.

Discussion

The AVAudioRecorder class in the AV Foundation framework facilitates audio recording in iOS applications. To start a recording, you need to pass various pieces of information to the initWithURL:settings:error: instance method of AVAudioRecorder:

The URL of the file where the recording should be saved
  This is a local URL. The AV Foundation framework will decide which audio format should be used for the recording based on the file extension provided in this URL, so choose the extension carefully.

The settings that must be used before and while recording
  Examples include the sampling rate, channels, and other information that help the audio recorder start the recording. This is a dictionary object.

The address of an instance of NSError where any initialization errors should be saved
  The error information could be valuable later, and you can retrieve it from this instance method in case something goes wrong.

The settings parameter of the initWithURL:settings:error: method is particularly interesting. There are many keys that can be saved in the settings dictionary, but we will discuss only some of the most important ones in this recipe:

AVFormatIDKey
  The format of the recorded audio. Some of the values that can be specified for this key are the following:

  - kAudioFormatLinearPCM
  - kAudioFormatAppleLossless

AVSampleRateKey
  The sample rate that needs to be used for the recording.

AVNumberOfChannelsKey
  The number of channels that must be used for the recording.

AVEncoderAudioQualityKey
  The quality with which the recording must be made. Here are some of the values that can be specified for this key:

  - AVAudioQualityMin
  - AVAudioQualityLow
  - AVAudioQualityMedium

- AVAudioQualityHigh

- AVAudioQualityMax

With all this information in hand, we can go on and write an application that can record audio input into a file and then play it using AVAudioPlayer. What we want to do, specifically, is this:

1. Start recording audio in Apple Lossless format.

2. Save the recording into a file named *Recording.m4a* in the application's *Documents* directory.

3. Five seconds after the recording starts, finish the recording process and immediately start playing the file into which we recorded the audio input.

We start by declaring the required properties in our view controller:

```
import UIKit
import AVFoundation

class ViewController: UIViewController,
AVAudioPlayerDelegate, AVAudioRecorderDelegate {

  var audioRecorder: AVAudioRecorder?
  var audioPlayer: AVAudioPlayer?

  <# rest of your code goes here #>

}
```

When the view inside the view controller is loaded for the first time, we will attempt to start the recording process and then stop the process after five seconds:

```
func startRecordingAudio(){

  var error: NSError?

  let audioRecordingURL = self.audioRecordingPath()

  audioRecorder = AVAudioRecorder(URL: audioRecordingURL,
    settings: audioRecordingSettings(),
    error: &error)

  if let recorder = audioRecorder{

    recorder.delegate = self
    /* Prepare the recorder and then start the recording */

    if recorder.prepareToRecord() && recorder.record(){

      println("Successfully started to record.")
```

```
    /* After 5 seconds, let's stop the recording process */
    let delayInSeconds = 5.0
    let delayInNanoSeconds =
    dispatch_time(DISPATCH_TIME_NOW,
      Int64(delayInSeconds * Double(NSEC_PER_SEC)))

    dispatch_after(delayInNanoSeconds, dispatch_get_main_queue(), {
      [weak self] in
      self!.audioRecorder!.stop()
      })

  } else {
    println("Failed to record.")
    audioRecorder = nil
  }

} else {
  println("Failed to create an instance of the audio recorder")
}

}

override func viewDidLoad() {
  super.viewDidLoad()

  /* Ask for permission to see if we can record audio */

  var error: NSError?
  let session = AVAudioSession.sharedInstance()

  if session.setCategory(AVAudioSessionCategoryPlayAndRecord,
    withOptions: .DuckOthers,
    error: &error){

      if session.setActive(true, error: nil){
        println("Successfully activated the audio session")

        session.requestRecordPermission{[weak self](allowed: Bool) in

          if allowed{
            self!.startRecordingAudio()
          } else {
            println("We don't have permission to record audio");
          }

        }
      } else {
        println("Could not activate the audio session")
      }

  } else {
```

```
      if let theError = error{
        println("An error occurred in setting the audio " +
          "session category. Error = \(theError)")
      }

    }
  }
```

The AVAudioSession class was introduced in the AV Foundation framework. Every iOS application has one audio session. This audio session can be accessed using the shared Instance type method of the AVAudioSession class.

After retrieving an instance of the AVAudioSession class, you can invoke the setCategory:error: instance method of the audio session object to choose among the different categories available to iOS applications. Different values that can be set as the audio session category of an application are listed here:

AVAudioSessionCategoryAmbient

This category will not stop the audio from other applications, but it will allow you to play audio over the audio being played by other applications, such as the Music app. The main UI thread of your application functions normally. The prepareToPlay and play instance methods of AVAudioPlayer return with the value true. The audio being played by your application stops when the user locks the screen. The silent mode silences the audio playback of your application only if your application is the only application playing an audio file. If you start playing audio while the Music app is playing a song, putting the device in silent mode does not stop your audio playback.

AVAudioSessionCategorySoloAmbient

This category is exactly like the AVAudioSessionCategoryAmbient category, except that this category stops the audio playback of all other applications, such as the Music app. When the device is put into silent mode, your audio playback is paused. This also happens when the screen is locked. This is the default category that iOS chooses for an application.

AVAudioSessionCategoryRecord

This stops other applications' audio (e.g., the music) and also does not allow your application to initiate an audio playback (e.g., using AVAudioPlayer). You can only record audio in this mode. Using this category, calling the prepareToPlay instance method of AVAudioPlayer returns true, and the play instance method returns false. The main UI interface functions as usual. The recording of your application continues even if the iOS device's screen is locked by the user.

AVAudioSessionCategoryPlayback

This category silences other applications' audio playback (such as the audio playback of music applications). You can then use the prepareToPlay and play instance methods of AVAudioPlayer to play a sound in your application. The main UI thread functions as normal. The audio playback continues even if the screen is locked by the user or if the device is in silent mode.

AVAudioSessionCategoryPlayAndRecord

This category allows audio to be played and recorded at the same time in your application. This stops the audio playback of other applications when your audio recording or playback begins. The main UI thread of your application functions as normal. The playback and the recording continues even if the screen is locked or the device is in silent mode.

AVAudioSessionCategoryAudioProcessing

This category can be used for applications that do audio processing, but not audio playback or recording. By setting this category, you cannot play or record any audio in your application. Calling the prepareToPlay and play instance methods of AVAudioPlayer returns false. Audio playback of other applications, such as the Music app, also stops if this category is set.

Users have to give permissions to apps that want to access the microphone. This is why we use AVAudioSession in our code snippet to ask the user for permission before attempting to use the microphone.

In the startRecordingAudio method of the view controller, we attempt to instantiate an object of type AVAudioRecorder and assign it to the audioRecorder property that we declared in the same view controller earlier.

We are using an instance method called audioRecordingPath to determine the local URL where we want to store the recording. This method is implemented like so:

```
func audioRecordingPath() -> NSURL{

  let fileManager = NSFileManager()

  let documentsFolderUrl = fileManager.URLForDirectory(.DocumentDirectory,
    inDomain: .UserDomainMask,
    appropriateForURL: nil,
    create: false,
    error: nil)

  return documentsFolderUrl!.URLByAppendingPathComponent("Recording.m4a")

}
```

The return value of this function is the document path of your application with the name of the destination file appended to it. For instance, if the document path of your application is:

```
file:///var/mobile/Containers/Data/Application/
<# Your Application ID #>/Documents/
```

the destination audio recording path will be:

```
file:///var/mobile/Containers/Data/Application/
<# Your Application ID #>/Documents/Recording.m4a
```

When instantiating the `AVAudioRecorder`, we are using a dictionary for the settings parameter of the initialization method of the audio recorder, as explained before. This dictionary is constructed using the `audioRecordingSettings` instance method, implemented in this way:

```
func audioRecordingSettings() -> NSDictionary{

    /* Let's prepare the audio recorder options in the dictionary.
    Later we will use this dictionary to instantiate an audio
    recorder of type AVAudioRecorder */

    return [
      AVFormatIDKey : kAudioFormatMPEG4AAC as NSNumber,
      AVSampleRateKey : 16000.0 as NSNumber,
      AVNumberOfChannelsKey : 1 as NSNumber,
      AVEncoderAudioQualityKey : AVAudioQuality.Low.rawValue as NSNumber
    ]

}
```

Our app also deliberately stopped the recording five seconds after it successfully started. Stopping called the `audioRecorderDidFinishRecording:successfully:` delegate method of our audio recorder delegate, informing it that the audio recorder finished its job. The `successfully` parameter of this method tells you whether the recording was successful or not.

Now that we have asked the audio recorder to stop recording, we will wait for its delegate messages to tell us when the recording has actually stopped. You shouldn't assume that the `stop` instance method of `AVAudioRecorder` instantly stops the recording. Instead, I recommend that you wait for the `audioRecorderDidFinishRecording:successful ly:` delegate method (declared in the `AVAudioRecorderDelegate` protocol) before proceeding.

When the audio recording has actually stopped, we will attempt to play what was recorded:

```
func audioRecorderDidFinishRecording(recorder: AVAudioRecorder!,
  successfully flag: Bool){

    if flag{

      println("Successfully stopped the audio recording process")
```

```
/* Let's try to retrieve the data for the recorded file */
var playbackError:NSError?
var readingError:NSError?

let fileData = NSData(contentsOfURL: audioRecordingPath(),
  options: .MappedRead,
  error: &readingError)

/* Form an audio player and make it play the recorded data */
audioPlayer = AVAudioPlayer(data: fileData, error: &playbackError)

/* Could we instantiate the audio player? */
if let player = audioPlayer{
  player.delegate = self

  /* Prepare to play and start playing */
  if player.prepareToPlay() && player.play(){
    println("Started playing the recorded audio")
  } else {
    println("Could not play the audio")
  }

} else {
  println("Failed to create an audio player")
}

} else {
  println("Stopping the audio recording failed")
}

/* Here we don't need the audio recorder anymore */
self.audioRecorder = nil;

}
```

After the audio player finishes playing the song (if it does so successfully), the audio
PlayerDidFinishPlaying:successfully: delegate method is called in the delegate
object of the audio player. We implement this method like so (this method is defined in
the AVAudioPlayerDelegate protocol):

```
func audioPlayerDidFinishPlaying(player: AVAudioPlayer!,
  successfully flag: Bool){

  if flag{
    println("Audio player stopped correctly")
  } else {
    println("Audio player did not stop correctly")
  }

  audioPlayer = nil

}
```

When playing audio files using `AVAudioPlayer`, we also need to handle interruptions (such as incoming phone calls) when deploying the application on an iOS device and before releasing the application to the App Store:

```
func audioPlayerBeginInterruption(player: AVAudioPlayer!) {
  /* The audio session is deactivated here */
}

func audioPlayerEndInterruption(player: AVAudioPlayer!,
  withOptions flags: Int) {
    if flags == AVAudioSessionInterruptionFlags_ShouldResume{
      player.play()
    }
}
```

12.3. Playing Video Files

Problem

You would like to be able to play video files in your iOS application.

Solution

Use an instance of the `MPMoviePlayerController` class.

 If you simply want to display a full-screen movie player, you can use the `MPMoviePlayerViewController` class and push your movie player view controller into the stack of view controllers of a navigation controller (for instance), or simply present your movie player view controller as a modal controller on another view controller using the `presentMoviePlayerViewControllerAnimated:` instance method of `UIViewController`. In this recipe, we use `MPMoviePlayer Controller` instead of `MPMoviePlayerViewController` in order to get full access to various settings that a movie player view controller does not offer, such as windowed-mode video playback (not full screen).

Discussion

The Media Player framework in the iOS SDK allows programmers to play audio and video files, among other interesting things. To be able to play a video file, we instantiate an object of type `MPMoviePlayerController` like so:

```
moviePlayer = MPMoviePlayerController(contentURL: url)
```

In this code, `moviePlayer` is a property of type `MPMoviePlayerController` defined for the current view controller. In older iOS SDKs, programmers had very little control over how movies were played using the Media Player framework. With the introduction of the iPad, the whole framework changed drastically to give more control to programmers and allow them to present their contents with more flexibility than before.

An instance of `MPMoviePlayerController` has a property called `view`. This view is of type `UIView` and is the view in which the media, such as video, will be played. As a programmer, you are responsible for inserting this view into your application's view hierarchy to present your users with the content being played. Because you get a reference to an object of type `UIView`, you can shape this view however you want. For instance, you can simply change the background color of this view to a custom color.

Many multimedia operations depend on the notification system. For instance, `MPMovie PlayerController` does not work with delegates; instead, it relies on notifications. This allows for a very flexible decoupling between the system libraries and the applications that iOS programmers write. For classes such as `MPMoviePlayerController`, we start listening for notifications that get sent by instances of that class. We use the default notification center and add ourselves as an observer for a notification.

To be able to test the recipe, we need a sample *.mov* file to play with the movie player. You can download an Apple-provided sample file from Apple Support (*http://bit.ly/ TtfcP7*). Make sure you download the H.264 file format. If this file is zipped, unzip it, and rename it to *Sample.m4v*. Now drag and drop this file into your application bundle in Xcode.

After doing this, we can go ahead and write a simple program that attempts to play the video file for us. Here are the declarations:

```
import UIKit
import MediaPlayer

class ViewController: UIViewController {

  var moviePlayer: MPMoviePlayerController?
  var playButton: UIButton?

  <# rest of the code goes here #>

}
```

Here is the implementation of the `startPlayingVideo` method:

```
func startPlayingVideo(){

    /* First let's construct the URL of the file in our application bundle
    that needs to get played by the movie player */
    let mainBundle = NSBundle.mainBundle()

    let url = mainBundle.URLForResource("Sample", withExtension: "m4v")

    /* If we already created a movie player,
    let's try to stop it */
```

```
if let player = moviePlayer{
  stopPlayingVideo()
}

/* Now create a new movie player using the URL */
moviePlayer = MPMoviePlayerController(contentURL: url)

if let player = moviePlayer{

  /* Listen for the notification that the movie player sends us
  whenever it finishes playing */
  NSNotificationCenter.defaultCenter().addObserver(self,
    selector: "videoHasFinishedPlaying:",
    name: MPMoviePlayerPlaybackDidFinishNotification,
    object: nil)

  println("Successfully instantiated the movie player")

  /* Scale the movie player to fit the aspect ratio */
  player.scalingMode = .AspectFit

  view.addSubview(player.view)

  player.setFullscreen(true, animated: false)

  /* Let's start playing the video in full-screen mode */
  player.play()

} else {
  println("Failed to instantiate the movie player")
}

}
```

As you can see, we manage the movie player's view ourselves. If we add the view of the movie player to the view controller's view, we have to remove the view manually. This view will not get removed from the view controller's view even if we release the movie player. The following method stops the video and then removes the associated view:

```
func stopPlayingVideo() {

  if let player = moviePlayer{
    NSNotificationCenter.defaultCenter().removeObserver(self)
    player.stop()
    player.view.removeFromSuperview()
  }

}
```

In the startPlayingVideo: instance method of the view controller, we are listening for the MPMoviePlayerPlaybackDidFinishNotification notification that MKMoviePlayer ViewController sends to the default notification center. We listen to this notification on the `videoHasFinishedPlaying:` instance method of the view controller. Here we can be notified when the movie playback has finished and perhaps dispose of the movie player object:

```
func videoHasFinishedPlaying(notification: NSNotification){

  println("Video finished playing")

  /* Find out what the reason was for the player to stop */
  let reason =
  notification.userInfo![MPMoviePlayerPlaybackDidFinishReasonUserInfoKey]
    as NSNumber?

  if let theReason = reason{

    let reasonValue = MPMovieFinishReason(rawValue: theReason.integerValue)

    switch reasonValue!{
    case .PlaybackEnded:
      /* The movie ended normally */
      println("Playback Ended")
    case .PlaybackError:
      /* An error happened and the movie ended */
      println("Error happened")
    case .UserExited:
      /* The user exited the player */
      println("User exited")
    default:
      println("Another event happened")
    }

    println("Finish Reason = \(theReason)")
    stopPlayingVideo()
  }

}
```

You might have noticed that we are invoking the `stopPlayingVideo:` instance method that we implemented in the `videoHasFinishedPlaying:` notification handler. We do this because the `stopPlayingVideo:` instance method takes care of unregistering the object from the notifications received by the media player and removes the media player from the superview. In other words, when the video stops playing, it does not necessarily mean that the resources we allocated for that player have been deallocated. We need to take care of that manually.

Now that the whole structure of our view controller is set up, we need to instantiate our `playButton` property by creating a new button and then adding it to our view controller. Pressing this button will then trigger the playback of the embedded video that we talked about earlier.

```
override func viewDidLoad() {
  super.viewDidLoad()

  playButton = UIButton.buttonWithType(.System) as? UIButton

  if let button = playButton{

    /* Add our button to the screen. Pressing this button
    starts the video playback */
    button.frame = CGRect(x: 0, y: 0, width: 70, height: 37)
    button.center = view.center

    button.autoresizingMask =
      .FlexibleTopMargin |
      .FlexibleLeftMargin |
      .FlexibleBottomMargin |
      .FlexibleRightMargin

    button.addTarget(self,
      action: "startPlayingVideo",
      forControlEvents: .TouchUpInside)

    button.setTitle("Play", forState: .Normal)

    view.addSubview(button)

  }

}
```

See Also

Recipe 12.4

12.4. Capturing Thumbnails from Video Files

Problem

You are playing a video file using an instance of the `MPMoviePlayerController` class and would like to capture a screenshot from the movie at a certain time.

Solution

Use the `requestThumbnailImagesAtTimes:timeOption:` instance method of `MPMovie PlayerController` like so:

```
/* Capture the frame at the third second into the movie */
let thirdSecondThumbnail = 3.0

/* We can ask to capture as many frames as we
```

want. But for now, we are just asking to capture one frame.
Ask the movie player to capture this frame for us */
player.requestThumbnailImagesAtTimes([thirdSecondThumbnail],
  timeOption: .NearestKeyFrame)

 It is of utmost importance that you set your time value as a double in Swift when you pass it to the aforementioned method. This is because the value will be eventually typecast to NSNumber when you create an array with the value. A double can be converted to that type, but not an Int. If in this example we had set our value to 3 instead of 3.0, we would have gotten an instance of the Int class, which is not typecastable.

Discussion

An instance of MPMoviePlayerController is able to capture thumbnails from the currently playing movie, synchronously and asynchronously. In this recipe, we are going to focus on asynchronous image capture for this class.

We can use the requestThumbnailImagesAtTimes:timeOption: instance method of MPMoviePlayerController to asynchronously access thumbnails. When I say "asynchronously," I mean that during the time the thumbnail is being captured and reported to your designated object (as we will soon see), the movie player will continue its work and will not block the playback. We must observe the MPMoviePlayerThumbnail ImageRequestDidFinishNotification notification message the movie player sends to the default notification center in order to find out when the thumbnails are available:

```
func startPlayingVideo(){

    /* First let's construct the URL of the file in our application bundle
    that needs to get played by the movie player */
    let mainBundle = NSBundle.mainBundle()

    let url = mainBundle.URLForResource("Sample", withExtension: "m4v")

    /* If we already created a movie player before,
    let's try to stop it */
    if let player = moviePlayer{
      stopPlayingVideo()
    }

    /* Now create a new movie player using the URL */
    moviePlayer = MPMoviePlayerController(contentURL: url)

    if let player = moviePlayer{

      /* Listen for the notification that the movie player sends us
      whenever it finishes playing */
      NSNotificationCenter.defaultCenter().addObserver(self,
```

```
    selector: "videoHasFinishedPlaying:",
    name: MPMoviePlayerPlaybackDidFinishNotification,
    object: nil)

  NSNotificationCenter.defaultCenter().addObserver(self,
    selector: "videoThumbnailIsAvailable:",
    name: MPMoviePlayerThumbnailImageRequestDidFinishNotification,
    object: nil)

  println("Successfully instantiated the movie player")

  /* Scale the movie player to fit the aspect ratio */
  player.scalingMode = .AspectFit

  view.addSubview(player.view)

  player.setFullscreen(true, animated: true)

  /* Let's start playing the video in full-screen mode */
  player.play()

  /* Capture the frame at the third second into the movie */
  let thirdSecondThumbnail = 3.0

  /* We can ask to capture as many frames as we
  want. But for now, we are just asking to capture one frame.
  Ask the movie player to capture this frame for us */
  player.requestThumbnailImagesAtTimes([thirdSecondThumbnail],
    timeOption: .NearestKeyFrame)

} else {
  println("Failed to instantiate the movie player")
}

}
```

You can see that we are asking the movie player to capture the frame at the third second into the movie. When this task is completed, the videoThumbnailIsAvailable: instance method of the view controller will be called. Here is how we can access the captured image:

```
func videoThumbnailIsAvailable(notification: NSNotification){

  if let player = moviePlayer{
    println("Thumbnail is available")

    /* Now get the thumbnail out of the user info dictionary */
    let thumbnail =
    notification.userInfo![MPMoviePlayerThumbnailImageKey] as? UIImage

    if let image = thumbnail{
```

```
        /* We got the thumbnail image. You can now use it here */
        println("Thumbnail image = \(image)")

    }
  }

}
```

Since we started listening to the `MPMoviePlayerThumbnailImageRequestDidFinishNo` `tification` notifications when we instantiated the movie player object in the `start` `PlayingVideo:` method, we must also stop listening for this notification whenever we stop the movie player (or whenever you believe is appropriate, depending on your application architecture).

```
NSNotificationCenter.defaultCenter().removeObserver(self)
```

When calling the `requestThumbnailImagesAtTimes:timeOption:` instance method of `MPMoviePlayerController`, we can specify one of two values for `timeOption`: `MPMo` `vieTimeOptionExact` or `MPMovieTimeOptionNearestKeyFrame`. The former gives us the frame playing at the exact point we requested in the timeline of the video, whereas the latter is less exact but uses fewer system resources and offers better performance when capturing thumbnails from a video. `MPMovieTimeOptionNearestKeyFrame` is usually adequate in terms of precision because it is just a couple of frames off.

12.5. Accessing the Music Library

Problem

You want to access an item that your user picks from her music library.

Solution

Use the `MPMediaPickerController` class.

Discussion

`MPMediaPickerController` is a view controller that the Music app displays to the user. By instantiating `MPMediaPickerController`, you can present a standard view controller to your users to allow them to select whatever item they want from the library and then transfer the control to your application. This is particularly useful in games, for instance, where the user plays the game and can have your application play his favorite tracks in the background.

You can get information from the media picker controller by becoming its delegate (conforming to `MPMediaPickerControllerDelegate`):

```
import UIKit
import MediaPlayer

class ViewController: UIViewController, MPMediaPickerControllerDelegate {

  var mediaPicker: MPMediaPickerController?

  <# rest of your code goes here #>

}
```

Inside your displayMediaPicker: selector, implement the code required to display an instance of the media picker controller and present it to the user as a modal view controller:

```
func displayMediaPicker(){

  mediaPicker = MPMediaPickerController(mediaTypes: .Any)

  if let picker = mediaPicker{

    println("Successfully instantiated a media picker")
    picker.delegate = self
    picker.allowsPickingMultipleItems = false

    presentViewController(picker, animated: true, completion: nil)

  } else {
    println("Could not instantiate a media picker")
  }

}

override func viewDidAppear(animated: Bool) {
  super.viewDidAppear(animated)
  displayMediaPicker()
}
```

The allowsPickingMultipleItems property of the media picker controller lets you specify whether users can pick more than one item from their library before dismissing the media picker controller. This takes a BOOL value, so for now we just set it to false; we will later see what this looks like. Now let's implement the various delegate messages defined in the MPMediaPickerControllerDelegate protocol:

```
func mediaPicker(mediaPicker: MPMediaPickerController!,
  didPickMediaItems mediaItemCollection: MPMediaItemCollection!){

  for thisItem in mediaItemCollection.items as [MPMediaItem]{

    let itemUrl = thisItem.valueForProperty(MPMediaItemPropertyAssetURL)
      as? NSURL
```

```
    let itemTitle =
    thisItem.valueForProperty(MPMediaItemPropertyTitle)
      as? String

    let itemArtist =
    thisItem.valueForProperty(MPMediaItemPropertyArtist)
      as? String

    let itemArtwork =
    thisItem.valueForProperty(MPMediaItemPropertyArtwork)
      as? MPMediaItemArtwork


    if let url = itemUrl{
      println("Item URL = \(url)")
    }

    if let title = itemTitle{
      println("Item Title = \(title)")
    }

    if let artist = itemArtist{
      println("Item Artist = \(artist)")
    }

    if let artwork = itemArtwork{
      println("Item Artwork = \(artwork)")
    }

  }

  mediaPicker.dismissViewControllerAnimated(true, completion: nil)

}
```

You can access different properties of each selected item using the `valueForProper ty:` instance method of `MPMediaItem`. Instances of this class will be returned to your application through the `mediaItemCollection` parameter of the `mediaPicker:did PickMediaItems:` delegate message.

Now let's write a program with a very simple GUI that allows us to ask the user to pick one music item from his Music library. After he picks the music file, we will attempt to play it using an `MPMusicPlayerController` instance. The GUI has two simple buttons: "Pick and Play," and "Stop Playing." The first button asks the user to pick an item from his Music library to play, and the second button stops the audio playback (if we are playing the song). We will start with the design of the UI of the application. Let's create it in a simple way, as shown in Figure 12-1.

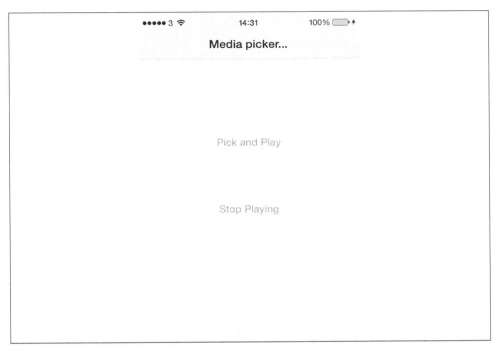

Figure 12-1. A very simple UI for the media picker and AV Audio Player

Now let's go ahead and define these two buttons in our view controller:

```
import UIKit
import MediaPlayer
import AVFoundation

class ViewController: UIViewController,
MPMediaPickerControllerDelegate, AVAudioPlayerDelegate {

  var myMusicPlayer: MPMusicPlayerController?
  var buttonPickAndPlay: UIButton?
  var buttonStopPlaying: UIButton?
  var mediaPicker: MPMediaPickerController?

  <# rest of the code #>

}
```

When the view loads up, we instantiate these two buttons and place them on the view:

```
override func viewDidLoad() {
  super.viewDidLoad()

  title = "Media picker..."
```

```
buttonPickAndPlay = UIButton.buttonWithType(.System) as? UIButton

if let pickAndPlay = buttonPickAndPlay{
  pickAndPlay.frame = CGRect(x: 0, y: 0, width: 200, height: 37)
  pickAndPlay.center = CGPoint(x: view.center.x, y: view.center.y - 50)
  pickAndPlay.setTitle("Pick and Play", forState: .Normal)
  pickAndPlay.addTarget(self,
    action: "displayMediaPickerAndPlayItem",
    forControlEvents: .TouchUpInside)
  view.addSubview(pickAndPlay)
}

buttonStopPlaying = UIButton.buttonWithType(.System) as? UIButton

if let stopPlaying = buttonStopPlaying{
  stopPlaying.frame = CGRect(x: 0, y: 0, width: 200, height: 37)
  stopPlaying.center = CGPoint(x: view.center.x, y: view.center.y + 50)
  stopPlaying.setTitle("Stop Playing", forState: .Normal)
  stopPlaying.addTarget(self,
    action: "stopPlayingAudio",
    forControlEvents: .TouchUpInside)
  view.addSubview(stopPlaying)
}

}
```

The two most important methods in the view controller are the displayMediaPicker
AndPlayItem and stopPlayingAudio:

```
func stopPlayingAudio(){

  NSNotificationCenter.defaultCenter().removeObserver(self)

  if let player = myMusicPlayer{
    player.stop()
  }

}

func displayMediaPickerAndPlayItem(){

  mediaPicker = MPMediaPickerController(mediaTypes: .AnyAudio)

  if let picker = mediaPicker{


    println("Successfully instantiated a media picker")
    picker.delegate = self
    picker.allowsPickingMultipleItems = true
    picker.showsCloudItems = true
    picker.prompt = "Pick a song please..."
    view.addSubview(picker.view)
```

```
          presentViewController(picker, animated: true, completion: nil)

     } else {
       println("Could not instantiate a media picker")
     }

   }
```

When the media picker controller succeeds, the `mediaPicker:didPickMediaItems`
message will be called in the delegate object (in this case, the view controller). On the
other hand, if the user cancels the media player, we'll get the `mediaPicker:mediaPick`
`erDidCancel` message. The following code implements the method that will be called
in each case:

```
func mediaPicker(mediaPicker: MPMediaPickerController!,
  didPickMediaItems mediaItemCollection: MPMediaItemCollection!){

    println("Media Picker returned")

    /* Instantiate the music player */

    myMusicPlayer = MPMusicPlayerController()

    if let player = myMusicPlayer{
      player.beginGeneratingPlaybackNotifications()

      /* Get notified when the state of the playback changes */
      NSNotificationCenter.defaultCenter().addObserver(self,
        selector: "musicPlayerStateChanged:",
        name: MPMusicPlayerControllerPlaybackStateDidChangeNotification,
        object: nil)

      /* Get notified when the playback moves from one item
      to the other. In this recipe, we are only going to allow
      our user to pick one music file */
      NSNotificationCenter.defaultCenter().addObserver(self,
        selector: "nowPlayingItemIsChanged:",
        name: MPMusicPlayerControllerNowPlayingItemDidChangeNotification,
        object: nil)

      /* And also get notified when the volume of the
      music player is changed */
      NSNotificationCenter.defaultCenter().addObserver(self,
        selector: "volumeIsChanged:",
        name: MPMusicPlayerControllerVolumeDidChangeNotification,
        object: nil)

      /* Start playing the items in the collection */
      player.setQueueWithItemCollection(mediaItemCollection)
      player.play()

      /* Finally dismiss the media picker controller */
```

```
        mediaPicker.dismissViewControllerAnimated(true, completion: nil)

    }

}

func mediaPickerDidCancel(mediaPicker: MPMediaPickerController!) {
  /* The media picker was cancelled */
  println("Media Picker was cancelled")
  mediaPicker.dismissViewControllerAnimated(true, completion: nil)
}
```

We are listening for the events that the music player generates through the notifications
that it sends. Here are the three methods that are responsible for handling the notifications we are listening to for the music player:

```
func musicPlayerStateChanged(notification: NSNotification){

  println("Player State Changed")

  /* Let's get the state of the player */
  let stateAsObject =
  notification.userInfo!["MPMusicPlayerControllerPlaybackStateKey"]
    as? NSNumber

  if let state = stateAsObject{

    /* Make your decision based on the state of the player */
    switch MPMusicPlaybackState(rawValue: state.integerValue)!{
    case .Stopped:
      /* Here the media player has stopped playing the queue. */
      println("Stopped")
    case .Playing:
      /* The media player is playing the queue. Perhaps you
      can reduce some processing that your application
      that is using to give more processing power
      to the media player */
      println("Paused")
    case .Paused:
      /* The media playback is paused here. You might want
      to indicate by showing graphics to the user */
      println("Paused")
    case .Interrupted:
      /* An interruption stopped the playback of the media queue */
      println("Interrupted")
    case .SeekingForward:
      /* The user is seeking forward in the queue */
      println("Seeking Forward")
    case .SeekingBackward:
      /* The user is seeking backward in the queue */
      println("Seeking Backward")
    }
```

```
    }
  }

  func nowPlayingItemIsChanged(notification: NSNotification){

    println("Playing Item Changed")

    let key = "MPMusicPlayerControllerNowPlayingItemPersistentIDKey"

    let persistentID =
    notification.userInfo![key] as? NSString

    if let id = persistentID{
      /* Do something with Persistent ID */
      println("Persistent ID = \(id)")
    }

  }

  func volumeIsChanged(notification: NSNotification){
    println("Volume Changed")
    /* The userInfo dictionary of this notification is normally empty */
  }
```

By running the application and pressing the "Pick and Play" button on the view controller, we will be presented with the media picker controller. When the picker view controller is displayed, the same Music UI will be presented to the user. After the user picks an item (or cancels the whole dialog), we will get appropriate delegate messages called in the view controller (because the view controller is the delegate of the media picker). After the items are picked (we allow only one item in this recipe, though), we will start the music player and start playing the whole collection.

If you want to allow your users to pick more than one item at a time, simply set the allowsPickingMultipleItems property of your media picker controller to true:

```
mediaPicker.allowsPickingMultipleItems = true
```

 Sometimes when working with the media picker controller (MPMedia PickerController), the "MPMediaPicker: Lost connection to iPod library" message will be printed to the console screen. This is because the media picker has been interrupted by an event, such as syncing with iTunes while the picker was being displayed to the user. Immediately, your mediaPickerDidCancel: delegate message will be called as well.

CHAPTER 13

Address Book

13.0. Introduction

On an iOS device, the Contacts application allows users to add contacts to, remove contacts from, and manipulate their address books. An address book can be a collection of people and groups. Each person can have properties such as first name, last name, phone number, and email address. Some properties can have a single value, and some can have multiple values. For instance, the first name of a person is one value, but the phone number can be multiple values (e.g., if the user has two home phone numbers).

The AddressBook.framework framework in the iOS SDK allows you to interact with the address book database on the device. You can get the array of all entities in the user's address book, insert and change values, and much more.

To use the address book-related functions in your application using the latest LLVM compiler features, all you have to do is import the following frameworks into your source code:

```
import UIKit
import AddressBook
import AddressBookUI

@UIApplicationMain
class AppDelegate: UIResponder, UIApplicationDelegate {

  var window: UIWindow?

}
```

You can use the Address Book framework on iOS Simulator, and you will be happy to know that Apple has already prepopulated the Contacts database on the simulator so that you don't have to do that by yourself (see Figure 13-1).

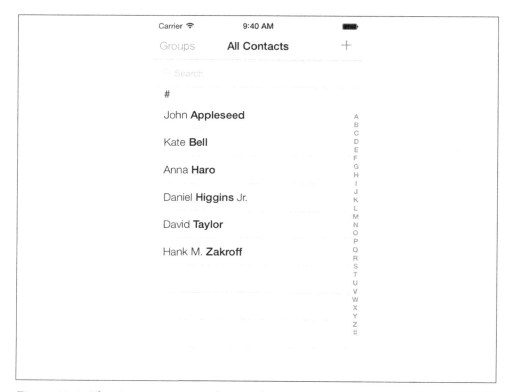

Figure 13-1. The Contacts app on the simulator already contains prepopulated information

 The examples in this chapter don't try to handle all the different types of errors that an Address Book API can throw. We simply check whether an API succeeds or fails. In your app, however, you might need to check these errors; for this reason, the code examples retrieve the references to errors that might happen during calls to each of the Address Book methods, just for your reference.

13.1. Retrieving a Person Entity with System UI

Problem

You want to ask iOS for help in allowing the users of your application to pick a contact from the Contacts.app on their device, without having to go into too much detail with Address Book and the low-level Core Foundation functions.

Solution

Use the `ABPeoplePickerNavigationController` class to ask iOS to prepare a system UI for the user where he can pick a contact or a property of a contact (such as a phone number). You don't have set up any Address Book objects or deal with permission requests to access user's contacts.

The interface for this navigation controller when displayed on the screen is nothing more than what we saw in Figure 13-1. From there, the user can pick a user or a property of the user, depending on which delegate methods of the `ABPeoplePickerNavigation Controller` class you implemented.

If you want to allow the user to pick a contact from their address book, you must implement the `peoplePickerNavigationController:didSelectPerson:` method of the `ABPeoplePickerNavigationControllerDelegate` protocol. The first parameter to this method will be the instance of your people picker navigation controller, which we seldom use but is valuable, for instance, if you have more than one people picker navigation controller in the same view controller. The second parameter will be of type `ABRecord Ref`, which is the record/person that the user picked from his address book.

 The reason that using the `ABPeoplePickerNavigationController` class does not prompt the user for permission to the address book from your app is that this class never gives you direct access to the data that the user might choose in the address book. Your app will always get a copy of the chosen data. Therefore, any changes that you make to that data will not affect the user's address book and contacts.

If you want to go into a bit more detail and allow the user to pick a property of a contact in his address book, such as a contact's phone number or email address, you must implement the `peoplePickerNavigationController:didSelectPerson:proper ty:identifier:` method of the `ABPeoplePickerNavigationControllerDelegate` protocol. The `property` parameter of this method will then be of type `ABPropertyID`, which can be set to any available value such as `kABPersonEmailProperty` or `kABPersonBirth dayProperty`. The last parameter to this method is of type `ABMultiValueIdentifier`, which we use to extract the selected information (such as a phone number) from the contact.

In order to set things up, you first need to import the appropriate framework into your project:

```
import AddressBookUI
```

This framework imports the AddressBook framework as well, so you do not have to do that manually. Then you need to ensure that you initialized an instance of `ABPeople PickerNavigationController` in your view controller and also ensure that your view controller conforms to the `ABPeoplePickerNavigationControllerDelegate` protocol. This protocol will be used by the `ABPeoplePickerNavigationController` class to inform you of user actions.

```
import UIKit
import AddressBookUI

class ViewController: UIViewController,
ABPeoplePickerNavigationControllerDelegate {

  let personPicker: ABPeoplePickerNavigationController

  required init(coder aDecoder: NSCoder) {
    personPicker = ABPeoplePickerNavigationController()
    super.init(coder: aDecoder)
    personPicker.peoplePickerDelegate = self
  }

  <# rest of the code #>

}
```

Now that our address book picker UI is set up, because we have conformed to the appropriate protocol, we need to implement the methods that are required from us, plus some optional ones that are needed in this recipe. The first method that we have to implement is the `peoplePickerNavigationControllerDidCancel:` method of the delegate, which gets called when the user cancels and closes the picker UI. Even though you might not exactly be interested in receiving this event, it is a required method in the protocol, so you need to implement it:

```
func peoplePickerNavigationControllerDidCancel(
  peoplePicker: ABPeoplePickerNavigationController!){
  /* Mandatory to implement */
}
```

The next method that we are going to implement in the protocol is the `peoplePicker NavigationController:didSelectPerson:property:identifier:` method. For now, we will just put the skeleton in our app like so:

```
func peoplePickerNavigationController(
  peoplePicker: ABPeoplePickerNavigationController!,
  didSelectPerson person: ABRecordRef!,
  property: ABPropertyID,
```

```
    identifier: ABMultiValueIdentifier){

    /* A property in a person was picked */

}
```

Next stop, in our UI, we place a little button that says "Pick a Property" and link it to a method in our view controller's code, like so:

```
@IBAction func performPickPerson(sender : AnyObject) {
    self.presentViewController(personPicker, animated: true, completion: nil)
}
```

When the button is pressed, this method gets called and we invoke the `presentView Controller:animated:completion:` method of our view controller to present the address book picker to the user.

OK, all of that is great, but how do we now go and retrieve the phone number that the user picked from a contact in the address book? Well, we need to implement our code for the `peoplePickerNavigationController:didSelectPerson:` method. Even though we are going to see how all this is done in the rest of this chapter, I want to just give you a preview of how this code appears in a simple application:

```
func peoplePickerNavigationController(
    peoplePicker: ABPeoplePickerNavigationController!,
    didSelectPerson person: ABRecordRef!) {

    /* Do we know which picker this is? */
    if peoplePicker != personPicker{
      return
    }

    /* Get all the phone numbers this user has */

    let phones: ABMultiValueRef = ABRecordCopyValue(person,
      kABPersonPhoneProperty).takeRetainedValue()

    let countOfPhones = ABMultiValueGetCount(phones)

    for index in 0..<countOfPhones{
      let phone = ABMultiValueCopyValueAtIndex(phones,
        index).takeRetainedValue() as String

      println(phone)

    }

}
```

You can now go ahead and run this code on your device and have a play with it. You will notice that the user is not asked for permission for our app to access the address book, as planned, but is presented with a system UI in which he can pick any of the contacts in her address book. When the contact is selected, the system picker UI disappears and the control comes back to our app. We then extract all the phone numbers that the selected user has in the database and print them out to the screen.

Discussion

The people picker controller is a great bridge to the address book for any app that doesn't need very detailed control over the address book database. For instance, if you are trying to do any of the following, the `ABPeoplePickerNavigationController` is the perfect match for your app:

1. Allow the user to pick a contact from their list and get read access in your app to properties of that contact.
2. Ask the user to pick a specific property of a contact from their address book.

After the user has picked a person from the list of people in his address book, the control is now in your hands. You can use the `ABRecordCopyValue` function to grab a specific property from the person's record. In our example, we saw how to get all the phone numbers from the user's entity. Let's have a look at another example. Let's say that we want to grab all email addresses that are associated with a selected user.

When the user is done picking a contact from the list, our `peoplePickerNavigation Controller:didSelectPerson:` delegate message is called. Here we attempt to copy the value of the `kABPersonEmailProperty` property first:

```
let emails: ABMultiValueRef = ABRecordCopyValue(person,
    kABPersonEmailProperty).takeRetainedValue() as ABMultiValueRef
```

Then we grab all the values out of the array of email messages that we just received, using the `ABMultiValueCopyArrayOfAllValues` function. This function also gives us an unmanaged object, which we have to turn into a memory-managed object immediately. The memory-managed version of this Core Foundation object will be of type `NSArray`, which will be the array that contains all the selected user's email addresses:

```
let allEmails = ABMultiValueCopyArrayOfAllValues(
    emails).takeRetainedValue() as NSArray
```

Last but not least, we will go through all the email addresses and print them to the screen:

```
for email in allEmails{
    println(email)
}
```

See Also

Recipe 13.5

13.2. Retrieving a Property of a Person Entity with System UI

Problem

You want to allow the user to pick a specific property of a contact from their address book and you want your app to retrieve the value of that property, without bugging the user with address book permissions. You just really want to use the system UI to display the address book instead of creating the UI yourself.

Solution

Follow what we talked about in Recipe 13.1, but instead of listening for the `peoplePick erNavigationController:didSelectPerson:` delegate method of the `ABPeoplePick erNavigationControllerDelegate` protocol, listen to the `peoplePickerNavigation Controller:didSelectPerson:property:identifier:` method of that protocol.

Discussion

When you implement the `peoplePickerNavigationController:didSelectPer son:property:identifier:` method, you will receive two very important properties of a person that has been selected. One is a value of type `ABPropertyID`, which gives you direct access to the property of the contact that the user tapped on. For instance, if this is one of the addresses that the contact has, you will be able to copy its value directly using the `ABRecordCopyValue` function. The other parameter that you will receive is of type `ABMultiValueIdentifier` and contains the index of the selected property. For instance, if the contact has three addresses assigned to her, this parameter will be 0 for the first address, 1 for the second, etc. Then you can use a function like `ABMultiValue CopyValueAtIndex` to get the value of a field at that specific index.

Don't worry if this all sounds very complicated. Let's instead have a look at an example. I am going to assume that you reset your iPhone Simulator at this point to get all the default contacts shipped with the simulator. What we are going to do in this recipe is bring up the people picker navigation controller, which we talked about in Recipe 13.1, but allow the user to pick an address for any of the contacts in her contact list. Then we are going to display the country, city, and street address of the selected address.

What we should do first is use the `displayedProperties` property of our controller. This is an array of `Int` instances that will determine which properties of each contact the user can see in the people picker. You can, for instance, add the value `kABPersonAd dressProperty` to this array to have the user see only the address properties of contacts in her contact list:

```
import UIKit
import AddressBookUI

class ViewController: UIViewController,
ABPeoplePickerNavigationControllerDelegate {

  let personPicker: ABPeoplePickerNavigationController

  required init(coder aDecoder: NSCoder) {
    personPicker = ABPeoplePickerNavigationController()
    super.init(coder: aDecoder)
    personPicker.displayedProperties = [
      Int(kABPersonAddressProperty)
      ]
    personPicker.peoplePickerDelegate = self
  }

  <# rest of the code #>

}
```

When we present this controller to the user and the user taps on a contact, she will only be able to see the address properties that are assigned to that contact, as you can see in Figure 13-2.

The user then taps on an address and we receive our `peoplePickerNavigationCon troller:didSelectPerson:property:identifier:` delegate method. In this method, we first copy the value of the chosen field (addresses). This gives us an array of addresses. We later have to get the selected address out of the array. So for now, we get all the addresses:

```
let addresses: ABMultiValueRef = ABRecordCopyValue(person,
  property).takeRetainedValue()
)
```

This gives us all the addresses for the current contact. Then we get the index of the selected address using the `identifier` parameter that we passed, which is basically an integer:

```
let index = Int(identifier) as CFIndex
```

Next, we actually copy the value of the selected address, which gives us a dictionary:

```
let address: NSDictionary = ABMultiValueCopyValueAtIndex(addresses,
  index).takeRetainedValue() as NSDictionary
```

Once you have your address dictionary, you can carve into it and get the country value with the `kABPersonAddressCountryKey` key or the city value with the `kABPersonAd dressCityKey` key:

```
let country = address[kABPersonAddressCountryKey as String] as String
let city = address[kABPersonAddressCityKey as String] as String
```

```
let street = address[kABPersonAddressStreetKey as String] as String

println("Country = \(country)")
println("City = \(city)")
println("Street = \(street)")
```

Returning to the user's addresses that we saw in Figure 13-2, if I pick the user's second address, I get the following values printed to the console:

```
Country = USA
City = Atlanta
Street = 1234 Laurel Street
```

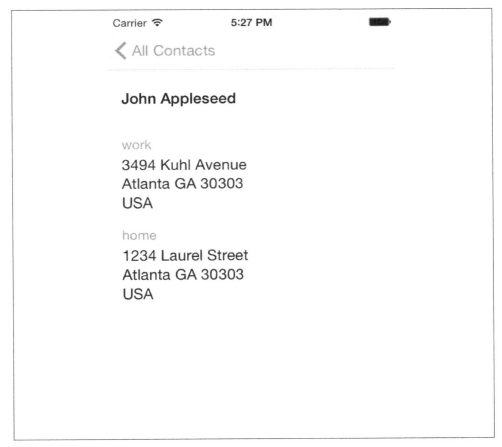

Figure 13-2. Only addresses are visible to the user

See Also

Recipe 13.1

13.3. Requesting Access to the Address Book

Problem

You want to start accessing the user's address book, which requires the user to have granted your app access to her address book database. You want to check whether you have access so that you don't receive a runtime error when you attempt access.

Solution

In order to find the current authorization state of your app, call the function `ABAddressBookGetAuthorizationStatus` in the Address Book framework. This function can return any of the following values:

`kABAuthorizationStatusNotDetermined`
> The user has not yet decided whether she would like to grant access to your application.

`kABAuthorizationStatusDenied`
> The user has explicitly denied your application from having access to the address book.

`kABAuthorizationStatusAuthorized`
> The user has authorized your application to have access to the address book on her device.

`kABAuthorizationStatusRestricted`
> Parental controls or other permissions configured on the iOS device prevent your app from accessing and interacting with the address book database on the device.

If you find out that the status that you received from the `ABAddressBookGetAuthorizationStatus` function is `kABAuthorizationStatusNotDetermined`, you can use the `ABAddressBookRequestAccessWithCompletion` function to ask for permission to access the user's address book database. You have to pass two parameters to this function:

An address book reference of type `ABAddressBookRef`
> The instance of the address book that you want to access.

A completion block of type `ABAddressBookRequestAccessCompletionHandler`
> After you call this function, iOS will ask the user if she wants to grant access to your application. Regardless of whether the user says yes or no, this block object will be called and you will then, via a Boolean parameter, get to know whether the answer was yes or no.

Discussion

Starting with iOS 6, Apple is quite rightly putting restrictions on how apps can access users' personal data, such as their contact information. This is done through a user interface designed by Apple that asks the users explicitly whether they allow these apps to access certain parts of their device and data, such as their address book database. Because we are all good iOS-land citizens, we will adhere to these rules and make sure that we access the user's address book only if we have been granted permission to do so.

Regardless of what you want to do with the address book, whether to read from it or write to it, you need to make sure that you have been granted sufficient privileges. If you are not sure about whether you can access the address book, simply call the `ABAddressBookGetAuthorizationStatus` function as demonstrated in this recipe.

Here is a little example of what to do depending on what the `ABAddressBookGetAuthorizationStatus` function returns to your application. In this example, we will call the aforementioned function and query the system about the authorization status of our app with regards to the address book database. If we are authorized to access it, fine. If we have been denied access, or if there is a system-wide restriction on address book access, we will display an alert view on the screen. If we have not yet been given access, we will ask the user for her permission to access the address book:

```
import UIKit
import AddressBook

@UIApplicationMain
class AppDelegate: UIResponder, UIApplicationDelegate {

  var window: UIWindow?
  var addressBook: ABAddressBookRef?

  func createAddressBook(){
    var error: Unmanaged<CFError>?

    addressBook = ABAddressBookCreateWithOptions(nil,
      &error).takeRetainedValue()

    /* You can use the address book here */

  }

  func application(application: UIApplication!,
    didFinishLaunchingWithOptions launchOptions:
    [NSObject : AnyObject]?) -> Bool {

      switch ABAddressBookGetAuthorizationStatus(){
      case .Authorized:
        println("Already authorized")
        createAddressBook()
        /* Now you can use the address book */
```

```
case .Denied:
  println("You are denied access to address book")

case .NotDetermined:
  createAddressBook()
  if let theBook: ABAddressBookRef = addressBook{
    ABAddressBookRequestAccessWithCompletion(theBook,
      {(granted: Bool, error: CFError!) in

        if granted{
          println("Access is granted")
        } else {
          println("Access is not granted")
        }

      })
  }

case .Restricted:
  println("Access is restricted")

default:
  println("Unhandled")
}

return true
  }

}
```

Now, when the user opens your app for the first time, undoubtedly, the authorization status that will come back from ABAddressBookGetAuthorizationStatus will be equal to kABAuthorizationStatusNotDetermined. At this point, we attempt to request permission using the ABAddressBookRequestAccessWithCompletion procedure. This will cause the user to see something similar to Figure 13-3 on her screen, and she can choose whether to grant or deny permission.

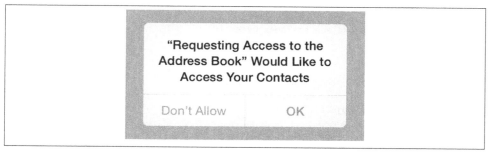

Figure 13-3. Our app asking for permission to access the address book database

---

13.4. Retrieving All the People in the Address Book

Problem

You want to retrieve all the contacts in the user's address book.

Solution

Use the `ABAddressBookCopyArrayOfAllPeople` function to retrieve an array of all contacts:

```
func readFromAddressBook(addressBook: ABAddressBookRef){

  /* Get all the people in the address book */
  let allPeople = ABAddressBookCopyArrayOfAllPeople(
    addressBook).takeRetainedValue() as NSArray

  for person: ABRecordRef in allPeople{
    println(person)
  }

}
```

Discussion

After accessing the user's address book database, we can call the `ABAddressBook CopyArrayOfAllPeople` function to retrieve an array of all the contacts in that address book. The return value of this function is an immutable array of type `CFArrayRef`. You can't work with this type of array as you would work with instances of `NSArray`, but you have two ways to traverse a `CFArrayRef` array. First, it natively supports two functions:

`CFArrayGetCount`
:   Gets the number of items in an instance of `CFArrayRef`. This is similar to the `count` instance method of an `NSArray`.

`CFArrayGetValueAtIndex`
:   Retrieves an item at a specific location of an instance of `CFArrayRef`. This is similar to the `objectAtIndex:` instance method of an `NSArray`.

Second, the `CFArrayRef` Core Foundation object is one of the objects that supports toll-free bridging to its `NS` counterpart, `NSArray`. This means that we can simply bridge this Core Foundation array and typecast it to an instance of `NSArray`. Just as a reminder, all local variables are strong variables, meaning that they will retain their contents. In this case, the `ABAddressBookCopyArrayOfAllPeople` function returns a Core Foundation array of all people in an address book.

The items that are put in an array of all people, retrieved by calling the `ABAddressBook CopyArrayOfAllPeople` function, are of type `ABRecordRef`. In Recipe 13.5, you will see how to access different properties of the entries, such as a person's entry, in the address book database.

13.5. Retrieving Properties of Address Book Entries

Problem

You retrieved a reference to an item in the address book, such as a person's entry, and you want to retrieve that person's properties, such as first and last names.

Solution

Use the `ABRecordCopyValue` function on the person's Address Book record.

Discussion

The records in the address book database are of type `ABRecordRef`. Each record could be either a group or a person. We have not discussed groups yet, so let's focus on people. Each person could have various types of information assigned to him, such as his first name, last name, email address, and so on. Bear in mind that many of these values are optional, and at the time of creating a new contact in the address book database, the user can simply leave out fields such as phone number, middle name, email address, URL, and so forth.

`ABRecordCopyValue` accepts an address book record and the property that has to be retrieved as its two parameters. The second parameter is the property of the record that we want to retrieve. Here are some of the common properties (all of these properties are defined as constant values in the *ABPerson* file):

kABPersonFirstNameProperty
> This value retrieves the first name of the given person. The return value is of type `CFStringRef`, which can be cast to `NSString` with a bridge cast, so you can do just about anything you want with the results.

kABPersonLastNameProperty
> This value retrieves the last name of the given person. Like the first name property, the return value will be of type `CFStringRef`, which again can be cast to `NSString`.

kABPersonMiddleNameProperty
> This value retrieves the middle name of the given person. Like the first name and the last name, the return value will be of type `CFStringRef`.

kABPersonEmailProperty
> This retrieves the given person's email address. The return value in this case will be of type `ABMultiValueRef`. This is a data type that can contain multiple values inside it, like an array, but *not exactly* like an array. This type of data will be discussed next.

Some of the values that we retrieve from the `ABRecordCopyValue` function are straightforward, generic types, such as `CFStringRef`. But this function can also return more complicated values, such as the email of a contact. The email could be further broken down into home email address, work email address, and so on. Values that can be further broken down like this are called *multivalues* in the Address Book framework. Various functions allow us to work with multiple values (which are of type `ABMultiValueRef`):

`ABMultiValueGetCount`
> Returns the number of value/label pairs that are inside the multivalue.

`ABMultiValueCopyLabelAtIndex`
> Returns the label associated with a multivalue item at a specific index (indexes are zero-based). For instance, if the user has three email addresses, such as work, home, and test addresses, the index of the first (work) email address in the email multivalue would be 0. This function will then retrieve the label associated with that address (in this example, *work*). Please bear in mind that multivalues do not necessarily need labels. Make sure you check for `nil` values.

`ABMultiValueCopyValueAtIndex`
> Returns the string value associated with a multivalue item at a specific index (indexes are zero-based). Suppose the user has work, home, and test email addresses. If we provide the index 0 to this function, it will retrieve the given contact's work email address.

> All Core Foundation array indexes are zero-based, just like their Cocoa counterpart array indexes.

Now let's go ahead and write a simple method that can retrieve all the people in the address book and print out their first name, last name, and email address objects, and place it in our app delegate:

```
func readAllPeopleInAddressBook(addressBook: ABAddressBookRef){

  /* Get all the people in the address book */
  let allPeople = ABAddressBookCopyArrayOfAllPeople(
    addressBook).takeRetainedValue() as NSArray

  for person: ABRecordRef in allPeople{

    let firstName = ABRecordCopyValue(person,
      kABPersonFirstNameProperty).takeRetainedValue() as String

    let lastName = ABRecordCopyValue(person,
      kABPersonLastNameProperty).takeRetainedValue() as String
```

```
    let email: ABMultiValueRef = ABRecordCopyValue(person,
      kABPersonEmailProperty).takeRetainedValue()

    println("First name = \(firstName)")
    println("Last name = \(lastName)")
    println("Email = \(email)")

  }

}
```

We will obviously first ask for permission from the user whether or not we can access the device's address book database. When permission is granted, we will call this method. I will not be repeating the code that requests for permission again, as we have already seen this code a few times in this chapter. Please refer to Recipe 13.3 for more information.

If you run this app in iOS Simulator for the latest iOS SDK, which has predefined contacts in the Contacts app, you will get the following printed to the console window:

```
First name = Kate
Last name = Bell
Email = ABMultiValueRef 0x7876f600 with 2 value(s)
    0: _$!<Work>!$_ (0x7876cf90) - kate-bell@mac.com (0x7876c950)
    1: _$!<Work>!$_ (0x7876cc20) - www.icloud.com (0x7876d520)

First name = Daniel
Last name = Higgins
Email = ABMultiValueRef 0x78952940 with 1 value(s)
    0: _$!<Home>!$_ (0x78952b10) - d-higgins@mac.com (0x78951460)
```

It's immediately visible that the multivalue field (email) cannot be read as a plain string object. So, using the functions that we just learned, let's go ahead and implement a method to accept an object of type ABRecordRef, read that record's multivalue email field, and print the values out to the console:

```
func readEmailsForPerson(person: ABRecordRef){

  let emails: ABMultiValueRef = ABRecordCopyValue(person,
    kABPersonEmailProperty).takeRetainedValue()

  for counter in 0..<ABMultiValueGetCount(emails){

    let email = ABMultiValueCopyValueAtIndex(emails,
      counter).takeRetainedValue() as String

    println(email)

  }

}
```

```
func readAllPeopleInAddressBook(addressBook: ABAddressBookRef){

    /* Get all the people in the address book */
    let allPeople = ABAddressBookCopyArrayOfAllPeople(
      addressBook).takeRetainedValue() as NSArray

    for person: ABRecordRef in allPeople{

      let firstName = ABRecordCopyValue(person,
        kABPersonFirstNameProperty).takeRetainedValue() as String
      let lastName = ABRecordCopyValue(person,
        kABPersonLastNameProperty).takeRetainedValue() as String

      println("First name = \(firstName)")
      println("Last name = \(lastName)")

      readEmailsForPerson(person)

    }
}
```

See Also

Recipe 13.4

13.6. Inserting a Person Entry into the Address Book

Problem

You want to create a new person contact and insert it into the user's address book.

Solution

Use the ABPersonCreate function to create a new person. Set the person's properties using the ABRecordSetValue function, and add the person to the address book using the ABAddressBookAddRecord function.

Discussion

After accessing the address book database using the ABAddressBookCreate function, you can start inserting new group and person records into the database. In this recipe, we will concentrate on inserting new person records. For information about inserting new groups into the address book, please refer to Recipe 13.7.

Use the ABPersonCreate function to create a new person record. Bear in mind that calling this function is not enough to add the person record to the address book. You must save the address book for your record to appear in the database.

By calling the `ABPersonCreate` function, you get a Core Foundation reference to a value of type `ABRecordRef`. Now you can call the `ABRecordSetValue` function to set the various properties of a new person entry. When you are done, you must add the new person record to the database. You can do this using the `ABAddressBookAddRecord` function. After doing this, you must also save any unsaved changes to the address book database in order to truly preserve your new person record. Do this by using the `ABAddressBook Save` function.

So let's combine all of this into a method that allows us to insert a new person entry into the address book:

```
func newPersonWithFirstName(firstName: String,
  lastName: String,
  inAddressBook: ABAddressBookRef) -> ABRecordRef?{

  let person: ABRecordRef = ABPersonCreate().takeRetainedValue()

  let couldSetFirstName = ABRecordSetValue(person,
    kABPersonFirstNameProperty,
    firstName as CFTypeRef,
    nil)

  let couldSetLastName = ABRecordSetValue(person,
    kABPersonLastNameProperty,
    lastName as CFTypeRef,
    nil)

  var error: Unmanaged<CFErrorRef>? = nil

  let couldAddPerson = ABAddressBookAddRecord(inAddressBook, person, &error)

  if couldAddPerson{
    println("Successfully added the person.")
  } else {
    println("Failed to add the person.")
    return nil
  }

  if ABAddressBookHasUnsavedChanges(inAddressBook){

    var error: Unmanaged<CFErrorRef>? = nil
    let couldSaveAddressBook = ABAddressBookSave(inAddressBook, &error)

    if couldSaveAddressBook{
      println("Successfully saved the address book.")
    } else {
      println("Failed to save the address book.")
    }
  }

  if couldSetFirstName && couldSetLastName{
```

```
    println("Successfully set the first name " +
       "and the last name of the person")
  } else {
    println("Failed to set the first name and/or " +
       "the last name of the person")
  }

  return person

}
```

In our app delegate, we will first check if we have permission to access the user's address book database. We have already seen this code in Recipe 13.3, so we won't repeat it here. Once you have access, you can then call the `createNewPersonInAddressBook:` method that we have written and pass the instance of the address book object to this method.

The `newPersonWithFirstName:lastName:inAddressBook:` method that we implemented creates a new person entry in the address book database. After invoking this function, you will see the results (as shown in Figure 13-4) in the Contacts application on iOS Simulator.

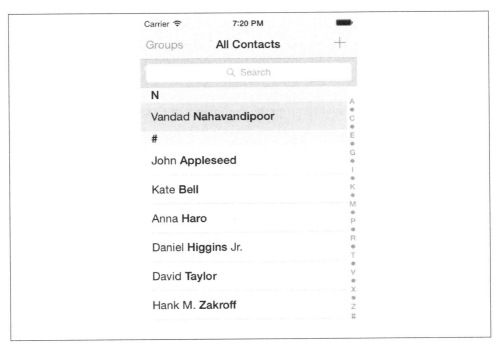

Figure 13-4. A new person record is added to the address book

13.7. Inserting a Group Entry into the Address Book

Problem

You want to categorize your contacts into groups.

Solution

Use the `ABGroupCreate` function.

Bear in mind that, as mentioned before, Core Foundation memory management is more complex than what Xcode's static analyzer could process. Therefore, attempting to use the LLVM compiler to compile Core Foundation code with static analysis turned on might give you a lot of warnings. You can ignore these and test the code with Instruments to make sure your code does not leak, but I encourage you to familiarize yourself with memory management in Core Foundation by reading Apple's "Memory Management Programming Guide for Core Foundation" document, as mentioned in the previous section.

Discussion

After retrieving the reference to the address book database, you can call the `ABGroupCreate` function to create a new group entry. However, you must perform a few more operations before you can insert this group into the address book operation. The first thing you have to do is set the name of this group using the `ABRecordSetValue` function with the `kABGroupNameProperty` property, as shown in the example code.

After the name of the group is set, add it to the address book database just like you add a new person's entry—using the `ABAddressBookAddRecord` function. For more information about adding a new person's entry to the address book database, please read Recipe 13.6.

 Inserting a new group with a name that already exists in the address book database creates a new group with the same name but with no group members. In later recipes, we learn how to avoid doing this by first finding the groups in the database and making sure a group with that name doesn't already exist.

After adding the group to the address book, you also need to save the address book's contents using the `ABAddressBookSave` function.

So, with all this in mind, let's go ahead and implement a method that allows us to create a new group with any desired name in the Address Book database:

```
func newGroupWithName(name: String, inAddressBook: ABAddressBookRef) ->
  ABRecordRef?{

    let group: ABRecordRef = ABGroupCreate().takeRetainedValue()

    var error: Unmanaged<CFError>?
    let couldSetGroupName = ABRecordSetValue(group,
      kABGroupNameProperty, name, &error)

    if couldSetGroupName{

      error = nil
      let couldAddRecord = ABAddressBookAddRecord(inAddressBook,
        group,
        &error)

      if couldAddRecord{

        println("Successfully added the new group")

        if ABAddressBookHasUnsavedChanges(inAddressBook){
          error = nil
          let couldSaveAddressBook =
          ABAddressBookSave(inAddressBook, &error)
          if couldSaveAddressBook{
            println("Successfully saved the address book")
          } else {
            println("Failed to save the address book")
            return nil
          }
        } else {
          println("No unsaved changes")
          return nil
        }
      } else {
        println("Could not add a new group")
        return nil
      }
    } else {
      println("Failed to set the name of the group")
      return nil
    }

    return group

}

func createNewGroupInAddressBook(addressBook: ABAddressBookRef){

  let personalCoachesGroup: ABRecordRef? =
  newGroupWithName("Personal Coaches",
    inAddressBook: addressBook)
```

```
if let group: ABRecordRef = personalCoachesGroup{
  println("Successfully created the group")
} else {
  println("Could not create the group")
}

}
```

All we have to do now is call the `createNewGroupInAddressBook:` method when our app delegate starts, to make sure that it works as expected. Before you attempt to call this method, though, do make sure that your app has the required permission to access the user's address book database. To read more about this, please have a look at Recipe 13.3.

After running your code, you will see results like those shown in Figure 13-5 (you might have created other groups already, so your address book might not look exactly like that shown in the figure).

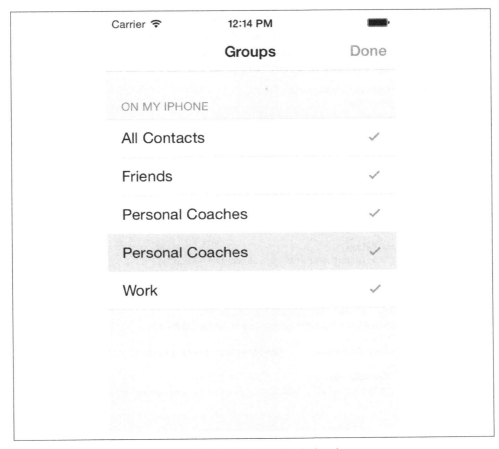

Figure 13-5. A new group created in the address book database

13.8. Adding Persons to Groups

Problem

You want to assign a person entry in the address book to a group.

Solution

Use the `ABGroupAddMember` function.

Discussion

We learned to insert person entries (in Recipe 13.6) and group entries (in Recipe 13.7) into the address book database. In those recipes, we implemented two custom methods named `newPersonWithFirstName:lastName:inAddressBook:` and `newGroupWith Name:inAddressBook:`. Now we want to add the person entry to the group we created and save the information to the address book database. Combining these three recipes, we can use the following code to achieve our goal:

```
func addPerson(person: ABRecordRef,
  toGroup: ABRecordRef,
  saveToAddressBook: ABAddressBookRef) -> Bool{

    var error: Unmanaged<CFErrorRef>? = nil
    var added = false

    /* Now attempt to add the person entry to the group */
    added = ABGroupAddMember(toGroup,
      person,
      &error)

    if added == false{
      println("Could not add the person to the group")
      return false
    }

    /* Make sure we save any unsaved changes */
    if ABAddressBookHasUnsavedChanges(saveToAddressBook){
      error = nil
      let couldSaveAddressBook = ABAddressBookSave(saveToAddressBook,
        &error)
      if couldSaveAddressBook{
        println("Successfully added the person to the group")
        added = true
      } else {
        println("Failed to save the address book")
      }
    } else {
      println("No changes were saved")
    }

    return added

}

func addPersonsAndGroupsToAddressBook(addressBook: ABAddressBookRef){

  let richardBranson: ABRecordRef? = newPersonWithFirstName("Richard",
    lastName: "Branson",
    inAddressBook: addressBook)

  if let richard: ABRecordRef = richardBranson{
    let entrepreneursGroup: ABRecordRef? = newGroupWithName("Entrepreneurs",
      inAddressBook: addressBook)

    if let group: ABRecordRef = entrepreneursGroup{
```

```
    if addPerson(richard, toGroup: group, saveToAddressBook: addressBook){
      println("Successfully added Richard Branson to the group")
    } else {
      println("Failed to add Richard Branson to the group")
    }

  } else {
    println("Failed to create the group")
  }

} else {
  println("Failed to create an entity for Richard Branson")
}

}
```

When your app starts, you need to make sure it has permission to access and update the user's address book. For more information about this, please see Recipe 13.3. When you are sure that you have permission, you can call the addPersonsAndGroupsToAd dressBook: method and pass the instance of address book that you retrieved from the system as a parameter to this method. Now we can see that the person entry we added to the "Entrepreneurs" group and to the database is, in fact, now inside this address book group, as shown in Figure 13-6.

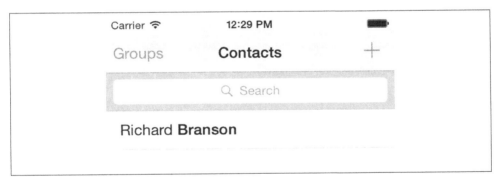

Figure 13-6. Adding a person to a group

See Also

Recipe 13.7

13.9. Searching the Address Book

Problem

You want to find a specific person or group in the address book database.

Solution

Use the `ABAddressBookCopyArrayOfAllPeople` and `ABAddressBookCopyArrayO fAllGroups` functions to find all people and groups in the address book. Traverse the returned arrays to find the information you are looking for. Alternatively, you can use the `ABAddressBookCopyPeopleWithName` function to find an entry about a person with a specific name.

Discussion

Up to this point, we have been inserting group and person entries into the address book without checking whether such a group or person already exists. We can use the `AB AddressBookCopyArrayOfAllPeople` and `ABAddressBookCopyArrayOfAllGroups` functions to get an array of all people and groups in the address book and search in the array to see whether the person or group entries we are about to insert into the address book already exist. When we check whether strings match, we also have to check for `nil` strings (which we assume mean that the contacts match). Here are two methods that make use of these functions and can also be used in other recipes:

```
func doesPersonExistWithFirstName(firstName paramFirstName: String,
  lastName paramLastName: String,
  inAddressBook addressBook: ABAddressBookRef) -> Bool{

    var exists = false
    let people = ABAddressBookCopyArrayOfAllPeople(
      addressBook).takeRetainedValue() as NSArray as [ABRecordRef]

    for person: ABRecordRef in people{

      let firstName = ABRecordCopyValue(person,
        kABPersonFirstNameProperty).takeRetainedValue() as String

      let lastName = ABRecordCopyValue(person,
        kABPersonLastNameProperty).takeRetainedValue() as String

        if firstName == paramFirstName &&
          lastName == paramLastName{
            return true
        }

    }
    return false
}
```

Similarly, we can check the existence of a group by first retrieving the array of all the groups in the address book database, using the `ABAddressBookCopyAr rayOfAllGroups` function:

```
func doesGroupExistWithGroupName(name: String,
  inAddressBook addressBook: ABAddressBookRef) -> Bool{

    let groups = ABAddressBookCopyArrayOfAllGroups(
      addressBook).takeRetainedValue() as NSArray as [ABRecordRef]

    for group: ABRecordRef in groups{

      let groupName = ABRecordCopyValue(group,
        kABGroupNameProperty).takeRetainedValue() as String

      if groupName == name{
        return true
      }

    }
    return false
}
```

As we saw earlier, there are two ways of finding a person in the address book database:

- Retrieve the array of all people in the address book, using the `ABAddressBookCopy ArrayOfAllPeople` function. Next, get each record inside the array and compare the first and last name properties of each person with the strings you are looking for. You can search any of the properties assigned to that person in the address book, including first name, last name, email, phone number, and so on.

- Ask the Address Book framework to perform the search based on a composite name. This is done using the `ABAddressBookCopyPeopleWithName` function.

Here is an example of using the `ABAddressBookCopyPeopleWithName` function to search for a contact with a specific name:

```
func doesPersonExistWithFullName(fullName: String,
  inAddressBook addressBook: ABAddressBookRef) -> Bool{

    let people = ABAddressBookCopyPeopleWithName(addressBook,
      fullName as NSString as CFStringRef).takeRetainedValue() as NSArray

    if people.count > 0{
      return true
    }

    return false

}
```

Using this function, you don't have to know the full name to be able to find a contact in the address book. You can pass a part of the name—for instance, just the first name—in order to find all the contacts with that specific first name.

The search performed by the `ABAddressBookCopyPeopleWithName` function is case-insensitive.

13.10. Retrieving and Setting a Person's Address Book Image

Problem

You want to be able to retrieve and set the images of address book entries.

Solution

Use one of the following functions:

`ABPersonHasImageData`
  Use this function to find out if an address book entry has an image set.

`ABPersonCopyImageData`
  Use this function to retrieve the image data (if any).

`ABPersonSetImageData`
  Use this function to set the image data for an entry.

Discussion

As mentioned in this recipe's Solution, we can use the `ABPersonCopyImageData` function to retrieve the data associated with an image of a person entry in the address book. We can use this function in a method of our own to make it more convenient to use:

```
func imageForPerson(person: ABRecordRef) -> UIImage?{

    let data = ABPersonCopyImageData(person).takeRetainedValue() as NSData

    let image = UIImage(data: data)
    return image
}
```

The `ABPersonSetImageData` function sets the image data for a person entry in the address book. Because this function uses data, not the image itself, we need to get NSData from UIImage. If we want the data pertaining to a PNG image, we can use the `UIImagePNGRepresentation` function to retrieve the PNG NSData representation of the image of type UIImage. To retrieve JPEG image data from an instance of UIImage, use the `UIImageJPEGRepresentation` function. Here is the method that allows you to set the image of a person entry in the address book database:

```
func setImageForPerson(person: ABRecordRef,
  inAddressBook addressBook: ABAddressBookRef,
  imageData: NSData) -> Bool{

    var error: Unmanaged<CFErrorRef>? = nil

    let couldSetPersonImage =
    ABPersonSetImageData(person, imageData as CFDataRef, &error)

    if couldSetPersonImage{
      println("Successfully set the person's image. Saving...")
      if ABAddressBookHasUnsavedChanges(addressBook){
        error = nil

        let couldSaveAddressBook = ABAddressBookSave(addressBook, &error)

        if couldSaveAddressBook{
          println("Successfully saved the address book")
          return true
        } else {
          println("Failed to save the address book")
        }
      } else {
        println("There are no changes to be saved!")
      }
    } else {
      println("Failed to set the person's image")
    }

    return false

}
```

CHAPTER 14

Files and Folder Management

14.0. Introduction

iOS is based on OS X, which itself is based on the Unix operating system. In iOS, the operating system's full directory structure is not visible to an app because each app, written by an iOS app developer, lives in its own sandbox. A sandbox environment is exactly what it sounds like: a sanctioned area where only the app that owns the sandbox can access the contents of the folder. Every app has its own sandbox folder and the sandbox folders by default have subfolders that apps can access.

When an iOS app is installed on the device, the folder structure shown in Figure 14-1 will be created for that app by the system.

Name.app
> Despite the odd name with the *.app* extension, this is a folder. The contents of your main bundle all go in here. For instance, all your app icons, your app binary, your different branding images, fonts, sounds, etc., are placed in this folder automatically when iOS installs your app on a device. The *name* is the product name that you set for your app. So if your app is called MyApp, the *.app* folder will be called *MyApp.app*.

Documents/
> This folder is the destination for all user-created content. Content that your app has populated, downloaded, or created should not be stored in this folder.

Library/
> You use this directory to store cached files, user preferences, and so on. Usually, this folder on its own does not contain files. It contains other folders that contain files.

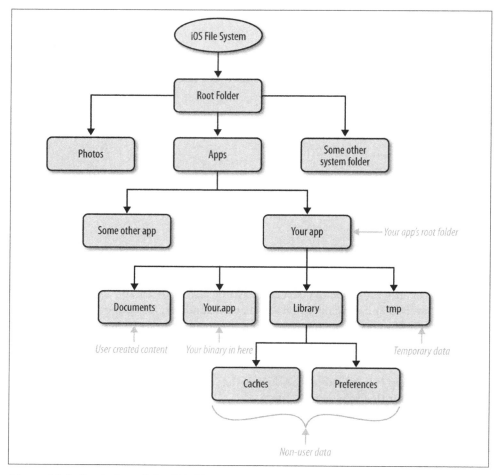

Figure 14-1. Depiction of the iOS filesystem

The root folder of every application contains various other folders, which I explain here:

Library/Caches/

The folder where you store data that your app can later re-create, if need be. The contents of this folder are not backed up by iOS. Also, iOS might remove the contents of this folder if the device is running out of disk space while your app is not running! So do not allow your app to rely on the contents of this folder too much; be prepared to re-create this content. Once again: the contents of this folder will not be backed up by iOS and can be deleted while your app is suspended.

For instance, if your app relies on files and folders that are to be created on disk, this folder is not be the best place to store this data. You are better off storing such files and folders in the */tmp* folder.

Library/Preferences/

As the name indicates, this folder contains the preferences that your app wants to remember between launches. We talk about this in detail later. iOS does back up the contents of this folder.

Library/Application Support/

The data that your app creates, not including the data created by the user, must be stored in this folder. It is good to know that iOS backs up the contents of this folder. This folder might not be created for you automatically, and you'll have to create it yourself if it doesn't exist. We talk about folder creation later in this chapter.

tmp/

These are temporary files that your app creates, downloads, and so on. The contents of this folder are not backed up by iOS. For instance, you can download a few photos from the Internet and store them in this folder in order to increase the performance of your application, so that you won't have to download the files every time the user opens your app. This folder serves exactly this purpose. Make sure that you are not storing any user-created documents or files in this folder.

Now you know the folders that iOS creates for you when your app is installed on an iOS device. The next thing you want to do is find the path of the rest of the useful folders that we just talked about, using the APIs that Apple has exposed to you (these are explained in this chapter).

14.1. Finding the Paths of the Most Useful Folders on Disk

Problem

You want to be able to find the path of some of the most useful folders that your app has access to (e.g., the folders that we talked about in this chapter's Introduction), so that you can access their content or create new content in those folders.

Programmers need to use APIs that are exposed in the iOS SDK to find the path of folders and/or files. In other words, you should never assume the path of a folder or a file. For example, you should always make sure that you use the appropriate APIs to find the paths that you are looking for, such as the *Documents* folder. Never, ever assume that this folder will be called *Documents* in your app's bundle. Simply use the appropriate APIs to find this path and, if you want to add or access files in the folder, attach your filenames to the end of this path.

Solution

Use the `URLsForDirectory:inDomains:` instance method of the `NSFileManager` class.

Discussion

The `NSFileManager` class offers a lot of file- and folder-related operations that you can do with iOS, right inside your apps, simply by making an instance of the class. I advise against using the shared file manager provided by this class through the `defaultMan ager` type method because it is not thread-safe. It is best to create and manage an instance of the `NSFileManager` class for yourself.

The `URLsForDirectory:inDomains:` instance method of the `NSFileManager` class allows you to search for specific directories on the iOS filesystem, mostly in your app's sandbox. There are two parameters to this method:

`URLsForDirectory:`
> This is the directory that you want to search for. Pass a value of type `NSSearchPath Directory` enumeration to this parameter. I will talk more about this soon.

`inDomains`
> This is *where* you look for the given directory. The value to this parameter must be of type `NSSearchPathDomainMask` enumeration.

Suppose you want to find the path to your app's *Documents* folder. This is how easily you can find it:

```
let fileManager = NSFileManager()
let urls = fileManager.URLsForDirectory(
  NSSearchPathDirectory.DocumentDirectory,
  inDomains: NSSearchPathDomainMask.UserDomainMask) as [NSURL]

if urls.count > 0{
  let documentsFolder = urls[0]
  println("\(documentsFolder)")
} else {
  println("Could not find the Documents folder")
}
```

As you can see, after creating our own instance of `NSFileManager`, we passed the `NSDo cumentDirectory` value as the folder we are looking for and `NSUserDomainMask` as the domain. Let's go through some of the most important values that you can pass to each one of the parameters to the `URLsForDirectory:inDomains:` instance method of the `NSFileManager` class:

`URLsForDirectory`
  `NSLibraryDirectory`
> The library folder for the app.

NSCachesDirectory
> The caches folder, as explained before.

NSDocumentDirectory
> The documents folder.

inDomains
NSUserDomainMask
> Specifies that the search be performed in the current user's folder. On OS X, this folder would be ~/.

Using this method, you can then find other folders such as the *caches* folder, as shown here:

```
let fileManager = NSFileManager()
let urls = fileManager.URLsForDirectory(
  NSSearchPathDirectory.CachesDirectory,
  inDomains: NSSearchPathDomainMask.UserDomainMask) as [NSURL]

if urls.count > 0{
  var documentsFolder = urls[0]
  println("\(documentsFolder)")
} else {
  println("Could not find the Documents folder")
}
```

If you want to find the *tmp* folder, use the NSTemporaryDirectory function like so:

```
if let tempDirectory = NSTemporaryDirectory(){
  println("\(tempDirectory)")
  } else {
  println("Could not find the temp directory")
  }
```

See Also

Recipe 14.0, "Introduction"

14.2. Writing to and Reading from Files

Problem

You want to be able to save information to disk (e.g., text, data, images, etc.).

Solution

Cocoa classes that allow you to store information, such as NSString, UIImage, and NSData, all expose instance methods that allow you to store their data to disk under a given path.

Discussion

In order to store text to disk, assuming that your text is stored in an instance of NSString (or the immutable version of this class), you can use the writeToFile:atomically:encoding:error: instance method of this class. This method works with strings that represent the destination path. Here are the parameters:

writeToFile
: The path of the file to write to, as a string.

atomically
: A Boolean that, if set to true, will first write the file to a temporary space and then move the temporary file to the destination that you chose. This ensures that the content of the file will be saved to disk first and then saved to its destination, so that if iOS crashes before the file is saved to the final destination, your content will still be saved later when the OS is back up again. It is recommended to set this value to true when storing information that you don't want to lose under any circumstance while your app is running.

encoding
: Encoding of the text that you want to write to the path. Programmers usually use UTF8 for the encoding, using the NSUTF8StringEncoding value.

error
: Takes a pointer to an NSError object so that if the saving operation fails, you will be able to find the error that happened during the process. You can pass nil to this parameter if you are not interested in knowing about the errors that might occur during the saving process. Bear in mind that this function returns a Boolean value and you can simply use this value to find out whether an error has occurred.

For instance, if you have some text that you want to temporarily store in your app, and you don't want it to be backed up by iOS, you can do the following:

```
let someText = NSString(string: "Put some string here")
let destinationPath = NSTemporaryDirectory() + "MyFile.txt"
var error:NSError?

let written = someText.writeToFile(destinationPath,
  atomically: true,
  encoding: NSUTF8StringEncoding,
  error: &error)

if written{
  println("Successfully stored the file at path \(destinationPath)")
} else {
  if let errorValue = error{
    println("An error occurred: \(errorValue)")
  }
}
```

Also, after you are done, to make sure things went fine, you can attempt to read the same string back into memory from the destination file, using the `stringWithContentsOfFile:encoding:error:` type method of the `NSString` class. This returns the autorelease string that is the contents of the specified file. If you want to explicitly instantiate an object of type `NSString` with the contents of the file, simply use the `initWithContentsOfFile:encoding:error:` constructor of the `NSString` class like so:

```
var error:NSError?
let path = NSTemporaryDirectory() + "MyFile.txt"

let succeeded = "Hello, World!".writeToFile(path,
  atomically: true,
  encoding: NSUTF8StringEncoding,
  error: &error)

if (succeeded){
  /* Now read from the same file */
  let readString = NSString(contentsOfFile: path,
    encoding: NSUTF8StringEncoding, error: nil) as String
  println("The read string is: \(readString)")
} else {
  if let theError = error{
    println("Could not write. Error = \(theError)")
  }
}
```

As you can see in this example code, we are using Swift's String class instead of `NSString` to save the string to the disk. Because Swift's String class is bridged automatically to Foundation's `NSString` class, we don't really have to do anything when using both of the aforementioned classes together, and we can use them interchangeably without any problems at all.

What we have done is create two convenient methods that allow us to write text to and read text from a specified location. In our app delegate, then, we use these two methods to write some text to the *temp* folder and then read the same text back to memory in order to make sure our methods are working fine.

If you want to work with URLs encapsulated in instances of `NSURL` (or the mutable version of it), you can use the `writeToURL:atomically:encoding:error:` instance method instead.

Instances of `NSURL` can point to resources (files, directories, etc.) locally or remotely. For example, an instance of `NSURL` can represent a local file in the *Documents* folder of your app as easily as it can represent the website URL for www.apple.com. This class simply provides functionality to access and work with URLs, regardless of which type of URL they are.

Other classes in foundation have methods similar to those of NSString. Let's take NSArray as an example. You can save the contents of an array using the writeToFile:atomically: instance method of NSArray. In order to read the contents of an array from disk, you can simply allocate an instance of the array and then initialize it using the initWithContentsOfFile: constructor of the array. Here is an example of both of these:

```
let path = NSTemporaryDirectory() + "MyFile.txt"
let arrayOfNames:NSArray = ["Steve", "John", "Edward"]

if arrayOfNames.writeToFile(path, atomically: true){
  let readArray:NSArray? = NSArray(contentsOfFile: path)
  if let array = readArray{
    println("Could read the array back = \(array)")
  } else {
    println("Failed to read the array back")
  }
}
```

 The writeToFile:atomically: instance method of NSArray class can only save an array that contains objects of the following type:

- NSString

- NSDictionary

- NSArray

- NSData

- NSNumber

- NSDate

If you attempt to insert any other objects in the array, your data will not be saved to disk, because this method first makes sure all the objects in the array are of one of the aforementioned types. This is simply because the Objective-C runtime will not otherwise have any idea how to store your data to disk. For instance, suppose you create a class called Person and create a first name and last name property for the class, then instantiate an instance and add it to an array. How can an array then save your person to disk? It simply cannot do that, as it won't know what it has to save to disk. This is a problem known as *marshalling*, and is solved by iOS only for the data types just listed.

Dictionaries are also very similar to arrays and have the same way of saving their data to disk and reading data back into the dictionary. The method names are exactly the same, and the rules of saving an array also apply to dictionaries. Here is an example:

```
let path = NSTemporaryDirectory() + "MyFile.txt"
let dict:NSDictionary = [
```

```
    "first name" : "Steven",
    "middle name" : "Paul",
    "last name" : "Jobs",
  ]

  if dict.writeToFile(path, atomically: true){

    let readDict:NSDictionary? = NSDictionary(contentsOfFile: path)
    if let dict = readDict{
      println("Read the dictionary back from disk = \(dict)")
    } else {
      println("Failed to read the dictionary back from disk")
    }
  } else {
    println("Failed to write the dictionary to disk")
  }
```

As you can see, this example writes the dictionary to disk and then reads it back from the same location. After reading, we compare the read dictionary to the one we saved to disk in order to make sure they both contain the same data.

Up to now, we have been using high-level classes such as NSString and NSArray to save our contents to disk. Now, what if we want to store a raw array of bytes to disk? That's easy, too. Suppose we have an array of four characters and we want to save that to disk:

```
let chars = [
  CUnsignedChar("a"),
  CUnsignedChar("b"),
  CUnsignedChar("c"),
  CUnsignedChar("d")
]
```

The easiest way of saving this raw array of bytes to disk is to encapsulate it in another high-level data structure like NSData and then use the relevant methods of NSData to write to and read from the disk. The saving and loading methods for NSData are virtually the same as those for NSArray and NSDictionary. Here is an example of saving raw data to disk and reading it back from the disk:

```
let path = NSTemporaryDirectory() + "MyFile.txt"
let chars = [CUnsignedChar("a"), CUnsignedChar("b")]
let data = NSData(bytes: chars, length: 2)
if data.writeToFile(path, atomically: true){
  println("Wrote the data")
  let readData = NSData(contentsOfFile: path)
  if readData!.isEqualToData(data){
    println("Read the same data")
  } else {
    println("Not the same data")
  }
} else {
  println("Could not write the data")
}
```

See Also

Recipe 14.0

14.3. Creating Folders on Disk

Problem

You want to be able to create folders on disk to save some of your app's files in them.

Solution

Use the `createDirectoryAtPath:withIntermediateDirectories:attributes:er ror:` instance method of the `NSFileManager` class, as shown here:

```
let tempPath = NSTemporaryDirectory()
let imagesPath = tempPath.stringByAppendingPathComponent("images")
var error:NSError?
let fileManager = NSFileManager()

if fileManager.createDirectoryAtPath(imagesPath,
  withIntermediateDirectories: true,
  attributes: nil,
  error: nil){
  println("Created the directory")
} else {
  println("Could not create the directory")
}
```

Discussion

The APIs exposed by `NSFileManager` are very easy to use, and it's no surprise that you can use them to create folders on disk in a few lines. The `createDirectoryAtPath:with IntermediateDirectories:attributes:error:` method may look scary at first, but it's not that bad. I will explain the different parameters that you can pass to it:

createDirectoryAtPath
  The path to the folder that has to be created.

withIntermediateDirectories
  A Boolean parameter that, if set to `true`, will create all the folders in the middle before it creates the final folder. For instance, if you want to create a folder named *images* in another folder named *data* inside the *tmp* folder of your app, but the *data* folder doesn't exist yet, you could easily ask to create the *tmp/data/images/* folder and set the `withIntermediateDirectories` parameter to `true`. This will make the system create the *data* for you as well as the *images* folder.

---

attributes

A dictionary of attributes that you can pass to the system in order to affect how your folder will be created. We won't be using these here, to keep things simple, but you can change things such as the modification date and time, the creation date and time, and other attributes of the created folder if you want to.

error

This parameter accepts a pointer to an error object of type `NSObject`, which will be populated with any errors that happen while the folder is being created. It's generally a good idea to pass an error object to this parameter, so that if the method fails (returns `false`), you can access the error and determine what went wrong.

See Also

Recipe 14.1

14.4. Enumerating Files and Folders

Problem

You want to enumerate folders within a folder or you want to enumerate the list of files inside a folder. The act of enumerating means that you simply want to list all the folders and/or files within another folder.

Solution

Use the `contentsOfDirectoryAtPath:error:` instance method of the `NSFileManager` class as shown here. In this example, we are enumerating all the files, folders, and symlinks under our app's bundle folder:

```
var error:NSError?
let fileManager = NSFileManager()
let bundleDir = NSBundle.mainBundle().bundlePath
let bundleContents = fileManager.contentsOfDirectoryAtPath(bundleDir,
  error: &error)!

if let contents = bundleContents{
  if contents.count == 0{
    println("The app bundle is empty!")
  } else {
    println("The app bundle contents = \(bundleContents)")
  }
} else if let theError = error {
  println("Could not read the contents. Error = \(theError)")
}
```

Discussion

In some of your iOS apps, you might need to enumerate the contents of a folder. Let me give you an example, in case this is a bit vague right now. Imagine that the user asked you to download 10 images from the Internet and cache them in your app. You go ahead and save them, say, in the *tmp/images/* folder that you manually created. Now the user closes your app and reopens it, and in your UI, you want to display the list of already-downloaded files in a table view. How can you achieve this? Well, it's easy. All you have to do is enumerate the contents of the aforementioned folder using the `NSFile Manager` class. As you saw in the Solution section of this recipe, the `contentsOfDirec toryAtPath:error:` instance method of the `NSFileManager` class returns an array of `NSString` objects that represents the files, folders, and symlinks within the given folder. However, it is not easy to say which one is a folder, which one is a file, and so on. To get more finely grained detail from the file manager, invoke the `contentsOfDirectoryA tURL:includingPropertiesForKeys:options:error:`. Let's go through the different parameters that you need to pass to this method:

`contentsOfDirectoryAtURL`
> The path of the folder that you want to inspect. This path should be provided as an instance of `NSURL`. Don't worry about it if you don't know how to construct this instance. We will talk about it soon.

`includingPropertiesForKeys`
> This is an array of properties that you would like iOS to fetch for every file, folder, or item that it finds in the given directory. For instance, you can specify that you want the creation date of the items to be returned in the results, as part of the URL instance that is returned to you (in instances of `NSURL` that you get back from the framework). Here is a list of some of the most important values that you can place in this array:

`NSURLIsDirectoryKey`
> Allows you to determine later whether one of the URLs returned is a directory.

`NSURLIsReadableKey`
> Allows you to determine later whether the returned URL is readable by your app's process.

`NSURLCreationDateKey`
> Returns the creation date of the item in the returned URL.

`NSURLContentAccessDateKey`
> Returns the last content access date in the returned results.

`NSURLContentModificationDateKey`
> As its name indicates, this allows you to determine the last-modified date for the returned URLs.

options

Only 0 or NSDirectoryEnumerationSkipsHiddenFiles can be entered for this parameter. If the latter value is entered, as the name of the value shows, all hidden items will be skipped during the enumeration.

error

A reference to an object that will be filled with an error should this method fail to execute its job. It's usually a good idea to provide error objects to these methods if you can. You get more control over why things fail, should they ever fail.

Now that we have more control over how the items are enumerated, let's enumerate all the items in the *.app* folder and print out the creation, last-modified, and last-accessed dates. We also print out whether the items are hidden or not, and whether we have read access to the files or not. The last thing we print out is whether the items are directories or not. Let's go:

```
func contentsOfAppBundle() -> [NSURL]{

  let propertiesToGet = [
    NSURLIsDirectoryKey,
    NSURLIsReadableKey,
    NSURLCreationDateKey,
    NSURLContentAccessDateKey,
    NSURLContentModificationDateKey
  ]

  var error:NSError?
  let fileManager = NSFileManager()
  let bundleUrl = NSBundle.mainBundle().bundleURL
  let result = fileManager.contentsOfDirectoryAtURL(bundleUrl,
    includingPropertiesForKeys: propertiesToGet,
    options: nil,
    error: &error) as [NSURL]

  if let theError = error{
    println("An error occurred")
  }

  return result

}

func stringValueOfBoolProperty(property: String, url: NSURL) -> String{
  var value:AnyObject?
  var error:NSError?
  if url.getResourceValue(
    &value,
    forKey: property,
    error: &error) && value != nil{
      let number = value as NSNumber
```

```swift
      return number.boolValue ? "YES" : "NO"
  }

  return "NO"
}

func isUrlDirectory(url: NSURL) -> String{
  return stringValueOfBoolProperty(NSURLIsDirectoryKey, url: url)
}

func isUrlReadable(url: NSURL) -> NSString{
  return stringValueOfBoolProperty(NSURLIsReadableKey, url: url)
}


func dateOfType(type: String, url: NSURL) -> NSDate?{
  var value:AnyObject?
  var error:NSError?
  if url.getResourceValue(
    &value,
    forKey: type,
    error: &error) && value != nil{
      return value as? NSDate
  }
  return nil
}

func printUrlPropertiesToConsole(url: NSURL){
  println("URL name = \(url.lastPathComponent)")
  println("Is a Directory? \(isUrlDirectory(url))")
  println("Is Readable? \(isUrlReadable(url))")

  if let creationDate = dateOfType(NSURLCreationDateKey, url: url){
    println("Creation Date = \(creationDate)")
  }

  if let accessDate = dateOfType(NSURLContentAccessDateKey, url: url){
    println("Access Date = \(accessDate)")
  }

  if let modificationDate =
    dateOfType(NSURLContentModificationDateKey, url: url){
    println("Modification Date = \(modificationDate)")
  }

  println("---------------------------------")

}

let appBundleContents = contentsOfAppBundle()

for url in appBundleContents{
```

```
            printUrlPropertiesToConsole(url)
    }
```

The output of this program will be something similar to that shown here:

```
URL name = Enumerating Files and Folders
Is a Directory? NO
Is Readable? YES
Creation Date = 2014-06-23 07:54:17 +0000
Access Date = 2014-06-23 07:54:19 +0000
Modification Date = 2014-06-23 07:54:17 +0000
----------------------------------
URL name = Frameworks
Is a Directory? YES
Is Readable? YES
Creation Date = 2014-06-23 06:53:35 +0000
Access Date = 2014-06-23 07:43:02 +0000
Modification Date = 2014-06-23 07:54:18 +0000
----------------------------------
URL name = Info.plist
Is a Directory? NO
Is Readable? YES
Creation Date = 2014-06-23 06:53:34 +0000
Access Date = 2014-06-23 07:54:19 +0000
Modification Date = 2014-06-23 06:53:34 +0000
----------------------------------
URL name = LaunchImage-700-568h@2x.png
Is a Directory? NO
Is Readable? YES
Creation Date = 2014-06-23 06:53:34 +0000
Access Date = 2014-06-23 07:54:18 +0000
Modification Date = 2014-06-23 06:53:34 +0000
----------------------------------
URL name = PkgInfo
Is a Directory? NO
Is Readable? YES
Creation Date = 2014-06-23 06:53:34 +0000
Access Date = 2014-06-23 07:53:03 +0000
Modification Date = 2014-06-23 06:53:34 +0000
----------------------------------
```

 The important thing to note about this app is that we are using the getResourceValue:forKey:error: instance method of the NSURL class to get the value of each one of the keys that we are querying from the file manager, such as the creation and modification date. We pass these requirements to the file manager, asking it to fetch this information for us. And then, once we have our URLs, we use the aforementioned method to retrieve the different properties from the resulting URLs.

So let's have a look at the different parts of this app. I will explain what each method we wrote does:

contentsOfAppBundle
> This method searches the *.app* folder for all items (files, folders, symlinks, etc.) and returns the result as an array. All items in the array will be of type NSURL and contain their creation date, last modification date, and other attributes that we talked about before.

stringValueOfBoolProperty:ofURL:
> This method will fetch the string equivalent (`true` or `false`) of a Boolean property of a URL. For instance, information about whether a URL is a directory or not is stored as a binary, Boolean value. However, if we want to print this Boolean value out to the console, we need to convert it to a string. We have two query items for each URL that will return instances of NSNumber containing a Boolean value: NSUR LIsDirectoryKey and NSURLIsReadableKey. So instead of writing this conversion code twice, methods are available to do the conversion of NSNumber to a string of `true` or `false` for us.

isURLDirectory:
> Takes in a URL and inspects it to see whether it is a directory. This method internally uses the `stringValueOfBoolProperty:ofURL:` method and passes the NSURLIsDir ectoryKey key to it.

isURLReadable:
> Determines whether your app has read access to a given URL. This method also internally uses the `stringValueOfBoolProperty:ofURL:` method and passes the NSURLIsReadableKey key to it.

dateOfType:inURL:
> Since we are going to inspect three types of properties in each URL that will be of type NSDate, we simply encapsulated the relevant code in this method, which takes the key and returns the date associated with that key in a given URL.

OK, that's about it, really. You now know how to enumerate folders and retrieve all items within the folder. You even know how to retrieve different attributes for different items.

See Also

Recipe 14.1; Recipe 14.2

14.5. Deleting Files and Folders

Problem

You created some files and/or folders on disk and no longer need them, so you want to delete them.

Solution

Use the `removeItemAtPath:error:` or the `removeItemAtURL:error:` instance method of the `NSFileManager` class. The former method takes the path as a string, and the latter takes the path as a URL.

Discussion

Deleting files and folders is perhaps one of the easiest operations that you can perform using a file manager. In iOS, you need to be mindful of where you store your files and folders and you need to get rid of files and folders when you no longer need them. For instance, let's create five text files in the *tmp/text* folder and then delete them after we are done. In the meantime, we can enumerate the contents of the folder before and after the deletion just to make sure things are working fine. Also, as you know, the *tmp/* folder exists when your app is installed, but the *tmp/text* folder doesn't. So we need to create it first. When we are done with the files, we will delete the folder as well:

```
let fileManager = NSFileManager()

func createFolderAtPath(path: String){

  var error:NSError?

  if fileManager.createDirectoryAtPath(path,
    withIntermediateDirectories: true,
    attributes: nil,
    error: &error) == false && error != nil{
      println("Failed to create folder at \(path), error = \(error!)")
  }

}

/* Creates 5 .txt files in the given folder, named 1.txt, 2.txt, etc. */
func createFilesInFolder(folder: String){

  for counter in 1...5{
    let fileName = NSString(format: "%lu.txt", counter)
    let path = folder.stringByAppendingPathComponent(fileName)
    let fileContents = "Some text"
    var error:NSError?
    if fileContents.writeToFile(path,
```

```
        atomically: true,
        encoding: NSUTF8StringEncoding,
        error: &error) == false{
          if let theError = error{
            println("Failed to save the file at path \(path)" +
              " with error = \(theError)")
          }
      }
    }

  }

  /* Enumerates all files/folders in a given path */
  func enumerateFilesInFolder(folder: String){

    var error:NSError?
    let contents = fileManager.contentsOfDirectoryAtPath(
      folder,
      error: &error)!

    if let theError = error{
      println("An error occurred \(theError)")
    } else if contents.count == 0{
      println("No content was found")
    } else {
      println("Contents of path \(folder) = \(contents)")
    }

  }

  /* Deletes all files/folders in a given path */
  func deleteFilesInFolder(folder: String){

    var error:NSError?
    let contents = fileManager.contentsOfDirectoryAtPath(folder,
      error: &error) as [String]

    if let theError = error{
      println("An error occurred = \(theError)")
    } else {
      for fileName in contents{
        let filePath = folder.stringByAppendingPathComponent(fileName)
        if fileManager.removeItemAtPath(filePath, error: nil){
          println("Successfully removed item at path \(filePath)")
        } else {
          println("Failed to remove item at path \(filePath)")
        }
      }
    }

  }
```

```
/* Deletes a folder in a given path */
func deleteFolderAtPath(path: String){

  var error:NSError?
  if fileManager.removeItemAtPath(path, error: &error){
    println("Successfully deleted the path \(path)")
  } else {
    if let theError = error{
      println("Failed to remove path \(path) with error \(theError)")
    }
  }

}
```

Now we execute these methods in order to see the results in action:

```
let txtFolder = NSTemporaryDirectory().stringByAppendingPathComponent("txt")

createFolderAtPath(txtFolder)
createFilesInFolder(txtFolder)
enumerateFilesInFolder(txtFolder)
deleteFilesInFolder(txtFolder)
enumerateFilesInFolder(txtFolder)
deleteFolderAtPath(txtFolder)
```

This example code combines a lot of the things that you learned in this chapter, from enumerating to creating to deleting files. It's all in this example. As you can see from the app's starting point, we are performing six main tasks, all of which have their associated methods to take care of them:

1. Create the *tmp/txt* folder. We know the *tmp* folder will be created by iOS for every app, but the *txt* doesn't come already created by iOS when your app is installed on the device.

2. Create five text files in the *tmp/txt* folder.

3. Enumerate all the files in the *tmp/txt* folder just to prove that we successfully created all five files in that folder.

4. Delete the files that we created to prove the point of this recipe.

5. Enumerate the files again in the *tmp/txt* folder to demonstrate that the deletion mechanism worked just fine.

6. Delete the *tmp/txt* folder, as we no longer need it. Again, as I mentioned before, be mindful of what folders and files you create on disk. Disk space doesn't grow on trees! So if you don't need your files and folders any longer, delete them.

Now you not only know how to create files and folders, but how to get rid of them when you no longer need them.

See Also

Recipe 14.2

14.6. Saving Objects to Files

Problem

You added a new class to your project, and you want to be able to save this object to disk as a file and then read it back from disk whenever required.

Solution

Make sure that your class conforms to the NSCoding protocol and implement all the required methods of this method. Don't worry; I will walk you through this in the Discussion section of this recipe.

Discussion

There are two really handy classes in iOS SDK for this specific purpose, which in the programming world is known as *marshalling*. They are called:

NSKeyedArchiver

> A class that can archive or save the contents of an object or object tree by keys. Each value in the class, let's say each property, can be saved to the archive, using a key that the programmer chooses. You will be given an archive file (we will talk more about this) and you will just save your values using keys that you choose. Just like a dictionary!

NSKeyedUnarchiver

> This class does the reverse of the archiver class. It simply gives you the unarchived dictionary and asks you to read the values into your object's properties.

In order for the archiver and the unarchiver to work, you need to make sure that the objects you are asking them to archive or unarchive conform to the NSCoding protocol. Let's start with a simple Person class. Here is the implementation of our class:

```
class Person: NSObject{
  var firstName: String
  var lastName: String
  init(firstName: String, lastName: String){
    self.firstName = firstName
    self.lastName = lastName
    super.init()
  }
}
```

Now if you don't write any code for the implementation of this class and try to compile your code, you will see that the compiler throws warnings that you have not conformed to the NSCoding protocol and have not implemented its required methods. The methods that we have to implement are as follows:

func encodeWithCoder(aCoder: NSCoder)

This method gives you a coder. You use the coder just like you would use a dictionary. Simply store your values in it using keys that you choose.

init(coder aDecoder: NSCoder!)

This method gets called on your class when you try to unarchive your class using NSKeyedUnarchiver. Simply read your values back from the NSCoder instance passed to this method.

Now, using this information, let's implement our class:

```
@objc(Person) class Person: NSObject, NSCoding{
  var firstName: String
  var lastName: String

  struct SerializationKey{
    static let firstName = "firstName"
    static let lastName = "lastName"
  }

  init(firstName: String, lastName: String){
    self.firstName = firstName
    self.lastName = lastName
    super.init()
  }

  convenience override init(){
    self.init(firstName: "Vandad", lastName: "Nahavandipoor")
  }

  required init(coder aDecoder: NSCoder) {
      self.firstName = aDecoder.decodeObjectForKey(SerializationKey.firstName)
        as String

      self.lastName = aDecoder.decodeObjectForKey(SerializationKey.lastName)
        as String
  }

  func encodeWithCoder(aCoder: NSCoder) {
    aCoder.encodeObject(self.firstName, forKey: SerializationKey.firstName)
    aCoder.encodeObject(self.lastName, forKey: SerializationKey.lastName)
  }

}
```

As you can see in the first line of the class, it inherits from NSObject, an Objective-C class. Therefore, we use the @ojc(*name*) marker to ensure that the name of this class is the same in both Swift and Objective-C runtimes, ensuring in turn that the archiver can easily archive and unarchive it.

We are also going to implement an equity operator overload on our class so that later we can compare two instances of the Person class and see whether they have the same first name and last name, from which we can conclude that they are equal:

```
func == (lhs: Person, rhs: Person) -> Bool{
  return lhs.firstName == rhs.firstName &&
    lhs.lastName == rhs.lastName ? true : false
}
```

You can see that the way we are using the instance of the NSCoder class is really similar to that of a dictionary except that, instead of setValue:forKey: in a dictionary, we use encodeObject:forKey:, and instead of objectForKey: in a dictionary, we use deco deObjectForKey:. All in all, very similar to the way we use dictionaries.

We are done with this class. So let's implement the archiving and unarchiving mechanism using the two aforementioned classes. Our plan is to first instantiate an object of type Person, archive it, get rid of it in memory, read it back from file, and see whether the unarchived value matches the value that we originally put in the class. We will be implementing this in our app delegate, because it's the easiest place to do this:

```
let path = NSTemporaryDirectory() + "person"
var firstPerson = Person()
NSKeyedArchiver.archiveRootObject(firstPerson, toFile: path)

var secondPerson = NSKeyedUnarchiver.unarchiveObjectWithFile(path)
  as Person!

if firstPerson == secondPerson{
  println("Both persons are the same")
} else {
  println("Could not read the archive")
}
```

So the archiving simply uses the archiveRootObject:toFile class method of the NSKeyedArchiver class, which takes an object and a file on which the content of the file has to be saved. Simple and easy. How about unarchiving? That is as easy as the archiving process. All you have to do is just pass the archived file path to the unarchiveObject WithFile: class method of the NSKeyedUnarchiver class, and that class will do the rest for you.

See Also

Recipe 14.1

CHAPTER 15

Camera and the Photo Library

15.0. Introduction

Most devices running iOS, such as the iPhone, are equipped with cameras. The most recent iPhone has two cameras, and some iPhones might only have one. Some iOS devices might not even have a camera. The `UIImagePickerController` class allows programmers to display the familiar Camera interface to their users and ask them to take a photo or shoot a video. The photos taken or the videos shot by the user with the `UIImagePickerController` class become accessible to the programmer.

In this chapter, you learn how to let users take photos and shoot videos from inside applications, access these photos and videos, and access the photos and videos that are placed inside the photo library on an iOS device, such as the iPod Touch and iPad.

 iOS Simulator does not support the Camera interface. Please test and debug all your applications that require a Camera interface on a real iOS device with a camera.

In this chapter, we first attempt to determine whether a camera is available on the iOS device running the application. You can also determine whether the camera allows you (the programmer) to capture videos, images, or both. To do this, make sure you have added the *MobileCoreServices* framework to your target. Simply import its umbrella framework into your application.

We then move to other topics, such as accessing videos and photos from different albums on an iOS device. These are the same albums that are accessible through the Photos application built into iOS.

Accessing photos inside albums is more straightforward than accessing videos, however. For photos, we will be given the address of the photo and we can simply load the data of the image either in an instance of NSData or directly into an instance of UIImage. For videos, we won't be given a file address on the filesystem from which to load the data of the video. Instead, we will be given an address such as this:

```
assets-library://asset/asset.MOV?id=1000000004&ext=MOV
```

For addresses such as this, we need to use the Assets Library framework. The Assets Library framework allows us to access the contents accessible through the Photos application, such as videos and photos shot by the user. You can also use the Assets Library framework to save images and videos on the device. These photos and videos will then become accessible by the user as well as other applications that wish to access these contents.

To make sure the recipes in this chapter compile correctly, ensure that both the Assets Library and the Mobile Core Services frameworks are always included in your source files. You can do this by simply importing them into your source codes.

To access the data of an asset given the URL to the asset, follow these steps:

1. Allocate and initialize an object of type ALAssetsLibrary. The Assets Library object facilitates the bridge that you need in order to access the videos and photos accessible by the Photos application.

2. Use the assetForURL:resultBlock:failureBlock instance method of the Assets Library object (allocated and initialized in step 1) to access the asset. An asset could be an image, a video, or any other resource that Apple might later decide to add to it. This method works with block objects. For more information about block objects and GCD, please refer to Chapter 7.

3. Release the Assets Library object allocated and initialized in step 1.

At this point, you might be wondering: how do I access the data for the asset? The resultBlock parameter of the assetForURL:resultBlock:failureBlock instance method of the Assets Library object will need to point to a block object that accepts a single parameter of type ALAsset. ALAsset is a class provided by the Assets Library that encapsulates an asset available to Photos and any other iOS application that wishes to use these assets. For more information about storing photos and videos in the photo library, please refer to Recipes 15.4 and 15.5. If you want to learn more about retrieving photos and videos from the photo library and the Assets Library, please refer to Recipe 15.6.

15.1. Detecting and Probing the Camera

Problem

You want to know whether the iOS device running your application has a camera that you can access. This is an important check to make before attempting to use the camera, unless you are sure your application will never run on a device that lacks one.

Solution

Use the `isSourceTypeAvailable:` class method of `UIImagePickerController` with the `UIImagePickerControllerSourceTypeCamera` value, like so:

```
import UIKit

class ViewController: UIViewController {

  func isCameraAvailable() -> Bool{

    return UIImagePickerController.isSourceTypeAvailable(.Camera)

  }

  override func viewDidLoad() {
    super.viewDidLoad()

    print("Camera is ")

    if isCameraAvailable() == false{
      print("not ")
    }

    println("available")

  }

}
```

Discussion

Before attempting to display an instance of `UIImagePickerController` to your user for taking photos or shooting videos, you must detect whether the device supports that interface. The `isSourceTypeAvailable:` class method allows you to determine three sources of data:

- The camera, by passing the `UIImagePickerControllerSourceTypeCamera` value to this method.

- The photo library, by passing the value `UIImagePickerControllerSourceTypePho` `toLibrary` to this method. This browses the root folder of the *Photos* directory on the device.

- The Camera Roll folder in the *Photos* directory, by passing the `UIImagePick` `erControllerSourceTypeSavedPhotosAlbum` value to this method.

If you want to check the availability of any of these facilities on an iOS device, you must pass these values to the `isSourceTypeAvailable:` class method of `UIImagePicker` `Controller` before attempting to present the interfaces to the user.

Now we can use the `isSourceTypeAvailable:` and `availableMediaTypesForSource` `Type:` class methods of `UIImagePickerController` to determine first if a media source is available (camera, photo library, etc.), and if so, whether media types such as image and video are available on that media source:

```
import UIKit
import MobileCoreServices

class ViewController: UIViewController {

  func cameraSupportsMedia(mediaType: String,
    sourceType: UIImagePickerControllerSourceType) -> Bool{


    let availableMediaTypes =
    UIImagePickerController.availableMediaTypesForSourceType(sourceType)
      as [String]

    for type in availableMediaTypes{
      if type == mediaType{
        return true
      }
    }

    return false
  }

  func doesCameraSupportShootingVideos() -> Bool{
    return cameraSupportsMedia(kUTTypeMovie as NSString, sourceType: .Camera)
  }

  func doesCameraSupportTakingPhotos() -> Bool{
    return cameraSupportsMedia(kUTTypeImage as NSString, sourceType: .Camera)
  }

  override func viewDidLoad() {
    super.viewDidLoad()

    if doesCameraSupportTakingPhotos(){
      println("The camera supports taking photos")
```

```
  } else {
    println("The camera does not support taking photos")
  }

  if doesCameraSupportShootingVideos(){
    println("The camera supports shooting videos")
  } else {
    println("The camera does not support shooting videos")
  }

}

}
```

Some iOS devices can have more than one camera. The two cameras might be called the front and the rear cameras. To determine whether these cameras are available, use the isCameraDeviceAvailable: class method of UIImagePickerController, like so:

```
func isFrontCameraAvailable() -> Bool{
  return UIImagePickerController.isCameraDeviceAvailable(.Front)
}

func isRearCameraAvailable() -> Bool{
  return UIImagePickerController.isCameraDeviceAvailable(.Rear)
}
```

By calling these methods on an older iPhone with no rear camera, you will see that the isFrontCameraAvailable method returns false and the isRearCameraAvailable method returns true. Running the code on an iPhone with both front and rear cameras proves that both methods return true, as iPhone 5s devices are equipped with both front- and rear-facing cameras.

If detecting which camera is present on a device isn't enough for your application, you can retrieve other settings using the UIImagePickerController class. One such setting is whether flash capability is available for a camera on the device. You can use the isFlashAvailableForCameraDevice: class method of UIImagePickerController to determine the availability of a flash capability on the rear or front camera. Please bear in mind that the isFlashAvailableForCameraDevice: class method of UIImagePickerController checks the availability of the given camera device before checking the availability of a flash capability on that camera. Therefore, you can run these methods on devices that do not have front or rear cameras without a need to first check if the camera is available.

```
func isFlashAvailableOnFrontCamera() -> Bool{
  return UIImagePickerController.isFlashAvailableForCameraDevice(.Front)
}

func isFlashAvailableOnRearCamera() -> Bool{
  return UIImagePickerController.isFlashAvailableForCameraDevice(.Front)
}
```

Now if we take advantage of all the methods that we wrote in this recipe and test them in your app, we can see the results on different devices:

```
if isFrontCameraAvailable(){
  println("The front camera is available")
  if isFlashAvailableOnFrontCamera(){
    println("The front camera is equipped with a flash")
  } else {
    println("The front camera is not equipped with a flash")
  }
} else {
  println("The front camera is not available")
}

if isRearCameraAvailable(){
  println("The rear camera is available")
  if isFlashAvailableOnRearCamera(){
    println("The rear camera is equipped with a flash")
  } else {
    println("The rear camera is not equipped with a flash")
  }
} else {
  println("The rear camera is not available")
}

if doesCameraSupportTakingPhotos(){
  println("The camera supports taking photos")
} else {
  println("The camera does not support taking photos")
}

if doesCameraSupportShootingVideos(){
  println("The camera supports shooting videos")
} else {
  println("The camera does not support shooting videos")
}
```

Here are the results when we run the application on the new iPhone:

```
The front camera is available
The front camera is not equipped with a flash
The rear camera is available
The rear camera is equipped with a flash
The camera supports taking photos
The camera supports shooting videos
```

Here is the output of the same code when run on iPhone Simulator:

```
The front camera is not available
The rear camera is not available
The camera does not support taking photos
The camera does not support shooting videos
```

15.2. Taking Photos with the Camera

Problem

You want to ask the user to take a photo with the camera on his iOS device, and then you want to access that photo.

Solution

Instantiate an object of type `UIImagePickerController` and present it as a modal view controller on your current view controller. Here is our view controller's declaration:

```
import UIKit
import MobileCoreServices

class ViewController: UIViewController,
UINavigationControllerDelegate, UIImagePickerControllerDelegate {

    /* We use this variable to determine if the viewDidAppear:
    method of our view controller has been called or not. If not, we
    display the camera view */
    var beenHereBefore = false
    var controller: UIImagePickerController?

    <# rest of the code goes here #>

}
```

The delegate of an instance of `UIImagePickerController` must conform to the `UINavigationControllerDelegate` and `UIImagePickerControllerDelegate` protocols. If you forget to include them in your source file(s), you'll get warnings from the compiler when assigning a value to the delegate property of your image picker controller. Please bear in mind that you can still assign an object to the delegate property of an instance of `UIImagePickerController` where that object does not explicitly conform to the `UIImagePickerControllerDelegate` and `UINavigationControllerDelegate` protocols, but implements the required methods in these protocols. However, I suggest that you give a hint to the compiler that the delegate object does, in fact, conform to the aforementioned protocols in order to avoid getting compiler warnings.

In our view controller, we will attempt to display an image picker controller as a modal view controller, like so:

```
override func viewDidAppear(animated: Bool) {
  super.viewDidAppear(animated)

  if beenHereBefore{
    /* Only display the picker once as the viewDidAppear: method gets
    called whenever the view of our view controller is displayed */
    return;
```

```
  } else {
    beenHereBefore = true
  }

  if isCameraAvailable() && doesCameraSupportTakingPhotos(){

    controller = UIImagePickerController()

    if let theController = controller{
      theController.sourceType = .Camera

      theController.mediaTypes = [kUTTypeImage as NSString]

      theController.allowsEditing = true
      theController.delegate = self

      presentViewController(theController, animated: true, completion: nil)
    }

  } else {
    println("Camera is not available")
  }

}
```

 We are using the isCameraAvailable and doesCameraSupportTak
ingPhotos methods in this example. These methods are implemented and explained in Recipe 15.1.

In this example, we are allowing the user to take photos using the image picker. You must have noticed that we are setting the delegate property of the image picker to self, which refers to the view controller. For this, we have to make sure we implemented the methods defined in the UIImagePickerControllerDelegate protocol, like so:

```
func imagePickerController(picker: UIImagePickerController!,
  didFinishPickingMediaWithInfo info: [NSObject : AnyObject]!){

    println("Picker returned successfully")

    let mediaType:AnyObject? = info[UIImagePickerControllerMediaType]

    if let type:AnyObject = mediaType{

      if type is String{
        let stringType = type as String

        if stringType == kUTTypeMovie as NSString{
          let urlOfVideo = info[UIImagePickerControllerMediaURL] as? NSURL
          if let url = urlOfVideo{
```

```
            println("Video URL = \(url)")
          }
        }

        else if stringType == kUTTypeImage as NSString as NSString{
          /* Let's get the metadata. This is only for images--not videos */
          let metadata = info[UIImagePickerControllerMediaMetadata]
            as? NSDictionary
          if let theMetaData = metadata{
            let image = info[UIImagePickerControllerOriginalImage]
              as? UIImage
            if let theImage = image{
              println("Image Metadata = \(theMetaData)")
              println("Image = \(theImage)")
            }
          }
        }

      }
    }

    picker.dismissViewControllerAnimated(true, completion: nil)
}

func imagePickerControllerDidCancel(picker: UIImagePickerController!) {
  println("Picker was cancelled")
  picker.dismissViewControllerAnimated(true, completion: nil)
}
```

Discussion

There are a couple of important things you must keep in mind about the image picker controller's delegate. First, two delegate messages are called on the delegate object of the image picker controller. The `imagePickerController:didFinishPickingMediaWithInfo:` method gets called when the user finishes execution of the image picker (e.g., takes a photo and presses a button at the end), whereas the `imagePickerControllerDidCancel:` method gets called when the image picker's operation is cancelled.

Also, the `imagePickerController:didFinishPickingMediaWithInfo:` delegate method contains information about the item that was captured by the user, be it an image or a video. The `didFinishPickingMediaWithInfo` parameter is a dictionary of values that tell you what the image picker captured and the metadata of that item, along with other useful information. The first thing you have to do in this method is to read the value of the `UIImagePickerControllerMediaType` key in this dictionary. The object for this key is an instance of `NSString` that could be one of these values:

kUTTypeImage
    For a photo that was shot by the camera

```
kUTTypeMovie
```
For a movie/video that was shot by the camera

The kUTTypeImage and kUTTypeMovie values are available in the Mobile Core Services framework and are of type CFStringRef. You can simply typecast these values to NSString if needed.

After determining the type of resource created by the camera (video or photo), you can access that resource's properties using the didFinishPickingMediaWithInfo dictionary parameter again.

For images (kUTTypeImage), you can access these keys:

```
UIImagePickerControllerMediaMetadata
```
This key's value is an object of type NSDictionary. This dictionary contains a lot of useful information about the image that was shot by the user. A complete discussion of the values inside this dictionary is beyond the scope of this chapter.

```
UIImagePickerControllerOriginalImage
```
This key's value is an object of type UIImage containing the image that was shot by the user.

```
UIImagePickerControllerCropRect
```
If editing is enabled (using the allowsEditing property of UIImagePicker Controller), the object of this key will contain the rectangle of the cropped area.

```
UIImagePickerControllerEditedImage
```
If editing is enabled (using the allowsEditing property of UIImagePicker Controller), this key's value will contain the edited (resized and scaled) image.

For videos (kUTTypeMovie) that are shot by the user, you can access the UIImagePick erControllerMediaURL key in the didFinishPickingMediaWithInfo dictionary parameter of the imagePickerController:didFinishPickingMediaWithInfo: method. The value of this key is an object of type NSURL containing the URL of the video that was shot by the user.

After you get a reference to the UIImage instance that the user took with the camera, you can simply use that instance within your application.

The images shot by the image picker controller within your application are not saved to the Camera Roll by default.

See Also

Recipe 15.1

15.3. Taking Videos with the Camera

Problem

You want to allow your user to shoot a video using his iOS device, and you would like to be able to use that video from inside your application.

Solution

Use `UIImagePickerController` with the `UIImagePickerControllerSourceTypeCamera` source type and the `kUTTypeMovie` media type:

```
override func viewDidAppear(animated: Bool) {
  super.viewDidAppear(animated)

  if beenHereBefore{
    /* Only display the picker once as the viewDidAppear: method gets
    called whenever the view of our view controller gets displayed */
    return;
  } else {
    beenHereBefore = true
  }

  if isCameraAvailable() && doesCameraSupportShootingVideos(){

    controller = UIImagePickerController()

    if let theController = controller{
      theController.sourceType = .Camera

      theController.mediaTypes = [kUTTypeMovie as NSString]

      theController.allowsEditing = true
      theController.delegate = self

      presentViewController(theController, animated: true, completion: nil)
    }

  } else {
    println("Camera is not available")
  }

}
```

The `isCameraAvailable` and `doesCameraSupportShootingVideos` methods used in this sample code are implemented and discussed in Recipe 15.1.

We will implement the delegate methods of the image picker controller like so:

```swift
func imagePickerController(picker: UIImagePickerController!,
  didFinishPickingMediaWithInfo info: [NSObject : AnyObject]!){

    println("Picker returned successfully")

    let mediaType:AnyObject? = info[UIImagePickerControllerMediaType]

    if let type:AnyObject = mediaType{

      if type is String{
        let stringType = type as String

        if stringType == kUTTypeMovie as NSString{
          let urlOfVideo = info[UIImagePickerControllerMediaURL] as? NSURL
          if let url = urlOfVideo{

            println("Url of video = \(url)")

            var dataReadingError: NSError?
            let videoData = NSData(contentsOfURL: url,
              options: .MappedRead,
              error: &dataReadingError)

            if videoData!.length == 0{
              /* We were able to read the data */
              println("Successfully loaded the data")
            } else {
              /* We failed to read the data. Use the dataReadingError
              variable to determine what the error is */
              if let error = dataReadingError{
                println("Failed to load the data with error  = \(error)")
              }
            }
          }
        }
      }

    }

    picker.dismissViewControllerAnimated(true, completion: nil)
}
```

```
func imagePickerControllerDidCancel(picker: UIImagePickerController!) {
  println("Picker was cancelled")
  picker.dismissViewControllerAnimated(true, completion: nil)
}
```

Discussion

Once you detect that the iOS device your application is running on supports video recording, you can bring up the image picker controller with the `UIImagePickerCon` `trollerSourceTypeCamera` source type and `kUTTypeMovie` media type to allow the users of your application to shoot videos. When they are done, the `imagePickerControl` `ler:didFinishPickingMediaWithInfo:` delegate method is called, and you can use the `didFinishPickingMediaWithInfo` dictionary parameter to find out more about the captured video (the values that can be placed inside this dictionary are thoroughly explained in Recipe 15.2).

When the user shoots a video using the image picker controller, the video will be saved in a temporary folder inside your application's bundle, not inside the Camera Roll. The following is an example of such a URL:

```
file:///private/var/mobile/Containers/Data/Application/
F133B7F6-DCBC-4875-B67E-1D9BA1095EB4/
tmp/capture/capturedvideo.MOV
```

As the programmer, not only can you allow your users to shoot videos from inside your application, but you can also modify how the videos are captured. You can change two important properties of the `UIImagePickerController` class in order to modify the default behavior of video recording:

videoQuality
> This property specifies the quality of the video. You can choose a value such as `UIImagePickerControllerQualityTypeHigh` or `UIImagePickerControllerQuali` `tyTypeMedium` for the value of this property.

videoMaximumDuration
> This property specifies the maximum duration of the video. This value is measured in seconds.

For instance, if we were to allow the users to record high-quality videos for up to 30 seconds, we could simply modify the values of the aforementioned properties of the instance of `UIImagePickerController` like so:

```
override func viewDidAppear(animated: Bool) {
  super.viewDidAppear(animated)

  if beenHereBefore{
    /* Only display the picker once because the viewDidAppear: method gets
    called whenever the view of our view controller is displayed */
    return;
```

```
    } else {
      beenHereBefore = true
    }

    if isCameraAvailable() && doesCameraSupportShootingVideos(){

      controller = UIImagePickerController()

      if let theController = controller{
        theController.sourceType = .Camera

        theController.mediaTypes = [kUTTypeMovie as NSString]

        theController.allowsEditing = true
        theController.delegate = self

        /* Record in high quality */
        theController.videoQuality = .TypeHigh

        /* Only allow 30 seconds of recording */
        theController.videoMaximumDuration = 30.0

        presentViewController(theController, animated: true, completion: nil)
      }

    } else {
      println("Camera is not available")
    }

  }
```

See Also

Recipe 15.1

15.4. Storing Photos in the Photo Library

Problem

You want to be able to store a photo in the user's photo library.

Solution

Use the UIImageWriteToSavedPhotosAlbum procedure:

```
import UIKit
import MobileCoreServices

class ViewController: UIViewController,
UIImagePickerControllerDelegate, UINavigationControllerDelegate {
```

```
/* We will use this variable to determine if the viewDidAppear:
method of our view controller is already called or not. If not, we will
display the camera view */
var beenHereBefore = false
var controller: UIImagePickerController?

func imageWasSavedSuccessfully(image: UIImage,
  didFinishSavingWithError error: NSError!,
  context: UnsafeMutablePointer<()>){

    if let theError = error{
      println("An error happened while saving the image = \(theError)")
    } else {
      println("Image was saved successfully")
    }
}

func imagePickerController(picker: UIImagePickerController!,
  didFinishPickingMediaWithInfo info: [NSObject : AnyObject]!){

    println("Picker returned successfully")

    let mediaType:AnyObject? = info[UIImagePickerControllerMediaType]

    if let type:AnyObject = mediaType{

      if type is String{
        let stringType = type as String

        if stringType == kUTTypeImage as NSString{

          var theImage: UIImage!

          if picker.allowsEditing{
            theImage = info[UIImagePickerControllerEditedImage] as UIImage
          } else {
            theImage = info[UIImagePickerControllerOriginalImage] as UIImage
          }

          let selectorAsString =
          "imageWasSavedSuccessfully:didFinishSavingWithError:context:"

          let selectorToCall = Selector(selectorAsString)

          UIImageWriteToSavedPhotosAlbum(theImage,
            self,
            selectorToCall,
            nil)

        }
```

```
    }
  }

    picker.dismissViewControllerAnimated(true, completion: nil)
}

func imagePickerControllerDidCancel(picker: UIImagePickerController){

println("Picker was cancelled")
  picker.dismissViewControllerAnimated(true, completion: nil)

}

func isCameraAvailable() -> Bool{
  return UIImagePickerController.isSourceTypeAvailable(.Camera)
}

func cameraSupportsMedia(mediaType: String,
  sourceType: UIImagePickerControllerSourceType) -> Bool{

    let availableMediaTypes =
    UIImagePickerController.availableMediaTypesForSourceType(sourceType) as
      [String]?

    if let types = availableMediaTypes{
      for type in types{
        if type == mediaType{
          return true
        }
      }
    }

    return false
}

func doesCameraSupportTakingPhotos() -> Bool{
  return cameraSupportsMedia(kUTTypeImage as NSString, sourceType: .Camera)
}

override func viewDidAppear(animated: Bool) {
  super.viewDidAppear(animated)

  if beenHereBefore{
    /* Only display the picker once because the viewDidAppear: method gets
    called whenever the view of our view controller is displayed */
    return;
  } else {
    beenHereBefore = true
  }

  if isCameraAvailable() && doesCameraSupportTakingPhotos(){
```

```
    controller = UIImagePickerController()

    if let theController = controller{
      theController.sourceType = .Camera

      theController.mediaTypes = [kUTTypeImage as NSString]

      theController.allowsEditing = true
      theController.delegate = self

      presentViewController(theController, animated: true, completion: nil)
    }

  } else {
    println("Camera is not available")
  }

  }

}
```

 The isCameraAvailable and doesCameraSupportTakingPhotos methods used in this example are thoroughly explained in Recipe 15.1.

Discussion

Usually after a user takes a photo with her iOS device, she expects it to be saved into her photo library. However, applications that are not originally shipped with iOS can ask the user to take a photo using the UIImagePickerController class, and then process that image. In this case, the user will understand that the application might not save the photo to her photo library—it might simply use it internally. For instance, if an instant messaging application allows users to transfer their photos to each other's devices, the user will understand that a photo he takes inside the application will not be saved to his photo library but will instead be transferred over the Internet to the other user.

However, if you decide you want to store an instance of UIImage to the photo library on the user's device, you can use the UIImageWriteToSavedPhotosAlbum function. This function accepts four parameters:

1. The image

2. The object that is notified when the image is fully saved

3. A parameter that specifies the selector that has to be called on the target object (specified by the second parameter) when the save operation finishes

4. A context value that gets passed to the specified selector when the operation is done

Providing the second, third, and fourth parameters to this procedure is optional. If you do provide the second and third parameters, the fourth parameter still remains optional.

When you attempt to use the UIImageWriteToSavedPhotosAlbum procedure to save a photo in the user's photo library, if it's the first time your app is doing this on the device, iOS asks the user for permission. This allows the user to either allow or disallow your app from storing photos in her photo library; after all, it's her device, and we should not be doing anything on it without her consent. If the user gives permission, the UIImage WriteToSavedPhotosAlbum procedure continues to save the image. If the user does not give permission, our completion handler selector is still called, but the didFinishSa vingWithError parameter of it is set to a valid error instance (see Figure 15-1).

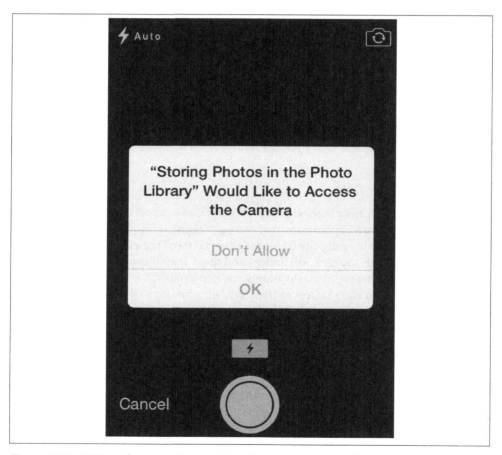

Figure 15-1. iOS is asking user's permission for our app to use the camera

If the user denies permission to your app (Figure 15-2), every subsequent call to the
UIImageWriteToSavedPhotosAlbum procedure will fail until the user manually changes
her device's settings.

Figure 15-2. The switch is turned off indicating that the user has denied our app access

 If the error parameter that you receive in this selector is equal to nil,
that means the image was saved in the user's photo library successfully. Otherwise, you can retrieve the value of this parameter to determine what the issue was.

15.5. Storing Videos in the Photo Library

Problem

You want to store a video accessible through a URL, such as a video in your application
bundle, to the photo library.

Solution

Use the writeVideoAtPathToSavedPhotosAlbum:completionBlock: instance method
of ALAssetsLibrary:

```
import UIKit
import AssetsLibrary

class ViewController: UIViewController {

  var assetsLibrary: ALAssetsLibrary?

  override func viewDidLoad(){
    super.viewDidLoad()
```

```
assetsLibrary = ALAssetsLibrary()

let videoURL = NSBundle.mainBundle().URLForResource("sample_iTunes",
  withExtension: "mov") as NSURL?

if let library = assetsLibrary{

  if let url = videoURL{

    library.writeVideoAtPathToSavedPhotosAlbum(url,
      completionBlock: {(url: NSURL!, error: NSError!) in

        if let theError = error{
          println("Error happened while saving the video")
          println("The error is = \(theError)")
        } else {
          println("no errors happened")
        }

    })
  } else {
    println("Could not find the video in the app bundle")
  }

}

}

}
```

Discussion

The Assets Library framework is a convenient bridge between developers and the photo library. As mentioned in Recipe 15.6, the iOS SDK provides built-in GUI components that you can use to access the contents of the photo library. However, you might sometimes require direct access to these contents. In such instances, you can use the Assets Library framework.

After allocating and initializing the Assets Library object of type ALAssetsLibrary, you can use the writeVideoAtPathToSavedPhotosAlbum:completionBlock: instance method of this object to write a video from a URL to the photo library. All you have to do is provide the URL of the video in NSURL form and a block object whose code will be called when the video is saved. The block object must accept two parameters of type NSURL and NSError.

If the error parameter is nil, the save process went well and you don't have to worry about anything.

The first parameter passed to the block object provided to the `writeVideoAtPathToSa vedPhotosAlbum:completionBlock:` method will point to the Assets Library URL of the stored video. A sample URL of this kind will look like this:

```
assets-library://asset/asset.mov?id=
7CD2D138-D035-4D3D-B2F6-AD510AFEF518&ext=mov
```

If it's the first time your app is attempting to use the photo library on the user's device, iOS will ask the user whether to allow or disallow this operation. If the user allows it, your call to the `writeVideoAtPathToSavedPhotosAlbum:completionBlock:` will be successful. If the user disallows the action, the error object inside your completion block will be a valid error object that you can inspect and act upon. If the user has previously disallowed your app from accessing her photo library, you won't be able to change that decision programmatically. Only she can allow access, by changing her decision in the Settings app on her device, under the Privacy section.

See Also

Recipe 15.6

15.6. Searching for and Retrieving Images and Videos

Problem

You want to be able retrieve photos and videos from the user's library.

Solution

Use the Photos framework to retrieve photos or videos from the user's library.

Discussion

The Photos framework is a modern framework that allows you to work with the user's Photos and Videos library and collections. The idea behind the Photos framework is to allow you to work in an asynchronous and intelligent way with the user's library. For instance, you can construct a fetch request and submit it to the framework and ask it to retrieve all of user's videos or photos. After you do so, you will not be given direct access to the data of those items. Instead, you will receive the metadata that represents those items. After you have the metadata, you can find out whether the fetched items are of interest to you. If they are not, you can just disregard them. If they are of interest to you, you can simply use another class to retrieve the data for those assets.

Let's have a look at a practical example. Let's say that we want to retrieve all the photos that the user has in her library and then retrieve the data for those photos. First, what we have to do is to ask the user to grant us access to her assets library like so:

```
/* Just a little method to help us display alert dialogs to the user */
func displayAlertWithTitle(title: String, message: String){
  let controller = UIAlertController(title: title,
    message: message,
    preferredStyle: .Alert)

  controller.addAction(UIAlertAction(title: "OK",
    style: .Default,
    handler: nil))

  presentViewController(controller, animated: true, completion: nil)

}

override func viewDidAppear(animated: Bool) {

  super.viewDidAppear(animated)

  PHPhotoLibrary.requestAuthorization{
    [weak self](status: PHAuthorizationStatus) in

    dispatch_async(dispatch_get_main_queue(), {

      switch status{
      case .Authorized:
        self!.retrieveImage()
      default:
        self!.displayAlertWithTitle("Access",
          message: "I could not access the photo library")
      }
      })

  }

}
```

If the user allows us to see her assets library, the previous code calls the retrieve
Image method of our view controller, which we are about to code next. In this method,
we will construct an object of type PHFetchOptions. This object will then define how
we want to retrieve our results. For instance, you can specify if you want your results to
be sorted by creation date or by modification date.

```
/* Retrieve the items in order of modification date, ascending */
let options = PHFetchOptions()
options.sortDescriptors = [NSSortDescriptor(key: "modificationDate",
  ascending: true)]
```

Then we need to retrieve all the assets whose type indicates they are images, using the
fetch options that we instantiated earlier. We can retrieve all the image assets in the user's
library using the fetchAssetsWithMediaType:options: type method of the PHAsset

class. The first parameter to this method is of type `PHAssetMediaType`, and we can pass the value of `.Image` to this parameter to retrieve all images:

```
/* Then get an object of type PHFetchResult that will contain
all our image assets */
let assetResults = PHAsset.fetchAssetsWithMediaType(.Image,
  options: options)
```

OK, now we have a collection of all the image assets in the user library. Let's check whether any results actually came back:

```
if assetResults == nil{
  println("Found no results")
  return
} else {
  println("Found \(assetResults.count) results")
}
```

The `fetchAssetsWithMediaType:options:` type method of the `PHAsset` class will give us an object of type `PHFetchResult` that supports fast enumeration. We can then enumerate through all the items in this object and find our assets. Every asset in this collection will be of type `PHAsset` and we can retrieve every asset's associated image data using an instance of the `PHCachingImageManager` class. So before we start enumerating all the assets that we fetched and trying to retrieve their data, let's create this manager object:

```
let imageManager = PHCachingImageManager()
```

Now we need to enumerate through the assets. Now that we have the instances of the `PHAsset`, we can retrieve their data using the `requestImageForAsset:targetSize:contentMode:options:resultHandler:` method of the `PHCachingImageManager` instance we just created:

```
assetResults.enumerateObjectsUsingBlock{(object: AnyObject!,
  count: Int,
  stop: UnsafeMutablePointer<ObjCBool>) in

  if object is PHAsset{
    let asset = object as PHAsset

    let imageSize = CGSize(width: asset.pixelWidth,
      height: asset.pixelHeight)

    /* For faster performance, and maybe degraded image */
    let options = PHImageRequestOptions()
    options.deliveryMode = .FastFormat

    imageManager.requestImageForAsset(asset,
      targetSize: imageSize,
      contentMode: .AspectFill,
      options: options,
      resultHandler: {(image: UIImage!,
```

```
    info: [NSObject : AnyObject]!) in

        /* The image is now available to us */

    })

    }

}
```

Now let's have a look at another example. Let's say that we want to retrieve all the videos in the user's library. The first thing that we have to do is change the way we call the `fetchAssetsWithMediaType:options:` type method of the `PHAsset` class and pass the value of `.Video` as the first parameter so that we retrieve videos instead of photos:

```
/* Then get an object of type PHFetchResult that will contain
all our video assets */
let assetResults = PHAsset.fetchAssetsWithMediaType(.Video,
  options: options)
```

Again we need to check whether we actually found any results:

```
if assetResults == nil{
  println("Found no results")
  return
} else {
  println("Found \(assetResults.count) results")
}
```

After we find that some videos came back in our search in the user's library, we attempt to play the first video. Let's start by getting the reference to this video:

```
/* Get the first video */
let object: AnyObject = assetResults[0]
```

Because the asset results array is an array of `AnyObject`, we need to find out whether we can typecast that to an object of type `PHAsset` like so:

```
if let asset = object as? PHAsset{

    <# do our work here #>

}
```

We also need to construct our video fetching options, of type `PHVideoRequestOp tions`, which we will then submit to the image manager to retrieve our image from the device or the cloud. Because we want to ask the system to download the image from the cloud if it currently doesn't exist on the device, we need to set the `networkAccessAl lowed` property of the video request options to `true`. Objects of type `PHVideoReques tOptions` also have a progress handler. Because items can be on the cloud and not on the device, you can submit your block object to this property. This leads to your progress

---

handler block being called and keeping you updated on the progress of downloading the video from the cloud before playback begins.

```
/* We want to be able to display a video even if it currently
resides only on the cloud and not on the device */
let options = PHVideoRequestOptions()
options.deliveryMode = .Automatic
options.networkAccessAllowed = true
options.version = .Current
options.progressHandler = {(progress: Double,
  error: NSError!,
  stop: UnsafeMutablePointer<ObjCBool>,
  info: [NSObject : AnyObject]!) in

  /* You can write your code here that shows a progress bar to the
  user and then using the progress parameter of this block object, you
  can update your progress bar. */

}
```

We now have our video request options and are ready to retrieve the video. To do so, we call the `requestAVAssetForVideo:options:resultHandler:` method of the `PHImageManager` class, of which `PHCachingImageManager` is a subclass. We submit a block object to to the result handler of this method. The first parameter of the block object is of type `AVAsset`. However, when you try to retrieve a video from the assets library, this item can come back of type `AVURLAsset`. This is great because we can then use the URL of this asset and construct a video player out of it using the `AVPlayer` class. After we have the video player, we need to construct a video player layer to attach to our view hierarchy and then play the player using its `play` method. Here is an example:

```
/* Now get the video */
PHCachingImageManager().requestAVAssetForVideo(asset,
  options: options,
  resultHandler: {[weak self](asset: AVAsset!,
    audioMix: AVAudioMix!,
    info: [NSObject : AnyObject]!) in

    /* This result handler is performed on a random thread, but
    we want to do some UI work, so let's switch to the main thread */

    dispatch_async(dispatch_get_main_queue(), {

      /* Did we get the URL to the video? */
      if let asset = asset as? AVURLAsset{
        let player = AVPlayer(URL: asset.URL)
        /* Create the layer now */
        let layer = AVPlayerLayer(player: player)
        layer.frame = self!.view.bounds
        self!.view.layer.addSublayer(layer)
        player.play()
      } else {
```

```
        println("This is not a URL asset. Cannot play")
    }

  })

}))
```

Perfect! Now give it a go on your own device and see how it goes. If you have at least one video that is accessible to the user, fetch that and attempt to display it on our view hierarchy.

See Also

Recipe 15.7

15.7. Reacting to Changes in Images and Videos

Problem

You want to be notified when an asset that you have a handle to, such as an image or a video, is changed under your feet. You would also like to be able to get the changed asset and update your user interface based on the changes that have occurred.

Solution

Register for change notifications on the photo library using the `registerChangeOb server:` method of the `PHPhotoLibrary` class. To unregister, invoke the `unregister ChangeObserver:` method.

Discussion

The way to use the `PHPhotoLibrary` class is through its `sharedPhotoLibrary` type method. This will return an object of type `PHPhotoLibrary`. Once you have the handle to the shared photo library, use its `registerChangeObserver:` method to register for changes.

So let's have a look at a real-life example. Let's say that we want to retrieve the newest photo in the user's library and then flip its hidden flag. So the photo will be hidden if it's not, and will be shown if it's hidden already. We will use the technique that we learned in Recipe 15.6 to retrieve the newest image in the user's library using the `creation Date` sort descriptor of our assets.

Then we will flip its hidden flag. All this time, we are waiting for asset-changed notifications that can be submitted by the `PHPhotoLibrary` class. We will also display this image on our view controller.

When the photo's visibility flag is changed, we receive a message from the `PHPhotoLibrary` class telling us that a change has occurred and we use the information that we are given to update our UI. So here are the variables that we are going to need in our view controller:

```
/* Handy extension on UIView to get the width and height */
extension UIView{
  var width: CGFloat{
  return CGRectGetWidth(self.bounds)
  }
  var height: CGFloat{
  return CGRectGetHeight(self.bounds)
  }
}

class ViewController: UIViewController, PHPhotoLibraryChangeObserver {

  /* This will represent the newest photo in our library */
  var lastPhoto: PHAsset?
  /* Pressing this button will flip the hidden flag of our asset */
  var buttonChange: UIButton!
  /* The image view that we will use to display the newest photo */
  var imageView: UIImageView?

  <# rest of the code #>

}
```

As you can see, we are going to enhance our user interface to add a button that, when pressed, will flip the hidden flag of our asset. Let's create this button and also listen to asset-changed notifications:

```
init(coder aDecoder: NSCoder!) {
  super.init(coder: aDecoder)
  buttonChange = UIButton.buttonWithType(.System) as UIButton
  buttonChange.frame = CGRect(x: 0, y: 0, width: 200, height: 50)
  buttonChange.setTitle("Change photo", forState: .Normal)
  buttonChange.addTarget(self,
    action: "performChangePhoto",
    forControlEvents: .TouchUpInside)
  PHPhotoLibrary.sharedPhotoLibrary().registerChangeObserver(self)
}

deinit{
  PHPhotoLibrary.sharedPhotoLibrary().unregisterChangeObserver(self)
}
```

When our view appears on the screen, we ask the user for permission to access her photo library, and if we are granted access, we attempt to retrieve the newest photo in her library and display it on our UI. If we are not given permission, we display a message to the user:

```
override func viewDidAppear(animated: Bool) {

  super.viewDidAppear(animated)

  PHPhotoLibrary.requestAuthorization{
    [weak self](status: PHAuthorizationStatus) in

    dispatch_async(dispatch_get_main_queue(), {

      switch status{
      case .Authorized:
        self!.retrieveAndDisplayNewestImage()
      default:
        self!.displayAlertWithTitle("Access",
          message: "I could not access the photo library")
      }
    })

  }

}
```

We are using our own displayAlertWithTitle:message: method here to display a message to the user if we are not given permission to access the assets library. This method has been defined and explained in Recipe 9.3. I suggest that you look at that recipe for the explanation and the code to this method.

If we are given permission to the assets library, we invoke our custom method of re trieveAndDisplayNewestImage, which will, as its name implies, attempt to retrieve the newest image in the user's assets library and display it on the screen:

```
func retrieveAndDisplayNewestImage(){
  /* Retrieve the items in order of creation date date, with the newest one
  on top */
  let options = PHFetchOptions()
  options.sortDescriptors = [NSSortDescriptor(key: "creationDate",
    ascending: false)]

  /* Then get an object of type PHFetchResult that will contain
  all our image assets */
  let assetResults = PHAsset.fetchAssetsWithMediaType(.Image,
    options: options)

  if assetResults == nil{
    println("Found no results")
    return
  } else {
    println("Found \(assetResults.count) results")
  }

  if let lastPhoto = assetResults[0] as? PHAsset{
    self.lastPhoto = lastPhoto
```

```
      retrieveImageForAsset(lastPhoto)

    }
  }
```

If everything goes well and we can find the newest image, we issue a call to the `retrie`
`veImageForAsset:` method, which in turn retrieves the image for the provided asset
that we found in the previous step and displays that image on the screen. If an image
was retrieved, it will also display the "Change Image" button on the screen. Pressing this
button invokes a method that we are going to see soon, which in turn flips the hidden
flag of our image. Let's have a look at the implementation of the `retrieveImageForAs`
`set:` method first:

```
func imageFetchingOptions() -> PHImageRequestOptions{
  /* Now retrieve the photo */
  let options = PHImageRequestOptions()
  options.deliveryMode = .HighQualityFormat
  options.resizeMode = .Exact
  options.version = .Current
  return options
}

func retrieveImageForAsset(asset: PHAsset){
  let imageSize = CGSize(width: view.width, height: view.height)

  PHCachingImageManager().requestImageForAsset(asset,
    targetSize: imageSize,
    contentMode: .AspectFit,
    options: imageFetchingOptions(),
    resultHandler: {[weak self] (image: UIImage!,
      info: [NSObject : AnyObject]!) in

      dispatch_async(dispatch_get_main_queue(), {

        if let theImageView = self!.imageView{
          theImageView.removeFromSuperview()
        }
        if image != nil{
          self!.imageView = UIImageView(image: image)
          if let imageView = self!.imageView{
            imageView.contentMode = .ScaleAspectFit
            imageView.frame = self!.view.bounds
            self!.view.addSubview(imageView)
            self!.buttonChange.center = self!.view.center
            self!.view.addSubview(self!.buttonChange)
          }

        } else {
          println("No image data came back")
```

```
        }
      })

    })
  }
```

As we saw, our "Change Photo" button calls the `performChangePhoto` method on our view controller. In this method, we want to perform a change on an asset of type `PHAsset`. We do this by first issuing the `canPerformEditOperation:` method on the asset itself. The parameter to this method will be the change that we are attempting to make. You can make changes to the properties of an asset, such as its creation date or hidden flag, or you can change the content of an asset altogether. The other type of change available is to delete the asset. So you get to specify how you would like to change the asset. In this example, we just want to flip the hidden flag on the asset. This flag is a property of the asset and won't change the content or delete this asset.

The `canPerformEditOperation:` method returns a Boolean value indicating whether you are allowed to make the changes that you want. If allowed, we will use the `perform Changes:` method of `PHPhotoLibrary`. The parameter that we have to provide to this method is a block object that performs the desired changes. The changes that we perform will be of type `PHAssetChangeRequest`, so we need to instantiate an object of this type and then do our work with it. Nothing else is required of us. Here is the implementation of the action of our button:

```
func performChangePhoto(){

  if let asset = lastPhoto{

    /* The hidden flag is a property of the asset, hence
    the .Properties value */
    if asset.canPerformEditOperation(.Properties){

      /* Make our changes here */
      PHPhotoLibrary.sharedPhotoLibrary().performChanges({

        /* Flip the hidden flag */
        let request = PHAssetChangeRequest(forAsset: asset)
        request.hidden = !asset.hidden
        }, completionHandler: {[weak self](success: Bool, error: NSError!) in

          if success{
            println("Successfully changed the photo")
          } else {
            dispatch_async(dispatch_get_main_queue(), {
              self!.displayAlertWithTitle("Failed",
                message: "Failed to change the photo properties")
              })
          }
```

```
      })

    } else {
      displayAlertWithTitle("Editing", message: "Could not change the photo")
    }

  }

}
```

Earlier you saw that our view controller conformed to the PHPhotoLibraryChangeOb
server protocol and that the observer parameter that we passed to the registerChan
geObserver: method of the PHPhotoLibrary class was our view controller instance. To
conform to this protocol, we need to implement the photoLibraryDidChange: method.
The parameter that is passed to this method is of type PHChange. Invoke the changeDe
tailsForObject: method on the PHChange instance to get an object of type PHOb
jectChangeDetails, which will let you know about the details of the change that occurred on an asset. The parameter that you need to pass to the aforementioned method
is your asset of type PHAsset. When you have the object change details, you can retrieve
a handle to the changed object and, if the object's contents have changed, reload
your UI:

```
func photoLibraryDidChange(changeInstance: PHChange!) {

  println("Image is changed now")

  dispatch_async(dispatch_get_main_queue(), {[weak self] in

    let change = changeInstance.changeDetailsForObject(self!.lastPhoto)
    if change != nil{
      self!.lastPhoto = change.objectAfterChanges as? PHAsset
      if change.assetContentChanged{
        self!.retrieveImageForAsset(self!.lastPhoto!)
      }
    }
  })

}
```

In this example, we listened to changes for a photo asset. The same techniques and
methods described in this recipe apply to video assets as well, as long as they are of type
PHAsset.

See Also

Recipe 15.6

15.8. Editing Images and Videos Right on the Device

Problem

You want to be able to edit an image that you pulled out of the user's assets library.

Solution

Invoke the `requestContentEditingInputWithOptions:completionHandler:` method of your instance of the `PHAsset` instance.

Discussion

 In this recipe, I assume that you reset your simulator to ensure that the photo library is reset to default settings, with all the original photos in it.

In this recipe, we are going to discuss a practical example of editing an image that we pulled out of the user's photo library. We are going to use the technique that we learned in Recipe 15.6 to retrieve an image. After we have the image, we are going to apply a "Posterize" filter on it and save it back to the user's library. The iOS simulator comes with a few photos preinstalled. We are going to take the photo that you see in Figure 15-3 and apply our "Posterize" filter on it to turn it into what you see in Figure 15-4.

Figure 15-3. Original photo to be edited

Figure 15-4. We applied the posterize filter to the image and saved it

Let's go ahead and add the required variables to our view controller:

```
import UIKit
import Photos
import OpenGLES
```

```
class ViewController: UIViewController {

  /* These two values are our way of telling the Photos framework about
  the identifier of the changes that we are going to make to the photo */
  let editFormatIdentifier = NSBundle.mainBundle().bundleIdentifier!
  /* Just an application-specific editing version */
  let editFormatVersion = "0.1"
  /* This is our filter name. We will use this for our Core Image filter */
  let filterName = "CIColorPosterize"


  <# rest of the code goes here #>

}
```

We are using the OpenGLES framework in this example because we will use that framework later to convert an image of type `CIImage` into its JPEG representation, so that we
can use the data of that JPEG image in order to save our changes. Here is our code for
this method:

```
/* This turns an image into its NSData representation */
func dataFromCiImage(image: CIImage) -> NSData{
  let glContext = EAGLContext(API: .OpenGLES2)
  let context = CIContext(EAGLContext: glContext)
  let imageRef = context.createCGImage(image, fromRect: image.extent())
  let image = UIImage(CGImage: imageRef, scale: 1.0, orientation: .Up)
  return UIImageJPEGRepresentation(image, 1.0)
}
```

The filter name that we are defining will also be used with our `CIFilter` class in order
to apply a filter to our `CIImage` instance. Now when our view appears on the screen, we
are going to retrieve the newest image in the user's library:

```
override func viewDidAppear(animated: Bool) {

  super.viewDidAppear(animated)

  PHPhotoLibrary.requestAuthorization{
    [weak self](status: PHAuthorizationStatus) in

    dispatch_async(dispatch_get_main_queue(), {

      switch status{
      case .Authorized:
        self!.retrieveNewestImage()
      default:
        self!.displayAlertWithTitle("Access",
          message: "I could not access the photo library")
      }
    })
```

```
    }

  }
```

Upon successful authorization to use the user's assets library, we are calling the `retrie`
`veNewestImage` method of our view controller. This method is similar to the `retrie`
`veAndDisplayNewestImage` method that we saw in Recipe 15.7, but here, after we find
the newest image in the user's library, we will attempt to edit it:

```
/* After this method retrieves the newest image from the user's assets
library, it will attempt to edit it */
func retrieveNewestImage() {

  /* Retrieve the items in order of creation date, with the newest one
  on top */
  let options = PHFetchOptions()
  options.sortDescriptors = [NSSortDescriptor(key: "creationDate",
    ascending: true)]

  /* Then get an object of type PHFetchResult that will contain
  all of our image assets */
  let assetResults = PHAsset.fetchAssetsWithMediaType(.Image,
    options: options)

  if assetResults == nil{
    println("Found no results")
    return
  } else {
    println("Found \(assetResults.count) results")
  }

  let imageManager = PHCachingImageManager()

  if let asset = assetResults[0] as? PHAsset{
    editAsset(asset)
  }

}
```

This method is calling the `editAsset:` method of our view controller that takes in a
parameter of type `PHAsset`. This method is the main topic of this recipe, so we are going
to keep our attention on this method for the remainder of this recipe.

We start our editing by telling the photos system service whether or not we are able to
handle any previous changes to the asset that we picked. Let me explain what this means.
Imagine an original image on the user's device. This image is untouched and unedited.
Then the user applies a sepia effect on the image and saves it. After that, our app goes
in (for example) and applies a posterize effect to the same image. Now the image has
two effects. It turns out that iOS keeps the original image but dynamically applies those
two effect on top of it when displaying the image to the user. Because the original is

intact, the user or our app can undo those edits. In short, every edit applied to an image leaves a trace in the system.

When we invoke the `requestContentEditingInputWithOptions:completionHan dler:` method on an asset of type `PHAsset`, the first parameter is an object of type `PHContentEditingInputRequestOptions`. This object has a property named `canHand leAdjustmentData` that can be set to a block object that takes in a parameter of type `PHAdjustmentData` and returns a Boolean value. This block object can be called multiple times, so you need to check the adjustment data's version information and identifier to check whether it is something that your app can handle.

The easiest way to write this block object is to check whether the adjustment data corresponds to an adjustment or editing that we did to the asset. Every adjustment is associatd with an identifier, a format version, and custom data. For the posterize adjustment that we are about to apply, we defined these values on top of our view controller as you saw earlier.

So we are going to start the implementation of our `editAsset:` method like so:

```
func editAsset(asset: PHAsset){

  /* Can we handle previous edits on this asset? */
  let requestOptions = PHContentEditingInputRequestOptions()
  requestOptions.canHandleAdjustmentData = {
    [weak self] (data: PHAdjustmentData!) -> Bool in
    /* Yes, but only if they are our edits */
    if data.formatIdentifier == self!.editFormatIdentifier &&
      data.formatVersion == self!.editFormatVersion{
        return true
    } else {
      return false
    }
  }

  <# rest of the code goes here #>
```

After we construct our editing options, we are going to start our editing process:

```
  /* Now ask the system if we are allowed to edit the given asset */
  asset.requestContentEditingInputWithOptions(requestOptions,
    completionHandler: {[weak self](input: PHContentEditingInput!,
      info: [NSObject : AnyObject]!) in
```

The input parameter of the completion handler block object that we passed to this method is of utmost importance to us. This value is of type `PHContentEditingInput` and is going to give us access to the image that we requested. We are going to get a URL to the image and also find its orientation. Using that information, we can construct an image of type `CIImage` so that later we will be able to apply our filter to it:

```
  /* Get the required information from the asset */
  let url = input.fullSizeImageURL
```

```
let orientation = input.fullSizeImageOrientation

/* Retrieve an instance of CIImage to apply our filter to */
let inputImage =
CIImage(contentsOfURL: url,
  options: nil).imageByApplyingOrientation(orientation)
```

Perfect, we have our image. Now what should we do with it? We should construct our posterize effect of type `CIFilter` and apply it to the image to receive a new image handle with the filter applied to it:

```
/* Apply the filter to our image */
let filter = CIFilter(name: self!.filterName)
filter.setDefaults()
filter.setValue(inputImage, forKey: kCIInputImageKey)
let outputImage = filter.outputImage
```

At this stage, feel free to grab a cup of coffee because things are going to get interesting. Before we can call the `performChanges:completionHandler:` method of our `PHPhoto Library` shared instance, we need to be able to construct a *content editing output* object that contains information about our changes. This output object is of type `PHContentE ditingOutput` and you will need to initialize it using the input that we were given earlier of type `PHContentEditingInput`.

After the instance is initialized, we need to set its `adjustmentData` property to an object of type `PHAdjustmentData`, which we construct using the adjustment identifier, version number, and data that we constructed in our view controller. This adjustment data represents the change that we are going to apply to the image.

The other very important thing that we need to do is convert our edited image to data of type `NSData` using the `dataFromCiImage:` method that we wrote earlier, and save that data to the URL specified by the `renderedContentURL` property of our `PHContentEdi tingOutput` instance. This might sound confusing, but what is happening is this: we are being given a URL that contains our image in the library. We then grab that image and apply a filter to it, and then save our changes as pure data. The `PHContentEditingOut put` class dictates where we have to save our changes for the system to be able to pick them up. This is really a protocol that Apple has decided to define for us programmers. The system saves the image to disk, then asks us to pick it up, edit it, and save it back to a location designated by an instance of the `PHContentEditingOutput` class. Simple, no?

```
/* Get the data of our edited image */
let editedImageData = self!.dataFromCiImage(outputImage)

/* The results of editing our image are encapsulated here */
let output = PHContentEditingOutput(contentEditingInput: input)
/* Here we are saving our edited image to the URL that is dictated
by the content editing output class */
editedImageData.writeToURL(output.renderedContentURL,
  atomically: true)
```

```
output.adjustmentData =
  PHAdjustmentData(formatIdentifier: self!.editFormatIdentifier,
    formatVersion: self!.editFormatVersion,
     data: self!.filterName.dataUsingEncoding(NSUTF8StringEncoding,
      allowLossyConversion: false))
```

Then we apply our changes like so:

```
/* Now perform our changes */
PHPhotoLibrary.sharedPhotoLibrary().performChanges({
  /* This is the change object and its output is the output object
  that we previously created */
  let change = PHAssetChangeRequest(forAsset: asset)
  change.contentEditingOutput = output
}, completionHandler: {[weak self] (success: Bool, error: NSError!) in

  self!.performOnMainThread{
    if success{
      self!.displayAlertWithTitle("Succeeded",
        message: "Successfully edited the image")
    } else {
      self!.displayAlertWithTitle("Failed",
        message: "Could not edit the image. Error = \(error)")
    }
  }

})
```

This code refers to a custom method called performOnMainThread: to perform a closure on the main thread, and we wrote this method like so:

```
/* A little handy method that allows us to perform a block
object on the main thread */
func performOnMainThread(block: dispatch_block_t){
  dispatch_async(dispatch_get_main_queue(), block)
}
```

See Also

Recipe 15.6; Recipe 15.7

CHAPTER 16

Notifications

16.0. Introduction

Notifications are objects that can carry data and be broadcast to multiple receivers. They are very good for decomposing work into different pieces of code, but can easily get out of hand if you misuse them. You should understand the limitations of notifications. We will talk more about their uses in this chapter and learn when you are better off without them.

Three types of notifications are available in iOS:

A normal notification (an instance of `NSNotification` *class)*
> This is a simple notification that your app can broadcast to all possible receivers inside your app. iOS also broadcasts notifications of this type to your app while your app is in the foreground, informing you of various system events that are happening, such as the keyboard showing or being hidden. These notifications are great for decoupling code, in that they can allow you to cleanly separate various components in a complex iOS application.

A local notification (an instance of `UILocalNotification` *class)*
> This is a notification that you schedule to be delivered to your app at a specific time. Your app can receive it even if the app is in the background or not running at all, and the app is started if the notification is delivered while your app is not running. You would normally schedule a local notification if you want to ensure that your app gets woken up (granted that the user permits this action, as we will see later) at a specific time of the day.

Push notifications
> This is a notification that is sent to an iOS device via a server. It is called a push notification because your app doesn't have to keep polling a server for notifications. iOS maintains a persistent connection to Apple Push Notification Services servers

(APNS servers), and whenever a new push message is available, iOS will process the message and send it to the app to which the push was designated.

 We will refer to normal notifications herein as notifications. The word *normal* is redundant in this context.

Local notifications are special in that they become visible to the user and the user can take action on them. Based on the user's action, your app will be notified by iOS to handle the action. On the other hand, notifications are invisible items that you can broadcast in your app and that your app has to handle. The user doesn't directly have to get involved unless you involve her as a result of receiving and processing the notification. For instance, your app may send a notification to another part of your app, which, upon receiving that notification, fires up an alert dialog. The user then has to get involved and press a button on the alert dialog to dismiss it (for instance). This is indirect involvement and is very much different from the direct involvement that local notifications demand from users.

Notifications are a big part of OS X and iOS. iOS sends system-wide notifications to all apps that are listening, and apps can send notifications as well. A system-wide, or *distributed*, notification can be delivered only by iOS.

A notification is a simple concept represented by the NSNotification class in the iOS SDK. A notification is posted by an object and can carry information. The object that sends the notification will identify itself to the notification center while posting the notification. The receiver of the notification can then probe the sender, perhaps using its class name, to find out more about the sender, which is called the *object* of the notification. A notification can also carry a user-info dictionary, which is a dictionary data structure that can carry extra information about the notification. If no dictionary is provided, this parameter is nil.

16.1. Sending Notifications

Problem

You want to decouple parts of your app and send a notification where it can be picked up by another component in your app.

Solution

Compose an instance of NSNotification and broadcast it to your app using the class's postNotification: method. You can get an instance of the notification center using its defaultCenter class method, like so:

```
import UIKit

class ViewController: UIViewController {

  let notificationName = "NotificationNameGoesHere"

  override func viewDidLoad() {
    super.viewDidLoad()

    let notification = NSNotification(name: notificationName,
      object: self,
      userInfo: [
        "Key1" : "Value1",
        "Key2" : 2]
    )

    NSNotificationCenter.defaultCenter().postNotification(notification)

  }

}
```

Discussion

A notification object is encapsulated in an instance of the NSNotification class. A notification object on its own is really nothing until it has been posted to the app using a notification center. A notification object has three important properties:

Name

> This is a string. When a listener starts listening for notifications, it has to specify the name of the notification, as we will see later in this chapter. If you are posting a notification in a class of yours, ensure that the name of that notification is well documented. We are going to see an example of this soon in this recipe.

Sender object

> You can optionally specify the object that is sending the notification. Usually this will be set to self. But why do we need to even specify the sender of a notification? This information is useful for the parts of the app that listen for notifications. Let's say that, in one of your classes, you are sending a notification with the name of *MyNotification* and another class in your application is sending a notification with the exact same name. When a listener starts listening for the *MyNotification* notification, the receiver can specify which notification source it is interested in. So the receiver can say that it wants to receive all notifications with the name of *MyNo*

tification coming from a specific object, but not from the second object. This way, the receiver can really be in control. Even though you can leave the Sender Object field as nil when posting a notification, it is much better to set this property to `self`, the object that is sending the notification.

User info dictionary

This is a dictionary object that you can attach to your notification object. The receiver can then read this dictionary when it receives the notification. Think of this as an opportunity to pass additional information to the receivers of your notification.

See Also

Recipe 16.0, "Introduction"

16.2. Listening for and Reacting to Notifications

Problem

You want to react to a notification that is being sent either by your app or by the system.

Solution

Listen to a particular notification by calling the `addObserver:selector:name:object:` method of the default notification center. This method has the following parameters:

`addObserver`

The object that observes a given notification. If this is the current class, put `self` here to point to the current instance of your class.

`selector`

The selector that receives the notification. This selector must have one parameter of type `NSNotification`.

`name`

The name of the notification that you want to listen to.

`object`

The object that sends you the notification. For instance, if a notification with the same name is being sent from two objects, you can narrow your target and only listen for the notification that comes from Object A instead of both Object A and Object B.

When you no longer want to receive notifications, issue the removeObserver: instance method of the NSNotificationCenter class. Make sure that you do this because the notification center retains instances of listener objects. You might encounter memory leaks or errors if the notification center retains an instance of your class after it has been released, so make sure that you remove yourself from the observers list.

Discussion

An example can make this whole thing very easy. Here, we create a class named Person and add two properties to it: a first name and a last name, both of type String. Then in our app delegate, we instantiate an object of type Person. Instead of setting the first name and the last name of the person, we send a notification to the notification center, and in the user info dictionary of the notification, we put the first name and the last name of type String. In the initialization method of our Person class, we listen for the notification that comes from the app delegate and then extract the first name and last name from its user info dictionary and set the person's properties to those values.

So here is the implementation of our app delegate:

```
import UIKit

@UIApplicationMain
class AppDelegate: UIResponder, UIApplicationDelegate {

  var window: UIWindow?

  /* The name of the notification that we are going to send */
  class func notificationName() -> String{
    return "SetPersonInfoNotification"
  }
  /* The first-name key in the user-info dictionary of our notification */
  class func personInfoKeyFirstName () -> String{
    return "firstName"
  }
  /* The last-name key in the user-info dictionary of our notification */
  class func personInfoKeyLastName() -> String{
    return "lastName"
  }

  func application(application: UIApplication,
    didFinishLaunchingWithOptions launchOptions:
    [NSObject : AnyObject]?) -> Bool {

    let steveJobs = Person()

    let userInfo = [
      self.classForCoder.personInfoKeyFirstName() : "Steve",
      self.classForCoder.personInfoKeyLastName() : "Jobs",
    ]
```

```
    let notification = NSNotification(
      name: self.classForCoder.notificationName(),
      object: self,
      userInfo: userInfo)

    /* The person class is currently listening for this
    notification. That class will extract the first name and last name
    from it and set its own first name and last name based on the
    userInfo dictionary of the notification. */
    NSNotificationCenter.defaultCenter().postNotification(notification)

    /* Here is proof */
    if let firstName = steveJobs.firstName{
      println("Person's first name is: \(firstName)")
    }
    if let lastName = steveJobs.lastName{
      println("Person's last name is: \(lastName)")
    }

    return true
  }

}
```

The important part is the implementation of the `Person` class:

```
import UIKit

class Person: NSObject{
  var firstName: String?
  var lastName: String?

  func handleSetPersonInfoNotification(notification: NSNotification){

    firstName = notification.userInfo![AppDelegate.personInfoKeyFirstName()]
      as? NSString

    lastName = notification.userInfo![AppDelegate.personInfoKeyLastName()]
      as? NSString

  }

  override init(){
    super.init()

    NSNotificationCenter.defaultCenter().addObserver(self,
      selector: "handleSetPersonInfoNotification:",
      name: AppDelegate.notificationName(),
      object: UIApplication.sharedApplication().delegate)
  }

  deinit{
    NSNotificationCenter.defaultCenter().removeObserver(self)
```

```
    }

}
```

 The value that you specify for the `object` parameter of the `addOb server:selector:name:object:` method is the object where you expect the notification to originate. If any other object sends a notification with the same name, your listener won't be asked to handle that. You would normally specify this object when you know exactly which object is going to send the notification you want to listen to. This may not always be possible, such as in a very complex application where a view controller in one tab has to listen for notifications from another view controller in another tab. In that case, the listener won't necessarily have a reference to the instance of the view controller from where the notification will originate, so in this case you can pass `nil` for the `parameter` of the aforementioned method.

When you run this app, you will see the following printed to the console:

```
Person's first name is: Steve
Person's last name is: Jobs
```

So this was a notification that we sent and received from within our app. What about system notifications? We will talk about them a bit more in detail later, but for now, while in Xcode, open the Swift file for the `UIWindow` class. Look for `UIKeyboardWill ShowNotification` and you will find a block of code like so:

```
let UIKeyboardWillShowNotification: NSString!
let UIKeyboardDidShowNotification: NSString!
let UIKeyboardWillHideNotification: NSString!
let UIKeyboardDidHideNotification: NSString!
```

That is Apple's code. We wrote our code in exactly the same way. Apple is exposing the notifications that the system sends and then documenting them. You need to do something similar. When creating notifications that are sent by components from within your app, make sure that you document them and tell programmers (maybe those on your team working on the same app) which values they should be expecting from the user info of your notification, along with anything else that they should know about your notifications.

16.3. Listening and Reacting to Keyboard Notifications

Problem

You allow the user to enter text in your UI by using a component such as a text field or a text view that requires the keyboard's presence. However, when the keyboard pops up on the screen, it obstructs a good half of your UI, rendering it useless. You want to avoid this situation.

Solution

Listen to the keyboard notifications and move your UI components up or down, or completely reshuffle them, so that although the keyboard is obstructing the screen, what is essential to the user is still visible. For more information about the actual notifications sent by the keyboard, please refer to "Discussion" on page 622.

Discussion

iOS devices do not have a physical keyboard. They have a software keyboard that pops up whenever the user has to enter some text into something like a text field (`UIText Field`, described further in Recipe 1.16) or a text view (`UITextView`, described further in Recipe 1.17). On the iPad, the user can even split the keyboard and move it up and down. These are some of the edge cases that you might want to take care of when designing your user interface. You can work with the UI designers in your company (if you have access to such experts) and let them know about the possibility of the user splitting the keyboard on the iPad. They will need to know about that before making the art and creatives. We will discuss that edge case in this recipe.

Let's have a look at the keyboard on the iPhone first. The keyboard can be displayed in portrait and landscape mode. In portrait, the keyboard on an iPhone looks like Figure 16-1.

The keyboard in landscape mode on an iPhone looks similar to that shown in Figure 16-2.

On the iPad, however, the keyboard is a bit different. The most obvious difference is that the keyboard is actually much bigger than the one on the iPhone, because the iPad screen is physically bigger. The landscape keyboard on an iPad is obviously wider, but contains the same keys as the portrait-mode keyboard. Also, the user can split the keyboard if she wants to. This gives users better control over the keyboard but introduces challenges for programmers and even more for UX and UI designers.

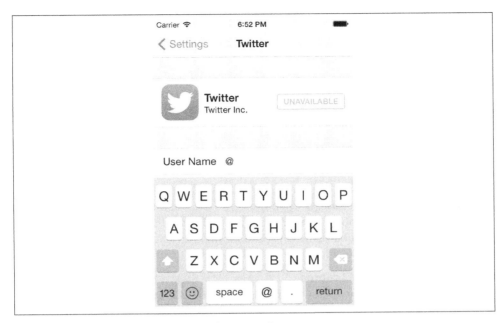

Figure 16-1. Portrait-mode keyboard on an iPhone

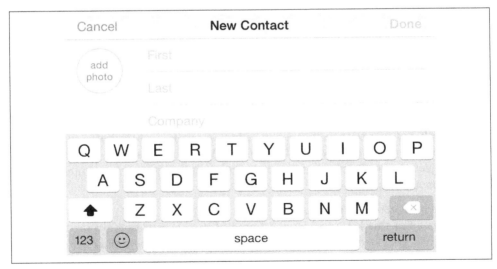

Figure 16-2. The keyboard in landscape mode on an iPhone

iOS broadcasts various notifications related to the display of the keyboard on the screen. Here is a list of these notifications and a brief explanation of each one:

UIKeyboardWillShowNotification

This notification is broadcast when the keyboard is about to be displayed on the screen. This notification carries a user-info dictionary that contains various information about the keyboard, the animation that the keyboard uses to be displayed on the screen, and more.

UIKeyboardDidShowNotification

This notification is broadcast when the keyboard is displayed on the screen.

UIKeyboardWillHideNotification

This notification is broadcast when the keyboard is about to be removed from the screen. This notification carries a user-info dictionary that contains various information about the keyboard, the keyboard's animation when it is hiding, the duration of the animation, etc.

UIKeyboardDidHideNotification

This notification is broadcast when the keyboard becomes fully hidden after being shown on the screen.

The UIKeyboardWillShowNotification and UIKeyboardWillHideNotification notifications carry a user-info dictionary. Here are the keys in those dictionaries that you might be interested in:

UIKeyboardAnimationCurveUserInfoKey

The value of this key specifies the type of animation curve the keyboard is using to show or hide itself. This key contains a value (encapsulated in an object of type NSValue) of type NSNumber that itself contains an unsigned integer of type NSUInteger.

UIKeyboardAnimationDurationUserInfoKey

The value of this key specifies the duration, in seconds, of the animation that the keyboard is using to show or hide itself. This key contains a value (encapsulated in an object of type NSValue) of type NSNumber that itself contains a double value of type double.

UIKeyboardFrameBeginUserInfoKey

The value of this key specifies the frame of the keyboard before the animation happens. If the keyboard is about to be displayed, this is the frame before the keyboard appears. If the keyboard is already displayed and is about to hide, it is the frame of the keyboard as it is on the screen before it animates out of the screen. This key contains a value (encapsulated in an object of type NSValue) of type CGRect.

`UIKeyboardFrameEndUserInfoKey`

The value of this key specifies the frame of the keyboard after the animation happens. If the keyboard is about to be displayed, this is the frame after the keyboard is animated fully displayed. If the keyboard is already displayed and is about to hide, it is the frame of the keyboard after it is fully hidden. This key contains a value (encapsulated in an object of type `NSValue`) of type `CGRect`.

The frames that get reported by iOS as the beginning and ending frames of the keyboard do not take into account the orientation of the device. You need to convert the reported `CGRect` values to a relevant orientation-aware coordinate, as we will see soon in this recipe.

Let's have a look at an example. We are going to create a simple single-view application that only runs on the iPhone and displays an image view and a text field. The text field is going to be located at the bottom of the screen. So when the user taps on the text field to enter some text into it, the keyboard pops up and blocks the text field completely. Our mission is to animate the contents of our view up to make them visible even if the keyboard is displayed on the screen. We are going to use storyboards for this app. In the view controller, we fill the view with a scroll view and place the image view and a text field in the scroll view, as shown in Figure 16-3.

The superview of the image view and the text field is a scroll view that fills the whole parent view's space.

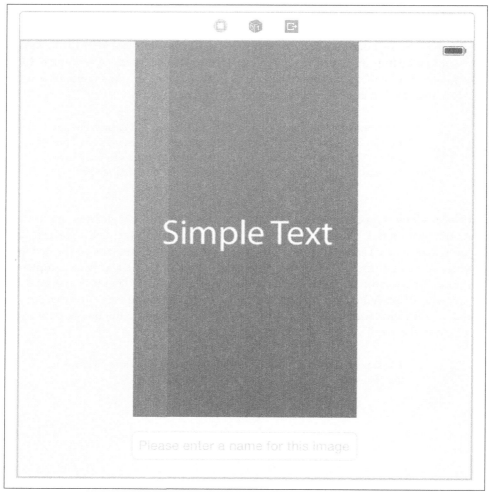

Figure 16-3. A simple storyboard with an image view and a text field

I hooked the scroll view, the image view, and the text field from the storyboard into the implementation of the view controller like so:

```
import UIKit

class ViewController: UIViewController {

    @IBOutlet weak var imageView: UIImageView!
    @IBOutlet weak var textField: UITextField!
    @IBOutlet weak var scrollView: UIScrollView!

    <# rest of the code #>
```

```
    }
```
Now we can start listening to keyboard notifications:
```
override func viewDidAppear(animated: Bool) {

    super.viewDidAppear(animated)

    let center = NSNotificationCenter.defaultCenter()

    center.addObserver(self,
        selector: "handleKeyboardWillShow:",
        name: UIKeyboardWillShowNotification,
        object: nil)

    center.addObserver(self,
        selector: "handleKeyboardWillHide:",
        name: UIKeyboardWillHideNotification,
        object: nil)

}

override func viewWillDisappear(animated: Bool) {
    super.viewWillDisappear(animated)

    NSNotificationCenter.defaultCenter().removeObserver(self)

}
```

 A common mistake programmers make is to keep listening for keyboard notifications when their view controller's view is not on the screen. They start listening for notifications in the viewDidLoad method and remove themselves as the observer in the destructor method. This is a problematic approach because when your view is off the screen and the keyboard is getting displayed on some other view, you should not be adjusting any components on your view controller. Keep in mind that keyboard notifications, just like any other notification, are broadcast to all observer objects within the context of your application, so you need to take extra care that you do not react to keyboard notifications while your view is off-screen.

In the previous code snippet, we started listening for keyboard-will-show notifications on the handleKeyboardWillShow: instance method of our view controller, and expect the keyboard-will-hide notifications on the handleKeyboardWillHide: method. These methods are not coded yet. Let's start with the first method, the handleKeyboardWill Show:. We need to detect the height of the keyboard using the UIKeyboardFrameEndU serInfoKey key inside the user-info dictionary that gets sent to us for this notification, and use that value to shift up our view's contents by the height of the keyboard. The good news is that we placed the contents of our view in a scroll view, so all we have to do is adjust its edge insets.

```
func handleKeyboardWillShow(notification: NSNotification){

  let userInfo = notification.userInfo

  if let info = userInfo{
    /* Get the duration of the animation of the keyboard for when it
    gets displayed on the screen. We will animate our contents using
    the same animation duration */
    let animationDurationObject =
    info[UIKeyboardAnimationDurationUserInfoKey] as NSValue

    let keyboardEndRectObject =
    info[UIKeyboardFrameEndUserInfoKey] as NSValue

    var animationDuration = 0.0
    var keyboardEndRect = CGRectZero

    animationDurationObject.getValue(&animationDuration)
    keyboardEndRectObject.getValue(&keyboardEndRect)

    let window = UIApplication.sharedApplication().keyWindow

    /* Convert the frame from the window's coordinate system to
    our view's coordinate system */
    keyboardEndRect = view.convertRect(keyboardEndRect, fromView: window)

    /* Find out how much of our view is being covered by the keyboard */
    let intersectionOfKeyboardRectAndWindowRect =
    CGRectIntersection(view.frame, keyboardEndRect);

    /* Scroll the scroll view up to show the full contents of our view */
    UIView.animateWithDuration(animationDuration, animations: {[weak self] in

      self!.scrollView.contentInset = UIEdgeInsets(top: 0,
        left: 0,
        bottom: intersectionOfKeyboardRectAndWindowRect.size.height,
        right: 0)

      self!.scrollView.scrollRectToVisible(self!.textField.frame,
        animated: false)

    })
  }

}
```

Our code is quite interesting and straightforward here. The only thing that might require explanation is the CGRectIntersection function. We are retrieving the rectangular shape (top, left, width, and height) of the keyboard at the end of its animation when it gets displayed on the screen. Now that we have the dimensions of the keyboard, using the CGRectIntersection function, we can detect how much of our view is getting covered by the keyboard. So we take the frame of the keyboard and the frame of our view to find out how much of our frame's view is obscured by the frame of the keyboard. The result is a structure of type CGRect, which is the rectangular area on our view that is obscured by the keyboard. Because we know the keyboard pops up from the bottom of the screen and animates up, the area of concern to us is vertical, so we retrieve the height of the intersection area and move up our contents by that much. We make the duration of our animation the same as the one used by the keyboard, so that our view and the keyboard move in sync.

The next stop is coding the handleKeyboardWillHide: method. This is where the keyboard will hide and no longer cover our view. In this method, we reset the edge insets of our scroll view, shifting everything down and back to its initial state:

```
func handleKeyboardWillHide(sender: NSNotification){

  let userInfo = sender.userInfo

  if let info = userInfo{
    let animationDurationObject =
    info[UIKeyboardAnimationDurationUserInfoKey]
      as NSValue

    var animationDuration = 0.0;

    animationDurationObject.getValue(&animationDuration)

    UIView.animateWithDuration(animationDuration, animations: {
      [weak self] in
      self!.scrollView.contentInset = UIEdgeInsetsZero
    })
  }

}
```

Last but not least, because our view controller is the delegate of the text field, we need to ensure that the keyboard dismisses when the user presses the Return key on her keyboard after typing something into the text field:

```
func textFieldShouldReturn(textField: UITextField!) -> Bool {
  textField.resignFirstResponder()
  return true
}
```

Now if you run your application and then start editing the text in your text field, you will notice that the scroll view magically moves everything in it up to allow you to see the text field you are editing (Figure 16-4):

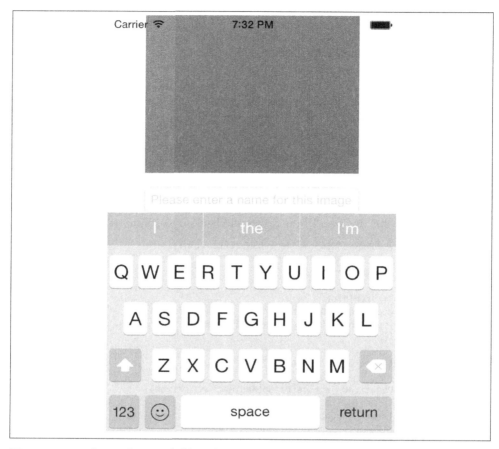

Figure 16-4. Editing the text field pushes our content up

See Also

Recipe 1.16; Recipe 1.17

16.4. Scheduling Local Notifications

Problem

You are developing an app, such as an alarm clock or a calendar app, that needs to inform the user of an event at a specific time, even if your app is not running or is in the background.

Solution

Instantiate an object of type UILocalNotification, configure it, and schedule it using the scheduleLocalNotification: instance method of the UIApplication class. You can get the instance of your application object using the sharedApplication class method of the UIApplication class.

Discussion

A *local notification* is what gets presented to the user if your application is running in the background or not running at all. You can schedule the delivery of a local notification using the scheduleLocalNotification: instance method of UIApplication. If your app is running in the *foreground* and a scheduled local notification is fired, no alert is displayed to the user. Instead, iOS will silently, through an app delegate message, let you know that the notification was fired. Don't worry about this for now; we will go into details about all this quite soon.

You can ask iOS to deliver a local notification to the user in the future when your application is not even running. These notifications could also be recurring—for instance, every week at a certain time. However, extra care must be taken when you are specifying the *fire date* for your notifications.

The cancelAllLocalNotifications instance method cancels the delivery of all pending local notifications from your app.

A notification of type UILocalNotification has many properties. The most important properties of a local notification are the following:

fireDate
> This is a property of type NSDate that dictates to iOS when the instance of the local notification has to be fired. This is required.

timeZone
> This property is of type NSTimeZone and tells iOS in the time zone in which the given fire-date is specified. You can get the current time zone using the timeZone instance method of the NSCalendar class, and you can get the current calendar using the currentCalendar class method of the aforementioned class.

alertBody
> This property is of type NSString and dictates the text that has to be displayed to the user when your notification is displayed on screen.

hasAction
> A Boolean property that tells iOS whether your app wants to take action when the notification happens. If you set this to true, iOS displays the dialog specified by your alertAction property (described next) to the user. If you set this to false, iOS just displays a dialog to the user indicating that the notification arrived.

alertAction

>   If the hasAction property is set to true, this property has to be set to a localized
>   string that represents the action that the user can take on your local notification,
>   should the notification be fired when the user doesn't have your app open in the
>   foreground. iOS will subsequently display the message in the notification center or
>   in the lock screen. If the hasAction property has the value of false, the alertAc
>   tion property's value has to be nil.

applicationIconBadgeNumber

>   If this local notification is required to change your app's icon badge number upon
>   being fired, this property can be set to the desired badge number for your app icon.
>   The value must be an integer. The proper way of assigning a value to this property
>   is to set it to the current app's icon badge number, plus 1. You can get your app's
>   current icon badge number using the applicationIconBadgeNumber property of
>   UIApplication class.

userInfo

>   This is an NSDictionary instance that can get attached to your notification and
>   received back by your app when the notification is delivered. We usually use these
>   dictionaries to include more information about the local notification, which can be
>   useful for us when we have the notification delivered to our app.

The hasAction and alertAction properties combine to allow the user to swipe on your
local notification in the notification center and make iOS open your app. That is how a
user can take action on a local notification. This is extremely useful, especially if you
are developing a calendar-like app where, for instance, you display a local notification
to the user when the birthday of her friend is approaching in a few days. You can then
allow her to take action on the notification. Perhaps, when she opens your app, you
could even present some virtual gift options that she could send to her friend on his
birthday.

The one thing that many programmers have issues with is the time zone of a local
notification. Let's say the time is now 13:00 in London, the time zone is GMT+0, and
your application is currently running on a user's device. You want to be able to deliver
a notification at 14:00 to your user, even if your application is not running at that time.
Now your user is on a plane at London's Gatwick Airport and plans to fly to Stockholm,
where the time zone is GMT+1. If the flight takes 30 minutes, the user will be in Stockholm at 13:30 GMT+0 (London time) and at 14:30 GMT+1 (Stockholm time). However,
when she lands, the iOS device will detect the change in the time zone of the system and
change the user's device time to 14:30. Your notification was supposed to occur at 14:00
(GMT+0), so as soon as the time zone is changed, iOS detects that the notification is
due to be displayed (30 minutes earlier, in fact, with the new time zone) and will display
your notification.

The issue is that your notification was supposed to be displayed at 14:00 GMT+0 or 15:00 GMT+1, and not 14:30 GMT+1. To deal with occasions such as this (which may be more common than you think, with modern travel habits), when specifying the date and time for your local notifications to be fired, you should also specify the time zone.

Let's put all this to the test and develop an app that can deliver a simple local notification 8 seconds after the user opens the app for the first time. Before we begin scheduling a local notification, we need to ask the user to allow us to display one. We will do this using the `registerUserNotificationSettings:` method of our application object. This method takes in a parameter of type `UIUserNotificationSettings`. The notification settings object can be constructed simply by specifying the type of notification that you want to display to the user. So here is our code to ask the user for permission to send her local notifications:

```
func application(application: UIApplication,
  didFinishLaunchingWithOptions launchOptions: [NSObject : AnyObject]?) -> Bool {

    /* First ask the user if we are
    allowed to perform local notifications */
    let settings = UIUserNotificationSettings(forTypes: .Alert,
      categories: nil)

    application.registerUserNotificationSettings(settings)

    return true
}
```

After we ask for permission to send notifications, iOS displays a dialog similar to that shown in Figure 16-5.

After the user accepts or denies our request, iOS will call the `application:didRegis terUserNotificationSettings:` method of our app delegate. The second parameter of this method is of type `UIUserNotificationSettings`. If the user accepted our request, this parameter will be a valid notification settings object equal to what we created before. But if the user denied permission, the `types` and the `categories` properties of this notification settings object will both be nil.

```
func application(application: UIApplication,
  didRegisterUserNotificationSettings
  notificationSettings: UIUserNotificationSettings!){

    if notificationSettings.types == nil{
      /* The user did not allow us to send notifications */
      return
    }

    let notification = UILocalNotification()

    /* Time and timezone settings */
```

```
notification.fireDate = NSDate(timeIntervalSinceNow: 8)
notification.timeZone = NSCalendar.currentCalendar().timeZone

notification.alertBody = "A new item is downloaded"

/* Action settings */
notification.hasAction = true
notification.alertAction = "View"

/* Badge settings */
notification.applicationIconBadgeNumber++

/* Additional information, user info */
notification.userInfo = [
  "Key 1" : "Value 1",
  "Key 2" : "Value 2"
]

/* Schedule the notification */
application.scheduleLocalNotification(notification)

}
```

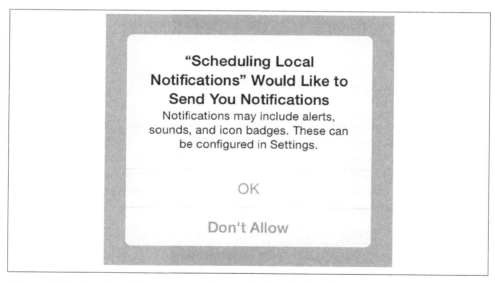

Figure 16-5. Local notification permissions dialog displayed to the user

After we schedule the notification and send our app to the background, iOS will deliver our notification to the user in a form similar to that shown in Figure 16-6.

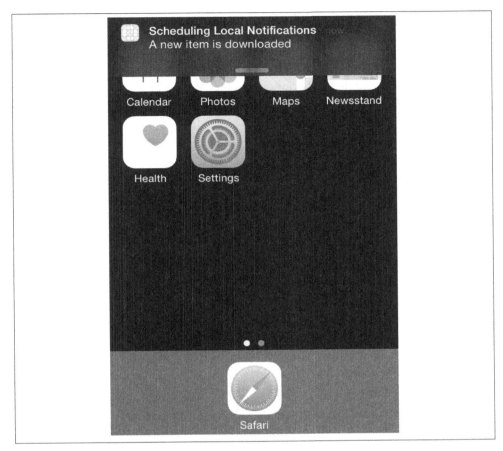

Figure 16-6. Our local notification is delivered to the user

This is all good, but local notifications are quite useless if we don't know how to react to them when they are fired. Read Recipe 16.5 to find out how to handle these notifications.

See Also

Recipe 16.0, "Introduction"

16.5. Listening for and Reacting to Local Notifications

Problem

You know how to schedule local notifications (see Recipe 16.4), but now you have to react to them when they are delivered to your app.

Solution

Implement and read the `UIApplicationLaunchOptionsLocalNotificationKey` key of your app's launching options dictionary when the `application:didFinishLaunching WithOptions:` method gets called on your app delegate. Read the Discussion section of this recipe for more information on why you have to handle a local notification in two places instead of one.

Discussion

How you handle a local notification depends on the state of your app when it is delivered and acted upon. Here are the different situations in which iOS may deliver a scheduled local notification to your app:

The user has the app open in front of her while the local notification is delivered
> In this case, the `application:didReceiveLocalNotification:` method is called when the notification is delivered.

The user has sent the app to the background and the local notification is delivered
> When the user taps on the notification, iOS can launch your app. In this case, again, the `application:didReceiveLocalNotification:` method of your app delegate is called.

The app is not open or active when the local notification is delivered
> In this case, the `application:didFinishLaunchingWithOptions:` method of your app delegate is called and the `UIApplicationLaunchOptionsLocalNotification Key` key inside the `didFinishLaunchingWithOptions` dictionary parameter of this method contains the local notification that caused your app to be woken up.

The local notification is delivered while the user's device is locked, whether the app is active in the background or is not running at all
> This will fire one of the previously mentioned ways of iOS opening your app, depending on whether your app was in the background while the user attempted to open your app using the notification.

Let's build on top of the example code that we learned about in Recipe 16.4. Regardless of the state of our app when the notification is fired, we'll handle it by displaying an alert to the user. First, we are going to put what we learned in Recipe 16.4 into a separate method so that we can call that method and schedule a new local notification. The reason for doing this is so that when our app opens, we can check whether it opened as a result of the user tapping on a local notification in the notification center of iOS. If yes, we *won't* fire another local notification. Instead, we will act on the existing one. However, if a local notification did not open our app, we will schedule a new one. Here is the method that schedules new local notifications to be delivered to our app eight seconds after the method is called:

```
func scheduleLocalNotification(){

    let notification = UILocalNotification()

    /* Time and timezone settings */
    notification.fireDate = NSDate(timeIntervalSinceNow: 8.0)
    notification.timeZone = NSCalendar.currentCalendar().timeZone

    notification.alertBody = "A new item is downloaded."

    /* Action settings */
    notification.hasAction = true
    notification.alertAction = "View"

    /* Badge settings */
    notification.applicationIconBadgeNumber =
      UIApplication.sharedApplication().applicationIconBadgeNumber + 1

    /* Additional information, user info */
    notification.userInfo = [
      "Key 1" : "Value 1",
      "Key 2" : "Value 2"
    ]

    /* Schedule the notification */
    UIApplication.sharedApplication().scheduleLocalNotification(notification)

}

func askForNotificationPermissionForApplication(application: UIApplication){
    /* First ask the user if we are
    allowed to perform local notifications */
    let settings = UIUserNotificationSettings(forTypes: .Alert | .Badge,
      categories: nil)

    application.registerUserNotificationSettings(settings)

}
```

This method is called `scheduleLocalNotification`. It simply creates the notification object and asks iOS to schedule it. Don't confuse our custom method named `scheduleLocalNotification` with the iOS method on `UIApplication` named `scheduleLocalNotification:` (note the colon at the end of the iOS method). You can think of our method as a handy utility method that does the hard work of scheduling a local notification by creating the notification and delegating the scheduling activity to iOS.

Now, in our `application:didFinishLaunchingWithOptions` method, we check whether an existing notification was the reason our app opened in the first place. If yes, we act upon the existing local notification. If no, we schedule a new one:

```
func application(application: UIApplication,
  didFinishLaunchingWithOptions launchOptions: [NSObject : AnyObject]?) -> Bool {

    if let options = launchOptions{

      /* Do we have a value? */
      let value =
      options[UIApplicationLaunchOptionsLocalNotificationKey]
        as? UILocalNotification

      if let notification = value{
        self.application(application ,
          didReceiveLocalNotification: notification)
      }
    } else {
      askForNotificationPermissionForApplication(application)
    }

    return true
  }
```

In the preceding code, when an existing local notification caused our app to launch, we redirected the local notification to the `application:didReceiveLocalNotification:` method, where we acted upon the existing notification. Here is our simple implementation of the aforementioned method:

```
func application(application: UIApplication,
  didReceiveLocalNotification notification: UILocalNotification!) {

    let key1Value = notification.userInfo!["Key 1"] as? NSString
    let key2Value = notification.userInfo!["Key 2"] as? NSString

    if key1Value != nil && key2Value != nil{
      /* We got our notification */
    } else {
      /* This is not the notification that we composed */
    }

  }
```

Give it a go now. You can try different combinations. Open the app and then keep it in the foreground, send it to the background, or even close it permanently. Take a look at how the app behaves in the various conditions you put it in.

See Also

Recipe 16.0, "Introduction"; Recipe 16.4

16.6. Handling Local System Notifications

Problem

When your application is brought to the foreground, you want to be able to get notifications about important system changes, such as the user's locale changes.

Solution

Simply listen to one of the many system notifications that iOS sends to waking applications. Some of these notifications are listed here:

NSCurrentLocaleDidChangeNotification

This notification is delivered to applications when the user changes her locale; for instance, if the user switches her iOS device's language from English to Spanish in the Settings page of the device.

NSUserDefaultsDidChangeNotification

This notification is fired when the user changes the application's settings in the Settings page of the iOS device (if any settings are provided to the user).

UIDeviceBatteryStateDidChangeNotification

This notification gets sent whenever the state of the battery of the iOS device is changed. For instance, if the device is plugged into a computer when the application is in the foreground, and then unplugged when in the background, the application will receive this notification (if the application has registered for this notification). The state can then be read using the batteryState property of an instance of UIDevice.

UIDeviceProximityStateDidChangeNotification

This notification gets sent whenever the state of the proximity sensor changes. The last state is available through the proximityState property of an instance of UIDevice.

Discussion

When your application is in the background, a lot of things can happen! For instance, the user might suddenly change the language of her iOS device through the Settings page from English to Spanish. Applications can register themselves for such notifications. These notifications will be coalesced and then delivered to a waking application.

Let me explain what I mean by the term *coalesced*. Suppose your application is in the foreground and you have registered for UIDeviceOrientationDidChangeNotifica tion notifications. Now the user presses the Home button and your application gets sent to the background. The user then rotates the device from portrait to landscape right, back to portrait, and then to landscape left. When the user brings your application to the foreground, you will receive only *one* notification of type UIDeviceOrientation DidChangeNotification. This is coalescing. All the other orientations that happened along the way are not important (because your application isn't in the foreground) and the system will not deliver them to your application. However, the system will deliver at least one notification for each aspect of the system, such as orientation, and you can then detect the most up-to-date orientation of the device.

Here is the implementation of a simple view controller that takes advantage of this technique to determine changes in orientation:

```
import UIKit

class ViewController: UIViewController {

  func orientationChanged(notification: NSNotification){
    println("Orientation Changed")
  }

  override func viewDidAppear(animated: Bool) {
    super.viewDidAppear(animated)

    /* Listen for the notification */
    NSNotificationCenter.defaultCenter().addObserver(self,
      selector: "orientationChanged:",
      name: UIDeviceOrientationDidChangeNotification,
      object: nil)

  }

  override func viewDidDisappear(animated: Bool) {
    super.viewDidDisappear(animated)
    /* Stop listening for the notification */
    NSNotificationCenter.defaultCenter().removeObserver(self,
      name: UIDeviceOrientationDidChangeNotification,
      object: nil)

  }

}
```

Run the application on the device now. After the view controller displays, press the Home button to send the application to the background. Now try changing the orientation of the device a couple of times, and then relaunch the application. Observe the results, and you will see that initially when your application opens, at most, one notification has been sent to the `orientationChanged:` method. You might get a second call, though, if your view hierarchy supports orientation changes.

Now let's say that your application exposes a settings bundle to the user. You want to be notified of the changes the user makes to your application's settings (while the application is in the background) as soon as your application is brought to the foreground. To do this, you should register for the `NSUserDefaultsDidChangeNotification` notification.

Applications written for iOS can expose a bundle file for their settings. These settings are available to users through the Settings application on their device. To get a better understanding of how this works, let's create a settings bundle:

1. In Xcode, choose File → New File.
2. Make sure the iOS category is selected on the left.
3. Choose the Resources subcategory.
4. Choose Settings Bundle as the file type and click Next.
5. Set the filename to *Settings.bundle*.
6. Click Save.

Now you have a file in Xcode named *Settings.bundle*. Leave this file as it is, without modifying it. Press the Home button on the device and go to the device's Settings application. If you named your application Foo, you will see Foo in the Settings application (the name of the sample application I created is "Handling Local System Notifications").

Tap on your application's name to see the settings your application exposes to the user. We want to know when the user changes these settings, so that we can adjust our application's internal state if required. Let's go ahead and start listening for the `NSUserDefaultsDidChangeNotification` notification in our app delegate. When our app terminates, obviously, we will remove our app delegate from the notification chain:

```
import UIKit

@UIApplicationMain
class AppDelegate: UIResponder, UIApplicationDelegate {

  var window: UIWindow?

  func handleSettingsChanged(notification: NSNotification){

    println("Settings changed")

    if let object:AnyObject = notification.object{
      println("Notification Object = \(object)")
    }
```

```
    }

    func application(application: UIApplication,
      didFinishLaunchingWithOptions launchOptions:
      [NSObject : AnyObject]?) -> Bool {

        NSNotificationCenter.defaultCenter().addObserver(self,
          selector: "handleSettingsChanged:",
          name: NSUserDefaultsDidChangeNotification,
          object: nil)

        return true
    }

}
```

Now try to change some of these settings while your application is running in the background. After you are done, bring the application to the foreground, and you will see that only one NSUserDefaultsDidChangeNotification notification will be delivered to your application. The object attached to this notification will be of type NSUser Defaults and will contain your application's settings user defaults.

16.7. Setting Up Your App for Push Notifications

Problem

You want to configure your application so that you can push notifications from a server to various devices.

Solution

Follow these steps:

1. Set up a provision profile for your app with push notifications enabled.

2. In your app, register the device for push notifications for your app.

3. Collect the device's push notifications identifier for your app and send that to a server.

In this recipe, we are going to discuss setting up and registering your app for push notifications. We are not going to talk about the server side of things yet. We will discuss that part in another recipe.

Discussion

Push notifications are similar to local notifications in that they allow you to communicate something with the user even when your app is not running. Although local notifications are scheduled by your app, push notifications are configured and sent by a server to Apple, and Apple will push the notifications to various devices around the world. The server part of things needs to be done by us. We then compose the push notifications and send them to Apple Push Notification Services servers (APNS). APNS will then attempt to deliver our push notifications through a secure channel to devices that we designated.

For iOS apps to be able to receive push notifications, they have to have a valid ropvision profile with push notifications enabled. To configure your profile properly, follow these steps:

 I assume that you have already set up your development and distribution certificates in your developer portal. You can use Xcode's new Accounts settings to automatically configure your certificates. Simply go to Xcode's Preferences and then open the Accounts pane. Add your Apple ID to the Accounts list and allow Xcode to configure your certificates for you.

1. Log into the iOS Dev Center (*http://bit.ly/19h9aLw*).

2. Navigate to the Certificates, Identifiers & Profiles section on the righthand side.

3. In the Identifiers section, create a new App ID for yourself with a valid Explicit App ID such as *com.pixolity.ios.Setting-Up-Your-App-for-Push-Notifications*. Note that I chose a reverse domain style name for this example app. Pick a reverse domain-style App ID that makes sense to you or your organization.

4. Under the App Services section of the new App ID page, ensure that you've enabled the Push Notifications box as shown in Figure 16-7.

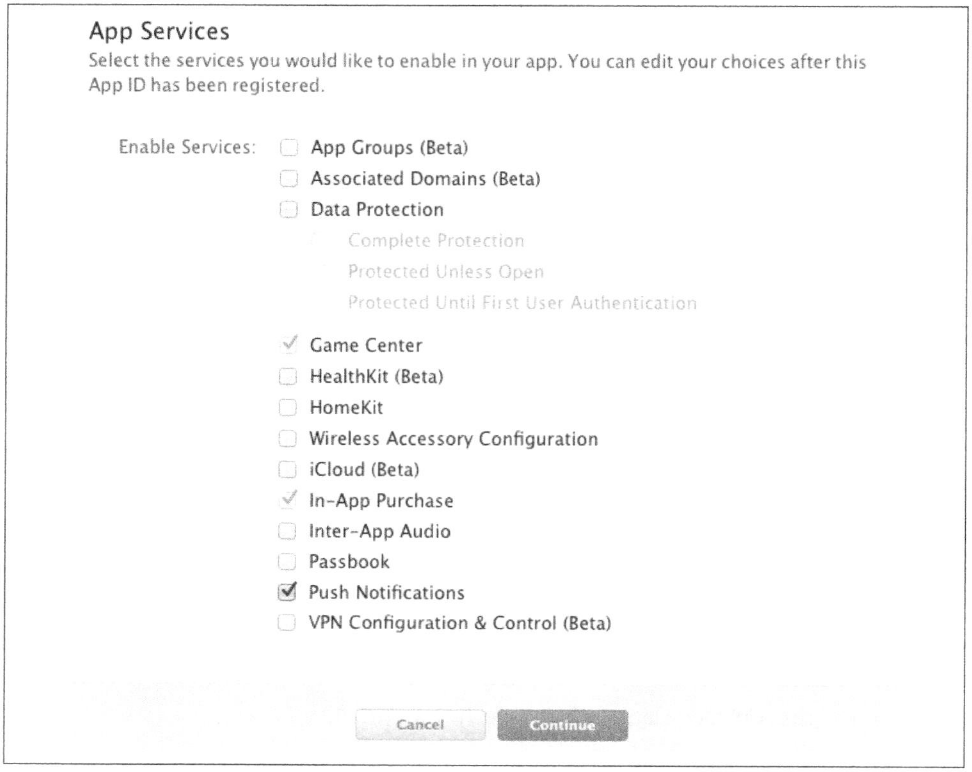

Figure 16-7. Enabling push notifications for an App ID

5. When you are happy with the configuration of your App ID (see Figure 16-8), submit the App ID to Apple.

6. After you set all your App ID configurations, generate your App ID and then navigate to the Provisioning Profiles section of the iOS portal.

7. Create a Development provision profile for your app. You can create the Ad Hoc and the App Store versions later, but for now you just need the Development provision profile to get started. The process is the same for Ad Hoc and App Store profiles, so don't worry. You can simply come back to this step when you are ready to submit your app to the App Store, and you will be able to generate the Ad Hoc and the App Store profiles.

Ensure that your new development provision profile is linked to the App ID that you generated earlier. This is the first question that you will be asked when generating the provision profile.

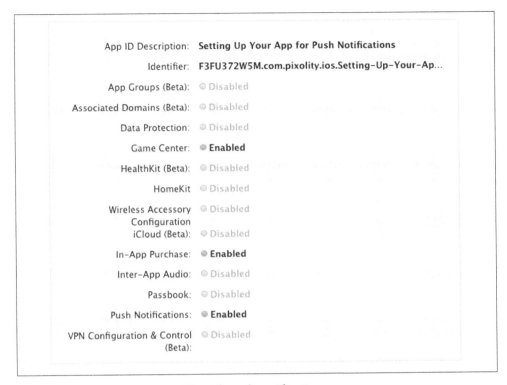

App ID Description: **Setting Up Your App for Push Notifications**

Identifier: **F3FU372W5M.com.pixolity.ios.Setting-Up-Your-Ap...**

App Groups (Beta): ⊙ Disabled

Associated Domains (Beta): ⊙ Disabled

Data Protection: ⊙ Disabled

Game Center: ⦿ **Enabled**

HealthKit (Beta): ⊙ Disabled

HomeKit: ⊙ Disabled

Wireless Accessory Configuration: ⊙ Disabled

iCloud (Beta): ⊙ Disabled

In-App Purchase: ⦿ **Enabled**

Inter-App Audio: ⊙ Disabled

Passbook: ⊙ Disabled

Push Notifications: ⦿ **Enabled**

VPN Configuration & Control (Beta): ⊙ Disabled

Figure 16-8. Creating an App ID with push notifications

8. When your profile is ready, download it and drag and drop it into iTunes on your computer to install it. Avoid double-clicking on the profile to install it. Doing so will change the name of the installed profile's filename to the MD5 hash name of the profile, which is very difficult to identify on disk. If you drag and drop the profile in iTunes, iTunes will install the profile with its original name.

9. In your app's build settings in Xcode, simply select to build with the provision profile that you just created. Ensure that you are using this profile for Development and use the App Store or Ad Hoc profile that you'll create later for the Release scheme.

10. Drag and drop your provision profile into a text editor, such as TextEdit, on OS X and find the Entitlements key in there. The entire section in my provision profile looks like this:

```
<key>Entitlements</key>
<dict>
  <key>application-identifier</key>
  <string>F3FU372W5M.com.pixolity.ios.
    Setting-Up-Your-App-for-Push-Notifications</string>
  <key>aps-environment</key>
```

```
      <string>development</string>
      <key>com.apple.developer.team-identifier</key>
      <string>F3FU372W5M</string>
      <key>get-task-allow</key>
      <true/>
      <key>keychain-access-groups</key>
      <array>
        <string>F3FU372W5M.*</string>
      </array>
    </dict>
```

11. Create a new plist in your Xcode project and name it *Entitlements.plist*. Right-click that file in Xcode and select Open As and then Source Code. Your file's contents will initially look like this:

```
<?xml version="1.0" encoding="UTF-8"?>
<!DOCTYPE plist PUBLIC "-//Apple//DTD PLIST 1.0//EN"
"http://www.apple.com/DTDs/PropertyList-1.0.dtd">
<plist version="1.0">
<dict/>
</plist>
```

12. Put the entitlements of your provision profile right into the *Entitlements.plist* file so that its contents look like this:

```
<?xml version="1.0" encoding="UTF-8"?>
<!DOCTYPE plist PUBLIC "-//Apple//DTD PLIST 1.0//EN"
"http://www.apple.com/DTDs/PropertyList-1.0.dtd">
<plist version="1.0">
<dict>
  <key>application-identifier</key>
  <string>F3FU372W5M.com.pixolity.ios.
    Setting-Up-Your-App-for-Push-Notifications</string>
  <key>aps-environment</key>
  <string>development</string>
  <key>com.apple.developer.team-identifier</key>
  <string>F3FU372W5M</string>
  <key>get-task-allow</key>
  <true/>
  <key>keychain-access-groups</key>
  <array>
    <string>F3FU372W5M.*</string>
  </array>
</dict>
</plist>
```

The values shown here in our code snippets relate to the profiles that *I* created. The profile that you create will have different values and certainly a different App ID, so follow the previous steps to create your App ID and profile properly, then grab the entitlements for *your* profile and place them in the *Entitlements.plist* file in your project.

13. You might need to choose All in your Xcode settings in order to see all of your settings. By default, the Basic settings are shown. If you attempt to find the Entitlements section in the Basic settings, you will not succeed.

    Now go to the build settings of your project, and in the Code Signing Entitlements section, enter the value of *$(SRCROOT)/$(TARGET_NAME)/Entitlements.plist* if you created your entitlements file under your project's target folder, or enter *$ (SRCROOT)/Entitlements.plist* if you created the entitlements file under the root folder of your source codes. If you are confused, simply try these two values, and after setting them, try to build your project. If Xcode complains that it cannot find the entitlements file, try the other value, and it should work. The Code Signing Entitlements build setting requires the relative path of the entitlements file from the root folder of your source code. So if you placed this file into another folder, you'll have to manually calculate the path to the file and feed it to this field.

14. Build your project and make sure no error is thrown by Xcode. If you are getting an error, it is probably because you did not set the proper provision profile to use or entered the wrong path for the Code Signing Entitlements in your build settings.

15. In your app delegate, invoke the `registerForRemoteNotifications` method of your `UIApplication:`, like so:

```
func application(application: UIApplication,
    didFinishLaunchingWithOptions launchOptions:
    [NSObject : AnyObject]?) -> Bool {

    application.registerForRemoteNotifications()

    return true
}
```

    This will ensure that your app is registered to receive push notifications that can carry alert messages, badge number modifications to your app icon, and also sounds. Don't worry about this for now. Just register your app for push notifications, as shown before. When you do this, iOS will ask the user for permission to register your app for push notifications and upon getting this permission, will send a push notification registration request to APNS.

16. Now implement the `application:didRegisterForRemoteNotificationsWithDeviceToken:` method of your app delegate. This method is called when iOS suc-

---

cessfully registers this device with the APNS and assigns a token to it. This token is only for this app and this device.

17. Next, implement the `application:didFailToRegisterForRemoteNotifications WithError:` method of your app delegate. This method is called if iOS fails to register your app for push notifications. This could happen if your profile is set up incorrectly or the device doesn't have an Internet connection, among other reasons. The `didFailToRegisterForRemoteNotificationsWithError` parameter will give you an error of type `NSError` that you can analyze to find the source of the problem.

That's all you need to know to set up your app to receive push notifications.

See Also

Recipe 16.0, "Introduction"

16.8. Delivering Push Notifications to Your App

Problem

You want to be able to send push notifications to users' devices that are registered for push notifications.

Solution

Ensure that you have collected their push notification token identifiers (see Recipe 16.7). Then generate the SSL certificates that will be used by your web services to send push notifications to devices. When that is done, create a simple web service to send push notifications to registered devices.

 This recipe is a follow-up to Recipe 16.7. Ensure that you have read and understood that recipe before proceeding with this one.

Discussion

In order to be able to communicate with the APNS, your web services need to do *handshaking* with the APNS using an Apple-issued SSL certificate. To generate this certificate, follow these steps:

1. Log in to the iOS Dev Center (*http://bit.ly/19h9aLw*).

2. Navigate to the Certificates, Identifiers & Profiles section on the righthand side.

---

3. In the App IDs section, find the App ID for your app that has push notifications set up for it, select that App ID, and press the Settings button to configure it, as shown in Figure 16-9.

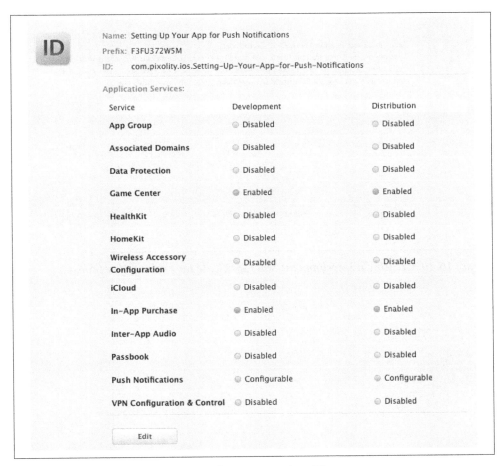

Figure 16-9. Modifying the settings of an existing App ID

4. In the Push Notifications section of the settings, under the Development SSL Certificate section, press the Create Certificate button (see Figure 16-10) and follow the guidance that Apple provides to create your certificate. We are creating the Development push notification SSL certificate for now, because we are solely focusing on the development part. Later, when you are ready to ship your app to the App Store, simply go through a similar process to create the Distribution version of the SSL certificates.

5. When your certificate is ready (see Figure 16-11), download it onto your computer and double-click it to import it into your keychain.

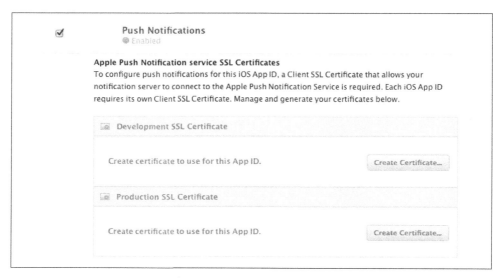

Figure 16-10. Creating a Development SSL Certificate for push notifications

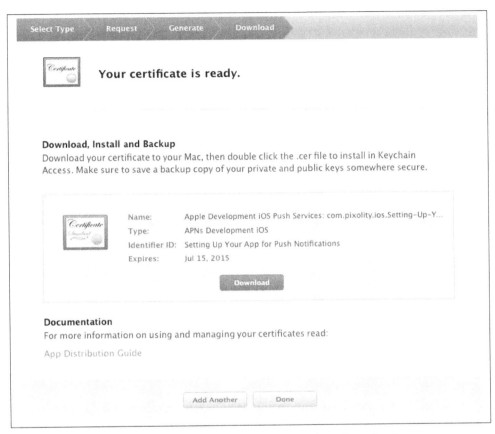

Figure 16-11. Development APNS SSL certificate is ready to download

6. Now open Keychain Access on OS X and go to the Login keychain (if that's your default keychain). Under the My Certificates section, find the certificate that you just imported into the keychain and expand it by clicking the little arrow button on its left, in order to reveal the associated private key for that certificate (see Figure 16-12).

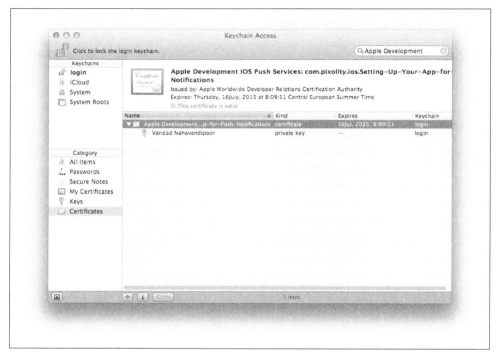

Figure 16-12. The push notifications development certificate and its private key

7. Right-click the certificate and export it as a *.cer* certificate file (as opposed to a *.p12* file) and give it the name of *PushCertificate.cer*.

8. Right-click the private key and export it as a *.p12* file (as opposed to a certificate file) and give it the name of *PushKey.p12*. You will be asked to specify a password for the private key. Make sure that you give it a password that you will remember later.

Great stuff. Now, for the purpose of this recipe and for the sake of simplicity, we are going to use PHP to send a simple push notification to our device, which has already been set up for push notifications in Recipe 16.7. Because setting up PHP on an Apache server is not really the topic of this book, we are going to take a shortcut and use MAMP (*http://www.mamp.info*). MAMP will install Apache and PHP on your machine if you don't already have them, so follow the instructions on the MAMP website. When you install MAMP, the root folder of your PHP files will be */Applications/MAMP/htdocs/*. If the folder changes in a future installation, open MAMP and navigate to the Preferences section, and then navigate to Apache. You can then find the root folder of Apache there.

For our PHP script to be able to communicate with APNS, we need to feed it the SSL certificate that we generated earlier in the iOS development portal. This is why we extracted the *.cer* certification and the *.p12* private key files, which we now need to feed to our PHP script. The way this works is that we will use the *openssl* in Terminal to combine the certificate and the *.p12* private key into a PEM file. A discussion about PEM files lies outside the scope of this book. In fact, you could write a whole book on this subject. I will, however, let you know that you can get more information about the subject by reading RFC 1421 (*http://bit.ly/rfc-1421*).

To create the PEM file, assuming that the *PushKey.p12* and the *PushCertificate.cer* files are exported on your desktop as you were instructed earlier, follow these steps:

1. Open Terminal in OS X.

2. Type the following command:

   ```
   openssl x509 -in PushCertificate.cer -inform der -out PushCertificate.pem
   ```

3. Then type the following command to convert your *.p12* file into a PEM file:

   ```
   openssl pkcs12 -nocerts -in PushKey.p12 -out PushKey.pem
   ```

4. You will be asked to enter the password that you specified for this private key when you exported it from Keychain Access. Also, after the importing password is checked and verified, you will be asked by OpenSSL to specify a passphrase for the resulting PEM file. The password needs to be at least four characters. Go ahead with that and make sure you remember this password for later.

5. Now you have two PEM files on your desktop: *PushCertificate.pem* and *Push Key.pem*. You need to combine them into a single PEM file, the format recognized by PHP. Use the following command to accomplish this task:

   ```
   cat PushCertificate.pem PushKey.pem > PushCertificateAndKey.pem
   ```

6. Now let's test if we can connect to the sandbox (test version, for development purposes) APNS server using the generated *.pem* files. Issue the following command in Terminal:

   ```
   openssl s_client -connect gateway.sandbox.push.apple.com:2195 \
       -cert PushCertificate.pem -key PushKey.pem
   ```

If everything goes well, you will be asked to enter the passphrase for your private key file. Remember it? OK, then, enter that here. If your connection is successful, you will see OpenSSL waiting for some input characters before closing the connection. Type in something random and press the Enter key. The connection is then closed. This means that your connection to the APNS server is successful with the given certificate and private key.

It is now time to set up a simple PHP script to push a simple notification to our device. But before we move forward any further, we need to get our device's push notification token in a format that can be understood by PHP. iOS encapsulates the push notification token in an instance of NSData, but PHP has no notion of what that means. We need to convert that token into a string that we can use in our PHP script. To do that, we will read every byte in the token and convert each into its hexadecimal-string representation:

```
func application(application: UIApplication,
    didRegisterForRemoteNotificationsWithDeviceToken deviceToken: NSData!) {

    /* Each byte in the data will be translated to its hex value like 0x01 or
    0xAB excluding the 0x part; so for 1 byte, we will need 2 characters to
    represent that byte, hence the * 2 */
    var tokenAsString = NSMutableString()

    /* Create a buffer of UInt8 values and then get the raw bytes
    of the device token into this buffer */
    var byteBuffer = [UInt8](count: deviceToken.length, repeatedValue: 0x00)
    deviceToken.getBytes(&byteBuffer)

    /* Now convert the bytes into their hex equivalent */
    for byte in byteBuffer{
      tokenAsString.appendFormat("%02hhX", byte)
    }

    println("Token = \(tokenAsString)")

}
```

Run your app and see that the device token is printed to the console. Take note of this device token, because we are going to use it in our PHP script:

```
<?php

/* We are using the sandbox version of the APNS for development. For production
  environments, change this to ssl://gateway.push.apple.com:2195 */
$apnsServer = 'ssl://gateway.sandbox.push.apple.com:2195';

/* Make sure this is set to the password that you set for your private key
  when you exported it to the .pem file using openssl on your OS X */
$privateKeyPassword = '1234';

/* Put your own message here if you want to */
$message = 'Welcome to iOS Push Notifications';

/* Put your device token here */
$deviceToken =
    '05924634A8EB6B84437A1E8CE02E6BE6683DEC83FB38680A7DFD6A04C6CC586E';

/* Replace this with the name of the file that you placed by your PHP
  script file, containing your private key and certificate that you generated
  earlier */
```

```php
$pushCertAndKeyPemFile = 'PushCertificateAndKey.pem';

$stream = stream_context_create();

stream_context_set_option($stream,
                          'ssl',
                          'passphrase',
                          $privateKeyPassword);

stream_context_set_option($stream,
                          'ssl',
                          'local_cert',
                          $pushCertAndKeyPemFile);

$connectionTimeout = 20;
$connectionType = STREAM_CLIENT_CONNECT | STREAM_CLIENT_PERSISTENT;
$connection = stream_socket_client($apnsServer,
                                   $errorNumber,
                                   $errorString,
                                   $connectionTimeout,
                                   $connectionType,
                                   $stream);

if (!$connection){
    echo "Failed to connect to the APNS server. Error no = $errorNumber<br/>";
    exit;
} else {
    echo "Successfully connected to the APNS. Processing...</br>";
}

$messageBody['aps'] = array('alert' => $message,
                            'sound' => 'default',
                            'badge' => 2,
                            );

$payload = json_encode($messageBody);

$notification = chr(0) .
                pack('n', 32) .
                pack('H*', $deviceToken) .
                pack('n', strlen($payload)) .
                $payload;

$wroteSuccessfully = fwrite($connection, $notification, strlen($notification));

if (!$wroteSuccessfully){
    echo "Could not send the message<br/>";
}
else {
    echo "Successfully sent the message<br/>";
}
```

```
fclose($connection);
```

Go through this script, even if you are not a PHP programmer, and read the comments. Ensure that you replace the values in the PHP script with the correct values for you. For instance, the device token used here is for my personal device. Use the device token that you retrieved for your own device earlier in this recipe. The passphrases and the *.pem* file locations may be different for you. What I did in this recipe to make sure things are easier is to place my PHP script in the same folder where I placed my private key and certificate *.pem* file (*PushCertificateAndKey.pem*) so that I can access the *.pem* file using a simple filename.

If you did everything right and followed the advice of this recipe, you should now be able to open your PHP script in a web browser and see the notifications on your device. The script sends the notification to the APNS server, which delivers it to the device.

See Also

Recipe 16.7

16.9. Reacting to Push Notifications

Problem

You can deliver push notifications to your app after reading Recipe 16.8, but don't know how to react to them in your app.

Solution

Implement the `application:didReceiveRemoteNotification:` method of your app delegate.

Discussion

The `application:didReceiveRemoteNotification:` method of your app delegate gets called whenever a push notification is delivered to iOS and the user acts upon it in a way that opens your app. This method gets called if your app is either in the foreground or the background, but not completely terminated. For instance, the user can ignore the push notification. In that case, the aforementioned method is not called. If the user presses the push notification, which in turn opens your app, iOS opens your app and bring it to the foreground, after which the aforementioned method is called on your app delegate.

If your app is fully terminated and not in the background, the push notification that triggers your app to wake up will be encapsulated by iOS in the launch options that are passed to the `application:didFinishLaunchingWithOptions:` method of your app delegate. To retrieve the notification object, simply query the `didFinishLaunchingWithOptions` parameter of this method (which is of type `NSDictionary`) and look for the `UIApplicationLaunchOptionsRemoteNotificationKey` key. The value of this key will be the push notification object that started your app.

The `didReceiveRemoteNotification` parameter of this property carries a dictionary of type `NSDictionary`. This dictionary will contain a root object called `aps`, and under this object, you will have a dictionary with the following keys, depending on how the server created the push notification (the server may not send all of these at once):

badge
: The value of this key is a number indicating the badge number that has to be set for your app's icon.

alert
: The message inside the push notification, of type `String`. The server might decide to send you a modified version of this key's value, which itself will be a dictionary containing the keys `body` and `show-view`. If this modified version of the alert is sent to you, the `body` key will contain the actual text of the body of the alert, and the `show-view` key will contain a Boolean value indicating whether the action button of the notification should be displayed to the user. The Action button allows the user to tap the notification in the notification center in order to open your app.

sound
: This is a string indicating the name of the sound file that your app needs to play.

content-available
: The value of this key is a number. If set to 1, it indicates that there is new content available for the application to download from the server. The server can send this to your app to request that it fetches from the server to retrieve a list of new items. Your app doesn't have to comply. Rather, this is a protocol between the server and the client, and you can use it if it makes sense in your app.

See Also

Recipe 16.8

CHAPTER 17

Core Data

17.0. Introduction

Core Data is a powerful framework on the iOS SDK that allows programmers to store and manage data in an object-oriented way. Traditionally, programmers had to store their data on disk using the archiving capabilities of Objective-C, or write their data to files and manage them manually. With the introduction of Core Data, programmers can simply interact with its object-oriented interface to manage their data efficiently. In this chapter, you learn how to use Core Data to create the model of your application (in the model-view-controller software architecture).

Core Data interacts with a persistent store at a lower level that is not visible to the programmer. iOS decides how the low-level data management is implemented. All the programmer needs to know is the high-level API she is provided with. But understanding the structure of Core Data and how it works internally is very important. Let's create a Core Data application to understand this a bit better.

With the new LLVM compiler, the only thing you have to do in order to include Core Data into your project is to include the umbrella header file, like so:

```
import UIKit
import CoreData
```

To be able to work with Core Data, you need to understand that a Core Data stack is based on the following concepts:

Persistent store
> The object that represents the actual database on disk. We never use this object directly.

Persistent store coordinator

The object that coordinates reading and writing of information from and to the persistent store. The coordinator is the bridge between the managed object context and the persistent store.

Managed object model (MOM)

This is a simple file on disk that will represent our data model. Think about it as your database schema.

Managed object

This class represents an entity that we want to store in Core Data. Traditional database programmers know such entities as *tables*. A managed object is of type NSManagedObject, and its instances are placed on managed object contexts. They adhere to the schema dictated by the managed object model, and they are saved to a persistent store through a persistent store coordinator.

Managed object context (MOC)

This is a virtual board. That sounds strange, right? But let me explain. We create Core Data objects in memory and set their properties and play with them. All this playing is done on a managed object context. The context keeps track of all the things we are doing with our managed objects and even allows us to undo those actions. Think of your managed objects on a context as toys that you put on a table to play with. You can move them around, break them, move them out of the table, and bring new toys in. That table is your managed object context, and you can save its state when you are ready. When you save the state of the managed object context, this save operation will be communicated to the persistent store coordinator to which the context is connected. Then the persistent store coordinator will store the information to the persistent store and subsequently to disk.

To add Core Data to your project and start using all the cool features that it has to offer, simply create a project and when asked whether to add Core Data to it or not, check the relevant box, as shown in Figure 17-1.

After you create your project with Core Data, your app delegate will have some new properties such as managedObjectModel and persistentStoreCoordinator. You should already know these from the description earlier in this chapter. The context is our playing table, the model is the schema of our database, and the coordinator is the object that will help us save our context to disk. Plain and easy. OK then, let's proceed with the rest of this chapter.

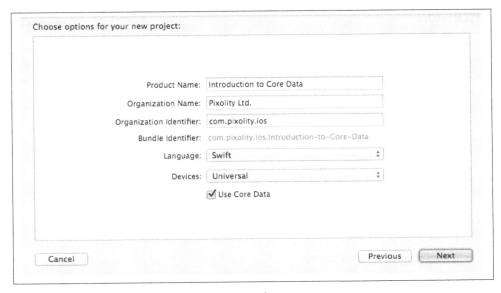

Figure 17-1. Adding Core Data to a new Xcode project

17.1. Performing Batch Updates on Core Data

Problem

You want to perform batch updates on your Core Data model objects without having to fetch them in advance.

Solution

Use the `NSBatchUpdateRequest` class. First, instantiate an object of this type. Set its `propertiesToUpdate` property to a dictionary of changes that you want to apply. For instance, if you have a model class called `Person` with an attribute that is called `age` of type `Int`, create a dictionary whose key is just the string "age" and whose value is the age that you want to set on your data.

Then define which one of the model objects have to be updated by your batch updating using the `predicate` property of your batch update instance. Please see Recipe 17.8 for information about predicates.

After you have your batch update object, you need to execute that on your managed object context using the context's `executeRequest:error:` method.

Discussion

Let's say that we have populated our Core Data stack with 1,000 person entities whose ages are random values between 0 and 120. We will write a method called `populateDa tabase` in our app delegate. This method will create our person entities and set their age to a random number:

```
import UIKit
import CoreData

@UIApplicationMain
class AppDelegate: UIResponder, UIApplicationDelegate {

  var window: UIWindow?
  let entityName = NSStringFromClass(Person.classForCoder())

  func populateDatabase(){

    for counter in 0..<1000{

      let person = NSEntityDescription.insertNewObjectForEntityForName(
        entityName,
        inManagedObjectContext: managedObjectContext!) as Person

      person.firstName = "First name \(counter)"
      person.lastName = "Last name \(counter)"
      person.age = NSNumber(unsignedInt: arc4random_uniform(120))

    }

    var savingError: NSError?
    if managedObjectContext!.save(&savingError){
      println("Managed to populate the database")
    } else {
      if let error = savingError{
        println("Failed to populate the database. Error = \(error)")
      }
    }

  }

  <# rest of the code #>

}
```

When our app is executed, we will populate the Core Data stack with all these person entities. Our person entity is defined like so:

```
import Foundation
import CoreData

@objc(Person) class Person: NSManagedObject {
```

```
    @NSManaged var age: NSNumber
    @NSManaged var firstName: String
    @NSManaged var lastName: String

}
```

What we want to do is to create a batch request that can find all the person entities whose age is currently less than 18, and change that to 18. That means that eventually, none of the users in our stack will have their age as less than 18. Here is our code:

```
func application(application: UIApplication,
    didFinishLaunchingWithOptions launchOptions: [NSObject : AnyObject]?) -> Bool {

    let batch = NSBatchUpdateRequest(entityName: entityName)
    batch.propertiesToUpdate = ["age" : 18]
    batch.predicate = NSPredicate(format: "age < %@", 18 as NSNumber)
    batch.resultType = .UpdatedObjectsCountResultType

    var batchError: NSError?
    let result = managedObjectContext!.executeRequest(batch,
      error: &batchError)

    if result != nil{
      if let theResult = result as? NSBatchUpdateResult{
        if let numberOfAffectedPersons = theResult.result as? Int{
          println("Number of people who were previously younger than " +
            "18 years old and whose age is now set to " +
            "18 is \(numberOfAffectedPersons)")
        }
      }
    } else {
      if let error = batchError{
        println("Could not perform batch request. Error = \(error)")
      }
    }

    return true
}
```

We are utilizing the `resultType` propety of our batch update instance. This property is of type `NSBatchUpdateRequestResultType` and we have currently set that property's value to `NSUpdatedObjectsCountResultType`. This means that we are asking the Core Data stack to perform our batch update and to return how many records were updated as a result.

You might have noted that the return value of the `executeRequest:error:` method of our managed object context is of type `NSPersistentStoreResult`, which is a very generic type. In your request, the return value will differ depending on the `result Type` property of your request. In our case, since we chose the `NSUpdatedObjectsCoun` tResultType result type, the return value of the aforementioned function will be of type NSBatchUpdateResult.

A value of this type has a property called result, which is of type AnyObject. But again, because our result type is set to NSUpdatedObjectsCountResultType, this property will carry a value of type Int, which is basically the number of items that were updated in our Core Data stack.

See Also

Recipe 17.3; Recipe 17.8

17.2. Writing to Core Data

Problem

You have already created a managed object, and you want to instantiate it and insert that instance into your app's Core Data context.

Solution

You can use the insertNewObjectForEntityForName:inManagedObjectContext: class method of NSEntityDescription to create a new object of a type specified by the first parameter of this method. When the new entity (the managed object) is created, you can modify it by changing its properties. After you are done, save your managed object context using the save: instance method of the managed object context.

I'll assume that you have created a universal application in Xcode with the name *Creating and Saving Data Using Core Data*. Now follow these steps to insert a new managed object into the context:

1. Find the implementation file of your app delegate.

 Person is the entity we created in our model in Xcode.

2. In the application:didFinishLaunchingWithOptions: method of your shared application delegate, write this code:

```
func application(application: UIApplication,
    didFinishLaunchingWithOptions launchOptions:
```

```
[NSObject : AnyObject]?) -> Bool {

    let entityName = NSStringFromClass(Person.classForCoder())

    let person = NSEntityDescription.insertNewObjectForEntityForName(
        entityName,
        inManagedObjectContext: managedObjectContext!) as Person

    person.firstName = "First name"
    person.firstName = "Last name"
    person.age = NSNumber(unsignedInt: arc4random_uniform(120))

    var savingError: NSError?

    if managedObjectContext!.save(&savingError){
        println("Successfully saved the new person")
    } else {
        if let error = savingError{
            println("Failed to save the new person. Error = \(error)")
        }
    }

    return true
}
```

Discussion

Previous recipes showed how to create entities and generate code based on them using the editor in Xcode. The next thing we need to do is start using those entities and instantiate them. For this, we use `NSEntityDescription` and call its `insertNewObject` `ForEntityForName:inManagedObjectContext:` class method. This will look up the given entity (specified by its name as `NSString`) in the given managed object context. If the entity is found, the method will return a new instance of that entity. This is similar to creating a new row (managed object) in a table (entity) in a database (managed object context).

 Attempting to insert an unknown entity into a managed object context will raise an exception of type `NSInternalInconsistencyExcep` `tion`.

After inserting a new entity into the context, we must save the context. This will flush all the unsaved data of the context to the persistent store. We can do this using the `save:` instance method of our managed object context. If the Boolean return value of this method is `true`, we can be sure that our context is saved. In Recipe 17.3, you will learn how to read the data back to memory.

17.3. Reading Data from Core Data

Problem

You want to be able to read the contents of your entities (tables) using Core Data.

Solution

Use an instance of NSFetchRequest:

```
func createNewPersonWithFirstName(firstName: String,
  lastName :String,
  age: Int) -> Bool{

  let newPerson =
  NSEntityDescription.insertNewObjectForEntityForName("Person",
    inManagedObjectContext: managedObjectContext!) as Person

  (newPerson.firstName, newPerson.lastName, newPerson.age) =
    (firstName, lastName, age)

  var savingError: NSError?

  if managedObjectContext!.save(&savingError){
    return true
  } else {
    if let error = savingError{
      println("Failed to save the new person. Error = \(error)")
    }
  }

  return false

}

func application(application: UIApplication,
  didFinishLaunchingWithOptions launchOptions: [NSObject : AnyObject]?) -> Bool {

  /* Create the entities first */
  createNewPersonWithFirstName("Anthony", lastName: "Robbins", age: 52)
  createNewPersonWithFirstName("Richard", lastName: "Branson", age: 62)

  /* Tell the request that we want to read the
  contents of the Person entity */
  /* Create the fetch request first */
  let fetchRequest = NSFetchRequest(entityName: "Person")

  var requestError: NSError?

  /* And execute the fetch request on the context */
  let persons = managedObjectContext!.executeFetchRequest(fetchRequest,
```

```
        error: &requestError) as [Person!]

    /* Make sure we get the array */
    if persons.count > 0{

        var counter = 1
        for person in persons{

            println("Person \(counter) first name = \(person.firstName)")
            println("Person \(counter) last name = \(person.lastName)")
            println("Person \(counter) age = \(person.age)")

            counter++
        }

    } else {
        println("Could not find any Person entities in the context")
    }

    return true
}
```

Bear in mind that our `Person` model object is defined like so:

```
import Foundation
import CoreData

@objc(Person) class Person: NSManagedObject {

    @NSManaged var firstName: String
    @NSManaged var lastName: String
    @NSManaged var age: NSNumber

}
```

In this code, we are using a counter variable inside a fast-enumeration block. The reason we need the counter in this fast-enumeration is for use in `println` debugging messages that we are printing in order to see the index of the current enumerated person object in the array. An alternative to this solution is to use a classic for-loop with a counter variable.

For more information about fetch requests, please refer to this recipe's Discussion.

Discussion

For those of you who are familiar with database terminology, a *fetch request* is similar to a `SELECT` statement. In the `SELECT` statement, you specify which rows, with which conditions, have to be returned from which table. With a fetch request, we do the same thing. We specify the entity (table) and the managed object context (the database layer). We can also specify sort descriptors for sorting the data we read. But first we'll focus on reading the data to make it simpler.

To be able to read the contents of the Person entity (which is an entity that we assumed to have already created), we must set the target entity name, in this case *Person*, in the fetch request by using the initWithEntityName: method. After the fetch request is constructed successfully, the only thing left to do is execute the fetch request as we saw in this recipe's Solution.

The return value of the executeFetchRequest:error: instance method of NSManagedObjectContext is either nil (in case of an error) or an array of Person managed objects. If no results are found for the given entity, the returned array will be empty.

17.4. Deleting Data from Core Data

Problem

You want to delete a managed object (a row in a table) from a managed object context (your database).

Solution

Use the deleteObject: instance method of NSManagedObjectContext:

```
func application(application: UIApplication,
    didFinishLaunchingWithOptions launchOptions: [NSObject : AnyObject]?) -> Bool {

    /* Create the entities first */
    createNewPersonWithFirstName("Anthony", lastName: "Robbins", age: 52)
    createNewPersonWithFirstName("Richard", lastName: "Branson", age: 62)

    /* Tell the request that we want to read the
    contents of the Person entity */
    /* Create the fetch request first */
    let fetchRequest = NSFetchRequest(entityName: "Person")

    var requestError: NSError?

    /* And execute the fetch request on the context */
    let persons = managedObjectContext!.executeFetchRequest(fetchRequest,
        error: &requestError) as [Person!]

    /* Make sure we get the array */
    if persons.count > 0{

        /* Delete the last person in the array */
        let lastPerson = (persons as NSArray).lastObject as Person
```

```
    managedObjectContext!.deleteObject(lastPerson)

    var savingError: NSError?
    if managedObjectContext!.save(&savingError){
      println("Successfully deleted the last person in the array")
    } else {
      if let error = savingError{
        println("Failed to delete the last person. Error = \(error)")
      }
    }

  } else {
    println("Could not find any Person entities in the context")
  }

  return true
}
```

 In this example code, we are using the `createNewPersonWithFirst`
`Name:lastName:age:` method that we coded in Recipe 17.3.

Discussion

You can delete managed objects (records of a table in a database) using the `deleteOb`
`ject:` instance method of `NSManagedObjectContext`.

This method doesn't return an error to you in any of its parameters, nor does it return
a `BOOL` value, so you really have no good way of knowing whether an object was successfully deleted using the managed object context. The best way to determine this is to
use that managed object's `deleted` method.

With this information, let's change the code that we wrote previously in this recipe:

```
func application(application: UIApplication,
  didFinishLaunchingWithOptions launchOptions: [NSObject : AnyObject]?) -> Bool {

  /* Create the entities first */
  createNewPersonWithFirstName("Anthony", lastName: "Robbins", age: 52)
  createNewPersonWithFirstName("Richard", lastName: "Branson", age: 62)

  /* Tell the request that we want to read the
  contents of the Person entity */
  /* Create the fetch request first */
  let fetchRequest = NSFetchRequest(entityName: "Person")

  var requestError: NSError?

  /* And execute the fetch request on the context */
```

```
    let persons = managedObjectContext!.executeFetchRequest(fetchRequest,
      error: &requestError) as [Person!]

    /* Make sure we get the array */
    if persons.count > 0{

      /* Delete the last person in the array */
      let lastPerson = (persons as NSArray).lastObject as Person

      managedObjectContext!.deleteObject(lastPerson)

      if lastPerson.deleted{
        println("Successfully deleted the last person...")

        var savingError: NSError?
        if managedObjectContext!.save(&savingError){
          println("Successfully saved the context")
        } else {
          if let error = savingError{
            println("Failed to save the context. Error = \(error)")
          }
        }

      } else {
        println("Failed to delete the last person")
      }

    } else {
      println("Could not find any Person entities in the context")
    }

    return true
}
```

When you run the app, you will get results similar to this printed to the console window:

```
Successfully deleted the last person...
Successfully saved the context
```

17.5. Sorting Data in Core Data

Problem

You want to sort the managed objects (records) that you fetch from a managed object context (database).

Solution

Create instances of NSSortDescriptor for each attribute (column, in the database world) of an entity that has to be sorted. Add the sort descriptors to an array and assign the array to an instance of NSFetchRequest using the setSortDescriptors: instance method. In this example code, Sorting_Data_in_Core_DataAppDelegate is the class that represents the app delegate in a universal app:

```
func application(application: UIApplication,
  didFinishLaunchingWithOptions launchOptions: [NSObject : AnyObject]?) -> Bool {

    /* Create the entities first */
    createNewPersonWithFirstName("Anthony", lastName: "Robbins", age: 52)
    createNewPersonWithFirstName("Richard", lastName: "Branson", age: 62)

    /* Create the fetch request first */
    let fetchRequest = NSFetchRequest(entityName: "Person")

    let ageSort = NSSortDescriptor(key: "age", ascending: true)

    let firstNameSort = NSSortDescriptor(key: "firstName", ascending: true)

    fetchRequest.sortDescriptors = [ageSort, firstNameSort]

    var requestError: NSError?

    /* And execute the fetch request on the context */
    let persons = managedObjectContext!.executeFetchRequest(fetchRequest,
      error:&requestError) as [Person!]

    for person in persons{

      println("First Name = \(person.firstName)")
      println("Last Name = \(person.lastName)")
      println("Age = \(person.age)")

    }

    return true
}
```

Discussion

An instance of NSFetchRequest can carry with itself an array of NSSortDescriptor instances. Each sort descriptor defines the attribute (column) on the current entity that has to be sorted and whether the sorting has to be ascending or descending. For instance, the Person entity that we are assumed to have created has firstName, lastName, and age attributes. If we want to read all the persons in a managed object context and sort them from youngest to oldest, we create an instance of NSSortDescriptor with the age key and set it to ascending:

```
let ageSort = NSSortDescriptor(key: "age", ascending: true)
```

You can assign more than one sort descriptor to one fetch request. The order in the array determines the order in which descriptors are provided. In other words, the output is sorted according to the first descriptor of the array, and within that order, entries are sorted according to the second descriptor of the array, etc.

See Also

Recipe 17.3

17.6. Boosting Data Access in Table Views

Problem

In an application that uses table views to present managed objects to the user, you want to be able to fetch and present the data in a more fluid and natural way than managing your data manually.

Solution

Use fetched results controllers, which are instances of `NSFetchedResultsController`.

Discussion

Fetched results controllers work in the same way as table views. Both have sections and rows. A fetched results controller can read managed objects from a managed object context and separate them into sections and rows. Each section is a group (if you specify it), and each row in a section is a managed object. You can then easily map this data to a table view and display it to the user. There are a few very important reasons why you might want to modify your application to use fetched results controllers:

- After a fetched results controller is created on a managed object context, any change (insertion, deletion, modification, etc.) will immediately be reflected on the fetched results controller as well. For instance, you could create your fetched results controller to read the managed objects of the `Person` entity. Then in some other place in your application, you might insert a new `Person` managed object into the context (the same context the fetched results controller was created on). Immediately, the new managed object will become available in the fetched results controller. This is just magical!

- With a fetched results controller, you can manage cache more efficiently. For instance, you can ask your fetched results controller to keep only N number of managed objects in memory per controller instance.

- Fetched results controllers are exactly like table views in the sense that they have sections and rows, as explained before. You can use a fetched results controller to present managed objects in the GUI of your application with table views with ease.

Here are some of the important properties and instance methods of fetched results controllers (all are objects of type `NSFetchedResultsController`):

`sections` *(property, of type* `NSArray`*)*
A fetched results controller can group data together using a key path. The designated constructor of the `NSFetchedResultsController` class accepts this grouping filter through the `sectionNameKeyPath` parameter. The `sections` array will then contain each grouped section. Each object in this array conforms to the `NSFetche dResultsSectionInfo` protocol.

`objectAtIndexPath:` *(instance method, returns a managed object)*
Objects fetched with a fetched results controller can be retrieved using their section and row index. Each section's rows are numbered 0 through *N-1*, where *N* is the total number of items in that section. An index path object comprises a section and row index and perfectly matches the information needed to retrieve objects from a fetched results controller. The `objectAtIndexPath:` instance method accepts index paths. Each index path is of type `NSIndexPath`. If you need to construct a table view cell using a managed object in a fetched results controller, simply pass the index path object in the `cellForRowAtIndexPath` parameter of the `tableView:cell ForRowAtIndexPath:` delegate method of a table view. If you want to construct an index path anywhere else in your application, use the `indexPathForRow:inSec tion:` class method of `NSIndexPath`.

`fetchRequest` *(property, of type* `NSFetchRequest`*)*
If at any point in your application you believe you have to change the fetch request object for your fetched results controllers, you can do so using the `fetchRequest` property of an instance of `NSFetchedResultsController`. This is useful, for example, if you want to change the sort descriptors (refer to Recipe 17.5 for information about this) of the fetch request object after you have allocated and initialized your fetched results controllers.

A fetched results controller also tracks the changes that happen in the context to which it is bound. For instance, let's say you created your fetched results controller on View Controller A, and on View Controller B you are deleting an object from your context. As soon as you do that on View Controller B, your first view controller that owns the fetched results controller will get notified, assuming that View Controller A is the delegate of the fetched results controller. This is great and will come in handy. Imagine the situation where you are developing an app and your app displays two view controllers to the user. The root view controller is a table view controller that lists all the user's contacts, and the second view controller allows the user to add a new contact. As soon as the user presses the Save button on the second view controller and goes back to the list of her contacts, she finds the list updated because of the delegation mechanism of the fetched results controller.

In the previously described application, you would declare your table view controller that lists all the user's contacts in this way:

```
import UIKit
import CoreData

class PersonsListTableViewController: UITableViewController,
NSFetchedResultsControllerDelegate {

  struct TableViewConstants{
    static let cellIdentifier = "Cell"
  }

  var barButtonAddPerson: UIBarButtonItem!
  var frc: NSFetchedResultsController!

  var managedObjectContext: NSManagedObjectContext?{
  return (UIApplication.sharedApplication().delegate
    as AppDelegate).managedObjectContext
  }

  func addNewPerson(sender: AnyObject){
    /* This is a custom segue identifier that we defined in our
    storyboard that simply does a "Show" segue from our view controller
    to the "Add New Person" view controller */
    performSegueWithIdentifier("addPerson", sender: nil)
  }

  required init(coder aDecoder: NSCoder) {
    super.init(coder: aDecoder)

    barButtonAddPerson = UIBarButtonItem(barButtonSystemItem: .Add,
      target: self,
      action: "addNewPerson:")

  }

  <# rest of the code #>

}
```

The bar button declared in the code will be a simple + button on the navigation bar that allows the user to go to the Add Person view controller, where he will be able to add a new contact to our managed object context. The fetched results controller will also be used to actually fetch the persons from context and assist us in displaying them on our table view.

This is how we construct our fetched results controller:

```
/* Create the fetch request first */
let fetchRequest = NSFetchRequest(entityName: "Person")

let ageSort = NSSortDescriptor(key: "age", ascending: true)

let firstNameSort = NSSortDescriptor(key: "firstName", ascending: true)

fetchRequest.sortDescriptors = [ageSort, firstNameSort]

frc = NSFetchedResultsController(fetchRequest: fetchRequest,
  managedObjectContext: managedObjectContext!,
  sectionNameKeyPath: nil,
  cacheName: nil)

frc.delegate = self
var fetchingError: NSError?
if frc.performFetch(&fetchingError){
  println("Successfully fetched")
} else {
  println("Failed to fetch")
}
```

You can see that the fetched results controller is choosing the current table view controller as its own delegate. The delegate of the fetched results controller has to conform to the NSFetchedResultsControllerDelegate protocol. Here are some of the most important methods in this protocol:

controllerWillChangeContent:
> Gets called on the delegate to let it know that the context that is backing the fetched results controller has changed and that the fetched results controller is about to change its contents to reflect that. We usually use this method to prepare our table view for updates by calling the beginUpdates method on it.

controller:didChangeObject:atIndexPath:forChangeType:newIndexPath:
> Gets called on the delegate to inform the delegate of specific changes made to an object on the context. For instance, if you delete an object from the context, this method gets called, and its forChangeType parameter will contain the value NSFetchedResultsChangeDelete. Alternatively, if you insert a new object into the context, this parameter will contain the value NSFetchedResultsChangeInsert.
>
> This method also gets called on your fetched results controller's delegate method when a managed object is updated, after the context is saved using the save: method of the context.

controllerDidChangeContent:
> Gets called on the delegate to inform it that the fetched results controller was refreshed and updated as a result of an update to a managed object context. Generally, programmers issue an endUpdates call on their table view within this method to

ask the table view to process all the updates that they submitted after a beginUp dates method.

Here is a typical implementation of the aforementioned methods in the app whose concept was explained earlier:

```
func controllerWillChangeContent(controller: NSFetchedResultsController!) {
  tableView.beginUpdates()
}

func controller(controller: NSFetchedResultsController,
  didChangeObject anObject: AnyObject,
  atIndexPath indexPath: NSIndexPath?,
  forChangeType type: NSFetchedResultsChangeType,
  newIndexPath: NSIndexPath?) {

    if type == .Delete{
      tableView.deleteRowsAtIndexPaths([indexPath!],
        withRowAnimation: .Automatic)
    }

    else if type == .Insert{
      tableView.insertRowsAtIndexPaths([newIndexPath!],
        withRowAnimation: .Automatic)
    }

}

func controllerDidChangeContent(controller: NSFetchedResultsController!) {
  tableView.endUpdates()
}
```

Now, obviously, we also talked about providing information to a table view using various methods of the fetched results controller, such as the objectAtIndexPath: method. A simple implementation of this method in a table view could look like this:

```
override func tableView(tableView: UITableView,
  numberOfRowsInSection section: Int) -> Int {

    let sectionInfo = frc.sections![section] as NSFetchedResultsSectionInfo
    return sectionInfo.numberOfObjects

}

override func tableView(tableView: UITableView,
  cellForRowAtIndexPath indexPath: NSIndexPath) -> UITableViewCell{

    let cell = tableView.dequeueReusableCellWithIdentifier(
      TableViewConstants.cellIdentifier,
      forIndexPath: indexPath) as UITableViewCell

    let person = frc.objectAtIndexPath(indexPath) as Person
```

```
    cell.textLabel.text = person.firstName + " " + person.lastName
    cell.detailTextLabel!.text = "Age: \(person.age)"

    return cell

}
```

In this code, we are telling our table view controller to display as many cells as there are instances of managed objects in our fetched results controller. While displaying each cell, we retrieve the `Person` managed object from the fetched results controller and configure our cell accordingly. Our table view controller, with no items in the managed object context, might look like Figure 17-2.

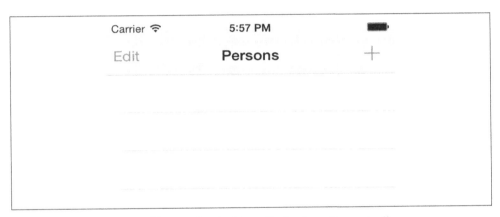

Figure 17-2. An empty table view backed by a fetched results controller

Now in the second view controller, where the user is allowed to add a new `Person` instance to the managed object context, we use the following method:

```
import UIKit
import CoreData

class AddPersonViewController: UIViewController {

  var textFieldFirstName: UITextField!
  var textFieldLastName: UITextField!
  var textFieldAge: UITextField!
  var barButtonAdd: UIBarButtonItem!

  func createNewPerson(sender: AnyObject){

    let appDelegate = UIApplication.sharedApplication().delegate
      as AppDelegate

    let managedObjectContext = appDelegate.managedObjectContext
```

```
    let newPerson =
    NSEntityDescription.insertNewObjectForEntityForName("Person",
      inManagedObjectContext: managedObjectContext!) as? Person

    if let person = newPerson{
      person.firstName = textFieldFirstName.text
      person.lastName = textFieldLastName.text
      if let age = textFieldAge.text.toInt(){
        person.age = age
      } else {
        person.age = 18
      }

      var savingError: NSError?

      if managedObjectContext!.save(&savingError){
        navigationController!.popViewControllerAnimated(true)
      } else {
        println("Failed to save the managed object context")
      }

    } else {
      println("Failed to create the new person object")
    }

  }

  <# rest of the code #>

}
```

This method reads the first name, last name, and age of the person to be created from three text fields on the view controller. We don't have to worry about the implementation of those text fields, as that has nothing to do with what we are trying to learn in this recipe. After this method is called, we call the `save:` method on our managed object context. This triggers the change in our fetched results controller in the first table view controller, which refreshes the table view.

We will also go ahead and create our UI components on the screen:

```
override func viewDidLoad() {
  super.viewDidLoad()

  title = "New Person"

  var textFieldRect = CGRect(x: 20,
    y: 80,
    width: view.bounds.size.width - 40,
    height: 31)

  textFieldFirstName = UITextField(frame: textFieldRect)
```

```
    textFieldFirstName.placeholder = "First Name"
    textFieldFirstName.borderStyle = .RoundedRect
    textFieldFirstName.autoresizingMask = .FlexibleWidth
    textFieldFirstName.contentVerticalAlignment = .Center
    view.addSubview(textFieldFirstName)

    textFieldRect.origin.y += 37
    textFieldLastName = UITextField(frame: textFieldRect)
    textFieldLastName.placeholder = "Last Name"
    textFieldLastName.borderStyle = .RoundedRect
    textFieldLastName.autoresizingMask = .FlexibleWidth
    textFieldLastName.contentVerticalAlignment = .Center
    view.addSubview(textFieldLastName)

    textFieldRect.origin.y += 37
    textFieldAge = UITextField(frame: textFieldRect)
    textFieldAge.placeholder = "Age"
    textFieldAge.borderStyle = .RoundedRect
    textFieldAge.autoresizingMask = .FlexibleWidth
    textFieldAge.keyboardType = .NumberPad
    textFieldAge.contentVerticalAlignment = .Center
    view.addSubview(textFieldAge)

    barButtonAdd = UIBarButtonItem(title: "Add",
      style: .Plain,
      target: self,
      action: "createNewPerson:")

    navigationItem.rightBarButtonItem = barButtonAdd

  }

  override func viewDidAppear(animated: Bool) {
    super.viewDidAppear(animated)
    textFieldFirstName.becomeFirstResponder()
  }
```

One last thing is how we can allow the user to delete items on the first table view controller:

```
override func tableView(tableView: UITableView,
  commitEditingStyle editingStyle: UITableViewCellEditingStyle,
  forRowAtIndexPath indexPath: NSIndexPath){

    let personToDelete = self.frc.objectAtIndexPath(indexPath) as Person

    managedObjectContext!.deleteObject(personToDelete)

    if personToDelete.deleted{
      var savingError: NSError?

      if managedObjectContext!.save(&savingError){
        println("Successfully deleted the object")
```

```
      } else {
        if let error = savingError{
          println("Failed to save the context with error = \(error)")
        }
      }
    }

  }
```

This code won't even touch the fetched results controller directly, but it deletes the selected person from the managed object context, which will refresh the fetched results controller, which, in turn, refreshes the table view. To learn more about table views, please refer to Chapter 6. The interface of our table view controller in deletion mode might look like that shown in Figure 17-3.

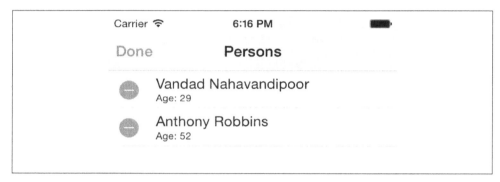

Figure 17-3. Deletion mode of a table view controller that uses a fetched results controller

17.7. Implementing Relationships in Core Data

Problem

You want to be able to link your managed objects to each other, such as linking a Person to the Home he lives in.

Solution

Use inverse relationships in the model editor.

Discussion

Relationships in Core Data can be one-to-one, inverse one-to-many, or inverse many-to-many. Here is an example of each type of relationship:

One-to-one relationship

An example is the relationship between a person and her nose. Each person can have only one nose, and each nose can belong to only one person.

Inverse one-to-many relationship

An example is the relationship between an employee and his manager. The employee can have only one direct manager, but his manager can have multiple employees working for her. Here, the relationship of the employee with the manager is one-to-one, but from the manager's perspective, the relationship is one (manager) to many (employees); hence the word *inverse*.

Inverse many-to-many relationship

An example is the relationship between a person and a car. One car can be used by more than one person, and one person can have more than one car.

In Core Data, you can create one-to-one relationships, but I highly recommend that you avoid doing so because, going back to the example in the preceding list, the person will know what nose she has, but the nose will not know who it belongs to. Please note that this is a different one-to-one model than what you might have seen in other database management systems where Object A and Object B are linked together when they have a one-to-one relationship. In a Core Data one-to-one relationship, Object A will know about Object B, but not the other way around. In an object-oriented programming language such as Objective-C, it is always best to create inverse relationships so that child elements can refer to parent elements of that relationship. In a one-to-many relationship, the object that can have associations with many other objects will retain a set of those objects. The set will be of type NSSet. However, in a one-to-one relationship, objects on both sides of the fence keep a reference to one another using the proper class names of one another because, well, the relationship is one-to-one and an instance of one object in another object can easily be represented with the class name of that object.

Let's go ahead and create a data model that takes advantage of an inverse one-to-many relationship:

1. In Xcode, find the *xcdatamodel* file that was created for you when you started your Core Data project.

2. Open the data model file in the editor by clicking on it.

3. Remove any entities that were created for you previously by selecting them and pressing the Delete key on your keyboard.

4. Create a new entity and name it Employee. Create three attributes for this entity, named firstName (of type String), lastName (of type String), and age (of type Integer 32), as shown in Figure 17-4.

Figure 17-4. The Employee entity with three attributes

5. Create another entity named `Manager` with the same attributes you created for the `Employee` entity (`firstName` of type `String`, `lastName` of type `String`, and `age` of type `Integer 32`). See Figure 17-5.

Figure 17-5. The Manager entity with three attributes

6. Create a new relationship for the `Manager` entity by first selecting the Manager entity in the list and then pressing the + button in the bottom of the Relationships box (see Figure 17-6).

Figure 17-6. We have added a new relationship to the Manager entity

7. Set the name of the new relationship to `employees` (see Figure 17-7).

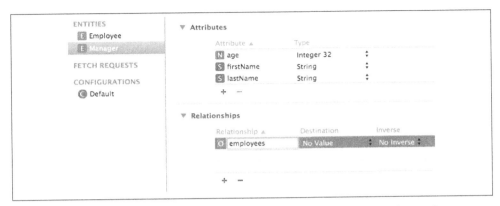

Figure 17-7. Changing the name of the new Manager-to-Employees relationship

8. Select the `Employee` entity and create a new relationship for it. Name the relationship `manager` (see Figure 17-8).

Figure 17-8. Changing the name of the new Employee-to-Manager relationship

9. Choose the `Manager` entity, and then select the `employees` relationship for the `Manager`. In the Relationships box, choose Employee in the Destination drop-down menu (because we want to connect a `Manager` to an `Employee` entity through this relationship), set the Inverse box's value to `manager` (because the `manager` relationship of the `Employee` will link an employee to her `Manager`), and tick the To-Many Relationship box in Data Model inspector. The results are shown in Figure 17-9.

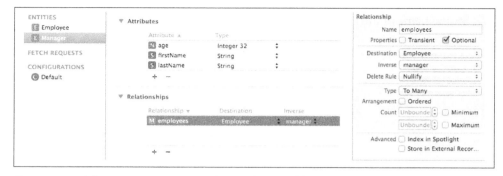

Figure 17-9. The Manager inverse relationship established with employees

10. Select both your `Employee` and `Manager` entities, select File → New File, and create the managed object classes for your model.

11. When you are asked whether you want to create a bridging header to Objective-C, press No in that dialog (see Figure 17-10).

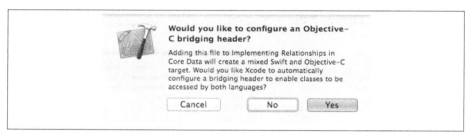

Figure 17-10. No bridging required for our model classes

12. Open your *Employee.swift* file and add the `@objc` keyword to it as shown here:

```
import Foundation
import CoreData

@objc(Employee) class Employee: NSManagedObject {

    @NSManaged var age: NSNumber
    @NSManaged var firstName: String
    @NSManaged var lastName: String
    @NSManaged var manager: Manager

}
```

13. Do the same for your *Manager.swift* file:

```
import Foundation
import CoreData
```

```
@objc(Manager) class Manager: NSManagedObject {

    @NSManaged var age: NSNumber
    @NSManaged var firstName: String
    @NSManaged var lastName: String
    @NSManaged var employees: NSSet

}
```

After creating the inverse one-to-many relationship, open the *Employee.swift* file and have a look at its contents. You can see that a new property has been added to this file. The property is named `manager` and its type is `Manager`, meaning that from now on, if we have a reference to any object of type `Employee`, we can access its `manager` property to access that specific employee's `Manager` object (if any). Let's have a look at the *Manager.swift* file now. The `employees` property is also created for the `Manager` entity. The data type of this object is `NSSet`. This simply means that the `employees` property of any instance of the `Manager` entity can contain 1 to *N* number of `Employee` entities (a one-to-many relationship: one manager, many employees).

Another type of relationship that you might want to create is a many-to-many relationship. Going back to the `Manager` to `Employee` relationship, with a many-to-many relationship, any manager could have *N* number of employees, and one employee could have *N* number of managers. To do this, follow the same instructions for creating a one-to-many relationship, but select the `Employee` entity and then the `manager` relationship. Change this name to `managers` and tick the To-Many Relationship box, as shown in Figure 17-11. Now the arrow has double arrowheads on both sides.

Figure 17-11. Creating a Many-to-Many relationship between the Manager and Employee entities

Now if you open the *Employee.swift* file, the contents will be different:

```
import Foundation
import CoreData
```

```
class Employee: NSManagedObject {

    @NSManaged var age: NSNumber
    @NSManaged var firstName: String
    @NSManaged var lastName: String
    @NSManaged var managers: NSSet

}
```

You can see that the managers property of the Person entity is now a set. Because the relationship from the employee to her managers is a set and so is the relationship from the manager to the employees, this creates a many-to-many relationship in Core Data.

In your code, for a one-to-many relationship, you can simply create a new Manager managed object (read how you can insert objects to a managed object context in Recipe 17.2), save it to the managed object context, and then create a couple of Employee managed objects and save them to the context as well. Now, to associate the manager with an employee, set the value of the manager property of an instance of Employee to an instance of the Manager managed object. Core Data will then create the relationship for you.

If you would like to retrieve all employees (of type Employee) that are associated to a manager object (of type Manager), all you have to do is use the allObjects instance method of the employees property of our manager object. This object is of type NSSet, so you can use its allObjects instance method to retrieve the array of all employee objects associated with a particular manager object.

17.8. Fetching Data in the Background

Problem

You want to perform fetches in your Core Data Stack, all in the background. This is great if you want to ensure that you have a responsive user interface.

Solution

Before performing background fetches, create a new managed object context with the concurrency type of NSPrivateQueueConcurrencyType. Then use the performBlock: method of your new background context to perform your fetches in the background. When you are done and ready to use your fetched objects in your UI, go back to the UI thread using dispatch_async (see Recipe 7.1) and for every object that you fetched in the background, issue the objectWithID: method on your main context. This will bring those background-fetched objects to your foreground context, ready to be used in your UI thread.

Discussion

Fetching on the main thread is not a good idea unless you have a very limited number of items in your Core Data stack, because a fetch generally issues a search call to Core Data. It then has to fetch some data for you, usually using a predicate. To make your UI more responsive, it's best that you issue your fetches on a background context.

You can have as many contexts as you want in your app, but there is one golden rule here. You cannot pass managed objects between contexts on different threads, because the objects are not thread-safe. That means that if you fetch objects on a background context, you cannot use them on the main thread. The correct way of passing managed objects between threads is to fetch them on a background thread, and then bring them into the main context (running on the main thread) using the `objectWithID:` method of your main context. This method accepts an object of type `NSManagedObjectID`, so in your background thread, instead of actually fetching the full managed objects, just fetch their persistent IDs and then pass those IDs to the main context to get the full object for you. This means that you do your actual searches and fetches in the background, grab the IDs of the objects that you found, and then pass those IDs to the main context for retrieval. This way, the main context will get a persistent ID to the objects, and the retrieval of those objects from the persistent store will be much faster than actually doing your whole search on the main context.

For the purpose of this recipe, I'm going to assume that you've already created a managed object model object named `Person` similar to that shown in Figure 17-12:

Figure 17-12. Our simple Core Data model for this recipe

With this model, before attempting to fetch anything from the stack, I'm going to populate the stack with 1,000 `Person` objects like so:

```
func populateDatabase(){

  for counter in 0..<1000{
    let person = NSEntityDescription.insertNewObjectForEntityForName(
      NSStringFromClass(Person.classForCoder()),
      inManagedObjectContext: managedObjectContext!) as Person

    person.firstName = "First name \(counter)"
    person.lastName = "Last name \(counter)"
```

```
      person.age = counter
    }

    var savingError: NSError?
    if managedObjectContext!.save(&savingError){
      println("Managed to populate the database")
    } else {
      if let error = savingError{
        println("Failed to populate the database. Error = \(error)")
      }
    }

}
```

Note how I use the NSStringFromClass to change the name of the Person class into a string and then instantiate objects of that type. Some programmers prefer just to type "Person" as a literal string, but the problem with hardcoding your string in such a manner is that, if you change your mind later and want to change the name of the Person in your Core Data stack, the hardcoded string will stay there and you might get crashes in your app at *runtime* because the model object named Person no longer exists. But if you use the aforementioned function to change the name of a class to a string, if that class's name changed or that class doesn't exist anymore, you'll get *compile-time* errors; and before you ship your app, you'll know that you have to fix those errors.

Before going any further with this recipe, I'm going to assume that you've already used the method that we just wrote to populate your database. So here is the general idea of how we are going to go about fetching our objects on a background context:

1. We create a background context using the initWithConcurrencyType: constructor of the NSManagedObjectContext class and pass the value of NSPrivateQueueCon currencyType to this method. This gives us a context that has its own private dispatch queue, so if you call the performBlock: block on the context, the block will be executed on a private background queue.

2. We then set the value of the persistentStoreCoordinator property of our background context to the instance of our persistent store coordinator. This binds our background context with our persistent store coordinator so that if you issue a fetch on the background context, it will be able to fetch the data right from disk or wherever the coordinator is storing the data.

3. We issue a performBlock: call on our background context and then issue a fetch request to look for all persons in the Core Data stack whose ages are between 100 and 200. Remember that the point of this exercise is not how realistic the data is. We are just trying to demonstrate a background fetch. When constructing the fetch

request, we set its `resultType` property's value to `NSManagedObjectIDResult Type`. This ensures that the results that come back from this fetch request are not actual managed objects, but just the object IDs. As explained before, we don't want to fetch managed objects because they are fetched on the background context and therefore can't be used on the main thread. So we fetch their IDs on the background context and then turn those IDs into real managed objects on the main context, after which the objects can be used on the main thread.

This is how we construct our fetch request:

```
func newFetchRequest() -> NSFetchRequest{

  let request = NSFetchRequest(entityName:
    NSStringFromClass(Person.classForCoder()))

  request.fetchBatchSize = 20
  request.predicate = NSPredicate(format: "(age >= 100) AND (age <= 200)")

  request.resultType = .ManagedObjectIDResultType
  return request

}
```

And this is how we go about creating our background context and then issue the fetch request on it:

```
func application(application: UIApplication,
  didFinishLaunchingWithOptions launchOptions: [NSObject : AnyObject]?) -> Bool {

    /* Set up the background context */
    let backgroundContext = NSManagedObjectContext(
      concurrencyType: .PrivateQueueConcurrencyType)

    backgroundContext.persistentStoreCoordinator =
    persistentStoreCoordinator

    /* Issue a block on the background context */
    backgroundContext.performBlock{[weak self] in

      var fetchError: NSError?
      let personIds = backgroundContext.executeFetchRequest(
        self!.newFetchRequest(),
        error: &fetchError) as [NSManagedObjectID]

      if fetchError == nil{

        let mainContext = self!.managedObjectContext

        /* Now go on the main context and get the objects on that
        context using their IDs */
        dispatch_async(dispatch_get_main_queue(), {
```

```
              for personId in personIds{
                let person = mainContext!.objectWithID(personId) as Person
                self!.mutablePersons.append(person)
              }
              self!.processPersons()
              })
          } else {
            println("Failed to execute the fetch request")
          }

        }

        return true
    }
```

This code collects all the managed objects in an array and then calls the processPer
sons method on our app delegate to process the results in the array. We will develop
this method like so:

```
import UIKit
import CoreData

@UIApplicationMain
class AppDelegate: UIResponder, UIApplicationDelegate {

  var window: UIWindow?
  var mutablePersons = [Person]()

  func processPersons(){

    /* Do your work here using the mutablePersons property of your app*/

  }

  <# rest of the code #>

}
```

See Also

Recipe 7.1; Recipe 17.3; Recipe 17.5

17.9. Using Custom Data Types in Your Core Data Model

Problem

You believe the choice of data types provided by Core Data doesn't suit your needs. You
may need to use more data types, such as UIColor, in your model objects, but Core Data
doesn't offer that data type out of the box.

Solution

Use transformable data types.

Discussion

Core Data allows you to create properties on your model objects and assign data types to those properties. Your choice is quite limited: a data type can be used in Core Data only if it can be turned into an instance of NSData and back again. By default, there are a number of popular classes, such as UIColor, that you cannot use for your properties. So what is the way around it? The answer is *transformable properties*. Let me explain the concept to you first.

So let's say that we want to create a model object in Core Data and name that model object Laptop. This object is going to have two properties: a model of type String and a color that we want to be of type UIColor. Core Data does not offer that data type, so we have to create a subclass of the NSValueTransformer class. Let's name our class ColorTransformer. Here are the things you have to do in the implementation of your class:

1. Override the allowsReverseTransformation class method of your class and return true from it. This will tell Core Data that you can turn colors into data and data back into colors.

2. Override the transformedValueClass class method of your class and return the class name of NSData from it. The return value of this class method tells Core Data what class you are transforming your custom value to. In this case, you are turning UIColor to NSData, so we need to return the class name of NSData from this method.

3. Override the transformedValue: instance method of your transformer. In your method, take the incoming value (which will in this case be an instance of UIColor), transform it to NSData, and return that data back from this method.

4. Override the reverseTransformedValue: instance method of your transformer to do the opposite: take the incoming value, which will be data, and transform it to color.

Given this information, we are going to proceed to implementing our transformer as follows. We store a color as data simply by breaking it into integer components and storing them in an array:

```
import UIKit

class ColorTransformer: NSValueTransformer {

  override class func allowsReverseTransformation() -> Bool{
    return true
  }
```

```swift
override class func transformedValueClass() -> AnyClass{
  return NSData.classForCoder()
}

override func transformedValue(value: AnyObject!) -> AnyObject {

  /* Transform color to data */

  let color = value as UIColor

  var red: CGFloat = 0
  var green: CGFloat = 0
  var blue: CGFloat = 0
  var alpha: CGFloat = 0
  color.getRed(&red, green: &green, blue: &blue, alpha: &alpha)

  var components = [red, green, blue, alpha]
  let dataFromColors = NSData(bytes: components,
    length: sizeofValue(components))

  return dataFromColors

}

override func reverseTransformedValue(value: AnyObject!) -> AnyObject {

  /* Transform data to color */
  let data = value as NSData
  var components = [CGFloat](count: 4, repeatedValue: 0.0)
  data.getBytes(&components, length: sizeofValue(components))

  let color = UIColor(red: components[0],
    green: components[1],
    blue: components[2],
    alpha: components[3])

  return color

}

}
```

Now let's go to our data model to create the Laptop managed object and create its attributes/properties. Ensure that the color attribute is transformable, and while this attribute is selected, press Alt+Command+3 on your keyboard to open the Model Inspector for this attribute. In the name field of the transformable class, enter the name of your custom transformer—in this case, ColorTransformer—as shown in Figure 17-13.

Figure 17-13. Setting up our model with a transformable attribute

Generate the class file for the `Laptop` managed object. After doing that, go into the implementation of this managed object and you'll notice that the `color` attribute of your class is of type `AnyObject`.

```
import Foundation
import CoreData

@objc(Laptop) class Laptop: NSManagedObject {

    @NSManaged var model: String
    @NSManaged var color: AnyObject

}
```

This is good, but to make it better and help the compiler catch issues for us if we assign values of the incorrect type to this property, let's manually change this data type to `UIColor`:

```
import Foundation
import CoreData
import UIKit

@objc(Laptop) class Laptop: NSManagedObject {

    @NSManaged var model: String
    @NSManaged var color: UIColor

}
```

In order for you to be able to set the data type of the `color` property to `UIColor`, you must ensure that you have imported the `UIKit` framework into the model class. The `UIColor` class is defined in the `UIKit` framework, and if that framework is missing from your model class, you will get a compilation error.

So now we are going to put all the things we learned here to use. In our app delegate, we create an instance of `Laptop` and set its color to red. Then we insert that into our

Core Data stack and try to read it back to see whether the color could successfully be saved and then retrieved from the database:

```
import UIKit
import CoreData

@UIApplicationMain
class AppDelegate: UIResponder, UIApplicationDelegate {

  var window: UIWindow?

  func application(application: UIApplication,
    didFinishLaunchingWithOptions launchOptions:
    [NSObject : AnyObject]?) -> Bool {

      /* Save the laptop with a given color first */
      let laptop = NSEntityDescription.insertNewObjectForEntityForName(
        NSStringFromClass(Laptop.classForCoder()),
        inManagedObjectContext: managedObjectContext!) as Laptop

      laptop.model = "model name"
      laptop.color = UIColor.redColor()

      var savingError: NSError?
      if managedObjectContext!.save(&savingError) == false{
        if let error = savingError{
          println("Failed to save the laptop. Error = \(error)")
        }
      }

      /* Now find the same laptop */
      let fetch = NSFetchRequest(entityName:
        NSStringFromClass(Laptop.classForCoder()))
      fetch.fetchLimit = 1
      fetch.predicate = NSPredicate(format: "color == %@", UIColor.redColor())

      var fetchingError: NSError?
      let laptops = managedObjectContext!.executeFetchRequest(fetch,
        error: &fetchingError) as [AnyObject]!

      /* Check for 1 because out fetch limit is 1 */
      if laptops.count == 1 && fetchingError == nil{

        let fetchedLaptop = laptops[0] as Laptop

        if fetchedLaptop.color == UIColor.redColor(){
          println("Right colored laptop was fetched")
        } else {
          println("Could not find the laptop with the given color")
        }

      } else {
```

```
      if let error = fetchingError{
        println("Could not fetch the laptop with the given color. " +
          "Error = \(error)")
      }
    }

    return true
  }

  <# the rest of the code #>

}
```

CHAPTER 18

Dates, Calendars, and Events

18.0. Introduction

The Event Kit and Event Kit UI frameworks allow iOS developers to access the Calendar database on an iOS device. You can insert, read, and modify events using the Event Kit framework. The Event Kit UI framework allows you to present built-in SDK GUI elements that allow the user to manipulate the Calendar database manually. In this chapter, we focus on the Event Kit framework first and then learn about the Event Kit UI framework.

With the Event Kit framework, a programmer can modify the user's Calendar database without the user knowing. However, this is not a very good practice. In fact, Apple prohibits programmers from doing so and asks us to always notify users about any changes that the program makes to the Calendar database. Here is a quote from Apple:

> If your application modifies a user's Calendar database programmatically, it must get confirmation from the user before doing so. An application should never modify the Calendar database without specific instruction from the user.

iOS comes with a built-in Calendar app that can work with different types of calendars, such as local, CalDAV, and so forth. In this chapter, we will be working with different types of calendars as well. To make sure you are prepared to run the code in some of the recipes in this chapter, please create an iCloud account and log in to that account using your iOS device. Now that you have your iCloud account, pull out your iOS device, head over to the Settings app, and choose iCloud. There, you can log into your iCloud account using the credentials that you created for your account earlier. This will bring all your iCloud calendars into your device.

To run the example code in this chapter, you must add the Event Kit framework, and in some cases the Event Kit UI framework, to your application. Using the Modules feature in the new LLVM compiler, the only thing you need to do to include these two frameworks into your projects is to import their appropriate umbrella headers into your source code, like so:

```
import UIKit
import EventKit
import EventKitUI
```

 iOS Simulator does not simulate the Calendar app. To test the recipes in this chapter, you must run and debug your program on a real iOS device. All examples in this chapter have been tested on a real device.

18.1. Constructing Date Objects

Problem

You want to construct an object of type NSDate using various components such as year, month, week, and day of week.

Solution

Use the dateWithEra:year:month:day:hour:minute:second:nanosecond: method of the NSCalendar class like so:

```
enum GregorianEra: Int{
  case BC = 0
  case AD
}

let date = NSCalendar.currentCalendar().dateWithEra(GregorianEra.AD.rawValue,
  year: 2014,
  month: 12,
  day: 25,
  hour: 10,
  minute: 20,
  second: 30,
  nanosecond: 40)

if date != nil{
  println("The date is \(date)")
} else {
  println("Could not construct the date")
}
```

Discussion

The `dateWithEra:year:month:day:hour:minute:second:nanosecond:` method of the `NSCalendar` class is very straightforward. In fact, all its parameters are quite easy to understand and are self-explanatory. The only parameter that might need a bit of explanation is `era` (the first parameter). This is an integer value that if set to 0, specifies the BC era and if set to 1, specifies the AD era in the Gregorian Calendar.

Another way of creating an instance of the `NSDate` class is by adding a date component to another date object—for instance, adding the equivalent of three days to a date object that is already of type `NSDate`. You can achieve this by calling the `dateByAddingU nit:value:toDate:options:` method of the `NSCalendar` class. The first parameter to this method is of type `NSCalendarUnit`, which is an enumeration that has been defined by Apple. This enumeration contains items such as `CalendarUnitHour` and `Calendar UnitMinute`. This parameter defines which part of the given date we want to add another component to. For instance, if you want to add two hours to an existing date object, specify the `CalendarUnitHour` value for this parameter. Here is an example:

```
let now = NSDate()

println(now)

let newDate = NSCalendar.currentCalendar().dateByAddingUnit(
  .CalendarUnitHour,
  value: 10,
  toDate: now,
  options:.MatchNextTime)

println(newDate)
```

In this example code, we add 10 hours to the current date and time, after which we print the current date and time as well as the modified date and time to the console. The result is something similar to that shown here:

```
2014-06-23 19:16:33 +0000
2014-06-24 05:16:33 +0000
```

See Also

Recipe 18.0

18.2. Retrieving Date Components

Problem

You want to retrieve the year, month, week, and other components of an instance of the `NSDate` class.

Solution

Use the `componentsInTimeZone:fromDate:` method of the `NSCalendar` class.

```
let now = NSDate()
let components = NSCalendar.currentCalendar().componentsInTimeZone(
  NSTimeZone.localTimeZone(), fromDate: now)

dump(components)
```

Discussion

The aforementioned method on the `NSCalendar` class allows you to retrieve an instance of the `NSDateComponents` class. This class has properties that you can extract and use, such as `era` (defined in Recipe 18.1), `year`, `month`, and `year`. Once you have date components in an instance of `NSDateComponents`, you can use that to construct dates as well, using the `dateFromComponents:` method of the `NSCalendar` class. Here is an example:

```
var components = NSDateComponents()
components.year = 2015
components.month = 3
components.day = 20
components.hour = 10
components.minute = 20
components.second = 30
let date = NSCalendar.currentCalendar().dateFromComponents(components)
println(date)
```

See Also

Recipe 18.1

18.3. Requesting Permission to Access Calendars

Problem

You want to add events or make other changes to the user's calendar, but this requires the user to give your app permission.

Solution

Invoke the `authorizationStatusForEntityType:` class method of the `EKEventStore` class and pass one of the following values to it as its parameter:

`EKEntityTypeEvent`
Permission to access/add/delete/modify events in the user's calendars.

EKEntityTypeReminder

Permission to access/add/delete/modify reminders in the user's calendars.

The method returns one of the following values:

EKAuthorizationStatusAuthorized

Your app is authorized to access the given type of items (events or reminders).

EKAuthorizationStatusDenied

The user has previously denied your app's access to the event store, and this remains in force.

EKAuthorizationStatusNotDetermined

Your app has not attempted to access the event store before, so the user has not been asked to grant or reject permission. In this case, you need to ask for permission from the user to access the event store on her device using the requestAccessToEntityType:completion: instance method of the EKEventStore class.

EKAuthorizationStatusRestricted

Due to some other restrictions on the device, such as parental controls, your app cannot access the event store on the device.

Here is a code snippet that handles all these cases for us:

```
let eventStore = EKEventStore()

switch EKEventStore.authorizationStatusForEntityType(EKEntityTypeEvent){

case .Authorized:
  extractEventEntityCalendarsOutOfStore(eventStore)
case .Denied:
  displayAccessDenied()
case .NotDetermined:
  eventStore.requestAccessToEntityType(EKEntityTypeEvent, completion:
    {[weak self] (granted: Bool, error: NSError!) -> Void in
      if granted{
        self!.extractEventEntityCalendarsOutOfStore(eventStore)
      } else {
        self!.displayAccessDenied()
      }
    })
case .Restricted:
  displayAccessRestricted()
}
```

This code snippet uses methods that will be described in the Discussion section of this recipe.

Discussion

The more Apple works on iOS, the more it pays attention to the user's privacy. So it is no shock that apps that want to access the user's event store, which contains all the calendars that have events and reminders, have to ask the user for permission first. In fact, if you don't ask for permission and then attempt to access the user's calendars, iOS blocks the execution of your app and displays a dialog to the user asking for permission. This dialog looks similar to the one shown in Figure 18-1.

Figure 18-1. Asking the user to grant or reject permission to an app wanting to access the event store on her device

Now as good citizens of the iOS land, it's best that we ask the Event Kit framework for permission to access the user's event store *before* attempting to make the requests. The `requestAccessToEntityType:completion:` instance method of the `EKEventStore` class is the best way to do that. The `requestAccessToEntityType` parameter can be either `EKEntityTypeEvent` or `EKEntityTypeReminder`, depending on whether you want to access the events or the reminders, respectively, and the `completion` parameter needs to be a block object of the following type:

```
typealias EKEventStoreRequestAccessCompletionHandler = (Bool, NSError!) -> Void
```

When you call this method, iOS asks the user to grant permission to your app to access the event store on her iOS device. Depending on her decision, your app may or may not get access. You can find that out by reading the value of the `granted` Boolean parameter of the `completion` block. If this value is `false`, you can then read the value of the `error` parameter to determine what went wrong.

In the Solution section code snippet, we call some instance methods that are supposed to display an error message to the user for the `EKAuthorizationStatusDenied` and the `EKAuthorizationStatusRestricted` return values of the `authorizationStatusForEn tityType:` type method of the `EKEventStore` class. The implementation of these two methods is extremely simple:

```
func displayAccessDenied(){
    println("Access to the event store is denied.")
```

```
    }

    func displayAccessRestricted(){
      println("Access to the event store is restricted.")
    }
```

The methods just display a message to the user letting her know that your app cannot access the event store because it is being denied access. Now under the EKAuthoriza tionStatusNotDetermined status, if the granted value is true, we call the extractE ventEntityCalendarsOutOfStore: instance method of our class. This is a method that will take the instance of our event store and then try to use its calendarsForEntity Type: instance method to get a list of calendars for that specific event type. The parameter to this method again can be either EKEntityTypeEvent or EKEntityTypeRe minder, and the return value that comes back from this method will be an array of calendars that can handle events or reminders, respectively. The objects in the returned array will be of type EKCalendar.

Instances of EKCalendar represent a calendar, as their name shows, in the user's event store. As you saw in in the Introduction of this chapter, the user may have different accounts on her device and under each account, she might have different calendars. For instance, you can create multiple calendars under your iCloud account. Each instance of the EKCalendar class represents one calendar object on the user's device.

Instances of the EKCalendar class have some interesting properties, such as the following:

title
:   A string value that is set to the title of the calendar, such as "Birthdays."

type
:   The type of the calendar. This value is of type EKCalendarType and can be equal to EKCalendarTypeLocal, EKCalendarTypeCalDAV, etc. This is the type of the calendar. For instance, iCloud calendars can be CalDAV calendars, so by querying this value, you can find out what type of calendar object you are dealing with. The type of calendar will in turn tell you what you can and cannot do with that calendar.

CGColor
:   This is the color of the calendar. This is a Core Graphics color, and you can convert it to UIColor by using the colorWithCGColor: class method of the UIColor class.

allowsContentModifications
:   This property tells you if the current calendar allows you to make any modifications to it. A modification could be an insertion, deletion, or simple change of an existing event or reminder in that calendar.

As you saw earlier, we were calling the extractEventEntityCalendarsOutOfStore: instance method of our app delegate, which we are now going to implement. Using what you have learned about calendar objects, you can now understand the implementation of this method:

```swift
func extractEventEntityCalendarsOutOfStore(eventStore: EKEventStore){

let calendarTypes = [
  "Local",
  "CalDAV",
  "Exchange",
  "Subscription",
  "Birthday",
]

let calendars = eventStore.calendarsForEntityType(EKEntityTypeEvent)
  as [EKCalendar]

for calendar in calendars{

  println("Calendar title = \(calendar.title)")
  println("Calendar type = \(calendarTypes[Int(calendar.type.value)])")

  let color = UIColor(CGColor: calendar.CGColor)
  println("Calendar color = \(color)")

  if calendar.allowsContentModifications{
    println("This calendar allows modifications")
  } else {
    println("This calendar does not allow modifications")
  }

  println("-------------------------")

}

}
```

When you run this code on your device, depending on how many calendars you set up on your iCloud account and other calendars that may have been linked to your computer, you will get results similar to those shown here, printed to your console:

```
Calendar title = vandad.np@gmail.com
Calendar type = CalDAV
Calendar color = UIDeviceRGBColorSpace 0.160784 0.321569 0.639216 1
This calendar allows modifications
-------------------------
Calendar title = init Mobile Calendar
Calendar type = CalDAV
Calendar color = UIDeviceRGBColorSpace 0.0941176 0.172549 0.341176 1
This calendar allows modifications
-------------------------
Calendar title = UK Holidays
Calendar type = Subscription
```

```
Calendar color = UIDeviceRGBColorSpace 1 0.584314 0 1
This calendar does not allow modifications
-------------------------
Calendar title = Schedule
Calendar type = CalDAV
Calendar color = UIDeviceRGBColorSpace 1 0.584314 0 1
This calendar allows modifications
-------------------------
```

See Also

Recipe 18.0, "Introduction"

18.4. Retrieving Calendar Groups on an iOS Device

Problem

The user has different calendar accounts, such as an iCloud account and a separate CalDAV account, and a calendar named *Calendar* under both of these accounts. You want to create an event under the calendar appropriately titled "Calendar" that belongs to the user's iCloud account, and not the other accounts that she might have on her iOS device.

Solution

Find the event sources in the user's event store by going through the `sources` array property in an instance of `EKEventStore`. This array will contain objects of type `EK Source`, each of which represents a group of calendars in the event store on the user's device.

Discussion

Let's not make anything complicated here. To make a long story short, users can have different accounts (iCloud, Exchange, etc.). Each of these accounts, if they support calendars, is treated as an *event source*. An event source will then contain calendars.

To find a specific calendar with a given title, you first have to find that calendar in the correct event source. For instance, the following code snippet attempts to find the event source titled *iCloud* on the user's device:

```swift
func findIcloudEventSource(){
  var icloudEventSource: EKSource?

  let eventStore = EKEventStore()
  for source in eventStore.sources() as [EKSource]{
    if source.sourceType.value == EKSourceTypeCalDAV.value &&
      source.title.lowercaseString == "icloud"{
```

```
        icloudEventSource = source
    }
  }

  if let source = icloudEventSource{
    println("The iCloud event source was found = \(source)")
  } else {
    println("Could not find the iCloud event source")
  }

}
```

 By following the instructions in Recipe 18.3, ensure that you have already asked the user for permission to access the calendars on her device.

If you look closely, you will see that we are also checking the type of the event source. This is because we know that iCloud calendars are CalDAV; hence, finding the source not only by the title "iCloud," but also by its type gives us more precision in pinpointing the correct event source.

After you find your target EKSource event source, you can enumerate and go through the different calendar objects that it holds by invoking the calendarsForEntityType: instance method on it. As its parameter, pass EKEntityTypeEvent to look for calendars that support events, or EKEntityTypeReminder to look for calendars that support reminders. Bear in mind that the return value of the aforementioned method is of type NSSet, not an array. But you can enumerate the items in that set just like you would an array:

```
func findIcloudEventSource(){
  var icloudEventSource: EKSource?

  let eventStore = EKEventStore()
  for source in eventStore.sources() as [EKSource]{
    if source.sourceType.value == EKSourceTypeCalDAV.value &&
      source.title.lowercaseString == "icloud"{
        icloudEventSource = source
    }
  }

  if let source = icloudEventSource{
    println("The iCloud event source was found = \(source)")

    let calendars = source.calendarsForEntityType(EKEntityTypeEvent)

    for calendar in calendars.allObjects as [EKCalendar]{
      println(calendar)
```

```
    }
  } else {
    println("Could not find the iCloud event source")
  }

}
```

See Also

Recipe 18.3

18.5. Adding Events to Calendars

Problem

You want to create new events in users' calendars.

Solution

Find the calendar you want to insert your event into (please refer to Recipe 18.3 and
Recipe 18.4). Create an object of type EKEvent using the eventWithEventStore: class
method of EKEvent and save the event into the user's calendar using the saveE
vent:span:error: instance method of EKEventStore:

```
func createEventWithTitle(
    title: String,
    startDate: NSDate,
    endDate: NSDate,
    inCalendar: EKCalendar,
    inEventStore: EKEventStore,
    notes: String) -> Bool{

    /* If a calendar does not allow modification of its contents,
    then we cannot insert an event into it */
    if inCalendar.allowsContentModifications == false{
      println("The selected calendar does not allow modifications.")
      return false
    }

    /* Create an event */
    var event = EKEvent(eventStore: inEventStore)
    event.calendar = inCalendar

    /* Set the properties of the event such as its title,
    start date/time, end date/time, etc. */
    event.title = title
    event.notes = notes
    event.startDate = startDate
```

```
    event.endDate = endDate

    /* Finally, save the event into the calendar */
    var error:NSError?

    let result = inEventStore.saveEvent(event,
      span: EKSpanThisEvent,
      error: &error)

    if result == false{
      if let theError = error{
        println("An error occurred \(theError)")
      }
    }

    return result
}
```

As you can see, this method expects a calendar object and an event store to create the event in. In Recipe 18.4, we learned how to find event sources and the calendars that are associated with those sources. We are therefore going to create some handy methods that can search in all the available event sources, and all the available calendars in those sources, for the specific calendar we are looking for. So here are our methods:

```
func sourceInEventStore(
  eventStore: EKEventStore,
  type: EKSourceType,
  title: String) -> EKSource?{

    for source in eventStore.sources() as [EKSource]{
      if source.sourceType.value == type.value &&
        source.title.caseInsensitiveCompare(title) ==
        NSComparisonResult.OrderedSame{
          return source
      }
    }

    return nil
}

func calendarWithTitle(
  title: String,
  type: EKCalendarType,
  source: EKSource,
  eventType: EKEntityType) -> EKCalendar?{

    for calendar in source.calendarsForEntityType(eventType).allObjects
      as [EKCalendar]{
      if calendar.title.caseInsensitiveCompare(title) ==
        NSComparisonResult.OrderedSame &&
        calendar.type.value == type.value{
          return calendar
```

```
        }
    }

    return nil
}
```

The `sourceInEventStore:sourceType:sourceTitle:` is able to find an event source with a given type and title. For instance, you can find the iCloud event source by passing EKSourceTypeCalDAV as the type and iCloud as the title and you will get the event source, if it is present on the device. After you have the event source, use the `calendarWithTitle:type:inSource:forEventType:` method to get a specific calendar inside a given event source. So if you want to find an iCloud calendar titled *Calendar*, assuming that you've already found the event source, pass EKCalendarTypeCalDAV as the type of the calendar and EKEntityTypeEvent as the event type.

Now that you have these handy methods at your disposal, you can create a new event as shown here:

```
func insertEventIntoStore(store: EKEventStore){

  let icloudSource = sourceInEventStore(store,
    type: EKSourceTypeCalDAV,
    title: "iCloud")

  if icloudSource == nil{
    println("You have not configured iCloud for your device.")
    return
  }

  let calendar = calendarWithTitle("Calendar",
    type: EKCalendarTypeCalDAV,
    source: icloudSource!,
    eventType: EKEntityTypeEvent)

  if calendar == nil{
    println("Could not find the calendar we were looking for.")
    return
  }

  /* The event starts from today, right now */
  let startDate = NSDate()

  /* And the event ends this time tomorrow.
  24 hours, 60 minutes per hour and 60 seconds per minute
  hence 24 * 60 * 60 */
  let endDate = startDate.dateByAddingTimeInterval(24 * 60 * 60)

  if createEventWithTitle("My Concert",
    startDate: startDate,
    endDate: endDate,
    inCalendar: calendar!,
```

```
    inEventStore: store,
    notes: ""){
    println("Successfully created the event.")
  } else {
    println("Failed to create the event.")
  }

}
```

Discussion

To programmatically create a new event in a calendar on an iOS device, we must do the following:

1. Allocate and initialize an instance of `EKEventStore`.

2. Find the calendar we want to save the event to (please refer to Recipe 18.4). We must make sure the target calendar supports modifications by checking that the calendar object's `allowsContentModifications` property is `true`. If it is not, you must choose a different calendar or forgo saving the event.

3. When you find your target calendar, create an event of type `EKEvent` using the `eventWithEventStore:` type method of `EKEvent`.

4. Set the properties of the new event such as its `title`, `startDate`, and `endDate`.

5. Associate your event with the calendar that you found in step 2 using the `calendars` property of an instance of `EKEvent`.

6. When you are done setting the properties of your event, add that event to the calendar using the `saveEvent:span:error:` instance method of `EKEventStore`. The return value of this method (a `BOOL` value) indicates whether the event was successfully inserted into the Calendar database. If the operation fails, the `NSError` object passed to the `error` parameter of this method will contain the error that occurred in the system while inserting this event.

If you attempt to insert an event without specifying a target calendar, or if you insert an event into a calendar that cannot be modified, the `saveEvent:span:error:` instance method of `EKEventStore` will fail with an error similar to this:

```
Error Domain=EKErrorDomain Code=1 "No calendar has been set."
UserInfo=0x15d860 {NSLocalizedDescription=No calendar has been set.}
```

Running our code on an iOS device, we will see an event created in the Calendar database, as shown in Figure 18-2.

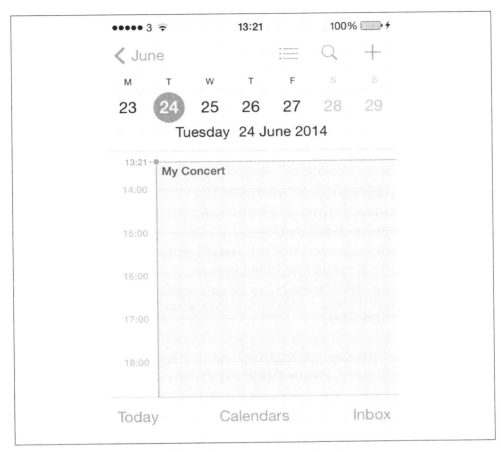

Figure 18-2. Programmatically adding an event to a calendar

iOS syncs online calendars with the iOS calendar. These calendars could be Exchange, CalDAV, and other common formats. Creating an event on a CalDAV calendar on an iOS device will create the same event on the server. The server changes are also reflected in the iOS Calendar database when the Calendar database is synced with the server.

See Also

Recipe 18.3

18.6. Accessing the Contents of Calendars

Problem

You want to retrieve events of type EKEvent from a calendar of type EKCalendar on an iOS device.

Solution

Follow these steps:

1. Instantiate an object of type EKEventStore.

2. Using the techniques that you learned earlier in this chapter, find the calendar object that you want to inspect and read from.

3. Determine the time and date where you want to start the search in the calendar and the time and date where the search must stop.

4. Pass the calendar object (found in step 2), along with the two dates you found in step 3, to the predicateForEventsWithStartDate:endDate:calendars: instance method of EKEventStore.

5. Pass the predicate created in step 4 to the eventsMatchingPredicate: instance method of EKEventStore. The result of this method is an array of EKEvent objects (if any) that fell between the given dates (step 3) in the specified calendar (step 2).

This code illustrates the preceding steps:

```
func readEvents(){

  /* Instantiate the event store */
  let eventStore = EKEventStore()

  let icloudSource = sourceInEventStore(eventStore,
    type: EKSourceTypeCalDAV,
    title: "iCloud")

  if icloudSource == nil{
    println("You have not configured iCloud for your device.")
    return
  }

  let calendar = calendarWithTitle("Calendar",
    type: EKCalendarTypeCalDAV,
    source: icloudSource!,
    eventType: EKEntityTypeEvent)

  if calendar == nil{
    println("Could not find the calendar we were looking for.")
```

```
    return
}

/* The event starts from today, right now */
let startDate = NSDate()

/* The end date will be 1 day from today */
let endDate = startDate.dateByAddingTimeInterval(24 * 60 * 60)

/* Create the predicate that we can later pass to the
event store in order to fetch the events */
let searchPredicate = eventStore.predicateForEventsWithStartDate(
  startDate,
  endDate: endDate,
  calendars: [calendar!])

/* Fetch all the events that fall between
the starting and the ending dates */
let events = eventStore.eventsMatchingPredicate(searchPredicate)
  as [EKEvent]

if events.count == 0{
  println("No events could be found")
} else {

  /* Go through all the events and print their information
  out to the console */
  for event in events{
    println("Event title = \(event.title)")
    println("Event start date = \(event.startDate)")
    println("Event end date = \(event.endDate)")
  }
}

}
```

 This code uses the methods we learned in Recipe 18.5 to find an iCloud calendar. I highly encourage you to review that recipe if you have not already done so or if you are having difficulty understanding how this code works.

Discussion

As mentioned in this chapter's Introduction, an iOS device can be configured with different types of calendars using CalDAV (for iCloud, etc.), Exchange, and so on. Each calendar that is accessible by the Event Kit framework is encompassed within an EKCalendar object. You can fetch events inside a calendar in different ways, but the easiest way is to create and execute a specially formatted specification of dates and times, called a *predicate*, inside an event store.

A predicate of type `NSPredicate` that we can use in the Event Kit framework can be created using the `predicateForEventsWithStartDate:endDate:calendars:` instance method of an `EKEventStore`. The parameters to this method are the following:

`predicateForEventsWithStartDate`
    The starting date and time from when the events have to be fetched.

`endDate`
    The ending date up until which the events will be fetched.

`calendars`
    The array of calendars to search for events between the starting and ending dates.

Be sure to ask the user for permission before attempting to access events or any other objects in her calendars. You can learn more about this in Recipe 18.3.

See Also

Recipe 18.3

18.7. Removing Events from Calendars

Problem

You want to be able to delete a specific event or series of events from users' calendars.

Solution

Use the `removeEvent:span:commit:error:` instance method of `EKEventStore`.

Discussion

The `removeEvent:span:commit:error:` instance method of `EKEventStore` can remove an instance of an event or all instances of a recurring event. For more information about recurring events, please refer to Recipe 18.8. In this recipe, we only remove an instance of the event and not the other instances of the same event in the calendar.

The parameters that we can pass to this method are the following:

`removeEvent`
    This is the `EKEvent` instance to be removed from the calendar.

`span`
    This is the parameter that tells the event store whether we want to remove only this event or all the occurrences of this event in the calendar. To remove only the current event, specify the `EKSpanThisEvent` value for the `removeEvent` parameter. To re-

move all occurrences of the same event from the calendar, pass the `EKSpanFu`
`tureEvents` value for the parameter.

`commit`
A Boolean value that tells the event store if the changes have to be saved on the
remote/local calendar immediately or not.

`error`
This parameter can be given a reference to an `NSError` object that will be filled with
the error (if any), when the return value of this method is `false`.

To demonstrate this, let's use the event creation method that we implemented in
Recipe 18.5. Then we can create an event in our iCloud calendar and attempt to delete
it from the event store:

```
func createAndDeleteEventInStore(store: EKEventStore){

  let icloudSource = sourceInEventStore(store,
    type: EKSourceTypeCalDAV,
    title: "iCloud")

  if icloudSource == nil{
    println("You have not configured iCloud for your device.")
    return
  }

  let calendar = calendarWithTitle("Calendar",
    type: EKCalendarTypeCalDAV,
    source: icloudSource!,
    eventType: EKEntityTypeEvent)

  if calendar == nil{
    println("Could not find the calendar we were looking for.")
    return
  }

  /* The event starts from today, right now */
  let startDate = NSDate()

  /* The end date will be 1 day from today */
  let endDate = startDate.dateByAddingTimeInterval(24 * 60 * 60)

  let eventTitle = "My Event"

  if createEventWithTitle(eventTitle,
    startDate: startDate,
    endDate: endDate,
    inCalendar: calendar!,
    inEventStore: store,
    notes: ""){
    println("Successfully created the event")
```

```
    } else {
      println("Could not create the event")
      return
    }

    if removeEventWithTitle(eventTitle,
      startDate: startDate,
      endDate: endDate,
      store: store,
      calendar: calendar!,
      notes: ""){
        println("Successfully created and deleted the event")
    } else {
      println("Failed to delete the event")
    }
  }
}
```

The `sourceInEventStore:sourceType:sourceTitle:` and `calendarWithTi
tle:type:inSource:forEventType:` methods that we are using in this example code
were described in Recipe 18.5. So I suggest you have a look at that recipe before proceeding with this one. In this code, after finding our target calendar, we create a dummy
event in the calendar using the method described in Recipe 18.5. After that, we attempt
to remove that event. The method that allows us to remove an existing event is coded
this way:

```
func removeEventWithTitle(
    title: String,
    startDate: NSDate,
    endDate: NSDate,
    store: EKEventStore,
    calendar: EKCalendar,
    notes: String) -> Bool{

  var result = false

  /* If a calendar does not allow modification of its contents,
  then we cannot insert an event into it */
  if calendar.allowsContentModifications == false{
    println("The selected calendar does not allow modifications.")
    return false
  }

  let predicate = store.predicateForEventsWithStartDate(startDate,
    endDate: endDate,
    calendars: [calendar])

  /* Get all the events that match the parameters */
  let events = store.eventsMatchingPredicate(predicate) as [EKEvent]

  if events.count > 0{

    /* Delete them all */
```

```
    for event in events{
      var error:NSError?

      if store.removeEvent(event,
        span: EKSpanThisEvent,
        commit: false,
        error: &error) == false{
          if let theError = error{
            println("Failed to remove \(event) with error = \(theError)")
          }
        }
    }

    var error:NSError?
    if store.commit(&error){
      println("Successfully committed")
      result = true
    } else if let theError = error{
      println("Failed to commit the event store with error = \(theError)")
    }

  } else {
    println("No events matched your input.")
  }

  return result

}
```

Because this method takes, as parameters, the calendar and the event store that the deletion has to occur on, it only has to do minimal processing. It just takes the start and end dates that we provide and creates a predicate to find the event that we are asking it to delete. After the event is found, it invokes the removeEvent:span:commit:error: instance method of the event store. This method, as explained previously, can delete a single event or an occurrence of events. For instance, you might have set an alarm on your device to wake you up every day at 6 o'clock in the morning. This is a recurring event. With what you learned here, you can delete *one* of the occurrences of that event but not all of them. But don't worry, we will soon learn about deleting recurring events in this chapter.

In this example, we are not committing the deletion of every event one by one. We are simply setting the commit parameter of the removeEvent:span:commit:error: method to false. After we are done, we are invoking the commit: method of the event store explicitly. The reason for this is that we don't really want to commit every single deletion. That would create a lot of overhead. We can delete as many events as we need to and then commit them all in one batch.

See Also

Recipe 18.3; Recipe 18.6

18.8. Adding Recurring Events to Calendars

Problem

You want to add a recurring event to a calendar.

Solution

In this example, we create an event that occurs on the same day, every month, for an entire year. The steps are as follows:

1. Create an instance of `EKEventStore`.

2. Find a modifiable calendar inside the event store, as we saw in Recipe 18.5.

3. Create an object of type `EKEvent` (for more information, refer to Recipe 18.5).

4. Set the appropriate values for the event, such as its `startDate` and `endDate` (for more information, refer to Recipe 18.5).

5. Instantiate an object of type `NSDate` that contains the exact date when the recurrence of this event ends. In this example, this date is one year from today's date.

6. Use the `recurrenceEndWithEndDate:` class method of `EKRecurrenceEnd` and pass the `NSDate` you created in step 5 to create an object of type `EKRecurrenceEnd`.

7. Allocate and then instantiate an object of type `EKRecurrenceRule` using the `initRecurrenceWithFrequency:interval:end:` method of `EKRecurrenceRule`. Pass the recurrence end date that you created in step 6 to the end parameter of this method. For more information about this method, please refer to this recipe's Discussion.

8. Assign the recurring event that you created in step 7 to the `recurringRule` property of the `EKEvent` object that was created in step 3.

9. Invoke the `saveEvent:span:error:` instance method with the event (created in step 3) as the `saveEvent` parameter and the value `EKSpanFutureEvents` for the span parameter. This will create our recurring event for us.

The following code illustrates these steps:

```
func createRecurringEventInStore(store: EKEventStore, calendar: EKCalendar)
    -> Bool{

    let event = EKEvent(eventStore: store)
```

```
/* Create an event that happens today and happens
every month for a year from now */
let startDate = NSDate()

 /* The event's end date is one hour from the moment it is created */
let oneHour:NSTimeInterval = 1 * 60 * 60
let endDate = startDate.dateByAddingTimeInterval(oneHour)

/* Assign the required properties, especially
the target calendar */
event.calendar = calendar
event.title = "My Event"
event.startDate = startDate
event.endDate = endDate

/* The end date of the recurring rule
is one year from now */
let oneYear:NSTimeInterval = 365 * 24 * 60 * 60;
let oneYearFromNow = startDate.dateByAddingTimeInterval(oneYear)

/* Create an Event Kit date from this date */
let recurringEnd = EKRecurrenceEnd.recurrenceEndWithEndDate(
  oneYearFromNow) as EKRecurrenceEnd

/* And the recurring rule. This event happens every
month (EKRecurrenceFrequencyMonthly), once a month (interval:1)
and the recurring rule ends a year from now (end:RecurringEnd) */

let recurringRule = EKRecurrenceRule(
  recurrenceWithFrequency: EKRecurrenceFrequencyMonthly,
  interval: 1,
  end: recurringEnd)

/* Set the recurring rule for the event */
event.recurrenceRules = [recurringRule]

var error:NSError?

if store.saveEvent(event, span: EKSpanFutureEvents, error: &error){
  println("Successfully created the recurring event.")
  return true
} else if let theError = error{
  println("Failed to create the recurring " +
    "event with error = \(theError)")
}

return false

}
```

In this code, we are using some of the methods and code snippets that we learned in Recipe 18.5. Have a look at the aforementioned recipe if you are unfamiliar with adding nonrecurring events to a calendar object.

When you run this code on your device and go to the Calendar app and tap on the created event, you will see something similar to that shown in Figure 18-3.

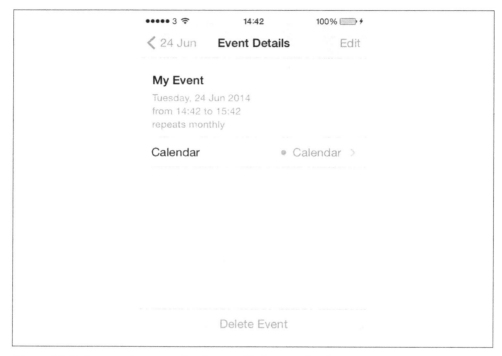

Figure 18-3. A recurring event has been added to a calendar

Discussion

A recurring event is an event that happens more than once. We can create a recurring event just like a normal one. Please refer to Recipe 18.5 for more information about inserting normal events into the Calendar database. The only difference between a recurring event and a normal event is that you apply a recurring rule to a recurring event. A recurring rule tells the Event Kit framework how the event has to occur in the future.

We create a recurring rule by instantiating an object of type `EKRecurrenceRule` using the `initRecurrenceWithFrequency:interval:end:` initialization method. Here are the parameters for this method:

initRecurrenceWithFrequency

Specifies whether you want the event to be repeated daily (EKRecurrenceFrequen cyDaily), weekly (EKRecurrenceFrequencyWeekly), monthly (EKRecurrenceFre quencyMonthly), or yearly (EKRecurrenceFrequencyYearly).

interval

A value greater than zero that specifies the interval between each occurrence's start and end period. For instance, if you want to create an event that happens every week, specify the EKRecurrenceFrequencyWeekly value with an interval of 1. If you want this event to happen every other week, specify EKRecurrenceFrequency Weekly with an interval of 2.

end

A date of type EKRecurrenceEnd that specifies the date when the recurring event ends in the specified calendar. This parameter is not the same as the event's end date (the endDate property of EKEvent). The end date of an event specifies when that specific event ends in the calendar, whereas the end parameter of the initRe currenceWithFrequency:interval:end: method specifies the final occurrence of the event in the database.

By editing this event (see Figure 18-4) in the Calendar application on an iOS device, you can see that the event is truly a recurring event that happens every month, on the same day the event was created, for a whole year.

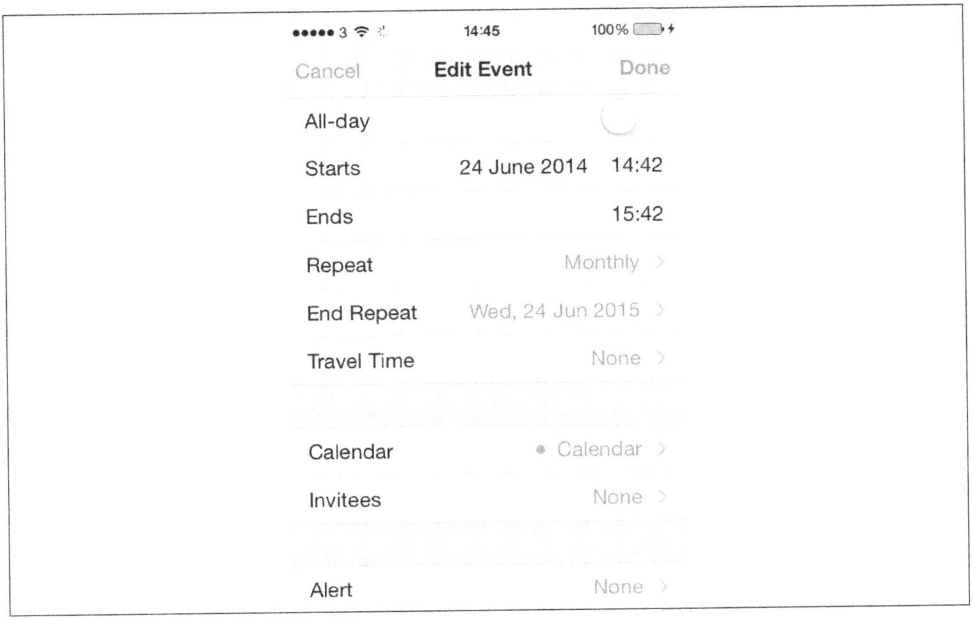

Figure 18-4. Editing a recurring event in the Calendar app on an iOS device

See Also

Recipe 18.5

18.9. Retrieving the Attendees of an Event

Problem

You want to retrieve the list of attendees for a specific event.

Solution

Use the `attendees` property of an instance of `EKEvent`. This property is of type `NSArray` and includes objects of type `EKParticipant`.

The example code that follows retrieves all the events that happen today (whatever the day may be) and print out useful event information, including the attendees of that event, to the console window:

```
func enumerateTodayEventsInStore(store: EKEventStore, calendar: EKCalendar){

  /* The event starts from today, right now */
  let startDate = NSDate()

  /* The end date will be 1 day from now */
  let endDate = startDate.dateByAddingTimeInterval(24 * 60 * 60)

  /* Create the predicate that we can later pass to
  the event store in order to fetch the events */
  let searchPredicate = store.predicateForEventsWithStartDate(
    startDate,
    endDate: endDate,
    calendars: [calendar])

  /* Fetch all the events that fall between the
  starting and the ending dates */
  let events = store.eventsMatchingPredicate(searchPredicate) as [EKEvent]

  /* Array of NSString equivalents of the values
  in the EKParticipantRole enumeration */
  let attendeeRole = [
    "Unknown",
    "Required",
    "Optional",
    "Chair",
    "Non Participant",
  ]

  /* Array of NSString equivalents of the values
  in the EKParticipantStatus enumeration */
```

```
let attendeeStatus = [
  "Unknown",
  "Pending",
  "Accepted",
  "Declined",
  "Tentative",
  "Delegated",
  "Completed",
  "In Process",
]

/* Array of NSString equivalents of the values
in the EKParticipantType enumeration */
let attendeeType = [
  "Unknown",
  "Person",
  "Room",
  "Resource",
  "Group"
]

/* Go through all the events and print their information
out to the console */

for event in events{

  println("Event title = \(event.title)")
  println("Event start date = \(event.startDate)")
  println("Event end date = \(event.endDate)")

  if event.attendees.count == 0{
    println("This event has no attendees")
    continue
  }

  for attendee in event.attendees as [EKParticipant]{
    println("Attendee name = \(attendee.name)")

    let role = attendeeRole[Int(attendee.participantRole.value)]
    println("Attendee role = \(role)")

    let status = attendeeStatus[Int(attendee.participantStatus.value)]
    println("Attendee status = \(status)")

    let type = attendeeStatus[Int(attendee.participantType.value)]
    println("Attendee type = \(type)")

    println("Attendee URL = \(attendee.URL)")

  }

}
```

```
}
```

 In this code snippet, we use vocabulary such as *stores*. If you are not familiar with stores and how you can retrieve calendar objects, please have a read through Recipe 18.4 before proceeding with this recipe.

Discussion

Different types of calendars, such as iCloud (CalDAV), can include participants in an event. iOS allows users to add participants to a calendar on the server, although not to the calendar on the iOS device. You can do this using iCloud, for instance.

Once the user adds participants to an event, you can use the `attendees` property of an instance of `EKEvent` to access the participant objects of type `EKParticipant`. Each participant has properties such as the following:

name
    This is the name of the participant. If you just specified the email address of a person to add him to an event, this field will be that email address.

URL
    This is usually the "mailto" URL for the attendee.

participantRole
    This is the role the attendee plays in the event. Different values that can be applied to this property are listed in the `EKParticipantRole` enumeration.

participantStatus
    This tells us whether this participant has accepted or declined the event request. This property could have other values, all specified in the `EKParticipantStatus` enumeration.

participantType
    This is of type `EKParticipantType`, which is an enumeration and, as its name implies, specifies the type of participant, such as group (`EKParticipantTypeGroup`) or individual person (`EKParticipantTypePerson`).

See Also

Recipe 18.5; Recipe 18.6

18.10. Adding Alarms to Calendars

Problem

You want to add alarms to the events in a calendar.

Solution

Use the `alarmWithRelativeOffset:` class method of `EKAlarm` to create an instance of `EKAlarm`. Add the alarm to an event using the `addAlarm:` instance method of `EKEvent`, like so:

```
func addAlarmToCalendarWithStore(store: EKEventStore, calendar: EKCalendar){

  /* The event starts 60 seconds from now */
  let startDate = NSDate(timeIntervalSinceNow: 60.0)

  /* And end the event 20 seconds after its start date */
  let endDate = startDate.dateByAddingTimeInterval(20.0)

  let eventWithAlarm = EKEvent(eventStore: store)
  eventWithAlarm.calendar = calendar
  eventWithAlarm.startDate = startDate
  eventWithAlarm.endDate = endDate

  /* The alarm goes off 2 seconds before the event happens */
  let alarm = EKAlarm(relativeOffset: -2.0)

  eventWithAlarm.title = "Event with Alarm"
  eventWithAlarm.addAlarm(alarm)

  var error:NSError?
  if store.saveEvent(eventWithAlarm, span: EKSpanThisEvent, error: &error){
    println("Saved an event that fires 60 seconds from now.")
  } else if let theError = error{
    println("Failed to save the event. Error = \(theError)")
  }

}
```

For information about event stores and calendars and the way to retrieve instances to them, please see Recipe 18.4.

Discussion

An event of type `EKEvent` can have multiple alarms. Simply create the alarm using either the `alarmWithAbsoluteDate:` or `alarmWithRelativeOffset:` class method of `EKAlarm`. The former method requires an absolute date and time (you can use the `CFAbsoluteTimeGetCurrent` function to get the current absolute time), whereas the latter method requires a number of seconds relative to the start date of the event when the alarm must be fired. For instance, if the event is scheduled for today at 6:00 a.m., and we go ahead and create an alarm with the relative offset of –60 (which is counted in units of seconds), our alarm will be fired at 5:59 a.m. the same day. Only zero and negative numbers are allowed for this offset. Positive numbers will automatically be changed to zero by iOS. Once an alarm is fired, iOS will display the alarm to the user, as shown in Figure 18-5.

Figure 18-5. iOS displaying an alert on the screen when an alarm is fired

You can use the removeAlarm: instance method of EKEvent to remove an alarm associated with that event instance.

See Also

Recipe 18.3

CHAPTER 19

Graphics and Animations

19.0. Introduction

You've certainly seen applications with beautiful graphics effects on iOS devices. And you've probably also encountered impressive animations in games and other apps. Working together, the iOS runtime and Cocoa programming frameworks make possible an amazing variety of graphics and animation effects with relatively simple coding. The quality of these graphics and animations depends partly, of course, on the aesthetic sensitivities of the programmer and artistic collaborators. But in this chapter, you'll see how much you can accomplish with modest programming skills.

I'll dispense with conceptual background, preferring to introduce ideas such as color spaces, transformation, and the graphics context as we go along. I'll just mention a few basics before leaping into code.

In Cocoa Touch, an app is made up of *windows* and *views*. An app with a UI has at least one window that contains, in turn, one or more views. In Cocoa Touch, a window is an instance of UIWindow. Usually, an app will open to the main window and the programmer will then add views to the window to represent different parts of the UI: parts such as buttons, labels, images, and custom controls. All these UI-related components are handled and drawn by UIKit.

Some of these things might sound relatively difficult to understand, but I promise you that as we proceed through this chapter, you will understand them with the many step-by-step examples I provide.

Apple has provided developers with powerful frameworks that handle graphics and animations in iOS and OS X. Here are some of these frameworks and technologies:

UIKit

The high-level framework that allows developers to create views, windows, buttons, and other UI-related components. It also incorporates some of the low-level APIs into an easier-to-use high-level API.

Quartz 2D

The main engine running under the hood to facilitate drawing in iOS; UIKit uses Quartz.

Core Graphics

A framework that supports the graphics context (more on this later), loading images, drawing images, and so on.

Core Animation

A framework that, as its name implies, facilitates animations in iOS.

When drawing on a screen, one of the most important concepts to grasp is the relation between points and pixels. I'm sure you're familiar with pixels, but what are *points*? They're the device-independent counterpart of pixels. Simply put, when writing your iOS apps and asked to provide a width/height or any other measurements like these, iOS reads your provided values as points, instead of pixels. For instance, if you want to fill the whole screen on an iPhone 5, you will say that you want a width of 320 and height of 568. However, we all know that the actual screen resolution of an iPhone 5 is 640 by 1136. This is the beauty of points: they take *content scale factor* into account.

Let me clarify what content scale factor is. It's a simple floating point number that allows iOS to calculate the actual number of pixels on the screen by looking at the logical number of points that it can render on that screen. On an iPhone 5, the content scale factor is 2.0, which tells iOS to multiply 320 by 2 to get the actual number of pixels that the device can render horizontally and to multiply 568 by 2 to get the number of pixels that the device can render vertically.

 The origin point of the screen on an iOS device is the top-left corner. Screens whose drawing origin is on the top-left corner are also referred to as upper left origin, or ULO, screens. This means that point (0, 0) is the topmost and leftmost point on the screen, and that positive values of the x-axis extend toward the right, while positive values of the y-axis extend toward the bottom. In other words, an x position of 20 is farther right on the screen than a position of 10 is. On the y-axis, point 20 is farther down than point 10.

In this chapter, we will be using view objects of type UIView to draw shapes, strings, and everything else that's visible on the screen.

I assume you have the latest Xcode from Apple. If not, open App Store on your OS X installation and search for and download Xcode.

In order to be able to incorporate some of these code snippets in an application, I will first show you the required steps to create a new project in Xcode and subclass UI View, where we can place the code:

1. Open Xcode.
2. From the File menu, select New → Project.
3. On the left side of the screen, make sure the iOS category is selected. Select Application under that category (see Figure 19-1).
4. On the right side of the screen, select single-view application, and press Next (see Figure 19-1).

Figure 19-1. Creating a single-view application for iOS in Xcode

5. In the Product Name box (Figure 19-2), select a name for your project.

6. In the Organization Name box, enter the name of your company. For a limited company in any country, this would usually be the name of the company without any suffixes (such as Ltd., AB, etc.).

7. In the Organization Identifier box, enter a bundle identifier prefix, which will be prepended to the Product Name you chose. This is usually com.company.

8. In the Device Family, select Universal, and then press Next.

9. On the next screen, select where you want to save your project and press Create.

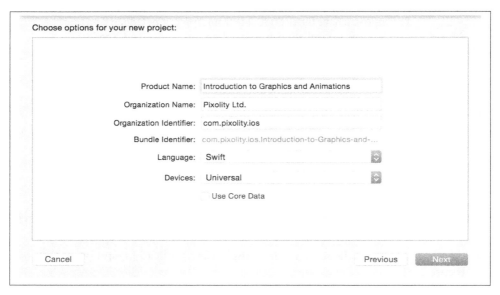

Choose options for your new project:

Product Name:	Introduction to Graphics and Animations
Organization Name:	Pixolity Ltd.
Organization Identifier:	com.pixolity.ios
Bundle Identifier:	com.pixolity.ios.Introduction-to-Graphics-and-...
Language:	Swift
Devices:	Universal
	Use Core Data

Cancel   Previous   Next

Figure 19-2. Setting the options for a new project in Xcode

Now your Xcode project is open. On the left side of Xcode, expand your project files to see all the files that Xcode created when you created the project. Now we will create a view object for the view controller. Please follow these steps to do so:

1. Right-click the root folder of your project group in Xcode and select New File....

2. In the New File dialog box, make sure iOS is selected as the category on the left side, and select Source as the subcategory (see Figure 19-3).

3. On the right side, select Cocoa Touch Class, and then press Next (see Figure 19-3).

4. On the next screen (Figure 19-4), make sure that the Subclass box has *UIView* written inside it, and set your class name to **View**. Proceed to saving your file on disk.

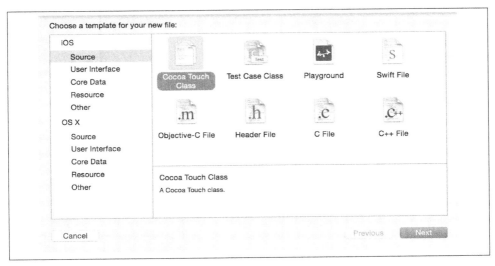

Figure 19-3. Creating a new Cocoa Touch Class in Xcode

Figure 19-4. Creating a subclass of UIView

5. Now open your storyboard file for iPhone and select the view of your view controller. Expand the Utilities section of the Interface Builder and change the class name of the view of your view controller to View, as shown in Figure 19-5.

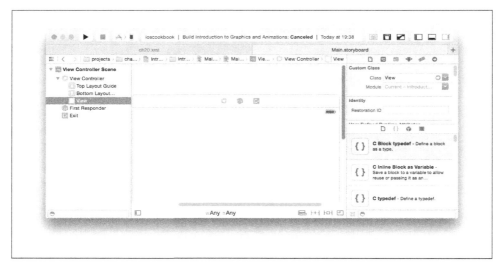

Figure 19-5. Changing the class name of a view controller in storyboard

Now we are ready to start coding. What we did was simply create a view class of type UIView so that later in this chapter, we can change the code in that class. Then we used Interface Builder to set the view controller's view class to the same view object that we created. This means that the view controller's view will now be an instance of the View class that we created.

You have probably already looked at the contents of the view class that Xcode generated. One of the most important methods inside this class is drawRect:. Cocoa Touch automatically calls this method whenever it is time to draw the view and uses it to ask the view object to draw its contents on the graphical context that Cocoa Touch automatically prepares for the view. A graphical context can be thought of as a canvas, offering an enormous number of properties, such as pen color, pen thickness, etc. Given the context, you can start *painting* straight away inside the drawRect: method, and Cocoa Touch will make sure that the attributes and properties of the context are applied to your drawings. We will talk more about this later, but for now, let's move on to more interesting subjects.

19.1. Drawing Text

Problem

You want to be able to draw text on the screen of an iOS device.

Solution

Use the `drawAtPoint:withFont:` method of `NSString`.

Discussion

To draw text, we can use some really handy methods built into the `NSString` class, such as `drawAtPoint:withAttributes:`. Before we proceed further, make sure that you followed the instructions in this chapter's Introduction. You should now have a view object, subclassed from `UIView`, named `View`. Open that file. If the `drawRect:` instance method of the view object is commented out, remove the comments until you have that method in your view object:

```
import UIKit

class View: UIView {

  init(frame: CGRect) {
    super.init(frame: frame)
    // Initialization code
  }

  override func drawRect(rect: CGRect)
  {

  }

}
```

The `drawRect:` method is where we'll do the drawing, as mentioned before. Here we can start loading the font, and then draw a simple string on the screen at point 40 on the x-axis and 180 on the y-axis (Figure 19-6):

```
import UIKit

class View: UIView {

  override func drawRect(rect: CGRect)
  {
    let fontName = "HelveticaNeue-Bold"
    let helveticaBold = UIFont(name: fontName, size: 40.0)
    let string = "Some String" as NSString
    string.drawAtPoint(CGPointMake(40.0, 180.0),
      withAttributes: [NSFontAttributeName : helveticaBold!])
  }

}
```

In this code, we are simply loading a bold Helvetica font at size 40, and using it to draw the text Some String at point (40, 180).

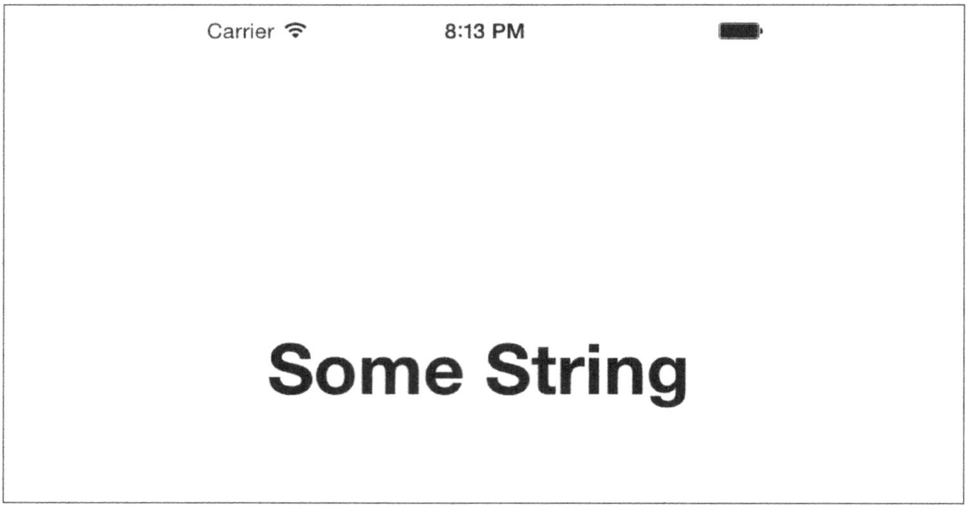

Carrier 🛜   8:13 PM

Some String

Figure 19-6. A random string drawn on the graphical context of a view

19.2. Drawing Images

Problem

You want to be able to draw images on the screen of an iOS device.

Solution

Use the `UIImage` class to load an image and then use the `drawInRect:` method of the image to draw it on a graphics context.

Discussion

UIKit helps you draw images with ease. All you have to do is load your images in instances of type `UIImage`. The `UIImage` class provides various class and instance methods to load your images. Here are some of the important ones in iOS:

`imageNamed:` *class method*
> Loads the image (and caches the image if it can load it properly). The parameter to this method is the name of the image in the bundle, such as *Tree Texture.png*.

`imageWithData:` *class method*
> Loads an image from the data encapsulated in an instance of an `NSData` object that was passed as the parameter to this method.

`initWithContentsOfFile:` *instance method (for initialization)*

Uses the given parameter as the path to an image that has to be loaded and used to initialize the image object.

This path should be the full path to the image in the app bundle.

`initWithData:` *instance method (for initialization)*

Uses the given parameter of type `NSData` to initialize the image. This data should belong to a valid image.

Please follow these steps to add an image to your Xcode project:

1. Find where the image is located in your computer.
2. Drag and drop the image into your image category, usually named *Images.xcassets*. Xcode will do the rest for you.

You can retrieve Safari's icon by following these steps:

1. Find the Safari app in the Finder.
2. Press Command-I in the Finder to get information on it.
3. Click the icon in the upper left of the Xcode Info window.
4. Press Command-C to copy it.
5. Open the Preview app.
6. In the File menu now in Preview, choose New from Clipboard.
7. You will now have an ICNS file with separate pages, each of which will have a different resolution and quality. Choose the highest quality image (usually the one on the top), export it to a PNG file, and name it *Safari@2x.png*. Then duplicate the same image and this time, resize it to 50% of the original size and save the new image as *Safari.png*. Now we have two images on disk, one for retina resolution and another for normal resolution displays.

We will be drawing this image on a graphics context to demonstrate how to draw images in this section of the book. I've already found the file, and dragged and dropped that image into my iOS app. Now I have an image called *Safari.png* in my app project's asset category.

Here is the code for *loading* an image:

```
let image = UIImage(named: "Safari")
```

For the remainder of this section, I assume you have this image in your project's asset category. Feel free to place other images in your app and refer to those images instead of *Safari.png*, which I will be using in example code.

The two easiest ways to draw an image of type UIImage on a graphics context are:

drawAtPoint: *instance method of* UIImage *class*
> Draws the image at its original size at the given point. Construct the point using the CGPoint constructor.

drawInRect: *instance method of* UIImage *class*
> Draws the image in the given rectangular space. To construct this rectangular space, use the CGRect constructor:

```
override func drawRect(rect: CGRect)
{
  let image = UIImage(named: "Safari")
  image!.drawAtPoint(CGPoint(x: 0, y: 20))
  image!.drawInRect(CGRect(x: 50, y: 10, width: 40, height: 35))
}
```

The drawAtPoint: call shown in this code snippet draws the image at its full size at point (0, 20), and the drawInRect: call draws the image at point (50, 10) at 40×35 points, as shown in Figure 19-7.

 Aspect ratio is the ratio between the width and the height of an image (or a computer screen). Let's assume you have an image that is 100×100 pixels. If you draw this image at point (0, 0) with a size of (100, 200), you can immediately see on the screen that the image is stretched in height (200 pixels instead of 100). The drawInRect: instance method of UIImage leaves it up to you how you want to draw your images. In other words, it is *you* who has to specify the *x*, *y*, width, and height of your image as it appears on the screen.

Figure 19-7. Drawing an image on a graphics context can be accomplished with two different methods

See Also

Recipe 15.6

19.3. Constructing Resizable Images

Problem

You want to be able to save some memory and disk space by creating resizable images for your UI components. You might also want to be able to create different sizes of the same UI component, such as a button, using only a single background image.

 Resizable images refer to simple PNG or JPEG images that can be loaded into an instance of `UIImage`.

Solution

Create a resizable image using the `resizableImageWithCapInsets:` instance method of the `UIImage` class.

Discussion

Resizable images might sound a bit strange at first, but they make sense when you understand the different display needs of your app. For instance, you might be working on an iOS app where you want to provide a background image for your buttons. The bigger the text in the button, the wider the button. So you now have two options on how you want to provide the background images of your buttons:

- Create one image per size of button. This will add to the size of your bundle, consume more memory, and require much more work from you. In addition, any change to the text requires a new image to make the button fit.

- Create one resizable image and use that throughout the app for all the buttons.

Without a doubt, the second option is much more appealing. So what are resizable images? They are simply images that are divided into two virtual areas:

- An area that will not be stretched.

- An area that will be stretched to fit any size.

As you can see in Figure 19-8, we created an image for a button. After a better look at the image, you can clearly see that it is made out of a gradient. The area that I drew a rectangle around is the area that can be cut out of the image. You might be wondering why. Have a closer look! If I cut that area and made it only one pixel wide and as tall as it is now, I could, in my app, put as many of those vertical slices that I cut together to form the same area that is highlighted in this photo. See Figure 19-9.

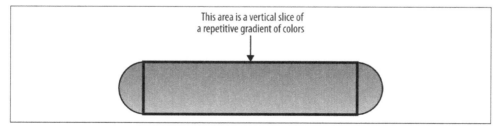

Figure 19-8. An image with a redundant area is a great candidate for a resizable image

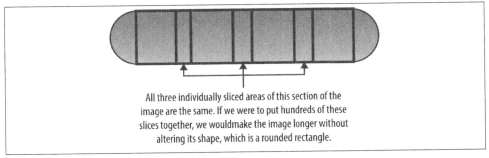

Figure 19-9. Individual slices of the center section of the image are all the same

So how can you make this image smaller and still be able to construct a button out of it? The answer is simple. In this case, where the image is consistently the same across the length of it, we simply cut the center of it into a slice that is one point wide while keeping it as tall as it is right now. Figure 19-10 shows what our image will look like after this operation.

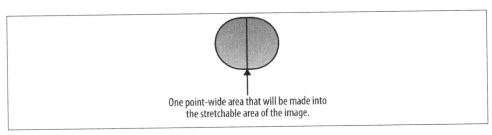

Figure 19-10. The resizable area of the image is made into a one-point-wide area

Now comes the interesting part! How can we tell the iOS SDK which part of the image to keep intact and which part to stretch? It turns out that iOS SDK has already taken care of this. First, load your image into memory using the UIImage APIs that you learned in this chapter. After constructing an instance of UIImage with an image that you know you can stretch, transform the image instance into a resizable image using the resiza bleImageWithCapInsets: instance method of the same instance. The parameter that this method takes is of type UIEdgeInsets, which is defined in this way:

```
struct UIEdgeInsets {
    var top: CGFloat
    var left: CGFloat
    var bottom: CGFloat
    var right: CGFloat
}
```

Edge insets are there to allow us to create what Apple calls *nine-part images*. A nine-part image is an image that has the following nine components:

- Upper-left corner
- Top edge
- Upper-right corner
- Right edge
- Lower-right corner
- Bottom edge
- Lower-left corner
- Left edge
- Center

Figure 19-11 illustrates this concept much better than words can.

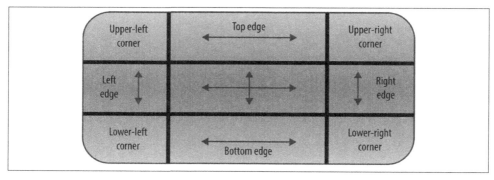

Figure 19-11. Illustration of a nine-part image

The purpose of storing an image as a nine-part image is that programmers can resize it vertically and horizontally to pretty much any size they want. When the programmer requires the image to be resized, some of these components will stay unchanged and some will be resized. The parts that stay unchanged are the corners, which aren't resized at all. The other parts of the image will be resized as follows:

Top edge
  This part of the image will be resized in its width but not in its height.

Right edge
  This part of the image will be resized in its height but not in its width.

Bottom edge
  This part of the image, just like the top edge, will be resized in its width, but not in its height.

Left edge

Just like the right edge, this part of the image will be resized in its height, but not in its width.

Center

Will be resized in both its width and its height.

The top, left, bottom, and right values of the inset mark the area that you don't want to stretch. For instance, if you specified the value of 10 for the left, 11 for the top, 14 for the right, and 5 for the bottom, you are telling iOS to put a vertical *line* on the image at 10 points from the left, a horizontal line at 11 points from the top, another vertical line at 14 points from the right, and a final horizontal line at 5 points from the bottom. The rectangular area *trapped* between these virtual lines is the resizable area of the image and the area outside this rectangle is not stretched. This might sound a bit confusing, but imagine a rectangle (your image) and then imagine that you draw another rectangle inside it. The inner rectangle is resizable but the outer rectangle stays intact. I think looking at a picture demonstrating these values will clarify this (Figure 19-12).

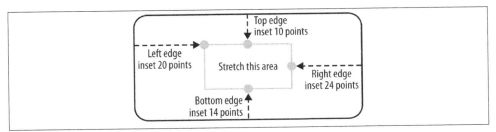

Figure 19-12. The stretchable portion of the image is defined by the edge insets

 The left and right distances are really the same in Figure 19-12. So are the top and the bottom distances. I only set them to different values to make the edge inset construction a bit more straightforward and easier to understand. If all the values were the same, when we construct the edge insets later, you may ask: which one is which?!

For an image like Figure 19-12, we should construct the edge inset like so:

```
let edgeInsets = UIEdgeInsets(top: 10.0,
    left: 20.0,
    bottom: 14.0,
    right: 24.0)
```

OK, now let's go back to our example code. What we are trying to do here is use the stretchable image that we created in Figure 19-10 for a real application. We will create a button and place it at the center of our only view controller's view. The button's text will read "Stretched Image on Button" and its size will be 200 points wide and 44 points tall. Here is our code:

```swift
override func viewDidLoad() {
    super.viewDidLoad()

    /* Instantiate the button */
    let button = UIButton.buttonWithType(.Custom) as UIButton
    button.frame = CGRect(x: 0, y: 0, width: 200, height: 44)


    /* Set the title of the button */
    button.setTitle("Stretched Image on Button", forState: .Normal)

    /* Adjust the font for our text */
    button.titleLabel!.font = UIFont.systemFontOfSize(15)

    /* Construct the stretchable image */
    let image = UIImage(named: "Button")!.resizableImageWithCapInsets(
      UIEdgeInsets(top: 0, left: 14, bottom: 0, right: 14))

    /* Set the background image of the button */
    button.setBackgroundImage(image, forState: .Normal)
    button.center = self.view.center

    self.view.addSubview(button)

}
```

Now if you run the app, you will see something similar to Figure 19-13.

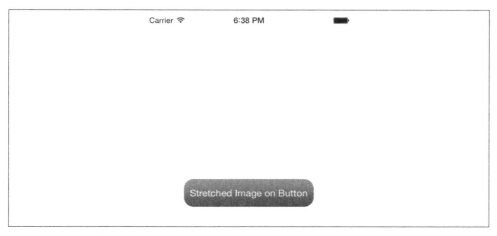

Figure 19-13. A button is displayed on the screen with a stretchable background image

See Also

Recipe 19.2

19.4. Drawing Lines

Problem

You simply want to be able to draw lines on a graphics context.

Solution

Retrieve the handle to your graphics context and then use the `CGContextMoveToPoint` and the `CGContextAddLineToPoint` functions to draw your line.

Discussion

When we talk about drawing shapes in iOS or OS X, we are implicitly talking about *paths*. What are paths, you may ask? A path is constructed from one or more series of points drawn on a screen. There is a big difference between paths and lines. A path can contain many lines, but a line cannot contain many paths. Think of paths as series of points—it's as simple as that.

Lines have to be drawn using paths. Specify the start and end points, and then ask Core Graphics to fill that path for you. Core Graphics recognizes that you created a line on that path and will paint that path for you using the color that you specified.

We will be talking about paths in more depth later (see Recipe 19.5), but for now let's focus on using paths to create straight lines. To do this, follow these steps:

1. Choose a color on your graphics context.
2. Retrieve the handle to the graphics context, using the `UIGraphicsGetCurrentCon text` function.
3. Set the starting point for your line using the `CGContextMoveToPoint` procedure.
4. Move your pen on the graphics context using the `CGContextAddLineToPoint` procedure to specify the ending point of your line.
5. Create the path that you laid out using the `CGContextStrokePath` procedure. This procedure will draw the path using the current color that has been set on the graphics context.

Optionally, you can use the `CGContextSetLineWidth` procedure to set the width of the lines that you are drawing on a given graphics context. The first parameter to this procedure is the graphics context that you are drawing on, and the second parameter is the width of the line, expressed as a floating-point number (CGFloat).

 In iOS, the line width is measured in logical points.

Here is an example:

```
override func drawRect(rect: CGRect)
{

    /* Set the color that we want to use to draw the line */
    UIColor.brownColor().set()

    /* Get the current graphics context */
    let context = UIGraphicsGetCurrentContext()

    /* Set the width for the line */
    CGContextSetLineWidth(context, 5)

    /* Start the line at this point */
    CGContextMoveToPoint(context, 50, 10)

    /* And end it at this point */
    CGContextAddLineToPoint(context, 100, 200)

    /* Use the context's current color to draw the line */
    CGContextStrokePath(context)

}
```

Running this code in iOS Simulator displays results similar to Figure 19-14.

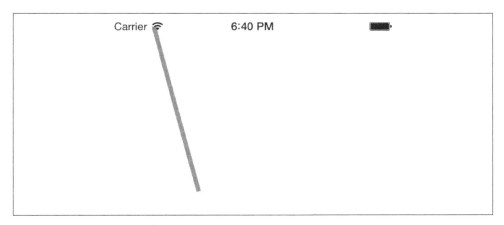

Figure 19-14. Drawing a line on a current graphics context

Let me show you another example. As mentioned earlier, the CGContextAddLineTo Point procedure specifies the end point of the current line. Now what if we have already drawn a line from point (20, 20) to point (100, 100), and want to draw a line from (100, 100) to (300, 100)? You might think that after drawing the first line, we have to move the pen to point (100, 100) using the CGContextMoveToPoint procedure, and then draw the line to point (300, 100) using the CGContextAddLineToPoint procedure. While that will work, there is a more efficient way to do this. After you call the CGContextAddLi neToPoint procedure to specify the ending point of your current line, your pen's position will change to what you pass to this method. In other words, after you issue a method using the pen, it leaves the pen's position at the ending point of whatever it drew. So to draw another line from the current ending point to another point, all you have to do is call the CGContextAddLineToPoint procedure again with another ending point. Here is an example:

```
override func drawRect(rect: CGRect) {
  /* Set the color that we want to use to draw the line */
  UIColor.brownColor().set()

  /* Get the current graphics context */
  let context = UIGraphicsGetCurrentContext()

  /* Set the width for the line */
  CGContextSetLineWidth(context, 5)

  /* Start the line at this point */
  CGContextMoveToPoint(context, 50, 10)

  /* And end it at this point */
  CGContextAddLineToPoint(context, 100, 100)

  /* Extend the line to another point */
```

```
    CGContextAddLineToPoint(context, 300, 100);

    /* Use the context's current color to draw the line */
    CGContextStrokePath(context)
}
```

The results are shown in Figure 19-15. You can see that both lines are successfully drawn without us having to move the pen for the second line.

The point where two lines meet is, not surprisingly, called a join. With Core Graphics, you can specify what type of join you want to have between lines that are connected to each other. To make your choice, you must use the `CGContextSetLineJoin` procedure. It takes two parameters: a graphics context on which you are setting the join type, and the join type itself, which must be of type `CGLineJoin`. `CGLineJoin` is an enumeration of the following values:

`kCGLineJoinMiter`
    Joins will be made out of sharp corners. This is the default join type.

`kCGLineJoinBevel`
    Joins will be squared off on the corner.

`kCGLineJoinRound`
    As the name implies, this makes round joins.

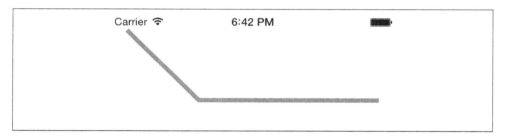

Figure 19-15. Drawing two lines at once

Let's look at an example. Let's say we want to write a program that can draw "rooftops" on a graphics context (three of them, one for each join type), and also draws text below each rooftop describing the type of join it is using. Something similar to Figure 19-16 will result.

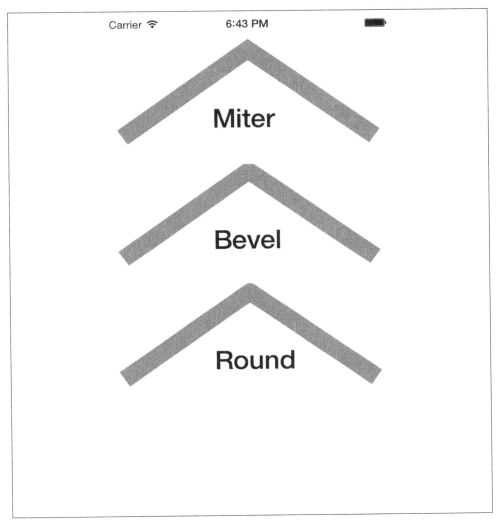

Figure 19-16. Three types of line joins in Core Graphics

To accomplish this, I've written a method named `drawRooftopAtTopPointOf:textTo
Display:lineJoin:`, which takes three parameters:

1. A point at which the top of the rooftop should be placed.
2. The text to display inside the rooftop.
3. The join type to be used.

The code is as follows:

```
func drawRooftopAtTopPointOf(point: CGPoint,
  textToDisplay: NSString,
  lineJoin: CGLineJoin){

    /* Set the color that we want to use to draw the line */
    UIColor.brownColor().set()

    /* Set the color that we want to use to draw the line */
    let context = UIGraphicsGetCurrentContext()

    /* Set the line join */
    CGContextSetLineJoin(context, lineJoin)

     /* Set the width for the lines */
    CGContextSetLineWidth(context, 20)

    /* Start the line at this point */
    CGContextMoveToPoint(context, point.x - 140, point.y + 100)

    /* And end it at this point */
    CGContextAddLineToPoint(context, point.x, point.y)

    /* Extend the line to another point to make the rooftop */
    CGContextAddLineToPoint(context, point.x + 140, point.y + 100)

    /* Use the context's current color to draw the lines */
    CGContextStrokePath(context)

    /* Draw the text in the rooftop using a black color */
    UIColor.blackColor().set()

    /* Now draw the text */
    let drawingPoint = CGPoint(x: point.x - 40, y: point.y + 60)
    let font = UIFont.boldSystemFontOfSize(30)
    textToDisplay.drawAtPoint(drawingPoint,
      withAttributes: [NSFontAttributeName : font])
}
```

Now let's call this method in the drawRect: instance method of the view object where
we have a graphics context:

```
override func drawRect(rect: CGRect){

  drawRooftopAtTopPointOf(CGPoint(x: 160, y: 40),
    textToDisplay: "Miter",
    lineJoin: kCGLineJoinMiter)

  drawRooftopAtTopPointOf(CGPoint(x: 160, y: 180),
    textToDisplay: "Bevel",
    lineJoin: kCGLineJoinBevel)

  drawRooftopAtTopPointOf(CGPoint(x: 160, y: 320),
    textToDisplay: "Round",
```

```
        lineJoin: kCGLineJoinRound)

    }
```

See Also

Recipe 19.5

19.5. Constructing Paths

Problem

You want to be able to draw any shape that you want on a graphics context.

Solution

Construct and draw paths.

Discussion

A series of points placed together can form a shape. A series of shapes put together builds a path. Paths can easily be managed by Core Graphics. In Recipe 19.4, we worked indirectly with paths using `CGContext` functions. But Core Graphics also has functions that work directly with paths, as we shall soon see.

Paths belong to whichever graphics context they are drawn on. Paths do not have boundaries or specific shapes, unlike the shapes we draw on them. But paths do have bounding boxes. Please bear in mind that boundaries are not the same as bounding boxes. Boundaries are limits above which you cannot draw on a canvas, while the bounding box of a path is the smallest rectangle that contains all the shapes, points, and other objects that have been drawn on that specific path. Think of paths as stamps, and think of your graphics context as the envelope. Your envelope could be the same every time you mail something to your friend, but what you put on that context (the stamp or the path) can be different.

After you finish drawing on a path, you can then draw that path on the graphics context. Developers familiar with game programming know the concept of *buffers*, which draw their scenes and, at appropriate times, *flush* the images onto the screen. Paths are those buffers. They are like blank canvases that can be drawn on graphics contexts when the time is right.

The first step in directly working with paths is to create them. The method creating the path returns a handle that you use whenever you want to draw something on that path, passing the handle to Core Graphics for reference. After you create the path, you can add different points, lines, and shapes to it and then draw the path. You can either fill the path or paint it with a stroke on a graphics context. Here are the methods you have to work with:

CGPathCreateMutable *function*

Creates a new mutable path of type CGMutablePathRef and returns its handle. We should dispose of this path after we are done with it, as you will soon see.

CGPathMoveToPoint *procedure*

Moves the current pen position on the path to the point specified by a parameter of type CGPoint.

CGPathAddLineToPoint *procedure*

Draws a line segment from the current pen position to the specified position (again, specified by a value of type CGPoint).

CGContextAddPath *procedure*

Adds a given path (specified by a path handle) to a graphics context, ready for drawing.

CGContextDrawPath *procedure*

Draws a given path on the graphics context.

CGPathAddRect *procedure*

Adds a rectangle to a path. The rectangle's boundaries are specified by a CGRect structure.

There are three important drawing methods that you can ask the CGContextDrawPath procedure to perform:

kCGPathStroke

Draws a line (stroke) to mark the boundary or edge of the path, using the currently selected stroke color.

kCGPathFill

Fills the area surrounded by the path with the currently selected fill color.

kCGPathFillStroke

Combines stroke and fill. Uses the currently selected fill color to fill the path and the currently selected stroke color to draw the edge of the path. We'll see an example of this method in the following section.

Let's have a look at an example. We will draw a blue line from the top-left to the bottom-right corner, and another from the top-right to the bottom-left corner, to create a gigantic X across the screen.

For this example, I removed the status bar from the application in iOS Simulator. If you don't want to bother doing this, please continue to the example code. With a status bar, the output of this code will be only slightly different from the screenshot I'll show. To hide the status bar, find the *Info.plist* file in your Xcode project and add a key to it named `UIStatusBarHidden` with the value of `true`, as shown in Figure 19-17. You will also need to set the value of the key `UIView ControllerBasedStatusBarAppearance` to NO. After you do so, view controllers will not dictate the status bar appearance and the rules that you set in the plist file will always take over. This will force your app's status bar to be hidden when it opens.

Key		Type	Value
▼ Information Property List	⊙	Dictionary	(14 items)
Localization native development region	↕	String	en
Executable file	↕	String	${EXECUTABLE_NAME}
Status bar is initially hidden	↕ ⊙ ⊖	Boolean	⬦ YES
View controller-based status bar appearance	↕	Boolean	NO
Bundle identifier	↕	String	com.pixolity.ios.${PRODUCT_NAME:rfc1034identifier}
InfoDictionary version	↕	String	6.0
Bundle name	↕	String	${PRODUCT_NAME}
Bundle OS Type code	↕	String	APPL
Bundle versions string, short	↕	String	1.0
Bundle creator OS Type code	↕	String	????
Bundle version	↕	String	1
Application requires iPhone environment	↕	Boolean	YES
Main storyboard file base name	↕	String	Main
▶ Required device capabilities	↕	Array	(1 item)

Figure 19-17. Hiding the status bar in an iOS app using the Info.plist file

```
override func drawRect(rect: CGRect) {

  /* Create the path */
  let path = CGPathCreateMutable()

  /* How big is our screen? We want the X to cover the whole screen */
  let screenBounds = UIScreen.mainScreen().bounds

  /* Start from top-left */
  CGPathMoveToPoint(path,
    nil,
    screenBounds.origin.x,
    screenBounds.origin.y)

  /* Draw a line from top-left to bottom-right of the screen */
  CGPathAddLineToPoint(path,
    nil,
    screenBounds.size.width,
    screenBounds.size.height)
```

```
/* Start another line from top-right */
CGPathMoveToPoint(path,
  nil,
  screenBounds.size.width,
  screenBounds.origin.y)

/* Draw a line from top-right to bottom-left */
CGPathAddLineToPoint(path,
  nil,
  screenBounds.origin.x,
  screenBounds.size.height)

/* Get the context that the path has to be drawn on */
let context = UIGraphicsGetCurrentContext()

/* Add the path to the context so we can
draw it later */
CGContextAddPath(context, path)

/* Set the blue color as the stroke color */
UIColor.blueColor().setStroke()

/* Draw the path with stroke color */
CGContextDrawPath(context, kCGPathStroke)
```

 The nil parameters getting passed to procedures such as CGPathMove
ToPoint represent possible transformations that can be used when
drawing the shapes and lines on a given path. For information about
transformations, refer to the recipe Recipe 19.9.

You can see how easy it is to draw a path on a context. All you really have to remember
is how to create a new mutable path (CGPathCreateMutable), add that path to your
graphics context (CGContextAddPath), and draw it on a graphics context (CGContext
DrawPath). If you run this code, you will get an output similar to that shown in
Figure 19-18.

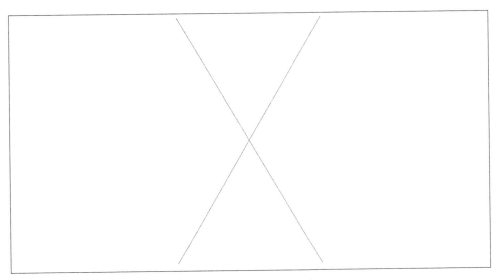

Figure 19-18. Drawing on a graphics context using paths

See Also

Recipe 19.4; Recipe 19.9

19.6. Drawing Rectangles

Problem

You want to be able to draw rectangles on a graphics context.

Solution

Use the `CGPathAddRect` to add a rectangle to a path and then draw that path on a graphics context.

Discussion

As we learned in Recipe 19.5, you can construct and use paths quite easily. One of the procedures that you can use on paths in Core Graphics is `CGPathAddRect`, which lets you draw rectangles as part of paths. Here is an example:

```
override func drawRect(rect: CGRect) {

    /* Create the path first. Just the path handle. */
    let path = CGPathCreateMutable()
```

```
/* Here are our rectangle boundaries */
let rectangle = CGRect(x: 10, y: 30, width: 200, height: 300)

/* Add the rectangle to the path */
CGPathAddRect(path, nil, rectangle)

/* Get the handle to the current context */
let currentContext = UIGraphicsGetCurrentContext()

/* Add the path to the context */
CGContextAddPath(currentContext, path)

/* Set the fill color to cornflower blue */
UIColor(red: 0.20, green: 0.60, blue: 0.80, alpha: 1.0).setFill()

/* Set the stroke color to brown */
UIColor.brownColor().setStroke()

/* Set the line width (for the stroke) to 5 */
CGContextSetLineWidth(currentContext, 5)

/* Stroke and fill the path on the context */
CGContextDrawPath(currentContext, kCGPathFillStroke)
```

Here we are drawing a rectangle on the path, filling it with cornflower blue, and stroking the edges of the rectangle with brown. Figure 19-19 shows how the output will look when we run the program.

Figure 19-19. Drawing a rectangle using paths

If you have multiple rectangles to draw, you can pass an array of CGRect objects to the
CGPathAddRects procedure. Here is an example:

```
override func drawRect(rect: CGRect) {
  /* Create the path first. Just the path handle. */
  let path = CGPathCreateMutable()

  /* Here are our first rectangle boundaries */
  let rectangle1 = CGRect(x: 10, y: 30, width: 200, height: 300)

  /* And the second rectangle */
  let rectangle2 = CGRect(x: 40, y: 100, width: 90, height: 300)

  /* Put both rectangles into an array */
  let rectangles = [rectangle1, rectangle2]

  /* Add the rectangles to the path */
  CGPathAddRects(path, nil, rectangles, 2)

  /* Get the handle to the current context */
  let currentContext = UIGraphicsGetCurrentContext()

  /* Add the path to the context */
  CGContextAddPath(currentContext, path)
```

```
/* Set the fill color to cornflower blue */
UIColor(red: 0.20, green: 0.60, blue: 0.80, alpha: 1.0).setFill()

/* Set the stroke color to black */
UIColor.blackColor().setStroke()

/* Set the line width (for the stroke) to 5 */
CGContextSetLineWidth(currentContext, 5)

/* Stroke and fill the path on the context */
CGContextDrawPath(currentContext, kCGPathFillStroke)
```

Figure 19-20 shows how the output of this code will look when run in iOS Simulator. The parameters that we pass to the CGPathAddRects procedure are (in this order):

1. The handle to the path where we will add the rectangles.

2. The transformation, if any, to use on the rectangles. (For information about transformations, refer to the recipe Recipe 19.9.)

3. A reference to the array holding the CGRect rectangles.

4. The number of rectangles in the array that we passed in the previous parameter. It is very important that you pass exactly as many rectangles as you have in your array, to avoid unknown behavior by this procedure.

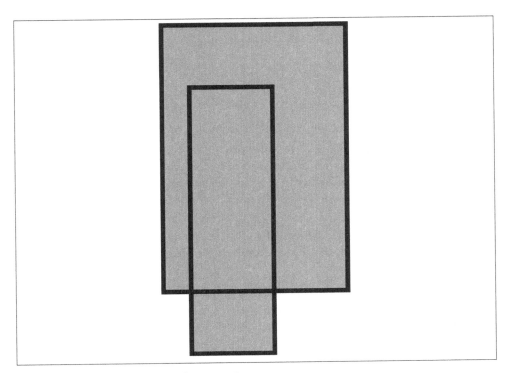

Figure 19-20. Drawing multiple rectangles at once

See Also

Recipe 19.5; Recipe 19.9

19.7. Adding Shadows to Shapes

Problem

You want to be able to apply shadows to shapes that you draw on graphic contexts.

Solution

Use the CGContextSetShadow procedure.

Discussion

It is easy to draw shadows using Core Graphics. The graphics context is the element that bears the shadow. What that means is that you need to apply the shadow to the context, draw the shapes that need the shadow, and then remove the shadow from the context (or set a new context). We will see an example of this soon.

In Core Graphics, we can use two procedures to apply a shadow to a graphics context:

`CGContextSetShadow` *procedure*

This procedure, which creates black or gray shadows, accepts three parameters:

- The graphics context on which the shadow has to be applied.

- The offset, specified by a value of type `CGSize`, from the right and the bottom part of each shape where the shadow has to be applied. The greater the *x* value of this offset is, the farther to the right of each shape the shadow will extend. The greater the *y* value of this offset is, the lower the shadow will extend.

- The blur value that has to be applied to the shadow, specified as a floating-point value (`CGFloat`). Specifying `0.0f` will cause the shadow to be a solid shape. The higher this value goes, the more blurred the shadow will get. We will see an example of this soon.

`CGContextSetShadowWithColor` *procedure*

This procedure accepts the exact same parameters as `CGContextSetShadow`, with one addition. This fourth parameter, of type `CGColorRef`, sets the color of the shadow.

At the beginning of this section, I mentioned that the graphics context retains its shadow properties until we explicitly remove the shadow. Let me make that point clearer by showing you an example. Let us go ahead and write code that allows us to draw two rectangles, the first one with a shadow and the second one without a shadow. We will draw the first one in this way:

```
func drawRectAtTopOfScreen(){
  /* Get the handle to the current context */
  let currentContext = UIGraphicsGetCurrentContext()

  let offset = CGSizeMake(10, 10)

  CGContextSetShadowWithColor(currentContext,
    offset,
    20,
    UIColor.grayColor().CGColor)

  /* Create the path first. Just the path handle. */
  let path = CGPathCreateMutable()

  /* Here are our rectangle boundaries */
  let firstRect = CGRect(x: 55, y: 60, width: 150, height: 150)

  /* Add the rectangle to the path */
  CGPathAddRect(path, nil, firstRect)
```

```
/* Add the path to the context */
CGContextAddPath(currentContext, path)

/* Set the fill color to cornflower blue */
UIColor(red: 0.20, green: 0.60, blue: 0.80, alpha: 1.0).setFill()

/* Fill the path on the context */
CGContextDrawPath(currentContext, kCGPathFill)
```

If we call this method in the `drawRect:` instance method of the view object, we will see
the rectangle drawn on the screen with a nice shadow just like we wanted it, as shown
in Figure 19-21.

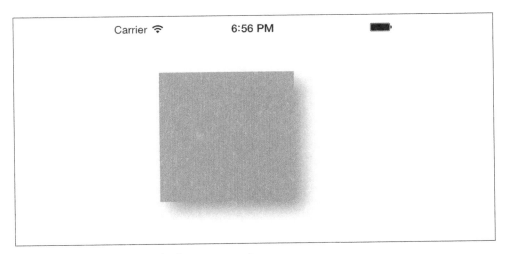

Figure 19-21. Shadow applied to a rectangle

Now let's go ahead and draw a second rectangle after the first one. We won't ask for a
shadow, but we'll leave the shadow property of the graphics context as it was for the first
rectangle:

```
func drawRectAtBottomOfScreen(){
  /* Get the handle to the current context */
  let currentContext = UIGraphicsGetCurrentContext()

  let secondPath = CGPathCreateMutable()

  let secondRect = CGRect(x: 150, y: 250, width: 100, height: 100)

  CGPathAddRect(secondPath, nil, secondRect)

  CGContextAddPath(currentContext, secondPath)

  UIColor.purpleColor().setFill()
```

```
    CGContextDrawPath(currentContext, kCGPathFill)

}

override func drawRect(rect: CGRect) {
  drawRectAtTopOfScreen()
  drawRectAtBottomOfScreen()
}
```

The drawRect: method first calls the drawRectAtTopOfScreen method, and right after that calls the drawRectAtBottomOfScreen method. We haven't asked for a shadow for the drawRectAtBottomOfScreen rectangle, yet if you run the app, you will see something similar to Figure 19-22.

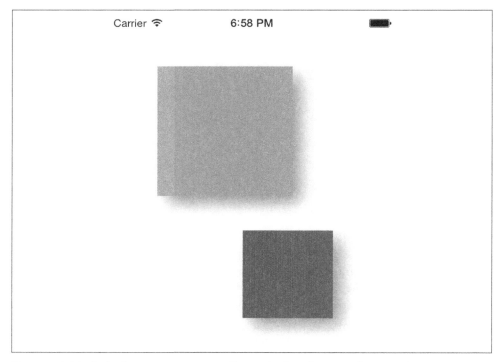

Figure 19-22. A shadow is unintentionally applied to the second rectangle

It's immediately obvious that the shadow is applied to the second rectangle at the bottom of the screen. To avoid this, we save the state of the graphics context *before* applying the shadow effect and then restore the state when we want to remove the shadow effect.

Broadly speaking, saving and restoring the state of a graphics context is not limited to shadows only. Restoring the state of a graphics context restores everything (fill color, font, line thickness, etc.) to the values they had before you set them. So for instance, if you applied fill and stroke colors, those colors will be reset.

You can save the state of a graphics context through the `CGContextSaveGState` procedure and restore the previous state through the `CGContextRestoreGState` procedure. So if we modify the `drawRectAtTopOfScreen` procedure by saving the state of the graphics context before applying the shadow, and restore that state after drawing the path, we will have different results, shown in Figure 19-23:

```
func drawRectAtTopOfScreen(){
  /* Get the handle to the current context */
  let currentContext = UIGraphicsGetCurrentContext()

  CGContextSaveGState(currentContext)

  let offset = CGSizeMake(10, 10)

  CGContextSetShadowWithColor(currentContext,
    offset,
    20,
    UIColor.grayColor().CGColor)

  /* Create the path first. Just the path handle. */
  let path = CGPathCreateMutable()

  /* Here are our rectangle boundaries */
  let firstRect = CGRect(x: 55, y: 60, width: 150, height: 150)

  /* Add the rectangle to the path */
  CGPathAddRect(path, nil, firstRect)

  /* Add the path to the context */
  CGContextAddPath(currentContext, path)

  /* Set the fill color to cornflower blue */
  UIColor(red: 0.20, green: 0.60, blue: 0.80, alpha: 1.0).setFill()

  /* Fill the path on the context */
  CGContextDrawPath(currentContext, kCGPathFill)

  /* Restore the context to how it was when we started */
  CGContextRestoreGState(currentContext)
```

Figure 19-23. Saving the state of the graphics context for accurate shadows

19.8. Drawing Gradients

Problem

You want to draw gradients on graphics contexts, using different colors.

Solution

Use the `CGGradientCreateWithColor` function.

Discussion

Core Graphics allows programmers to create two types of gradients: axial and radial. (We only discuss axial gradients in this book.) Axial gradients are gradients that start from one point with one color and end at another point with another color (although they can start and stop with the same color, which does not make them much of a gradient). "Axial" means relating to an axis. The two points (start and end point) create a line segment, which will be the axis on which the gradient will be drawn. An example of an axial gradient is shown in Figure 19-24.

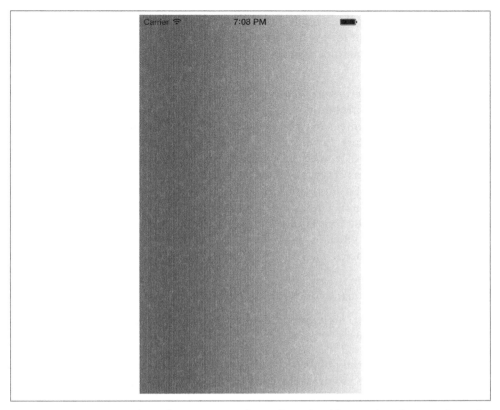

Figure 19-24. An axial gradient starting from the color blue and ending in the color green

In order to create an axial gradient, you must call the `CGGradientCreateWithCol orComponents` function. The return value of this function will be the new gradient of type `CGGradientRef`. This is the handle to the gradient.

The `CGGradientCreateWithColorComponents` function takes four parameters:

A color space

This is a container for a range of colors and must be of type `CGColorSpaceRef`. For this parameter, we can just pass the return value of the `CGColorSpaceCreateDevi ceRGB` function, which will give us an RGB color space.

An array of color components

This array has to contain red, green, blue, and alpha values, all represented as `CGFloat` values. The number of elements in the array is tightly linked to the next two parameters. Essentially, you have to include enough values in this array to specify the number of locations in the fourth parameter. So if you ask for two locations (the start and end point), you have to provide two colors in the array here. And because each color is made out of red, green, blue, and alpha, this array has to have 2×4 items: four for the first color and four for the second. Don't worry if you didn't get all this; you will eventually understand it through the examples that follow in this section.

Locations of colors in the array of colors
This parameter controls how quickly the gradient shifts from one color to another. The number of elements must be the same as the value of the fourth parameter. If we ask for four colors, for example, and we want the first color to be the starting color and the last color to be the ending color in the gradient, we have to provide an array of two items of type `CGFloats`, with the first item set to `0.0f` (as in the *first* item in the array of colors) and the second item set to `3.0f` (as in the *fourth* item in the array of colors). The values of the two intermediate colors determine how the gradient actually inserts colors to get from the start to the end. Again, don't worry if this is too difficult to grasp. I will give you many examples to help you fully understand the concept.

Number of locations
This specifies how many colors and locations we want.

Let's have a look at an example. Suppose we want to draw the same gradient we saw in Figure 19-24. Here's how:

1. Pick the start and end points of the gradient—the axis along which it will shift. In this case, I've chosen to move from left to right. Think of this as changing color as you move along a hypothetical horizontal line. Along that line, we will spread the colors so that every perpendicular line to this horizontal line contains only one color. In this case, the perpendicular lines would be every vertical line in Figure 19-24. Look at those vertical lines closely. Every single one contains only one color, which runs all the way from the top to the bottom. That's how axial gradients work. OK, that's enough theory—let's go to the second step.

2. Now we have to create a color space to pass to the first parameter of the `CGGra dientCreateWithColorComponents` function, as mentioned before:

   ```
   let colorSpace = CGColorSpaceCreateDeviceRGB()
   ```

 We will release this color space after we are done with it.

3. Select blue as the starting point (left) and green as the ending point (right), according to the colors chosen in Figure 19-24. The names I've selected (`startColorCom ponents` and `endColorComponents`) are arbitrarily chosen to help us remember what we're doing with each color. We'll actually use array positions to specify which one is the start and which one is the end:

```
let startColor = UIColor.blueColor()
let startColorComponents = CGColorGetComponents(startColor.CGColor)

let endColor = UIColor.greenColor()
let endColorComponents = CGColorGetComponents(endColor.CGColor)
```

4. After retrieving the components of each color, we place them all in one flat array to pass to the `CGGradientCreateWithColorComponents` function:

```
let colorComponents = [

    /* Four components of the orange color (RGBA) */
    startColorComponents[0],
    startColorComponents[1],
    startColorComponents[2],
    startColorComponents[3], /* First color = blue */


    /* Four components of the blue color (RGBA) */
    endColorComponents[0],
    endColorComponents[1],
    endColorComponents[2],
    endColorComponents[3], /* Second color = green */

]
```

5. Because we have only two colors in this array, we need to specify that the first is positioned at the very beginning of the gradient (position 0.0) and the second at the very end (position 1.0). So let's place these indices in an array to pass to the `CGGradientCreateWithColorComponents` function:

```
let colorIndices = [
    0.0, /* Color 0 in the colorComponents array */
    1.0, /* Color 1 in the colorComponents array */
] as [CGFloat]
```

6. Now all we have to do is actually call the `CGGradientCreateWithColorCompo nents` function with all these values that we generated:

```
let gradient = CGGradientCreateWithColorComponents(colorSpace,
    colorComponents,
    colorIndices,
    2)
```

Now we'll use the `CGContextDrawLinearGradient` procedure to draw the axial gradient on a graphics context. This procedure takes five parameters:

Graphics context
Specifies the graphics context on which the axial gradient will be drawn.

Axial gradient
The handle to the axial gradient object. We created this gradient object using the `CGGradientCreateWithColorComponents` function.

Start point
A point on the graphics context, specified by a `CGPoint`, that indicates the start point of the gradient.

End point
A point on the graphics context, specified by a `CGPoint`, that indicates the end point of the gradient.

Gradient drawing options
Specifies what happens if your start or end point isn't at the edge of the graphical context. You can use your start or end color to fill the space that lies outside the gradient. Specify one of the following values for this parameter:

`kCGGradientDrawsAfterEndLocation`
Extends the gradient to all points after the ending point of the gradient

`kCGGradientDrawsBeforeStartLocation`
Extends the gradient to all points before the starting point of the gradient

`0`
Does not extend the gradient in any way

The output of this code will obviously look similar to Figure 19-24. Because we started the gradient from the leftmost point of the view and stretched it all the way to the rightmost point, we couldn't take advantage of all the values that could be passed to the final *gradient drawing options* parameter of the `CGContextDrawLinearGradient` procedure. Let's remedy that, shall we? How about we draw a gradient that looks similar to that shown in Figure 19-25?

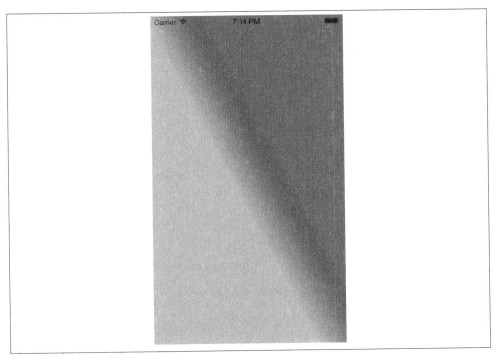

Figure 19-25. An axial gradient with start and end point color extensions

We will use the same procedure explained earlier in this section to code the result:

```
override func drawRect(rect: CGRect) {

    let currentContext = UIGraphicsGetCurrentContext()
    let colorSpace = CGColorSpaceCreateDeviceRGB()

    let startColor = UIColor.blueColor()
    let startColorComponents = CGColorGetComponents(startColor.CGColor)

    let endColor = UIColor.greenColor()
    let endColorComponents = CGColorGetComponents(endColor.CGColor)

    let colorComponents = [

        /* Four components of the orange color (RGBA) */
        startColorComponents[0],
        startColorComponents[1],
        startColorComponents[2],
        startColorComponents[3], /* First color = orange */


        /* Four components of the blue color (RGBA) */
```

```
    endColorComponents[0],
    endColorComponents[1],
    endColorComponents[2],
    endColorComponents[3], /* Second color = blue */

]

let colorIndices = [
  0.0, /* Color 0 in the colorComponents array */
  1.0, /* Color 1 in the colorComponents array */
] as [CGFloat]

let gradient = CGGradientCreateWithColorComponents(colorSpace,
  colorComponents,
  colorIndices,
  2)

let screenBounds = UIScreen.mainScreen().bounds

let startPoint = CGPoint(x: 0, y: screenBounds.size.height / 2)

let endPoint = CGPoint(x: screenBounds.size.width, y: startPoint.y)

CGContextDrawLinearGradient (currentContext,
gradient,
startPoint,
endPoint,
0)
```

See Also

Recipe 19.2

19.9. Transforming Views

Problem

You want to move everything that is drawn on a graphics context to a new location, without changing your drawing code—or you would simply like to displace your context's contents with ease.

Solution

Use various flavors of the `CGAffineTransformMake...` function to create an affine transformation.

Discussion

Recipe 19.6 mentioned transformations. These are exactly what the name suggests: changes to the way a graphic is displayed. Transformations in Core Graphics are objects that you apply to shapes before they are drawn. For instance, you can create a translation transformation. "Translating what?", you might be ask. A translation transformation is a mechanism by which you can *displace* a shape or a graphics context.

Other types of transformations include rotation and scaling. These are all examples of *affine* transformations, which map each point in the origin to another point in the final version. All the transformations we discuss in this book are affine transformations.

A translation transformation *translates* the current position of a shape on a path or graphics context to another relative place. For instance, if you draw a point at location (10, 20), apply a translation transformation of (30, 40) to it, and then draw it, the point will be drawn at (40, 60), because 40 is the sum of 10+30 and 60 is the sum of 20+40.

In order to create a new translation transformation, we must use the `CGAffineTrans formMakeTranslation` function, which will return an affine transformation of type `CGAffineTransform`. The two parameters to this function specify the x and the y translation in points.

In Recipe 19.6, we saw that the `CGPathAddRect` procedure accepts, as its second parameter, a transformation object of type `CGAffineTransform`. To displace a rectangle from its original place to another, you can simply create an affine transformation specifying the changes you want to make in the x and y coordinates and pass the transformation to the second parameter of the `CGPathAddRect` procedure as shown here:

```
override func drawRect(rect: CGRect) {

  /* Create the path first. Just the path handle. */
  let path = CGPathCreateMutable()

  /* Here are our rectangle boundaries */
  let rectangle = CGRect(x: 10, y: 30, width: 200, height: 300)

  /* We want to displace the rectangle to the right by
  100 points but want to keep the y position
  untouched */
  var transform = CGAffineTransformMakeTranslation(100, 0)

  /* Add the rectangle to the path */
  CGPathAddRect(path, &transform, rectangle)

  /* Get the handle to the current context */
  let currentContext = UIGraphicsGetCurrentContext()

  /* Add the path to the context */
  CGContextAddPath(currentContext, path)
```

```
/* Set the fill color to cornflower blue */
UIColor(red: 0.20, green: 0.60, blue: 0.80, alpha: 1.0).setFill()

/* Set the stroke color to brown */
UIColor.brownColor().setStroke()

/* Set the line width (for the stroke) to 5 */
CGContextSetLineWidth(currentContext, 5)

/* Stroke and fill the path on the context */
CGContextDrawPath(currentContext, kCGPathFillStroke)
```

Figure 19-26 shows the output of this block of code when placed inside a view object.

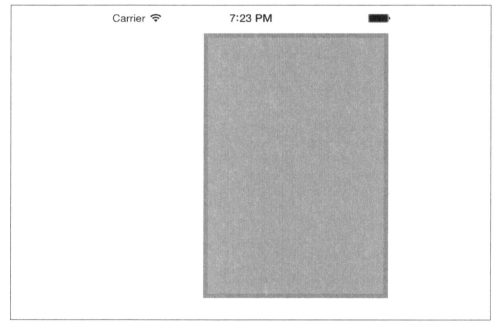

Figure 19-26. A rectangle with an affine translation transformation

Compare Figure 19-26 with Figure 19-19. Can you see the difference? Check the source code for both figures and you'll see that the *x* and *y* points specified for both rectangles in both code blocks are the same. It is just that in Figure 19-26, we applied an affine translation transformation to the rectangle when we added it to the path.

In addition to applying transformations to shapes that get drawn to a path, we can apply transformations to graphics contexts using the CGContextTranslateCTM procedure. This applies a translation transformation on the current transformation matrix

(CTM). The current transformation matrix, although its name might be complex, is quite simple to understand. Think of CTM as how your graphics context's center is set up and how each point that you draw gets projected onto the screen. For instance, when you ask Core Graphics to draw a point at (0, 0), Core Graphics finds the center of the screen by looking at the CTM. The CTM will then do some calculations and tell Core Graphics that point (0, 0) is indeed at the top-left corner of the screen. Using procedures such as CGContextTranslateCTM, you can change how CTM is configured and subsequently force every shape drawn on the graphics context to be shifted to another place on the canvas. Here is an example where we achieve the exact same effect we saw in Figure 19-26 by applying a translation transformation to the CTM instead of directly to the rectangle:

```
override func drawRect(rect: CGRect) {

    /* Create the path first. Just the path handle. */
    let path = CGPathCreateMutable()

    /* Here are our rectangle boundaries */
    let rectangle = CGRect(x: 10, y: 30, width: 200, height: 300)

    /* Add the rectangle to the path */
    CGPathAddRect(path, nil, rectangle)

    /* Get the handle to the current context */
    let currentContext = UIGraphicsGetCurrentContext()

    /* Save the state of the context to revert
    back to how it was at this state, later */
    CGContextSaveGState(currentContext);

    /* Translate the current transformation matrix
    to the right by 100 points */
    CGContextTranslateCTM(currentContext, 100, 0)

    /* Add the path to the context */
    CGContextAddPath(currentContext, path)

    /* Set the fill color to cornflower blue */
    UIColor(red: 0.20, green: 0.60, blue: 0.80, alpha: 1.0).setFill()

    /* Set the stroke color to brown */
    UIColor.brownColor().setStroke()

    /* Set the line width (for the stroke) to 5 */
    CGContextSetLineWidth(currentContext, 5)

    /* Stroke and fill the path on the context */
    CGContextDrawPath(currentContext, kCGPathFillStroke)
```

```
/* Restore the state of the context */
CGContextRestoreGState(currentContext)
```

After running this program, you will notice that the results are exactly like those shown in Figure 19-26.

One of the transformations that you can apply is scaling. You can easily ask Core Graphics to scale a shape, such as a circle, to 100 times its original size.

To create an affine scale transformation, use the `CGAffineTransformMakeScale` function, which returns a transformation object of type `CGAffineTransform`. If you want to apply a scale transformation directly to a graphics context, use the `CGContextSca leCTM` procedure to scale the current transformation matrix (CTM).

Scale transformation functions take two parameters: one to scale the *x*-axis and the other to scale the *y*-axis. Take another look at the rectangle in Figure 19-19. If we want to scale this rectangle to half its normal length and width, we can simply scale the *x*- and the *y*- axis by 0.5 (half their original value), as shown here:

```
/* Scale the rectangle to half its size */
let transform = CGAffineTransformMakeScale(0.5, 0.5)

/* Add the rectangle to the path */
CGPathAddRect(path, &transform, rectangle);
```

Figure 19-27 shows what we see after applying the scale transformation to the code we wrote in Recipe 19.6.

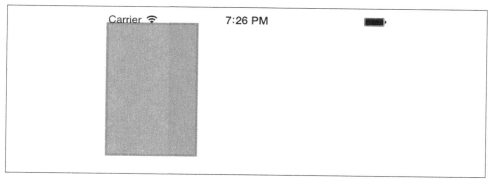

Figure 19-27. Scaling a rectangle

In addition to the `CGAffineTransformMakeScale` function, you can use the `CGCon textScaleCTM` procedure to apply a scale transformation to a graphics context. The following code will achieve the exact same effect as the previous example, as you can see in Figure 19-27:

```
override func drawRect(rect: CGRect) {
```

```
/* Create the path first. Just the path handle. */
let path = CGPathCreateMutable()

/* Here are our rectangle boundaries */
let rectangle = CGRect(x: 10, y: 30, width: 200, height: 300)

/* Add the rectangle to the path */
CGPathAddRect(path, nil, rectangle)

/* Get the handle to the current context */
let currentContext = UIGraphicsGetCurrentContext()

/* Scale everything drawn on the current
graphics context to half its size */
CGContextScaleCTM(currentContext, 0.5, 0.5)

/* Add the path to the context */
CGContextAddPath(currentContext, path)

/* Set the fill color to cornflower blue */
UIColor(red: 0.20, green: 0.60, blue: 0.80, alpha: 1.0).setFill()

/* Set the stroke color to brown */
UIColor.brownColor().setStroke()

/* Set the line width (for the stroke) to 5 */
CGContextSetLineWidth(currentContext, 5)

/* Stroke and fill the path on the context */
CGContextDrawPath(currentContext, kCGPathFillStroke)
```

Just like scaling and translation, you can apply rotation translation to shapes drawn on paths and graphics contexts. You can use the CGAffineTransformMakeRotation function and pass the rotation value in radians to get back a rotation transformation of type CGAffineTransform. You can then apply this transformation to paths and shapes. If you want to rotate the whole context by a specific angle, you must use the CGContextRota teCTM procedure.

Let's rotate the same rectangle we had in Figure 19-19 45 degrees clockwise (see Figure 19-28). The values you supply for rotation must be in radians. Positive values cause clockwise rotation, while negative values cause counterclockwise rotation:

```
/* Rotate the rectangle 45 degrees clockwise */
var transform = CGAffineTransformMakeRotation((45.0 * M_PI) / 180.0)

/* Add the rectangle to the path */
CGPathAddRect(path, &transform, rectangle)
```

As we saw in Recipe 19.9, we can also apply a transformation directly to a graphics context using the CGContextRotateCTM procedure.

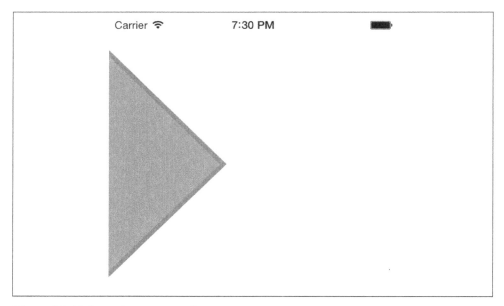

Figure 19-28. Rotating a rectangle

See Also

Recipe 19.6; Recipe 19.9

19.10. Animating Views

Problem

You want to animate the displacement of views.

Solution

Use the animation methods of UIView while displacing your views.

Discussion

There are various ways of performing animations in iOS: capabilities are provided at a relatively low level, but also at a higher level. The highest level we can get is through UIKit, which is what we will be discussing in this section. UIKit includes some low-level Core Animation functionalities and presents us with a really clean API to work with.

The starting point for performing animations in UIKit is to call the `animateWithDura tion:animations:completion:` type method of the UIView class. Its first parameter is the duration of the animation in seconds, the second parameter is a block object that dictates what animation should be performed, and the last parameter is another block object that gets called by UIKit whenever the animation is finished.

As we saw in Recipe 19.2, I included in my assets category an image called *Safari.png*. This is Safari's icon, which I showed you how to extract manually out of Safari's bundle. Now, in my view controller, I want to place this image in an image view of type UIImage View and then move that image view from the top-left corner of the screen to the bottom-right corner.

Here are the steps that complete this task:

1. Open the Swift file for your view controller.
2. Define an instance of UIImageView as a property of the view controller, and call it safariImageView, like so:

```
import UIKit

class ViewController: UIViewController {

  var safariImageView:UIImageView
  let safariImage = UIImage(named: "Safari")

  override init(nibName nibNameOrNil: String!,
    bundle nibBundleOrNil: NSBundle!) {
    safariImageView = UIImageView(image: safariImage)
    super.init(nibName: nibNameOrNil, bundle: nibBundleOrNil)
  }

  required init(coder aDecoder: NSCoder) {
    safariImageView = UIImageView(image: safariImage)
    super.init(coder: aDecoder)
  }

}
```

3. After your view is loaded, position the image view correctly and add it to your view.

```
override func viewDidLoad() {
  super.viewDidLoad()

  /* Just set the size to make the image smaller */
  self.safariImageView.frame = CGRect(x: 0, y: 30, width: 100, height: 100)

  self.view.addSubview(self.safariImageView)

}
```

4. Figure 19-29 shows how the view will look when we run the program in iOS Simulator.

Carrier 📶   6:16 PM   🔋

Figure 19-29. Adding an image view to a view object

5. Now when the view appears on the screen, in the `viewDidAppear:` instance method of the view controller, we will start the animation block for the image view and start an animation that moves the image from its initial location at the top-left corner of the screen to the bottom-right corner. We will make sure this animation happens over a five-second time period:

```
override func viewDidAppear(animated: Bool) {
  super.viewDidAppear(animated)

  /* Start from top-left corner */
  self.safariImageView.frame = CGRect(x: 0, y: 30, width: 100, height: 100)
  let endRect = CGRect(x: self.view.bounds.size.width - 100,
    y: self.view.bounds.size.height - 100,
    width: 100,
    height: 100)

  UIView.animateWithDuration(5.0, animations: {[weak self] in
    self!.safariImageView.frame = endRect
    }, completion: {
    [weak self] (completed: Bool) in
    println("Finished the animation")
    })
}
```

Now if you run the app, you will notice that as soon as your view gets displayed, the image shown in Figure 19-29 will start moving toward the bottom-right corner, as shown in Figure 19-30, over a period of five seconds.

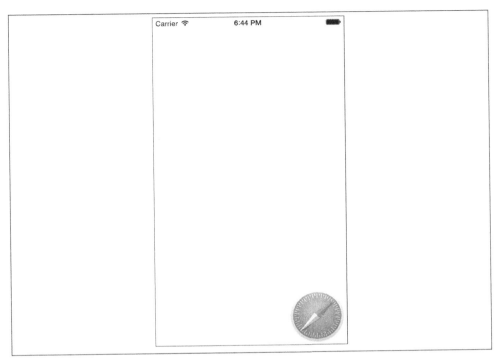

Figure 19-30. The image is animated to the bottom-right corner of the screen

Now let's look at another animation. In this example code, I want to have two image views (both displaying the same image) appear on the screen at the same time: one at the top-left corner and the other at the bottom-right corner, as shown in Figure 19-31.

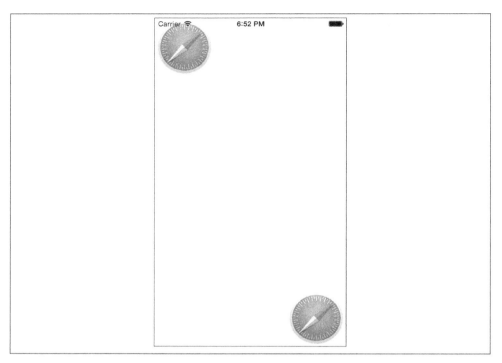

Figure 19-31. The starting position of the animation

In this section, I will call the top-left image *image 1* and the bottom-right image *image 2*.

In this code, we are going to create two images, as mentioned, in the top-left and bottom-right corners. Next, we want image 1 to start moving toward image 2 over a three-second period, and then fade away. While image 1 is approaching image 2, we want image 2 to start its animation and move toward the top-left corner of the screen, where image 1 used to be. We also want image 2 to complete its animation over a three-second time period and fade away at the end. This will look *really* cool when you run it on a device or on iOS Simulator. Let me show you how to code it:

1. On top of your view controller, define two image views:

```
var safariImageView1:UIImageView!
var safariImageView2:UIImageView!
```

2. In the `viewDidLoad` instance method of your view controller, initialize both of the image views and place them on your view:

```swift
var safariImageView1:UIImageView
var safariImageView2:UIImageView

var bottomRightRect:CGRect{
get{
  return CGRect(
    x: self.view.bounds.size.width - 100,
    y: self.view.bounds.size.height - 100,
    width: 100,
    height: 100)
}
}

let topLeftRect = CGRect(x: 0, y: 0, width: 100, height: 100)
let image = UIImage(named: "Safari")

override init(nibName nibNameOrNil: String!, bundle nibBundleOrNil:
    NSBundle!) {
  safariImageView1 = UIImageView(image: image)
  safariImageView2 = UIImageView(image: image)
  super.init(nibName: nibNameOrNil, bundle: nibBundleOrNil)
}

init(coder aDecoder: NSCoder!) {
  safariImageView1 = UIImageView(image: image)
  safariImageView2 = UIImageView(image: image)
  super.init(coder: aDecoder)
}

override func viewDidLoad() {
  super.viewDidLoad()

  safariImageView1.frame = topLeftRect
  safariImageView2.frame = bottomRightRect
  self.view.addSubview(safariImageView1)
  self.view.addSubview(safariImageView2)
}
```

3. Implement an instance method called `startTopLeftImageViewAnimation` for your view controller. This method, as its name suggests, will carry out the animation for image 1, moving it from the top-left corner of the screen to the bottom-right corner while fading it out. Fading is accomplished simply by setting the alpha value to 0:

```swift
func startTopLeftImageViewAnimation(){

  /* Start from top left corner */
  safariImageView1.frame = topLeftRect
```

```
        safariImageView1.alpha = 1

        UIView.animateWithDuration(3, animations: {
          [weak self] in
          self!.safariImageView1.frame = self!.bottomRightRect
          self!.safariImageView1.alpha = 0
          }, completion: {
          [weak self] (finished: Bool) in
            self!.safariImageView1.removeFromSuperview()
          })

    }
```

4. When the animation for any of these image views stops, we intend to remove those image views from their parent views, as they are not useful anymore. For this, we will use the completion block of our animation. This block will get called when the animations for image 1 (as we saw before) and for image 2 (as we will soon see) stop.

5. We also need a method that will animate image 2. There is a little difference between how I've written the animation method for image 2 as compared to that for image 1. I want to be able to start image 2's animation *almost* as image 1 is finishing its animation. So if image 1 performs its animation in three seconds, I want image 2 to start its animation at second 2.0 in image 1's animation, so that I can see image 2 starting to animate before image 1 gets to the bottom-right corner of the screen and fades away. To accomplish this, I start both animations at the same time, but the animation for image 2 will include a two-second delay at the beginning. So if I start both animations at 1 p.m., image 1 starts its animation at 13:00:00 and finishes at 13:00:03, while image 2 starts at 13:00:02 and finishes at 13:00:05. Here is how we will animate image 2:

```
    func startBottomRightViewAnimationAfterDelay(paramDelay: CGFloat){

      /* Start from bottom right corner */
      safariImageView2.frame = bottomRightRect

      safariImageView2.alpha = 1

      UIView.animateWithDuration(3, delay: NSTimeInterval(paramDelay),
        options: UIViewAnimationOptions(rawValue: 0),
        animations: {
          [weak self] in
          self!.safariImageView2.frame = self!.topLeftRect
          self!.safariImageView2.alpha = 0
        },
        completion: {[weak self] (finished: Bool) in
          self!.safariImageView2.removeFromSuperview()
        })
```

```
        }
```

6. Last but not least, we have to fire both the `startTopLeftImageViewAnimation` and the `startBottomRightViewAnimationAfterDelay:` methods at the same time when the view becomes visible:

```
override func viewDidAppear(animated: Bool){
  super.viewDidAppear(animated)

  startTopLeftImageViewAnimation()
  startBottomRightViewAnimationAfterDelay(2)

}
```

In order to rotate a view while animating it, you must apply a rotation transformation to it while in an animation block (see Recipe 19.9). Let's have a look at some sample code that will make this clearer. Let's say we have an image named *Safari.png*, and we want to display it in the center of the screen. After the image is displayed, we want to rotate it 90 degrees over a five-second time period and then rotate it back to its original orientation. So when the view appears on the screen, let's rotate the image view 90 degrees clockwise:

```
var safariImageView:UIImageView
let image = UIImage(named: "Safari")

override init(nibName nibNameOrNil: String!, bundle nibBundleOrNil: NSBundle!) {
  safariImageView = UIImageView(image: image)
  super.init(nibName: nibNameOrNil, bundle: nibBundleOrNil)
}

init(coder aDecoder: NSCoder!) {
  safariImageView = UIImageView(image: image)
  super.init(coder: aDecoder)
}

override func viewDidLoad() {
  self.view.addSubview(safariImageView)
}

override func viewDidAppear(animated: Bool) {
  super.viewDidAppear(animated)

  safariImageView.center = self.view.center

  /* Begin the animation */

  UIView.animateWithDuration(5, animations: {[weak self] in
    if let strongSelf = self{
      strongSelf.safariImageView.transform =
        CGAffineTransformMakeRotation(
```

```
        CGFloat((90.0 * M_PI) / 180.0))
    }

  }) {[weak self] (finished: Bool) in

    if let strongSelf = self{
      UIView.animateWithDuration(5, animations: {
        strongSelf.safariImageView.transform =
        CGAffineTransformIdentity
      })
    }
  }

}
```

 In the animation's completion block, we are rotating the image view counterclockwise back to 0 degrees (where it originally was) over a five-second time period.

there are many ways to animate views (direct or indirect subclasses of UIView) and many properties that you can modify while carrying out your animations. Be creative and inspect other properties in UIView that you might have not previously known about. You might also want to take a look at the documentation for UIView in Xcode Organizer.

In order to scale a view while animating it, you can either apply a scale transformation to it within an animation block, or just increase the view's width and/or height.

Let's have a look at scaling an image view by applying a scale transformation to it:

```
var safariImageView:UIImageView
let image = UIImage(named: "Safari")

override init(nibName nibNameOrNil: String!, bundle nibBundleOrNil: NSBundle!) {
  safariImageView = UIImageView(image: image)
  super.init(nibName: nibNameOrNil, bundle: nibBundleOrNil)
}

init(coder aDecoder: NSCoder!) {
  safariImageView = UIImageView(image: image)
  super.init(coder: aDecoder)
}

override func viewDidLoad() {
  self.view.addSubview(safariImageView)
}

override func viewDidAppear(animated: Bool) {
  super.viewDidAppear(animated)
```

```
/* Place the image view at the center of
the view of this view controller */
safariImageView.center = self.view.center

/* Make sure no translation is applied to this image view */
safariImageView.transform = CGAffineTransformIdentity;


/* Make the image view twice as large in
width and height */

/* Begin the animation */
UIView.animateWithDuration(5, animations: {
  [weak self] in
  /* Rotate the image view 90 degrees */
  self!.safariImageView.transform =
    CGAffineTransformMakeScale(2, 2)
  })
}
```

This code uses an affine scale transformation to scale the image view to become twice as big as it originally was. The best thing about applying scale transformations to a view is that the width and height are scaled using the center of the view as the center of the scaling. Suppose that the center of your view is at point (100, 100) on the screen, and you scale your view to be twice as big in width and height. The resulting view will have its center remain at point (100, 100) on the screen, while being twice as big in each direction. If you were to scale a view by increasing its frame's width and height explicitly, you would end up with the final view being located somewhere else on the screen. That's because when changing the frame of the image view to scale the width and height, you are also changing the value of the x and the y of the frame, whether you want to or not. Because of that, your image view will not be scaled up from its center. Fixing this issue is outside the scope of this book, but feel free to play with it for a while, and maybe you will find the solution. One hint that I *will* give you is that you can run two animations at the same time in parallel: one for changing the width and height, and the other for changing the center of the image view!

CHAPTER 20

Core Motion

20.0. Introduction

iOS devices are usually equipped with accelerometer hardware. Some iOS devices might also include a gyroscope, such as the new iPhone and the new iPad. Before attempting to use either the accelerometer or the gyroscope in your iOS applications, you must check the availability of these sensors on the iOS device on which your app runs. Recipe 20.3 and Recipe 20.4 include techniques you can use to detect the availability of the accelerometer and gyroscope. With a gyroscope, iOS devices are able to detect motion in six axes.

Let's go through a situation that will show you the value of the gyroscope. The accelerometer cannot detect the rotation of the device around its vertical axis if you are holding the device perfectly still in your hands, sitting in a computer chair, and rotating your chair in a clockwise or counterclockwise fashion. From the standpoint of the floor or the Earth, the device is rotating around the vertical axis, but it's not rotating around its own y-axis which is the vertical center of the device. So, the accelerometer does not detect any motion.

However, the gyroscope included in some iOS devices allows us to detect such movements. This allows more fluid and flawless movement detection routines. This is typically useful in games, where the developers need to know not only whether the device is moving on the x-, y-, and z-axes (information they can get from the accelerometer), but also whether it is changing in relation to the Earth along these directions, which requires a gyroscope.

Programmers can use the Core Motion framework to access both the accelerometer data and the gyroscope data (if available). All recipes in this chapter make use of the Core Motion framework. With the new features in the LLVM compiler, the only thing you need to do to link your app with a system framework is to simply import that framework on top of your header/implementation files and the compiler will do the actual importing of the framework into your app for you.

iOS Simulator does not simulate the accelerometer or the gyroscope hardware. However, you can generate a *shake* with iOS Simulator using Hardware → Shake Gesture (see Figure 20-1).

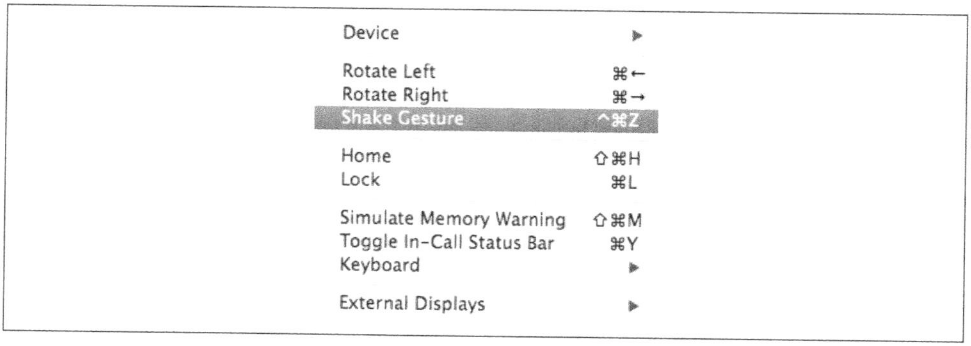

Device		▶
Rotate Left	⌘ ←	
Rotate Right	⌘ →	
Shake Gesture	^⌘Z	
Home	⇧⌘H	
Lock	⌘L	
Simulate Memory Warning	⇧⌘M	
Toggle In-Call Status Bar	⌘Y	
Keyboard		▶
External Displays		▶

Figure 20-1. The Shake Gesture option in iOS Simulator

20.1. Retrieving Altitude Data

Problem

You want to retrieve the user's relative altitude: the difference in height from point A to point B in time, where point A is where you start monitoring for altitude and point B is when you stop monitoring for altitude. Point A is referred to as the *reference point* because the relative altitude that we will receive at any point between A to B will be relative to point A. Point A will always have the relative altitude of 0. If the user goes up, the relative altitude in relation to point A will be positive, and if he goes down, this number will be negative.

Solution

Use the `CMAltimeter` class. This class has a type method called `isRelativeAltitudeA vailable` that returns a Boolean value. If the return value is `true`, the current device on which your code is running allows it to retrieve relative altitude data. You should never attempt to retrieve altitude data before checking the value of this propety and ensuring that it is set to `true`. Once you are sure relative altitude data is available, you can instantiate an object of type `CMAltimeter` and use its `startRelativeAltitudeUpdates ToQueue:withHandler:` method to start monitoring relative altitude changes. The first parameter that you need to provide to this method is an operation queue that will be used by iOS to report relative altitude updates to you, and the second parameter of this method is a closure of type CMAltitudeHandler that is defined like so:

```
typealias CMAltitudeHandler = (CMAltitudeData!, NSError!) -> Void
```

The first parameter of this block object will receive the altitude data. This data contains a property called relativeAltitude, a number you can read that represents the relative altitude data of the device from point A until the moment you read it, in meters.

Discussion

Let's have a look at an example where as soon as our app becomes active, we determine whether we are able to retrieve relative altitude data from the device. If yes, we start accumulating the changes in altitude to a queue. As soon as the app becomes inactive, we stop the relative altitude monitoring mechanism that we built into our app.

 Ensure that every call to the startRelativeAltitudeUpdatesTo Queue:withHandler: method is balanced with a call to the stopRela tiveAltitudeUpdates method of your instance of the CMAltimeter class.

```
import UIKit
import CoreMotion

@UIApplicationMain
class AppDelegate: UIResponder, UIApplicationDelegate {

  var window: UIWindow?
  /* The altimeter instance that will deliver our altitude updates if they
  are available on the host device */
  lazy var altimeter = CMAltimeter()
  /* A private queue on which altitude updates will be delivered to us */
  lazy var queue = NSOperationQueue()

  func application(application: UIApplication,
    didFinishLaunchingWithOptions launchOptions:
    [NSObject : AnyObject]?) -> Bool {
    return true
  }

  /* Start altitude updates if possible */
  func applicationDidBecomeActive(application: UIApplication) {
    if CMAltimeter.isRelativeAltitudeAvailable(){
      altimeter.startRelativeAltitudeUpdatesToQueue(queue,
        withHandler: {(data: CMAltitudeData!, error: NSError!) in

        println("Relative altitude is \(data.relativeAltitude) meters")

      })
```

```
      }
    }

    /* Stop altitude updates */
    func applicationWillResignActive(application: UIApplication) {
      altimeter.stopRelativeAltitudeUpdates()
    }

}
```

See Also

Recipe 20.3; Recipe 20.5; Recipe 20.2

20.2. Retrieving Pedometer Data

Problem

You want to query the following information from an iOS device:

- Number of steps that the user has taken from point A to B in time
- Number of floors climbed or descended from point A to B in time
- Distance travelled by the user in meters from point A to B in time

Solution

Use the CMPedometer class. If you want to detect the number of steps that the user takes from one point to another point in time, first invoke the isStepCountingAvailable type method of the aforementioned class to find out whether step counting is available on the host device. If yes, instantiate an object of type CMPedometer and invoke the startPedometerUpdatesFromDate:withHandler: method of that object. This method will accept a date as its first parameter. This date is the date when you would like to start querying the user's pedometer information. If you want to start from right now, pass a newly initialized instance of the NSDate class to this parameter. The second parameter to this method is a closure of type CMPedometerHandler that will get called whenever new pedometer information is available. The first parameter of this closure is of type CMPedometerData that, depending on the capabilities of the device and the pedometer on that device, can contain information such as the number of steps travelled, number of floors climbed or descended, and distance travelled by the user.

To detect whether the pedometer on the host machine can detect the floors climbed or descended by the user, invoke the isFloorCountingAvailable type method the CMPedometer class. This method returns a Boolean value indicating whether floor counting is available. Also, if you want to detect whether distance counting is enabled, invoke the `isDistanceAvailable` type method of the aforementioned class to get a Boolean value that indicates whether this functionality can be used at present on the host device.

Discussion

A pedometer is a device that is able to detect a person's footsteps. When a pedometer detects a step and has gathered (through user caliberation or direct input) information about how long each step is, it can detect the distance travelled by the user. iOS devices mix functionality from variety of sensors such as the accelerometer and the gyroscope to detect various movements by the user, including the number of stairs climbed or descended.

Pedometer functionality is available through the `CMPedometer` class. Let's say that we want to detect the number of steps the user takes as soon as our app is started up:

```
import UIKit
import CoreMotion

@UIApplicationMain
class AppDelegate: UIResponder, UIApplicationDelegate {

  var window: UIWindow?
  lazy var pedometer = CMPedometer()

  func application(application: UIApplication,
    didFinishLaunchingWithOptions launchOptions:
    [NSObject : AnyObject]?) -> Bool {
      return true
  }

  func applicationDidBecomeActive(application: UIApplication) {
    if CMPedometer.isStepCountingAvailable(){

      pedometer.startPedometerUpdatesFromDate(NSDate(), withHandler: {
        (data: CMPedometerData!, error: NSError!) in

        println("Number of steps = \(data.numberOfSteps)")

      })

    } else {
      println("Step counting is not available")
    }
  }

  func applicationWillResignActive(application: UIApplication) {
    pedometer.stopPedometerUpdates()
  }

}
```

As you can see, we are checking whether step counting is available and, if yes, we start pedometer updates from our `CMPedometer` instance. The pedometer data, encapsulated in the `CMPedometerData` instance passed to our closure, will include the `numberOf Steps` property that is expressed in meters.

Now let's say that we want to detect the distance travelled by the user from yesterday until right now. In order to query pedometer data from a certain date to another date, we need to use the `queryPedometerDataFromDate:toDate:withHandler:` method of our pedometer instance. The first two parameters are of type `NSDate`, which will define the starting and ending date, and the third parameter is of type `CMPedometerHandler`, which we have already talked about. So let's have a look at this example:

```
import UIKit
import CoreMotion

/* A really simple extension on NSDate that gives us convenience methods
for "now" and "yesterday" */
extension NSDate{
  class func now() -> NSDate{
    return NSDate()
  }
  class func yesterday() -> NSDate{
    return NSDate(timeIntervalSinceNow: -(24 * 60 * 60))
  }
}

@UIApplicationMain
class AppDelegate: UIResponder, UIApplicationDelegate {

  var window: UIWindow?
  lazy var pedometer = CMPedometer()

  func application(application: UIApplication,
    didFinishLaunchingWithOptions launchOptions:
    [NSObject : AnyObject]?) -> Bool {
      return true
  }

  func applicationDidBecomeActive(application: UIApplication) {

    /* Can we ask for distance updates? */
    if CMPedometer.isDistanceAvailable(){

      pedometer.queryPedometerDataFromDate(NSDate.yesterday(),
        toDate: NSDate.now(),
        withHandler: {(data: CMPedometerData!, error: NSError!) in

        println("Distance travelled from yesterday to now " +
          "= \(data.distance) meters")

      })
```

```
    } else {
      println("Distance counting is not available")
    }
  }

  func applicationWillResignActive(application: UIApplication) {
    pedometer.stopPedometerUpdates()
  }

}
```

The other example that we can have a look at is to ask our pedometer instance to detect the number of floors that were climbed from 10 minutes ago to now. We will use the isFloorCountingAvailable type method of our pedometer class to detect whether floor counting is enabled. If floor counting is enabled, we use the queryPedometerData taFromDate:toDate:withHandler: method to query this data. The data that comes back to us will be of type CMPedometerData, of course. We will then be able to read the floor counting information using the floorsAscended and the floorsDescended properties of this data. The names of these properties kind of describe what they are all about, so I won't attempt to over-explain that. Here is our example:

```
import UIKit
import CoreMotion

extension NSDate{
  class func now() -> NSDate{
    return NSDate()
  }
  class func tenMinutesAgo() -> NSDate{
    return NSDate(timeIntervalSinceNow: -(10 * 60))
  }
}

@UIApplicationMain
class AppDelegate: UIResponder, UIApplicationDelegate {

  var window: UIWindow?
  lazy var pedometer = CMPedometer()

  func application(application: UIApplication,
    didFinishLaunchingWithOptions launchOptions:
    [NSObject : AnyObject]?) -> Bool {
      return true
  }

  func applicationDidBecomeActive(application: UIApplication) {

    /* Can we ask for floor climb/descending updates? */
    if CMPedometer.isFloorCountingAvailable(){
```

```
      pedometer.queryPedometerDataFromDate(NSDate.tenMinutesAgo(),
        toDate: NSDate.now(),
        withHandler: {(data: CMPedometerData!, error: NSError!) in

          println("Floors ascended = \(data.floorsAscended)")
          println("Floors descended = \(data.floorsAscended)")

      })

    } else {
      println("Floor counting is not available")
    }
  }

  func applicationWillResignActive(application: UIApplication) {
    pedometer.stopPedometerUpdates()
  }

}
```

See Also

Recipe 20.1; Recipe 20.3

20.3. Detecting the Availability of an Accelerometer

Problem

In your program, you want to detect whether the accelerometer hardware is available.

Solution

Use the `accelerometerAvailable` property of `CMMotionManager` to detect the accelerometer hardware. The `accelerometerActive` property can also be used to detect whether the accelerometer hardware is currently sending updates to the program.

Let's first make sure we imported the required header files:

```
import UIKit
import CoreMotion

@UIApplicationMain
class AppDelegate: UIResponder, UIApplicationDelegate
```

Next, go on to detect the availability of an accelerometer in the app delegate:

```
import UIKit
import CoreMotion

@UIApplicationMain
```

```
class AppDelegate: UIResponder, UIApplicationDelegate {

  var window: UIWindow?

  func application(application: UIApplication,
    didFinishLaunchingWithOptions launchOptions:
    [NSObject : AnyObject]?) -> Bool {

    let motionManager = CMMotionManager()

    if motionManager.accelerometerAvailable{
      println("Accelerometer is available")
    } else{
      println("Accelerometer is not available")
    }

    if motionManager.accelerometerActive{
      println("Accelerometer is active")
    } else {
      println("Accelerometer is not active")
    }

    return true
  }

}
```

Accelerometer hardware might be available on the iOS device running your program. This, however, does not mean the accelerometer hardware is sending updates to your program. If the accelerometer or gyroscope *is* sending updates to your program, we say it is *active* (which requires you to define a delegate object, as we will soon see).

If you run this code on iOS Simulator, you will get values similar to these in the console window:

```
Accelerometer is not available
Accelerometer is not active
```

Running the same code on the new iPhone, you will get values similar to these:

```
Accelerometer is available
Accelerometer is not active
```

Discussion

An iOS device could have a built-in accelerometer. Because we don't yet know which iOS devices have accelerometer hardware built in and which don't, it is best to test the availability of the accelerometer before using it.

You can detect the availability of this hardware by instantiating an object of type CMMotionManager and accessing its isAccelerometerAvailable method. This method is of type BOOL and returns `true` if the accelerometer hardware is available and `false` if not.

In addition, you can detect whether the accelerometer hardware is currently sending updates to your application (whether it is active) by issuing the `isAccelerometerAc tive` method of `CMMotionManager`. You will learn about retrieving accelerometer data in Recipe 20.5.

See Also

Recipe 20.5

20.4. Detecting the Availability of a Gyroscope

Problem

You want to find out whether the current iOS device that is running your program has gyroscope hardware available.

Solution

Use the `gyroAvailable` property of an instance of `CMMotionManager` to detect the gyroscope hardware. The `gyroActive` property is also available if you want to detect whether the gyroscope hardware is currently sending updates to your program (in other words, whether it is active):

```
import UIKit
import CoreMotion

@UIApplicationMain
class AppDelegate: UIResponder, UIApplicationDelegate {

  var window: UIWindow?

  func application(application: UIApplication,
    didFinishLaunchingWithOptions launchOptions:
    [NSObject : AnyObject]?) -> Bool {

      let motionManager = CMMotionManager()

      if motionManager.gyroAvailable{
        println("Gryro is available")
      } else {
        println("Gyro is not available")
      }

      if motionManager.gyroActive{
        println("Gryo is active")
```

```
        } else {
          println("Gryo is not active")
        }

        return true
    }

  }
```

iOS Simulator does not have gyroscope simulation in place. If you run this code on the simulator, you will receive results similar to these in the console window:

```
Gyro is not available
Gyro is not active
```

If you run this code on an iOS device with a gyroscope, such as the new iPhone, the results could be different:

```
Gyro is available
Gyro is not active
```

Discussion

If you plan to release an application that makes use of the gyroscope, you must make sure other iOS devices without this hardware can run your application. If you are using the gyroscope as part of a game, for instance, you must make sure other iOS devices that are capable of running your application can play the game, although they might not have a gyroscope installed. Not all iOS devices have a gyroscope. This recipe shows you how to determine whether a device has a gyroscope.

To achieve this, you must first instantiate an object of type `CMMotionManager`. After this, you must access the `gyroAvailable` property (of type `Bool`) and see whether the gyroscope is available on the device running your code. You can also use the `gyroActive` property of the `CMMotionManager` instance to find out whether the gyroscope is currently sending your application any updates. For more information about this, please refer to Recipe 20.7.

See Also

Recipe 20.7

20.5. Retrieving Accelerometer Data

Problem

You want to ask iOS to send accelerometer data to your application.

Solution

Use the `startAccelerometerUpdatesToQueue:withHandler:` instance method of `CMMotionManager`. Here is our view controller that utilizes `CMMotionManager` to get accelerometer updates:

```
import UIKit
import CoreMotion

class ViewController: UIViewController {

  lazy var motionManager = CMMotionManager()

}
```

We will now implement our view controller and take advantage of the `startAccelerometerUpdatesToQueue:withHandler:` method of the `CMMotionManager` class:

```
import UIKit
import CoreMotion

class ViewController: UIViewController {

  lazy var motionManager = CMMotionManager()

  override func viewDidLoad() {
    super.viewDidLoad()

    if motionManager.accelerometerAvailable{
      let queue = NSOperationQueue()
      motionManager.startAccelerometerUpdatesToQueue(queue, withHandler:
        {(data: CMAccelerometerData!, error: NSError!) in

          println("X = \(data.acceleration.x)")
          println("Y = \(data.acceleration.y)")
          println("Z = \(data.acceleration.z)")

        }
      )
    } else {
      println("Accelerometer is not available")
    }

  }

}
```

Discussion

The accelerometer reports three-dimensional data (three axes) that iOS reports to your program as *x*, *y*, and *z* values. These values are encapsulated in a CMAcceleration structure:

```
struct CMAcceleration {
    var x: Double
    var y: Double
    var z: Double
}
```

If you hold your iOS device in front of your face with the screen facing you in portrait mode:

- The *x*-axis runs from left to right at the horizontal center of the device, with values ranging from –1 to +1 from left to right.
- The *y*-axis runs from bottom to top at the vertical center of the device, with values ranging from –1 to +1 from bottom to top.
- The *z*-axis runs from the back of the device, through the device toward you, with values ranging from –1 to +1 from back to front.

The best way to understand the values reported from the accelerometer hardware is by taking a look at a few examples. Here is one: let's assume you have your iOS device facing you with the bottom of the device pointing to the ground and the top pointing up. If you hold it perfectly still without tilting it in any specific direction, the values you have for the *x*-, *y*-, and *z*-axes will be (x: 0.0, y: –1.0, z: 0.0). Now try the following while the screen is facing you and the bottom of the device is pointing to the ground:

1. Turn the device 90 degrees clockwise. The values at that moment are (x: +1.0, y: 0.0, z: 0.0).

2. Turn the device a further 90 degrees clockwise. Now the top of the device must be pointing to the ground. The values you have at this moment are (x: 0.0, y: +1.0, z: 0.0).

3. Turn the device a further 90 degrees clockwise. Now the top of the device is pointing to the left. The values you have right now are (x: –1.0, y: 0.0, z: 0.0).

4. Finally, if you rotate the device a further 90 degrees clockwise, where the top of the device once again points to the sky and the bottom of the device points to the ground, the values will be as they were originally (x: 0.0, y: –1.0, z: 0.0).

So, from these values, we can conclude that rotating the device around the *z*-axis changes the *x* and *y* values reported by the accelerometer, but not the *z* value.

Let's conduct another experiment. Hold the device again so it's facing you with its bottom pointing to the ground and its top pointing to the sky. The values that a program will get from the accelerometer, as you already know, are (x: 0.0, y: −1.0, z: 0.0). Now try these movements:

1. Tilt the device backward 90 degrees around the x-axis so that its top is pointing backward. In other words, hold it as though it is sitting face-up on a table. The values you get at this moment are (x: 0.0, y: 0.0, z: −1.0).

2. Now tilt the device backward 90 degrees so that its back is facing you, its top is facing the ground, and its bottom is facing the sky. The values you get at this moment are (x: 0.0, y: 1.0, z: 0.0).

3. Tilt the device backward 90 degrees so that it's facing the ground with its back facing the sky and its top pointing toward you. The reported values at this moment are (x: 0.0, y: 0.0, z: 1.0).

4. And finally, if you tilt the device one more time in the same direction, so the device is facing you and its top is facing the sky, the values you get are the same values you started with.

Therefore, we can observe that rotating the device around the x-axis changes the values of the y- and z-axes, but not x. I encourage you to try the third type of rotation—around the y-axis (pointing from top to bottom)—and observe the changes in the values reported for the x- and the z-axes.

To be able to receive accelerometer updates, you have two options:

- The `startAccelerometerUpdatesToQueue:withHandler:` instance method of `CMMotionManager`.

  This method will deliver accelerometer updates on an operation queue (of type `NSOperationQueue`) and will require a basic knowledge of blocks that are used extensively in Grand Central Dispatch (GCD). For more information about blocks, please refer to Chapter 7.

- The `startAccelerometerUpdates` instance method of `CMMotionManager`.

  When you call this method, the accelerometer (if available) will start updating accelerometer data in the motion manager object. You need to set up your own thread to continuously read the value of the `accelerometerData` property (of type `CMAccelerometerData`) of `CMMotionManager`.

In this recipe, we are using the first method (with blocks). I highly recommend that you first read Chapter 7 before proceeding with this recipe. The block we provide to the `startAccelerometerUpdatesToQueue:withHandler:` instance method of `CMMotionManager` must be of type `CMAccelerometerHandler`:

```
typealias CMAccelerometerHandler = (CMAccelerometerData!, NSError!) -> Void
```

In other words, we must accept two parameters on the block. The first one must be of type `CMAccelerometerData`, and the second must be of type `NSError`, as implemented in our example code.

See Also

Recipe 20.3

20.6. Detecting Shakes on an iOS Device

Problem

You want to know when

the user shakes an iOS device.

Solution

Use the `motionEnded:withEvent:` method of any object in your application that is of type `UIResponder`. This could be your view controller(s) or even your main window object.

Discussion

The `motionEnded:withEvent:` method of a responder object gets called whenever a motion has been captured by iOS. The simplest implementation of this method is this:

```
override func motionEnded(motion: UIEventSubtype,
  withEvent event: UIEvent) {

    /* Handle the motion here */

}
```

The `motion` parameter, as you can see, is of type `UIEventSubtype`. One of the values of type `UIEventSubtype` is `UIEventSubtypeMotionShake`, which is what we are interested in. As soon as we detect this event, we know that the user has shaken her iOS device. Now go to the implementation of your view controller and handle the `motionEnded:withEvent:` method:

```
override func motionEnded(motion: UIEventSubtype,
  withEvent event: UIEvent) {

    if motion == .MotionShake{
      let controller = UIAlertController(title: "Shake",
        message: "The device is shaken",
```

```
        preferredStyle: .Alert)

    controller.addAction(UIAlertAction(title: "OK",
        style: .Default,
        handler: nil))

    presentViewController(controller, animated: true, completion: nil)

    }

}
```

If you now simulate a shake event, even if you are on iOS Simulator (see this chapter's Introduction), you will see that our application displays an alert controller to the user, similar to that shown in Figure 20-2.

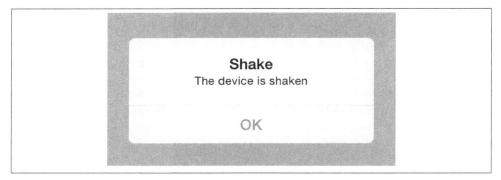

Figure 20-2. Shake gesture is detected

20.7. Retrieving Gyroscope Data

Problem

You want to be able to retrieve information about the device's motion from the gyroscope hardware on an iOS device.

Solution

Follow these steps:

1. Find out whether the gyroscope hardware is available on the iOS device. Please refer to Recipe 20.4 for directions on how to do this.

2. If the gyroscope hardware is available, make sure it is not already sending you updates. Please refer to Recipe 20.4 for directions.

3. Use the `gyroUpdateInterval` property of `CMMotionManager` to set the number of updates you want to receive per second. For instance, for 20 updates per second (one second), set this value to 1.0/20.0.

4. Invoke the `startGyroUpdatesToQueue:withHandler:` instance method of `CMMotionManager`. The queue object could simply be the main operation queue (as we will see later), and the handler block must follow the `CMGyroHandler` format.

The following code implements these steps:

```
import UIKit
import CoreMotion

@UIApplicationMain
class AppDelegate: UIResponder, UIApplicationDelegate {

  var window: UIWindow?
  lazy var manager = CMMotionManager()
  lazy var queue = NSOperationQueue()

  func application(application: UIApplication,
    didFinishLaunchingWithOptions launchOptions:
    [NSObject : AnyObject]?) -> Bool {


      if manager.gyroAvailable{

        if manager.gyroActive == false{

          manager.gyroUpdateInterval = 1.0 / 40.0

          manager.startGyroUpdatesToQueue(queue,
            withHandler: {(data: CMGyroData!, error: NSError!) in

              println("Gyro Rotation x = \(data.rotationRate.x)")
              println("Gyro Rotation y = \(data.rotationRate.y)")
              println("Gyro Rotation z = \(data.rotationRate.z)")

          })
        } else {
          println("Gyro is already active")
        }

      } else {
        println("Gyro isn't available")
      }

      return true
  }

}
```

Discussion

With `CMMotionManager`, application programmers can attempt to retrieve gyroscope updates from iOS. You must first make sure the gyroscope hardware is available on the iOS device on which your application is running (please refer to Recipe 20.4). After doing so, you can use the `gyroUpdateInterval` property of `CMMotionManager` to set the number of updates you would like to receive per second for updates from the gyroscope hardware. For instance, if you want to be updated N times per second, set this value to $1.0/N$.

After you set the update interval, you can call the `startGyroUpdatesToQueue:withHan` `dler:` instance method of `CMMotionManager` to set up a handler block for the updates. For more information about blocks, please refer to Chapter 7. Your block object must be of type `CMGyroHandler`, which accepts two parameters:

data
> The data that comes from the gyroscope hardware, encompassed in an object of type `CMGyroData`. You can use the `rotationRate` property of `CMGyroData` (a structure) to get access to the x, y, and z values of the data, which represent all three Euler angles known as roll, pitch, and yaw, respectively. You can learn more about these by reading about flight dynamics.

error
> An error of type `NSError` that might occur when the gyroscope is sending updates.

If you do not want to use block objects, you must call the `startGyroUpdates` instance method of `CMMotionManager` instead of the `startGyroUpdatesToQueue:withHan` `dler:` instance method and set up your own thread to read the gyroscope hardware updates posted to the `gyroData` property of the instance of `CMMotionManager` you are using.

See Also

Recipe 20.4

CHAPTER 21

Cloud

21.0. Introduction

One of the really great frameworks in the iOS SDK is CloudKit. Using this framework, you can store public and private information on the cloud with ease. One of the key concepts in CloudKit is *containers*, which are virtual boxes that encapsulate public and private databases.

Before I go into more details about all this jargon, let's imagine a simple scenario. Your app is running on an iOS device and the owner of that device has an iCloud account already set up for herself. Every app that runs on that device has its own CloudKit container and multiple apps can share containers if they are set up in a specific way. Your default container is your app's own container, but you can find a container for another app if you know its unique identifier in the cloud. Containers are represented by the CKContainer class in CloudKit.

Every container (and therefore every app that uses a container) has two databases: one public and the other private. When you use the private database and store information there, the information is saved in the user's iCloud account and is private to her on that device for your app. If you use the public database, the user doesn't need an iCloud account to be able to read that information. So all users of your app can use information from the public database.

 Information that is stored in the public database for your app counts against your iCloud storage quota, so be very careful about tracking its size. The information stored by a user in her private database counts against the user's iCloud quota, which is why the user has to be logged into her iCloud account before using the private database.

Databases in CloudKit are represented by the CKDatabase class.

CloudKit contains records, like traditional databases, embodying items of information along with metadata. Key Value Coding is used to store your information in records. That means you can use subscripting to set the value of a particular key in the record and then save that record to a private or a public database. Records are of type `CKRecord`.

Every record must be stored in a *zone*, which is like a table in the database. Record zones are represented with the `CKRecordZone` class. Zones act like silos for records, letting you separate different types of data in that database. But every database has a default zone, so if your data structure is simple, you can just use the default zone and dispense with creating new zones in your databases.

Each record in a database has a unique identifier. This is similar to the primary key of a record in a table inside a relational database. This record identifier has a record name and a record zone as its properties.

The *record name* is a name that you designate for every record. For instance, if you want to store information for a Volvo V50 car as a record, you could use "Volvo V50" for the record identifier's record name. The record zone could be nil to use the default record zone, or you could pass an instance of an existing record zone to this identifier class. You can use record identifiers to fetch objects from your databases, as we will see later in this chapter. Record identifiers are represented by the `CKRecordID` class.

CloudKit also has the concept of *references*. As their name suggests, references are means of connecting two records to each other in some kind of a relationship. For instance, your Volvo V50 has four wheels (at least I hope so!) and each wheel belongs to the car, so you can create a reference from each wheel to the car. Apple recommends that you create backwards references from the child to the parent rather than from the parent to the child in CloudKit. References are represented with the `CKReference` class.

On top of all this, CloudKit also has the concept of *assets*. These are large files that you can associate with records. Going back to our Volvo V50 example, if you want to store a photo of the car, it is best to create an asset out of that image and then associate that asset with your records. We will see how to do this later in this chapter. Assets in CloudKit are represented by the `CKAsset` class.

CloudKit, as its name suggest, sits on top of iCloud and uses iCloud for all data storage and transportation. Now that we have learned the structure and concepts about Cloud-Kit, let's have a look at what iCloud is and how we might be able to use it in our apps. Remember, to use CloudKit, you do not have to know anything about iCloud at all. You can write fully functional cloud-based apps using CloudKit without having any knowledge whatsoever about iCloud, but I do encourage you to read the rest of this chapter's introduction to familiarize yourself with iCloud as well.

iCloud is Apple's cloud infrastructure. A cloud is a name given to a service that stores information on a centralized location, where the user cannot physically access the disk/memory that stores the information. For instance, an iCloud storage space could be allocated by Apple in California, and all iPhone devices in New York could have all their iCloud traffic go to the California iCloud data center.

The purpose of using iCloud, from a programmer's perspective, is to give users the ability to seamlessly transfer their app data from one machine to another. Let's have a look at a real-life example of when iCloud comes in very handy. Imagine that you have developed an app called Game XYZ. Sarah is a hypothetical user of your game, and she purchased it through the App Store. Your game is a universal app and hence can be run on both the iPhone and the iPad. It just so happens that Sarah has an iPad and an iPhone and has installed your game on both devices. She is playing your game at the office and is at level 12. She goes back home and picks up her iPad to play some more, only to discover that the game starts from level 1 on her iPad because she was playing on her iPhone all along. This is definitely not a pretty situation. What is better is for your game to be intelligent enough to save its state and resume that state when your users restart the game, regardless of which device they have been running it on. To handle this situation, you could use iCloud to store Sarah's game state on her iPhone and let iCloud synchronize this data to the data centers that are maintained by Apple. When she picks her iPad up, you could use your app to contact iCloud and find out if there is a recent game state saved for Sarah. If yes, then you can load that state for her to give her the feeling that she didn't even leave your game. She just switched devices. This is a bit more work for you, but in the end you will get really happy customers.

Before being able to use iCloud services, you first need to enable your app for iCloud. This requires creating the correct provisioning profiles in iOS Provisioning Portal and then enabling the correct entitlements in your project. You can read more about this in Recipe 21.1.

 I use the terms "folder" and "directory" interchangeably throughout this chapter.

21.1. Setting Up Your App for CloudKit

Problem

You want to use CloudKit in your application.

Solution

Follow these steps:

1. Ensure that you set up a valid profile for your project that supports iCloud by following the steps described in Recipe 1.22.

2. Navigate to the Capabilities tab of your project settings and turn on the iCloud option.

3. If you don't already have a team or multiple teams set up in your Xcode, you will be asked to set one up or choose an existing one as shown in Figure 21-1. Click Choose.

Figure 21-1. Choose a team to fetch iCloud profiles from

4. Now tick the CloudKit box and choose the "Specify custom containers" box as well, as shown in Figure 21-2. Then choose the containers that you want your app to be able to access. Every app has its own container as we mentioned before, and these containers can be created and managed in the iOS Dev Center portal.

Figure 21-2. Selecting the containers this app needs to access

If you want to use the default container for your app that is associated with the provision profile, and hence the bundle identifier that your app is set up to use, simply leave "Use default container" selected, as it is in Figure 21-2.

Discussion

Now that we have set up our app to use its default container, let's experiment a little bit with CloudKit. One of the main functionalities that you should get used to when using CloudKit is to find out whether the current user is logged into iCloud. You might decide that your app requires that the user be signed into her iCloud account in order for you to store some of her private information into a private database in your app's default container. You can do so by first accessing the default container.

Start by querying the value of the `defaultContainer` type method of the `CKContainer` class. This method will return your default container of type `CKContainer`. Once you have the default container, issue the `accountStatusWithCompletionHandler:` method on the container to find the status of the user in regards to iCloud and whether she is currently logged in. The completion handler that you pass to this method will receive the status of type `CKAccountStatus` and an error object. If the error object is nil, you can proceed to find out more about the status.

So let's look at an example. We will find out whether the current user is currently logged into her iCloud account, and then subscribe to the `NSUbiquityIdentityDidChangeNotification` notification to be notified whenever the user logs out or logs back in with a different iCloud account. You always need to do this if you are storing information in the user's private database. Imagine a scenario where you continue to store information in another user's private database thinking it is the previous user. That would be bad.

Let's begin by importing our frameworks and a variable that will be our container:

```
import UIKit
import CloudKit

class ViewController: UIViewController {

    let container = CKContainer.defaultContainer()

    <#rest of the code #>
}
```

Then as soon as our view controller is loaded, we want to find out whether the user's iCloud status is going to change. We need to find out when our app becomes active so that we start listening for iCloud account changes, and when the app becomes inactive, we stop listening for these changes. But because we are in a view controller and not in our app delegate, we need to listen for app notifications:

```
/* Start listening for iCloud user change notifications */
func applicationBecameActive(notification: NSNotification){
  NSNotificationCenter.defaultCenter().addObserver(self,
    selector: "handleIdentityChanged:",
    name: NSUbiquityIdentityDidChangeNotification,
    object: nil)
}
```

```
/* Stop listening for those notifications when the app becomes inactive */
func applicationBecameInactive(notification: NSNotification){
  NSNotificationCenter.defaultCenter().removeObserver(self,
    name: NSUbiquityIdentityDidChangeNotification,
    object: nil)
}

override func viewDidLoad() {
  super.viewDidLoad()

  /* Find out when the app is becoming active and inactive
  so that we can find out when the user's iCloud logging status changes.*/
  NSNotificationCenter.defaultCenter().addObserver(self,
    selector: "applicationBecameActive:",
    name: UIApplicationDidBecomeActiveNotification,
    object: nil)

  NSNotificationCenter.defaultCenter().addObserver(self,
    selector: "applicationBecameInactive:",
    name: UIApplicationWillResignActiveNotification,
    object: nil)

}
```

When the app becomes active, the notification will be sent to the `applicationBeca`
`meActive:` method of our view controller. In that method, we start listening for the
`NSUbiquityIdentityDidChangeNotification` notification. When the app becomes inactive, the system calls the `applicationBecameInactive:` method of our view controller, which unsubscribes from this notification. We don't need to listen for it anymore if
we are inactive.

When the user's iCloud identity changes, the `handleIdentityChanged:` method of our
view controller is called. In this method, we query the `ubiquityIdentityToken` property
of an instance of `NSFileManager` that represents the currently logged-in user in iCloud.
If this property is nil, that means the user has logged out of iCloud. If this token is non-
nil, that means a new user is logged into iCloud:

```
func handleIdentityChanged(notification: NSNotification){

  let fileManager = NSFileManager()

  if let token = fileManager.ubiquityIdentityToken{
    println("The new token is \(token)")
  } else {
    println("User has logged out of iCloud")
  }

}
```

Next stop, when our view is displayed on the screen, we will find information about the user and whether she is currently logged into iCloud.

```
override func viewDidAppear(animated: Bool) {
  super.viewDidAppear(animated)

  container.accountStatusWithCompletionHandler{
    [weak self] (status: CKAccountStatus, error: NSError!) in

    /* Be careful, we might be on a different thread now so make sure that
    your UI operations go on the main thread */
    dispatch_async(dispatch_get_main_queue(), {

      var title: String!
      var message: String!

      if error != nil{
        title = "Error"
        message = "An error occurred = \(error)"
      } else {

        title = "No errors occurred"

        switch status{
        case .Available:
          message = "The user is logged in to iCloud"
        case .CouldNotDetermine:
          message = "Could not determine if the user is logged" +
          " into iCloud or not"
        case .NoAccount:
          message = "User is not logged into iCloud"
        case .Restricted:
          message = "Could not access user's iCloud account information"
        }

        self!.displayAlertWithTitle(title, message: message)

      }

    })

  }

}

deinit{
  NSNotificationCenter.defaultCenter().removeObserver(self)
}
```

We are using the `displayAlertWithTitle:message:` method in our view controller in order to display an alert to the user. To find the implementation of this method and avoid having to take space in the book to redeclare this method, have a look at the

Recipe 9.3 recipe for more information. Now run the application on a device and see it for yourself.

See Also

Recipe 1.22

21.2. Storing Data with CloudKit

Problem

You want to store records on the public or private database of your app's container in CloudKit.

Solution

Follow these steps:

1. Instantiate an object of type `CKRecord`.
2. Set each value with a key into the record using its `setObject:forKey:` method.
3. When you are done storing all your values, save the record using the `saveRecord:completionHandler:` method of your database of type `CKDatabase`.

```
import UIKit
import CloudKit

class ViewController: UIViewController {

  let database = CKContainer.defaultContainer().publicCloudDatabase

  override func viewDidLoad() {
    super.viewDidLoad()

    /* Store information about a Volvo V50 car */
    let volvoV50 = CKRecord(recordType: "Car")
    volvoV50.setObject("Volvo", forKey: "maker")
    volvoV50.setObject("V50", forKey: "model")
    volvoV50.setObject(5, forKey: "numberOfDoors")
    volvoV50.setObject(2015, forKey: "year")

    /* Save this record publicly */
    database.saveRecord(volvoV50, completionHandler: {
      (record: CKRecord!, error: NSError!) in

      if error != nil{
        println("Error occurred. Error = \(error)")
      } else {
```

```
        println("Successfully saved the record in the public database")
    }

    })

  }

}
```

Discussion

Your records will be stored asynchronously on CloudKit. If you haven't noticed already, using CloudKit, you do not need to explicitly specify your records' schema. In relational databases, administrators and programmers know that they have to create their databases and tables, each table with a detailed schema, but this isn't true in CloudKit. In a sense, CloudKit will actually create your schema based on the keys that you provided.

Now, if you want to find out whether CloudKit properly saved your record, go to iCloud's developer portal (*https://icloud.developer.apple.com*) and log in with the same Apple ID that you used to create your provision profile for the app that created the record. Find the Record Types section and browse it. You will then see that your record of type Car was created and its metadata was saved on CloudKit, as shown in Figure 21-3.

🗑 ＋				Vandad Nahavandipoor ⌄

Car

Created:	Modified:	Security:	Metadata Index:
Jul 18 2014 16:26	Jul 18 2014 16:26	Roles ⌄	Fields ⌄

Attribute Name	Attribute Type	Index
maker	String	Sort, Search, Query ⌄
model	String	Sort, Search, Query ⌄
numberOfDoors	String	Sort, Search, Query ⌄
year	String	Sort, Search, Query ⌄

Figure 21-3. The record is saved

The information that you can see in the aforementioned website is not the data itself, but the schema of the record that you created. When we instantiated our record, we were asked to provide a record type. The type in this case is equal to the schema. So when we passed Car as the type, this tells CloudKit that we want to have a schema named Car and the keys with values that you set in the record define the schema.

Now let's look at creating some record IDs for our records. As mentioned before, record IDs are similar to primary keys in a database, in that they define the record in a unique way, usually using a record zone and a record name. Let's say that we want to store three cars into iCloud. Two of them are estate/family/combi cars and one of them is a typical hatchback that you see on the roads.

This is a great chance for us to start using record zones. We will save our estate cars into a zone that we name Estate and our hatchback car into a zone that is appropriately named Hatchback. Then we will save our records into them using the same method you've already seen.

 Bear in mind that record zones can be created only in the user's private database.

We start by defining a structure that shows the different types of cars that we have. Our structure can also return a CloudKit zone ID and a zone to us depending to what it is set to:

```
import UIKit
import CloudKit

class ViewController: UIViewController {

  let database = CKContainer.defaultContainer().privateCloudDatabase

  enum CarType: String{
    case Hatchback = "Hatchback"
    case Estate = "Estate"

    func zoneId() -> CKRecordZoneID{
      let zoneId = CKRecordZoneID(zoneName: self.rawValue,
        ownerName: CKOwnerDefaultName)
      return zoneId
    }

    func zone() -> CKRecordZone{
      return CKRecordZone(zoneID: self.zoneId())
    }
```

```
        }

    <# rest of the code #>

    }
```

You can see that the structure is using its own value of Hatchback or Estate to create the zone ID, and then creates the zone based on that ID for us. Easy stuff. We need a method that can return a new record that represents a car, depending on the type of the car:

```
func carWithType(type: CarType) -> CKRecord{
    let uuid = NSUUID().UUIDString
    let recordId = CKRecordID(recordName: uuid, zoneID: type.zoneId())
    let car = CKRecord(recordType: "MyCar", recordID: recordId)
    return car
}
```

It is obvious that we are using the NSUUID class to create a random identifier for every record that we create. You can opt to create some sort of other ID for your records, but here, the ID is important only because it allows us to define the zone for our data. A simple, essentially random ID is sufficient.

This method only takes care of creating the record for us in memory, but doesn't set all the values that we need on it, so let's create a method that uses the previous method but actually sets the keys and values in it based on the maker, the model of the car, the number of doors, and the year it was manufactured.

```
func carWithType(type: CarType,
    maker: String,
    model: String,
    numberOfDoors: Int,
    year: Int) -> CKRecord{

    let record = carWithType(type)

    record.setValue(maker, forKey: "maker")
    record.setValue(model, forKey: "model")
    record.setValue(numberOfDoors, forKey: "numberOfDoors")
    record.setValue(year, forKey: "year")

    return record

}
```

This method takes the car type, so for every car type we want to create, we need to specify the type. That is great, but what would be better is if we had two convenience methods that could create either a hatchback or an estate car for us like so:

```
func hatchbackCarWithMaker(maker: String,
    model: String,
    numberOfDoors: Int,
    year: Int) -> CKRecord{
```

```
        return carWithType(.Hatchback,
          maker: maker,
          model: model,
          numberOfDoors: numberOfDoors,
          year: year)
    }

    func estateCarWithMaker(maker: String,
      model: String,
      numberOfDoors: Int,
      year: Int) -> CKRecord{
        return carWithType(.Estate,
          maker: maker,
          model: model,
          numberOfDoors: numberOfDoors,
          year: year)
    }
```

We are going to create four cars in this example, so we need to save them all. Let's create a method that takes in an array of records and saves them one after the other:

```
func saveCarClosure(record: CKRecord!, error: NSError!){

    /* Be careful, we might be on a non-UI thread */

    if error != nil{
      println("Failed to save the car. Error = \(error)")
    } else {
      println("Successfully saved the car with type \(record.recordType)")
    }

}

func saveCars(cars: [CKRecord]){
    for car in cars{
      database.saveRecord(car, completionHandler: saveCarClosure)
    }
}
```

The closure that we provided to the completion handler only prints out the success or the failure of the saving operation. Make sure that you do not perform any UI-related operations here in this closure, as it may be called on a non-UI thread. After this is done, we eventually need to create the cars:

```
func saveEstateCars(){

    let volvoV50 = estateCarWithMaker("Volvo",
      model: "V50",
      numberOfDoors: 5,
      year: 2016)

    let audiA6 = estateCarWithMaker("Audi",
      model: "A6",
```

```
      numberOfDoors: 5,
      year: 2018)

    let skodaOctavia = estateCarWithMaker("Skoda",
      model: "Octavia",
      numberOfDoors: 5,
      year: 2016)

    println("Saving estate cars...")
    saveCars([volvoV50, audiA6, skodaOctavia])

  }

  func saveHatchbackCars(){

    let fordFocus = hatchbackCarWithMaker("Ford",
      model: "Focus",
      numberOfDoors: 6,
      year: 2018)

    println("Saving hatchback cars...")
    saveCars([fordFocus])

  }
```

This is very simple stuff. We created our records with our values and then saved them.
When our view displays on the screen, we check whether the user is logged into her
iCloud account. We do this because in this example, we are using a zone called Hatchback to store hatchback cars and another zone called Estate to save the estate cars and
as mentioned before, zones are available only on private databases saved on the user's
iCloud account. So if the user has not logged into her iCloud account, we will not be
able to proceed with any saving operations on her private database.

After we check to make sure she is logged into her iCloud account, we attempt to fetch
the existing zones in her private database using the `fetchAllRecordZonesWithComple`
`tionHandler:` method of the database object. The completion handler parameter will
then receive an array of zones that we need to go through and find whether the zones
we are trying to access have already been created. If they have been created, we proceed
to save our records in them. If they haven't been created, we create them and then
proceed to saving the records:

```
    override func viewDidAppear(animated: Bool) {
      super.viewDidAppear(animated)

      if isIcloudAvailable(){
        displayAlertWithTitle("iCloud", message: "iCloud is not available." +
          " Please sign into your iCloud account and restart this app")
        return
      }
```

```
database.fetchAllRecordZonesWithCompletionHandler{[weak self]
  (zones:[AnyObject]!, error: NSError!) in

  if error != nil{
    println("Could not retrieve the zones")
  } else {

    var foundEstateZone = false
    var foundHatchbackZone = false

    for zone in zones as [CKRecordZone]{

      if zone.zoneID.zoneName == CarType.Hatchback.rawValue{
        foundHatchbackZone = true
      }
      else if zone.zoneID.zoneName == CarType.Estate.rawValue{
        foundEstateZone = true
      }
    }

    self!.useOrSaveZone(zoneIsCreatedAlready: foundEstateZone,
      forCarType: .Estate)

    self!.useOrSaveZone(zoneIsCreatedAlready: foundHatchbackZone,
      forCarType: .Hatchback)

  }

}

}
```

The `isIcloudAvailable` method is defined like so:

```
func isIcloudAvailable() -> Bool{
  if let token = NSFileManager.defaultManager().ubiquityIdentityToken{
    return true
  } else {
    return false
  }
}
```

The `useOrSaveZone:` method that we used when our view is displayed on the screen either creates a new record zone or, if it already exists, saves our records on it:

```
func saveCarsForType(type: CarType){
  switch type{
  case .Hatchback:
    saveHatchbackCars()
  case .Estate:
    saveEstateCars()
  default:
    println("Unknown car state is given")
```

```
    }
  }

  func performOnMainThread(block: dispatch_block_t){
    dispatch_async(dispatch_get_main_queue(), block)
  }

  func useOrSaveZone(#zoneIsCreatedAlready: Bool, forCarType: CarType){

    if zoneIsCreatedAlready{
      println("Found the \(forCarType.rawValue) zone. " +
        "It's been created already")
      saveCarsForType(forCarType)
    } else {
      database.saveRecordZone(forCarType.zone(),
        completionHandler: {[weak self]
          (zone: CKRecordZone!, error: NSError!) in
          if error != nil{
            println("Could not save the hatchback zone. Error = \(error)")
          } else {
            println("Successfully saved the hatchback zone")
            self!.performOnMainThread{self!.saveCarsForType(forCarType)}
          }
      })
    }

  }
```

OK, now give this a go in your own application. If you run it for the first time, you will
see that your zones are created first, followed by your records. But if you run the app
for the second time you will see something similar to the following printed to the screen,
showing that you didn't have to re-create the zones:

```
Found the Estate zone. It's been created already
Saving estate cars...
Found the Hatchback zone. It's been created already
Saving hatchback cars...
Successfully saved the car with type MyCar
Successfully saved the car with type MyCar
Successfully saved the car with type MyCar
Successfully saved the car with type MyCar
```

See Also

Recipe 1.22; Recipe 21.1

21.3. Retrieving Data with CloudKit

Problem

You have the identifier of your record and would like to fetch it back from the server.

Solution

Use the `fetchRecordWithID:completionHandler:` method of your CloudKit database and pass a valid record identifier to it. This identifier must be assigned to an object that you have successfully stored in CloudKit.

Discussion

In Recipe 21.2, we saw how you could create record identifiers. In this recipe, we are going to store the information for a Volvo V50 in the user's private iCloud database, in the default zone. This means that we don't have to define a custom zone. This recipe is based on what we learned in the aforementioned recipe, so I recommend that you read that recipe before proceeding with this one.

There are various ways to find the records. This recipe fetches a record using its identifier. Therefore, we need to store a record first and keep the record's identifier somewhere handy so that the next time our app runs, we can hand this identifier to CloudKit and ask it to fetch the record for us. The following recipe will show how to search a database and retrieve items using their attributes.

In Recipe 21.2, we defined a structure called `CarType` and we are going to use the same structure here. However, we want to save only an Estate Volvo V50 into the user's database, so we are going to strip that structure down into just an Estate car:

```
import UIKit
import CloudKit

class ViewController: UIViewController {

  let database = CKContainer.defaultContainer().privateCloudDatabase

  /* Defines our car types */
  enum CarType: String{
    case Estate = "Estate"

    func zoneId() -> CKRecordZoneID{
      let zoneId = CKRecordZoneID(zoneName: self.rawValue,
        ownerName: CKOwnerDefaultName)
      return zoneId
    }

  }
```

```
/* Check whether the user is logged into her iCloud account */
func isIcloudAvailable() -> Bool{
  if let token = NSFileManager.defaultManager().ubiquityIdentityToken{
    return true
  } else {
    return false
  }
}

<# rest of the code #>

}
```

Now we'll define a method that can generate an identifier for our new record and refer to the identifier again the next time it's called. We will use NSUserDefaults to store this identifier so that the next time this method is called, we can retrieve it and give it to CloudKit to fetch for us. If we change this identifier every time, we will never be able to find an old record! Here is a simple implementation of the method:

```
/* This method generates a record ID and keeps it in the system defaults
so that the second time it is called, it generates the exact same record
ID as before, which we can use to find the stored record in the database */
func recordId() -> CKRecordID{

  /* The key into NSUserDefaults */
  let key = "recordId"

  var recordName =
  NSUserDefaults.standardUserDefaults().stringForKey(key)

  func createNewRecordName(){
    println("No record name was previously generated")
    println("Creating a new one...")
    recordName = NSUUID().UUIDString
    NSUserDefaults.standardUserDefaults().setValue(recordName, forKey: key)
    NSUserDefaults.standardUserDefaults().synchronize()
  }

  if let name = recordName{
    if countElements(name) == 0{
      createNewRecordName()
    } else {
      println("The previously generated record ID was recovered")
    }
  } else {
    createNewRecordName()
  }

  return CKRecordID(recordName: recordName, zoneID: CarType.Estate.zoneId())

}
```

When our view appears on the screen, we first check whether the user has already signed into iCloud. If not, we display a message to her about this. If she has, we attempt to first fetch an existing record using the identifier of that record. If we find the record, we print it out to the console. If we don't find it, we attempt to create it using our method named saveRecordWithCompletionHandler:, which is defined like so:

```
func saveRecordWithCompletionHandler(completionHandler:
  (succeeded: Bool, error: NSError!) -> Void){

    /* Store information about a Volvo V50 car */
    let volvoV50 = CKRecord(recordType: "MyCar", recordID: recordId())
    volvoV50.setObject("Volvo", forKey: "maker")
    volvoV50.setObject("V50", forKey: "model")
    volvoV50.setObject(5, forKey: "numberOfDoors")
    volvoV50.setObject(2015, forKey: "year")

    /* Save this record publicly */
    database.saveRecord(volvoV50, completionHandler: {
      (record: CKRecord!, error: NSError!) in
      completionHandler(succeeded: (error == nil), error: error)
      })

}
```

We have the ability to save a record if it doesn't exist. Next stop: fetching the existing record.

```
override func viewDidAppear(animated: Bool) {
  super.viewDidAppear(animated)

  if isIcloudAvailable(){
    displayAlertWithTitle("iCloud", message: "iCloud is not available." +
      " Please sign into your iCloud account and restart this app")
    return
  }

  println("Fetching the record to see if it exists already...")

  /* Attempt to find the record if we saved it already */
  database.fetchRecordWithID(recordId(), completionHandler:{[weak self]
    (record: CKRecord!, error: NSError!) in

    if error != nil{
      println("An error occurred")

      if error.code == CKErrorCode.UnknownItem.rawValue{
        println("This error means that the record was not found.")
        println("Saving the record...")

        self!.saveRecordWithCompletionHandler{
          (succeeded: Bool, error: NSError!) in
```

```
      if succeeded{
        println("Successfully saved the record")
      } else {
        println("Failed to save the record. Error = \(error)")
      }

    }

  } else {
    println("I don't understand this error. Error = \(error)")
  }

} else {
  println("Seems like we had previously stored the record. Great!")
  println("Retrieved record = \(record)")
}

})

}
```

Here, Apple has taken quite a strange approach in how they call the completion handler in the `fetchRecordWithID:completionHandler:` method. You would think that if the record could not be found, both the error and the record will be nil. The error would be nil because the communication to the server was successful even though the record could not be found, and the record would be nil because, well, it could not be found! However, instead, if a record cannot be found, Apple returns a valid error with the code equal to `CKErrorUnknownItem`. So we are checking that error and then creating our record. After the record is created, we simply close our app and open it again to see the results.

For the implementation of the `displayAlertWithTitle:message:` method in our view controller, have a look at the Recipe 9.3 recipe.

When you fetch an existing record from the server, the returning value is exactly what you previously saved in CloudKit. What this means is that you can take the record, make modifications to it using what we learned in Recipe 21.2 and then save it back. So let's expand upon our previous example and, when we retrieve the previously saved car, add a new color value to it and save it back. It is noteworthy that the identifier of your record will stay the same even if you make changes to that record and save it back.

For this example, we are going to create a string enumeration that represents our colors. The enumerations will also be able to give us a random color. So when we fetch our existing item and find it, we will just give it a new random color:

```
enum Color : String{
  case Red = "Red"
  case Blue = "Blue"
  case Green = "Green"
  case Yellow = "Yellow"

  static let allColors = [Red, Blue, Green, Yellow]

  static func randomColor() -> Color{
    let colorIndex = Int(arc4random_uniform(UInt32(allColors.count)))
    return Color.allColors[colorIndex]
  }

}
```

When our view appears on the screen and we are able to find the record, we will generate the new color, place it in the record that we just fetched, and save the record back to CloudKit like so:

```
override func viewDidAppear(animated: Bool) {
  super.viewDidAppear(animated)

  if isIcloudAvailable(){
    displayAlertWithTitle("iCloud", message: "iCloud is not available." +
      " Please sign into your iCloud account and restart this app")
    return
  }

  println("Fetching the record to see if it exists already...")

  /* Attempt to find the record if we saved it already */
  database.fetchRecordWithID(recordId(), completionHandler:{[weak self]
    (record: CKRecord!, error: NSError!) in

    if error != nil{
      println("An error occurred")

      if error.code == CKErrorCode.UnknownItem.rawValue{
        println("This error means that the record was not found.")
        println("Saving the record...")

        self!.saveRecordWithCompletionHandler{
          (succeeded: Bool, error: NSError!) in

          if succeeded{
            println("Successfully saved the record")
          } else {
            println("Failed to save the record. Error = \(error)")
          }

        }
```

```
      } else {
        println("I don't understand this error. Error = \(error)")
      }

    } else {
      println("Seems like we had previously stored the record. Great!")
      println("Retrieved record = \(record)")

      /* Now make your changes to the record */
      let colorKey = "color"
      let newColor = Color.randomColor().rawValue
      var oldColor = record.valueForKey(colorKey) as? String
      if oldColor == nil{
        oldColor = "Unknown"
      }
      println("Changing the car color from \(oldColor) to \(newColor)")
      record.setValue(newColor, forKey:colorKey)
      self!.database.saveRecord(record, completionHandler:
        {(record:CKRecord!, error: NSError!) in

          if error == nil{
            println("Successfully modified the record")
          } else {
            println("Failed to modify the record. Error = \(error)")
          }

      })

    }

  })

}
```

You will then be able to see results similar to those shown here, printed to the console:

```
Fetching the record to see if it exists already...
The previously generated record ID was recovered
Seems like we had previously stored the record. Great!
Retrieved record = <CKRecord: 0x146844b0; recordType=MyCar,
  recordID=91CE379E-DF9C-4C4F-81E5-BC17DD1B0AAF:
  (Estate:__defaultOwner__), recordChangeTag=7, values={
    Color = Green;
    maker = Volvo;
    model = V50;
    numberOfDoors = 5;
    year = 2015;
}>
Changing the car color from Green to Red
Successfully modified the record
```

See Also

Recipe 21.2; Recipe 1.22; Recipe 21.1

21.4. Querying the Cloud with CloudKit

Problem

You want to search for specific records in CloudKit using some information that is relevant to the records, such as the attributes we learned to store in every record in Recipe 21.2.

Solution

Follow these steps:

1. Form a predicate of type NSPredicate that specifies what you are looking for in CloudKit.

2. Form an instance of the CKQuery class with your predicate and the record type you are looking for.

3. Invoke the performQuery:inZoneWithID:completionHandler: method of your database, which is of type CKDatabase.

 This recipe is based on what we learned in Recipe 21.2. We will attempt to query the data that we stored in the user's private database in that recipe. So before continuing, I recommend that you read that recipe.

Discussion

Queries in CloudKit work the same way that they work in various places in Cocoa Touch. For instance, let's say that you have an array of Person instances. We will define this class like so:

```
@objc(Person) class Person: NSObject{
  var firstName: NSString
  var lastName: NSString

  init(firstName: NSString, lastName: NSString){
    self.firstName = firstName
    self.lastName = lastName
  }

}
```

This class subclasses `NSObject`, because we want to add instances of it to an instance of `NSArray` and this array accepts only objects that directly or indirectly subclass `NSObject`. So let's move on and create an array of this type:

```
let richard = Person(firstName: "Richard", lastName: "Branson")
let vandad = Person(firstName: "Vandad", lastName: "Nahavandipoor")
let anthony = Person(firstName: "Anthony", lastName: "Robbins")

let persons = [richard, vandad, anthony]
```

Our array is now created and all we have to do is issue a predicate on it. What we are going to do here is find all the Person instances in this array whose first name has six or fewer letters. Our predicate will then be created like so:

```
let longestAcceptableFirstNameLetters = 6
let predicate = NSPredicate(format: "firstName.length <= %@",
  longestAcceptableFirstNameLetters as NSNumber)
```

Every predicate has a format and an optional list of arguments. The format will contain the formatting, of course, and if there are variables in the format, you can provide the values of those variables in the list of arguments. In our example, the formatting specifies that the length of the first name of items we are looking for has to be less than or equal to a variable that is set to the value of `longestAcceptableFirstNameLetters`.

To execute our predicate on the array of persons, we will use the `filteredArrayUsing Predicate:` method of the `NSArray` class to get a filtered array back like so:

```
if let array = filteredArray{
  for person in array{
    println("Found a person with first name equal or less than 6 letters")
    println("First name = \(person.firstName)")
    println("Last name = \(person.lastName)")
  }
} else {
  println("Could not find any items in the filtered array")

}
```

Not surprisingly, after running the application, the results will be similar to those shown here:

```
Found a person with first name equal or less than 6 letters
First name = Vandad
Last name = Nahavandipoor
```

Now that you have a basic understanding of predicates, let's have a look at predicates and queries in CloudKit. In Recipe 21.2, we stored some cars in the user's private database. Each car had a model, a year it was manufactured, the number of doors that it had, etc. In this recipe, we want to go through all the cars that we stored in the user's database and find the ones made by a specific maker (in this example, Volvo) whose manufacturing year was a certain year and higher, which is our way of determining the car's age.

Here is our code for this mission:

```
override func viewDidAppear(animated: Bool) {
  super.viewDidAppear(animated)

  if isIcloudAvailable(){
    displayAlertWithTitle("iCloud", message: "iCloud is not available." +
      " Please sign into your iCloud account and restart this app")
    return
  }

  let makerToLookFor = "Volvo"
  let smallestYearToLookFor = 2013

  let predicate = NSPredicate(format: "maker = %@ AND year >= %@",
    makerToLookFor, smallestYearToLookFor as NSNumber)

  let query = CKQuery(recordType: "MyCar", predicate: predicate)

  database.performQuery(query, inZoneWithID: nil, completionHandler: {
    (records: [AnyObject]!, error: NSError!) in

    if error != nil{
      println("An error occurred while performing the query.")
      println("Error = \(error)")
    } else {
      println("\(records.count) record(s) came back")
      for record in records as [CKRecord]{
        println("Record = \(record)")
      }
    }

  })

}
```

 For the implementation of the isIcloudAvailable method, please refer to Recipe 21.2.

So first we defined what we were looking for in the form of variables; then we formed our predicate, and then the query. After the query is created and you run your app and test it to ensure that CloudKit understands your predicate, you can perform your query using the performQuery:inZoneWithID:completionHandler: method of your database object. If CloudKit doesn't understand your query format, it will throw an exception as soon as you attempt to create the CKQuery instance.

The performQuery:inZoneWithID:completionHandler: method of the database takes three parameters:

1. The query, of type CKQuery.
2. The zone in which to issue the query. If you want to query in the default zone, pass nil to this parameter.
3. The completion handler to execute when the query is done.

The completion handler passed as the last parameter defines a block that will report back an array of CKRecord objects. These will be actual data of the records, and you can simply read them or modify them and save them back to the database as we learned in Recipe 21.3.

You may have already thought about how to handle large data sets, but let me just bring this matter up. Suppose you have one million records in the user's private database and you want to query that database. Also assume that your query will match about half of those records. That is a lot of records that CloudKit has to retrieve for you, so it doesn't make sense for it to send you all the data in one go. If you are sure that only a small subset of data will come back from your query, use a simple query as we talked about before. If you know that your query could return an unknown or a large number of values from the database, you need to approach the issue in a different way. What we need to do is this:

1. Create your predicate of type NSPredicate like we did before.
2. Create the query like before, with the CKQuery class.
3. Instead of executing the query directly on the database, instantiate an object of type CKQueryOperation with the query as a parameter. Then issue the operation just as you would execute any other instance of the NSOperation, as we learned in Recipe 7.6.
4. When the operation is ready, add it to an operation queue and let it get executed.

When executed as a CKQueryOperation, a query is divided up and executed by the system one part at a time. The system determines how many records it can reasonably return at a time, gives you those records, and waits for you to restart the query. So the way to handle results from CKQueryOperation is to handle each record as it comes back, then reissue the operation until the system tells you all the records matching your query have been returned.

Operations of type CKQueryOperation have two really important properties, both containing methods.

recordFetchedBlock
This closure gets executed for each record fetched by the query operation.

queryCompletionBlock

This completion closure is called after the `recordFetchedBlock` has run for all records retrieved in this part of the queue. This completion block will receive a parameter of type `CKQueryCursor`. If the value is nil, it means that the operation found all the records it could and there are no more records to search through. Otherwise, the parameter will be a valid cursor of type `CKQueryCursor`. This means there are more values left for you to peek at. If you want to retrieve them, create another instance of the `CKQueryOperation` class in this completion block and pass this cursor to the constructor of this class. Then add this new operation to your operation queue and spin it off just like you do with other operations, to read the rest of the records.

So let's complete our example and start querying all the cars in the database that are from 2013 or newer, made by Volvo:

```
func recordFetchBlock(record: CKRecord!){

  println("Fetched a record = \(record)")

}

override func viewDidAppear(animated: Bool) {
  super.viewDidAppear(animated)

  if isIcloudAvailable(){
    displayAlertWithTitle("iCloud", message: "iCloud is not available." +
      " Please sign into your iCloud account and restart this app")
    return
  }

  let makerToLookFor = "Volvo"
  let smallestYearToLookFor = 2013

  let predicate = NSPredicate(format: "maker = %@ AND year >= %@",
    makerToLookFor, smallestYearToLookFor as NSNumber)

  let query = CKQuery(recordType: "MyCar", predicate: predicate)

  let operation = CKQueryOperation(query: query)
  operation.recordFetchedBlock = recordFetchBlock
  operation.queryCompletionBlock = {[weak self]
    (cursor: CKQueryCursor!, error: NSError!) in
    if cursor != nil{
      /* There is so much data that a cursor came back to us and we will
      need to fetch the rest of the results in a separate operation */
      println("A cursor was sent to us. Fetching the rest of the records...")
      let newOperation = CKQueryOperation(cursor: cursor)
      newOperation.recordFetchedBlock = self!.recordFetchBlock
      newOperation.queryCompletionBlock = operation.queryCompletionBlock
      self!.operationQueue.addOperation(newOperation)
```

```
    } else {
      println("No cursor came back. We've fetched all the data")
    }
  }

  operationQueue.addOperation(operation)

}
```

In this code, `operationQueue` is just a lazy property of our view controller:

```
lazy var operationQueue = NSOperationQueue()
```

See Also

Recipe 21.2; Recipe 21.5

21.5. Observing Changes to Records in CloudKit

Problem

You want to ask CloudKit to observe changes to your databases and inform you through push notifications of any change that occurs without you having to perform the kind of manual queries we learned how to do in Recipe 21.4.

Solution

Use subscriptions in CloudKit by following these steps:

1. Specify a string that will become the unique identifier of your subscription.

2. Call the `fetchSubscriptionWithID:completionHandler:` method of your database object. This will attempt to find a subscription object with the given identifier. If this subscription is already found, you are good to go.

3. If this subscription object is not found, instantiate a subscription object of type `CKSubscription` for the creation, deletion, or update of items and add it to your database using the `saveSubscription:completionHandler:` method of the database. You will also need to set the value of the `notificationInfo` property of your subscription instance to a valid instance of the `CKNotificationInfo` that dictates to CloudKit how you would like to receive your subscription's push notifications.

Discussion

Queries, as we learned in Recipe 21.4, are a fantastic way to poll information from CloudKit. You can use predicates to find records in the cloud using `NSPredicate`, which is attached to a query of type `CKQuery`. As great as queries are, they are quite heavy on resources because they fetch the results for you from the cloud. They also work in a poll-based fashion, in that your app has to issue those queries to the cloud and wait for the results. Wouldn't it be great if CloudKit could observe deletions, additions, and updates to the cloud data on your behalf and inform you whenever something is changed, added, or deleted? CloudKit does exactly this using the CKSubscription class.

Because this type of subscription is based on push notifications and your app's ability to receive push notifications, you need to enable push notifications on your app using the instructions in Recipe 16.7. The following is our app delegate that asks the user for permission to receive push notifications:

```
class func goAheadWithSubscriptionCreationNotificationName() -> String{
  return "\(__FUNCTION__)"
}

func goAheadWithSubscriptionCreation(){
  NSNotificationCenter.defaultCenter().postNotificationName(
    AppDelegate.goAheadWithSubscriptionCreationNotificationName(),
    object: nil)
}

func application(application: UIApplication,
  didRegisterForRemoteNotificationsWithDeviceToken deviceToken: NSData!) {

    println("Successfully registered for remote notifications")
    goAheadWithSubscriptionCreation()

}

func application(application: UIApplication,
  didFailToRegisterForRemoteNotificationsWithError error: NSError!){
    println("Failed to receive remote notifications")
}

func application(application: UIApplication,
  didRegisterUserNotificationSettings
  notificationSettings: UIUserNotificationSettings!) {

    if notificationSettings.types == nil{
      /* The user did not allow us to send notifications */
      return
    }

    if application.isRegisteredForRemoteNotifications() == false{
      println("Not registered for push notifications. Registering now...")
      application.registerForRemoteNotifications()
    } else {
      println("We are already registered for push notifications")
      goAheadWithSubscriptionCreation()
    }
}
```

```
func application(application: UIApplication,
  didFinishLaunchingWithOptions launchOptions: [NSObject : AnyObject]?) -> Bool {

    var needToRequestSettingChanges = true
    if let settings = application.currentUserNotificationSettings(){
      if settings.types != nil{
        needToRequestSettingChanges = false
      }
    }

    if needToRequestSettingChanges{
      let settings = UIUserNotificationSettings(forTypes: .Alert | .Badge,
        categories: nil)

      println("Requesting change to user notification settings...")
      application.registerUserNotificationSettings(settings)
    } else {

      println("We've already set the notification settings.")

      if application.isRegisteredForRemoteNotifications() == false{
        println("Not registered for push notifications. Registering now...")
        application.registerForRemoteNotifications()
      } else {
        println("We are already registered for push notifications")
        goAheadWithSubscriptionCreation()
      }

    }

    return true
}
```

When we are able to register for push notifications, we call the `goAheadWithSubscrip`
`tionCreation` method of our app delegate. This method simply sends a simple notification to the rest of the app to let any subscribers (to this notification) know that our
app is set up properly for push notifications. In our view controller, we observe this
notification and then create a CloudKit subscription that monitors the creation of records in the default zone of the user's private database for our app.

Let's go to our view controller and define our properties and other required values:

```
import UIKit
import CloudKit

class ViewController: UIViewController {

  let database = CKContainer.defaultContainer().privateCloudDatabase
  let recordType = "MyCar"
  let maker = "carmaker"
  let model = "Some model name"
```

```
let subscriptionId = "MySubscriptionIdentifier"
let backgroundTaskName = "saveNewCar"

/* The background task identifier for the task that will save our
record in the database when our app goes to the background */
var backgroundTaskIdentifier: UIBackgroundTaskIdentifier =
UIBackgroundTaskInvalid

<# rest of the code #>

}
```

The make and model are the values that we use to create our subscription, based on insertions into the database for cars with the given make and model. We will use this to retrieve a subscription with that name if we've already created it before. You cannot create two subscriptions in the same zone with the same name.

Four properties of the CKNotificationInfo instance need to be set before you create your subscription object:

alertLocalizationKey

> The key in your localization string table, whose value is set as the alert's body that will be displayed to the user whenever you receive the push notification for your subscription from Apple.

shouldBadge

> A Boolean value that indicates to the subscription whether the push that comes from Apple should increase your app's badge count.

desiredKeys

> The keys that have to come back from the push notification for the record that was updated, deleted, or added. These are the keys into your schema for your objects.

alertActionLocalizationKey

> A localizable key to your localization string table for the alert's action button. The user will be able to press this button to be redirected to your app if your app isn't running and if the user has enabled alerts instead of notification bars.

So this is how we create our subscription object:

```
func subscription() -> CKSubscription{

  var predicate = NSPredicate(format: "maker == %@", maker)

  let subscription = CKSubscription(recordType: recordType,
    predicate: predicate,
    subscriptionID: subscriptionId,
    options: .FiresOnRecordCreation)

  let notificationInfo = CKNotificationInfo()
  notificationInfo.alertLocalizationKey = "creationAlertBodyKey"
```

```
notificationInfo.shouldBadge = false
notificationInfo.desiredKeys = ["model"]
notificationInfo.alertActionLocalizationKey = "creationAlertActionKey"

subscription.notificationInfo = notificationInfo

return subscription
}
```

Please note the value that we passed to the `options` parameter of the `CKSubscription` class's constructor. This parameter tells CloudKit what type of event it has to create a notification for. In this case, we are interested to hear when a new record is inserted into our CloudKit container with a given record type and predicate. You can opt in to receiving these notifications for update, deletion, and creation events.

When our app appears on the screen, we will do a few things. First we will opt in to system notifications when the app comes to the foreground after having been sent to the background. When it goes to the background, we will attempt to borrow time from iOS to save a record into CloudKit so that we get to see a proper notification appear on the screen. If our app is in the foreground and we attempt to insert a new record that causes our subscription to fire a notification, iOS will not display the notification because our app is already running and is on the user's screen. We will also find out whether we have to wait for the app delegate to register us for push notifications. If we are already registered for push notifications, we will continue with the creation of our subscription object:

```
override func viewDidAppear(animated: Bool) {
  super.viewDidAppear(animated)

  if isIcloudAvailable(){
    displayAlertWithTitle("iCloud", message: "iCloud is not available." +
      " Please sign into your iCloud account and restart this app")
    return
  }

  NSNotificationCenter.defaultCenter().addObserver(self,
    selector: "appWentToBackground:",
    name: UIApplicationDidEnterBackgroundNotification,
    object: nil)

  NSNotificationCenter.defaultCenter().addObserver(self,
    selector: "appCameToForeground:",
    name: UIApplicationWillEnterForegroundNotification,
    object: nil)

  /* If we are already registered for push notifications, we don't have
  to wait for the app delegate to inform us that we can go ahead */
  if UIApplication.sharedApplication().isRegisteredForRemoteNotifications(){
    goAheadAfterPushNotificationRegistration(nil)
  } else {
```

```
      NSNotificationCenter.defaultCenter().addObserver(self,
        selector: "goAheadAfterPushNotificationRegistration:",
        name: AppDelegate.goAheadWithSubscriptionCreationNotificationName(),
        object: nil)
    }

  }

  override func viewDidDisappear(animated: Bool) {
    NSNotificationCenter.defaultCenter().removeObserver(self)
  }
```

Now we write the chunk of code that creates the new car in the background and that ends the background task when the app is brought to the foreground:

```
func createAndSaveANewCar(){

  let recordName = NSUUID().UUIDString

  let recordId = CKRecordID(recordName: recordName)

  let newCar = CKRecord(recordType: recordType, recordID: recordId)

  newCar.setValue(maker, forKey: "maker")
  newCar.setValue(model, forKey: "model")
  newCar.setValue(5, forKey: "numberOfDoors")
  newCar.setValue(2016, forKey: "year")
  newCar.setValue("Orange", forKey: "color")

  println("Saving the new car...")
  database.saveRecord(newCar, completionHandler: {[weak self]
    (record: CKRecord!, error: NSError!) in

    if error != nil{
      println("Failed to save the car. Error = \(error)")
    } else {
      println("Successfully saved the car")
    }

    if self!.backgroundTaskIdentifier != UIBackgroundTaskInvalid{
      UIApplication.sharedApplication().endBackgroundTask(
        self!.backgroundTaskIdentifier)
      self!.backgroundTaskIdentifier = UIBackgroundTaskInvalid
    }

    })

}

func appWentToBackground(notification: NSNotification){

  println("Going to the background...")
```

```
/* Start a background task that saves a new car record
into the database */
self.backgroundTaskIdentifier =
  UIApplication.sharedApplication().beginBackgroundTaskWithName(
    backgroundTaskName,
    expirationHandler: {[weak self] in
      println("Background task is expired now")
    })

println("App is in the background so let's create the car object")
self.createAndSaveANewCar()

}

func appCameToForeground(notification: NSNotification){

  println("Application came to the foreground")

  if self.backgroundTaskIdentifier != UIBackgroundTaskInvalid{
    println("We need to invalidate our background task")
    UIApplication.sharedApplication().endBackgroundTask(
      self.backgroundTaskIdentifier)
    self.backgroundTaskIdentifier = UIBackgroundTaskInvalid
  }
}
```

Last but not least, when we are ready with our push notification registration process, we can proceed to create our subscription object. First we will attempt to find an existing subscription object with the given identifier. If one doesn't exist, we will create one:

```
func goAheadAfterPushNotificationRegistration(notification: NSNotification!){

  println("We are asked to proceed because notifications are registered...")

  println("Trying to find the subscription...")
  database.fetchSubscriptionWithID(subscriptionId, completionHandler: {
    [weak self] (subscription: CKSubscription!, error: NSError!) in

    if error != nil{
      if error.code == CKErrorCode.UnknownItem.rawValue{
        println("This subscription doesn't exist. Creating it now...")

        self!.database.saveSubscription(self!.subscription(),
          completionHandler:
          {(subscription: CKSubscription!, error: NSError!) in

            if error != nil{
              println("Could not save the subscription. Error = \(error)")
            } else {
              println("Successfully saved the subscription")
            }
```

```
            })

        } else {
            println("An unknown error occurred. Error = \(error)")
        }
    } else {

        println("Found the subscription already. No need to create it.")

    }

    })

}
```

Go ahead and run your application. You will see logs similar to the following printed to the console if you have already created your subscription before. In other words, these are the logs that you will see if you ran this application at least once before:

```
We've already set the notification settings.
We are already registered for push notifications
We are asked to proceed because notifications are registered...
Trying to find the subscription...
Found the subscription already. No need to create it.
```

Now send the app to the background to see the following logs:

```
Going to the background...
App is in the background so let's create the car object
Saving the new car...
Successfully saved the car
```

Wait a few seconds for the push notification to appear on your screen, as shown in Figure 21-4.

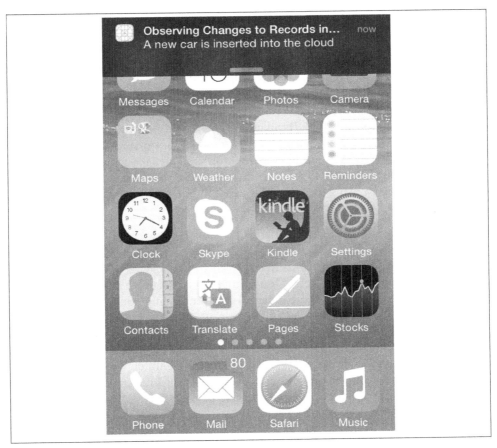

Figure 21-4. Subscription push notification is delivered to our app

See Also

Recipe 21.4; Recipe 21.2

21.6. Retrieving User Information from CloudKit

Problem

You want to learn some information about the currently logged-in iCloud user in your app. You might even be interested in finding information about the user's contacts and their iCloud account-related information, all the while knowing that no personal information will be shared with you via CloudKit.

Solution

Use the `fetchUserRecordIDWithCompletionHandler:` method of your container to retrieve the user identifier of type `CKRecordID`. This will be a unique identifier that identifies the logged-in user. If there is an error in the process, you will receive a valid instance of `NSError` in your app and the code for this error will be of type `CKErrorCode`. If the user is not logged into iCloud, your error code will be equal to `CKErrorNotAuthenticated`, so you need to catch that. If the user's ID is found, you can pass that ID to the `fetchRecordWithID:completionHandler:` method of your private or public database and ask CloudKit to retrieve the user's record if you want to make changes to that record. For instance, you might want to retrieve the user record, add some data to it, and save it back to the database using the technique that you learned in Recipe 21.2.

Discussion

CloudKit has information about all iCloud users. The `fetchRecordWithID:completionHandler:` method of your container's private or public database can find the currently logged-in iCloud user from CloudKit. After you retrieve the record, you can simply add some data to it and save it back. However, usually, you just want to receive an identifier for the user, in which case you can use the `fetchUserRecordIDWithCompletionHandler:` method of the container. The identifier that comes back from this method remains the same for the current user for your app. Any other app that accesses the user ID on the same device will receive a different identifier. Your app running on various devices that belong to the same user with the same iCloud credentials will receive the same identifier. This identifier is not the user's email address. It is a UUID that you can use to identify the user if you wish to.

Based on this information, you can write a method that retrieve's the user's identifier and record like so:

```
func retrieveUserInformation(){

  println("Retrieving user information...")

  let container = CKContainer.defaultContainer()
  let database = CKContainer.defaultContainer().publicCloudDatabase

  container.fetchUserRecordIDWithCompletionHandler{
    (recordId: CKRecordID!, error: NSError!) in

    if error != nil{
      println("Could not receive the record ID")

      if error.code == CKErrorCode.NotAuthenticated.rawValue{
        println("This user is not logged into iCloud")
      } else {
        println("I cannot understand this error = \(error)")
```

```
      }

    } else {

    println("Fetched the user ID")
    println("Record Name = \(recordId.recordName)")

    database.fetchRecordWithID(recordId,
      completionHandler: {(record: CKRecord!, error: NSError!) in

        if error != nil{
          println("Error in fetching user. Error = \(error)")
        } else {

          if record.recordType == CKRecordTypeUserRecord{
            println("Successfully fetched the user record")

            /* You can add some objects to this user if you want to
            and save it back to the database */

            println(record)

          } else {
            println("The record that came back is not a user record")
          }

        }

    })

    }

  }

}
```

If you run this code while the user is logged into iCloud on the current device, you will see messages similar to these, printed to the console:

```
Retrieving user information...
Fetched the user ID
Record Name = _60b7e74d63cddba3f2536cfb2fd38898
Successfully fetched the user record
```

Another thing you can do with user-identity APIs in CloudKit is to create an iCloud login flow for your user. You can first determine whether the user is logged in using the code just thrown, and if she is not logged in, you can ask for her username and employ that to fetch her user information from CloudKit. However, before you attempt to discover the user record or identifier based on her email address, you need to ask the user for permission to do so. The reason for this permission request is that if the user provides her email address and you fetch her identity, your app has access to both pieces of this information and you can potentially use this information in ways with which the user may not be comfortable. Hence the permission request.

Before you decide to ask a user for permission to access her user information, you must issue the `statusForApplicationPermission:completionHandler:` method of the container to find out whether your app has been given permission to query the user's personal information. The first parameter to this method is of type `CKApplicationPer missions` and you must pass the value of `CKApplicationPermissionUserDiscovera bility` to it to get your permission. The completion handler will then be called with a status of type `CKApplicationPermissionStatus` and an error of type `NSError`.

First check whether an error came back and, if so, handle it. If no error occured, go on and use the status to find out if you are authorized. If you aren't authorized, then use the `requestApplicationPermission:completionBlock:` method of your container to ask for permission. This method has the same type and number of parameters and completion block as the `statusForApplicationPermission:completionBlock:` method, but instead asks for permission.

When your app asks for permission to access the user's iCloud information, the user will see a dialog similar to that shown in Figure 21-5 appear on her screen. She can then make a decision whether to allow the permission or not.

Figure 21-5. Our app asks for permission to access user's cloud information

Let's have a look at an example. When our app starts, we are going to want to see whether we have permission to access the user's information. If not, we will ask for permission. Here is the first step in defining our constants and variables:

```
import UIKit
import CloudKit

class ViewController: UIViewController {

  let container = CKContainer.defaultContainer()

  <# rest of the code #>

}
```

Then we are going to ask for permission as soon as our view appears on the screen:

```
override func viewDidAppear(animated: Bool) {
  super.viewDidAppear(animated)

  if isIcloudAvailable(){
    displayAlertWithTitle("iCloud", message: "iCloud is not available." +
      " Please sign into your iCloud account and restart this app")
    return
  }

  println("Retrieving permissions...")
  container.statusForApplicationPermission(.PermissionUserDiscoverability,
    completionHandler: {[weak self]
      (status: CKApplicationPermissionStatus, error: NSError!) in

      if error != nil{
        println("Error happened = \(error)")
      } else {

        switch status{
        case .Granted:
          println("Access is granted. Processing...")
          self!.retrieveUserInformation()
        case .InitialState:
          self!.requestPermissionToAccessUserInformation()
        default:
          println("We do not have permission to user's information")
        }

      }

    })

}
```

If the permission is not granted (initial state), we invoke our view controller's `reques tPermissionToAccessUserInformation` method, which will use the `requestApplica tionPermission:completionHandler:` method of the container to ask for permission:

```
func requestPermissionToAccessUserInformation(){

  println("Requesting permission to access user's information...")

  container.requestApplicationPermission(.PermissionUserDiscoverability,
    completionHandler: {[weak self]
      (status: CKApplicationPermissionStatus, error: NSError!) in

      if error != nil{
        println("Error happened = \(error)")
      } else {

        switch status{
        case .Granted:
          println("Access is granted. Processing...")
          self!.retrieveUserInformation()
        default:
          println("We do not have permission to user's information")
        }

      }

    })
}
```

Then, if the access is granted by the user (see Figure 21-5), we call the `retrieveUser Information` method of the view controller. In this method, we first retrieve the user record identifier using the `fetchUserRecordIDWithCompletionHandler:` method of our container. Then if no error occurred, we call the `discoverUserInfoWithUserRe cordID:completionHandler:` of the container and pass the discovered record ID to this method to find out information about the user.

The completion handler that we pass to this method will receive two parameters. The first has user information and is of type `CKDiscoveredUserInfo`, whereas the second is an error of type `NSError`. If there is no error present, you can use the given user information object of type `CKDiscoveredUserInfo` to read user's details, such as her first name, last name, and user ID:

```
func retrieveUserInformation(){

  println("Retrieving user information...")
  container.fetchUserRecordIDWithCompletionHandler{[weak self]
    (recordId: CKRecordID!, error: NSError!) in

    if error != nil{
      println("Could not receive the record ID. Error = \(error)")
    } else {
```

```
      println("Fetched the user ID")
      println("Record Name = \(recordId.recordName)")

      self!.container.discoverUserInfoWithUserRecordID(recordId,
        completionHandler: {
          (userInfo: CKDiscoveredUserInfo!, error: NSError!) in

          if error != nil{
            println("Error in fetching user. Error = \(error)")
          } else {

            /* You have access to the record ID as well in
            userInfo.userRecordID */

            println("First name = \(userInfo.firstName)")
            println("Last name = \(userInfo.lastName)")

          }

      })

    }

  }

}
```

In addition to retrieving the user's iCloud information, you might also want to retrieve the user's contacts' iCloud information. You would want to do this purely from a discoverability point of view. For instance, you might want to display a list of the user's contacts who are also using your application. You can do this using the `discoverAll ContactUserInfosWithCompletionHandler:` method of the container object. This method will not ask the user for permission to access her contacts list, because in reality, your app is not getting any access to the user's contact list. CloudKit is doing that for you. Then the whole list is encrypted and sent to Apple for processing. This method only returns information about contacts who have run your app and have granted discoverability permission to your app. Those users must also exist in the current user's address book before you can discover them by running this method on the current user's container.

The completion handler that you pass to this method will return an array of `CKDisco veredUserInfo` objects and an error. First check the error to make sure everything is fine. Then you can go through the `CKDiscoveredUserInfo` objects just like we saw before:

```
func retrieveUserContactInformation(){

  println("Discovering all user's contacts' iCloud information...")
```

```
container.discoverAllContactUserInfosWithCompletionHandler{
  (userInfos: [AnyObject]!, error: NSError!) in

  if error != nil{
    println("An error occurred. Error = \(error)")
  } else {

    println("\(userInfos.count) resuls came back")

    for userInfo in userInfos as [CKDiscoveredUserInfo]{

      println("Found contact's information")
      println("First name = \(userInfo.firstName)")
      println("Last name = \(userInfo.lastName)")

    }
  }

}

}
```

See Also

Recipe 21.2

21.7. Storing and Synchronizing Dictionaries in iCloud

Problem

You want to store key-value data in dictionary form in iCloud and seamlessly read and write to this centralized and synchronized dictionary from various devices and from various iCloud accounts.

Solution

Use the NSUbiquitousKeyValueStore class.

The data that you store in iCloud using the NSUbiquitousKeyValueStore is uniquely created in iCloud using the provision profile with which you sign the app and the end user's iCloud account. In other words, you simply store values in iCloud using the NSUbiquitousKeyValueStore class, not worrying if one user's data is going to clash with another user's data. iCloud does that separation for you.

In Recipe 21.1, we used the Capabilities tab of our target settings to enable CloudKit for our app. However, to use the NSUbiquitousKeyValueStore class, we need to enable the key-value store for iCloud as well. This can be done from the same Capabilities tab of your target settings. In the Capabilities tab, expand the iCloud section if it's not already expanded, and then ensure that the "Use key-value store" option is ticked.

Discussion

The `NSUbiquitousKeyValueStore` class works very similar to the `NSUserDefaults` class. It can store string, Boolean, integer, float, and other values. Each one of the values must have a key associated with it. You can then read the values by passing the keys to this class. The difference between the `NSUbiquitousKeyValueStore` and the `NSUser Defaults` class is that the former synchronizes its dictionary data with iCloud, whereas the latter only stores the dictionary locally to a *.plist* file—this data will be deleted when the app is deleted from the user's device.

An instance of your application uses a unique identifier to store data in iCloud. This unique identifier is made up of three key pieces:

Team ID
> This is the unique identifier for your iOS Developer Program. When you sign up for the iOS Developer Program, Apple automatically generates a unique identifier for your account. To retrieve this identifier, simply log into Developer Center (*http:// bit.ly/Qdj3FC*) and select Your Account from the top menu items. Then choose Account Summary from the menus on the left. On the screen to the right, your Team ID is displayed under the *Developer Account Summary* section. No two iOS Developer accounts can have the same Team ID.

Reverse-domain-style company identifier
> This string is usually in the form of *com.COMPANYNAME*, where *COMPANYNAME* is the name of your company and *APPNAME* is the name of your app. For instance, my company name is `Pixolity`, so my reverse-domain-style company identifier will be *com.pixolity*.

App identifier and optional suffix
> This is the string that gets attached as the suffix to the reverse-domain-style company identifier.

The Team ID is always bound to the provision profile with which you will sign your app. You do *not* have to enter this value into your project settings. For instance, if my company name is *Pixolity* and I set the reverse-domain-style name for my app to *com.pixolity* and my App ID to *icloudapp*, the name that iCloud will use in the entitlements is *$(TeamIdentifierPrefix)$(CFBundleIdentifier)*.

The `$(TeamIdentifierPrefix)` value is the Team ID, which will be resolved to my actual Team ID when Xcode compiles my application and signs it with a provision profile. The `$(CFBundleIdentifier)` value will be resolved, at compile time, to the bundle identifier of my target.

Now that we are sure we set up the project properly and entitlements are set up as well, we can move on to using the `NSUbiquitousKeyValueStore` class to store keys and values in iCloud. There are various methods that the `NSUbiquitousKeyValueStore` class exposes so we can save the values in iCloud. Some of these methods are explained here:

`setString:forKey:`
Sets a string value for the given key. The string must be of type `NSString`. Obviously, classes that subclass `NSString`, such as `NSMutableString` can also be stored in iCloud using this method.

`setArray:forKey:`
Sets an array value for the given key. The array can be either a mutable or an immutable array.

`setDictionary:forKey:`
Sets a mutable or an immutable dictionary for the given key.

`setBool:forKey:`
Sets a Boolean value of type `BOOL` for the given key.

`setData:forKey:`
Sets a mutable or an immutable data for the given key.

None of these methods will actually do the saving for you. If you are done setting the values, then you must call the `synchronize` method of `NSUbiquitousKeyValueStore` for your settings to be flushed first to iOS and then synchronized with iCloud.

All the work that we do with the `NSUbiquitousKeyValueStore` is done through the `defaultStore` class method of this class. This class method will return an instance of the `NSUbiquitousKeyValueStore` class, that is ready to use.

Obviously, after setting the values for keys, we are going to want to retrieve those values at some point during the runtime of the app. We can do this using some of the methods that the NSUbiquitousKeyValueStore provides. Some of these methods are listed here:

stringForKey:
Returns the string associated with the given key, or nil if that key cannot be found. This will be an immutable string even if you used this key to store a mutable string in iCloud.

arrayForKey:
Returns the array associated with the given key, or nil if that key cannot be found. This will be an immutable array even if the original array you stored in iCloud for this key was mutable.

dictionaryForKey:
Returns the dictionary associated with the given key, or nil if that key cannot be found. The dictionary returned by this method will be immutable even if the original dictionary you stored in iCloud for this key was mutable.

boolForKey:
Returns the Boolean value of type BOOL associated with the given key, or nil if that key cannot be found.

dataForKey:
Returns the data of type NSData associated with the given key, or nil if that key cannot be found. The data returned by this method will be immutable even if the original data stored in iCloud for this key was mutable.

So let's have a look at how we can perhaps use this class in the apps. As you already know, iCloud's power really proves handy when you are sharing data between two or more devices for the same user. For instance, if the user starts reading a book on his iPhone, and then picks up his iPad, the app that presents the book sees the last page the user was at and opens the book right there. In effect, we have two devices pretending to be one, for the sake of usability for the end user. For this example, we will store a string and a Boolean value in iCloud using the NSUbiquitousKeyValueStore class. We will place a check to see if those values had already been stored in iCloud; if yes, we will read their value. I can then build this app, run it on my iPhone and then on my iPad, and see what happens:

```
func application(application: UIApplication,
  didFinishLaunchingWithOptions launchOptions: [NSObject : AnyObject]?) -> Bool {

  if isIcloudAvailable() == false{
    println("iCloud is not available")
    return true
  }

  let kvoStore = NSUbiquitousKeyValueStore.defaultStore()
```

```
var stringValue = "My String"
let stringValueKey = "MyStringKey"

var boolValue = true
let boolValueKey = "MyBoolKey"

var mustSynchronize = false

if kvoStore.stringForKey(stringValueKey) == nil{
  println("Could not find the string value in iCloud. Setting...")
  kvoStore.setString(stringValue, forKey: stringValueKey)
  mustSynchronize = true
} else {
  stringValue = kvoStore.stringForKey(stringValueKey)!
  println("Found the string in iCloud = \(stringValue)")
}

if kvoStore.boolForKey(boolValueKey) == false{
  println("Could not find the Boolean value in iCloud. Setting...")
  kvoStore.setBool(boolValue, forKey: boolValueKey)
  mustSynchronize = true
} else {
  println("Found the Boolean in iCloud, getting...")
  boolValue = kvoStore.boolForKey(boolValueKey)
}

if mustSynchronize{
  if kvoStore.synchronize(){
    println("Successfully synchronized with iCloud.")
  } else {
    println("Failed to synchronize with iCloud.")
  }
}

return true
}
```

For the implementation of the isIcloudAvailable method, please refer to Recipe 21.2.

After setting up the correct provision profiles, enabling entitlements for this project, and running this app on an iOS device that has already been set up with an iCloud account, we can observe these results printed to the console screen:

```
Could not find the string value in iCloud. Setting...
Could not find the boolean value in iCloud. Setting...
Successfully synchronized with iCloud.
```

Now I will leave my device sitting here for a minute or two just to make sure that iCloud has enough time to synchronize my data with the cloud. I will then run the same code on another device that has been linked to the same iCloud account as the first device to see what happens:

```
Found the string in iCloud = My String
Found the boolean in iCloud, getting...
```

Fantastic. This demonstrates that iCloud is indeed synchronizing the data for multiple iOS devices that are hooked to the same iCloud account.

21.8. Creating and Managing Files and Folders in iCloud

Problem

You want to store specific files into specific folders within the user's iCloud storage for your app.

Solution

Follow these steps:

1. Make sure your app is set up to use iCloud (see Recipe 21.1).

2. Now instantiate an object of type NSFileManager and pass the path that you created in the previous two steps to the URLForUbiquityContainerIdentifier: method of this class. The return value of this method will be the *local* address for iCloud storage on the device that is running your app. Let's call this path *Root iCloud Path*.

3. Append the folder name that you want to create to the Root iCloud Path (see previous step). Keep the resulting path in a string or an instance of NSURL.

4. Invoke the fileExistsAtPath:isDirectory: method of your file manager. If this method returns false, then go on to create the folder using the createDirector yAtPath:withIntermediateDirectories:attributes:error:method of the file manager. If the return value of the fileExistsAtPath:isDirectory: method is true, check whether the Boolean value that comes out of the isDirectory parameter is false. If it is false, then you must create your folder again as instructed, because the path that was found by the fileExistsAtPath:isDirectory: method was not a directory, but a file.

Discussion

One of the things that can make iCloud *sound* complicated to developers is that they assume that because it is a cloud storage, they have to deal with URLs outside their apps or URLs on the Internet. Well, this is not true. With iCloud, the URLs that you deal with are actually iOS-related. By that, I mean that the URLs are local to the device connected to iCloud. iCloud will then synchronize these local URLs and their data with the iCloud storage hosted by Apple in the cloud. The developer doesn't really have to worry about this part, unless there are conflicts that need to be resolved because two devices running your app and using the same iCloud account simultaneously modified a resource that cannot automatically be merged. We will talk about this later; let's just focus on creating folders in iCloud for now.

So let's now implement what we learned in the Solution section of this chapter:

```swift
import UIKit

@UIApplicationMain
class AppDelegate: UIResponder, UIApplicationDelegate {

  var window: UIWindow?
  let fileManager = NSFileManager()
  var documentsDirectory: String?

  func doesDocumentsDirectoryExist() -> Bool{
    var isDirectory = false as ObjCBool
    var mustCreateDocumentsDirectory = false

    if let directory = documentsDirectory{
      if fileManager.fileExistsAtPath(directory,
        isDirectory: &isDirectory){
          if isDirectory{
            return true
          }
      }
    }

    return false
  }

  func createDocumentsDirectory(){
    println("Must create the directory.")

    var directoryCreationError: NSError?

    if let directory = documentsDirectory{
      if fileManager.createDirectoryAtPath(directory,
        withIntermediateDirectories:true,
        attributes:nil,
        error:&directoryCreationError){
          println("Successfully created the folder")
      } else {
        if let error = directoryCreationError{
          println("Failed to create the folder with error = \(error)")
        }
      }
    }
```

```
  } else {
    println("The directory was nil")
  }

}

func application(application: UIApplication,
  didFinishLaunchingWithOptions launchOptions:
  [NSObject : AnyObject]?) -> Bool {

    let containerURL =
    fileManager.URLForUbiquityContainerIdentifier(nil)

    documentsDirectory =
    containerURL!.path!.stringByAppendingPathComponent("Documents")

    if doesDocumentsDirectoryExist(){
      println("This folder already exists.")
    } else {
      createDocumentsDirectory()
    }

    return true
  }

}
```

 The Container Identifier that Xcode sets up by default for your application is contructed from the string "iCloud" and a bundle identifier. If you want, you can specify your own string. One of the great features of iCloud for developers is that the container identifiers that you specify for your app's iCloud storage don't have to be linked in any way to your app or your app's bundle identifier. If you believe the default identifier is confusing, just change it to something that makes more sense to you and your team.

OK, now that we know about creating directories in the iCloud container of our app, we can go ahead and save a resource into the Documents folder for the current user's iCloud storage for the app:

```
func storeFile(){
  println("Storing a file in the directory...")

  if let directory = documentsDirectory{

    let path =
    documentsDirectory!.stringByAppendingPathComponent("File.txt")

    var writingError: NSError?
```

```
      if "Hello, World!".writeToFile(path,
        atomically: true,
        encoding: NSUTF8StringEncoding,
        error: &writingError){
          println("Successfully saved the file")
      } else {
        if let error = writingError{
          println("An error occurred while writing the file = \(error)")
        }
      }

  } else {
    println("The directory was nil")
  }

}
```

 Saving a file in a cloud URL does not explicitly tell iOS that the file has to be placed in cloud storage.

If you run this app on an iPhone that has been set up to back up data and files to an iCloud account, you can go to the Settings app on the device, find your app's iCloud storage information, and notice that the file we stored has really been saved in our app's iCloud container (see Figure 21-6).

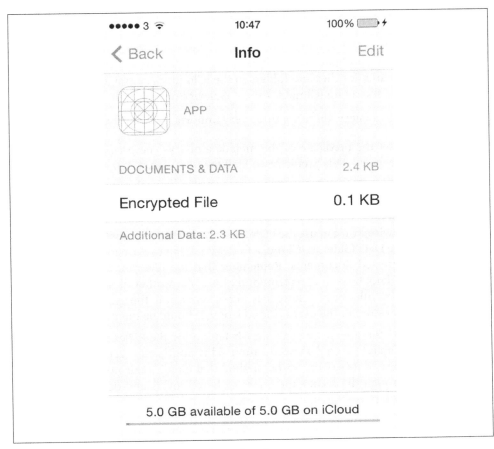

Figure 21-6. Our file is indeed saved in iCloud

See Also

Recipe 21.1; Recipe 21.7

21.9. Searching for Files and Folders in iCloud

Problem

You want to search for files and/or folders inside the current iCloud user's cloud space allocated for your app.

Solution

Use the `NSMetadataQuery` class.

Discussion

OS X developers are probably familiar with the `NSMetadataQuery` class. This class allows developers to query Spotlight items, whether they are files or folders. In iOS, we will use this class to search for files and folders in the iCloud space assigned to the app for the current user, if she set up iCloud for the iOS device on which the app is running.

To set up a metadata query, there are three very important things that we need to do:

1. We need to set the predicate of the metadata query. The *predicate* is the search criteria of the query. This predicate will tell the query what items we are searching for.

2. We also need to set the query's search scope. In order to search in the user's iCloud Documents folder, we set this scope to `NSMetadataQueryUbiquitousDocuments Scope`. Otherwise, you can use the `NSMetadataQueryUbiquitousDataScope`, which represents the Data folder in iCloud, a folder your app can use to store data related to the user-created documents. Remember that the files you store in the user's iCloud should not be your app's temporary files or any other files that your app can retrieve in some other way if those files weren't present in the user's iCloud storage. Items that you store in the user's iCloud storage should be the user's creations.

3. After we start the query, we shall start listening for the `NSMetadataQueryDidFi nishGatheringNotification` notification. This notification gets called when the query has finished its search. In the method that handles this notification, we can then look through the results the query gathered for us and determine if any of those files/folders are the ones we're looking for.

The `setPredicate:` instance method of `NSMetadataQuery` class allows us to set the predicate of the query. The predicate must be of type `NSPredicate`. We will use the `predicateWithFormat:` type method of `NSPredicate` class to initialize the predicate. Remember, the predicate will tell the query what to search for. The `predicate WithFormat:` accepts a format string in the following format:

```
QUERY_ITEM COMPARISON_CRITERIA PATTERN
```

The *QUERY_ITEM* part of the format of the predicate can be any of the `NSMetadataItem` constant values. For instance, we can use the `NSMetadataItemFSNameKey` constant value to tell the predicate that the search pattern targets the filesystem name of the items in the cloud. Because the format provided to the `predicateWithFormat:` method can be a variable number of arguments, with the first argument dictating the format of the rest of the arguments, you can pass `%K` as the *QUERY_ITEM*. For instance, the following two predicates are basically the same in terms of how they supply input to the metadata query:

```
let predicate = NSPredicate(format: "%K like %@",
NSMetadataItemFSNameKey,
```

```
"*")

let samePredicate = NSPredicate(format: "NSMetadataItemFSNameKey like %@",
"*")
```

The *COMPARISON_CRITERIA* part of the format of the predicate can be any of the following values:

>

To indicate that you are searching for query items that are bigger in value than your criteria patterns. For instance, you can search in the Documents folder in the iCloud container of an app for all files whose size is bigger than X kilobytes, where X is defined by you.

<

This comparison criteria is similar to the previous criteria. This criteria looks for items in the iCloud container of an app whose size (as an example) is smaller than the file size that you specified in the pattern.

like

This comparison criteria is used for searching for filenames and display names of files. You can even use wildcards with this criteria; for instance, looking for all files whose names start with a specific character.

We can go on and on about this, but I suggest we dive into the development piece to get a better understanding of how metadata queries work. For this example, here is what we will do:

1. When the app loads (in the app delegate), we simply search for *all* files in the app's iCloud container.

2. We then log the names of all the files that we found to the console, using `println`.

3. At the end of every search, we create a new file whose name is generated randomly using a random integer. We then make sure that file doesn't already exist in the iCloud container for the app. If it doesn't, we save it to the iCloud container. Simple, isn't it? This way, whenever the app opens up, we create a new file to the user's iCloud storage.

 Storing unnecessary files in users' iCloud storage is a really bad practice. Make sure, as stated before, that you use iCloud only to store files that have been directly created by your user, such as documents or creative images. For this example, because we need to find files/folders in the user's iCloud container to prove that the solution works, we need to at least have something stored in the iCloud container for the app.

Save files into iCloud using the `setUbiquitous:itemAtURL:destinationURL:error:` instance method of `NSFileManager`. Here are the parameters for this method:

setUbiquitous
This is a Boolean value that you set to `true` if you want to move a file to iCloud.

itemAtURL
The parameter passed to this method is the `NSURL` pointing to the file in your app's bundle that needs to be moved to iCloud.

destinationURL
This is the URL where the source file has to be copied in the user's iCloud storage. This URL must be an iCloud URL.

error
A pointer to an `NSError` object that will get set to an error, if one occurs during the process.

What we are going to do now is this:

1. Create the Documents folder for our app's iCloud container if this folder doesn't exist already.

2. Save a file into our app bundle's temporary directory.

3. Move the file in our bundle into iCloud.

4. Start a query to look for files in our iCloud container.

5. Print all the results for our query to make sure our file could be found.

We start by defining our required variables:

```
import UIKit

class ViewController: UIViewController {

  let metadataQuery = NSMetadataQuery()
  let fileManager = NSFileManager()
  var cloudDocumentsDirectory: String?
  let fileName = "MyFileName.txt"

  <# rest of the code #>

}
```

Then when our view controller is instantiated, we find the Documents directory in the cloud:

```
init(coder aDecoder: NSCoder!) {
  super.init(coder: aDecoder)

  let containerURL =
```

```
    fileManager.URLForUbiquityContainerIdentifier(nil)

    cloudDocumentsDirectory =
      containerURL!.path!.stringByAppendingPathComponent("Documents")

}
```

When our view appears on the screen, we subscribe to the `NSMetadataQueryDidFinish`
`GatheringNotification` notification that our query sends to us after it finishes searching our iCloud container. We also create the file in our app bundle and then move it to
our iCloud container:

```
override func viewDidAppear(animated: Bool) {
  super.viewDidAppear(animated)

  println("Listening for notifications...")
  /* Listen for a notification that gets fired when the metadata query
  has finished finding the items we were looking for */
  NSNotificationCenter.defaultCenter().addObserver(self,
    selector: "handleMetadataQueryFinished:",
    name: NSMetadataQueryDidFinishGatheringNotification,
    object: nil)

  if doesDocumentsDirectoryExist(){
    println("This folder already exists.")
    /* Now store the file */
    storeFile()
  } else {
    createDocumentsDirectory()
  }

}

override func viewDidDisappear(animated: Bool) {
  super.viewDidDisappear(animated)
  NSNotificationCenter.defaultCenter().removeObserver(self)
}
```

When our view appears, we use the `doesDocumentsDirectoryExist` method of our view
controller to detect whether the Documents directory already exists in the cloud. If not,
we create it using the `createDocumentsDirectory` method. That method not only creates the documents folder, but also calls the `storeFile` method of our view controller,
as we are going to see soon. This method stores the file first in the app bundle and then
moves it into the cloud:

```
func storeFile(){
  println("Storing a file in the directory...")

  if let directory = cloudDocumentsDirectory{

    let pathInAppBundle =
    NSTemporaryDirectory().stringByAppendingPathComponent(fileName)
```

```
    let pathInCloud =
    directory.stringByAppendingPathComponent(fileName)

    var writingError: NSError?

    if "Hello, World!".writeToFile(pathInAppBundle,
      atomically: true,
      encoding: NSUTF8StringEncoding,
      error: &writingError){
        println("Successfully saved the file in the app bundle")

        println("Now moving this file into the cloud...")

        let sourceUrl = NSURL(fileURLWithPath: pathInAppBundle)
        let destinationUrl = NSURL(fileURLWithPath: pathInCloud)

        var savingError: NSError?
        if fileManager.setUbiquitous(true,
          itemAtURL: sourceUrl!,
          destinationURL: destinationUrl!,
          error: &savingError){
            println("Successfully moved the file to the cloud...")
        } else {
          if let error = savingError{
            println("Failed to move the file to the cloud = \(error)")
          }
        }

    } else {
      if let error = writingError{
        println("An error occurred while writing the file = \(error)")
      }
    }
    startQuery()
  } else {
    println("The directory was nil")
  }

}

func doesDocumentsDirectoryExist() -> Bool{
  var isDirectory = false as ObjCBool
  var mustCreateDocumentsDirectory = false

  if let directory = cloudDocumentsDirectory{
    if fileManager.fileExistsAtPath(directory,
      isDirectory: &isDirectory){
        if isDirectory{
          return true
        }
    }
```

```
    }

    return false
}

func createDocumentsDirectory(){
  println("Must create the directory.")

  var directoryCreationError: NSError?

  if let directory = cloudDocumentsDirectory{
    if fileManager.createDirectoryAtPath(directory,
      withIntermediateDirectories:true,
      attributes:nil,
      error:&directoryCreationError){
        println("Successfully created the folder")
        /* Now store the file */
        storeFile()
    } else {
      if let error = directoryCreationError{
        println("Failed to create the folder with error = \(error)")
      }
    }
  } else {
    println("The directory was nil")
  }

}
```

After the file is saved, we call the `startQuery` method of the view controller. This method simply kicks off the metadata query of items in our documents folder in the cloud:

```
func startQuery(){
  println("Starting the query now...")

  metadataQuery.searchScopes = [NSMetadataQueryUbiquitousDocumentsScope]
  let predicate = NSPredicate(format: "%K like %@",
    NSMetadataItemFSNameKey,
    "*.*")

  metadataQuery.predicate = predicate
  if metadataQuery.startQuery(){
    println("Successfully started the query.")
  } else {
    println("Failed to start the query.")
  }
}
```

After the query is done, the `NSMetadataQueryDidFinishGatheringNotification` notification is called by the system. We are catching that notification in the `handleMeta dataQueryFinished:` method of our view controller, which simply goes through all the items that were discovered:

```
func handleMetadataQueryFinished(sender: NSMetadataQuery){

  println("Search finished");

  /* Stop listening for notifications because we are not expecting
  anything more */
  NSNotificationCenter.defaultCenter().removeObserver(self)

  /* We are done with the query; let's stop the process now */
  metadataQuery.disableUpdates()
  metadataQuery.stopQuery()

  for item in metadataQuery.results as [NSMetadataItem]{

    let itemName = item.valueForAttribute(NSMetadataItemFSNameKey)
      as String

    let itemUrl = item.valueForAttribute(NSMetadataItemURLKey)
      as NSURL

    let itemSize = item.valueForAttribute(NSMetadataItemFSSizeKey)
      as Int

    println("Item name = \(itemName)")
    println("Item url = \(itemUrl)")
    println("Item size = \(itemSize)")

  }

}
```

See Also

Recipe 1.22

Index

Symbols

++ operator, 7
== operator, 6
=== operator, 6

A

ABAddressBookAddRecord function, 541, 544
ABAddressBookCopyArrayOfAllGroups function, 550–551
ABAddressBookCopyArrayOfAllPeople function, 537–538, 550–551
ABAddressBookCopyPeopleWithName function, 550–551
ABAddressBookGetAuthorizationStatus function, 534–536
ABAddressBookRequestAccessWithCompletion function, 534
ABAddressBookSave function, 542, 544
ABGroupAddMember function, 547–549
ABGroupCreate function, 544–546
ABMultiValueCopyArrayOfAllValues function, 530
ABPeoplePickerNavigationController class, 527–530
ABPeoplePickerNavigationControllerDelegate protocol, 527, 531
ABPersonCopyImageData function, 552
ABPersonCreate function, 541–543

ABPersonHasImageData function, 552
ABPersonSetImageData function, 552
ABRecordCopyValue function, 530, 538–540
ABRecordSetValue function, 541, 544
accelerometers
    about, 787
    detecting availability, 794–796
    retrieving data from, 797–801
action extensions, 107, 137–144
action sheets
    with destructive buttons, 36
    displaying, 31–37
actions, assigning to triggers, 28
activity view controllers, 57–67, 107
Address Book framework
    about, 525
    adding persons to groups, 547–549
    images of address book entries, 552
    inserting group entry, 544–546
    inserting person entry, 541–543
    requesting address book access, 534–536
    retrieving a person entity, 527–530
    retrieving all contacts, 537–538
    retrieving all properties of entries, 538–540
    retrieving property of a person entity, 531–533
    searching address book, 549–551
alarms, adding to calendar events, 725–727
ALAsset class, 578

We'd like to hear your suggestions for improving our indexes. Send email to index@oreilly.com.

ALAssetsLibrary class, 578, 595–597
alert views, displaying, 31–37
altitude, relative, 788–790
animation and animators
    about, 247
    animating components with push, 257–262
    animating views, 776–785
APNS (Apple Push Notification Services)
    servers, 615, 648
App IDs
    creating, 103, 377
    data protection and, 399–403
    modifying settings of, 649
    push notifications and, 643
Apple Push Notification Services (APNS)
    servers, 615, 648
array indexes, zero-based, 539
arrays, creating and using, 2
assets (CloudKit), 806
Assets Library framework, 578
asynchronous connections
    CloudKit and, 813
    downloading data, 479–482
    handling timeouts, 483–484
attachment behavior, 262–266
Audience button, 122–129
audio files
    playing, 499–501, 503
    playing in background, 357–360
    recording, 501–509
authenticating users with Touch ID, 373–376
authorization
    accessing address book, 534–536
    accessing health information, 155, 158, 171,
        176
    accessing location services, 416, 418
AV Foundation framework
    about, 499
    playing audio files, 358, 499–501
    recording audio, 501–509
AVAsset class, 601
AVAudioPlayer class
    handling interruptions, 509
    playing audio files, 499–501, 503
    playing audio in background, 358–360
    prepare to play settings, 505
AVAudioPlayerDelegate protocol, 508
AVAudioRecorder class, 502–509
AVAudioRecorderDelegate protocol, 507

AVAudioSession class, 505
AVPlayer class, 601
AVURLAsset class, 601

B

Background Fetch capability, 348–356
background tasks
    adding background fetch to apps, 348–356
    completing long-running, 345–348
    downloading data, 473–476
    fetching data, 686–690
    handling location changes, 360–362
    handling network connections, 363–365
    local notifications and, 631
    playing audio files, 357–360
batch updates on Core Data, 661–664
behavior classes, 247
birthdate, setting, 173–177
BLE (Bluetooth Low Energy), 409–415
block objects, 317
Bluetooth Low Energy (BLE), 409–415
Bluetooth technology
    HomeKit codes and, 233
    iBeacons and, 409–415
    soft keyboards and, 87
blur effects, adding to views, 9–12
buffers, 751
buttons
    adding to navigation bars, 70–75
    adding to user interface, 27–30
    choosing audience, 122–129
    destructive, 36

C

calendars
    about, 697
    accessing contents of, 712–714
    adding alarms to, 725–727
    adding events to, 707–711
    adding recurring events to, 718–721
    date picker control, 46
    deleting events from, 714–717
    requesting permission to access, 700–704
    retrieving groups on iOS devices, 705–706
calories burned information, 183–196
camera
    about, 577–578
    customizing map views with a, 440–443

detecting and probing, 579–582
taking photos with, 583–586
taking video with, 587–589
Camera Roll folder, 580
category data type, 156
CBPeripheralManager class, 409
CBUUID class, 411
CDSA (Common Data Security Architecture), 367
certificate signing requests, 100
CertificateSigningRequest.certSigningRequest file, 101
CFDataRef data type, 384
CFDictionaryRef data type, 384
CGAffineTransformMakeRotation function, 450, 775
CGAffineTransformMakeScale function, 307, 461, 774
CGAffineTransformMakeTranslation function, 771
CGContextAddLineToPoint function, 745
CGContextAddPath procedure, 752
CGContextDrawLinearGradient procedure, 768
CGContextDrawPath procedure, 752
CGContextMoveToPoint function, 745
CGContextRestoreGState procedure, 763
CGContextRotateCTM procedure, 775
CGContextSaveGState procedure, 763
CGContextScaleCTM procedure, 774
CGContextSetLineJoin procedure, 748
CGContextSetLineWidth procedure, 745
CGContextSetShadow procedure, 759–763
CGContextSetShadowWithColor procedure, 760
CGContextStrokePath procedure, 745
CGContextTranslateCTM procedure, 772
CGFloat data structure, 285
CGGradientCreateWithColor function, 764
CGGradientCreateWithColorComponents function, 765
CGLineJoin enumeration, 748
CGPathAddLineToPoint procedure, 752
CGPathAddRect function, 755–758
CGPathAddRect procedure, 771
CGPathCreateMutable function, 752
CGPathMoveToPoint procedure, 752
CGPoint data structure, 252
CGRect data structure, 39
CGRectIntersection function, 628

characteristic data type
about, 156
assigning to dynamic effects, 269–272
HomeKit and, 202
manipulating with HomeKit, 206–209
parental lock, 209
retrieving values, 172–177
CIFilter class, 610
CIImage class, 113, 610
CKAsset class, 806
CKContainer class, 805, 809
CKDatabase class, 805, 812, 826
CKDiscoveredUserInfo class, 844
CKErrorCode enumeration, 840
CKNotificationInfo class, 831, 834
CKQuery class, 826, 828, 831
CKQueryCursor class, 830
CKQueryOperation class, 829
CKRecord class, 812
CKRecordID class, 806, 840
CKRecordZone class, 806
CKReference class, 806
CKSubscription class, 831, 835
classes, grouping functionality with, 4
CLBeaconRegion class, 409
CLFloor class, 408
CLGeocoder class, 435
CLLocation class, 408
CLLocationManager class
detecting user in building, 408
handling location changes in background, 360
pinpointing device location, 415–420
processing iBeacons, 409
CLLocationManagerDelegate protocol, 415
Clock app, 41
closures (block objects), 317
CloudKit framework
about, 805–807
observing record changes in, 831–838
querying the cloud, 826–831
retrieving data with, 820–825
retrieving user information from, 839–845
setting up apps for, 807–812
storing data with, 812–819
CLPlacemark class, 436
CMAcceleration data structure, 799
CMAccelerometerData class, 801
CMAltimeter class, 788–790

CMGyroHandler delegate, 803–804
CMMotionManager class
    detecting accelerometer availability, 794–796
    detecting gyroscope availability, 796–797
    retrieving accelerometer data, 798–801
    retrieving gyroscope data, 803
CMPedometer class, 790–794
CMPedometerData class, 792
Cocoa Touch, 729, 826
code signing request file, 102
collection views
    about, 275–277
    adding custom interactions to, 312–314
    feeding custom cells for rendering, 297–302
    handling events in, 303–307
    headers and footers in, 307–312
    providing basic content to, 292–296
collision behavior
    about, 248
    detecting and reacting to, 250–257
    gravity behavior and, 251
    push behavior and, 259
colors
    custom map view pins, 424
    tint, 40
Common Data Security Architecture (CDSA), 367
completion handlers, 159
components
    about, 42
    adding gravity behavior to, 249
    adding snap effect to, 266–269
    animating with push, 257–262
    attaching multiple items to each other, 262–266
    collision behavior and, 250–257
    segmented controls, 54–56, 74
concurrency, 315
    (see also GCD)
    about, 315
    creating with operations, 335–339
    performing non-UI-related tasks, 321–329
    performing UI-related tasks, 319–321
concurrent queues (dispatch), 316
constants, defining, 2
Contacts app
    about, 525
    adding persons to groups, 547–549
    inserting entries, 541–543

    inserting group entry, 544–546
    person's address book image, 552
    picking a contact from, 527–530
    picking property of a contact, 531–533
    retrieving all contacts, 537–538
    retrieving all properties of entries, 538–540
container apps, 109
containers, 805
content scale factor, 730
content size, 88
continuous gesture recognizers, 446
controllers
    boilerplate code in, 111
    date picker, 46–49
    defining labels, 21
    displaying alert, 32–37
    displaying temporary information, 12
    extensions and, 107
    implementing range pickers, 50–53
    in MVC architecture, 1
    navigation, 68–75
    presenting sharing options, 57–67
    segmented controls, 53–56, 74
converting between measurement units, 196–199
Core Animation framework, 730, 776–785
Core Data framework
    about, 659–686
    adding to projects, 660
    boosting data access, 672–680
    custom data types, 690–694
    deleting data from, 668–670
    fetching data in background, 686–690
    implementing relationships in, 680
    performing batch updates on, 661–664
    reading data from, 666–668
    sorting data in, 670–671
    writing to, 664–665
Core Foundation framework
    memory management, 544
    zero-based indexes, 539
Core Graphics framework
    about, 452, 730
    applying shadows, 760–763
    constructing paths, 751–754
    creating affine transformations, 307, 461
    drawing gradients, 764–769
    drawing lines, 745–750
    drawing rectangles, 755–758

transforming views, 771–775
Core Location framework
    about, 407
    detecting user in building, 407–408
    handling location changes in background,
        360–362
    pinpointing device location, 415–420
Core Motion framework
    about, 787
    detecting accelerometer availability, 794–796
    detecting gyroscope availability, 796–797
    retrieving accelerometer data, 797–801
    retrieving altitude data, 788–790
    retrieving gyroscope data, 802–804
    retrieving pedometer data, 790–794
correlation data type, 157
CTM (current transformation matrix), 773
cumulative value types, 157
current transformation matrix (CTM), 773
custom keyboard extension, 129–137

D

date and time
    constructing date objects, 698–699
    local notifications and, 632
    picking, 46–49
date of birth, setting, 173–177
deadlocks, 318
default keychain, 368
DELETE request (HTTP), 488–491
deleting
    data from Core Data, 668–670
    events from calendars, 714–717
    existing values in keychains, 390–391
    files and folders, 571–573
    table view cells, 281–282
deserializing JSON objects, 491–495
destructive buttons, 36
development certificates, 102
development profiles, 100–106
device registration, 104
dictionaries
    accessing, 3
    creating, 492
    defining, 3
    storing and synchronizing in iCloud, 846–
        851
discrete gesture recognizers, 446
discrete value types, 157

dispatch queues, 315–316
dispatch_ keyword, 316
dispatch_after function, 329–330
dispatch_async function, 319, 321–329, 686
dispatch_get_global_queue function, 316, 323
dispatch_get_main_queue function, 316, 319–
    321
dispatch_group_async function, 333
dispatch_group_create function, 332–334
dispatch_group_notify function, 333
dispatch_once function, 331–332
dispatch_queue_create function, 316
dispatch_sync function, 319, 321–329
dispatch_time function, 330
downloading data
    array of URLs, 338
    asynchronously, 479–482
    audio files, 358
    in background, 473–476
    NSURLSession and, 465–472
    synchronously, 484–487
drag gestures, 445
drawing
    gradients, 764–769
    images, 736–738
    lines, 745–750
    paths, 751–754
    rectangles, 755–758
    shadows, 759–763
    text on device screen, 734–735
drawRect: method, 734, 735, 761
drawRectAtBottomOfScreen method, 762
drawRectAtTopOfScreen method, 762
dynamic user interfaces (see UI Dynamics)

E

edge insets, 741
editing photos, 110–118
EKAlarm class, 725–727
EKCalendar class, 703, 712
EKEvent class
    accessing contents of calendars, 712–714
    adding alarms to calendars, 725–727
    adding events to calendars, 707
    adding recurring events, 718
    deleting events from calendars, 714
    retrieving list of attendees, 722–724
EKEventStore class
    accessing contents of calendars, 712–714

adding events to calendars, 707–711
deleting events from calendars, 714
permission accessing calendars, 700–703
retrieving calendar groups, 705
EKParticipant class, 722–724
EKParticipantStatus enumeration, 724
EKRecurrenceEnd class, 718
EKRecurrenceRule class, 718
EKSource class, 705
energy formatters, 186, 196–199
entitlements (app), 371, 376–380, 393–396, 807
enumerations, declaring and using, 8
error handling, 565
Event Kit framework, 697
Event Kit UI framework, 697
events
    adding alarms to calendars, 725–727
    adding recurring to calendars, 718–721
    adding to calendars, 707–711
    creating, 709–711
    deleting from calendars, 714–717
    handling in collection views, 303–307
    retrieving list of attendees, 722–724
extension containers, 109
extension context, 109
extensions
    about, 107–110
    action, 107, 137–144
    custom keyboard, 129–137
    photo editing, 110–118
    sharing, 107, 118–129
    Today, 144–153
    uppercase, 138

F

fetch requests, 667
fetched results controllers, 672–680
FIFO (first-in-first-out), 316
file and folder management
    creating folders on disk, 564–565
    deleting files and folders, 571–573
    enumerating files and folders, 565–570
    folder structure, 555–557
    in iCloud, 851–854
    paths for useful folders, 557–559
    reading from files, 559–563
    saving objects to files, 574–576
    searching in iCloud, 855–861
    storing files in app sandbox, 399–403

writing to files, 559–563
first-in-first-out (FIFO), 316
folders (see file and folder management)
footers
    in collection views, 307–312
    in table views, 282–288

G

GCD (Grand Central Dispatch)
    about, 315–319
    adding background fetch capabilities, 348–356
    completing tasks in background, 345–348
    creating concurrency with operations, 335–339
    creating dependency between operations, 340–342
    firing periodic tasks, 342–344
    grouping tasks together, 332–334
    handling location changes in background, 360–362
    handling network connections in background, 363–365
    performing non-UI-related tasks, 321–329
    performing tasks after a delay, 329–330
    performing tasks only once, 331–332
    performing UI-related tasks, 319–321
    playing audio in background, 357–360
gesture recognizers
    about, 445–447
    adding customized to collection views, 312–314
    long-press gestures, 455–457
    pan gestures, 452–454
    pinch gestures, 460–461
    rotation gestures, 449–452
    screen edge pan gestures, 462–463
    swipe gestures, 447–449
    tap gestures, 458–459
gestures (see specific gestures)
GET request (HTTP), 488–491
gradients, drawing, 764–769
Grand Central Dispatch (see GCD)
gravity behavior
    about, 247
    adding to UI components, 249
    collision behavior and, 251
grep command, 368, 372

group entry (Address Book), 544–546
    adding persons to, 547–549
    searching for, 549–551
gyroscopes
    about, 787
    detecting availability, 796–797
    retrieving data, 802–804

H

headers
    in collection views, 307–312
    in table views, 282–288
health management application
    about, 155
    converting between units, 196–199
    observing changes to information, 177–183
    retrieving user characteristics, 172–177
    setting up apps for HealthKit, 155–159
    total calories burned information, 183–196
    user's height information, 165–172
    user's weight information, 160–165
HealthKit framework
    about, 155
    converting between units, 196–199
    observing changes to information, 177–183
    retrieving user characteristics, 172–177
    setting up apps for, 155–159
    total calories burned information, 183–196
    user's height information, 165–172
    user's weight information, 160–165
height information, accessing and modifying, 165–172
HKCategorySample class, 161
HKCategoryType class, 156
HKCharacteristicType class, 156, 173
HKHealthStore class, 156
HKMetricPrefix enumeration, 160
HKObjectType class, 156
HKObserverQuery class, 177
HKQuantity class, 160, 196
HKQuantitySample class, 160, 192
HKQuantityType class, 160, 165
HKQuantityTypeIdentifier enumeration, 157, 183–196
HKQuery class, 178
HKSample class, 161
HKSampleQuery class, 160, 161–165
HKSampleType class, 156, 164, 178

HKUnit class
    about, 155
    converting between units example, 196
    user's height example, 167
    user's weight example, 160
HKUpdateFrequency enumeration, 180
HKWorkoutType class, 156
HMAccessory class, 202
HMAccessoryBrowser class, 229
HMAccessoryBrowserDelegate protocol, 229
HMCharacteristic class, 235–242
HMHome class, 202
HMHomeDelegate protocol, 220
HMHomeManager class, 202, 212
HMHomeManagerDelegate protocol, 212
HMRoom class, 219, 225
HMService class, 202
HMServiceGroup class, 202, 242
HMZone class, 202, 226
home appliance management
    about, 201–203
    adding rooms to home, 219
    grouping services of HomeKit accessories, 242–245
    interacting with accessories, 234–242
    managing HomeKit accessories, 229–234
    managing in HomeKit, 212–219
    simulating HomeKit accessories, 203–211
    specifying zones in home, 224
HomeKit Accessory Simulator
    about, 203
    adding accessories, 210
    adding characteristic, 206–209
    adding services, 205
    creating accessories, 203
    displaying accessory information, 204
HomeKit framework
    about, 201–203
    adding rooms to home, 219
    grouping services of accessories, 242–245
    interacting with accessories, 234–242
    managing accessories, 229–234
    managing user's home in, 212–219
    simulating accessories, 203–211
    specifying zones in home, 224
host applications, 109
HTTP requests, 488–491

I

IBAction, 138
iBeacons, defining and processing, 409–415
IBOutlet, 298
iCloud account
    loading calendars on device, 697
    Sign Out button, 27
    synchronizing data, 807
    user login notification, 809
    writing to and reading data from, 397–399
iCloud structure
    CloudKit and, 806
    managing files and folders in, 851–854
    searching for files and folders in, 855–861
    storing and synchronizing dictionaries in,
        846–851
image picker controllers, 583
image sharing extensions, 119–129
images, 597
    (see also photos)
    adding blur effects, 9–12
    adding editing capabilities for, 110–118
    displaying on navigation bars, 68–70
    displaying with UIImageView, 17–20
    drawing, 736–738
    editing on device, 608
    implementing range pickers, 52
    nine-part, 741
    person's address book, 552
    reacting to changes in, 602–607
    resizable, 739–744
    Retina displays, 65, 70
    searching for and retrieving, 597–602
indexes, zero-based, 539
indicators, scroll views and, 90
inserting, 544
Interface Builder, 76, 297–302, 307–312, 734
Internet connections, 229
inverse many-to-many relationship (Core Data),
    681, 685
inverse one-to-many relationship (Core Data),
    681–686
iOS Dev Center portal, 808, 847
iOS Simulator
    accelerator data and, 795
    background location processing, 362
    gyroscope data and, 797
    playing audio in background and, 357
    Shake Gesture option, 788

J

jailbreaking process, 367
JSON objects, 491–495

K

kCGPathFill method, 752
kCGPathFillStroke method, 752
kCGPathStroke method, 752
key-value observing (KVO) compliance, 319
key: value syntax, 3, 370
keyboards
    Bluetooth, 87
    building custom, 129–137
    listening and reacting to notifications, 621–
        629
Keychain Access
    about, 367
    iOS and, 369, 371–373
    Mac OS X and, 369–371
    opening, 651
    provision profiles and, 100–104
keychain access groups, 393–396
keychains
    about, 367–373
    deleting existing values in, 390–391
    enabling app security, 376–380
    finding values in, 383–386
    sharing data between apps, 392–396
    storing values in, 381–383
    updating existing values in, 386–390
    writing to and reading data from iCloud,
        397–399
kilocalories, 187
kSecAttrAccessGroup attribute, 392–396
kSecAttrAccount attribute
    deleting values in keychain example, 390
    finding values in keychain example, 383
    storing keychain values example, 381
kSecAttrComment attribute, 390
kSecAttrService attribute
    deleting values in keychain example, 390
    finding values in keychain example, 383
    sharing keychain data example, 392
    storing keychain values example, 381
kSecAttrSynchronizable attribute, 397–399
kSecClass attribute
    deleting values in keychain example, 390
    finding values in keychain example, 383

storing keychain values example, 381
kSecClassGenericPassword attribute
    deleting values in keychain example, 390
    inding values in keychain example, 383
    storing keychain values example, 381
kSecMatchLimit attribute, 386
kSecMatchLimitAll attribute, 386
kSecReturnAttributes attribute, 383
kSecReturnData attribute, 383
kSecValueData attribute, 381, 386–390
KVO (key-value observing) compliance, 319

L

layout object, 276
let keyword, 2
lines, drawing, 745–750
LLVM compiler
    including frameworks, 499, 525, 659, 787
    Modules feature, 697
    static analysis and, 544
local notifications
    about, 615, 631
    handling, 639–642
    listening and reacting to, 636
    scheduling, 630–638
location (see Core Location framework)
long-press gestures, 445, 455–457

M

main instance method, 318
main queue (dispatch), 316
managed object context (MOC), 660
managed object model (MOM), 660
managed objects, 660
Map Kit framework
    about, 407
    customizing map views with a camera, 440–443
    displaying custom pins on map views, 423–428
    displaying directions on maps, 434
    displaying pins on map views, 420–422
    searching on map views, 429–434
map views
    customizing with a camera, 440–443
    displaying custom pins on, 423–428
    displaying directions, 434
    displaying pins on, 420–422

searching on, 429–434
Maps app, 434
marshalling process, 562, 574
measurement, unit (see HealthKit framework)
Media Player framework
    about, 499
    accessing music library, 516–523
    capturing thumbnails from video files, 513–516
    playing video files, 509–512
medical data (see health management application)
memory management, 544
metadata, 597, 806
MKAnnotation protocol, 420
MKAnnotationView class, 423–428
MKDirections class, 434
MKDirectionsRequest class, 434
MKDirectionsResponse class, 434
MKLocalSearch class, 430–434
MKLocalSearchRequest class, 429
MKLocalSearchResponse class, 429
MKMapCamera class, 440–443
MKMapItem class, 434, 434
MKMapView class, 421
MKPinAnnotationView class, 424
MKPlacemark class, 435
Mobile Core Services framework, 577
MOC (managed object context), 660
model-view-controller (MVC) architecture, 1
models (MVC architecture), 1
MOM (managed object model), 660
MPMediaItem class, 518
MPMediaPickerController class, 516–523
MPMediaPickerControllerDelegate protocol, 516
MPMoviePlayerController class
    capturing thumbnails from video files, 513–516
    playing video files, 509–512
MPMoviePlayerViewController class, 509
MPMusicPlayerController class, 518
multimedia (see audio files; video files)
multitasking, 315
    (see also GCD)
music library, accessing, 516–523
MVC (model-view-controller) architecture, 1

N

navigation bars
    adding buttons to, 70–75
    displaying images on, 68–70
NCWidgetProviding protocol, 144
network connections
    about, 465
    customizing URL requests, 487
    deserializing JSON objects, 491–495
    downloading asynchronously, 479–482
    downloading data in the background, 473–476
    downloading date from URL, 465–472
    downloading synchronously, 484–487
    handling in background, 363–365
    handling timeouts, 483–484
    sending HTTP requests, 488–491
    serializing JSON objects, 491–495
    uploading data, 477–478
New File dialog box, 732
nine-part images, 741
normal notifications (see notifications)
Notification Center, adding widgets to, 144–153
notifications
    about, 615–616
    delivering to apps, 648–656
    handling local system, 639–642
    listening and reacting to keyboard, 621–629
    listening and reacting to local, 636
    listening for and reacting to, 618–621
    on photo library, 602
    reacting to push, 656–657
    scheduling local, 630–638
    sending, 616–618
    setting up for push, 642–648
    user iCloud account login, 809
NSArray class
    about, 3, 66
    Address Book and, 530, 537
    file destination paths and, 562
    JSON objects and, 492
    listing event attendees, 722
    querying cloud example, 827
NSBatchUpdateRequest class, 661–664
NSBatchUpdateRequestResultType enumeration, 663
NSBatchUpdateResult class, 664
NSBlockOperation class, 337
NSBundle class, 501

NSCalendar class
    constructing date objects, 698–699
    retrieving date components, 700
NSCalendarUnit enumeration, 699
NSCoding protocol, 574–576
NSCurrentLocaleDidChangeNotification, 639
NSData class
    downloading audio files, 358
    downloading data example, 470, 480, 484
    file destination paths and, 559
    image data and, 578
    JSON objects and, 493
    loading audio files, 501
    loading web pages example, 95
    person's address book image and, 552
    push notifications and, 654
    transformable data types and, 691
    uploading data example, 477
NSDate class
    calculating beginning of day, 188
    constructing date objects, 698–699
    identifying date of birth, 173
    identifying date of type, 570
    pedometer data and, 792
    recurring events and, 718
    retrieving date components, 699
    storing data in arrays, 290
NSDateComponents class, 700
NSDictionary class
    about, 3
    file destination paths and, 563
    images and, 586
    JSON objects and, 492
    keyboard boundaries and, 85
    notifications and, 632, 657
NSEntityDescription class, 664–665
NSError class
    accelerometer data and, 801
    deleting events from calendars and, 715
    downloading data example, 480
    gyroscope data and, 804
    iCloud searches and, 858
    map directions example, 436
    push notifications and, 648
    recording audio example, 502
    storing videos example, 596
    user's health information example, 180
    user's home example, 217, 225, 226
NSExtensionContext class, 109

NSExtensionItem class, 109, 124, 139
NSFetchedResultsController class, 672–680
NSFetchedResultsControllerDelegate protocol, 675
NSFetchedResultsSectionInfo protocol, 673
NSFetchRequest class, 666–668, 671
NSFileManager class
    creating folders on disk, 564–565
    deleting files and folders, 571–573
    enumerating files and folders, 565–570
    iCloud and, 851, 858
    moving file locations, 468
    storing files securely, 400
    user iCloud account logins and, 810
NSFileProtectionKey attribute, 400
NSIndexPath class, 673
NSInternalInconsistencyException, 665
NSItemProvider class, 139
NSJSONSerialization class, 492–495
NSKeyedArchiver class, 574
NSKeyedUnarchiver class, 574
NSLengthFormatterUnit enumeration, 197
NSLocationWhenInUseUsageDescription attribute, 418
NSManagedObject class, 660
NSManagedObjectContext class, 668–670, 688
NSManagedObjectID class, 687
NSMassFormatterUnit enumeration, 197
NSMetadataItem class, 856
NSMetadataQuery class, 855–861
NSMetadataQueryDidFinishGatheringNotification, 856
NSMutableArray class, 495
NSMutableAttributedString class, 25
NSMutableDictionary class, 495
NSMutableString class, 495
NSMutableURLRequest class
    customizing URL requests and, 487
    downloading data and, 480
    HTTP requests and, 488–491
    uploading data and, 478
NSNotification class, 615, 617–618
NSNotificationCenter class, 619
NSNull class, 492
NSNumber class, 492, 514, 570
NSNumberFormatter class, 166
NSNumberFormatterStyle class, 166
NSObject class
    error handling and, 565

inheritance and, 576
    pins on map view example, 420
    querying cloud example, 827
NSOperation class, 318, 335–339, 340, 829
NSOperationQueue class, 318, 335–339, 468
NSPersistentStoreResult class, 663
NSPredicate class
    accessing calendars example, 714
    CKQuery and, 831
    querying the cloud and, 826, 856
    user's health information example, 178
NSSecureCoding protocol, 139
NSSet class, 156, 681
NSShadow class, 25
NSSortDescriptor class, 160, 670
NSString class
    Address Book and, 538
    asynchronous connections and, 480
    displaying pins on map views example, 420
    displaying static text example, 25
    drawing text, 735
    file destination paths and, 559
    finding values in keychains and, 384
    image pickers and, 585
    JSON objects and, 492
    loading web pages example, 95
    picking values example, 45
    sharing options example, 61, 64
    social sharing and, 496
    table views and, 287
NSTableView class, 326
NSTextAlignment enumeration, 77
NSThread class, 321
NSTimer class, 343–344, 346
NSUbiquitousKeyValueStore class, 846–851
NSURL class
    asynchronous connections and, 480
    file destination paths and, 561
    getting key values, 569
    iCloud and, 851
    loading web pages and, 91
    storing videos example, 596
NSURLConnection class
    about, 465
    downloading asynchronously, 479–482
    downloading synchronously, 484–487
    handling network connections in background, 363–365
    handling timeouts, 483–484

sending HTTP requests, 488–491
NSURLRequest class
    downloading data example, 480
    handling timeouts example, 483
    loading web pages example, 91, 95
    uploading data example, 478
NSURLResponse class, 480
NSURLSession class
    about, 465
    downloading data in the background, 473–476
    downloading data using, 465–472, 482
    extensions and, 109, 125
    uploading data using, 477–478
NSURLSessionConfiguration class
    downloading data example, 466
    downloading data in background example, 473
    uploading data example, 477
NSURLSessionDataDelegate protocol, 470
NSURLSessionDataTask class, 466, 478
NSURLSessionDownloadTask class, 466
NSURLSessionUploadTask class, 478
NSUserDefaults class, 821, 847
NSUserDefaultsDidChangeNotification, 639
NSUUID class, 207, 411, 815
NSValue class, 85
NSValueTransformer class, 691

O

observer queries, 177–183
On/Off controls, 38–41
one-to-one relationship (Core Data), 681
opaque data type, 384
OpenGLES framework, 610
operation objects, 318–319
operation queues, 317–319
operators
    about, 5–7
    overriding, 6

P

pan gestures, 445, 452–454
parental lock characteristic, 209
passwords, default keychain and, 368
paths, drawing, 751–754
pedometer data, retrieving, 790–794
PEM files, 653

persistent store, 659
persistent store coordinator, 660
person entity (Address Book)
    adding to groups, 547–549
    inserting, 541–543
    inserting group entry, 544–546
    person's image data, 552
    retrieving, 527–530
    retrieving all contacts, 537–538
    retrieving all properties of, 538–540
    retrieving property of, 531–533
    searching for, 549–551
PHAdjustmentData class, 113, 612
PHAsset class, 598, 606, 608
PHAssetChangeRequest class, 606
PHAssetMediaType enumeration, 599
PHCachingImageManager class, 599
PHChange class, 607
PHContentEditingController protocol, 110
PHContentEditingInput class, 110, 612, 613
PHContentEditingOutput class, 113, 613
PHFetchOptions class, 598
PHFetchResult class, 599
PHImageManager class, 601
photo editing extensions, 110–118
photo library
    checking availability of, 580
    notifications on, 602
    storing photos in, 590–595
    storing videos in, 595–597
PhotoEditingViewController class, 111
photos, 590
    (see also images)
    editing on device, 608
    reacting to changes in, 602–607
    searching for and retrieving, 597–602
    storing in photo library, 590–595
    taking with camera, 583–586
Photos app
    adding photo editing capabilities to, 110–118
    providing custom sharing extensions, 119–129
Photos framework, 597–602
PHPhotoLibrary class, 602–607, 613
PHPhotoLibraryChangeObserver protocol, 607
PHVideoRequestOptions class, 600
picker views
    picking date and time, 46–49
    picking values, 41–46

pinch gestures, 445, 460–461
pixels versus points, 730
placeholder text, 81
points versus pixels, 730
popup controllers, 12–17, 58
POST request (HTTP), 488–491
private keys, 100, 101
progress bars, 96–99
projects, creating in Xcode, 731
properties, transformable, 691–694
provision profiles
    app entitlements and, 371, 376–380, 393–
      396, 807
    creating, 99–106
    push notifications and, 643
    supporting HomeKit, 203
push behavior
    animating components with, 257–262
    collision behavior and, 259
    simulating, 248
push notifications
    about, 615
    CloudKit record changes, 831–838
    delivering to apps, 648–656
    reacting to, 656–657
    setting up for, 642–648
PUT request (HTTP), 488–491

Q

quantity data type, 156
Quartz 2D drawing engine, 730
querying user data
    about, 161–165
    CloudKit support, 826–831
    iCloud support, 855–861
    observing changes to user information, 177–
      183

R

random identifiers, 815
range pickers, 49–53
rawValue property, 8
reading
    data from Core Data, 666–668
    from files, 559–563
    keychain data from iCloud, 397–399
record names (CloudKit), 806
record zones, 806, 814

rectangles
    drawing, 755–758
    rotating, 775
recurring events, adding to calendars, 718–721
reference points, 788
reference views, 248
references (CloudKit), 806
refresh control for table views, 288–292
registering devices, 104
relationships in Core Data, 680
relative altitude, 788–790
resizable images, 739–744
Retina displays (iOS devices), 65, 70
RFRC 1421, 653
root view controllers, 15
rotating rectangles, 775
rotation gestures, 445, 446, 449–452
rows, deleting from table views, 281–282

S

Safari's icon
    adding blur effects, 10–12
    animating, 777–785
    displaying, 17–20
sandbox environment, 399–403, 555
scheduling local notifications, 630–638
screen edge pan gestures, 462–463
scrollable content
    creating with UIScrollView, 88–91
    displaying long lines of text, 83–87
searching
    address book, 549–551
    for files and folders in iCloud, 855–861
    for images and videos, 597–602
    on map views, 429–434
SecItemAdd function, 381–383, 392–396, 397
SecItemCopyMatching function, 383–386
SecItemDelete function, 390–391
SecItemUpdate function, 386–390
security
    about, 367–373
    accessing user calendars, 700–704
    authenticating users with Touch ID, 373–376
    deleting existing values in keychains, 390–
      391
    enabling for apps, 376–380
    finding values in keychains, 383–386
    sharing keychain data between apps, 392–
      396

storing files in app sandbox, 399–403
storing values in keychains, 381–383
updating existing values in keychains, 386–390
user interface and, 403
writing to and reading data from iCloud, 397–399
security command
cms argument, 372
dump-keychain argument, 368
find-generic password argument, 371
segmented controls, 53–56, 74
segue names, 213
SELECT statement, 667
serial queues (dispatch), 316
serializing JSON objects, 491–495
service groups (HomeKit), 202, 242–245
services
creating within apps, 137–144
HomeKit and, 202, 205
shadows, adding to shapes, 759–763
shake events, detecting, 801
shapes, adding shadows to, 759–763
sharing content, presenting options, 57–67
sharing extensions, 107, 118–129
Sign Out button, 27
Siri (iOS devices), 202, 242–245
SLComposeServiceViewController class, 119
SLComposeSheetConfigurationItem class, 126
SLComposeViewController class, 495–498
sliders
implementing range pickers, 49–53
volume, 50
snap effect
about, 248
adding to components, 266–269
Social framework, 495–498
sorting data in Core Data, 670–671
SSL certificates, 649
start instance method, 318
states
controller restoration of, 171
gesture recognizers, 447
static text, displaying with UILabel, 21–26
storyboards, 138, 625
structures, grouping functionality with, 4
subclassing classes, 275
subscriptions in CloudKit, 831–838
Swift programming language, 1

swipe gestures, 445, 447–449
switch statement, 8
switches, manipulating, 37–41
synchronous connections
blocking threads, 479, 484
downloading data, 479, 484–487
system notifications, 639–642

T

table view controllers
displaying popovers, 13–17
refresh control, 289–292
table views
about, 275–277
boosting data access in, 672–680
deleting rows from, 281–282
displaying temporary information, 12–17
headers and footers in, 282–288
populating with data, 277–280
refresh control for, 288–292
tap gestures, 445, 446, 458–459
task management (see GCD)
temporary views, 12–17
text fields
about, 75
accepting user input, 75–83
placeholder text in, 81
text views
creating scrollable content, 88–91
displaying long lines of text, 83–87
reacting to notifications, 622
text, drawing on device screen, 734–735
thumb (sliders), 51
thumbnails from video files, 513–516
time (see date and time)
timeouts, handling in asynchronous connections, 483–484
timers
creating and scheduling, 346
firing periodic tasks, 342–344
tint colors, 40
Today extension, 144–153
Today view (Notification Center), 144–153
total calories burned information, 183–196
touch events (see gesture recognizers)
Touch ID, 373–376
transformable properties, 691–694
transformations, 770–775
triggers, assigning actions to, 28

U

UDID (devices), 104
UI Dynamics
  about, 247–248
  adding gravity to components, 249
  adding snap effect to components, 266–269
  animating components with push, 257–262
  assigning characteristics to effects, 269–272
  attaching multiple items to each other, 262–266
  collision behavior and, 250–257
UIActivity class, 59, 63
UIActivityItemSource protocol, 59
UIActivityViewController class
  displaying extensions, 107, 137
  presenting sharing options, 57–67
  presenting sharing options and, 119
UIAlertAction class, 32
UIAlertController class, 31–37, 217
UIAlertControllerStyle enumeration, 34
UIApplication class
  backgroundTimeRemaining property, 360
  completing long-running tasks in background, 345–348
  push notifications and, 647
  scheduling notifications, 631
  setNetworkActivityIndicatorVisible: method, 96
  setting background-fetch capabilities, 349–356
UIAttachmentBehavior class, 262
UIBarButtonItem class, 12, 70–75
UIBarButtonSystemItem enumeration, 73
UIBezierPath class, 252
UIBlurEffect class, 9
UIBlurEffectStyle enumeration, 11
UIButton class, 27–30, 133
UICollectionReusableView class, 308
UICollectionView class, 294
UICollectionViewCell class, 292–296, 297, 304
UICollectionViewController class, 296, 305, 313
UICollectionViewDataSource protocol, 306
UICollectionViewDelegate protocol, 303
UICollectionViewDelegateFlowLayout protocol, 305
UICollectionViewFlowLayout class, 276
UICollisionBehavior class, 248, 250–257
UICollisionBehaviorDelegate protocol, 254

UIColor class
  converting colors, 703
  Core Data and, 691
  static text and, 25
  tint colors and, 40
UIControlContentVerticalAlignment enumeration, 77
UIControlEventValueChanged event, 40, 290
UIDatePicker class, 46–49
UIDatePickerMode enumeration, 47
UIDevice class, 639
UIDeviceBatteryStateDidChangeNotification, 639
UIDeviceOrientationDidChangeNotification, 640
UIDeviceProximityStateDidChangeNotification, 639
UIDynamicAnimator class
  about, 248
  dynamic effects and, 270
  gravity behavior and, 249
  push behavior and, 258
  snap effect and, 266
UIDynamicItem protocol
  collision behavior example, 251
  dynamic effects example, 269
  gravity behavior example, 249
  snap effect example, 267
UIDynamicItemBehavior class, 269
UIEventSubtype enumeration, 801
UIFont class, 25
UIGestureRecognizer class, 446
UIGraphicsGetCurrentContext function, 745
UIGravityBehavior class, 248, 249, 256
UIImage class
  applying filters, 112
  custom pins for map views, 423
  drawing images, 736–738
  file destination paths and, 559
  image pickers and, 586
  loading image data and, 578
  resizable images and, 740
  Retina displays and, 64
  retrieving image data, 552
UIImageJPEGRepresentation function, 552
UIImagePickerController class
  about, 577
  detecting and probing camera, 579–582
  taking photos with camera, 583–586

taking video with camera, 587–589
UIImagePickerControllerDelegate protocol, 583
UIImageView class, 17–20, 287, 777–785
UIImageWriteToSavedPhotosAlbum procedure, 590–595
UIInputViewController class, 129–137
UIKeyboardDidHideNotification, 624
UIKeyboardDidShowNotification, 624
UIKeyboardWillHideNotification, 624, 624
UIKeyboardWillShowNotification, 624, 624
UIKit framework, 693, 730, 776
UILabel class, 21–26, 82, 283
UILocalNotification class, 615, 631–638
UILongPressGestureRecognizer class, 455–457
UILongTapGestureRecognizer class, 456
UINavigationBar class, 71
UINavigationControllerDelegate protocol, 583
UINib class, 294, 298
UIPanGestureRecognizer class, 452–454, 462
UIPickerViewDataSource protocol, 43
UIPickerViewDelegate protocol, 44
UIPinchGestureRecognizer class, 460–461
UIPopoverArrowDirection enumeration, 17
UIPopoverController class, 12
UIProgressView class, 97–99
UIProgressViewStyle enumeration, 98
UIPushBehavior class, 248, 257
UIRectEdge enumeration, 462
UIRefreshControl class, 289–292
UIResponder class, 801
UIRotationGestureRecognizer class, 449–452
UIScreenEdgePanGestureRecognizer class, 462–463
UIScrollView class, 88–91, 275
UIScrollViewDelegate protocol, 89
UISegmentedControl class, 53–56
UISlider class, 49–53
UISnapBehavior class, 248, 266
UISwipeGestureRecognizer class, 447–449
UISwitch class, 37–41, 73
UITableView class, 275, 326
UITableViewCell class, 275, 278–280
UITableViewDataSource protocol, 275, 277–280, 283
UITableViewDelegate protocol, 275, 282, 283
UITapGestureRecognizer class, 458–459
UITextBorderStyle enumeration, 77
UITextField class, 75–83, 403, 622
UITextFieldDelegate protocol, 59, 77

UITextFieldViewMode enumeration, 83
UITextInputTraits protocol, 135
UITextView class, 83–87, 622
UIUserNotificationSettings class, 633
UIVibrancyEffect class, 12
UIView class
    animating views, 776–785
    assigning objects and, 70
    collection views and, 296
    custom keyboard extension and, 129
    displaying footers, 284
    drawing support, 734, 735
    gesture recognizers and, 445, 446
    subclassing, 734
    UIDynamicItem protocol and, 249, 251, 267, 269
    UIScrollView class and, 88
    UIVisualEffect class and, 9
    video files and, 510
UIViewContentMode enumeration, 19
UIViewController class, 31, 509
UIVisualEffect class, 12
UIVisualEffectView class, 9
UIWebView class, 94–97
UIWebViewDelegate protocol, 96
UIWindow class, 621
ULO (upper left origin) screens, 730
unit measurement (see HealthKit framework)
UPickerView class, 41–46
uploading data, 477–478
upper left origin (ULO) screens, 730
uppercase extension, 138
URLs
    customizing requests, 487
    downloading array of, 338
    downloading asynchronously from, 479–482
    downloading data from, 465–472
user input, accepting with UITextField, 75–83
UUIDs, 207, 411

V

var keyword, 2
varoiables, defining, 2
video files
    capturing thumbnails from, 513–516
    editing on device, 608
    playing, 509–512
    reacting to changes in, 602–607
    searching for and retrieving, 597–602

storing in photo library, 595–597

taking videos with camera, 587–589

view controllers, creating view object for, 732

views, 1

(see also specific views)

adding blur effects to, 9–12

animating, 776–785

Cocoa Touch support, 729

gesture recognizers and, 445

loading web pages, 91–97

in MVC architecture, 1

progress bars, 96–99

scrollable content in, 83–91

transforming, 770–775

volume sliders, 50

W

web pages

loading with UIWebView, 94–97

loading with WebKit, 91–94

Web Views, 24

WebKit framework, loading web pages with, 91–94

weight information, retrieving and modifying, 160–165

where clause (switch statement), 8

widgets, adding to Notification Center, 144–153

windows (Cocoa Touch), 729

WKNavigationDelegate protocol, 91

WKPreferences class, 91

WKWebView class, 91

WKWebViewConfiguration class, 91

writing

to Core Data, 664–665

to files, 559–563

keychain data to iCloud, 397–399

X

.xib file extension, 297–302, 307

Z

zero-based array indexes, 539

zones (house), 202, 224

About the Author

Vandad Nahavandipoor is an iOS and OS X programmer for an international media group with over 7,000 employees in more than 29 countries. Previously he worked for Lloyds Banking Group in England to deliver their iOS apps to millions of users in the UK. He has led an international team of more than 30 iOS developers, and some of the projects he has overseen include the NatWest and RBS iOS apps running on millions of iPhones and iPads in the UK. Vandad received his B.Sc and M.Sc in Information Technology for E-Commerce from the University of Sussex in England

Vandad's programming experience started when he first learned Basic on his father's Commodore 64. He then took this experience and applied it on his uncle's Intel 186 computer, running Basic on DOS. At this point, he found programming for personal computers exciting indeed and moved on to learn Object Pascal. This allowed him to learn Borland Delphi quite easily. He wrote a short 400-page book on Borland Delphi and dedicated the book to Borland. From then, he picked up x86 Assembly programming and wrote a hobby 32-bit operating system named Vandior. It wasn't until late 2007 when iOS programming became his main focus.

Aside from programming, Vandad is a road cyclist, enjoying friendly competition in cyclosportive events in England and traveling long distance on his bicycle to other European countries every now and then. He also enjoys tinkering with his piano and playing electric guitar. Some of his electric guitar performances are available on YouTube.

Colophon

The red-billed tropicbird (*Phaethon aethereus*) is also called the boatswain bird. Tropicbirds look like terns but are not genetically related to them; in fact, tropicbirds have no close living relative species, making them a bit of an evolutionary mystery. The red-billed tropicbird was featured on the Bermudan $50 bill starting in 2009, but it was subsequently replaced by the native white-tailed tropicbird, which has a higher population in Bermuda.

Red-billed tropicbirds are large, with long tails, white bodies, and the eponymous red bill that curves downward. With the tail feathers included, they are almost 40 inches long; a wingspan of one meter balances out their bodies and makes them graceful flyers. They have black markings on their flight feathers and in their eyes. Male and female birds look similar, but males can have longer tails. Red-billed tropicbirds' feet are located very far back on their bodies, so their movements on land are almost comically awkward and occur mostly on their bellies. They are not nimble swimmers either, but they move comfortably through the air over the ocean, where they hover in hopes of catching flying fish. Flying fish appear to be a favorite prey, but tropicbirds will eat other fish and even cephalopods as well.

Red-billed tropicbirds live in places like the Galapagos, the Cape Verde islands, the West Indies, and even the Persian Gulf. Despite their preference for warm, tropical waters, a particular single red-billed tropicbird keeps returning to Seal Island in coastal Maine every year. There is a large seabird population in that part of the state, but this individual is the only one of his kind to be found that far north. Some years ago, locals placed a wood decoy carving of a tropicbird out and the inexplicable visitor tried to court and mate with it. The chance of seeing this bird has meant good business for the boat charters that take birdwatchers out to see the puffins and black Guillemots that otherwise dominate the local bird scene.

The cover image is from the *Riverside Natural History*. The cover fonts are URW Typewriter and Guardian Sans. The text font is Adobe Minion Pro; the heading font is Adobe Myriad Condensed; and the code font is Dalton Maag's Ubuntu Mono.

Get even more for your money.

Join the O'Reilly Community, and register the O'Reilly books you own. It's free, and you'll get:

- $4.99 ebook upgrade offer
- 40% upgrade offer on O'Reilly print books
- Membership discounts on books and events
- Free lifetime updates to ebooks and videos
- Multiple ebook formats, DRM FREE
- Participation in the O'Reilly community
- Newsletters
- Account management
- 100% Satisfaction Guarantee

Signing up is easy:

1. Go to: oreilly.com/go/register
2. Create an O'Reilly login.
3. Provide your address.
4. Register your books.

Note: English-language books only

To order books online:
oreilly.com/store

For questions about products or an order:
orders@oreilly.com

To sign up to get topic-specific email announcements and/or news about upcoming books, conferences, special offers, and new technologies:
elists@oreilly.com

For technical questions about book content:
booktech@oreilly.com

To submit new book proposals to our editors:
proposals@oreilly.com

O'Reilly books are available in multiple DRM-free ebook formats. For more information:
oreilly.com/ebooks

O'REILLY®

Have it your way.

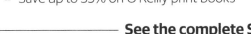

Lightning Source UK Ltd.
Milton Keynes UK
UKOW07f2201010615

252694UK00004B/22/P